Mount Everest, the highest point on the Earth, is about **29,035 feet** above sea level.

Mount Everest
8,846 m

Sea Level

Puerto Rico Trench
8,605 m

The deepest point in the Atlantic Ocean, in the Puerto Rico Trench, is more than **5 miles** below sea level.

Oceans cover about $\frac{7}{10}$ of Earth's surface.

They are about 6 feet long and can weigh 1,400 pounds.

Leatherbacks are the largest living sea turtles.

HSP Math

 **Harcourt**

SCHOOL PUBLISHERS

Visit *The Learning Site!*
www.harcourtschool.com

SCHOOL PUBLISHERS

Printed in the United States of America

ISBN 13: 978-0-15-341262-2
ISBN 10: 0-15-341262-3

4 5 6 7 8 9 10   0914   16 15 14 13 12 11 10 09

HSP Math

Mathematics Advisor

Tom Roby
Associate Professor of
    Mathematics
Director, Quantitative
    Learning Center
University of Connecticut
Storrs, Connecticut

Senior Authors

Evan M. Maletsky
Professor Emeritus
Montclair State University
Upper Montclair, New Jersey

Joyce McLeod
Visiting Professor, Retired
Rollins College
Winter Park, Florida

Authors

Karen S. Norwood
Associate Professor of
    Mathematics Education
North Carolina State University
Raleigh, North Carolina

Tom Roby
Associate Professor of
    Mathematics
Director, Quantitative
    Learning Center
University of Connecticut
Storrs, Connecticut

James A. Mendoza Epperson
Associate Professor
Department of Mathematics
The University of Texas
    at Arlington
Arlington, Texas

Juli K. Dixon
Associate Professor of
    Mathematics Education
University of Central Florida
Orlando, Florida

Janet K. Scheer
Executive Director
Create-A-Vision
Foster City, California

David G. Wright
Professor
Department of Mathematics
Brigham Young University
Provo, Utah

David D. Molina
Program Director, Retired
The Charles A. Dana Center
The University of Texas
    at Austin

Jennie M. Bennett
Mathematics Teacher
Houston Independent
    School District
Houston, Texas

Lynda Luckie
Director, K-12 Mathematics
Gwinnett County Public Schools
Suwanee, Georgia

Angela G. Andrews
Assistant Professor of
    Math Education
National Louis University
Lisle, Illinois

Vicki Newman
Classroom Teacher
McGaugh Elementary School
Los Alamitos Unified
    School District
Seal Beach, California

Barbara Montalto
Mathematics Consultant
Assistant Director
    of Mathematics, Retired
Texas Education Agency
Austin, Texas

Minerva Cordero-Epperson
Associate Professor of
    Mathematics and
Associate Dean of the
    Honors College
The University of Texas
    at Arlington
Arlington, Texas

Program Consultants and Specialists

Michael DiSpezio
Writer and On-Air Host,
    JASON Project
North Falmouth,
    Massachusetts

Valerie Johse
Elementary Math Specialist
Office of Curriculum
    & Instruction
Pearland I.S.D.
Pearland, Texas

Concepion Molina
Southwest Educational
    Development Lab
Austin, Texas

Lydia Song
Program Specialist–Mathematics
Orange County Department
    of Education
Costa Mesa, California

Rebecca Valbuena
Language Development
    Specialist
Stanton Elementary School
Glendora, California

Robin C. Scarcella
Professor and Director
Program of Academic English
    and ESL
University of California,
    Irvine
Irvine, California

Tyrone Howard
Assistant Professor
UCLA Graduate School
    of Education
Information Studies
University of California
    at Los Angeles
Los Angeles, California

Russell Gersten
Director, Instructional
    Research Group
Long Beach, California
Professor Emeritus of
    Special Education
University of Oregon
Eugene, Oregon

Understand Whole Numbers and Operations

Technology

Harcourt Mega Math: Chapter 1, pp. 6, 18; Chapter 2, p. 50; Chapter 3, p. 65; Extra Practice: pp. 24, 56, 80
The Harcourt Learning Site:
www.harcourtschool.com
Multimedia Math Glossary
www.harcourtschool.com/hspmath

THE WORLD ALMANAC FOR KIDS

Multiplication and Division Facts

4 Multiplication and Division Facts 90

5

Algebra: Use Multiplication and Division Facts — 116

MATH ON LOCATION

DVD from **FUTURES** with Chapter Projects and **VOCABULARY POWER** 89

READ Math WORKSHOP 101

WRITE Math WORKSHOP 121

GO ONLINE — Technology

Harcourt Mega Math: Chapter 4, p. 100; Chapter 5, p. 130; Extra Practice: pp. 110, 140
The Harcourt Learning Site: www.harcourtschool.com
Multimedia Math Glossary www.harcourtschool.com/hspmath

THE WORLD ALMANAC FOR KIDS

Money Around the World 146

UNIT 3

Time, Temperature, and Data

8 Interpret and Graph Data 202

MATH ON LOCATION

DVD from FUTURES Channel with Chapter Projects and **VOCABULARY POWER** 149

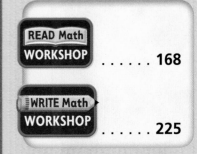

READ Math WORKSHOP 168

WRITE Math WORKSHOP 225

GO ONLINE — Technology

Harcourt Mega Math: Chapter 6, p. 170; Chapter 7, p. 191; Chapter 8, p. 212; Chapter 9, p. 237; Extra Practice: pp. 172, 196, 232
The Harcourt Learning Site: www.harcourtschool.com
Multimedia Math Glossary
www.harcourtschool.com/hspmath

THE WORLD ALMANAC FOR KIDS

Record High Temperatures **238**

Multiply by 1-Digit and 2-Digit Numbers

MATH ON LOCATION

DVD from with FUTURES Channel Chapter Projects and
VOCABULARY POWER 241

READ Math WORKSHOP 257

WRITE Math WORKSHOP 285

GO ONLINE **Technology**

The Harcourt Learning Site:
www.harcourtschool.com
Multimedia Math Glossary
www.harcourtschool.com/hspmath

Space Travel. 300

Divide by 1-Digit and 2-Digit Divisors

MATH ON LOCATION

DVD from **the FUTURES Channel** with Chapter Projects and
VOCABULARY POWER 303

READ Math WORKSHOP 313
WRITE Math WORKSHOP 381

GO ONLINE — Technology

Harcourt Mega Math: Chapter 11, p. 309; Chapter 12, p. 336; Chapter 13, p. 355; Chapter 14, p. 384; Extra Practice: pp. 324, 344, 364, 390
The Harcourt Learning Site: www.harcourtschool.com
Multimedia Math Glossary www.harcourtschool.com/hspmath

WORLD ALMANAC FOR KIDS

Amazing Collectibles . . . 396

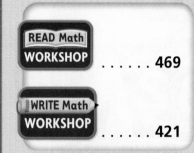

MATH ON LOCATION

DVD from _the_ **FUTURES** Channel
with
Chapter Projects and
**VOCABULARY
POWER** 399

**READ Math
WORKSHOP** 469

**WRITE Math
WORKSHOP** 421

GO ONLINE Technology

Harcourt Mega Math: Chapter
15, pp. 404, 408, 416; Chapter
16, pp. 433, 435; Chapter 17,
pp. 465, 468; Chapter 18,
pp. 489, 491; Extra Practice:
pp. 424, 450, 476, 500
The Harcourt Learning Site:
www.harcourtschool.com
Multimedia Math Glossary
www.harcourtschool.com/
hspmath

THE WORLD ALMANAC FOR KIDS

Cool Kites 506

Geometry

MATH ON LOCATION

DVD from 📽 **Futures** channel with Chapter Projects and **VOCABULARY POWER** 509

READ Math WORKSHOP 529

WRITE Math WORKSHOP 545

GO ONLINE — **Technology**

Harcourt Mega Math: Chapter 19, p. 522; Chapter 20, p. 544; Chapter 21, p. 572; Extra Practice: pp. 534, 562, 590
The Harcourt Learning Site: www.harcourtschool.com Multimedia Math Glossary www.harcourtschool.com/ hspmath

THE WORLD ALMANAC FOR KIDS

Looking at Toys 596

24 Probability   664

Student Handbook

MATH ON LOCATION

DVD from FUTURES channel with Chapter Projects and **VOCABULARY POWER** 599

READ Math **WORKSHOP** 653

WRITE Math **WORKSHOP** 675

GO ONLINE   Technology

Harcourt Mega Math: Chapter 22, p. 616; Chapter 23, pp. 638, 646; Chapter 24, pp. 674, 678, 681; Extra Practice: pp. 626, 654, 686
The Harcourt Learning Site:
www.harcourtschool.com
Multimedia Math Glossary
www.harcourtschool.com/
hspmath

THE WORLD ALMANAC FOR KIDS

Birthday
Rocks 692

TALK, READ, and WRITE
About Math

Mathematics is a language of numbers, words, and symbols.

This year you will learn ways to communicate about math as you **talk**, **read**, and **write** about what you are learning.

The table and the bar graph show the speeds of some of the fastest steel roller coasters in the United States.

Steel Roller Coasters		
Roller Coaster	**Park**	**Speed** (in miles per hour)
Kingda Ka	Six Flags Great Adventure Jackson, New Jersey	128
Top Thrill Dragster	Cedar Point Sandusky, Ohio	120
Superman: The Escape	Six Flags Magic Mountain Valencia, California	100
Millennium Force	Cedar Point Sandusky, Ohio	93
Titan	Six Flags Over Texas Arlington, Texas	85
Phantom's Revenge	Kennywood West Mifflin, Pennsylvania	82

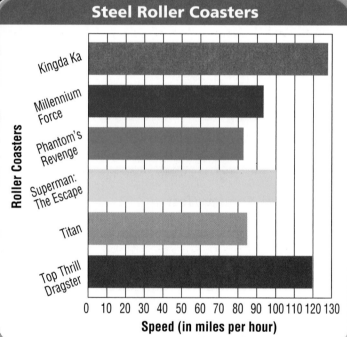

TALK Math

Talk about the table and the bar graph.

1. What information is in the table but is not in the bar graph?

2. What is the difference in the way the data are organized in the table and on the bar graph?

3. What do the numbers along the bottom of the bar graph represent?

4. Why is it important that the spaces between the numbers on the bar graph are the same size?

Read the data in the table and on the bar graph.

4. In what city and state is the fastest roller coaster located?

5. What is the difference in speed of Superman: The Great Escape and Phantom's Revenge?

6. What is the difference in speed of the two roller coasters in Sandusky, Ohio?

7. Which two roller coasters have a difference in speed of 35 miles per hour?

WRITE Math ▶

Write a problem about the bar graph.

This year you will write many problems. When you see **Pose a Problem**, you look at a problem on the page and use it to write your own problem.

> In your problem you can
> - change the numbers or some of the information.
> - exchange the known and unknown information.
> - write an open-ended problem that can have more than one correct answer.

These problems are examples of ways you can pose your own problem. Solve each problem.

Problem How much faster is the Kingda Ka than the Millennium Force?

- **Change the Numbers or Information**
  How much faster is the Millennium Force than the Titan?

- **Exchange the Known and Unknown Information**
  The speed of the Millennium Force is 93 miles per hour. Which roller coaster has a speed that is 27 miles per hour faster than the Millennium Force?

- **Make the Problem Open-Ended**
  Name a roller coaster with a speed between 90 and 125 miles per hour.

Pose a Problem Chose one of the three ways to write a new problem. Use the information in the table and on the bar graph.

Understand Whole Numbers and Operations

Math on Location

A DVD FROM
The Futures Channel

with
Chapter Projects

1 Flowers are packaged by the dozen and prepared for shipment to flower businesses.

2 Flowering plants must be watered and cared for until they are shipped to customers.

3 Florists make arrangements by combining specific numbers of different colors.

VOCABULARY POWER

TALK Math

What math is used in **Math on Location**? How could you find if there are more red flowers or yellow flowers prepared for shipment?

READ Math

REVIEW VOCABULARY You learned the words below last year. How do these words relate to **Math on Location**?

compare to describe whether numbers are equal to, less than, or greater than each other

estimate to find an answer that is close to the exact amount

greater than (>) a symbol used to compare two numbers, with the greater number given first

less than (<) a symbol used to compare two numbers, with the lesser number given first

WRITE Math

Copy and complete the table, using the word pairs shown below. Use what you know about numbers and operations.

addition, subtraction	addition, sum	sum, total
subtraction, count back	regroup, compare	addition, count on
digit, place value	fact family,	compare, order
subtraction, difference	number sentence	odd, even
greater than, less than	sum, difference	

Same	Opposite	Go Together	Not Related
	addition, subtraction		

Technology
Multimedia Math Glossary link at
www.harcourtschool.com/hspmath

1 Understand Place Value

FAST FACT

Lesser flamingos, the smallest type of flamingos, live in Africa. A large flock can eat 35 tons of water plants in one day. Sometimes as many as 1,000,000 flamingos live together in one flock!

Investigate

Many different types of animals live in Africa. How can the animal populations shown in the table be compared?

African Animals	
Animal	**Estimated Population**
Giraffe	110,000
Cheetah	10,500
Elephant	530,000
Flamingo	3,250,000
Lion	35,000
Rhinoceros	14,770

GO ONLINE

Technology
Student pages are available in the Student eBook.

Show What You Know

Check your understanding of important skills needed for success in Chapter 1.

▶ **Place Value Through Thousands**

Find the value of the underlined digit.

1. 8<u>2</u>4
2. 59<u>1</u>
3. <u>3</u>74
4. <u>5</u>,312

5. 1,04<u>3</u>
6. 9,<u>2</u>08
7. <u>2</u>,307
8. 7,<u>8</u>61

▶ **Read and Write Whole Numbers Through Thousands**

Write each number in standard form.

9. thirty-five
10. eight hundred four
11. seven thousand, two hundred twenty-one

12. seventy-eight
13. five hundred sixty-three
14. two thousand, forty-six

15. 600 + 40 + 9
16. 3,000 + 200 + 8
17. 5,000 + 700 + 50 + 1

▶ **Compare Whole Numbers Through Thousands**

Compare. Write <, >, or = for each ●.

18. 203 ● 230
19. 65 ● 56
20. 888 ● 881
21. 98 ● 103

22. 5,339 ● 5,393
23. 422 ● 4,222
24. 3,825 ● 5,283
25. 7,881 ● 7,881

VOCABULARY POWER

CHAPTER VOCABULARY

compare
digit
equal to (=)
expanded form
greater than (>)
less than (<)
millions
not equal to (≠)
order
period
place value
standard form
word form

WARM-UP WORDS

period each group of three digits separated by commas in a multidigit number

standard form a way to write numbers by using digits

expanded form a way to write numbers by showing the value of each digit

word form a way to write numbers by using words

1 Place Value Through Hundred Thousands

OBJECTIVE: Model, read, write, and identify the place value of whole numbers through hundred thousands.

Quick Review

Write in standard form.

1. 6 tens 5 ones
2. 4 hundreds 2 tens
3. 8 tens 9 ones
4. 7 hundreds 7 ones
5. 5 hundreds 3 tens 1 one

Learn

PROBLEM The cost of caring for a pet can really add up. Did you know that the average yearly cost to take care of a medium-sized dog is $1,115?

You can use base-ten blocks to show the cost.

Vocabulary

period

standard form

word form

expanded form

Activity

Materials ■ base-ten blocks

Model 1,115 in more than one way.

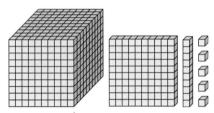

1 thousand 1 hundred 1 ten 5 ones shows 1,115.

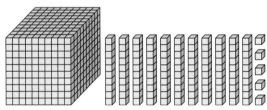

1 thousand 11 tens 5 ones shows 1,115.

Think: 1 hundred = 10 tens

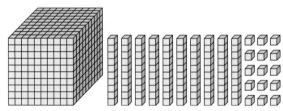

1 thousand 10 tens 15 ones shows 1,115.

Think: 1 ten = 10 ones

• Are these different ways to show 1,115 related? Explain.

Understand Place Value

In 2004, there were 146,692 Labrador retrievers registered with the American Kennel Club. What is the value of the digit 4 in 146,692?

A place-value chart can help you understand the value of each digit in a number. In the base-ten number system, each place value is ten times the place value to the right. The value of a digit depends on its place-value position in the number.

Example Use place value to find the value of a digit.

	PERIOD				
THOUSANDS			**ONES**		
Hundreds	Tens	Ones	Hundreds	Tens	Ones
1	4	6,	6	9	2

1 hundred thousand	4 ten thousands	6 thousands	6 hundreds	9 tens	2 ones
$1 \times 100,000$	$4 \times 10,000$	$6 \times 1,000$	6×100	9×10	2×1
100,000	40,000	6,000	600	90	2

← Multiply the digit by its place value to find the value of each digit.

So, the value of the digit 4 is 40,000.

Each group of three digits separated by commas in a multidigit number is called a **period**. Commas separate the periods. Each period has ones, tens, and hundreds in it. The number 146,692 has two periods, ones and thousands.

You can use place value and period names to read 146,692 and to write 146,692 in different forms.

Standard Form: 146,692

Word Form: one hundred forty-six thousand, six hundred ninety-two

Expanded Form: $100,000 + 40,000 + 6,000 + 600 + 90 + 2$

More Examples

Ⓐ **Standard Form:** 70,186

 Word Form: seventy thousand, one hundred eighty-six

 Expanded Form: $70,000 + 100 + 80 + 6$

Ⓑ **Standard Form:** 306,409

 Word Form: three hundred six thousand, four hundred nine

 Expanded Form: $300,000 + 6,000 + 400 + 9$

ERROR ALERT

When numbers have zeros, you do not need to write or represent the digit 0 in word form or expanded form.

Guided Practice

1. Name the number shown by the model. What are two other ways can you model this number?

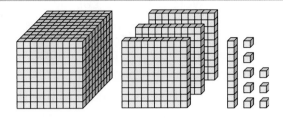

Write each number in two other forms.

☑ 2. four hundred seven thousand, fifty-one

☑ 3. 90,000 + 6,000 + 200 + 80 + 1

4. [TALK Math] Explain how you can use the standard form of a number to write the number in word form.

Independent Practice and Problem Solving

Write each number in two other forms.

5. 70,000 + 4,000 + 50 + 6

6. five hundred thousand, two hundred six

7. 981,416

8. 80,308

Complete.

9. 340,680 = three hundred forty __?__, six hundred eighty = ■ + 40,000 + ■ + 80

10. ■ + 6,000 + 400 + 3 = 56,4■■ = fifty-six thousand, four __?__ three

Write the value of the underlined digit in each number.

11. <u>4</u>35,258

12. 368,<u>1</u>09

13. 5<u>7</u>0,217

14. 129,<u>6</u>34

USE DATA For 15–16, use the table.

15. How many poodles were registered in 2004? Write the number in two other forms.

16. Represent the number of pointers in as many different ways as you can. Use models, pictures, or numbers.

17. ≡**FAST FACT** In 2001, an English mastiff set a world record for heaviest dog, with a weight of 282 pounds. Describe two different ways that you could use base-ten blocks to show this number.

18. [WRITE Math] ▸ **Reasoning** What number is 100 less than the greatest number you can make if you use the digits 2, 3, 4, 5, and 9 exactly once?

19. Cameron wrote this sequence of numbers: 437, 447, 457, 467. What pattern do you see?

Dogs Registered by the American Kennel Club in 2004		
	Breed	**Number Registered**
	Bulldogs	19,396
	Pointers	512
	Poodles	32,671
	Pomeranians	21,269

Extra Practice on page 24, Set A

Learn About) Ways Numbers are Used

You can name numbers in different ways.

The number of dog bones shown can be named as 1 thousand 3 hundreds 1 ten 2 ones or 500 + 500 + 100 + 100 + 100 + 10 + 2.

Examples

A Use numbers and words.

4,100

4 thousands 1 hundred

41 hundreds

410 tens

4,100 ones

B Use numbers and operation signs.

1,247

1,000 + 200 + 40 + 7

500 + 500 + 240 + 7

1,250 − 3

1,300 − 53

Try It

Name each number two ways using numbers and words.

20. 150   **21.** 705   **22.** 479   **23.** 862   **24.** 2,464

Name each number two ways using numbers and operation signs.

25. 308   **26.** 1,305   **27.** 2,300   **28.** 4,550   **29.** 576

Mixed Review and Test Prep

30. Find the next number in this pattern.
(Grade 3)

4, 8, 12, 16, 20, ■

31. Test Prep What is the value of the digit 8 in 382,425?

A 80

B 800

C 8,000

D 80,000

32. What number makes this number sentence true? (Grade 3)

8 + 4 = ■ × 3?

33. Test Prep A movie theater's weekend ticket sales totaled one hundred thousand, forty-six dollars. What is this number in standard form?

A 100,046   **C** 104,006

B 100,064   **D** 140,006

CD ROM **Technology**
Use Harcourt Mega Math, Fraction Action, *Number Line Mine,* Level A.

2 Model Millions

OBJECTIVE: Understand the magnitude of numbers through millions.

Investigate

Materials ■ 10-by-10 grid paper ■ crayons ■ tape

A stack of 1 million one-dollar bills is as tall as a nine-story building. One million is the next counting number after 999,999. One million is written as 1,000,000 in standard form.

A Draw a dot in each box in 1 column of the 10-by-10 grid paper. Each dot represents 1 one-dollar bill. How many one-dollar bills does this grid represent?

B Draw a dot in each box of the grid. How many one-dollar bills does one grid represent when filled?

C Tape your grid paper to other students' grid papers. Write the number of 1 one-dollar bills that are represented by the sheets of grid paper taped together.

- How many sheets of grid paper will you need to represent 1,000 one-dollar bills? 10,000 one-dollar bills? 100,000 one-dollar bills? 1,000,000 one-dollar bills?

Draw Conclusions

You can look for a pattern to find how many sheets of grid paper you will need to show 1,000,000 one-dollar bills. Copy and complete the table.

1. What pattern did you use to complete the table? Explain.

2. **Analysis** How can picturing what a model of 1 million looks like help you better understand the relative size of numbers?

Quick Review

Write the word form of each number.

1. 5,234   2. 72,806
3. 96,041   4. 352,629
5. 842,597

Vocabulary

millions

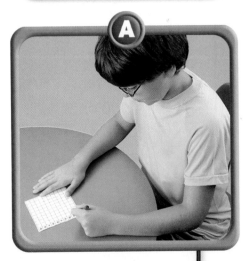

Model Millions	
Total Dollars	**Sheets of Paper**
100	1
1,000	10
10,000	100
100,000	■
1,000,000	■

The period to the left of thousands is **millions**.
One million is equal to 10 hundred thousands.

You can use place value and period names to help
you read numbers in millions.

In 1989, Pablo Picasso's painting entitled *Les Noces de Pierrette*
sold for $51,671,920. Look at the amount paid for the painting
in the place-value chart.

MILLIONS			THOUSANDS			ONES		
Hundreds	Tens	Ones	Hundreds	Tens	Ones	Hundreds	Tens	Ones
	5	1,	6	7	1,	9	2	0

The number 51,671,920 is read as fifty-one million, six
hundred seventy-one thousand, nine hundred twenty.

TALK Math

Would the population of a large country be counted in thousands or millions? Give some examples of things that can be counted in the millions.

Practice

Solve.

1. How many hundreds are in 1,000?

2. How many hundreds are in 10,000?

3. How many thousands are in 100,000?

✓4. How many thousands are in 1,000,000?

**Tell whether the number is large enough to be in the millions
or more. Write *yes* or *no*.**

5. the number of miles from Earth to the sun

✓6. the number of people in your class

7. the number of grains of sand on a beach

8. the number of bees living in a beehive

9. the number of students riding on a school bus

10. the number of people living in the United States

Choose the number in which the digit 7 has the greater value.

11. 7,500,000 or 75,000,000

12. 35,007,000 or 35,070,000

13. 19,070,000 or 700,000

14. 237,100,000 or 71,100,000

15. **WRITE Math** ▶ **Describe** how 10,000 sheets of 10-by-10 grid paper and 1,000 thousands blocks are related.

3 Place Value Through Millions

OBJECTIVE: Read, write, and identify the place value of numbers through millions.

Learn

PROBLEM You can write the number 92,955,628 in standard form, word form, and expanded form.

Example Use place value to write and read numbers in millions.

MILLIONS			THOUSANDS			ONES		
Hundreds	Tens	Ones	Hundreds	Tens	Ones	Hundreds	Tens	Ones
	9	2,	9	5	5,	6	2	8

Standard Form: 92,955,628

Word Form: ninety-two million, nine hundred fifty-five thousand, six hundred twenty-eight

Expanded Form: 90,000,000 + 2,000,000 + 900,000 + 50,000 + 5,000 + 600 + 20 + 8

The distance between the Earth and the sun is about 92,955,628 miles.

More Examples

A **Standard Form:** 5,200,007
Word Form: five million, two hundred thousand, seven
Expanded Form: 5,000,000 + 200,000 + 7

B **Standard Form:** 860,092,170
Word Form: eight hundred sixty million, ninety-two thousand, one hundred seventy
Expanded Form: 800,000,000 + 60,000,000 + 90,000 + 2,000 + 100 + 70

• How do you find the value of the digit 4 in 45,213,073?

Math Idea
You can use place value and period names to read and write numbers in three forms.

Guided Practice

1. How can you use place value and period names to write the number 5,324,904 in word form?

Write each number in two other forms.

2. ninety million, four hundred eight thousand, seventeen

3. 365,009,058

4. ⬭ TALK Math ⬭ Explain how you can use the expanded form of a number to write the number in standard form.

Independent Practice and Problem Solving

Write each number in two other forms.

5. forty-seven million, five hundred eight thousand

6. two hundred three million, forty thousand, six hundred nineteen

7. 60,570,020

8. 400,000,000 + 60,000 + 5,000 + 100

Use the number 63,145,973.

9. Write the name of the period that has the digits 145.

10. Write the name of the period that has the digits 63.

11. Write the digit in the millions place.

12. Write the value of the digit 6.

Find the sum. Then write the answer in standard form.

13. 4 thousands 3 hundreds 2 ones +
5 thousands 2 tens 4 ones

14. 3 ten thousands 4 hundreds 8 tens +
4 ten thousands

USE DATA For 15–16, use the Average Distance from the Sun picture.

Planet	Venus	Mars	Jupiter	Saturn
Distance from the Sun in miles	67,200,000	141,600,000	483,800,000	890,800,000

15. What is the average distance of Saturn from the sun?

16. Which planet has an average distance of four hundred eighty-three million, eight hundred thousand miles from the sun?

17. ⬭ WRITE Math ⬭ ▸ Explain how trading the position of the digit 2 and the digit 4 in 129,304,718 affects the value of the number.

Mixed Review and Test Prep

18. What is 100 more than 45,678? (p. 5)

19. There are 12 inches in 1 foot. How many inches are there in 3 feet? (Grade 3)

20. **Test Prep** What is the value of the digit 7 in 78,423,106?

A 70,000   **C** 7,000,000

B 700,000   **D** 70,000,000

Extra Practice on page 24, Set B

Compare Whole Numbers

OBJECTIVE: Compare numbers through millions using base-ten blocks, number lines, and place value.

Learn

PROBLEM Crystal Palace Cave in Alaska is 429 feet deep. French Creek Cave in Montana is 434 feet deep. Which is deeper, Crystal Palace Cave or French Creek Cave?

Example 1 Use base-ten blocks.

To find which cave is deeper, compare 429 and 434.

Compare the values of the blocks in each place-value position from left to right. Keep comparing the blocks until the values are different.

	Hundreds	Tens	Ones

Model 429.

Model 434.

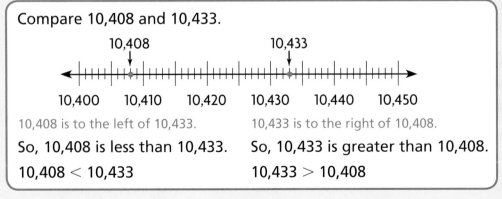

There are the same number of hundreds.

3 tens is greater than 2 tens.

434 > 429

So, French Creek Cave is deeper than Crystal Palace Cave.

Example 2 Use a number line.

Compare 10,408 and 10,433.

10,408   10,433

10,400   10,410   10,420   10,430   10,440   10,450

10,408 is to the left of 10,433.   10,433 is to the right of 10,408.

So, 10,408 is less than 10,433.   So, 10,433 is greater than 10,408.

10,408 < 10,433   10,433 > 10,408

Example 3 Use a place-value chart.

Mammoth Cave National Park in Kentucky had 1,898,822 visitors in 2002 and 1,888,126 visitors in 2004. In which year were there more visitors?

Compare 1,898,822 and 1,888,126.

MILLIONS			THOUSANDS			ONES		
Hundreds	Tens	Ones	Hundreds	Tens	Ones	Hundreds	Tens	Ones
		1,	8	9	8,	8	2	2
		1,	8	8	8,	1	2	6

Step 1

Start with the first place on the left. Compare the millions.

1,898,822
↓   1 = 1
1,888,126

There are the same number of millions.

Step 2

Compare the hundred thousands.

1,898,822
↓   8 = 8
1,888,126

There are the same number of hundred thousands.

Step 3

Compare the ten thousands.

1,898,822
↓   9 > 8
1,888,126

9 ten thousands are greater than 8 ten thousands.
So, 1,898,822 > 1,888,126.

> **Math Idea**
> To compare numbers, start at the left and compare the digits in each place-value position until the digits differ.

So, there were more visitors in 2002.

Example 4 Compare different numbers of digits.

Compare 21,623,785 and 103,317,256. Write <, >, or =.

  21,623,785
↑   0 < 1
103,317,256

So, 21,623,785 < 103,317,256.

Example 5 Compare to make a relationship true.

What numbers make this relationship true?

26■ ≠ 265   **Think:** What digits are not equal to 5?

Replace ■ with 0, 1, 2, 3, 4, 6, 7, 8, or 9.

260, 261, 262, 263, 264, 266, 267, 268, and 269 are **not equal to** 265.

So, the digits 0, 1, 2, 3, 4, 6, 7, 8, or 9 make the relationship true.

 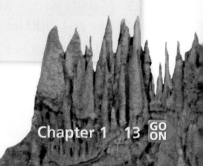

1. Use the base-ten blocks to compare 324 and 332. Write the lesser number.

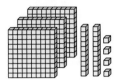 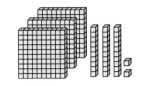

2. Use the number line to compare 5,327 and 5,341. Write the greater number.

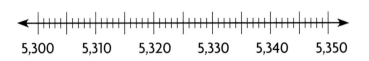

5,300   5,310   5,320   5,330   5,340   5,350

Compare. Write <, >, or = for each ●.

3. 45,595 ● 45,585   ✓ 4. $631,328 ● $640,009   ✓ 5. 528,807,414 ● 5,699,001

6. [TALK Math] Explain how to compare 79,308 and 79,354.

Independent Practice and Problem Solving

Use the number line to compare. Write the lesser number.

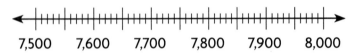

7,500   7,600   7,700   7,800   7,900   8,000

7. 7,710 or 7,680   8. 7,800 or 7,680   9. 7,584 or 7,616

Compare. Write <, >, or = for each ●.

10. $2,212 ● $2,600   11. 41,190 ● 41,090   12. 63,803 ● 6,409

13. 88,304 ● 88,304   14. $5,249,116 ● $41,090   15. 439,064 ● 440,000,438

16. 8,279,314 ● 8,279,299   17. 975,408 ● 912,005,300   18. 7,512,720 ● 8,510,001

★ **Algebra** Find all of the digits that can replace each ■.

19. 420 ≠ 4■0   20. 7,486 ≠ 7,48■   21. 3,■15 ≠ 3,129

USE DATA For 22–24, use the table.

22. Which ocean trench is deeper, Tonga or Marianas?

23. Which ocean trench has a depth less than 34,000 feet?

24. **Pose a Problem** Write a problem that compares two numbers from the Deepest Ocean Trenches table.

25. [WRITE Math] **Reasoning** Which is greater, the number that is 1,000 less than 16,892 or the number that is 10,000 less than 26,892? **Explain** how you know.

Deepest Ocean Trenches

Trench	Depth (in feet)
Bonin	32,786
Marianas	35,837
Philippine	34,436
Tonga	35,430

Learn About) Using Benchmarks to Estimate

A **benchmark** is a known number of things that helps you understand the size or amount of a different number of things.

Example

Use the benchmark to choose the best estimate for the number of bats it would take to cover the whole wall of the cave.

To cover the wall, it would take about 4 times the benchmark.

$10 + 10 + 10 + 10$, or $4 \times 10 = 40$

The most reasonable estimate for the number of bats it would take to cover the whole wall is 40 bats.

• Will your estimate be less than, more than, or the same amount as the actual number? Explain.

10 bats
Benchmark

10, 20, 30, or 40

Try It

Use the benchmark to choose the best estimate for each amount.

26.
1,000 worms
Benchmark
500, 750, 1,000, or 1,500

27.
20 beetles
Benchmark
10, 20, 60, or 120

28.
200 spiders
Benchmark
50, 100, 200, or 400

Mixed Review and Test Prep

29. Find the elapsed time. (Grade 3)
start: 4:10 P.M.
end: 6:40 P.M.

30. Test Prep Which number is greatest?

A 549,300

B 4,004,030

C 5,490,003

D 594,030

31. Name the customary unit you would use to measure the length of a butterfly.
(Grade 3)

32. Test Prep During a canned food drive, Ms. Ling's class set a goal to collect 1,200 cans each day. After 3 days they had collected 1,225 cans, 1,050 cans, and 1,243 cans. Which total was less than their daily goal?

A 1,243 cans   C 1,200 cans

B 1,225 cans   D 1,050 cans

LESSON 5

Order Whole Numbers

OBJECTIVE: Order numbers through millions using base-ten blocks, number lines, and place value.

Quick Review

Compare. Write <, >, or = for each ●.

1. 5,322 ● 5,330
2. 32,086 ● 9,002
3. 75,461 ● 75,461
4. 284,500 ● 285,111
5. 3,284,500 ● 662,796

Learn

PROBLEM Did you know that the giant sequoia is the world's largest kind of tree? Sequoia National Park in California is home to many of the largest sequoias. Three of the largest trees in the park are 275 feet tall, 241 feet tall, and 255 feet tall. Order the heights of the trees from greatest to least.

Example 1   Use base-ten blocks.

Order 275, 241, and 255 from greatest to least.

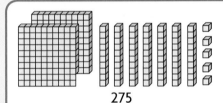

| 275 | 241 | 255 |

Step 1	**Step 2**	**Step 3**
Compare the hundreds. There are the same number of hundreds.	Compare the tens. The model for 275 has the most tens, so it is the greatest number.	Compare the tens in 241 and 255. The model for 255 has more tens, so it is greater than 241.

So, from greatest to least, the numbers are 275, 255, 241.

So, the heights of the trees, in order from greatest to least, are 275 feet, 255 feet, and 241 feet.

Example 2   Use a number line.

Order 20,650; 21,150; and 20,890 from greatest to least.

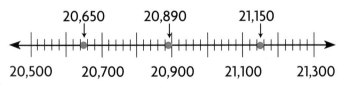

So, the numbers, in order from greatest to least, are 21,150; 20,890; and 20,650.

GENERAL SHERMAN

16

Example 3 Use place value.

The table shows the number of visitors to Sequoia National Park during three years.

You can order the number of visitors for each year by using a place-value chart.

Order 1,418,519; 1,552,258; and 1,520,835 from least to greatest.

Visitors to Sequoia National Park	
Year	Number of Visitors
2002	1,418,519
2003	1,552,258
2004	1,520,835

Math Idea

When you compare and order numbers, you must begin comparing at the greatest place-value position.

MILLIONS			THOUSANDS			ONES		
Hundreds	Tens	Ones	Hundreds	Tens	Ones	Hundreds	Tens	Ones
		1,	4	1	8,	5	1	9
		1,	5	5	2,	2	5	8
		1,	5	2	0,	8	3	5

Step 1

Start with the first place on the left. Compare the millions.

1,418,519
↓
1,552,258   1 = 1
↓
1,520,835

There are the same number of millions.

Step 2

Compare the hundred thousands.

1,418,519
↓
1,552,258   4 < 5
↓
1,520,835

Since 4 < 5, 1,418,519 is the least of the three numbers.

Step 3

Compare the ten thousands in the other two numbers.

1,552,258
↓   5 > 2
1,520,835

Since 5 > 2, 1,552,258 is greater than 1,520,835.

1,418,519 < 1,520,835 < 1,552,258

So, the number of visitors in order from least to greatest, is 1,418,519; 1,520,835; and 1,552, 258.

• Explain how you would order 102,535,458; 105,236,030; and 120,539,078 from greatest to least.

Guided Practice

1. Use the base-ten blocks to order 1,027; 1,105; and 1,041 from least to greatest.

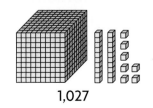
1,027

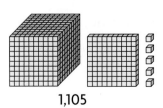
1,105

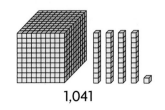
1,041

Solve.

2. Use the number line to order 4,788; 4,793; and 4,784 from least to greatest.

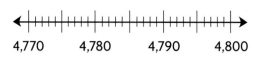

4,770   4,780   4,790   4,800

Write the numbers in order from least to greatest.

✓ 3. $55,997; $57,000; $56,038

✓ 4. 787,925; 1,056,000; 789,100

5. **TALK Math** **Explain** how knowing the number of digits in each number can help you order a set of whole numbers.

Independent Practice and Problem Solving

Write the numbers in order from greatest to least.

6. 8,523; 8,538; 8,519

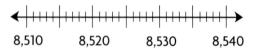

8,510   8,520   8,530   8,540

7. 43,050; 42,938; 42,951

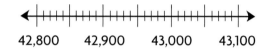

42,800   42,900   43,000   43,100

8. $623,096; $68,999; $621,960

9. 3,452,805; 3,542,805; 542,905

10. 7,122,890; 700,122,089; 70,122,098

11. $939,822; $9,398,820; $9,398,802

12. 430,000,459; 43,000,549; 403,000,456

13. 8,778; 870,780; 878,070; 807,870

⭐ **Algebra** **Write all of the digits that can replace each ■.**

14. $567 < 5\blacksquare5 < 582$

15. $3,408 < 3,\blacksquare30 < 3,540$

16. $52,780 > 5\blacksquare,790 > 50,120$

17. $4,464,545 > 4,4\blacksquare3,535 > 4,443,550$

USE DATA **For 18–20, use the map of California.**

18. Name the national parks in order from least number of acres to greatest number of acres.

19. Which park has less than 500,000 acres?

20. In a comparison of the number of acres in Yosemite National Park and in Joshua Tree National Park, in which place do the digits first differ?

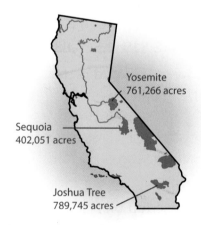

Yosemite 761,266 acres

Sequoia 402,051 acres

Joshua Tree 789,745 acres

21. **Reasoning** A number has 4 different odd digits. The difference between the greatest digit and the least digit is 6. The number is greater than 2,000 and less than 3,160. What is the number?

22. **WRITE Math** ▸ **What's the Question?** There are three numbers: 643,251; 633,512; and 633,393. The answer is 633,393.

Technology
Use Harcourt Mega Math, Fraction Action, *Number Line Mine*, Level B.

Numbers are used in many ways.

Examples

Counting	Measuring	Locating	Labeling
There are 2,256 books.	The room is 14 feet by 12 feet.	Apartment 605 is on the sixth floor.	The number on his soccer jersey is 17.

Try It

Tell which way each number is used.

23. The lake is 127 feet deep.

24. Ling lives in apartment 533.

25. Max wears the number 34 on his baseball uniform.

26. There were 53,000 fans at a football game.

27. Sam's family drove 345 miles during one day of their vacation.

28. Eliza's address is 10873 Woodbury Lane.

Mixed Review and Test Prep

29. What is a name for a polygon with exactly 4 sides? (Grade 3)

30. **Test Prep** Which shows the numbers in order from least to greatest?

    A 102,397; 102,395; 102,359

    B 216,001; 216,101; 216,010

    C 422,956; 422,596; 422,298

    D 575,029; 575,209; 575,290

31. Ellie bought a T-shirt for $8.95. She paid with a $10 bill. How much change did she receive? (Grade 3)

32. **Test Prep** Movie theater ticket sales for three days this week were $4,235; $6,478; and $5,049. Which amount is the greatest?

Problem Solving Workshop
Strategy: Use Logical Reasoning

OBJECTIVE: Solve problems by using the strategy *use logical reasoning*.

Learn the Strategy

Sometimes a problem has clues that help you find the solution.
Organizing the clues can help you use logical reasoning to draw
conclusions and solve the problem.

Sometimes, the clues can be organized in a list.

Kari, Nora, and June are the only runners
in a race. June finishes before Nora. Kari
is not last. June is not first.

In what position did each runner finish?

1st	2ND	3rd
Kari	~~Kari~~	~~Kari~~
~~Nora~~	~~Nora~~	Nora
~~June~~	June	~~June~~

Sometimes, the clues can be organized in a Venn diagram.

Ben is thinking of a number from 45 to 60.
The sum of the digits is greater than 10.
The product of the digits is less than 30.

What number is Ben thinking of?

Sum of Digits >10   Product of Digits <30

58 59 | 47 | 53 52
48 49 | | 60 54
56 57 | | 51 55
| | 50 46
| | 45

Sometimes, the clues can be organized in a table.

Max, Anya, and Troy each have a different
kind of pet. The pets are a dog, a cat, and a
fish. Troy's pet does not bark or swim. Anya
does not have a dog.

What pet does each person have?

	Dog	Cat	Fish
Max	Yes	No	No
Anya	No	No	Yes
Troy	No	Yes	No

TALK Math

Look at the third problem.
Which boxes can be filled
in using only the clue about
Troy's pet? Explain.

Use the Strategy

PROBLEM Baseball games were played on Friday, Saturday, and Sunday. The number of people who attended were 32,431; 44,462; and 44,064. The greatest number of people attended Saturday's game. Fewer than 40,000 people attended Sunday's game. How many people attended each day?

Read to Understand

Reading Skill

• Use a graphic aid to organize the clues.
• What information is given?

Plan

• **What strategy can you use to solve the problem?**
  You can use logical reasoning.

Solve

• **How can you use the strategy to solve the problem?**
  Look at one clue at a time. Make a table to record the information you know, and draw conclusions.

	32,431	44,462	44,064
Friday			
Saturday			
Sunday			

The greatest number of people went to Saturday's game. The greatest number in the problem is 44,462. So, write *yes* in Saturday's row for 44,462. Write *no* in the rest of the row for Saturday and the rest of the column for 44,462.

	32,431	44,462	44,064
Friday		no	
Saturday	no	yes	no
Sunday		no	

Fewer than 40,000 people went to Sunday's game. The only number that is less than 40,000 is 32,431. Write *yes* in Sunday's row for 32,431 and *no* in the rest of that row and column.

That leaves one number for Friday, 44,064. Write *yes* in the table to show this.

	32,431	44,462	44,064
Friday	no	no	yes
Saturday	no	yes	no
Sunday	yes	no	no

So, 44,064 people went to Friday's game; 44,462 people went to Saturday's game; and 32,431 people went to Sunday's game.

Check

• **Look back at the problem. Do your work and your answer make sense? Explain.**

Guided Problem Solving

1. Ed, Nick, Sandra, and Ty collect baseball cards. Ed has fewer than 500 cards. Sandra has more than 700 cards. Nick has more cards than Sandra. How many baseball cards does each person have?

   First, make a table to organize the information given in the problem.

   Then, use the information given in the problem to complete the table.

   Finally, use logical reasoning to answer the question.

	447	568	703	764
Ed	Yes	No	No	No
Nick	No			
Sandra	No			
Ty	No			

2. Leena, Theo, Chris, Ann, and Bob are waiting in line for hockey tickets. Leena is not first or last. Theo is behind Leena but is not last. Chris is in front of Leena. Ann is behind Bob. In what order are they standing in line?

3. **What if** a basketball team has a score that is a 2-digit number. The sum of the digits is 8. The difference between the digits is 2. The tens digit is less than the ones digit. What is the score?

Problem Solving Strategy Practice

Use logical reasoning to solve.

4. Copy and complete the magic square. Each row and column should have a sum of 12.

2	■	7
■	■	0
■	1	■

5. Look at the record crowds list. Richard forgot to write the name of the sport for each crowd. Use these clues to decide what the record crowd is for each sport.

   • Football did not have the smallest record crowd.

   • Soccer's record crowd is greater than 150,000 people.

   Record Crowds at a Single Football Game, Baseball Game, and Soccer Game

   199,854 people
   103,985 people
   92,706 people

6. **WRITE Math** ▶ Will, Rachel, Owen, and Kara are standing in line to enter the stadium to watch a track meet. Will is in front of Owen. Rachel is first. Kara is after Rachel. In what order are they standing in line? **Explain.**

Mixed Strategy Practice

USE DATA For 7–9, use the information about sports collectors' items shown in the art.

7. Mr. Clay, Mr. Juarez, and Ms. Michaels buy the Annika Sorenstam golf ball, the Tom Brady Super Bowl football, and the Larry Bird signed basketball. Mr. Juarez spends less than $300. Mr. Clay spends more than Ms. Michaels does. Which item does each person buy?

8. **Pose a Problem** Look back at Problem 7. Change the items that Mr. Clay wants to buy.

9. **Open-Ended** Mr. Krauss bought a Sandy Koufax baseball card for $135. He used $20-bills, $10-bills, and $5-bills to make exactly $135. The total number of bills that Mr. Krauss used is fewer than 12. What combination of bills might Mr. Krauss have used?

10. Tina saves money to buy a baseball card that costs $30. After 2 weeks, she has $10. After 3 weeks, she has $15. After 4 weeks, she has $20. How long do you think it will take her to save $30?

Choose a STRATEGY

Draw a Diagram or Picture
Make a Model or Act It Out
Make an Organized List
Find a Pattern
Make a Table or Graph
Predict and Test
Work Backward
Solve a Simpler Problem
Write an Equation
Use Logical Reasoning

Babe Ruth signed baseball
Price: $38,157

Wayne Gretzky hockey puck
Price: $494

Mickey Mantle game bat
Price: $37,604

Annika Sorenstam golf ball
Price: $287

Larry Bird signed basketball
Price: $326

Tom Brady signed Super Bowl XXIX football
Price: $499

CHALLENGE YOURSELF

More young people than ever before are playing sports. For example, in 2005, an average of 17,500,000 young people were playing soccer, 204,000 were playing lacrosse, and 2,200,000 young people were playing baseball.

11. Mariah plays lacrosse. Compared to soccer and baseball, is she part of a group that has the most young people participating or the least?

12. Al is writing down the number of young people who participate in each sport. He wrote down the number for football incorrectly. He knows that the number is less than the numbers for soccer and baseball, but more than the number for lacrosse. Could the number be 200,600 or 260,000? **Explain** how you know.

Extra Practice

Set A Write each number in two other forms. (pp. 4–7)

1. 700,000 + 3,000 + 600 + 4

2. 27,683

3. seventy-six thousand, four hundred thirty-two

4. eight hundred ninety-one thousand, two hundred fifty

5. 116,508,906

6. 60,000 + 800 + 90

Set B Use the number 827,916,401. (pp. 10–11)

1. Write the name of the period that has the digits 827.

2. Write the name of the period that has the digits 916.

3. Write the digit in the ten millions place.

4. Write the digit in the thousands place.

5. Write the value of the digit 8.

6. Write the value of the digit 9.

Set C Compare. Write <, >, or = for each ●. (pp. 12–15)

1. 1,409 ● 1,389

2. 6,794 ● 8,005

3. $56,006 ● $56,006

4. 37,106 ● 37,008

5. $10,006 ● $2,789

6. 6,807,043 ● 6,870,034

7. 4,345,119 ● 535,119

8. 88,416 ● 101,871,415

9. 2,124,156 ● 1,124,156

10. Doug's family drove 768 miles on Saturday and 524 miles on Sunday. On which day did they drive farther?

11. During the school book fair, 1,123 books were sold the first week and 1,032 books were sold the second week. During which week were fewer books sold?

Set D Write the numbers in order from least to greatest. (pp. 16–19)

1. 48,004; 48,040; 40,804

2. $30,004; $3,074; $3,704

3. $522,818; $55,945; $600,961

4. 437,408; 428,509; 420,320

5. 221,829,459; 283,000; 2,820,999

6. 5,408,517; 5,460,500; 4,558,590

7. Sales at Toy Mart for three days this week were $2,571; $1,897; and $3,342. Which amount is the greatest?

8. Theater attendance for performances on Friday was 16,207 people, for Saturday was 28,771 people, and for Sunday was 16,270 people. On which day was attendance the least?

Technology
Use Harcourt Mega Math, The Number Games, *Number Line Mine*, Levels A, B.

Climb the Math Mountain

Who's Climbing
2 or 3 players

Get Your Climbing Gear!
- Number cards (0–9, three of each)
- Coins (a different kind of coin for each player)
- Paper

the Top

Camp 7

Camp 5

Camp 6

Camp 4

Camp 3

Camp 2

Camp 1

Start Climbing!

■ Each player draws 6 horizontal lines on a sheet of paper. Each line needs to be long enough to fit a number card on it.

■ Each player selects a different kind of coin and places the coin on CAMP 1. Players shuffle the number cards and place them facedown in a stack.

■ The object of the game is to make the greatest number. Players take turns drawing a card and placing it on one of his or her 6 lines until each player has made a 6-digit number.

■ Once a player has placed a number card on a line, it cannot be moved.

■ The player with the greatest number moves his or her coin up the mountain to the next camp. If the numbers are the same, each player moves to the next camp.

■ Players return the number cards to the stack, shuffle them, and repeat the steps to play another round.

■ The first player to reach CAMP 7 wins.

Numbers in Other Cultures

Numeration Systems

Our numeration system uses Arabic numerals, or digits 0–9, and is based on groupings of ten. Some ancient cultures had numeration systems that used other numerals or symbols to represent numbers.

The table below compares Arabic, Roman, and Egyptian numerals.

Arabic	0	1	2	3	4	5	6	7	8	9	10	50	100	500	1000
Roman		I	II	III	IV	V	VI	VII	VIII	IX	X	L	C	D	M
Egyptian		I	II	III	IIII	IIIII	IIIIII	IIIIIII	IIIIIIII	IIIIIIIII	∩		℮		𓆼

To write Roman numerals as Arabic numerals:

- Add if the values of the symbols are the same or if they decrease from left to right. A symbol cannot repeat more than 3 times.
- Subtract if a symbol's value is less than the value of the symbol to its right.

Examples

A **Write CXIII in Arabic numerals.**

Think: C represents 100, X represents 10, and each I represents 1.

So, CXIII is 100 + 10 + 1 + 1 + 1, or 113.

B **Write MCD in Arabic numerals.**

Think: M represents 1,000, C represents 100, and D represents 500.

Since C < D, CD is 500 − 100, or 400.
So, MCD is 1,000 + 400, or 1,400.

To write Egyptian numerals as Arabic numerals: Find the sum of the symbols.

C **Write** 𓆼℮℮III **in Arabic numerals.**

Think: 𓆼 represents 1,000, ℮ represents 100, and I represents 1.

So, 𓆼℮℮III is 1,000 + 100 + 100 + 1 + 1 + 1, or 1,203.

D **Write** 𓆼𓆼∩∩∩ **in Arabic numerals.**

Think: 𓆼 represents 1,000, and ∩ represents 10.

So, 𓆼𓆼∩∩∩ is 1,000 + 1,000 + 10 + 10 + 10 + 10 + 10, or 2,060.

Try It

Write Roman numerals as Arabic numerals.

1. LXXXVIII
2. CCXCV
3. MCMXIV
4. MMDCIX

Write Egyptian numerals as Arabic numerals.

5. ∩IIII

6. ℮℮℮∩∩IIIIII

7. ℮℮℮℮ ∩∩ IIII

8. 𓆼𓆼℮℮∩∩∩

9. **WRITE Math** ▶ **Explain** the advantages in writing numbers using the Arabic numeration system compared with using the Roman and Egyptian numeration systems.

Chapter 1 Review/Test

Check Vocabulary and Concepts

Choose the best term from the box.

VOCABULARY
expanded form
million
period

1. One __?__ is equal to 10 hundred thousands. (p. 9)

2. In 549,167,001 the digits 1, 6, and 7 are in the same __?__. (p. 5)

Check Skills

Write each number in two other forms. (pp. 4–7, 10–11)

3. two hundred thirty-four thousand, one hundred forty-six

4. 78,091

5. 30,000,000 + 600,000 + 8,000 + 500 + 7

6. fifty-three million, seven hundred thousand, eighty

7. 702,655

8. 1,000,000 + 40,000 + 1,000 + 30

Write the value of the underlined digit in each number. (pp. 4–7)

9. 90,6̲59   10. 5̲01,462   11. 4,7̲15,001   12. 804̲,183,712   13. 3̲42,500,654

Compare. Write <, >, or = for each ●. (pp. 12–15)

14. 27,985 ● 28,064   15. 523,406 ● 523,406   16. 3,416,125 ● 3,408,926

Write numbers in order from least to greatest. (pp. 16–19)

17. 207,409; 270,210,009; 27,420

18. 7,029,400; 6,258,414; 6,285,484

Check Problem Solving

Solve. (pp. 20–23)

19. George is thinking of a number between 70 and 90. The sum of the digits is less than 12. The product of the digits is greater than 25. What is George's number?

20. **WRITE Math ▶** Matt and his 3 friends played an electronic game. Their scores are shown at the right. Tina had more than 10,000 points. Rosa had more points than Tina. Sam had less than 5,000 points. How many points did each friend have? **Show** a table or an organized list that supports your solution.

PLAYER A..........8,450

PLAYER B..........10,320

PLAYER C..........11,080

PLAYER D..........4,900

Standardized Test Prep
Chapter 1

Number and Operations

1. In 2002, the estimated number of cats in the United States was seventy-six million, four hundred thirty thousand. What is this number in standard form? (p. 10)

   A 76,430

   B 76,000,430

   C 76,430,000

   D 760,430,000

Test Tip **Understand the problem.**

See Item 2. Make sure you understand what the problem asks. Item 2 asks you to find a set of numbers that is in order from greatest to least. So, a list that is in order from least to greatest would be incorrect.

2. Which set of numbers is in order from greatest to least? (p. 16)

   A 736,849; 739,489; 1,725,089

   B 1,725,089; 736,849; 739,489

   C 1,725,089; 739,489; 736,849

   D 739,489; 736,849; 1,725,089

3. Which of the following represents the number 305,082? (p. 4)

   A $300,000 + 50,000 + 800 + 2$

   B $300,000 + 50,000 + 80 + 2$

   C $30,000 + 5,000 + 800 + 2$

   D $300,000 + 5,000 + 80 + 2$

4. **WRITE Math** ▶ Wendy says that the number 235,340 is exactly 1,000 less than the number 245,340. Do you agree? **Explain** how you know. (p. 4)

Algebraic Reasoning

5. The table below shows the number of players needed to make a certain number of volleyball teams.

Volleyball				
Number of Teams	1	2	3	4
Number of Players	6	12	18	24

   How many players are needed to make 8 volleyball teams? (Grade 3)

   A 6

   B 32

   C 36

   D 48

6. Ms. Gomez bought 24 pens. The pens came in 3 packages with the same number of pens in each. Which number sentence shows how to find the number of pens in each package? (Grade 3)

   A $24 - 3 = \blacksquare$

   B $24 \div 3 = \blacksquare$

   C $24 + 3 = \blacksquare$

   D $24 \times 3 = \blacksquare$

7. What symbol goes in the box to make this number sentence true? (Grade 3)

   $$4 \ \blacksquare \ 7 = 28$$

   A $\times$

   B $\div$

   C $+$

   D $-$

8. **WRITE Math** ▶ **Explain** how you can find the number that makes this number sentence true. (Grade 3)

   $$\blacksquare - 5 = 15$$

Geometry

9. Which of these is a pentagon? (Grade 3)

A

B

C

D

10. What is the area of this figure? (Grade 3)

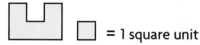 = 1 square unit

A 3 square units

B 4 square units

C 5 square units

D 6 square units

11. ▐WRITE Math▶ Raul says that an isosceles triangle can also be a right triangle. Do you agree? **Explain** your answer. (Grade 3)

Data Analysis and Probability

12. The bar graph shows the number of books Ed read during the past two months.

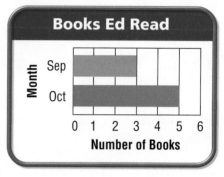

How many books did Ed read in the two months altogether? (Grade 3)

A 5   **C** 15

B 8   **D** 20

13. Look at the tally table.

Spinner Experiment	
Outcome	**Tally**
Red	|||
Yellow	||||
Blue	||||| ||||

In how many spins did the pointer not stop on blue? (Grade 3)

A 3   **C** 7

B 4   **D** 9

14. ▐WRITE Math▶ A bag has 3 yellow marbles, 4 red marbles, and 2 blue marbles, all of equal size. Which term best describes the probability of pulling a blue marble— *certain, likely, unlikely,* or *impossible?* **Explain** your answer. (Grade 3)

2 Add and Subtract Whole Numbers

Investigate

Every day, people visit the Statue of Liberty by taking ferries from New York City and Liberty Park, New Jersey. Use the data in the bar graph to write a daily tourist report. Use subtraction in your report to compare the number of passengers riding the different ferries.

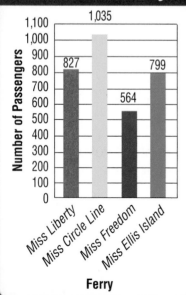

Ferries to the Statue of Liberty

Number of Passengers — Ferry:
Miss Liberty: 827
Miss Circle Line: 1,035
Miss Freedom: 564
Miss Ellis Island: 799

FAST FACT

The height of the Statue of Liberty from the ground to the tip of the torch is just over 305 feet. The index finger of the Statue of Liberty is 8 feet long.

GO ONLINE

Technology
Student pages are available in the Student eBook.

Show What You Know

Check your understanding of important skills needed for success in Chapter 2.

▶ Regroup Tens as Hundreds

Regroup. Write the missing numbers.

1.
12 tens = ■ hundred ■ tens

2.
23 tens = ■ hundreds ■ tens

3. 7 tens ■ ones = 8 tens 3 ones

4. ■ tens 28 ones = 6 tens 8 ones

▶ Regroup Hundreds as Tens

Regroup. Write the missing numbers.

5.
2 hundreds = ■ tens

6.
3 hundreds = ■ tens

7.
1 hundred 1 ten = ■ tens

▶ Two-Digit Addition and Subtraction

Find the sum or difference.

8. 29
   $+57$

9. 31
   $+49$

10. 87
    -28

11. 52
    $+36$

12. 73
    -24

13. 61
    -40

VOCABULARY POWER

CHAPTER VOCABULARY	WARM-UP WORDS
compatible numbers	**fact family** a set of related addition and su▯ equations
difference	
estimate	**inverse operations** Operation▯ Addition and subtraction a▯
fact family	
front-end estimation	**round** to replace a nu▯
inverse operations	tells about how many o▯
round	
sum	

Gu▯
1. Kei▯
17 p▯
and co▯
solve th▯

ALGEBRA
Relate Addition and Subtraction

OBJECTIVE: Use the inverse relationship between addition and subtraction to solve problems.

Quick Review

1. $9 + 4 = \blacksquare$
2. $12 - 6 = \blacksquare$
3. $7 + 8 = \blacksquare$
4. $11 - 4 = \blacksquare$
5. $5 + 8 = \blacksquare$

Vocabulary

inverse operations

fact family

Learn

PROBLEM Justin can do 8 pull-ups in a row. His older brother Marcus can do 15 pull-ups in a row. How many more pull-ups can Marcus do than Justin?

Addition and subtraction are opposites, or **inverse operations**. One operation undoes the other. A set of related addition and subtraction sentences using the same numbers is a **fact family**.

Example Use the inverse operation and a related fact.

Subtract. $15 - 8 = \blacksquare$

> Think: $8 + \blacksquare = 15$
> Use a fact family to solve the problem.
> $8 + 7 = 15$, so $15 - 8 = 7$.

Math Idea

You can use inverse operations and related facts to check answers to problems.

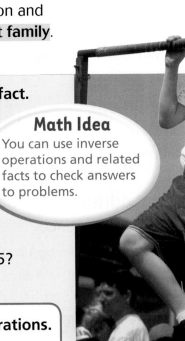

So, Marcus can do 7 more pull-ups than Justin.

• What are the facts in the fact family for 7, 8, and 15?

More Examples Find the missing number.

A Use related facts.

$13 - \blacksquare = 4$

Think: $13 - 4 = \blacksquare$

$13 - 4 = 9$, so $13 - 9 = 4$.

B Use inverse operations.

$\blacksquare - 5 = 6$

Think: $5 + 6 = \blacksquare$

$5 + 6 = 11$, so $11 - 5 = 6$.

• What operation can you use to solve the problem $\blacksquare + 8 = 12$? Explain.

ided Practice

...sha did 8 more push-ups than Tara did. Keisha did ...ush-ups. How many push-ups did Tara do? Copy ...mplete the related addition fact. Then use it to ...e problem.

$17 - 8 = \blacksquare$

$8 + \blacksquare = 17$

Check your understanding of important skills
needed for success in Chapter 2.

▶ **Regroup Tens as Hundreds**

Regroup. Write the missing numbers.

1.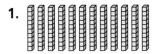

12 tens = ■ hundred ■ tens

2.

23 tens = ■ hundreds ■ tens

3. 7 tens ■ ones = 8 tens 3 ones

4. ■ tens 28 ones = 6 tens 8 ones

▶ **Regroup Hundreds as Tens**

Regroup. Write the missing numbers.

5.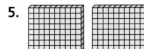

2 hundreds = ■ tens

6.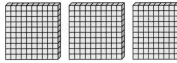

3 hundreds = ■ tens

7.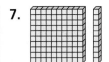

1 hundred 1 ten = ■ tens

▶ **Two-Digit Addition and Subtraction**

Find the sum or difference.

8.	9.	10.	11.	12.	13.
29 +57	31 +49	87 −28	52 +36	73 −24	61 −40

VOCABULARY POWER

CHAPTER VOCABULARY

compatible numbers
difference
estimate
fact family
front-end estimation
inverse operations
round
sum

WARM-UP WORDS

fact family a set of related addition and subtraction equations

inverse operations Operations that undo each other. Addition and subtraction are inverse operations.

round to replace a number with another number that tells about how many or how much

ALGEBRA

Relate Addition and Subtraction

OBJECTIVE: Use the inverse relationship between addition and subtraction to solve problems.

Quick Review

1. $9 + 4 = \blacksquare$
2. $12 - 6 = \blacksquare$
3. $7 + 8 = \blacksquare$
4. $11 - 4 = \blacksquare$
5. $5 + 8 = \blacksquare$

Vocabulary

inverse operations

fact family

Learn

PROBLEM Justin can do 8 pull-ups in a row. His older brother Marcus can do 15 pull-ups in a row. How many more pull-ups can Marcus do than Justin?

Addition and subtraction are opposites, or **inverse operations**. One operation undoes the other. A set of related addition and subtraction sentences using the same numbers is a **fact family**.

Example Use the inverse operation and a related fact.

Subtract. $15 - 8 = \blacksquare$

> Think: $8 + \blacksquare = 15$
> Use a fact family to solve the problem.
> $8 + 7 = 15$, so $15 - 8 = 7$.

Math Idea
You can use inverse operations and related facts to check answers to problems.

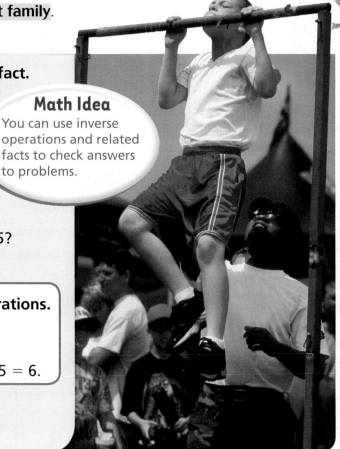

So, Marcus can do 7 more pull-ups than Justin.

• What are the facts in the fact family for 7, 8, and 15?

More Examples Find the missing number.

A Use related facts.
$13 - \blacksquare = 4$
Think: $13 - 4 = \blacksquare$
$13 - 4 = 9$, so $13 - 9 = 4$.

B Use inverse operations.
$\blacksquare - 5 = 6$
Think: $5 + 6 = \blacksquare$
$5 + 6 = 11$, so $11 - 5 = 6$.

• What operation can you use to solve the problem $\blacksquare + 8 = 12$? Explain.

Guided Practice

1. Keisha did 8 more push-ups than Tara did. Keisha did 17 push-ups. How many push-ups did Tara do? Copy and complete the related addition fact. Then use it to solve the problem.

$17 - 8 = \blacksquare$
$8 + \blacksquare = 17$

Write a related fact. Use it to complete the number sentence.

2. $14 - \blacksquare = 8$ **3.** $5 + \blacksquare = 12$ ✓**4.** $\blacksquare - 9 = 6$ ✓**5.** $\blacksquare + 4 = 11$

6. [TALK Math] **Explain** why the fact family with the numbers 8 and 16 has only two number sentences instead of four.

Independent Practice and Problem Solving

Write a related fact. Use it to complete the number sentence.

7. $11 - \blacksquare = 7$ **8.** $\blacksquare + 7 = 13$ **9.** $8 + \blacksquare = 12$ **10.** $\blacksquare + 5 = 11$

11. $\blacksquare - 9 = 8$ **12.** $6 + \blacksquare = 12$ **13.** $10 - \blacksquare = 7$ **14.** $\blacksquare - 3 = 8$

15. $\blacksquare - 4 = 8$ **16.** $3 + \blacksquare = 9$ **17.** $11 - \blacksquare = 2$ **18.** $\blacksquare + 4 = 13$

Write the fact family for each set of numbers.

19. 4, 7, 11   **20.** 5, 5, 10   **21.** 6, 7, 13   **22.** 3, 9, 12

For 23–24, use the pictograph.

23. How many more votes did jumping-jacks get than push-ups? What related facts can you use to solve this problem?

24. If sit-ups gets 4 more votes, how many votes will sit-ups and push-ups have in all?

25. [WRITE Math] ▸ **What's the Error?** Jan was asked to write a related fact for $7 + 4 = 11$. She wrote $7 - 4 = 3$. **Explain** why Jan's answer is incorrect. What is the correct answer?

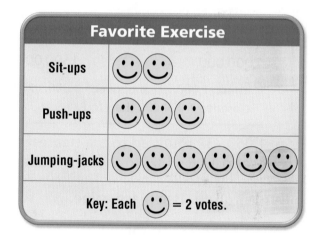

Mixed Review and Test Prep

26. A newspaper ad showed these prices: mini-van: $30,010; truck: $29,998; sports car: $30,100. List the prices in order from least expensive to most expensive. (p. 16)

27. Chan's website had 2,014 visitors and Lori's website had 1,987. Sheila's website had more visitors than Lori's, but fewer than Chan's. What are five possible numbers of visitors Sheila's website could have had? (p. 16)

28. Test Prep Which of the following sets of numbers cannot be used to make a fact family?

A 8, 9, 17

B 1, 3, 5

C 7, 7, 14

D 2, 7, 9

Extra Practice on page 56, Set A

Round Whole Numbers Through Millions

OBJECTIVE: Round whole numbers through millions.

Learn

PROBLEM In 2002, the United States welcomed 1,063,732 immigrants from around the world. A national newspaper stated that the United States welcomed about 1,000,000 immigrants. Is the newspaper's estimate reasonable?

When you **round** a number, you replace it with a number that tells about how many or how much. Rounded numbers are often easier to compute with. Round 1,063,732 to the nearest million.

ONE WAY Use a number line.

```
          1,063,732
              ↓
  ←|┼┼┼┼┼┼|┼┼┼┼┼┼|┼┼┼┼┼┼|┼┼┼┼┼┼|┼┼┼┼┼┼|┼┼┼┼┼┼→
  1,000,000          1,500,000          2,000,000
```

Think: 1,063,732 is between 1,000,000 and 2,000,000. 1,063,732 is closer to 1,000,000 than to 2,000,000.

So, 1,063,732 rounded to the nearest million is 1,000,000. 1,000,000 is close to 1,063,732, so the newspaper's estimate is reasonable.

ANOTHER WAY Use place value.

Round 1,063,732 to the nearest hundred thousand.

- Find the place to which you want to round.

- Look at the digit to the right. If the digit to the right is *less than 5*, the digit in the rounding place stays the same. If the digit is *5 or greater*, the digit in the rounding place increases by 1.

- Change all the digits to the right of the rounding place to zero.

Place to be rounded to: hundred thousands
↓
1,063,732

↓
1,063,732

The digit in the ten thousands place is 6. Since 6 > 5, the digit 0 increases by 1.

1,063,732 → 1,100,000

So, 1,063,732 rounded to the nearest hundred thousand is 1,100,000.

- When might you use rounded numbers instead of exact numbers? Explain.

Example

The table shows distances immigrants may travel to Houston, Texas, from different cities around the world. About how far do immigrants from London and Frankfurt travel to Houston?

Distances Immigrants Travel to Houston, Texas	
From	**Distance (in miles)**
Bangkok, Thailand	9,253
Frankfurt, Germany	5,245
London, England	4,860
New Delhi, India	8,366
Tel Aviv, Israel	7,079
Tokyo, Japan	6,682

Round the distances below to the nearest thousand miles.

London to Houston   4,860 → 5,000

Frankfurt to Houston   5,245 → 5,000

So, immigrants from London and Frankfurt travel about 5,000 miles to Houston.

More Examples

A **Round to the nearest ten thousand.**

45,278 is between 40,000 and 50,000.

place to be rounded to   Look at the thousands digit. Since 5 = 5, the digit 4 is increased by 1.
↓
45,278

So, 45,278 rounded to the nearest ten thousand is 50,000.

B **Round to the nearest thousand.**

45,278 is between 45,000 and 46,000.

place to be rounded to   Look at the hundreds digit. Since 2 < 5, the digit 5 stays the same.
↓
45,278

So, 45,278 rounded to the nearest thousand is 45,000.

C **Round to the nearest hundred.**

7,832 is between 7,800 and 7,900.

place to be rounded to   Look at the tens digit. Since 3 < 5, the digit 8 stays the same.
↓
7,832

So, 7,832 rounded to the nearest hundred is 7,800.

D **Round to the nearest ten dollars.**

$697 is between $690 and $700.

place to be rounded to   Look at the ones digit. Since 7 > 5, the digit 9 is increased by 1. Regroup 10 tens as 1 hundred.
↓
$697

So, $697 rounded to the nearest ten dollars is $700.

• How does understanding place value help you to round numbers?

ERROR ALERT

When you round a 9 to the next greater digit, remember to regroup to the next place value.

Guided Practice

1. In 2002, a total of 71,105 immigrants came to the United States from India. Use the number line to round this number to the nearest hundred.

71,105
↓

71,100   71,150   71,200

Round each number to the place value of the underlined digit.

2. 3<u>4</u>,567   **3.** $4<u>1</u>,267   **4.** $<u>2</u>34   ✅ **5.** 3,<u>4</u>76,321

Round each number to the nearest ten, thousand, hundred thousand, and million.

6. 1,657,809   **7.** 2,709,365   **8.** 16,442,896   ✅ **9.** 8,851,342

10. (TALK Math) Describe all the numbers that, when rounded to the nearest thousand, are 312,000.

Independent Practice and Problem Solving

Round each number to the place value of the underlined digit.

11. 7<u>6</u>9   **12.** <u>7</u>,507   **13.** <u>1</u>8,682   **14.** <u>5</u>7,945

15. <u>5</u>,645,408   **16.** 284,<u>7</u>92,300   **17.** $<u>9</u>21   **18.** $9<u>9</u>,814

Round each number to the nearest ten, thousand, hundred thousand, and million.

19. 6,144,683   **20.** 5,351,169   **21.** 7,826,431   **22.** 2,332,435

23. 1,943,232   **24.** 7,899,161   **25.** 43,346,561   **26.** 462,974,233

27. Write five numbers that round to 540,000.

28. What is the greatest whole number that rounds to 300,000? What is the least?

29. **Reasoning** Write a number that rounds to 47,000 when rounded to the nearest thousand and to 50,000 when rounded to the nearest ten thousand.

30. ☰**FAST FACT** In 2002, Michigan had 21,787 immigrants. Round this number to the nearest thousand and the nearest ten thousand. Which rounded number is closer to the original number?

USE DATA For 31–32, use the table.

31. Is the number of immigrants from China closer to 61,000 or 62,000?

32. What is the greatest place to which you might round all three numbers?

33. Euro's answer rounds to 7,000. Write three numbers that could be his exact answer.

34. (WRITE Math) Explain how to round 982,145 to the nearest hundred thousand.

Immigrants Welcomed to U.S. from Selected Countries, 2002	
Country	**Number**
China	61,282
Mexico	219,380
Philippines	51,308

Learn About Rounded or Exact Amounts

Sometimes rounded numbers are used because you do not need to know exact amounts or quantities. At other times, the exact amounts cannot be counted or measured, or they may change often.

Which numbers in the paragraph below are rounded?

Example

> The Ellis Island Immigration Museum is open between 9:30 A.M. and 5:15 P.M. Almost 2,000,000 people visit the museum each year. Many visitors take guided tours that last about 50 minutes. There are 3 floors of exhibits at the museum.
>
> **Think:** Words like *almost* and *about* tell you that a number is not exact.

So, the numbers 2,000,000 and 50 are rounded because they may change often.

Try It

Identify any rounded numbers. Explain why you think exact numbers are not used.

35. The museum has taped more than 1,300 interviews with immigrants who passed through Ellis Island. The oldest person interviewed was 106 years old, and the youngest was 46.

36. A ferry to Ellis Island costs $11.50 for adults and children 13 and older, $9.50 for seniors, and $4.50 for children 4–12. The ferry ride between Ellis Island and the Statue of Liberty takes about 10 minutes. Don's mother plans to bring $60 to buy ferry tickets for 5 people.

▲ Between 1892 and 1954, about 12,000,000 immigrants entered the U.S. through Ellis Island.

Mixed Review and Test Prep

37. Write two million, twenty thousand, two hundred ninety-seven in standard form. (p. 10)

38. Write a related number sentence and use it to find the missing number. (p. 32)

$$15 - \blacksquare = 7$$

39. **Test Prep** To which place do you round to find the rounded number that is closest to 3,264,587?

40. **Test Prep** Which number rounds to 300,000?

A 389,001

B 351,213

C 252,348

D 249,899

MENTAL MATH
Estimate Sums and Differences
OBJECTIVE: Estimate sums and differences.

Quick Review

Round to the place of the underlined digit.

1. <u>7</u>,286   2. 4,6<u>0</u>1
3. <u>2</u>8,099   4. 31,5<u>4</u>6
5. 1<u>9</u>,738

Learn

PROBLEM An Arctic tern flies 11,437 miles from Alaska to the South Pole for the winter. Then it flies 11,856 miles on a different route back to Alaska. About how many miles does the tern fly in all?

You can estimate to find about how many miles. An **estimate** is a number close to an exact amount.

Vocabulary

estimate

front-end estimation

compatible numbers

ONE WAY **Use rounding to estimate.** 11,437 + 11,856

11,437	→	11,000
+11,856	→	+12,000
		23,000

Round each number to the nearest thousand.

So, the Arctic tern flies about 23,000 miles in all.

OTHER WAYS

In **front-end estimation**, add the front digits of the addends. Write zeros for the other digits.

Ⓐ Use front-end estimation to estimate.
10,159 + 29,706

```
 10,159
+29,706
 30,000
```
So, the sum is about 30,000.

Alaska

South Pole

Compatible numbers are easy to compute with mentally. Use compatible numbers and properties to estimate a sum.

Ⓑ Use compatible numbers and properties to estimate.

Estimate the sum. 46 + 28 + 67

46 + 28 + 67	
40 + 28 + 60	Find compatible numbers. **Think:** 40 + 60 = 100
28 + 40 + 60	Use the Commutative Property.
28 + (40 + 60)	Use the Associative Property.
28 + 100 = 128	

So, the sum is about 128.

Remember

The Commutative Property of Addition states that you can add numbers in any order and the sum remains the same.
4 + 5 = 5 + 4
The Associative Property of Addition states that you can group numbers in different ways and the sum remains the same.
4 + (6 + 2) = (4 + 6) + 2

Estimate Differences

A mallard duck can fly at a height of 18,762 feet.
A bald eagle can fly at a height of 9,329 feet. About how
much higher can a mallard duck fly than a bald eagle?

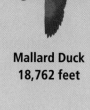

**Mallard Duck
18,762 feet**

ONE WAY   Use rounding to estimate. 18,762 − 9,329

$$\begin{array}{r} 18{,}762 \\ -\ 9{,}329 \\ \end{array} \quad \rightarrow \quad \begin{array}{r} 19{,}000 \\ -\ 9{,}000 \\ \hline 10{,}000 \end{array}$$
Round each number to the
nearest thousand.

So, a mallard can fly about 10,000 feet higher than a bald eagle.

You can find a closer estimate by rounding to a lesser place.

$$\begin{array}{r} 18{,}762 \\ -\ 9{,}329 \\ \end{array} \quad \rightarrow \quad \begin{array}{r} 18{,}800 \\ -\ 9{,}300 \\ \hline 9{,}500 \end{array}$$
Round each number to the
nearest hundred.

So, a closer estimate is 9,500 feet higher.

OTHER WAYS

Ⓐ Use front-end estimation to estimate. 29,028 − 15,783

$$\begin{array}{r} 29{,}028 \\ -15{,}783 \\ \hline 10{,}000 \end{array}$$
Subtract the front digit of each number.
Write zeros for the other digits.

So, the difference is about 10,000.

You can find a closer estimate by using the remaining digits.

$$\begin{array}{r} 9{,}028 \\ -5{,}783 \\ \hline 4{,}000 \end{array}$$
Estimate the difference
of the remaining digits.

$$\begin{array}{r} 10{,}000 \\ +\ 4{,}000 \\ \hline 14{,}000 \end{array}$$
Adjust the estimate
by adding.

So, a closer estimate is 14,000.

**Bald Eagle
9,329 feet**

Ⓑ Use compatible numbers to estimate. 17,324 − 5,642.

$$\begin{array}{r} 17{,}324 \\ -\ 5{,}642 \\ \end{array} \quad \rightarrow \quad \begin{array}{r} 15{,}000 \\ -\ 5{,}000 \\ \hline 10{,}000 \end{array}$$
Think: 15,000 − 5,000 is easy
to compute mentally.

So, the difference is about 10,000.

• Explain the difference between using compatible numbers
  and using rounding to estimate.

1. Alex estimated 37,782 + 41,255 as 70,000. Find an estimate that is closer to the actual sum by rounding each number to the nearest hundred.

Use rounding to estimate.

2. 12,591
    +36,284

3. 6,362
    −1,714

4. 76,368
    −31,842

5. 4,182,832
    +4,747,099

✓ 6. 9,362
    +5,781

Use front-end estimation to estimate.

7. 3,072
    +6,581

8. 5,639
    −2,147

9. 9,215,322
    −4,351,378

10. 42,137
    +19,205

✓ 11. 73,206
    −21,358

12. **TALK Math** **Describe** how to estimate the sum 3,718 + 6,524.

Independent Practice **and Problem Solving**

Use rounding to estimate.

13. 7,409
    +6,186

14. 8,932
    −5,341

15. 81,592
    −27,491

16. 26,372
    +54,949

17. 6,224,372
    −1,948,754

Use front-end estimation to estimate.

18. 259
    +684

19. 746
    −309

20. 9,472
    −2,612

21. 2,493,592
    +4,371,073

22. 58,942
    −35,172

Use compatible numbers to estimate.

23. 10,732 − 8,961

24. 1,070 − 508

25. 22,579 − 16,067

26. 384 + 225 + 587

27. 282 + 25 + 51 + 172

28. 2,467 + 511 + 1,124 + 542

Adjust the estimate to make it closer to the exact sum or difference.

29. 7,395 + 4,098
    Estimate: 11,000

30. 68,905 − 23,241
    Estimate: 50,000

31. 15,319 − 4,246
    Estimate: 10,000

32. 327 + 198
    Estimate: 500

33. 14,222 + 12,723
    Estimate: 26,000

34. 999 − 251
    Estimate: 700

35. Mr. Po drove 296 miles one way on his trip. Mrs. Han drove 482 miles one way on her trip. Estimate how many more miles round trip Mrs. Han drove than Mr. Po.

36. **WRITE Math** ▸ **Explain** how a rounded sum compares to the exact sum if the addends are rounded to a greater place value.

Extra Practice on page 56, Set C

Learn About) Underestimates and Overestimates

When you estimate, you get either an overestimate or an underestimate. An **underestimate** is less than the exact answer. An **overestimate** is greater than the exact answer.

Examples

Ⓐ Use front-end estimation.

67,516	→	67,516
+ 25,185	→	+ 25,185
		80,000

Only the front-end digits were added, so the estimate is an underestimate.

Ⓑ Round the addends.

67,516	→	70,000
+ 25,185	→	+ 30,000
		100,000

Both rounded addends are greater than the original addends. So, the estimate is an overestimate.

Try It

Tell why the estimate is an overestimate or an underestimate.

37. 7,524 + 1,632
Estimate: 10,000

38. 15,104 + 28,301
Estimate: 30,000

39. 2,714 + 1,906
Estimate: 3,000

40. 20,714 + 33,822
Estimate: 50,000

41. Morton has $1,523 and Joey has $2,714. They estimated that they have $3,000 altogether. Is this an underestimate or an overestimate? **Explain** how you know.

42. Reasoning Roxanne and Gerald need to buy enough boxes to pack and ship a cartload of apples. They need to estimate how many apples they have so they can buy the right number of boxes. Should they overestimate or underestimate the number of apples they have? **Explain.**

Mixed Review and Test Prep

43. Round $28,355 to the nearest $1,000.
(p. 34)

44. Test Prep A plane flying at 32,198 feet drops 14,824 feet. Which is the best estimate of how high the plane is flying now?

  A 10,000 feet   **C** 40,000 feet

  B 15,000 feet   **D** 50,000 feet

45. If the diameter of a circle is 54 centimeters, what is the radius? (Grade 3)

46. Test Prep This year, students sold 7,342 newspapers to raise money for their school. Last year they sold 943 fewer newspapers. About how many newspapers did they sell in all last year and this year? **Explain** how you got your answer.

Mental Math Strategies

OBJECTIVE: Use mental math strategies to find sums and differences.

Learn

PROBLEM The high school choir and orchestra are giving a concert. There are 56 students in the choir. There are 37 students in the orchestra. At the concert, each student has a chair on the stage. How many chairs are needed?

Sometimes you don't need paper and pencil to add or subtract. Use these strategies to help you add or subtract mentally.

ONE WAY Use the *Break Apart* Strategy.

A **Addition**

Find the sum. 56 + 37   Think: 56 = 50 + 6

		37 = 30 + 7
Add the tens.	50 + 30 = 80	
Add the ones.	6 + 7 = 13	
Add the sums.	80 + 13 = 93	

So, 93 chairs are needed.

B **Subtraction**

Find the difference. 76 − 42   Think: 76 = 70 + 6

		42 = 40 + 2
Subtract the tens.	70 − 40 = 30	
Subtract the ones.	6 − 2 = 4	
Add the differences.	30 + 4 = 34	

So, 76 − 42 = 34.

• Why do you think this strategy is called the break apart strategy?

More Examples

C **Addition**
Find the sum. 235 + 412
200 + 400 = 600
30 + 10 = 40
5 + 2 = 7
600 + 40 + 7 = 647

D **Subtraction**
Find the difference. 458 − 136
400 − 100 = 300
50 − 30 = 20
8 − 6 = 2
300 + 20 + 2 = 322

E **Use a *Friendly Number* Strategy.**

You can change one number to the nearest 10 and then adjust the other number to add or subtract mentally.

Subtraction is easier if the number you subtract is a friendly number. To get a friendly number, increase the number you subtract to the next ten. Then add the same amount to the other number to adjust the answer.

Find the difference. 56 − 38

Think: Add to 38 to make a number with 0 ones.

Add 2 to 38 to get 40. $38 + 2 = 40$

Add 2 to 56 to adjust the difference. $56 + 2 = 58$

Subtract. $58 - 40 = 18$

So, 56 − 38 = 18.

• Why do you use the next friendly ten for 38 instead of 56?

F **Use a *Swapping* Strategy.**

When you add numbers, you can swap digits with the same place value. Sometimes this helps you make a friendly number.

Find the sum. 239 + 194

Think: 194 is close to the friendly number 200.

Swap the ones digits. $234 + 199$

Add 1 to 199 to get 200. $199 + 1 = 200$

Subtract 1 from 234 to adjust the sum. $234 - 1 = 233$

Add. $200 + 233 = 433$

So, 239 + 194 = 433.

• Explain how to solve the problem by swapping the digits in a different place.

Guided Practice

1. Find 68 + 56 mentally. Add 2 to 68 to make the next friendly number. Subtract 2 from 56 to adjust the sum. What is the sum?

Add or subtract mentally. Tell the strategy you used.

2. 86 − 43   **3.** 72 + 39   **4.** 62 − 29   ☑ **5.** 867 − 425   ☑ **6.** 145 + 213

7. [**TALK Math**] Write a set of directions to find 478 − 215, using mental math.

Add or subtract mentally. Tell the strategy you used.

8. $94 - 57$ **9.** $16 + 58$ **10.** $95 + 36$ **11.** $38 + 75$ **12.** $93 - 46$

13. $152 - 79$ **14.** $238 + 431$ **15.** $286 - 159$ **16.** $723 + 142$ **17.** $442 - 238$

18. $758 - 426$ **19.** $384 + 218$ **20.** $276 + 79$ **21.** $576 - 98$ **22.** $726 - 314$

Find the sum or difference.

23. $462 - 18$ **24.** $79 - 42$ **25.** $134 + 112$ **26.** $27 + 335$ **27.** $86 + 63$

28. $656 - 429$ **29.** $64 + 58$ **30.** $47 - 39$ **31.** $211 + 725$ **32.** $137 - 19$

USE DATA For 33–35, use the table and mental math.

33. How many instruments make up the orchestra?

34. How many more strings are there than woodwinds and brass combined?

35. Alyvia has 100 instrument stands. How many more does she need so each instrument has a stand?

36. [WRITE Math] **Explain** how to find $87 - 53$ using the break apart and friendly number strategies. Which is easier to use?

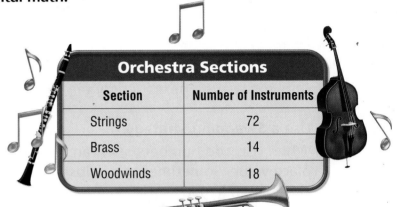

Orchestra Sections

Section	Number of Instruments
Strings	72
Brass	14
Woodwinds	18

Mixed Review and Test Prep

37. The number of people at a concert, rounded to the nearest hundred, was 5,400. What is the actual number of people if the digit in the tens place is 8 and the digit in the ones place is 2? (p. 34)

38. There were 623 people at the concert on Friday. On Saturday, 287 more people attended the concert than attended on Friday. About how many people attended the concert in all? (p. 38)

39. **Test Prep** Dan wants to buy an apple that costs 48¢ and a banana that costs 45¢. He adds 2¢ to 48¢ to find the total mentally. How should he adjust the sum to find the total?

A Add 2¢ to 45¢.

B Add 5¢ to 45¢.

C Subtract 2¢ from 45¢.

D Subtract 5¢ from 45¢.

Write to Explain

Writing to explain how you use mental math strategies can help you learn how to add and subtract greater numbers in your head.

Three groups of students are practicing for a dance concert. There are 19 students in the first group, 17 students in the second group, and 12 students in the third group. How many students are practicing?

Read the explanation Ryan gave for his solution.

Tips

To write an explanation:

- Your first sentence should tell what the problem is.
- Use words such as first, next, and finally to explain your steps.
- Use correct math vocabulary.
- Show your computations.
- Write a statement to summarize the answer.

I need to add $19 + 17 + 12$. First, I can use the friendly number strategy to add $19 + 17$. I add 1 to 19 to make 20 and subtract 1 from 17 to make 16 because I know that the sum of $20 + 16$ is the same as the sum of $19 + 17$. Add $20 + 16 = 36$.

Next, I need to find the sum of $36 + 12$. I use the break apart strategy. $36 = 30 + 6$ and $12 = 10 + 2$. So, I can add the tens and ones to find the sum.

I add $30 + 10 = 40$, $6 + 2 = 8$, and $40 + 8 = 48$. The sum is 48.
So, there are 48 students practicing.

Problem Solving Write to explain how you used mental math strategies to solve.

1. There are 18 fourth graders, 14 fifth graders, and 23 sixth graders in the choir. How many students are in the choir?

2. Would you use mental math to subtract $185 - 67$?

Problem Solving Workshop
Skill: Estimate or Exact Answer

OBJECTIVE: Solve problems by using the skill *estimate or exact answer*.

Use the Skill

PROBLEM The safe maximum flying weight of the plane is 1,600 pounds. The weights of some items are in the table below. Is the total weight of the plane, oil, fuel, extra equipment, baggage, and pilot less than 1,600 pounds? What is the maximum total weight the passengers can be?

Whether you need an estimate or exact answer depends on the situation.

Step 1 Find the total weight of the pilot and loaded plane.

You do not need to know the exact weight to find if it is less than 1,600 pounds. You can estimate this weight to compare to 1,600 pounds.	Round to the next ten pounds. Then add. $$973 + 15 + 20 + 146 + 95 + 150$$ $$\downarrow \quad \downarrow \quad \downarrow \quad \downarrow \quad \downarrow \quad \downarrow$$ $$980 + 20 + 20 + 150 + 100 + 150 = 1{,}420$$ 1,420 pounds $<$ 1,600 pounds

Step 2 Find how much weight is left for passengers.

Find the difference between the total weight of the loaded plane and the safe maximum flying weight. Find an exact answer.	Add to find the exact weight of the loaded plane. $$973 + 15 + 20 + 146 + 95 + 150 = 1{,}399$$ Subtract the exact weight from 1,600. $$1{,}600 - 1{,}399 = 201$$ There are 201 pounds left for passengers.

Light Plane Weights

Item	Weight (in pounds)
Empty Plane	973
Oil	15
Extra Equipment	20
Fuel	146
Baggage	95
Pilot/Adult	150
Safe Maximum Weight	1,600

So, the total weight of the loaded plane is less than 1,600 pounds, and the maximum total weight of the passengers is 201 pounds.

Think and Discuss

Explain whether to estimate or find an exact answer. Then solve.

a. If there were no baggage or extra equipment, what is the maximum total weight of passengers the loaded plane could hold?

b. Two bags weigh 95 pounds. If one of them weighs 47 pounds, about how much does the other bag weigh?

Guided Problem Solving

1. Horseshoe Falls in Australia is 502 feet high. Students measured their school and found that it was 210 feet long and 80 feet wide. Which is greater, the height of Horseshoe Falls or the distance around the outside of the school?

   First, decide if you need an estimate or an exact answer.

   Then, decide how you will compare the two numbers.

   Finally, make the comparison.

2. **What if** the students estimated that the school was about 200 feet long and about 100 feet wide? **Explain** why you should estimate or find an exact answer.

3. To be an airline pilot, you must fly a total of at least 1,500 hours. Dan flew 827 hours last year and 582 hours this year. How many more hours must he fly to be an airline pilot?

Mixed Applications

Explain whether to estimate or find an exact answer. Then solve the problem.

4. The school hallway is 190 feet long. If Carlos walks the length of the school hallway 3 times, will he have walked at least 500 feet? How far will he have walked?

5. The auditorium has 360 seats. There are 189 fourth-grade students and 170 fifth-grade students. If all the fifth-grade students sit in the auditorium, how many seats are left for fourth-grade students?

USE DATA For 6–8, use the bar graph.

6. How many degrees warmer was Meridien's highest January temperature than Greenville's?

7. The difference between the highest and lowest January temperatures at the Jackson station was 57°F. Find Jackson's lowest temperature in January.

8. In 2006, Vicksburg's highest January temperature was about 26°F warmer than normal. What was the normal temperature in Vicksburg in January?

9. **WRITE Math** **Explain** when you might need an exact answer and when you can estimate.

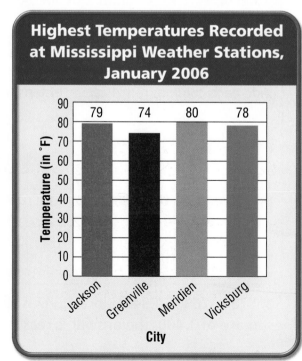

Highest Temperatures Recorded at Mississippi Weather Stations, January 2006

6 Add and Subtract 3-Digit and 4-Digit Numbers

OBJECTIVE: Add and subtract 3-digit and 4-digit numbers.

Learn

PROBLEM In spring, some monarch butterflies fly 1,718 miles from their winter home in Mexico to South Dakota. They fly another 1,042 miles to reach their summer home in Ontario, Canada. How far do the butterflies fly in all?

ONE WAY Use place value.

Add. 1,718 + 1,042   **Estimate.** 2,000 + 1,000 = 3,000

Step 1	Step 2	Step 3	Step 4
Add the ones. Regroup 10 ones.	Add the tens.	Add the hundreds.	Add the thousands.
$\begin{array}{r} {}^{1} \\ 1,7\,1\,8 \\ +1,0\,4\,2 \\ \hline 0 \end{array}$	$\begin{array}{r} {}^{1} \\ 1,7\,1\,8 \\ +1,0\,4\,2 \\ \hline 6\,0 \end{array}$	$\begin{array}{r} {}^{1} \\ 1,7\,1\,8 \\ +1,0\,4\,2 \\ \hline 7\,6\,0 \end{array}$	$\begin{array}{r} {}^{1} \\ 1,7\,1\,8 \\ +1,0\,4\,2 \\ \hline 2,7\,6\,0 \end{array}$

So, the butterflies fly 2,760 miles in all. Since 2,760 is close to the estimate of 3,000, the answer is reasonable.

ANOTHER WAY Use column addition.

Add. 578 + 769   **Estimate.** 600 + 800 = 1,400

Step 1	Step 2	Step 3	Step 4
Draw lines to separate each place. Add each column.	Regroup 17 ones as 1 ten 7 ones. 13 tens + 1 ten = 14 tens	Regroup 14 tens as 1 hundred 4 tens. 12 hundreds + 1 hundred = 13 hundreds	Regroup 13 hundreds as 1 thousand 3 hundreds.

Step 1:

	H	T	O
	5	7	8
+	7	6	9
	12	13	17

Step 2:

	H	T	O
	5	7	8
+	7	6	9
	12	13	17
	12	14	7

Step 3:

	H	T	O
	5	7	8
+	7	6	9
	12	13	17
	12	14	7
	13	4	7

Step 4:

		H	T	O
		5	7	8
+		7	6	9
		12	13	17
		12	14	7
		13	4	7
	1	3	4	7

So, 578 + 769 = 1,347. Since 1,347 is close to the estimate of 1,400, the answer is reasonable.

Subtract 3-Digit and 4-Digit Numbers

ONE WAY Use place value.

Subtract. 5,000 − 1,948 **Estimate.** 5,000 − 2,000 = 3,000

There are not enough ones, tens, or hundreds to subtract, so you have to regroup.

Step 1	**Step 2**	**Step 3**	**Step 4**
Subtract the ones. 8 > 0. Regroup 5 thousands as 4 thousands 9 hundreds 9 tens 10 ones.	Subtract the tens.	Subtract the hundreds and thousands.	Add to check.

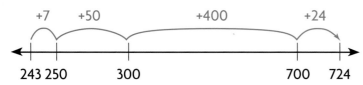

Step 1:
```
    9 9
 4 10 10 10
  5,0 0 0
 −1,9 4 8
        2
```

Step 2:
```
    9 9
 4 10 10 10
  5,0 0 0
 −1,9 4 8
       5 2
```

Step 3:
```
    9 9
 4 10 10 10
  5,0 0 0
 −1,9 4 8
  3,0 5 2
```

Step 4:
```
   1 11
   3,052
 + 1,948
   5,000
```

So, 5,000 − 1,948 = 3,052. Since 3,052 is close to the estimate of 3,000, the answer is reasonable.

ERROR ALERT

Remember that when the bottom digit is greater than the top digit, you need to regroup to subtract. Regroup from the next greater place value to the left that is not 0.

ANOTHER WAY Use a number line.

You can use a number line to find 724 − 243.

```
   +7    +50          +400        +24
  ⌒     ⌒       ⌒              ⌒
◄──┼──┼────────┼──────────────┼───┼──►
  243 250     300            700 724
```

Add the numbers above the number line to find the difference between 243 and 724.

7 + 50 + 400 + 24 = 481

So, 724 − 243 = 481.

More Examples

A
```
   7,8 4 9
 −3,6 1 8
  4,2 3 1
```

B
```
       11
   7  1 13
  8,2 3 9
 −   7 8 2
  7,4 5 7
```

C
```
        9
   8  10 17
  9,0 7 9
 −2,1 8 3
  6,8 9 6
```

- How can you use place value to add or subtract 4-digit numbers?

1. Copy each step of the problem at the right. Then tell what is happening in each step.

Step 1
$$\begin{array}{r} {}^{0\ 14}\!\!\not{7}\,\not{1}\,4 \\ -438 \\ \hline 6 \end{array}$$

Step 2
$$\begin{array}{r} {}^{6\ \not{0}\ 14}\!\!\not{7}\,\not{1}\,4 \\ -438 \\ \hline 76 \end{array}$$

Step 3
$$\begin{array}{r} {}^{6\ \not{0}\ 14}\!\!\not{7}\,\not{1}\,4 \\ -438 \\ \hline 276 \end{array}$$

Estimate. Then find the sum or difference.

2.
$$\begin{array}{r} 309 \\ +892 \\ \hline \end{array}$$

3.
$$\begin{array}{r} 3,007 \\ -1,432 \\ \hline \end{array}$$

4.
$$\begin{array}{r} 2,608 \\ +4,193 \\ \hline \end{array}$$

✓5.
$$\begin{array}{r} 726 \\ +2,643 \\ \hline \end{array}$$

✓6.
$$\begin{array}{r} 6,000 \\ -4,275 \\ \hline \end{array}$$

7. **TALK Math** Explain how you know which places to regroup to subtract.

Independent Practice and Problem Solving

Estimate. Then find the sum or difference.

8.
$$\begin{array}{r} 957 \\ +409 \\ \hline \end{array}$$

9.
$$\begin{array}{r} 7,345 \\ -1,213 \\ \hline \end{array}$$

10.
$$\begin{array}{r} 8,936 \\ +\ \ 385 \\ \hline \end{array}$$

11.
$$\begin{array}{r} 2,375 \\ +1,098 \\ \hline \end{array}$$

12.
$$\begin{array}{r} 9,000 \\ -4,217 \\ \hline \end{array}$$

13.
$$\begin{array}{r} 536 \\ -273 \\ \hline \end{array}$$

14.
$$\begin{array}{r} 4,892 \\ +\ \ 708 \\ \hline \end{array}$$

15.
$$\begin{array}{r} 8,400 \\ -2,785 \\ \hline \end{array}$$

16.
$$\begin{array}{r} 7,419 \\ -\ \ 846 \\ \hline \end{array}$$

17.
$$\begin{array}{r} 6,045 \\ +1,742 \\ \hline \end{array}$$

18.
$$\begin{array}{r} 908 \\ -726 \\ \hline \end{array}$$

19.
$$\begin{array}{r} 6,245 \\ +1,534 \\ \hline \end{array}$$

20.
$$\begin{array}{r} 8,300 \\ -\ \ 953 \\ \hline \end{array}$$

21.
$$\begin{array}{r} 7,962 \\ -2,358 \\ \hline \end{array}$$

22.
$$\begin{array}{r} 3,407 \\ +2,936 \\ \hline \end{array}$$

Algebra Find the missing digit.

23.
$$\begin{array}{r} 9\blacksquare 6 \\ +437 \\ \hline 1,383 \end{array}$$

24.
$$\begin{array}{r} 6,532 \\ -4,1\blacksquare 5 \\ \hline 2,407 \end{array}$$

25.
$$\begin{array}{r} \blacksquare,158 \\ -\ \ 437 \\ \hline 1,721 \end{array}$$

26.
$$\begin{array}{r} 3,657 \\ +\ \ 2\blacksquare 4 \\ \hline 3,901 \end{array}$$

27.
$$\begin{array}{r} 6\blacksquare 42 \\ -3,491 \\ \hline 2,551 \end{array}$$

USE DATA For 28–29, use the picture.

28. How many more butterflies roosted on September 2 than on September 3 and 4 combined?

29. **Pose a Problem** Write a problem like Problem 28 by changing the dates.

30. **Reasoning** Add an even 4-digit number and an odd 4-digit number. Is the sum odd or even? **Explain.**

31. **WRITE Math** ▸ **What's the Question?** Angelina's nature group counted 622 butterflies roosting on Monday. On Tuesday, they counted 458 butterflies. The answer is 164 butterflies.

Monarch Butterflies at Fall Roost

Date	Number of Butterflies
September 1	923
September 2	2,418
September 3	279
September 4	356

Traveling monarchs rest in large groups called roosts.

Technology
Use Harcourt Mega Math, The Number Games, *Tiny's Think Tank*, Levels B, C.

Extra Practice on page 56, Set E

Learn About) Finding Distance on a Number Line

You can use a number line to visualize a problem
and to help you solve the problem.

Example

Driving from Green Bay, Wisconsin, to Wheaton, Illinois,
on major highways, you go through Milwaukee, Wisconsin,
and Wheeling, Illinois.

Look at the distances on the number line. What is the
distance from Wheeling to Wheaton?

Add to find the distance from Green Bay to Wheeling. $119 + 97 = 216$

Subtract to find the distance from Wheeling to Wheaton. $243 - 216 = 27$

So, the distance from Wheeling to Wheaton is 27 miles.

Try It

**Draw a number line to find the distance. Label the letters on
the number line in alphabetical order.**

32. *A* to *D* is 185 miles. *B* to *C* is 57 miles.
C to *D* is 94 miles. Find *A* to *B*.

33. *A* to *D* is 278 miles. *A* to *B* is 43 miles.
C to *D* is 129 miles. Find *B* to *C*.

34. *A* to *D* is 723 miles. *A* to *B* is 36 miles.
B to *C* is 170 miles. Find *C* to *D*.

35. *A* to *D* is 1,483 miles. *B* to *C* is 214 miles.
C to *D* is 412 miles. Find *A* to *B*.

Mixed Review and Test Prep

36. What number makes this number
sentence true? (p. 32)
$$5 + \blacksquare = 12$$

37. Test Prep Greg has put 1,372 pieces of
his puzzle together. He has 1,128 pieces
left to finish the puzzle. How many pieces
are in the puzzle?

   A 244   **B** 256   **C** 2,490 **D** 2,500

38. When you add two odd numbers, is it
certain or impossible that the sum will
be odd? (Grade 3)

39. Test Prep Students collected 875 cans
during the first month of their aluminum
drive. The second month, they collected
2,155 cans. How many more cans did
they collect the second month than the
first month? **Explain.**

Choose a Method

OBJECTIVE: Choose paper and pencil, a calculator, or mental math to add and subtract to 7-digit numbers.

Learn

PROBLEM The planet Saturn has dozens of moons. Two of its moons are Titan and Iapetus. Titan is 1,221,850 kilometers from Saturn. Iapetus is 2,339,450 kilometers farther from Saturn than Titan is. How far is Iapetus from Saturn?

Examples

A **Use paper and pencil.**

Add. 1,221,850 + 2,339,450   **Estimate.** 1,000,000 + 2,000,000 = 3,000,000

Step 1	
Add the ones and tens. Regroup.	$\begin{array}{r} 1 \\ 1{,}221{,}850 \\ +2{,}339{,}450 \\ \hline 00 \end{array}$

Step 2	
Add the hundreds. Regroup.	$\begin{array}{r} 1\ 1 \\ 1{,}221{,}850 \\ +2{,}339{,}450 \\ \hline 300 \end{array}$

Step 3	
Add the thousands. Regroup.	$\begin{array}{r} 11\ 1 \\ 1{,}221{,}850 \\ +2{,}339{,}450 \\ \hline 1{,}300 \end{array}$

Step 4	
Add the ten thousands, hundred thousands, and millions.	$\begin{array}{r} 11\ 1 \\ 1{,}221{,}850 \\ +2{,}339{,}450 \\ \hline 3{,}561{,}300 \end{array}$

B **Use a calculator.**

So, Iapetus is 3,561,300 kilometers from Saturn. The answer is close to the estimate of 3,000,000, so 3,561,300 is reasonable.

- Is mental math a good method for finding the sum of these numbers? Explain.

Math Idea

You can find a sum or difference using paper and pencil, a calculator, or mental math. Choose the method that works best with the numbers in the problem.

C **Use mental math.**

Add. 41,570 + 4,020   **Estimate.** 42,000 + 4,000 = 46,000

Step 1	Step 2	Step 3
Break apart 4,020 to add. 4,020 = 4,000 + 20	Add the thousands. 41,570 + 4,000 = 45,570	Add the tens. 45,570 + 20 = 45,590

So, the sum is 45,590. The answer is close to the estimate of 46,000, so 45,590 is reasonable.

Subtract Greater Numbers

Saturn's diameter at its equator is 120,536 kilometers. Its diameter between the poles is 108,728 kilometers. How much greater is Saturn's diameter at the equator than between the poles?

Examples

D Use paper and pencil.

Subtract. 120,536 − 108,728   **Estimate.** 120,000 − 110,000 = 10,000

Step 1		Step 2	
Subtract the ones and tens. Regroup.	$\begin{array}{r} {}^{2\,16} \\ 120,5\cancel{3}\cancel{6} \\ -108,728 \\ \hline 08 \end{array}$	Subtract the hundreds. Regroup.	$\begin{array}{r} {}^{\,9} \\ {}^{1\ \,10\ 15\ 2\ 16} \\ 1\,\cancel{2}\,\cancel{0},\cancel{5}\,\cancel{3}\,\cancel{6} \\ -108,728 \\ \hline 808 \end{array}$

Step 3		Step 4	
Subtract the thousands, ten thousands, and hundred thousands.	$\begin{array}{r} {}^{\,9} \\ {}^{1\ \,10\ 15\ 2\ 16} \\ 1\,\cancel{2}\,\cancel{0},\cancel{5}\,\cancel{3}\,\cancel{6} \\ -108,728 \\ \hline 11,808 \end{array}$	Add to check.	$\begin{array}{r} {}^{11\ \ \ 1} \\ 108,728 \\ +\ 11,808 \\ \hline 120,536 \end{array}$

E Use a calculator.

1 2 0 5 3 6 − 1 0 8 7 2 8 =   = 11'808.

So, the diameter at the equator is 11,808 kilometers greater. The answer is close to the estimate of 10,000, so 11,808 is reasonable.

F Use mental math.

Subtract. 143,000 − 9,000   **Estimate.** 140,000 − 10,000 = 130,000

You can use the friendly number strategy.	
Add 1,000 to 9,000 to get 10,000.	9,000 + 1,000 = 10,000
Add 1,000 to 143,000 to adjust the difference.	143,000 + 1,000 = 144,000
Subtract.	144,000 − 10,000 = 134,000

So, the difference is 134,000. The answer is close to the estimate of 130,000, so 134,000 is reasonable.

• How do you decide which method to use when adding and subtracting greater numbers?

1. Tell which problem would be easier to solve using mental math. Then find the sum.

    a.   241,156
        +176,812

    b.   340,100
        +204,000

Find the sum or difference. Write the method you used.

2. 342,007
    +569,305

3. 706,300
    −401,000

✔ 4. 945,322
      −461,070

✔ 5. 6,280,000
      +1,300,000

6. **TALK Math** Explain why mental math is a better method for finding 170,000 + 25,300 than finding 170,000 − 25,300.

Independent Practice and Problem Solving

Find the sum or difference. Write the method you used.

7. 850,540
   −200,310

8. 3,287,004
   +2,069,506

9. 3,506,721
   +4,080,000

10. 4,528,300
    −2,175,700

11. 5,302,700
  +   410,000

12. 592,014
   −286,728

13. 632,004
  − 12,000

14. 5,838,672
   +3,415,059

⭐ **Algebra** **Find the missing digit.**

15. 43■,257
   +253,019
   ──────
   692,276

16. 892,■43
   −250,742
   ──────
   642,201

17. 538,627
  −2■4,394
  ──────
  274,233

18. 2,4■7,308
   +3,896,321
   ──────
   6,313,629

USE DATA For 19–22, use the information in the picture.

Average Distance From Saturn

Saturn

Pan	Pandora	Dione	Rhea
133,583 km	141,700 km	377,400 km	527,040 km

19. How much farther from Saturn is Rhea than Pan and Pandora combined?

20. **Pose a Problem** Write a problem like Problem 19 by changing the moons.

21. Helene orbits Saturn 243,817 kilometers farther away than Pan does. Which moon orbits Saturn at the same distance as Helene?

22. **WRITE Math** Explain which method to use to find how much closer Dione is to Saturn than Rhea is. Why is the method you chose the best one to use?

Learn About) Palindromes

A palindrome is a word that reads the same forward or backward. *Mom* and *radar* are word palindromes. There are also number palindromes such as 34,043, and 2,002. You can use addition to make number palindromes.

"Madam, I'm Adam" is a sentence palindrome.

Example

Step 2	Step 2	Step 3	Step 4

Write a number. 348	Reverse the digits. 843	Add the two numbers.
		
		   348
		+ 843
		――――
		1,191
			Keep reversing and adding until you make a palindrome.
			
			    348
			+ 843
			――――
			1,191
			+ 1,911
			――――
			3,102
			+ 2,013
			――――
			palindrome ⟶ 5,115

Try It

Use each number to make a number palindrome.

23. 421   **24.** 236   **25.** 48   **26.** 637   **27.** 1,384   **28.** 2,518

Mixed Review and Test Prep

29. Deb's and Sid's families went to Alabama. Deb's family traveled 1,757 miles and Sid's family traveled 563 miles. About how much farther did Deb's family travel? (p. 38)

30. Nick wants to score 5,000 points in a video game. He has scored 3,752 points. How many more points must he score to reach his goal? (p. 48)

31. Test Prep The United States has 9,161,923 square kilometers of land and 469,495 square kilometers of water. What is the total area of land and water in the United States?

32. Test Prep There are 135,663 kilometers of coastline that border the Pacific Ocean. There are 111,866 kilometers of coastline that border the Atlantic Ocean. How many more kilometers of coastline border the Pacific Ocean?

  A 23,797 kilometers

  B 24,203 kilometers

  C 24,807 kilometers

  D 247,529 kilometers

Extra Practice

Set A Write a related fact. Use it to complete the number sentence. (pp. 32–33)

1. $14 - \blacksquare = 8$ **2.** $12 - \blacksquare = 3$ **3.** $\blacksquare + 9 = 17$ **4.** $6 + \blacksquare = 13$

5. $\blacksquare - 5 = 6$ **6.** $\blacksquare + 9 = 15$ **7.** $8 + \blacksquare = 16$ **8.** $\blacksquare - 8 = 4$

Set B Round each number to the nearest ten, thousand, hundred thousand, and million. (pp. 34–37)

1. 2,325,602   **2.** 8,092,677   **3.** 4,588,491   **4.** 19,908,725

5. 3,409,718   **6.** 2,061,499   **7.** 12,947,173   **8.** 61,098,511

Set C Use rounding to estimate. (pp. 38–41)

1. $\begin{array}{r} 3,458 \\ +3,997 \\ \hline \end{array}$ **2.** $\begin{array}{r} 2,476 \\ -1,184 \\ \hline \end{array}$ **3.** $\begin{array}{r} 60,320 \\ +12,391 \\ \hline \end{array}$ **4.** $\begin{array}{r} 88,925 \\ -21,647 \\ \hline \end{array}$

5. Maria practiced the piano for 45 minutes on Monday, 50 minutes on Tuesday, and 60 minutes on Wednesday. Her goal was to practice for at least 130 minutes. Estimate to determine how long she practiced. Did she reach her goal?

Set D Add or subtract mentally. Tell the strategy you used. (pp. 42–45)

1. $89 - 37$ **2.** $590 + 275$ **3.** $497 - 308$ **4.** $752 + 244$ **5.** $609 - 297$

6. Mr. Chase is ordering 249 pencils and 290 erasers. Use mental math to determine the total number of items Mr. Chase is ordering. Tell what strategy you used.

Set E Estimate. Then find the sum or difference. (pp. 48–51)

1. $\begin{array}{r} 563 \\ +261 \\ \hline \end{array}$ **2.** $\begin{array}{r} 732 \\ -124 \\ \hline \end{array}$ **3.** $\begin{array}{r} 6,409 \\ +3,188 \\ \hline \end{array}$ **4.** $\begin{array}{r} 7,600 \\ -2,677 \\ \hline \end{array}$ **5.** $\begin{array}{r} 4,898 \\ -3,621 \\ \hline \end{array}$

Set F Find the sum or difference. Write the method you used. (pp. 52–55)

1. $\begin{array}{r} 430,002 \\ +250,091 \\ \hline \end{array}$ **2.** $\begin{array}{r} 675,966 \\ -350,521 \\ \hline \end{array}$ **3.** $\begin{array}{r} 4,900,275 \\ +\ \ \ 100,125 \\ \hline \end{array}$ **4.** $\begin{array}{r} 2,800,175 \\ -1,100,125 \\ \hline \end{array}$

Technology
Use Harcourt Mega Math, The Number Games, *Tiny's Think Tank*, Levels B, C.

Who's the Closest?

On Your Mark!
4 players and a referee

Get Set!
• Digit cards (0–9)
• Problem board

Go!

■ Players take turns being the referee. For each round, the referee decides
• whether to use addition or subtraction,
• how many digits each number will have,
• and what the goal will be. For example, the referee might choose the goal *closest to 0, closest to 500,* or *closest to 1,000.*

■ Choose a problem board based on the referee's decision.

■ Place the digit cards facedown in a stack.

■ The referee draws a digit card and reads the digit aloud. The players write the digit in a blank space on their boards. Once a digit has been written, it may not be erased.

■ The referee continues to draw digit cards, one at a time. Players fill in their boards as the digits are called.

■ When all the blank spaces on their board have been filled, each player solves his or her own problem. The referee checks to see who is closest to the goal. That player wins the round.

Use Logical Reasoning

WORK UP OR DOWN

In a number pyramid, each number is found by adding the two numbers below it. In the pyramid at the right, $25 = 10 + 15$, $10 = 2 + 8$, and $15 = 8 + 7$.

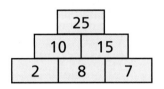

You can find missing numbers in a number pyramid by using addition and subtraction.

To find A: Think $121 + A = 238$,
so $A = 238 - 121 = 117$.

To find B: Think $A + B = 247$,
so $B = 247 - A = 247 - 117 = 130$.

To find C: Think $519 + 532 = C$, so $C = 1,051$.

Examples

A Find the missing numbers *M* and *N*.

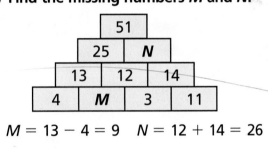

$M = 13 - 4 = 9$ $N = 12 + 14 = 26$

B Find the missing numbers *R*, *S*, and *T*.

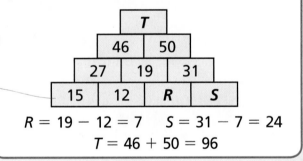

$R = 19 - 12 = 7$ $S = 31 - 7 = 24$
$T = 46 + 50 = 96$

Try It

Find the missing numbers.

1.

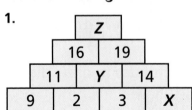

2.

3. **WRITE Math** ▸ **Explain** how you found each missing number in Problem 2.

Chapter 2 Review/Test

Check Vocabulary and Concepts

Choose the best term from the box.

1. Addition and subtraction are opposite, or __?__. (p. 32)

2. When you estimate by adding the front digit of each addend, it is called __?__. (p. 38)

> **VOCABULARY**
> compatible numbers
> front-end estimation
> inverse operations

Check Skills

Write a related fact. Use it to complete the number sentence. (pp. 32–33)

3. ■ − 8 = 6   4. 9 + ■ = 14   5. ■ + 4 = 11   6. 12 − ■ = 6

Round each number to the place value of the underlined digit. (pp. 34–37)

7. 7,5<u>6</u>7,231   8. 6,0<u>8</u>1,392   9. 7,40<u>9</u>,488   10. 8,9<u>7</u>8,004

Estimate by using rounding, front-end estimation, or compatible numbers. (pp. 38–41)

11.	321	12.	6,799	13.	34,893	14.	67,062
	+198		−3,856		−19,877		+23,219

Add or subtract mentally. Tell the strategy you used. (pp. 42–45)

15. 81 + 49   16. 497 − 206   17. 344 − 190   18. 499 + 99   19. 601 − 350

Estimate. Then find the sum or difference. (pp. 48–51)

20.	6,895	21.	9,084	22.	4,708	23.	6,053
	+2,156		−3,486		+3,795		−1,857

Check Problem Solving

Solve. Explain why an exact answer or an estimate is needed. (pp. 46–47)

24. There are 76 students in the third grade and 92 students in the fourth grade. Rachael buys 180 cookies. Does she have enough to give each student one cookie? If so, how many cookies will be left?

25. **WRITE Math** ▸ Mr. Sykes has $7,000 and wants to buy the items at the right. **Explain** how he can use estimation to find whether he has enough money.

$2,459 $2,359 $2,599

Standardized Test Prep
Chapters 1–2

Number and Operations

1. The first year's budget for the new zoo is $839,745. Which digit is in the ten thousands place? (p. 10)

   A 3   B 7   C 8   D 9

Test Tip **Look for important words.**

See Item 2. Look for the key words in the problem to help you decide whether to add or subtract.

2. The table below shows play attendance. How many more people attended on Friday than on Wednesday? (p. 48)

Play Attendance			
Day	Wed	Thu	Fri	Sat
Number	1,659	2,344	4,618	4,328

   A 2,669   C 5,987

   B 2,959   D 8,946

3. Which list shows the numbers 48, 29, 37, 54, and 18 in order from least to greatest? (p. 16)

   A 48, 29, 37, 54, 18

   B 54, 48, 37, 29, 18

   C 18, 37, 29, 48, 54

   D 18, 29, 37, 48, 54

4. **Explain** how to round 3,749 to the nearest hundred. (p. 34)

Measurement

5. Which rectangle has an area of 20 square units? (Grade 3)

   A

   B

   C

   D

6. What temperature is shown on the thermometer? (Grade 3)

   A 65°F

   B 55°F

   C 45°F

   D 35°F

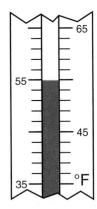

7. **Explain** how to read the time shown on the clock below.

   (Grade 3)

Algebraic Reasoning

8. Which number sentence is **NOT** part of the fact family that includes $4 \times 5 = 20$? (Grade 3)

  A $5 \times 4 = 20$

  B $20 \div 5 = 4$

  C $20 \div 4 = 5$

  D $5 + 4 = 9$

9. The table shows the relationship between the number of spiders and the number of legs. What is the missing number? (Grade 3)

Spider Legs				
Spiders	1	2	3	4
Legs	8	16	▧	32

  A 19

  B 20

  C 24

  D 28

10. What might the missing number be in the pattern? (Grade 3)

$$50, 46, 42, \blacksquare, 34$$

  A 36

  B 37

  C 38

  D 40

11. **WRITE Math** Bonnie says that $4 + 3 + 7 = 16 - 2$. **Explain** how to find if she is correct. (Grade 3)

Geometry

12. Which pair of figures below do **NOT** appear to be similar? (Grade 3)

A

B

C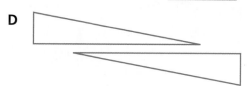

D

13. What is the name of the solid figure shown below? (Grade 3)

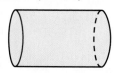

  A Cube

  B Circle

  C Rectangular prism

  D Cylinder

14. **WRITE Math** **Describe** how a rectangle and a square are alike and how they are different. (Grade 3)

3 Algebra: Use Addition and Subtraction

Investigate

Bowlers play 10 frames, or rounds. Each frame starts with 10 pins standing. A bowler may roll two balls in each frame to try to knock down all the pins. Suppose the first ball knocks down only some of the pins. If 4 pins are left standing, use the equation $4 + p = 10$ to find how many pins were knocked down. What addition or subtraction equations can you write to find the number of pins that could be knocked down by a first ball?

≡ **FAST FACT**

The 2003 Special Olympics World Summer Games in Dublin, Ireland, hosted 269 Special Olympics bowlers.

GO ONLINE

Technology
Student pages are available in the Student eBook.

Check your understanding of important skills needed for success in Chapter 3.

▶ **Addition and Subtraction**

Find the sum or difference.

1. $8 + 5 = $ ■   **2.** $12 + 7 = $ ■   **3.** $16 - 3 = $ ■

4. $12 - 9 = $ ■   **5.** $9 + 8 = $ ■   **6.** $15 + 7 = $ ■

7. $11 - 3 = $ ■   **8.** $14 + 5 = $ ■   **9.** $25 - 8 = $ ■

▶ **Find the Missing Number**

Find the missing number.

10. $5 + $ ■ $ = 11$ **11.** $16 - $ ■ $ = 9$ **12.** $8 + $ ■ $ = 15$

13. $13 - $ ■ $ = 4$ **14.** ■ $ + 4 = 9$ **15.** ■ $ - 7 = 4$

16. ■ $ - 8 = 5$ **17.** $17 - $ ■ $ = 8$ **18.** ■ $ + 6 = 14$

19. $3 + $ ■ $ = 10$ **20.** ■ $ - 5 = 9$ **21.** ■ $ + 2 = 11$

▶ **Number Patterns**

Predict the next number in the pattern.

22. 14, 21, 28, 35, ■   **23.** 6, 13, 20, 27, ■

24. 125, 225, 325, 425, ■   **25.** 88, 92, 96, 100, ■

26. 35, 30, 25, 20, ■   **27.** 253, 263, 273, 283, ■

VOCABULARY POWER

CHAPTER VOCABULARY

Associative Property of Addition
Commutative Property of Addition
equation
expression
Identity Property of Addition
inverse operations
parentheses
variable

WARM-UP WORDS

equation a number sentence which shows that two quantities are equal

expression a part of a number sentece that has numbers and operation signs but does not have an equal sign

variable a letter or symbol that stands for a number or numbers

1 Addition Properties

OBJECTIVE: Identify and use the properties of addition.

Quick Review

1. $90 + 30$ 2. $82 + 15$
3. $17 + 22$ 4. $9 + 7$
5. $45 + 13$

Vocabulary

Commutative Property

Identity Property

Associative Property

Learn

PROBLEM Jared and Savon collect swirled and clear marbles. They have the same number of marbles. Jared has 38 swirled marbles and 23 clear marbles. Savon has 23 swirled marbles. How many clear marbles does Savon have?

The **Commutative Property of Addition** states that numbers can be added in any order and the sum will be the same.

Example 1 Use the Commutative Property.

Jared's marbles				Savon's marbles			
38 swirled	plus	23 clear	equals	23 swirled	plus	■ clear	
↓	↓	↓	↓	↓	↓	↓	↓
38	+	23	=	23	+	■	

Since $38 + 23 = 23 + 38$, then ■ $= 38$.

So, Savon has 38 clear marbles.

The **Identity Property of Addition** states that when you add zero to any number, the sum is that number.

Example 2 Use the Identity Property.

If Savon has no other swirled marbles, how many swirled marbles does he have in all?	$23 + 0 = 23$ $0 + 23 = 23$

So, Savon has 23 swirled marbles in all.

The **Associative Property of Addition** states that the way addends are grouped does not change the sum.

Math Idea

Parentheses ( ) tell which operation to do first.

Example 3 Use the Associative Property.

Matilda has 16 red, 24 yellow, and 18 blue shooter marbles. How many shooter marbles does she have in all?

$16 + (24 + 18) = (16 + 24) + 18$
$16 + \quad 42 \quad = \quad 40 \quad + 18$
$\quad 58 \quad = \quad \quad 58$

So, Matilda has 58 marbles.

1. Which shows an example of the Commutative Property?

$(13 + 17) + 22 = 13 + (17 + 22)$ $46 + 21 = 21 + 46$ $67 + 0 = 67$

Find the missing number. Name the property you used.

2. $73 + \blacksquare = 73$ ✓3. $47 + \blacksquare = 56 + 47$ ✓4. $\blacksquare + (31 + 18) = (24 + 31) + 18$

5. **TALK Math** **Explain** how to use the Commutative and Associative Properties to add $62 + 79 + 38$ mentally.

Independent Practice and Problem Solving

Find the missing number. Name the property you used.

6. $93 + 28 = 28 + \blacksquare$ 7. $\blacksquare + 0 = 31$ 8. $35 + (42 + \blacksquare) = (35 + 42) + 56$

9. $69 = \blacksquare + 69$ 10. $59 + 85 = \blacksquare + 59$ 11. $(76 + 97) + 19 = 76 + (\blacksquare + 19)$

Change the order or group the addends so that you can add mentally. Find the sum. Name the property you used.

12. $450 + 83 + 50$ 13. $78 + 32 + 46$ 14. $125 + 62 + 75$ 15. $64 + 15 + 36 + 30$

USE DATA For 16–17, use the table.

16. Use the Associative Property to find the total number of green, red, and blue marbles that Serena has.

17. Serena has 10 fewer clay marbles than the total number of green and black marbles. How many clay marbles does she have?

18. **WRITE Math** **Explain** how you know which addition property to use to solve a problem.

Serena's Marbles	
Color	**Number**
Black	24
Blue	43
Green	26
Red	17

Mixed Review and Test Prep

19. What unit should Mary Jane use to measure the height of the classroom door? Tell why. (Grade 3)

20. Joe's trip is 2,035 miles long. He stops after 628 miles and again after 745 miles. How many miles are left? (p. 48)

21. **Test Prep** Jameson has 28 gold coins, 27 silver coins, and 12 bronze coins. **Explain** how to use addition properties to find the total number of coins Jameson has. Then solve the problem.

Extra Practice on page 80, Set A

Technology
Use Harcourt Mega Math, Ice Station Exploration, *Arctic Algebra*, Level Y.

Write and Evaluate Expressions

OBJECTIVE: Write and evaluate addition and subtraction expressions.

Quick Review

What is 5 more than each number?

1. 7   2. 10
3. 16   4. 23
5. 35

Vocabulary

expression

variable

Learn

PROBLEM Monica had $15 to go to the mall. Her mom gave her $5 more. She spent $7. How much money does she have left?

You can write an expression to show how much money Monica has left. An **expression** has numbers and operation signs, but does not have an equal sign.

$(15 + 5) - 7$ **Think:** $15 plus $5 minus $7

Find the value of $(15 + 5) - 7$.

$(15 + 5) - 7$ Add $15 and $5.
    ↓
$20 - 7$ Subtract $7 from $20.
       ↓
      $13

So, $(15 + 5) - 7$ is 13. Monica has $13 left.

Example 1 Write an expression to match the words. Then find the value of the expression.

A Marc earned $12. He spent $3 on a game and $5 on a shirt.

$12 - ($3 + $5)$ Add $3 and $5.
          ↓
$12 - 8 Subtract $8 from $12.
   ↓
  $4

So, the value of the expression is $4.

B Marc's uncle gave him $12. He spent $3 on a taco. Then he found $5.

$($12 - $3) + 5 Subtract $3 from $12.
   ↓
$9 + 5 Add $9 and $5.
    ↓
  $14

So, the value of the expression is $14.

C Jory had 17 toy cars. He gave 5 to Bill. Then, he gave 2 to Sam.

$(17 - 5) - 2$
     ↓
  $12 - 2$
       ↓
      10

So, the value of the expression is 10.

ERROR ALERT

Always do the operation in parentheses first, even if it comes second in the expression.

Expressions with Variables

Kyla buys a ticket to the water park. She spends $3 for lunch. What expression shows how much money she spends in all?

A **variable** is a letter or symbol that represents an unknown number. You can use a variable to show how much Kyla spends on the ticket.

price of ticket	plus	money spent for lunch
↓	↓	↓
■	+	3

So, the expression ■ + 3 shows how much money Kyla spends in all.

Example 2

Suppose admission to the water park costs $8. How much money does Kyla spend in all? Find the value of ■ + 3 when ■ = 8 to find how much she spends in all.

ONE WAY Use a model.

Use pattern blocks to model the expression ■ + 3. Let ⬡ represent the price of a ticket, and let ■ represent $1.

⬡ + ■ ■ ■

■ + 3

To find the value of ■ + 3 if ■ = 8, replace ⬡ with 8 ■s. Place the ■s in one group to show the value of the expression.

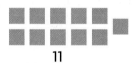

11

So, Kyla spends $11 in all.

ANOTHER WAY Use symbols.

Use the expression ■ + 3.

■ + 3	Replace ■ with 8, since the admission price is $8.
↓	
8 + 3	Add.
↓	
11	

So, Kyla spends $11 in all.

A letter can also be used as a variable.

Example 3 Find the value of the expression.

A $18 - n$ if $n = 6$.

$18 - n$	Replace n with 6.
↓	
$18 - 6$	Subtract 6 from 18.
↓	
12	

So, the value of the expression is 12.

B $9 + (y - 7)$ if $y = 15$.

$9 + (y - 7)$	Replace y with 15.
↓	
$9 + (15 - 7)$	Subtract 7 from 15.
↓	
$9 + 8$	Add.
↓	
17	

So, the value of the expression is 17.

1. There are 10 grapes in a bowl. Sara eats some of the grapes. Let g be the number of grapes she eats. Write an expression to show how many grapes are left.

Find the value of each expression.

2. $9 - (3 + 2)$ 3. $10 - (8 - 5)$ 4. $\blacksquare + 25$ if $\blacksquare = 7$ ✓ 5. $13 - n$ if $n = 6$

Write an expression with a variable. Tell what the variable represents.

6. Peter hangs 3 posters on the wall. Amber hangs some more posters on the wall.

✓ 7. Alisha found some shells on the beach. She gave 4 of them to Lance.

8. **TALK Math** Explain how to find the value of the expression $12 - (5 + m)$ if $m = 3$.

Independent Practice and Problem Solving

Find the value of each expression.

9. $14 + (7 + 3)$ 10. $17 - (6 - 5)$ 11. $\blacksquare - 18$ if $\blacksquare = 30$ 12. $20 - (5 - c)$ if $c = 3$
13. $(9 - 8) + 4$ 14. $(6 + 9) - 2$ 15. $8 - \blacksquare$ if $\blacksquare = 6$ 16. $(33 - m) + 3$ if $m = 11$

Write an expression to match the words.

17. Yara caught 15 fish. She caught 7 more. She threw 2 back.

18. Quan had 2 books. Lei gave her 3 and Barrey gave her 4.

Write an expression with a variable. Tell what the variable represents.

19. Denise had some rubber stamps. She loaned 6 rubber stamps to her teacher.

20. Jimmy has 16 model cars. He buys some more model cars.

21. Isis had 7 different collections. She started some more collections.

22. Ramiro had some money. He gave $20 to Anya.

USE DATA For 23–24, use the sign.

23. Keisha wants to buy 30 boxes of puppy treats for her local animal shelter. Will Keisha save more money if she buys 3 crates of 10 boxes, or 1 crate of 5 boxes and 1 crate of 25 boxes? How much will she save?

24. What is the least amount that it will cost Greg to buy 15 boxes?

25. Tyler had 50 boxes of treats. He gave some boxes to a local shelter. Write an expression to show how many boxes Tyler donated to the shelter.

Puppy Treats

Number of Boxes per Crate	Cost per Crate
5	$3
10	$5
25	$10
50	$18

26. Reasoning Place parentheses in the expression $16 - 7 - 4$ so the expression has a value of 13.

27. WRITE Math ▸ **What's the Error?** Taylor said the value of $20 - (9 + x)$ is 20 if $x = 9$. **Describe** how Taylor could have made the error. Find the correct value.

Learn About) Finding the Value of an Expression on a Number Line

You can use a number line to find the value of an expression that uses whole numbers.

Example

Use a number line to find the value of $(5 + 8) - 3$.

First, start at 5 and count on 8 spaces from 5.

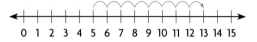

Then, count back 3 spaces. The number you end at is the value of the expression.

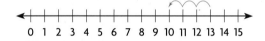

So, $(5 + 8) - 3 = 10$.

Try It

Use a number line to find the value of each expression.

28. $(6 + 5) - 4$ **29.** $(14 - 7) + 3$ **30.** $(13 - 4) - 5$ **31.** $8 + (7 - 4)$

Mixed Review and Test Prep

32. A bag holds 1 red tile, 1 green tile, and 5 blue tiles of the same size. Which color tile is Tia most likely to choose if she pulls a tile without looking? (Grade 3)

33. Test Prep There are 8 children around the table. Some of the children leave. Which expression shows the number of children still at the table?

   A $8 + c$ **C** $8 - c$

   B $c - 8$ **D** $c + 8$

34. On different days Josh sold 35, 27, and 15 tickets. Show how to use addition properties and mental math to find the total number of tickets Josh sold. (p. 42)

35. Test Prep There are 9 pears in a basket. Singh and Allie each take 2 pears. Write an expression that shows the number of pears left in the basket. How many pears are left in the basket?

3 Addition and Subtraction Equations

OBJECTIVE: Write and solve addition and subtraction equations.

Quick Review

1. $17 + 6$
2. $25 - 8$
3. $56 + 24$
4. $93 - 32$
5. $73 + 29$

Vocabulary

equation

Learn

PROBLEM A service dog has completed 4 months of its 9-month training program at Canine Companions. What equation can you write to show how many months the dog has left to finish its training?

An **equation** is a number sentence stating that two amounts are equal.

Example 1 Write an addition equation.

Match the words to write an equation. Use the variable m to show the number of months left to finish his training.

4 months	plus	months left	equals	9 months
↓	↓	↓	↓	↓
4	+	m	=	9

So, the equation is $4 + m = 9$.

Example 2 Write a subtraction equation.

There are 10 dog biscuits in a bowl. After the dogs eat some, there are 3 dog biscuits left.

Let b represent the number of dog biscuits eaten.

10 dog biscuits	minus	dog biscuits eaten	equals	3 dog biscuits left
↓	↓	↓	↓	↓
10	−	b	=	3

• **What if** there are 12 dog biscuits in the bowl? After some more dog biscuits are put in the bowl, there are 17 dog biscuits. How would the equation change?

Example 3 Write a problem for the equation $m - 3 = 4$.

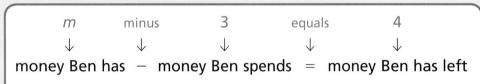

m	minus	3	equals	4
↓	↓	↓	↓	↓
money Ben has	−	money Ben spends	=	money Ben has left

After spending $3 for a dog bone, Ben has $4 left. How much money did Ben have to start with?

Solve Equations

An equation is true if the values on both sides of the equal sign are equal. You solve an equation when you find the value of the variable that makes the equation true.

In the problem, to find how many months the service dog has left to finish its training, you can solve the equation $4 + m = 9$.

 ONE WAY Use the strategy *predict and test*.

Materials ■ Equabeam® Balance

You can use the Equabeam® Balance to find the number that makes $4 + m = 9$ a true equation.

Step 1	**Step 2**
Show 4 on the left and 9 on the right.	Replace m with 4.　　Place 4 on the left side.
	$4 + 4 \stackrel{?}{=} 9$　　　$8 \neq 9$
	Replace m with 5.　　Place 5 on the left side.
	$4 + 5 \stackrel{?}{=} 9$　　　$9 = 9$ ✔

So, the service dog has 5 months left to finish its training.

ANOTHER WAY Use mental math.

Solve.	$14 - d = 8$	**Think:** 14 minus what number equals 8?
	$d = 6$	
Check:	$14 - 6 \stackrel{?}{=} 8$	Replace d with 6.
	$8 = 8$ ✔	The equation is true.

So, the value of d is 6.

Guided Practice

1. Which number, 8 or 9, makes the equation $n + 5 = 14$ true?

Write an equation. Use +, −, or = for each ●.

2. A box has 24 pens. There are some blue pens, p, and 8 red pens.

    $24 ● p ● 8$

✓3. Emil has 18 stamps. He uses some stamps, s, and now has 12 stamps left.

    $18 ● s ● 12$

Solve the equation.

4. $x + 9 = 17$ **5.** $c - 6 = 7$ **6.** $15 + \blacksquare = 21$ ✓**7.** $13 - n = 4$

8. (TALK Math) Explain how you can check that the equation
$20 + a = 29$ is true for $a = 9$.

Independent Practice and Problem Solving

Write an equation. Use +, −, or = for each ●.

9. There are 15 apples in the box. Some
are green apples, a, and 9 are red apples.

$$15 \bullet a \bullet 9$$

10. Andrea had some money, m. She spent
$8 and had $4 left.

$$m \bullet 8 \bullet 4$$

Solve the equation.

11. $4 + b = 16$ **12.** $\blacksquare - 5 = 20$ **13.** $m - 9 = 12$ **14.** $24 - n = 21$

Write words to match the equation.

15. $m + 5 = 13$ **16.** $15 - n = 4$ **17.** $12 - p = 8$ **18.** $y - 6 = 8$

USE DATA For 19–20, use the table.

19. How many more hearing dogs graduated than
service dogs?

20. The number of service dogs that graduated
in November is 6 less than the number of
service dogs that graduated in December.
Write and solve an equation to show the number
of service dogs that graduated in December.
Tell what the variable represents.

Graduating Dogs		
Month	Number of Hearing	Number of Service
February	8	2
May	5	4
November	9	4

21. Reasoning If $6 = m + 4$ and $c + m = 7$,
find m and c.

22. WRITE Math ▸ Compare the values of n
for $n + 8 = 12$ and $12 - n = 8$. **Explain**
how you solved each equation.

Mixed Review and Test Prep

23. A magazine has 207,620 readers. Write
the number of readers in word form. (p. 4)

24. A display has 35 dolls in it. Some of the
dolls are sold. Then 6 are returned. Write
an expression for the number of dolls in
the display now. (p. 66)

25. Test Prep Art class lasts 45 minutes.
Students work 35 minutes on their
projects. The rest of the time they clean
up. Which equation can be used to find
how long it takes to clean up?

A $35 + c = 45$ **C** $45 + c = 35$

B $35 - c = 45$ **D** $c - 45 = 35$

(Extra Practice) on page 80, Set C

Are We There Yet?

READ Math WORKSHOP

 Reading Skill Cause and Effect

Levi's and Cindy's families are meeting at Lake Ontario for vacation. Both families live the same distance from the lake. Levi's family drives 196 miles the first day and 223 miles the second day to reach the lake. Cindy's family drives 195 miles the first day. How far does Cindy's family drive on the second day to reach the lake?

Cause and effect can help you understand this problem.

Cause	Effect
The first day, Cindy's family drove fewer miles.	The second day, Cindy's family drives more miles than Levi's.

Write an equation that shows the distances each family travels. Let d represent the distance Cindy's family drives on the second day.

Levi's family		Cindy's family	
first day	second day	first day	second day
↓	↓	↓	↓

$$196 + 223 = 195 + d$$

Compare the numbers in the equation to solve. Use mental math to make an addend on the left side of the equation the same as the one on the right side.

Think: Since 196 is one more than 195, d has to be one more than 223 for the equation to be true.

▲ Lake Ontario, located north of New York, is 802 feet deep at its deepest point!

Problem Solving Use cause and effect to solve.

1. Solve the problem above.

2. Hannah's and Ravi's families plan to camp together near Lake Ontario. They live the same distance from the campground. Hannah's family drives 142 miles on the first day and the rest of the way on the second day. Ravi's family drives 143 miles on the first day and 176 miles on the second day. How far does Hannah's family drive on the second day? Write an equation. Tell what the variable represents and then solve.

Problem Solving Workshop
Strategy: Work Backward

OBJECTIVE: Solve problems using the strategy *work backward*.

Learn the Strategy

When you work backward to solve a problem, you start with the end result and use the facts in the problem to work back to the beginning of a problem.

Work backward from a total.

There are 16 pelicans at the pier. When more pelicans fly to the pier, there are 20 pelicans. How many more pelicans fly to the pier?

When you add to find a total, you can subtract to work backward to solve.

Write an addition equation to model the problem.

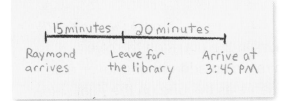

$16 + p = 20$ Let p = number of pelicans that fly to the pier.

To find the value of p, work backward.

$20 - 16 = p$

Work backward from an end time.

Raymond and Charity got to the library at 3:45 P.M. It takes 20 minutes to walk to the library from Charity's house, and Raymond got to Charity's house 15 minutes before they left for the library. At what time did Raymond arrive at Charity's house?

Use a model to find the time Raymond arrived at Charity's house.

15 minutes | 20 minutes

Raymond arrives | Leave for the library | Arrive at 3:45 PM

To find the time Raymond arrived at Charity's house, work backward.

TALK Math
How can you check your answer to the first problem?

74

Use the Strategy

PROBLEM A wildlife preserve in Zimbabwe, Africa, has a habitat for lions. The rangers released 8 lions back into the wild and then received 12 lions from another preserve. Now there are 24 lions at the preserve. How many lions did the preserve have before the release?

Read to Understand

- **What are you asked to find?**
- **What information will you use?**

Plan

- **What strategy can you use to solve the problem?**

  You can write an equation with a variable. Then solve the problem by working backward.

Solve

- **How can you use the strategy to solve the problem?**

  Write an equation with a variable to model the problem.

   Make sure the equation shows the sequence of events.

  Think: There were some lions before the release. Eight lions were released. Then the preserve received 12 lions. Now there are 24 lions.

  Choose a variable. Let b represent the number of lions before the release. To find the value of b, work backward.

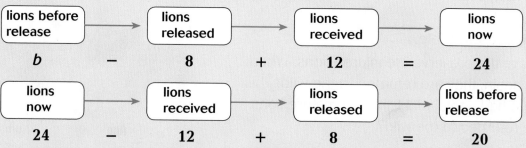

lions before release		lions released		lions received		lions now
b	$-$	8	$+$	12	$=$	24

lions now		lions received		lions released		lions before release
24	$-$	12	$+$	8	$=$	20

So, there were 20 lions before the release.

Check

- **Look back at the problem. Does the answer make sense for the problem? Explain.**

Guided Problem Solving

1. There are many volunteer teams that feed the lions at Léon Preserve. Another preserve needed help, so 10 volunteer teams left. The next day, 4 new volunteer teams arrived and now Léon Preserve has 15 teams. How many teams were there originally?

   First, choose a variable. Tell what the variable represents.

   Let v represent the original number of volunteer teams.

   Next, write an equation.

   $v - 10 + 4 = 15$

   Then, work backward.

   $15 - 4 + 10 = v$

   Finally, solve the equation.

   $\blacksquare = v$

2. **What if** 5 volunteer teams left and 11 arrived? How many teams were there originally?

3. Many volunteer teams must patrol and clean the lion preserve. Twelve teams leave the preserve on patrol. Seven teams arrive to clean. There are 23 teams at the preserve now. How many volunteer teams were there originally?

Problem Solving Strategy Practice

Work backward to solve.

4. It costs $2,900 to volunteer for 4 weeks at a lion breeding project. There is an extra cost for each additional week. It costs Jeff $3,500 to volunteer for 5 weeks. How much does each additional week cost?

USE DATA For 5–6, use the table.

5. The mature lions at the preserve are injured lions. When they are healthy again, they are returned to the wild. This year, the preserve had a total of 11 injured mature lions. How many were returned to the wild?

6. **WRITE Math** Last week, 7 cubs were moved to the adolescent group, and 4 cubs were born. **Explain** how to find how many cubs the preserve had last week.

7. **FAST FACT** The largest recorded African lion weighed 690 pounds. The difference in weight between the largest lion and an average lion is 120 pounds. How much does an average African lion weigh?

Preserve Lion Population

Age	Number
Cubs	18
Adolescents	14
Mature	2
Older	7

Mixed Strategy Practice

8. Daily duties for each animal include grooming, walking, and feeding. If a volunteer is in charge of 7 animals, how many daily duties will the volunteer do?

USE DATA For 9–10, use the bar graph.

9. There were more volunteers for the lion project during the summer than during the spring. If 105 people volunteered in the summer, how many more volunteers were there than in the spring?

10. During a two-week stay at the wildlife preserve in the summer, there were 17 fewer volunteers than the total number for the spring. How many volunteers were there in the two-week period?

11. **Pose a Problem** Look back at Problem 7. Write a similar problem by exchanging the known and unknown information.

12. **Open-Ended** Zawati Preserve had some volunteers. Some of the volunteers went to other preserves. Zawati Preserve has 12 volunteers left. How many volunteers might have been there to begin with and how many might have left for other preserves?

13. Volunteers rescued a lion, an elephant, and a leopard from traps. They rescued the lion before the leopard. The lion was not the first animal rescued. In what order did the volunteers rescue the animals?

CHALLENGE YOURSELF

Visitors to the wildlife preserve can take a guided tour to see the animals. There were 373 visitors to the preserve in January and 388 visitors in February.

14. Each month, the preserve had 15 more visitors than the month before. How many visitors did the preserve have in June, July, and August combined?

15. During January, 151 more children than adults visited the preserve. Draw a diagram to find how many adults visited the preserve during January.

Choose a STRATEGY

Draw a Diagram or Picture

Make a Model or Act It Out

Make an Organized List

Find a Pattern

Make a Table or Graph

Predict and Test

Work Backward

Solve a Simpler Problem

Write an Equation

Use Logical Reasoning

Spring Project Volunteers

5 Patterns: Find a Rule

OBJECTIVE: Find a rule for a number relationship and write an equation for the rule.

Quick Review

Add 12 to each number.

1. 6   2. 14
3. 23   4. 35
5. 60

Learn

PROBLEM A pattern of figures is made using a row of triangles 1 unit long on each side. The perimeter of the first figure is 3 units. The second figure has 2 triangles and a perimeter of 4 units. The third figure has 3 triangles and a perimeter of 5 units. Find a rule for the perimeter of a figure using the number of triangles in the figure.

Remember
Perimeter is the distance around a figure.

 Activity Materials ■ triangle pattern blocks

- Use pattern blocks to model the pattern.
- Make an input/output table. The input, *t*, is the number of triangles, and the output, *p*, is the perimeter.
- Find a pattern in the table.
  Pattern: The output is 2 more than the input.

Input	Output
t	*p*
1	3
2	4
3	5
4	■
5	■

So, the rule is the perimeter is 2 more than the number of triangles.

You can use the rule to write an equation. Use variables to show the input and output.

input   output
  ↓   ↓
$t + 2 = p$ **Think:** To find the value of *p*, add 2 to *t*.

Examples Find a rule. Write your rule as an equation. Use the equation to extend your pattern.

A

Input	*x*	8	10	12	14	16
Output	*y*	4	6	8	■	■

Rule: Subtract 4 from *x*.
Equation: $x - 4 = y$

Test your rule for each pair of numbers in the table.

$x - 4 = y$ $x - 4 = y$
$14 - 4 = 10$ $16 - 4 = 12$

So, the next two numbers are 10 and 12.

B

Input	*b*	9	17	25	33	■
Output	*c*	16	24	32	40	48

Rule: Add 7 to *b*.
Equation: $b + 7 = c$

Test your rule for each pair of numbers in the table.

$b + 7 = c$
$41 + 7 = 48$ **Think:** Work backward, $b = 48 - 7$.

So, the next number is 41.

✓ **1.** Rule: Add 15 to the input, r. The equation is: $r + 15 = s$.
What are the next two numbers in the pattern?

Input	r	7	9	12	16	20	23
Output	s	22	24	27	31	■	■

Find a rule. Write your rule as an equation. Use the equation to extend your pattern.

✓ **2.**

Input	a	12	25	31	43	59	62	74
Output	b	20	33	39	■	■	■	■

✓ **3.**

Input	m	62	58	47	31	24	17	9
Output	n	57	53	42	■	■	■	■

4. ⎾**TALK Math**⏌ **Explain** why it is important to test your rule with all the numbers in an input/output table.

Independent Practice and Problem Solving

Find a rule. Write your rule as an equation. Use the equation to extend your pattern.

5.

Input	x	35	42	63	75	80	97	98
Output	y	24	31	52	■	■	■	■

6.

Input	w	14	21	45	■	■	■	■
Output	x	34	41	65	73	92	100	123

Use the rule and equation to make an input/output table.

7. Add 16 to k.
$k + 16 = m$

8. Subtract 10 from b.
$b - 10 = c$

9. Add 23 to f.
$f + 23 = g$

10. Subtract 17 from x.
$x - 17 = y$

USE DATA For 11–12, use the table.

11. Find a rule. Write your rule as an equation for the information in the table. Use the equation to extend your pattern.

12. ▐WRITE Math▶ **What's the Question?** Mabel has $12 on Friday after buying lunch each day that week. The answer is $27.

Hot Lunch Accounts	
Before Lunch	After Lunch
$16	$13
$24	$21
$29	$26
$33	$30

Mixed Review and Test Prep

13. Channel 12 had 78,553 viewers on Sunday and 35,192 on Monday. About how many more viewers did Channel 12 have on Sunday? (p. 38)

14. Dan has $18. He buys a book and has $11 left. Write and solve an equation to find how much the book cost. (p. 70)

15. **Test Prep** Which equation describes the data in the table?

Input	r	14	23	31	39
Output	s	8	17	25	33

A $r + 6 = s$ **C** $s - 6 = r$

B $r - 6 = s$ **D** $r + s = 6$

Extra Practice on page 80, Set D

Extra Practice

Set A Find the missing number. Name the property you used. (pp. 64–65)

1. $62 + 46 = 46 +$ ■

2. $53 + (64 +$ ■$) = (53 + 64) + 19$

3. ■$+ 0 = 92$

4. $98 =$ ■$+ 98$

5. $(23 + 77) + 54 = 23 + ($■$+ 54)$

6. $79 + 63 = 63 +$ ■

Set B Find the value of each expression. (pp. 66–69)

1. $11 + (8 - 4)$

2. $24 - (7 + 9)$

3. $6 - (10 - 8)$

4. $13 + (15 - 8)$

5. ■$- 15$
   if ■$= 65$

6. $25 - (9 - c)$
   if $c = 4$

7. $53 +$ ■
   if ■$= 18$

8. $16 - (c + 4)$
   if $c = 7$

Write an expression with a variable. Tell what the variable represents.

9. Nikolai had some cookies. He gave 7 cookies to his friends.

10. Donna has 12 books. She buys some more at the book fair.

Set C Write an equation. Use +, −, or = for each ●. (pp. 70–73)

1. Garrett has 36 DVDs. Some are movies, and the other 9 are games.

$$36 \bullet m \bullet 9$$

2. Kristi spends $4 for a sandwich. She has $8 left.

$$w \bullet 4 \bullet 8$$

3. Fatima has 12 pairs of earrings. Four pairs are gold and the rest are silver.

$$4 \bullet s \bullet 12$$

4. Lachlan and his father used 3 cans of paint. They had 5 cans to begin with, and they have some left.

$$5 \bullet c \bullet 3$$

Solve the equation.

5. $9 + n = 17$

6. ■$- 8 = 15$

7. $n - 15 = 20$

8. $30 - b = 20$

9. $k - 33 = 7$

10. $g + 19 = 25$

11. $41 + m = 59$

12. $9 +$ ■$= 100$

Set D Find a rule. Write your rule as an equation.
Use your equation to extend your pattern. (pp. 78–79)

1.
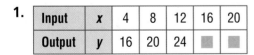

Input	x	4	8	12	16	20
Output	y	16	20	24	■	■

2.

Input	x	32	47	55	■	■
Output	y	23	38	46	73	88

3.

Input	x	19	27	38	46	72
Output	y	26	34	45	■	■

4.

Input	x	71	80	85	■	■
Output	y	68	77	82	89	95

TECHNOLOGY ★ CONNECTION

Spreadsheet: Graph Ordered Pairs

You can represent geometric patterns in tables and on graphs.

Materials ■ spreadsheet program ■ tiles

Step 1 Use square tiles to model the pattern of figures up to a figure with 10 blocks.

Step 2 Make an input/output table for the number of squares and the perimeter of each figure. Write ordered pairs for each input/output value.

Input (Number of Squares)	Output (Perimeter in units)	Ordered Pair
1	4	(1,4)
2	6	(2,6)
3	8	(3,8)
4	10	(4,10)
5	■	■

Step 3 Enter the input/output data into a spreadsheet. To move among cells in the spreadsheet, use the arrow keys or click on the desired cell.

	A	B
1	Number of Squares	Perimeter (in units)
2	1	4
3	2	6
4	3	8
5	4	10
6	5	12
7	6	14
8	7	16

Step 4 Make a graph of the input/output data. Enter a title and labels for the graph.

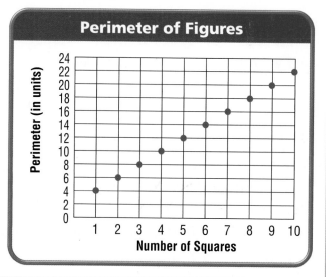

Try It

1. Which ordered pair corresponds to a figure with 10 blocks?

2. **Explore More   Explain**, in units, the relationship between the number of squares and the perimeter.

Use Relational Thinking

Baseball Cards

Mike has 27 baseball cards and buys 18 more cards. Laura has the same number of baseball cards as Mike after she buys 19 cards. How many baseball cards did Laura have before she bought 19 cards?

You can write an equation to find the number of baseball cards Laura had.

Mike's   **Laura's**

27 cards + 18 cards = x cards + 19 cards

27 + 18 = x + 19

Think: The value of the left side of an equation is the same as the value of the right side.

Use relational thinking to find the value of x without computing.

$27 + 18 = x + 19$
$27 + 18 = 26 + 19$ **Think:** 19 is 1 more than 18, so x is 1 less than 27.
$x = 26$

So, Laura had 26 baseball cards before she bought 19 cards.

Examples Use relational thinking.

A $12 + 9 = 10 + 8 + n$ **Think:** 10 is 2 less
$12 + 9 = 10 + 8 + 3$ than 12, and 8 is
1 less than 9.
$n = 3$

So, n is $2 + 1$, or 3.

B $75 - 36 = 75 - 35 - s$ **Think:** 75 is
$75 - 36 = 75 - 35 - 1$ equal to 75,
and 35 is 1
$s = 1$ less than 36.

So, s is 1.

Try It
Use relational thinking to find the value of the variable.

1. $8 + 5 = p + 6$

2. $85 - 25 = 75 - y$

3. $449 + 862 = 450 + b$

4. $100 - 77 = s - 79$

5. $4 + 38 = 4 + 36 + x$

6. $99 - 68 = 99 - 66 - t$

7. $55 + 59 = 50 + 50 + c$

8. $432 - 167 = 432 - 67 - n$

9. $87 + 56 = 86 + 55 + p$

10. **WRITE Math** ▸ **Explain** how you used relational thinking to solve Problem 7.

Chapter 3 Review/Test

Check Vocabulary and Concepts

Choose the best term from the box.

VOCABULARY

Associative Property
  of Addition
Commutative Property
  of Addition
equation

1. An __?__ is a number sentence stating that two amounts are equal. (p.70)

2. Numbers can be added in any order and the sum will be the same. This is called the __?__ . (p. 64)

Check Skills

Find the missing number. Name the property you used. (pp. 64–65)

3. $52 + 28 = 28 + \blacksquare$

4. $\blacksquare + 0 = 67$

5. $28 + (12 + \blacksquare) = (28 + 12) + 38$

Find the value of each expression. (pp. 66–69)

6. $16 + (9 - 5)$

7. $27 - (7 + 8)$

8. $25 + (11 - 7)$

9. $33 - (10 - 6)$

10. $\blacksquare - 12$
    if $\blacksquare = 52$

11. $45 - (d + 9)$
    if $d = 4$

12. $36 + (15 - y)$
    if $y = 7$

13. $14 + \blacksquare$
    if $\blacksquare = 25$

Solve the equation. (pp. 70–73)

14. $8 + d = 15$

15. $k - 7 = 35$

16. $n + 21 = 24$

17. $17 - b = 9$

18. $a + 7 = 23$

19. $8 + g = 21$

20. $m - 9 = 12$

21. $26 - w = 18$

Find a rule. Write your rule as an equation. Use your equation to extend the pattern. (pp. 78–79)

22.

Input	x	23	35	49	56	71
Output	y	36	48	62	■	■

23.

Input	x	26	34	46	■	■
Output	y	11	19	31	58	77

Check Problem Solving

Solve. (pp. 74–77)

24. Ellie had 37 stuffed animals in her collection. Her aunt gave her some more stuffed animals to add to her collection, so now she has 43. How many stuffed animals did her aunt give her?

25. **WRITE Math** ▸ Manuel saved $64 for a new bicycle, including the $18 he earned mowing lawns. Write an equation. **Explain** how to work backward to find how much money Manuel had before he mowed the lawns.

Unit Review/Test
Chapters 1–3

Multiple Choice

1. The table shows attendance at some amusement parks in 2004 and 2005.

Amusement Park Visitors	
Year	**Number of Visitors**
2004	328 million
2005	335 million

How many more amusement park visitors were there in 2005 than in 2004? (p. 48)

A 7 million

B 8 million

C 9 million

D 653 million

2. Which number is shown in expanded form? (p. 4)

$$90,000 + 3,000 + 600 + 40 + 3$$

A 99,643   **C** 93,064

B 93,643   **D** 90,364

3. Sherri found a grand piano that costs $29,445. To the nearest thousand, how much does the piano cost? (p. 34)

A $30,000   **C** $29,000

B $29,500   **D** $20,000

4. Which digit is in the millions place in 35,970,241? (p. 10)

A 9   **C** 5

B 7   **D** 3

5. A flight from New York to Austin costs $453 in July and $298 in October. About how much more does the flight cost in July than in October? (p. 38)

A $50   **C** $250

B $150   **D** $800

6. What is the value of the digit 8 in 48,213? (p. 4)

A 80,000   **C** 800

B 8,000   **D** 80

7. Jake had $43. He spent some on music and $3 on a magazine. Now he has $21 left. How much did he spend on music? (p. 74)

A $24   **C** $19

B $21   **D** $17

8. Which number sentence shows the inverse operation for $3 + 6 = 9$? (p. 32)

A $9 - 3 = 6$ **C** $6 + 3 = 9$

B $9 \div 3 = 3$ **D** $9 + 3 = 12$

9. Which equation describes the data in the table? (p. 78)

Input	x	5	7	9	11	13
Output	y	14	16	18	20	22

A $x + 8 = y$ **C** $x + 10 = y$

B $x + 9 = y$ **D** $x + 11 = y$

GO ONLINE **Technology** Use *Online Assessment.*

10. Marcos had some comic books. At Cory's Comics he bought 4 more. Now Marcos has 43 comic books in all. Which equation could be used to find how many comic books Marcos had before he went to Cory's Comics? (p. 70)

A $43 = \blacksquare + 4$

B $43 = \blacksquare - 43$

C $43 = \blacksquare - 4$

D $\blacksquare = 43 + 4$

11. The table shows the number of cars that use Exit 8 on Trans-State Parkway on different days.

Exit 8 Traffic	
Day	Number of Cars
Sunday	2,451
Monday	3,612
Tuesday	3,519

How many cars in all use Exit 8 on Sunday and Monday? (p. 48)

A 1,161

B 5,063

C 6,062

D 6,063

12. Which digit makes the number sentence true? (p. 12)

$$4,201,351 > 4,20\blacksquare,351$$

A 3

B 2

C 1

D 0

Short Response

13. Alma had 9 CDs. She gave some of the CDs to Ricky. Write an expression to show how many CDs Alma has left. (p. 66)

14. The first edition of the *Oxford English Dictionary* was published in 1928. The third edition was published online in 2000. How many years after the first edition was the third edition published? (p. 52)

15. Order the numbers from greatest to least. (p. 16)

$$12,413; \ 13,313; \ 12,213; \ 13,113$$

16. A music group printed 20,000 postcards. They handed out 16,263. About how many postcards were not handed out? (p. 38)

17. An online store received 8,827 orders on Monday. On Tuesday, just 1,993 orders were left to be shipped. How many orders were shipped on Monday? (p. 48)

Extended Response [WRITE Math]

18. Kathleen's computer stores 900 songs. She has 883 songs and wants to add 15 more. Will 15 more songs fit on Kathleen's computer? Do you need an exact answer or an estimate. **Explain.** (p. 46)

19. **Explain** how you know that this number sentence is true. (p. 64)

$$(14 + 3) + 5 = 14 + (3 + 5)$$

THE WORLD ALMANAC FOR KIDS

Languages We Speak

Languages at Home

No one is sure how many languages there are in the world, but there are certainly more than 4,000. Most people in the United States speak English. However, many people speak other languages, too.

Language Spoken at Home in the United States

Language	Number of Speakers over 5 Years Old
Chinese	2,193,000
English Only	214,809,000
French	1,379,000
German	1,094,000
Italian	782,000
Spanish	29,698,000

FACT·ACTIVITY

Use the table above to answer the questions.

❶ If you round to the nearest million, which languages have about 1 million speakers?

❷ Do more speakers over 5 years old speak German or French at home?

❸ Which language has a number of speakers with the digit 2 in the thousands place?

❹ Which language's number of speakers would round to 2,000,000?

❺ In which number does the digit 1 have the greatest value?

❻ Write the number of French speakers in word form.

❼ **WRITE Math** ▶ **Explain** how to round the number of Spanish speakers to the nearest hundred thousand.

23 18 9 20 9 14 7
9 14   3 15 4 5

Codes are like secret languages. Morse code allows people to communicate over long distances without speaking.

In 1838, the American inventor Samuel F. B. Morse developed a code for sending messages over electrical wires. His code used short pulses ("dots") and long pulses ("dashes") of electricity to represent letters and numbers.

Morse Code

A	B	C	D	E	F	G	H	I	J	K	L	M
.-	-...	-.-.	-..	.	..-.	--.	....	..	.---	-.-	.-..	--

N	O	P	Q	R	S	T	U	V	W	X	Y	Z
-.	---	.--.	--.-	.-.	...	-	..-	...-	.--	-..-	-.--	--..

1	2	3	4	5	6	7	8	9	0
.----	..---	...--	....-	.....	-....	--...	---..	----.	-----

Telegraph operators tap a key like this to send messages in Morse code.

FACT·ACTIVITY

Use codes to write messages.

1. Show your name and birth date in Morse code.

2. The title of this page is written in a simple number code. The chart to the right shows the code used. Use the code to find the title of this page.

3. Make up your own number code.

► Make a different code using the same 26 letters.

► How can you use number patterns to make a new code?

► How can you use what you know about place value to make up a new code?

► Write a message in your code. Do not put the solution on the page. Give it to a few classmates to see if they can crack the code!

Number Code

A = 1	B = 2	C = 3	D = 4
E = 5	F = 6	G = 7	H = 8
I = 9	J = 10	K = 11	L = 12
M = 13	N = 14	O = 15	P = 16
Q = 17	R = 18	S = 19	T = 20
U = 21	V = 22	W = 23	X = 24
Y = 25	Z = 26		

2 Multiplication and Division Facts

Save the Blackfooted Ferret

Math on Location

with
Chapter Projects

1

Many families like this baby black-footed ferret's family of 4 are protected and fed by scientists.

2

Family groups are prepared to live in divided areas in the wild by living in similar, but protected, areas.

3

Protection and preparation equal multiple strong families for a species once considered extinct.

VOCABULARY POWER

TALK Math

Look at the words below the first **Math on Location** photograph. If each family group in the protected area has the same number of ferrets as that family, how could you find the number of ferrets in 6 family groups?

READ Math

REVIEW VOCABULARY You learned the words below when you learned multiplication and division facts. How do these words relate to **Math on Location**?

divide to separate into equal groups; the opposite operation of multiplication

fact family a set of related multiplication and division, or addition and subtraction, number sentences

multiply when you combine equal groups, you can multiply to find how many in all; the opposite operation of division

WRITE Math ▶

Copy and complete the Venn diagram below. Use what you know about multiplication and division facts to complete the Venn diagram.

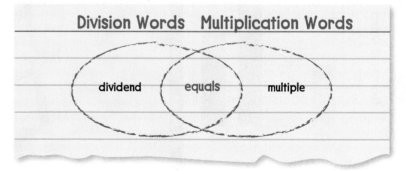

Division Words   Multiplication Words

dividend   equals   multiple

Technology
Multimedia Math Glossary link at
www.harcourtschool.com/hspmath

4 Multiplication and Division Facts

Investigate

Use the bar graph. Suppose there are at least 2 cars on each roller coaster train and that each train is filled with riders. What are the possible numbers of cars each train might have? Choose a roller coaster, and draw pictures of how the train could look.

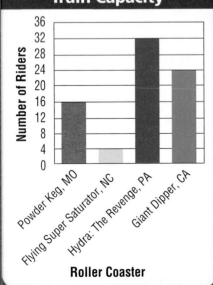

Roller Coaster Train Capacity

Number of Riders

36
32
28
24
20
16
12
8
4
0

Powder Keg, MO
Flying Super Saturator, NC
Hydra: The Revenge, PA
Giant Dipper, CA

Roller Coaster

≡FAST FACT

The roller coaster, Hydra: The Revenge, is in Pennsylvania. Its cars have no floor. The Hydra roller coaster has 3,198 feet of track. In one hour, 1,245 people can ride on it.

GO ONLINE

Technology
Student pages are available in the Student eBook.

Check your understanding of important skills
needed for success in Chapter 4.

▶ **Meaning of Multiplication**

Copy and complete each number sentence.

1.
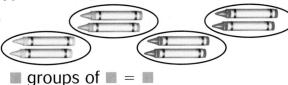

■ groups of ■ = ■

2.

■ rows of ■ = ■

3.

■ rows of ■ = ■

4.
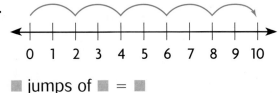

0 1 2 3 4 5 6 7 8 9 10

■ jumps of ■ = ■

▶ **Meaning of Division**

Answer the questions for each picture.

5. How many stars are there in all?
6. How many equal groups are there?
7. How many stars are in each group?

8. How many tiles are there in all?
9. How many equal rows are there?
10. How many tiles are in each row?

VOCABULARY POWER

CHAPTER VOCABULARY

addition	inverse
array	operations
divide	multiple
dividend	multiply
divisor	product
fact family	quotient
factor	square number
	subtraction

WARM-UP WORDS

divide to separate into equal groups; the opposite operation of multiplication

inverse operations operations, such as multiplication and division, that undo each other

multiply when you combine equal groups, you can multiply to find how many in all; the opposite operation of division

ALGEBRA
Relate Operations

OBJECTIVE: Relate repeated addition to multiplication and repeated subtraction to division.

Quick Review

1. $7 + 7$
2. $3 + 3 + 3$
3. $21 - 7$
4. $14 - 7$
5. $7 - 7$

Vocabulary

multiply   divide

Learn

When you **multiply**, you join equal-size groups. When you **divide**, you separate into equal-size groups or you find how many in each group.

PROBLEM The miniature train ride has 6 cars. Each car holds 4 people. How many people at a time can ride the train?

Example 1 Use repeated addition and multiplication.

Draw a picture to show 6 groups of 4.

Add to find how many in all.	Multiply to find how many in all.
Write: $4 + 4 + 4 + 4 + 4 + 4 = 24$	**Write:** $6 \times 4 = 24$, or $\begin{array}{r} 4 \\ \times 6 \\ \hline 24 \end{array}$
Read: 6 fours equal 24.	**Read:** 6 times 4 equals 24.

So, 24 people at a time can ride the train.

ERROR ALERT

Remember that the multiplication sign ($\times$) is different from the plus sign ($+$). 6×4 means 6 groups of 4. $6 + 4$ means 6 and 4 more.

Example 2 Use repeated subtraction and division.

There are 12 people waiting to ride the miniature train. Each car holds 4 people. How many cars will the 12 people fill?

Subtract to find how many equal-size groups there are. Start with 12. Take away groups of 4 until you reach zero.	Divide to find how many equal-size groups there are.
Count the number of times you subtract 4.	There are 3 groups of 4.
Write: $12 - 4 - 4 - 4 = 0$	**Write:** $12 \div 4 = 3$, or $4\overline{)12}\,^{3}$
Read: From 12 subtract 4 three times.	**Read:** 12 divided by 4 equals 3.

So, the 12 people will fill 3 cars.

Copy and complete.

1. ■ + ■ = ■
   ■ groups of ■ = ■
   ■ × ■ = ■

2. 6 − 2 − ■ − ■ = ■
   ■ ÷ ■ = ■

Write the related multiplication or division sentence. Draw a picture that shows the sentence.

3. 5 groups of 6 equal 30.   ✅ 4. 9 − 3 − 3 − 3 = 0   ✅ 5. 3 + 3 + 3 + 3 + 3 = 15

6. **TALK Math** A ride has 4 cars that hold 5 people each. How many people at a time can ride? Show two ways to solve this problem. **Explain** how the two ways are related.

Independent Practice and Problem Solving

Write the related multiplication or division sentence. Draw a picture that shows the sentence.

7. 14 − 7 − 7 = 0

8. 4 + 4 + 4 = 12

9. 12 − 6 − 6 = 0

Reasoning Tell whether the number sentence is *true* or *false*. If false, explain how you know.

10. $8 + 8 + 8 + 8 + 8 \stackrel{?}{=} 5 \times 8$ 11. $3 \times 7 \stackrel{?}{=} 14 + 7$ 12. $5 \times 4 \stackrel{?}{=} 4 + 4 + 4 + 4$

13. Thirty-six people at a time can ride the Scrambler. Each car holds 3 people. If 8 cars are full and the rest of the cars are empty, how many more people can get on?

14. Sara has 27 tickets. If each ride costs 3 tickets, how many different rides can she go on?

15. Andy says $10 \times 2 = 20$. How can he check his answer?

16. **WRITE Math** Is 2×3 equal to 3×2? Use related addition facts to **explain.**

Mixed Review and Test Prep

17. What polygon has exactly 3 sides?
    (Grade 3)

18. There were 26 people in line for a ride. After some people got on, 12 people were left in line. Write and solve an equation to find how many people got on the ride. (p. 70)

19. **Test Prep** A roller coaster can hold 21 people in 7 cars. How many people can each car hold?

    A 2   C 4

    B 3   D 6

Extra Practice on page 110, Set A

ALGEBRA
Relate Multiplication and Division

OBJECTIVE: Use the inverse relationship between multiplication and division to solve problems.

Learn

PROBLEM A box of crayons holds 2 rows of 8 crayons each. How many crayons does the box hold?

Example 1 Use repeated addition.

$2 \times 8 = n$ Think: $2 \times 8 = 8 + 8$, or 16.
     $\downarrow$
$2 \times 8 = 16$

So, the box holds 16 crayons.

Multiplication and division using the same number are opposite operations, or **inverse operations**. One operation undoes the other.

A **fact family**, a set of related multiplication and division sentences using the same numbers, shows this relationship.

factor	factor	**product**	**dividend**	**divisor**	**quotient**
2	× 8	= 16	16	÷ 8	= 2
8	× 2	= 16	16	÷ 2	= 8

← fact family for 2, 8, 16

Example 2 Use a related multiplication sentence.
Another box holds 16 crayons. There are 2 crayons of each color. How many colors of crayons are in the box?

$16 \div 2 = n$ Think: $8 \times 2 = 16$, so $16 \div 2 = 8$.
     $\downarrow$
$16 \div 2 = 8$

So, the box holds 8 colors of crayons.

Guided Practice

Copy and complete the fact family.

1. $4 \times 8 = 32$ $32 \div \blacksquare = 4$
   $8 \times \blacksquare = 32$ $\blacksquare \div 4 = 8$

Write the fact family for the set of numbers.

2. 2, 5, 10   **3.** 3, 4, 12   **4.** 2, 6, 12   ✓ **5.** 2, 3, 6   ✓ **6.** 1, 3, 3

7. (TALK Math) **Explain** how to use a fact family to write the related multiplication and division sentences.

Independent Practice and Problem Solving

Write the fact family for the set of numbers.

8. 2, 7, 14   **9.** 1, 4, 4   **10.** 3, 5, 15   **11.** 3, 3, 9   **12.** 5, 6, 30

Find the value of the variable. Then write a related sentence.

13. $24 \div 8 = n$ **14.** $3 \times 10 = c$ **15.** $8 \div 1 = y$ **16.** $36 \div m = 9$ **17.** $7 \times a = 28$

18. $6 \times 1 = b$ **19.** $35 \div 5 = p$ **20.** $18 \div 9 = n$ **21.** $8 \times c = 40$ **22.** $y \div 3 = 7$

USE DATA For 23–24, use the pictograph.

23. What if the crayon factory made 8 different shades of yellow? How many symbols would represent 8 shades in the pictograph?

24. How many different shades of crayon colors does the crayon factory make?

25. ≡**FAST FACT** The average American child will use up about 730 crayons by the age of 10, or about 6 crayons each month. About how many crayons will a child use up in 4 months?

26. (WRITE Math) ▸ **What's the Error?** Dale says that 2×6 is in the same fact family as $6 \div 2$. Is he right? **Explain** why or why not.

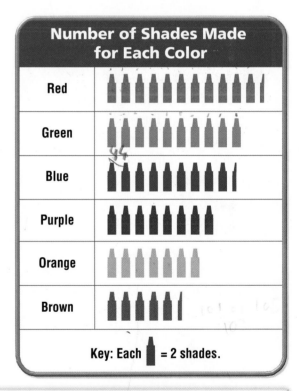

Number of Shades Made for Each Color

Red	
Green	
Blue	
Purple	
Orange	
Brown	

Key: Each ▐ = 2 shades.

Mixed Review and Test Prep

27. Use the pictograph above. How many more shades of green crayons does the crayon factory make than shades of purple crayons? (Grade 3)

28. There are 24 crayons in a box. Randee removes some crayons. Write an expression that shows the number of crayons left in the box. (p. 66)

29. **Test Prep** Suzy colored 3 pages in a coloring book. Don colored 6 times as many pages as Suzy colored. How many pages did Don color?

  A 3   **C** 9

  B 6   **D** 18

Extra Practice on page 110, Set B

3 Multiply and Divide Facts Through 5

OBJECTIVE: Multiply and divide facts from 0 through 5.

Quick Review

Write the fact family.

1. 2, 3, 6
2. 1, 3, 3
3. 3, 5, 15
4. 4, 7, 28
5. 2, 9, 18

Learn

Mr. Chen asked his students to use models to show that multiplication and division are inverse operations. This is how they showed their work.

A Amanda made 4 quilt blocks. How many rectangles did she use?

$4 \times 3 = 12$

$12 \div 4 = 3$

First, I made 4 groups of 3 rectangles to get 12 rectangles. Then, to check, I used 12 rectangles and separated them into 4 groups to get 3 in each group.

B Jon's quilt is 2 times as long as Mia's quilt. Mia's quilt is 4 blocks long. How long is Jon's quilt?

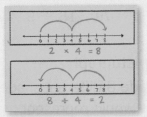

$2 \times 4 = 8$

$8 \div 4 = 2$

I started at 0 on a number line and made 2 jumps of 4 to land at 8. Then, to check, I started at 8 and took 2 jumps of 4 back to 0.

▲ In a rail fence quilt each quilt block is made by sewing 3 rectangular strips together.

C Paul's quilt has 20 blocks, with 4 blocks in each row. How many rows does his quilt have?

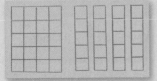

$5 \times 4 = 20$ $20 \div 4 = 5$

I made 5 rows of 4 blocks to make 20 blocks. Then, to check, I divided 20 blocks into 4 columns to get 5 in each column.

D Ella used 21 rectangles to make some quilt blocks with 3 rectangles in each. How many quilt blocks did she make?

Since there are 3 rectangles in each block, I found 21 by looking down column 3. Then I looked left to find the quotient, 7.

To check, I looked across row 7 and down column 3 to find the product, 21.

$21 \div 3 = 7$, so $7 \times 3 = 21$.

×	0	1	2	3	4	5
0	0	0	0	0	0	0
1	0	1	2	3	4	5
2	0	2	4	6	8	10
3	0	3	6	9	12	15
4	0	4	8	12	16	20
5	0	5	10	15	20	25
6	0	6	12	18	24	30
7	0	7	14	21	28	35
8	0	8	16	24	32	40
9	0	9	18	27	36	45

- **Reasoning** Use the multiplication table to show that $0 \div 5 = 0$. Then use the table to show that $5 \div 0 = 5$ does not make sense.

Guided Practice

Find the product or quotient. Then write a related multiplication or division sentence.

1. $2 \times 5 = n$

2. $6 \div 3 = n$

3. $2 \times 4 = n$

Find the product or quotient.

4. 6×1 **5.** $14 \div 2$ **6.** 8×3 **7.** $36 \div 4$ **8.** 3×3 **9.** $15 \div 5$

10. **TALK Math** **Explain** why division by a number is the inverse of multiplication by that number. Give an example. You may wish to draw a model.

Independent Practice and Problem Solving

Find the product or quotient.

11. 6×2 **12.** $10 \div 1$ **13.** 9×3 **14.** $28 \div 4$ **15.** $27 \div 3$ **16.** 6×5

17. 4×1 **18.** 10×5 **19.** $24 \div 4$ **20.** $16 \div 2$ **21.** 8×4 **22.** $40 \div 4$

★**Algebra** **Find the value of $n \times 4$ for each value of n.**

23. $n = 4$ **24.** $n = 1$ **25.** $n = 6$ **26.** $n = 10$ **27.** $n = 5$ **28.** $n = 0$

USE DATA For 29–31, use the quilt block.

29. Maya wants to make 4 quilt blocks like this one. She cut out 4 squares and 8 triangles. How many more triangles does she need to cut out?

30. Enrique's quilt is 2 quilt blocks by 2 quilt blocks. How many squares and triangles did he cut out?

31. **WRITE Math** **What's the Question?** Davis cut out 28 triangles. The answer is 7 squares.

Mixed Review and Test Prep

32. Which fact does **NOT** belong to the fact family for 1, 5, 5? (p. 94)

$5 \times 1 = 5$ $\qquad$ $5 \div 5 = 1$
$5 \div 1 = 5$ $\qquad$ $1 + 4 = 5$

33. Order 408, 98, 480, and 804 from least to greatest. (p. 16)

34. **Test Prep** A quilt is 3 quilt blocks wide and 5 quilt blocks long. How many quilt blocks does it have in all?

A 2 $\qquad\qquad$ **C** 15

B 8 $\qquad\qquad$ **D** 35

Extra Practice on page 110, Set C

Multiply and Divide Facts Through 10

OBJECTIVE: Multiply and divide facts through 10.

Learn

Using strategies can help you learn the multiplication and division facts that you do not know.

PROBLEM A checkerboard has 8 squares on each side. How many squares are on a checkerboard?

To find the product of 8 and 8, you can break apart one of the factors into products you know.

Activity **Use the break apart strategy.**
Materials ■ centimeter grid paper

Multiply. 8×8

Step 1	Step 2	Step 3
Draw a square array that is 8 units wide and 8 units long. Think of the area as 8×8.	Cut apart the array to make two smaller arrays for products you know.	Find the sum of the products of the two smaller arrays.

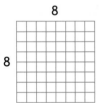

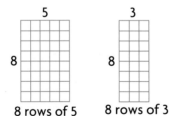

8 rows of 5   8 rows of 3

The factor 8 is now 5 plus 3.

$$8 \times 5 = 40$$
$$8 \times 3 = 24$$
$$40 + 24 = 64$$

So, there are 64 squares on a checkerboard.

• **What if** you cut apart the array horizontally? What other ways can you break apart the 8×8 array?

• Use grid paper and the break apart strategy to find 9×7.

• Does the break apart strategy always work? Explain.

Quick Review

Skip-count to find the missing number.
1. 3, 6, 9, ■, 15
2. 10, 8, 6, ■, 2
3. 4, 8, 12, ■, 20
4. 21, 18, 15, ■, 9
5. 25, 20, 15, ■, 5

More Strategies

Use a multiplication table.

Multiply. 5×7

Find the row for the factor 5. Find the column for the factor 7.
Look down column 7. The product is found where row 5 and
column 7 meet.

×	0	1	2	3	4	5	6	7	8	9	10
0	0	0	0	0	0	0	0	0	0	0	0
1	0	1	2	3	4	5	6	7	8	9	10
2	0	2	4	6	8	10	12	14	16	18	20
3	0	3	6	9	12	15	18	21	24	27	30
4	0	4	8	12	16	20	24	28	32	36	40
5	0	5	10	15	20	25	30	35	40	45	50
6	0	6	12	18	24	30	36	42	48	54	60
7	0	7	14	21	28	35	42	49	56	63	70
8	0	8	16	24	32	40	48	56	64	72	80
9	0	9	18	27	36	45	54	63	72	81	90
10	0	10	20	30	40	50	60	70	80	90	100

So, $5 \times 7 = 35$.

Math Idea
The Commutative Property
of Multiplication states that you
can multiply any two factors in any
order and get the same product. So,
if you know that $6 \times 9 = 54$,
you also know that $9 \times 6 = 54$.
You need to memorize only
half of the facts in the
multiplication table.

• How can you use the multiplication table to find $70 \div 10$?

Use inverse operations.
Divide. $63 \div 9$
Think: $9 \times 7 = 63$
So, $63 \div 9 = 7$.

Use a pattern.
Divide. $42 \div 6$
Count back from 42 by sixes.
Think: 42, 36, 30, 24, 18, 12, 6, 0
So, $42 \div 6 = 7$.

Use doubles.
Multiply. 8×9
Think: The factor 8 is an
even number. $4 + 4 = 8$
$$4 \times 9 = 36$$
$$4 \times 9 = 36$$
$$36 + 36 = 72$$
So, $8 \times 9 = 72$.

Guided Practice

1. Copy the sentences. Use the arrays to complete the sentences.

$6 \times 4 = \blacksquare$
$6 \times 5 = \blacksquare$
$6 \times 9 = \blacksquare + \blacksquare$
So, $6 \times 9 = \blacksquare$.

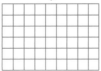

Find the product or quotient. Show the strategy you used.

2. 8×6 **3.** $63 \div 7$ **4.** $30 \div 6$ **5.** 7×6 ☑**6.** $50 \div 10$ ☑**7.** 3×9

8. **TALK Math** Explain two ways to use strategies to find 8×7.

Independent Practice and Problem Solving

Find the product or quotient. Show the strategy you used.

9. $40 \div 10$ **10.** 6×6 **11.** $8\overline{)64}$ **12.** $27 \div 9$ **13.** $56 \div 7$ **14.** 9×10

15. $7\overline{)49}$ **16.** $7\overline{)42}$ **17.** $9 \div 9$ **18.** 10×10 **19.** $8\overline{)80}$ **20.** 4×9

21. $\begin{array}{r} 3 \\ \times 7 \\ \hline \end{array}$ **22.** $\begin{array}{r} 10 \\ \times 6 \\ \hline \end{array}$ **23.** $\begin{array}{r} 0 \\ \times 8 \\ \hline \end{array}$ **24.** $\begin{array}{r} 4 \\ \times 7 \\ \hline \end{array}$ **25.** $\begin{array}{r} 9 \\ \times 9 \\ \hline \end{array}$ **26.** $\begin{array}{r} 2 \\ \times 6 \\ \hline \end{array}$

⭐**Algebra** Find the value of the coins.

27.

Nickels	5	6	7	8	9	10
Cents	25	▪	▪	▪	▪	▪

28.

Dimes	1	2	4	6	8	10
Cents	10	▪	▪	▪	▪	▪

USE DATA For 29–31, use the Game 1 Results.

29. In checkers, a king is 2 checkers stacked. Tanya has 3 kings. How many single checkers does she have?

30. What is the greatest number of kings that Jamal could have?

31. Ed had the same number of checkers left at the end of each game. He ends the checkers marathon with a total of 45 checkers left. How many games did Ed play?

Game 1 Results

ED   TANYA   JAMAL

32. **WRITE Math** ▸ Find the missing numbers. Describe the relationships between the products. **Explain** why this happened.

$6 \times 2 = \blacksquare$
$6 \times 4 = \blacksquare$
$6 \times 8 = \blacksquare$
$6 \times 16 = \blacksquare$

Mixed Review and Test Prep

33. What number makes the equation true? (p. 70)

$$11 + n = 19$$

34. Barb put 5 pictures on each of 3 pages of her scrapbook. How many pictures did Barb put in her scrapbook in all? (p. 96)

35. **Test Prep** Brett has 8 stacks of checkers. There are 7 checkers in each stack. How many checkers does Brett have? **Describe** the strategy you used to find the product.

Extra Practice on page 110, Set D

CD ROM **Technology** Use Harcourt Mega Math, The Number Games, *Up, Up, and Array,* Levels B, C, F, G.

Are You Game?

Reading Skill **Visualize**

A growing number of students are having fun playing chess. Many are joining clubs, playing in tournaments, and even competing online.

Maya's chess club has 6 members. The club will play 24 games this weekend. Each member plays the same number of games. How many games will each club member play this weekend?

Visualizing the information given in a problem can help you understand the situation. When you visualize, you picture something in your mind.

▼ In addition to being fun, chess sharpens both thinking and social skills. The United States Chess Federation has about 100,000 members, and more than half of them are students. More than 1,550 students from around the country competed in the 2005 National K–12/Collegiate Chess Championship.

Make a list of models that can be used to help solve the problem, and then picture each model in your mind.

↓

Think about which model best represents the situation.

↓

Picture the situation in your mind. Then draw a picture.

Models

groups of objects

number line

array

multiplication table

Problem Solving **Visualize to understand the problem.**

1. Solve the problem above.

2. Barney and Lauren are playing a card-matching game. Before they begin, they place 42 cards facedown in rows and columns. If they place 7 cards in each row, how many columns of cards do they have?

Chapter 4 101

5 Multiplication Table Through 12

OBJECTIVE: Multiply and divide facts through 12.

Investigate

Materials ■ blank multiplication table

You can use patterns and strategies to help you complete a multiplication table for the facts of 11 and 12. Copy the table.

Remember

The Zero Property states that the product of 0 and any number is 0. The Identity Property states that the product of 1 and any number is that number.

×	0	1	2	3	4	5	6	7	8	9	10	11	12
0	0	0	0	0	0	0	0	0	0	0	0	■	■
1	0	1	2	3	4	5	6	7	8	9	10	■	■
2	0	2	4	6	8	10	12	14	16	18	20	■	■
3	0	3	6	9	12	15	18	21	24	27	30	■	■
4	0	4	8	12	16	20	24	28	32	36	40	■	■
5	0	5	10	15	20	25	30	35	40	45	50	■	■
6	0	6	12	18	24	30	36	42	48	54	60	■	■
7	0	7	14	21	28	35	42	49	56	63	70	■	■
8	0	8	16	24	32	40	48	56	64	72	80	■	■
9	0	9	18	27	36	45	54	63	72	81	90	■	■
10	0	10	20	30	40	50	60	70	80	90	100	■	■
11	■	■	■	■	■	■	■	■	■	■	■	■	■
12	■	■	■	■	■	■	■	■	■	■	■	■	■

A Use the Zero Property to complete the row and column for 0. Use the Identity Property to complete the row and column for 1.

B Use doubles to complete the row and column for 2.

C Count forward to complete the rows and columns for 3 through 10.

D Use the break apart strategy to find 11×11, 11×12, and 12×12.

E Now complete the rest of the table.

Draw Conclusions

1. Compare your break apart strategy to find 12×12 with your classmates' break apart strategies. What can you conclude?

2. **Application** What strategy could you use to find the product of 20 and 5? Find the product. Describe the strategy you used.

You can also use a multiplication table to find the quotient in a division problem.

Divide. 56 ÷ 8 = ■

Think: 8 × ■ = 56

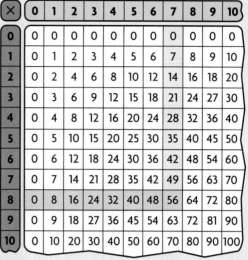

Step 1

Find the row for the given factor, 8.

Step 2

Look across to find the product, 56.

Step 3

Look up to find the missing factor, 7.

So, 56 ÷ 8 = 7.

In Step 1, the divisor is the given factor in the related multiplication fact. In Step 2, the dividend is the product. The quotient is the missing factor.

- How do you know that you can use the multiplication fact 8 × 7 = 56 to find 56 ÷ 8?

TALK Math

How do strategies and patterns help you learn multiplication facts?

Practice

Find the product or quotient. Show the strategy you used.

1. 6 × 11
2. 12 × 10
3. 77 ÷ 11
4. 10 × 11
5. 11 × 12
6. 48 ÷ 12
7. 3 × 12
8. 60 ÷ 12
9. 11 × 4
10. 11 × 3
11. 96 ÷ 12
12. 9 × 11
13. 132 ÷ 11
14. 5 × 11
15. 12 × 12
16. 121 ÷ 11
17. 6 × 12
18. 7 × 11

Algebra Use the rule to find the missing numbers.

19. Multiply the input by 11.

Input	Output
1	■
10	■
11	■
12	■

20. Multiply the input by 12.

Input	Output
2	■
■	48
5	■
■	120

21. Divide the input by 11.

Input	Output
22	■
44	■
66	■
■	8

22. Divide the input by 12.

Input	Output
36	■
72	■
■	9
■	12

23. **WRITE Math** What could be the missing factors in ★ × ▲ = 48? Find as many factor pairs as you can. **Explain** how you found these factors.

LESSON 6

Patterns on the Multiplication Table

OBJECTIVE: Identify patterns on the multiplication table.

Quick Review

Name the pattern unit.

1. 1, 2, 3, 1, 2, 3, 1, 2, 3
2. 2, 4, 2, 4, 2, 4, 2, 4
3. 3, 0, 7, 3, 0, 7, 3, 0, 7
4. 8, 5, 8, 5, 8, 5, 8, 5
5. 6, 5, 4, 6, 5, 4, 6, 5, 4

Vocabulary

square number

multiple

Learn

You can use a multiplication table to explore number patterns.

Activity   Materials ▪ multiplication table

- Find 4 × 4. Circle the product.
- Shade the squares for all the products above the row for 4 and to the left of the column for 4. Look at the array you shaded. What shape do you see?

A number that can be modeled with a square array is called a square number. A **square number** is a number that is the product of any number and itself.

- Continue multiplying to find the other square numbers in the table. Circle the square numbers. What do you see?
- Compare the number at the left and above each square number. What pattern do you see?

The product of two counting numbers is a **multiple** of each of those numbers. To find the multiples of 4, multiply by the counting numbers 1, 2, 3, and so on. Look at the row or the column for the factor 4.

- List the multiples of 4 shown in the table. What patterns do you see?
- Look at the multiples of 1, 3, 5, 7, 9, and 11. What patterns do you see?

×	0	1	2	3	4	5	6	7	8	9	10	11	12
0	0	0	0	0	0	0	0	0	0	0	0	0	0
1	0	1	2	3	4	5	6	7	8	9	10	11	12
2	0	2	4	6	8	10	12	14	16	18	20	22	24
3	0	3	6	9	12	15	18	21	24	27	30	33	36
4	0	4	8	12	(16)	20	24	28	32	36	40	44	48
5	0	5	10	15	20	25	30	35	40	45	50	55	60
6	0	6	12	18	24	30	36	42	48	54	60	66	72
7	0	7	14	21	28	35	42	49	56	63	70	77	84
8	0	8	16	24	32	40	48	56	64	72	80	88	96
9	0	9	18	27	36	45	54	63	72	81	90	99	108
10	0	10	20	30	40	50	60	70	80	90	100	110	120
11	0	11	22	33	44	55	66	77	88	99	110	121	132
12	0	12	24	36	48	60	72	84	96	108	120	132	144

Guided Practice

1. Use the array to find the square number. ▪ × ▪ = ▪

Find the square number.

2. 6 × 6   3. 2 × 2   4. 9 × 9   5. 1 × 1   6. 4 × 4   ✓7. 11 × 11

Use the multiplication table.

8. What pattern do you see in the multiples of 5?

🎯 9. Which multiples have only even numbers?

10. **TALK Math** **Explain** how patterns in the multiplication table can help you remember multiplication facts.

Independent Practice and Problem Solving

Find the square number.

11. 3×3 12. 6×6 13. 8×8 14. 10×10 15. 7×7 16. 12×12

Use the multiplication table.

17. What pattern do you see in the multiples of 8?

18. What pattern do you see in the first 9 multiples of 10?

19. What pattern do you see in the ones digits of multiples of 2?

20. What pattern do you see in the multiples of 4 and multiples of 12?

REASONING Write *true* or *false*. If the statement is false, explain why.

21. All of the multiples of 6 are multiples of 3.

22. For any multiple of 5, the ones digit is 5.

USE DATA For 23–25, use the Facts of Nine table.

Facts of Nine
$1 \times 9 = 9$
$2 \times 9 = 18$
$3 \times 9 = 27$
$4 \times 9 = 36$
$5 \times 9 = 45$
$6 \times 9 = 54$
$7 \times 9 = 63$
$8 \times 9 = 72$
$9 \times 9 = 81$
$10 \times 9 = 90$

23. How does the pattern of the tens digits in the products relate to the pattern of the factors?

24. How do the digits of each product relate to the factor 9?

25. **Explain** how you can use the patterns to find 9×9 without using the table.

26. Use the rule *3 less than 2 times the number* to make a pattern. Start with 4. What is the fifth number in the pattern?

27. **WRITE Math** ▸ What patterns do you see in the multiples of 2 and 4 in the multiplication table? **Compare** how they are alike and how they are different.

Mixed Review and Test Prep

28. Would you measure the length of a goldfish in inches, in feet, or in miles?
(Grade 3)

29. Find the missing number. (p. 64)

$$12 + 64 = \blacksquare + 12$$

30. **Test Prep** The multiples of which number are double the multiples of 3?

A 2   C 9

B 6   D 12

Extra Practice on page 110, Set E

Problem Solving Workshop
Skill: Choose the Operation

OBJECTIVE: Solve problems by using the skill *choose the operation*.

Use the Skill

PROBLEM Nancy is baking cookies to take to a party. There will be 12 people at the party. She mixes enough cookie dough for each person to have 4 cookies. Then she bakes the cookies on cookie sheets for 11 minutes. How many cookies will Nancy bake in all?

This chart will help you decide which operation you can use to solve the problem.

Add	Join groups of the same or different sizes
Subtract	Take away or compare groups
Multiply	Join equal-size groups
Divide	Separate into equal-size groups or find how many in each group

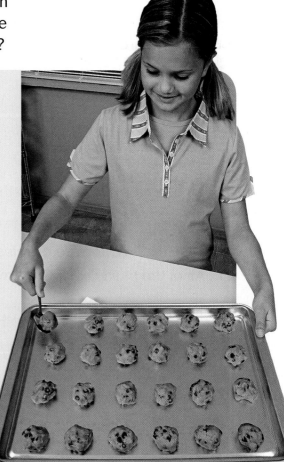

Since Nancy bakes 12 equal groups of 4 cookies, you can multiply to find how many cookies she will bake in all.

number of people	number of cookies for each person	total number of cookies
↓	↓	↓
12 ×	4 =	48

So, Nancy will bake 48 cookies in all.

• What other operation could you use to solve this problem? Explain how you solved the problem.

Think and Discuss

Tell which operation you would use to solve the problem.
Explain your choice. Solve the problem.

a. The Sandwich Shop served 3,275 lunches in May and served 4,250 lunches in June. How many lunches did the Shop serve in all?

b. Raul's class made $200 from this year's bake sale. Last year, the class made $178. How much more did the class make this year?

c. The cafeteria served 132 pizza lunches. Each pizza was cut into 12 slices. If each student received 1 slice, how many pizzas were served?

Guided Problem Solving

Tell which operation you would use to solve the problem.
Then solve the problem.

1. Russell made 36 ounces of trail mix to take on a hiking trip. He poured equal amounts of the trail mix into 4 bags. How many ounces of trail mix are in each bag?

   Think: What operation can you use to find how many ounces of trail mix are in each bag?

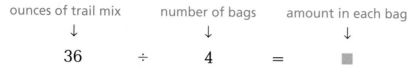

ounces of trail mix		number of bags		amount in each bag
↓		↓		↓
36	÷	4	=	■

2. **What if** Russell poured equal amounts of the trail mix into 6 bags? How many ounces of trail mix would be in each bag?

3. The hiking trip is on Friday. On Thursday, the high temperature was 67°F. Russell hopes that it will be 8 degrees warmer on Friday. What temperature is Russell hoping for?

Mixed Applications

USE DATA For 4–7, use the information in the picture.

4. Donald wants to place flower bouquets on 6 tables. How much will the flower bouquets cost in all?

5. Sonya bought 3 boxes of crackers. What number sentence can be used to find the amount of money Sonya spent on 1 box of crackers?

6. Art wants to send out 24 invitations for his party. How many boxes of cards will he need? How much will they cost?

7. Look at Mr. Hill's shopping list. What information is needed to find the total amount of money he spent at the grocery store?

8. **Pose a Problem** Write a word problem for the number sentence $48 \div 12 = n$. Then solve the problem.

9. **WRITE Math** ▸ Orange Park charges $11 per day per person. Deer Park charges $2 per hour per person. Help Lisa choose the less expensive park to hold her picnic if 12 people come to the picnic for 5 hours. **Explain** how you decided.

Mr. Hill's Shopping List

3 boxes of crackers
2 gallons of orange juice
2 loaves of bread
1 bouquet of flowers

ALGEBRA
Find Missing Factors

OBJECTIVE: Use multiplication and division to find missing factors.

Quick Review

Write the fact family.

1. 2, 5, 10   2. 3, 6, 18
3. 5, 7, 35   4. 6, 8, 48
5. 9, 9, 81

Learn

PROBLEM A basketball club has 10 members. How many teams of 5 players can play at the same time?

When you know the product and one factor, you can use a model or a fact family to help you find the missing factor.

■ × 5 = 10   **Think:** What number times 5 equals 10?

ONE WAY **Use a model.**

Draw 10 counters in rows of 5. Count the number of rows to find the missing factor. There are 2 rows of 5 counters.

ANOTHER WAY **Use a fact family.**

Use a related division sentence to find the missing factor.

$10 \div 5 = 2$, so $2 \times 5 = 10$. The missing factor is 2.

Remember
A variable is a symbol or letter that stands for a number or numbers you don't know.

So, 2 teams of 5 players can play at the same time.

More Examples **Find the missing factors.**

A $\star \times 8 = 56$ **Think:** What number times 8 equals 56?
  $\star = 7$

Check: $7 \times 8 \overset{?}{=} 56$ Replace $\star$ with 7.
  $56 = 56$ ✔   The sentence is true.

The missing factor is 7.

B $9 \times n = 45$ **Think:** 9 times what number equals 45?
  $n = 5$

Check: $9 \times 5 \overset{?}{=} 45$ Replace n with 5.
  $45 = 45$ ✔   The sentence is true.

The missing factor is 5.

• How could you use division to solve Examples A and B?

Guided Practice

1. The first factor in a multiplication sentence is 3, and the product is 30. Use the model to find the missing factor.

  $3 \times ■ = 30$

Find the missing factor.

2. $n \times 5 = 55$ **3.** $6 \times \blacktriangledown = 72$ ☑ **4.** $10 \times g = 70$ ☑ **5.** $\blacksquare \times 11 = 132$

6. (**TALK Math**) **Explain** the relationship between factors and products. Use an example to show what you mean.

Independent Practice (and Problem Solving

Find the missing factor.

7. $\blacksquare \times 2 = 18$ **8.** $12 \times p = 12$ **9.** $\bigstar \times 9 = 72$ **10.** $11 \times r = 110$

11. $g \times 10 = 120$ **12.** $4 \times d = 32$ **13.** $7 \times n = 63$ **14.** $c \times 10 = 50$

15. $\blacksquare \times 3 = 40 - 4$ **16.** $7 \times \blacksquare = 43 + 6$ **17.** $3 \times \blacksquare = 19 + 5$ **18.** $\blacksquare \times 8 = 20 - 4$

USE DATA **For 19–21, use the table.**

19. Each football team has 1 coach. Three teams and their coaches are arranged for a photograph. How many people are in the photograph?

20. **Reasoning** In a game, 2 basketball teams play against each other. You want to find out how many players are on the court during a game. In a multiplication sentence, will the answer be a product or a factor?

21. **Pose a Problem** Look back at Problem 19. Write a similar problem by exchanging the known and unknown numbers.

Sports Teams	
Sport	**Players**
Baseball	9
Basketball	5
Football	11
Ice Hockey	6
Soccer	11
Volleyball	6

22. High school basketball games last 32 minutes. There are 4 quarters in each game. Write a number sentence that can be used to find the number of minutes in each quarter.

23. (**WRITE Math** ▸ A sports team needs to reserve a field for a game. The players collect $88 in all to pay for the field. Each player paid $8. **Explain** how to find how many players are on the team.

Mixed Review and Test Prep

24. Which type of graph would best represent the Sports Team data in the table above? (Grade 3)

25. Nikki has some baseball tickets. She gave 2 tickets to her friends. Write an expression for the number of tickets Nikki has now. (p. 66)

26. **Test Prep** Mark buys 36 eggs. Each carton holds 12 eggs. Which number sentence can be used to find the number of egg cartons Mark buys?

A $\blacksquare \times 36 = 12$ **C** $\blacksquare \times 9 = 36$

B $\blacksquare \times 4 = 12$ **D** $\blacksquare \times 12 = 36$

(Extra Practice) on page 110, Set F

Extra Practice

Set A Write the related multiplication or division sentence.
Draw a picture that shows the sentence. (pp. 92–93)

1. $16 - 8 - 8 = 0$

2. $4 + 4 + 4 + 4 + 4 = 20$

3. $6 + 6 + 6 + 6 = 24$

4. $3 + 3 + 3 + 3 = 12$

5. $7 + 7 + 7 + 7 + 7 = 35$

6. $27 - 9 - 9 - 9 = 0$

Set B Write the fact family for the set of numbers. (pp. 94–95)

1. 4, 5, 20

2. 3, 4, 12

3. 5, 9, 45

4. 6, 7, 42

5. 8, 9, 72

Set C Find the product or quotient. (pp. 96–97)

1. 8×2

2. 6×4

3. $21 \div 3$

4. 8×5

5. $4 \div 4$

6. $18 \div 3$

7. A roller coaster at an amusement park has 8 cars.
Each car can hold 4 people. How many people can
ride the roller coaster on one trip?

Set D Find the product or quotient. Show the strategy you used. (pp. 98–101)

1. $36 \div 9$

2. 7×8

3. 7×6

4. $7\overline{)63}$

5. $30 \div 6$

6. 8×10

7. 5×9

8. $8\overline{)48}$

9. 9×8

10. $7\overline{)14}$

11. 9×9

12. $6\overline{)54}$

13. There are 49 students going on a field trip to the
planetarium. Each van can hold 7 students.
How many vans are needed?

Set E Use the multiplication table on page 104. (pp. 104–105)

1. What pattern do you see in the ones digits of multiples of 5?

2. What patterns do you see in the multiples of 3 and 9?

3. What patterns do you see in the multiples of 2 and 3?

Set F Find the missing factor. (pp. 108–109)

1. $2 \times m = 24$

2. $6 \times w = 36$

3. $c \times 9 = 72$

4. $g \times 6 = 66$

5. $\blacksquare \times 3 = 17 + 1$

6. $5 \times \bigstar = 33 - 3$

7. $4 \times \blacksquare = 32 + 4$

8. $8 \times \blacktriangle = 65 - 1$

9. Carlos read the same number of pages in his 60-page
book each day for 1 week. After the week, he still had
4 pages to read. How many pages did Carlos read
each day?

CD ROM Technology
Use Harcourt Mega Math, The Number Games,
Up, Up, and Array, Levels A, B, C, D, E, F, G, H.

HOPSCOTCH FACTS

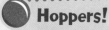

Hoppers!
2 teams, at least 2 players on each team

Get Set!
- Number cards (1–12, two sets)
- Two-color counters (1 for each team)

Hop!

- Players shuffle each set of number cards and place them facedown in two stacks.

- Teams take turns. A player chooses one card from each stack. A teammate uses those numbers to write a basic multiplication or division fact sentence.

- If the fact sentence is correct, the team places a counter on 1. The cards are placed in discard stacks.

- If a player makes an incorrect fact sentence on the first or second turn, that team loses a turn. If a player makes an incorrect fact sentence after his or her team has hopped past 2 on the game board, that team moves its counter back two spaces.

- On each turn, teammates trade roles.

- If all the number cards are used, players shuffle each set and place them facedown to use again.

- The first team to reach 10 wins.

 **Number Relationships**

Even or Odd?

Eric is making smoothies for his family. Some family members want 2 cups of blueberries, and some want 3 cups of blueberries in their smoothies. Will Eric use an even or odd number of cups when he makes the smoothies?

Is the product even or odd when you multiply two even numbers? two odd numbers? an even number and an odd number?

Examples

A Even × Even
2 × 2 = 4
2 × 4 = 8
2 × 6 = 12

B Odd × Odd
3 × 1 = 3
3 × 3 = 9
3 × 5 = 15

C Even × Odd
2 × 1 = 2
2 × 3 = 6
2 × 5 = 10

So, if Eric uses 2 cups for an even number of people, he will use an even number of cups in all. If he uses 3 cups for an odd number of people, he will use an odd number of cups in all. If he uses 2 cups for an odd number of people, he will use an even number of cups in all.

- Is the product even or odd when you multiply three even numbers?
- Is the product even or odd when you multiply three odd numbers?

Try It
Tell whether the product is *even* or *odd*.

1. 4 × 7   2. 5 × 9   3. 6 × 8   4. 9 × 7

5. 8 × 6   6. 8 × 4 × 6   7. 7 × 9 × 5   8. 4 × 6 × 2

9. Is the product even or odd when you multiply 5 by an even number? an odd number? **Explain.**

10. Is the product even or odd when you multiply two even numbers and an odd number? **Explain.**

11. [WRITE Math] ▶ **Explain** how you can tell whether a product of two or more numbers will be even or odd.

Chapter 4 Review/Test

Check Vocabulary and Concepts

Choose the best term from the box.

1. A __?__ is the product of any number and itself. (p. 104)

2. In $36 \div 9 = 4$, 4 is the __?__. (p. 94)

3. The answer to a multiplication problem is called the __?__. (p. 94)

VOCABULARY

divisor
product
quotient
square number

Check Skills

Write the related multiplication or division sentence.
Draw a picture that shows the sentence. (pp. 92–93)

4. $10 - 5 - 5 = 0$ 5. $3 + 3 + 3 = 9$ 6. $12 - 12 = 0$ 7. $2 + 2 + 2 = 6$

Find the value of the variable. (pp. 94–95, 108–109)

8. $24 \div 2 = y$ 9. $48 \div 6 = w$ 10. $56 \div 7 = a$ 11. $99 \div 9 = v$

12. $k \times 12 = 60$ 13. $108 \div 9 = b$ 14. $g \times 6 = 42$ 15. $72 \div e = 9$

Find the product or quotient. (pp. 96–97, 98–101, 102–103)

16. 3×6 17. 12×4 18. $4)\overline{28}$ 19. $60 \div 5$ 20. 6×6

21. 7×12 22. $33 \div 11$ 23. 5×3 24. 8×8 25. $8)\overline{96}$

26. 4×8 27. $5)\overline{50}$ 28. $9 \div 9$ 29. $9)\overline{45}$ 30. 7×6

Check Problem Solving

Solve. (pp. 106–107)

31. Ed collected cans for recycling. He collected 79 cans last week and 114 cans this week. How many more cans did he collect this week than last week?

32. Maria needs 8 ounces of nuts to make 1 batch of cookies. How many ounces of nuts will she need to make 4 batches of cookies?

33. **WRITE Math** There are 12 baseball bats in each shipping carton. Would you use addition or multiplication to find the number of baseball bats in 6 shipping cartons? **Explain.**

Standardized Test Prep
Chapters 1–4

Number and Operations

1. There are 9 spiders in the terrarium. Each spider has 8 legs. How many legs are there in all? (p. 98)

   A 72

   B 80

   C 88

   D 96

2. Round 3,219,754 to the nearest hundred. (p. 34)

   A 3,220,000

   B 3,219,800

   C 3,219,700

   D 3,200,000

3. The new baseball field has 5,213 seats. That is 3,928 more seats than the old field had. How many seats did the old field have? (p. 48)

   A 2,295

   B 2,285

   C 1,295

   D 1,285

4. **WRITE Math** ▸ Molly has 6 loaves of bread. Each loaf of bread has 10 slices. **Explain** how to find how many slices of bread there are in all. (p. 98)

Algebraic Reasoning

5. What is the value of the expression $24 + n$ if $n = 2$? (p. 66)

   A 48   C 22

   B 26   D 12

6. Look at the problem below.

   $$\blacksquare + 5 = \blacklozenge$$

   If $\blacklozenge = 16$, what is $\blacksquare$? (p. 70)

   A 9

   B 10

   C 11

   D 12

7. Find the missing factor. (p. 108)

   $$5 \times y = 40$$

   A 8

   B 9

   C 10

   D 12

8. **WRITE Math** ▸ Paula has 12 flowers. The table shows the number of petals in different numbers of flowers.

Flower Petals				
Flowers	2	4	6	7
Petals	22	44	66	77

   Explain how to find the total number of petals in Paula's flowers. (p. 102)

Geometry

9. Which statement is true about the right triangle shown below? (Grade 3)

   A The triangle has 1 obtuse angle.

   B The triangle has 1 right angle.

   C The triangle has 2 right angles.

   D The triangle has 3 acute angles.

10. The music room is shaped like a rectangle 30 feet wide and 20 feet long.

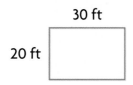

   What is the perimeter of the room? (Grade 3)

   A 30 feet   **C** 100 feet

   B 50 feet   **D** 600 feet

11. Which statement is **NOT** true? (Grade 3)

   A All right angles are congruent.

   B All circles are similar.

   C All squares are similar.

   D All circles are congruent.

12. **WRITE Math** ▸ **Describe** the difference between a cone and a pyramid. (Grade 3)

Data Analysis and Probability

Test Tip **Get the information you need.**

See Item 13. To solve the problem, you need to know how many different outcomes are possible when Marian tosses the coin.

13. Marian played a coin-tossing game. The table shows the results.

Coin Toss	
Outcome	**Number**
Heads	12
Tails	12

   If Marian tosses the coin again, what are the chances that the result will be heads? (Grade 3)

   A 1 out of 12   **C** 1 out of 3

   B 1 out of 4   **D** 1 out of 2

14. **WRITE Math** ▸ The pointer of Jack's spinner stopped on yellow 6 times, green 2 times, and red 4 times.

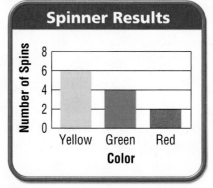

   Explain how you would change the graph to show the results. (Grade 3)

5 Algebra: Use Multiplication and Division Facts

FAST FACT

Scarlet macaws are large parrots that live in the tropical rain forests of Central and South America. Scarlet macaws are about 35 inches long and can live as many as 80 years.

Investigate

Macaws make their nests at the very tops of leafy trees in tropical rain forests. Choose a tree from the table. Write three different expressions that equal the total number of macaws in a tree, using two or more operations. Explain how you decided whether you should use parentheses.

Macaws in Four Trees	
Tree	Number of Macaws
A	24
B	16
C	20
D	12

Technology
Student pages are available in the Student eBook.

Check your understanding of important skills
needed for success in Chapter 5.

▶ **Use a Rule**

Copy and complete each table.

1.

Team	2	3	4	5	6
Players	12	18	24	■	■

Rule: Multiply the number of
teams by 6.

2.

Dimes	4	5	6	7	8
Pennies	40	50	■	70	■

Rule: Multiply the number of
dimes by 10.

3.

Legs	12	16	20	24	28
Cows	3	4	5	■	■

Rule: Divide the number of
legs by 4.

4.

Inches	12	24	36	48	60
Feet	1	2	■	4	■

Rule: Divide the number of
inches by 12.

▶ **Fact Families**

Copy and complete each number sentence.

5. $5 \times 3 = $ ■
$15 \div $ ■ $ = 3$

6. $6 \times 7 = $ ■
$42 \div $ ■ $ = 7$

7. $4 \times 9 = $ ■
$36 \div $ ■ $ = 9$

8. $7 \times 9 = $ ■
$63 \div $ ■ $ = 9$

▶ **Addition and Subtraction Equations**

Solve the equation by using mental math. Check your solution.

9. $n + 8 = 13$

10. $9 - n = 6$

11. $n + 6 = 14$

12. $12 - n = 3$

VOCABULARY POWER

CHAPTER VOCABULARY

Distributive Property   inequality
equation   parentheses
expression   variable
Associative Property of Multiplication
Commutative Property of Multiplication
Identity Property of Multiplication
order of operations
Zero Property of Multiplication

WARM-UP WORDS

Distributive Property the property that
states that multiplying a sum by a number
is the same as multiplying each addend by
the number and then adding the products

order of operations a special set of rules
that gives the order in which calculations
are done in an expression

Multiplication Properties

OBJECTIVE: Identify and use the properties of multiplication.

Learn

The properties of multiplication can help you find products of two or more factors.

MULTIPLICATION PROPERTIES

The **Zero Property** states that the product of 0 and any number is 0.

$$3 \times 0 = 0$$

The **Identity Property** states that the product of 1 and any number is that number.

$$1 \times 3 = 3$$

The **Commutative Property** states that you can multiply two factors in either order and get the same product.

$$2 \times 3 = 6 \qquad 3 \times 2 = 6$$

The **Associative Property** states that you can group factors in different ways and get the same product. Use parentheses ( ) to group the factors you multiply first.

$$(4 \times 2) \times 3 = 24 \qquad 4 \times (2 \times 3) = 24$$

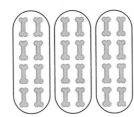 

- Use counters to show two ways you can group $3 \times 2 \times 5$ to find the product. Are the products the same? Explain how you know. Make a drawing to record your models.

Example 1 Use the properties to find the missing factor.

A ▪ $\times 12 = 0$
   $0 \times 12 = 0$ Zero Property

So, ▪ = 0.

B $9 \times$ ▪ $= 8 \times 9$
   $9 \times 8 = 8 \times 9$ Commutative Property

So, ▪ = 8.

The Distributive Property

PROBLEM At the pet store, the rabbits are in a pen that is 4 feet long by 12 feet wide. What is the area of the pen?

Activity Use the Distributive Property.
Materials ■ square tiles

The **Distributive Property** states that multiplying a sum by a number is the same as multiplying each addend by the number and then adding the products.

Multiply. 4×12

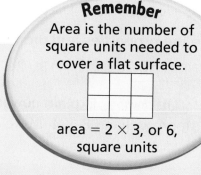

Remember
Area is the number of square units needed to cover a flat surface.

area = 2×3, or 6, square units

Step 1	**Step 2**	**Step 3**
Make a model to find 4×12. Use square tiles to build an array.	Break apart the array to make two smaller arrays for products you know.	Use the Distributive Property to show the sum of two products.

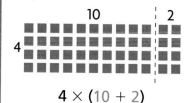

Step 1: 12 / 4 / $4 \times 12 =$ ■

Step 2: 10 · 2 / 4 / $4 \times (10 + 2)$

Step 3:
$(4 \times 10) + (4 \times 2)$
$\downarrow \qquad \downarrow$
$40 \quad + \quad 8 \quad = \quad 48$

So, the area of the pen is 48 square feet.

The properties can help you solve problems mentally.

Example 2 Use the properties and mental math.

Ⓐ Find 8×12.

$8 \times 12 = 8 \times (10 + 2)$ **Think:** $12 = 10 + 2$
$\quad\quad = (8 \times 10) + (8 \times 2)$ Distributive Property
$\quad\quad = 80 + 16$
$\quad\quad = 96$

Ⓑ Find $5 \times 5 \times 2$.

$5 \times 5 \times 2 = 5 \times (5 \times 2)$ Associative Property
$\quad\quad\quad\quad = 5 \times 10$
$\quad\quad\quad\quad = 50$

Ⓒ Find $2 \times 7 \times 5$.

$2 \times 7 \times 5 = 2 \times (5 \times 7)$ Commutative Property
$\quad\quad\quad\quad = (2 \times 5) \times 7$ Associative Property
$\quad\quad\quad\quad = 10 \times 7$
$\quad\quad\quad\quad = 70$

• How can you group the factors to multiply $5 \times 2 \times 8$?

• Is $27 \times (48 - 48) = 0$ true? Explain how you can easily see this.

1. Use the Associative Property to find the missing factor. $(12 \times \blacksquare) \times 4 = 12 \times (3 \times 4)$

Use the properties and mental math to find the product.

2. $1 \times 56 \times 1$ 3. $24 \times 0 \times 6$ ✓4. $8 \times 3 \times 3$ ✓5. 7×11

6. **TALK Math** Explain how the Commutative Property is true for 4×8 and 8×4. Make a model or draw a picture.

Independent Practice (and Problem Solving

Use the properties and mental math to find the product.

7. $9 \times 7 \times 0$ 8. $2 \times 4 \times 7$ 9. $8 \times 5 \times 2$ 10. $6 \times 9 \times 1$

Find the missing number. Name the property you used.

11. $8 \times 6 = 6 \times \blacksquare$ 12. $36 \times \blacksquare = 36$ 13. $5 \times 12 = (5 \times 10) + (5 \times \blacksquare)$

Make a model and use the Distributive Property to find the product.

14. 7×12 15. 3×12 16. 6×12 17. 12×9

Show two ways to group by using parentheses. Find the product.

18. $3 \times 2 \times 5$ 19. $8 \times 7 \times 1$ 20. $7 \times 0 \times 2$ 21. $2 \times 6 \times 2$

22. There are 2 tables, each with 3 tanks with 5 fish in each. There are also 3 tables, each with 2 tanks with 5 fish in each. Are the quantities the same? **Explain.**

23. There are 9 tanks with 11 tetras in each and 12 tanks with 7 mollies in each. Are there more tetras or mollies? How many more?

24. **Pose a Problem** Write a problem that can be solved using the product $(4 \times 2) \times 8$.

25. **WRITE Math** ▶ What's the Question? The product is 19. **Explain** how you know.

Mixed Review and Test Prep

26. Josh read 72 pages of a 200-page book. Then he read 39 more pages. How many pages are left to read? (p. 42)

27. There are 7 boxes and 42 books. Each box has the same number of books. How many books are in each box? (p. 98)

28. **Test Prep** A chef receives 2 boxes, each of which has 4 cartons of eggs. There are 12 eggs in each carton. How many eggs did the chef receive?

   A 50   **C** 72

   B 52   **D** 96

 Extra Practice on page 140, Set A

Write to Prove or Disprove

Sometimes, you must evaluate whether a number sentence or math idea is true or false. You can use what you know about operations and properties to prove or disprove whether the multiplication properties are true for division.

Sharon's group wants to know if the Commutative Property is true for division. The members of her group wrote this explanation to show what they learned.

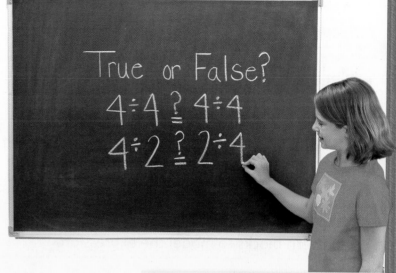

We can try different division problems to prove or disprove that the Commutative Property is true for division. We decided to try $4 \div 4$ and $4 \div 2$.

First, we asked if $4 \div 4 \stackrel{?}{=} 4 \div 4$. Both quotients equal 1. So, the number sentence is true, and the Commutative Property works for this division problem.

Next, we asked if $4 \div 2 \stackrel{?}{=} 2 \div 4$. In this example, the divisor and the dividend are different numbers. $4 \div 2 = 2$ and $2 \div 4 = \frac{2}{4}$. The quotients 2 and $\frac{2}{4}$ are not equal. So, this number sentence is false.

Finally, our group members agreed that since the second number sentence is false, division is not commutative.

Tips

To write to prove or disprove:

- Use correct math vocabulary.
- State the math idea you are proving or disproving.
- Decide on at least two examples to use to test your idea.
- Show your computations, and explain what you learned about each of your examples.
- To prove, every case needs to be tested. To disprove, only one false case is needed.
- Show your reasoning by making a conclusion about each example.
- Finally, write a conclusion that states whether you proved or disproved the math idea you were testing.

Problem Solving Write to prove or disprove each property for division.

1. Zero Property

2. Identity Property

Multiplication and Division Expressions

OBJECTIVE: Write and evaluate multiplication and division expressions.

Learn

PROBLEM Diana collects stamps. She has 5 times as many stamps in her collection now as when she started the collection. Write an expression for the number of stamps she has now. Then find how many stamps she has now if she started with 3 stamps.

Remember

An expression is part of a number sentence that has numbers and operation signs but does not have an equal sign. A variable can stand for any number. You can use any letter as a variable.

Example 1

ONE WAY Use a model.

Use pattern blocks to model the expression.

> Let ⬡ represent the number of stamps Diana started her collection with, and let ■ represent 1 stamp.
>
> ⬡ ⬡ ⬡ ⬡ ⬡   ← number of stamps she has now
>
> Since she started with 3 stamps, replace each ⬡ with 3 ■s.
>
> ⬡   ⬡   ⬡   ⬡   ⬡
> ↓   ↓   ↓   ↓   ↓
> ▦ ▦ ▦ ▦ ▦ = 15

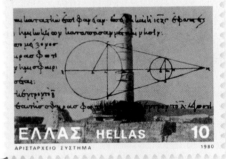

ANOTHER WAY Use a variable.

Write an expression with a variable.

> Let *n* represent the number of stamps Diana started her collection with.
>
> $5 \times n$ ← number of stamps she has now
>
> Find the value of $5 \times n$ if $n = 3$.
>
> $5 \times n$
> ↓
> 5×3 Replace *n* with 3, since she started with 3 stamps.
> ↓
> 15

So, Diana has 15 stamps in her collection now.

- How could you use the Associative Property to rewrite and then find the value of $(d \times 4) \times 3$ if $d = 6$?

Example 2

Carl keeps his stamps in a stamp album. He fills a page with 24 stamps in equal rows. Write an expression for the number of stamps in 1 row. Then find how many stamps are in each row if he puts the stamps in 4 rows.

ONE WAY **Use a model.**

Use pattern blocks to model the expression.

> Use 24 ■s to represent 24 stamps.
>
> Put the ■s into 4 equal rows.

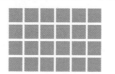

ANOTHER WAY **Use a variable.**

Write an expression with a variable.

> Let r represent the number of equal rows of stamps.
>
> $24 \div r$ ← number of stamps in each row
>
> Find the value of $24 \div r$ if $r = 4$.
>
> $24 \div r$
> ↓
> $24 \div 4$ Replace r with 4 since there are 4 equal rows.
> ↓
> 6

So, Carl put 6 stamps in each row.

READ Math

These multiplication phrases have the same meaning:

- 4 groups each with n objects
- $4 \times n$
- 4 times a number, n

These division phrases have the same meaning:

- n objects separated into 6 groups
- $n \div 6$
- a number, n, divided by 6

Example 3 Write an expression to match the words. Then find the value of the expression.

A Carl spent $10 on some stamps. Write an expression for the price of 1 stamp.

total cost ÷ among a number of stamps
   ↓   ↓
  10   ÷ s ← s is the number of stamps.

Suppose he bought 5 stamps.

$10 \div s$
↓
$10 \div 5$ Replace s with 5.
↓
2

So, Carl spent $2 on each stamp.

B Carl bought some $3 stamps. Write an expression for the total amount he spent.

a number of stamps × price of each stamp
        ↓   ↓
       s ×   3   ← s is the number of stamps.

Suppose he bought 8 stamps.

$s \times 3$
↓
8×3 Replace s with 8.
↓
24

So, Carl spent $24 for 8 stamps.

1. There are 2 boxes of crayons, with *c* crayons in each box. Find the total number of crayons, $2 \times c$, if $c = 8$.

Write an expression that matches the words.
Tell what the expression represents.

2. 3 times a number of words, *w*, in a spelling list

☑ 3. a handful of keys, *k*, divided equally and put on 4 key chains

Find the value of the expression.

4. $2 \times p$ if $p = 9$ 5. $6 \times w$ if $w = 7$ 6. $40 \div m$ if $m = 5$ ☑ 7. $s \div 3$ if $s = 27$

8. **TALK Math** Explain how to find the value of $8 \times k$ and $36 \div k$ if $k = 4$.

Independent Practice and Problem Solving

Write an expression that matches the words.
Tell what the expression represents.

9. the price of some toys, *t*, at $5 each

10. several pages, *p*, that have 10 stickers each

11. a number of books, *b*, divided equally and put on 6 shelves

12. 16 miniature cars divided equally into a number of display cases, *c*

Find the value of the expression.

13. $c \times 8$ if $c = 3$ 14. $9 \times y$ if $y = 7$ 15. $v \div 8$ if $v = 32$ 16. $25 \div q$ if $q = 5$

17. $a \div 2$ if $a = 12$ 18. $b \times 4$ if $b = 8$ 19. $72 \div b$ if $b = 9$ 20. $7 \times r$ if $r = 8$

Match the expression with the words.

21. $9 \div y$ 22. $6 \times (y \times 3)$ 23. $9 \times y$ 24. $(6 \div y) + 3$

  a. 6 times the product of *y* and 3   b. 9 divided by *y*

  c. 6 divided by *y*, and add 3   d. 9 times *y*

Find the value of each expression if *n* = 7. Then write <, >, or =.

25. $59 - 58$ ● $n \div 7$ 26. 9×3 ● $42 \div n$ 27. $4 \times n$ ● $26 + 4$

28. Angela buys some sheets of stamps. Each sheet has 10 stamps. Write an expression for the number of stamps she buys. How many more stamps are on 9 sheets than on 6 sheets?

29. **FAST FACT** In 1932, it cost 3¢ to mail a letter. By 2007, the price was 5 pennies more than 12 times as much. How much did it cost to mail a letter in 2007?

Extra Practice on page 140, Set B

30. Reasoning Use the Commutative and Associative Properties to rewrite and then to find $(5 \times n) \times 2$ if $n = 9$. **Explain** how you found your answer.

31. ▭WRITE Math ▸ **What's the Error?** Blaine claims that $w \times 8$ is 16 if $w = 8$. What error might Blaine have made? Write the correct answer.

Mixed Review and Test Prep

32. Mabel had some apple slices. She ate 3 of them. Write an expression for the number of apple slices Mabel has left. (p. 66)

33. Test Prep Cody has 40 postcards. He puts the cards into equal stacks. Write an expression for the number of cards in each stack. How many postcards are in each stack if he makes 5 stacks? **Explain.**

34. Show two ways to use parentheses to group $6 \times 2 \times 3$. Find the products. (p. 118)

35. Test Prep Dan has 6 times as many coins as Suzie. Let s represent the number of coins Suzie has. Which expression shows the number of coins Dan has?

A $6 + s$

B $6 - s$

C $6 \times s$

D $6 \div s$

Problem Solving connects to Art

Since 1934, the United States Postal Service has sold special stamps to raise money to buy wetlands for the National Wildlife Refuge System. Each year there is an art contest. The two winning pictures are used on Federal Duck Stamps. Each Federal Duck Stamp sells for $15. In 1989, the Junior Duck Stamp program was started for students from kindergarten through high school.

Write an expression that matches the words.

1. the total of 2 stamps on each Artist Commemorative card, c

2. the total price of a number of Federal Duck Stamps, s, that cost $15 each

Each Junior Duck Stamp, s, costs $5. Find the total cost for the number of stamps.

3. $s = 8$ **4.** $s = 5$ **5.** $s = 7$

▲ A winning stamp from 2005

LESSON 3 Order of Operations

OBJECTIVE: Use the order of operations to find the value of expressions.

Quick Review

1. 8×6
2. $56 \div 7$
3. $45 + 28$
4. $91 - 34$
5. $17 - (6 + 2)$

Vocabulary

order of operations

Learn

PROBLEM At the Eric Carle Museum of Picture Book Art, Corey buys 1 book for $6 and 2 books for $4 each. She pays with a $20 bill. How much money does she have left?

HANDS ON Activity

- Find the value of $20 - 1 \times 6 - 2 \times 4$.

- Compare the value you found with those of other classmates. Do all the values make sense? Explain.

- Compare how you found the value of the expression. What can you conclude? Explain.

▲ The Eric Carle Museum of Picture Book Art in Amherst, Massachusetts, is the first full-scale museum in the United States that is devoted to picture-book art.

When solving problems with more than one type of operation, you need to know which operation to do first. A special set of rules, called the **order of operations**, gives the order in which calculations are done in an expression.

First, perform any operations in parentheses.
Next, multiply and divide from left to right.
Then, add and subtract from left to right.

Step 1		Step 2		Step 3	
$20 - 1 \times 6 - 2 \times 4$ $20 - \quad 6 \quad - \quad 8$	There are no parentheses, so multiply from left to right.	$20 - 6 - 8$ $14 \quad - 8$	Next, subtract from left to right.	$14 - 8$ 6	Then, subtract again.

So, Corey has $6 left.

Examples Follow the order of operations.

A $15 + 24 \div 8 - 2$
$15 + \quad 3 \quad - 2$
$\quad 18 \quad\quad - 2$
$\quad\quad\quad 16$

There are no parentheses, so divide from left to right. Then add and subtract from left to right.

B $15 + 24 \div (8 - 2)$
$15 + 24 \div \quad 6$
$15 + \quad 4$
$\quad 19$

Do what is in the parentheses first. Next divide. Then add.

- How are the expressions in Examples A and B alike? How are they different?

126

1. To find the value of the expression $5 + 2 \times 8$, what step will you do first? What step is next? What is the value?

Follow the order of operations to find the value of each expression.

2. $3 \times 6 - (2 + 4) \div 2$ ✓ 3. $3 \times (6 - 2) + 4 \div 2$ ✓ 4. $3 \times (6 - 2 + 4) \div 2$

5. **TALK Math** Explain why the values of $8 + 6 \div 2$ and $(8 + 6) \div 2$ are different. What is the value of each expression?

Independent Practice and Problem Solving

Follow the order of operations to find the value of each expression.

6. $45 - 15 \div 5$ 7. $30 + 2 \times (6 - 4)$ 8. $36 - (4 + 8) \div 4 \times 2$

Write *correct* if the operations are listed in the correct order.
If not, write the correct order of operations.

9. $(4 + 5) \times 2$ Multiply, add   10. $20 \div (10 - 6)$ Subtract, divide

11. $32 - 8 \div 2$ Divide, subtract   12. $(16 + 8) \div 4 - 3$ Divide, add, subtract

Reasoning Use the numbers listed to make a true number sentence.

13. 2, 6, and 5   14. 4, 12, and 18   15. 8, 9, and 7

■ + ■ × ■ = 16   ■ − ■ ÷ ■ = 15   ■ × ■ − ■ = 47

16. Picture books in the museum shop are on sale for $3 off the original price. Owen buys 1 book that originally cost $7 and 2 books that originally cost $6 each. How much does he spend?

17. **Open-Ended** The expressions $9 + 9$ and 3×6 both equal 18. Write two other names for 18 that use only numbers less than 10 and at least three different operations.

18. **WRITE Math** Is $4 + 8 \times 3$ equal to $4 + 3 \times 8$? **Explain** how you know without finding the value of each expression.

19. Tessa buys 4 books for $4 each and a pen for $2. Sheri buys 3 books for $5 each and two pencils for $1 each. Who spends more money? How much more?

Mixed Review and Test Prep

20. Ken puts 6 cars in each of b boxes. Write an expression for the total number of cars.

(p. 122)

21. How many seconds are in 3 minutes?

(Grade 3)

22. **Test Prep** Find the value of $5 + 3 \times 6 - 2$.

A 17   C 32

B 21   D 46

Multiplication and Division Equations

OBJECTIVE: Write and solve multiplication and division equations.

Learn

PROBLEM Sofie is making a number of bracelets to sell at the school craft fair. Each bracelet uses 6 beads. She has 24 beads. What equation can you write to find the number of bracelets she can make?

Remember
An equation is a number sentence that shows that two amounts are equal.

Example 1 Write multiplication equations.

A The number of bracelets times 6 beads each is 24 beads.
$$b \times 6 = 24 \quad \leftarrow b \text{ is the number of bracelets.}$$

So, the equation is $b \times 6 = 24$.

If the missing information changes, the equation changes.

B 4 bracelets times the number of beads in each is 24 beads.
$$4 \times n = 24 \quad \leftarrow n \text{ is the number of beads.}$$

C 4 bracelets times 6 beads each is the total number of beads.
$$4 \times 6 = t \quad \leftarrow t \text{ is the total number of beads.}$$

Example 2 Write division equations.

Ethan pays $12 to make spin-art pictures. Each picture costs $4 to make. What equation can you write to find the number of pictures he can make?

A $12 divided equally among the number of pictures is $4.
$$12 \div p = 4 \quad \leftarrow p \text{ is the number of pictures.}$$

So, the equation is $12 \div p = 4$.

If the missing information changes, the equation changes.

B The total cost divided equally among 3 pictures is $4.
$$t \div 3 = 4 \quad \leftarrow t \text{ is the total cost of the pictures.}$$

C $12 divided equally among 3 pictures is the cost of each picture.
$$12 \div 3 = c \quad \leftarrow c \text{ is the cost for each picture.}$$

Solve Equations

You can solve equations by using different strategies and methods.

ONE WAY **Use the strategy *predict and test*.**

Materials ▪ Equabeam™ balance

Use the Equabeam balance to solve $10 \div n = 2$.

Place a weight on 10 on the left side.

Predict how many weights you need to place on 2 on the right side to restore balance.

Test your prediction. Repeat until you restore balance.

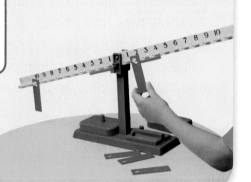

- How many weights do you need to place on 2? What is the value of n?

- Predict the value of b in $9 \times b = 18$. Test your prediction. What is the value of b?

ANOTHER WAY **Use the properties and mental math.**

Ⓐ $m \times 7 = 28$
$m = 4$

Think: What number times 7 equals 28?

Check: $4 \times 7 \overset{?}{=} 28$
$28 = 28$ ✔

Replace m with 4.
The equation is true.
The value of m is 4.

Ⓑ $32 \div g = 4$
$g = 8$

Think: 32 divided by what number equals 4?

Check: $32 \div 8 \overset{?}{=} 4$
$4 = 4$ ✔

Replace g with 8.
The equation is true.
The value of g is 8.

Ⓒ $4 \times h \times 2 = 16$
$4 \times 2 \times h = 16$ Commutative Property
$8 \times h = 16$ Associative Property
$h = 2$ **Think:** 8 times what number equals 16?

Check: $4 \times 2 \times 2 \overset{?}{=} 16$ Replace h with 2.
$16 = 16$ ✔   The equation is true.
The value of $h = 2$.

Guided Practice

1. Choose the equation that shows the total number of clay animals, a, divided equally among 4 shelves is 8 animals each.

   a. $4 \div a = 8$ **b.** $a \div 4 = 8$ **c.** $8 \div 4 = a$

Write an equation for each. Choose the variable for the unknown. Tell what the variable represents.

2. An equal amount of money for each of 6 hand-painted hats is a total of $30.

✓3. The total number of rings divided equally among 4 friends is 2 rings for each friend.

Solve the equation.

4. $3 \times n = 21$

5. $d \div 6 = 8$

6. $z \div 5 = 4$

✓7. $a \times 7 = 63$

8. **TALK Math** Jill buys 15 pins at the fair. Her sister buys 3 pins. To show how many times as many pins Jill buys than her sister, Jill writes $3 \times r = 15$, and her sister writes $15 \div r = 3$. Is the value of r the same in both equations? **Explain** how the equations are alike and how they are different.

Independent Practice and Problem Solving

Write an equation for each. Choose the variable for the unknown. Tell what the variable represents.

9. Three knitted scarves at an equal cost for each is a total cost of $27.

10. 12 potholders divided equally among a number of bags is 3 potholders each.

11. The total number of toys divided equally among 6 shelves is 9 toys on each shelf.

12. The same number of necklaces in each of 6 boxes makes a total of 42 necklaces.

Solve the equation.

13. $4 \times n = 32$

14. $c \div 7 = 7$

15. $p \times 5 = 35$

16. $9 = k \div 3$

17. $m \div 8 = 7$

18. $6 = 54 \div n$

19. $3 \times h \times 2 = 18$

20. $2 \times n \times 6 = 60$

USE DATA For 21–22, use the picture.

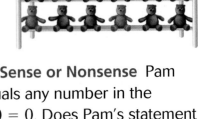
Tommy's Handmade Bears

21. **What if** Tommy made 12 more teddy bears? How could he arrange them on the shelves so that each shelf has the same number of bears?

22. Tommy sells 24 bears. He sells 8 bears each hour. Write an equation to find how many hours it takes him to sell the bears. Solve the equation.

23. **Reasoning** Find the values of a and b in these equations. **Explain** how you found the value of a and b.
    $a \times 6 = 18$ and $a \times b = 12$

24. **WRITE Math** ▸ Sense or Nonsense Pam says that n equals any number in the equation $n \times 0 = 0$. Does Pam's statement make sense? **Explain**.

Technology
Use Harcourt Mega Math, Ice Station Exploration, *Arctic Algebra*, Levels F, T.

Extra Practice on page 140, Set D

Learn About) Balancing Equations

Since the scale is balanced, the weight of the purse and hat on the left side is equal to the weight of the shoes and hat on the right side. Will the scale be balanced if you take away one hat from each side?

Balancing an equation is like balancing a scale. If both sides of the equation have the same value added, subtracted, multiplied, or divided (except by 0), the equation remains true.

Example
Write an equation for the weight of one purse.

Step 1	Step 3
Take away one hat from each side. 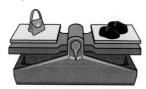 Both sides stay equal.	Let p represent one purse. Let s represent one shoe. 1 purse equals 2 shoes. $p = 2 \times s$

• **What if** one shoe weighs 3 ounces? How much will one purse weigh?

Try It
Use the art of the balance scale at the right.

25. Write an equation for the balance scale. Let d represent the weight of a doll and t represent the weight of a teddy bear.

26. What if one doll weighs 5 pounds? How much will one bear weigh?

Mixed Review and Test Prep

27. Maia used 4 green beads, 8 blue beads, and 12 yellow beads to make 1 necklace for the craft fair. Use this data to make a pictograph. (Grade 3)

28. Test Prep Some friends are at the movies. The friends pay $30 in all for admission. Each ticket costs $6. Write an equation to show how many friends are at the movies. Then solve the equation.

29. Megan has 27 buttons. Each shirt needs 3 buttons. How many shirts can she sew buttons on? (p. 96)

30. Test Prep In which equation does $n = 2$?

A $14 \div n = 12$ C $2 \div n = 4$

B $18 \div n = 9$ D $8 \div n = 2$

Problem Solving Workshop
Strategy: Predict and Test

OBJECTIVE: Solve problems using the strategy *predict and test*.

Learn the Strategy

Sometimes, you can make an educated prediction to solve a problem and then test your prediction to see whether it fits the problem conditions. It is a good strategy to use when one condition depends on another condition.

Make a list to record your predictions.

What are three consecutive numbers whose sum is 15?

Think: The sum is less than 20, so the addends must be 1-digit numbers.

Predict 1: 2+3+4=9 too low
Predict 2: 3+4+5=12 too low
Predict 3: 4+5+6=15 ✓

Make a table to record your predictions.

Mary is thinking of two numbers. The sum of the numbers is 15, and the difference of the numbers is 3. What are Mary's numbers?

Think: Write two equations, $m + n = 15$ and $m - n = 3$.

Predict	Test Sum: $m+n=15$	Test Difference: $m-n=3$	Does It Check?
m=8 n=7	8+7=15	8-7=1	The sum is 15. The difference is 1. too low
m=12 n=3	12+3=15	12-3=9	The sum is 15. The difference is 9. too high
m=9 n=6	9+6=15	9-6=3	The sum is 15. ✓ The difference is 3. ✓

Draw a picture to record your predictions.

Write 2, 3, 4, and 5 in each outer circle so the sums of the numbers across and down are equal.

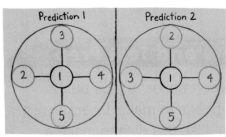

Prediction 1: $2 + 1 + 4 = 7$ and $3 + 1 + 5 = 9$

Prediction 2: $3 + 1 + 4 = 8$ and $2 + 1 + 5 = 8$ ✔

To use the strategy, make a prediction, test your prediction, and then revise the prediction until all conditions in the problem are met.

TALK Math

How can you use the first prediction to make a better prediction?

Use the Strategy

PROBLEM On rainy days, Raul likes to solve riddles. He found this riddle in a book about numbers.

The product of two numbers is 24. Their sum is 11. What are the numbers?

Read to Understand

- Identify the details given.
- Are there details you will not use? If so, what?

Plan

- **What strategy can you use to solve the problem?**

  You can predict and test to solve the problem.

Solve

- **How can you use the strategy to solve the problem?**

  Make a table to record your predictions.

  Think: What are the factors of 24? Write two equations to test your predictions.

  Use what you know about multiplication facts to make a prediction. Check your prediction and test another pair of factors, if needed. Predict and test until all the problem conditions are met.

  So, the numbers are 3 and 8.

Predict	Test		Does It Check?
	Product: $a \times b = 24$	**Sum:** $a + b = 11$	
$a = 2$ $b = 12$	$2 \times 12 = 24$	$2 + 12 = 14$	The product is 24. The sum is 14. too high
$a = 4$ $b = 6$	$4 \times 6 = 24$	$4 + 6 = 10$	The product is 24. The sum is 10. too low
$a = 3$ $b = 8$	$3 \times 8 = 24$	$3 + 8 = 11$	The product is 24. ✔ The sum is 11. ✔

Check

- **How do you know your answer is correct?**
- **What other strategy could you use to solve the problem?**

1. Erica is thinking of two numbers. The difference of the two numbers is 5. The product of the numbers is 24. What are Erica's numbers?

   First, make a table.

   Next, make a prediction based on the facts.

   Then, adjust and predict again until you find the two numbers.

Predict	Test		Does It Check?
	Difference $a - b = 5$	Product $a \times b = 24$	
$a = 6$ $b = 1$	$6 - 1 = 5$	$6 \times 1 = 6$	The difference is 5. The product is 6. too low

2. **What if** the product of the two numbers is 36? What would Erica's numbers be?

3. Marc likes to solve word scrambles and mazes. Yesterday he solved 10 word scrambles and mazes in all. He solved 2 more word scrambles than mazes. How many word scrambles did Marc solve yesterday?

Predict and test to solve.

4. Tina and Larry play a memory game. Tina scores twice as many points as Larry does. Together they score 30 points. How many points does Tina score?

5. Marie buys two puzzle books. Together the books cost $17. One book costs $3 more than the other. How much does each book cost?

USE DATA For 6–8, copy and complete the puzzle.

6. Write 2 in the center circle. Write 3, 4, 6, and 8 in the outer circles so that the products across and down are equal.

7. Write 3 in the center circle. Write 2, 4, 6, and 8 in the outer circles so the sums across and down are equal.

8. Write 4 in the center circle. Write 2, 3, 6, and 9 in the outer circles so the products across and down are equal.

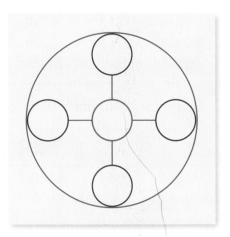

9. André is thinking of a number. The number times itself is less than 150 but greater than 75. The sum of the number and itself is less than 20. What is the number?

10. **WRITE Math** ▸ **Sense or Nonsense** Maria says that the sum of two numbers is 6 and their product is 5. Does Maria's statement make sense? **Explain.**

Mixed Strategy Practice

USE DATA For 11–15, copy and complete the table.

	Sum	Product	Difference	Two Numbers
11.	14	48	■	■, ■
12.	11	■	5	■, ■
13.	12	35	■	■, ■
14.	■	40	6	■, ■
15.	15	■	9	■, ■

16. Jimmy designed a maze made up of triangles. If you can move only forward, and never retrace your steps, how many different ways can you walk through his maze?

17. Patty, Rex, Jan, and Tara were waiting in line for their riddle cards at the corn maze. Tara was behind Rex. Patty was not next to Jan. Jan was first in line. Patty was between Rex and Tara. In what order were they standing in line?

18. **Pose a Problem** Look back at Problem 9. Write a similar riddle.

19. **Open-Ended** John is thinking of two odd numbers that add up to 26. What could John's numbers be?

Choose a STRATEGY

Draw a Diagram or Picture
Make a Model or Act It Out
Make an Organized List
Find a Pattern
Make a Table or Graph
Predict and Test
Work Backward
Solve a Simpler Problem
Write an Equation
Use Logical Reasoning

▼ Two and one-half miles of maze in the shape of Wisconsin was cut into 10 acres of corn near Janesville, Wisconsin.

CHALLENGE YOURSELF

Ryan is working on number puzzles in a book. It takes him 2 minutes to complete a puzzle rated *Easy*, and 3 minutes to complete one rated *Hard*.

20. On Monday, Ryan worked for 25 minutes and completed a total of 11 puzzles. How many *Hard* puzzles did he complete? How many *Easy* ones?

21. On Tuesday, Ryan worked for 30 minutes and completed the same number of *Easy* puzzles as *Hard* ones. **Explain** how you can find how many *Easy* and how many *Hard* puzzles Ryan completed on Tuesday.

6 Explore Inequalities

OBJECTIVE: Write, solve, and graph inequalities that include variables.

Quick Review

Find the value if $n = 8$.

1. $n + 7$ 2. $3 \times n$
3. $n - 5$ 4. $13 - n$
5. $n \div 2$

Vocabulary

inequality

less than or equal to ($\leq$)

greater than or equal to ($\geq$)

Learn

PROBLEM The New England aster is a wildflower often found in Illinois. Its seeds sprout in 8 or fewer days. In how many days can aster seeds possibly sprout?

An **inequality** is a mathematical sentence that uses the symbols $<$, $>$, $\leq$, $\geq$, or $\neq$, and shows a relationship between two quantities that are not equivalent.

READ Math

Read $<$ as "is less than."

Read $>$ as "is greater than."

Read $\leq$ as "is less than or equal to."

Read $\geq$ as "is greater than or equal to."

Read $\neq$ as "is not equal to."

HANDS ON

ONE WAY Use a model.

Materials ■ Equabeam balance

$d \leq 8$ shows the number of days, d, that the seeds can possibly take to sprout. Use a balance to show all the counting numbers less than or equal to 8.

Put a weight at 1 on the left side. Put a weight at 8 on the right side. What happens to the balance?

Move the weight on the left side to a number greater than 1. Repeat until you find all the counting numbers that are less than or equal to 8. What numbers did you find?

So, aster seeds can possibly sprout in 1, 2, 3, 4, 5, 6, 7, or 8 days.

OTHER WAYS

A **Use paper and pencil.**
Which of the numbers 2 and 3 makes this inequality true?

$$w \neq 12 - 9$$

Try 2. $\rightarrow$ $2 \neq 12 - 9$ Yes

Try 3. $\rightarrow$ $3 \neq 12 - 9$ No

So, 2 makes the inequality true.

B **Use a number line.**
$$s + 2 \geq 5$$

0 1 2 3 4 5 6

The blue arrow shows that all whole numbers greater than 6 also make the inequality true.

So, 3, 4, 5, and 6 are some of the whole numbers that make the inequality true.

- In Example A, are there other whole numbers that make this inequality true? Explain.

1. The number line shows the whole numbers that make the inequality $d + 2 < 6$ true. What are the whole numbers?

0 1 2 3 4 5 6 7

Which of the numbers 2, 3, 5, and 6 make the inequality true?

2. $q > 3$

3. $30 \div n \le 6$

✅ 4. $m - 2 \ge 3$

✅ 5. $a < 7$

6. ⌈TALK Math⌉ **Explain** how you know whether a whole number makes an inequality true.

Independent Practice and Problem Solving

Which of the numbers 1, 4, 7, and 9 make the inequality true?

7. $k \le 4$

8. $x < 7$

9. $q > 7$

10. $r + 3 \ne 7$

Draw a number line, and graph three whole numbers that make the inequality true.

11. $f < 5$

12. $p \times 3 > 6$

13. $a \ne 2$

14. $6 \le j + 6$

Write an inequality to match the words. Choose the variable for the unknown. Tell what the variable represents.

15. The plant grows 14 inches wide at the most.

16. There are more than 100 types of wild roses.

USE DATA For 17–18, use the information in the article.

17. Write an inequality to show the height, h, an aster grows.

18. **Challenge** The New England aster flowers have more petals than other asters. What are the number of petals each flower possibly may have?

19. ⌈WRITE Math⌉ ▸ **Explain** how the equation ■ $= 5$ and the inequality ■ > 5 are alike and how they are different.

New England Aster

Height up to 7 feet tall
Bloom August to October
Flowers Flower heads are 1 to 2 inches wide; ray flowers have 35 to 45 purple petals.

Mixed Review and Test Prep

20. Pam rides her bike 6 miles on Saturday. On Sunday, she rides 3 times as far. How many more miles does she ride on Sunday than on Saturday? (p. 96)

21. Find the value of $5 + 36 \div 4$. (p. 126)

22. **Test Prep** Which value of b makes the inequality true?

$$b - 2 \ge 3$$

A $b = 5$

B $b = 4$

C $b = 3$

D $b = 2$

⌈Extra Practice⌉ on page 140, Set E

Patterns: Find a Rule

OBJECTIVE: Find a rule for a number relationship and write an equation for the rule.

Quick Review

1. 5×7
2. 8×6
3. $32 \div 4$
4. $63 \div 9$
5. $3 \times 6 + 2$

Learn

PROBLEM One gallon of milk equals 4 quarts of milk, 2 gallons equal 8 quarts, and 3 gallons equal 12 quarts. How many quarts of milk do 4 gallons equal?

You can use an input/output table to find a rule that relates the number of gallons to the number of quarts.

▲ One cow can produce more than 188 gallons of milk in a month.

Input (gallons)	Output (quarts)
1	4
2	8
3	12
4	■

Find a pattern to help you find a rule.

Pattern: Each output is the input multiplied by 4.

Rule: Multiply the input by 4.

⟵ Input: 4   Output: $4 \times 4 = 16$

So, 4 gallons equal 16 quarts of milk.

You can write an equation to show the rule. Use variables to show the input and output.

input (gallons)   output (quarts)
↓   ↓
$$g \times 4 = q$$

Think of the equation as a rule.
To find the value of q, multiply g by 4.

ERROR ALERT

A rule must work for each pair of numbers in the table. Be sure to test your rule with each pair of numbers in the table.

Examples

Ⓐ Find a rule. Write your rule as an equation. Use the equation to find the next number in your pattern.

Input, b	Output, c	Think:
14	2	$14 \div 7 = 2$
28	4	$28 \div 7 = 4$
42	6	$42 \div 7 = 6$
56	■	⟵ $56 \div 7 = 8$

Pattern: Each output is the input divided by 7.
Rule: Divide b by 7.
Equation: $b \div 7 = c$

So, the next number in your pattern is 8.

Ⓑ Use the equation $(n \times 3) + 5 = p$ to complete the table.

First, multiply n by 3.
Then, add 5 to the result.

Input, n	4	5	6	7	8	9
Output, p	17	20	23	26	■	■

$(8 \times 3) + 5 = 29$
$(9 \times 3) + 5 = 32$

So, the next two numbers are 29 and 32.

Guided Practice

1. The rule is multiply w by 6. The equation is $w \times 6 = z$. What is the next number in the pattern?

Input, w	4	5	6	7	8
Output, z	24	30	36	42	■

Find a rule. Write your rule as an equation. Use your rule to find the missing numbers.

✓ 2.

Input, b	90	70	60	50	30	20	10
Output, c	9	7	6	■	■	■	■

✓ 3.

Input, r	2	3	5	6	8	9	10
Output, s	18	27	45	■	■	■	■

4. **TALK Math** Explain how to use the table to write an equation to find the distance in miles, d, a truck travels on g gallons of gas. Use the equation to complete the table.

Input, g	1	2	3	4
Output, d	12	24	36	■

Independent Practice and Problem Solving

Find a rule. Write your rule as an equation. Use your rule to find the missing numbers.

5.

Input, x	14	28	42	56	70	77	84
Output, y	2	4	6	■	■	■	■

6.

Input, d	3	4	6	■	■	■	11
Output, f	15	20	30	40	45	50	55

Use the rule and the equation to make an input/output table.

7. Divide k by 10.
$k \div 10 = m$

8. Multiply c by 12.
$c \times 12 = d$

9. Multiply f by 4, add 7.
$(f \times 4) + 7 = g$

10. Divide p by 5, subtract 2.
$(p \div 5) - 2 = q$

USE DATA For 11–12, use the food pyramid for kids.

11. How many cups of milk should a kid drink in 2, 3, 4, and 5 days? Make an input/output table. Write an equation to solve.

12. **WRITE Math** Explain how to find a rule and write an equation for the total number of ounces of grain a kid should eat in 3 days.

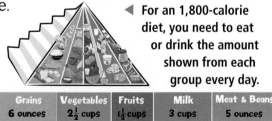

◄ For an 1,800-calorie diet, you need to eat or drink the amount shown from each group every day.

Grains	Vegetables	Fruits	Milk	Meat & Beans
6 ounces	$2\frac{1}{2}$ cups	$1\frac{1}{2}$ cups	3 cups	5 ounces

Mixed Review and Test Prep

13. What multiplication fact could you use to help you find $50 \div 10$? (p. 94)

14. Kay will read 48 pages. She will read 8 pages a day. Write an equation to find how many days, d, it will take her to read the pages. (p. 128)

15. **Test Prep** What equation shows a rule for the table?

Input, q (quarts)	3	6	9
Output, p (pints)	6	12	18

Extra Practice on page 140, Set F

Extra Practice

Set A Use the properties and mental math to find the product. (pp. 118–121)

1. $2 \times 7 \times 5$ 2. $2 \times 0 \times 31$ 3. $1 \times 6 \times 7$ 4. $3 \times 8 \times 2$

5. $8 \times 1 \times 7$ 6. $5 \times 2 \times 6$ 7. $5 \times 9 \times 2$ 8. $3 \times 0 \times 34$

9. A grocery store received a shipment of 2 crates, each with 10 cases of juice boxes. There are 5 juice boxes in each case. How many juice boxes did the grocery store receive?

Set B Find the value of the expression. (pp. 122–125)

1. $d \times 9$ if $d = 6$ 2. $f \div 7$ if $f = 49$ 3. $6 \times n$ if $n = 8$ 4. $56 \div q$ if $q = 7$

5. Allison pasted 10 pictures on each of n pages in her album. Write an expression to show the total number of pictures in the album.

Set C Follow the order of operations to find the value of each expression. (pp. 126–127)

1. $64 - 16 \div 4$ 2. $18 - 2 \times (5 + 4)$ 3. $24 \div (10 - 4) \times 8$ 4. $48 - (9 + 9) \div 2$

5. $6 \times 5 - 3$ 6. $24 + 36 \div 9$ 7. $16 + 8 \div 4$ 8. $35 \div (16 - 9)$

Set D Solve the equation. (pp. 128–131)

1. $3 \times n = 21$ 2. $c \div 9 = 1$ 3. $t \times 4 = 28$ 4. $h \div 4 = 10$

5. $r \div 6 = 5$ 6. $56 \div m = 7$ 7. $3 \times w \times 3 = 36$ 8. $3 \times n \times 4 = 24$

Set E Which of the numbers 1, 3, 6, and 8 make the inequality true? (pp. 136–137)

1. $k \neq 5$ 2. $n \leq 8$ 3. $r \geq 6$ 4. $g + 3 < 7$

5. In order to ride the roller coaster, a person must be at least 48 inches tall. Write an inequality to show the height, h, a person must be to ride the roller coaster.

Set F Find a rule. Write your rule as an equation. Use your rule to find the missing numbers. (pp. 138–139)

1.
Input, a	6	12	18	24	30
Output, b	1	2	3	▓	▓

2.
Input, m	4	5	6	▓	▓
Output, n	32	40	48	56	64

Technology
Use Harcourt Mega Math, Ice Station
Exploration, *Arctic Algebra*, Levels F, H, K, Q, T.

TECHNOLOGY CONNECTION

Calculator: Evaluate Expressions

A mail-order company sells boxes of holiday cards. The company charges $12 per box plus a flat shipping fee of $3. How much does an order of 7 boxes of holiday cards cost? 9 boxes?

You can use the TI-15 calculator to find the cost of an order. Find the value of the expression $(12 \times b) + 3$ if b is the number of boxes ordered.

Step I Press the following keys to prepare the calculator:

Now the calculator is programmed to first multiply by 12 and then to add 3.

Step 2	Step 3
Find the value of the expression $12 \times b + 3$ if $b = 7$.	Find the cost for an order of 9 boxes of holiday cards.

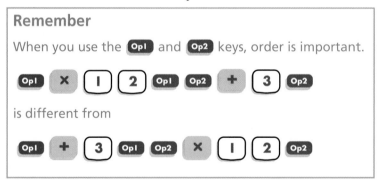

So, an order of 7 boxes of holiday cards costs $87, and an order of 9 boxes of holiday cards costs $111.

Remember

When you use the **Op1** and **Op2** keys, order is important.

is different from

Tips

Before entering a new problem, clear the stored operations. Press at the same time:

Try It

Use a TI-15 calculator to find the cost of each order.

1. 7 or 9 boxes of cards for $14 each plus a $5 shipping fee

2. 2 or 3 books for $23 each plus a $4 shipping fee

3. **Explore More** **Explain** how you would find the cost of an order of any number of the same item if shipping were included in the price.

Two-Step Equations

Keep Your Balance

Kim rode her bicycle 68 miles on the Wild Goose State Trail in one day. She rode the same number of miles each hour for the first 7 hours. After a short rest, she rode another 5 miles. How many miles did Kim ride in each of the first 7 hours?

You can write an equation and then use the strategy *work backward* to find the number of miles Kim rode in 1 hour.

Write an equation. Let *m* represent the number of miles.

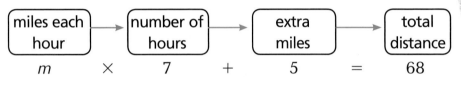

Reverse the operations and the order to work backward.

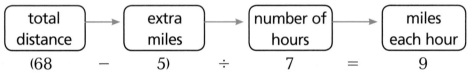

Check: $9 \times 7 + 5 \stackrel{?}{=} 68$ Replace *m* with 9.

$63 + 5 \stackrel{?}{=} 68$ Use the order of operations. Multiply. Then add.

$68 = 68$ ✔ The equation is true. The value of *m* is 9.

So, Kim rode 9 miles in 1 hour.

Example

Solve. $(y \div 2) - 3 = 9$
$(9 + 3) \times 2 = 24$ Work backward.

Check: $(24 \div 2) - 3 \stackrel{?}{=} 9$ Replace *y* with 24.
$12 - 3 \stackrel{?}{=} 9$ Divide. Then subtract.
$9 = 9$ ✔ The equation is true.

So, the value of **y** is 24.

Try It

Work backward to solve the equation. Check your answer.

1. $n \div 3 + 2 = 8$ **2.** $(8 \times e) - 6 = 58$ **3.** $(z \div 4) - 1 = 5$ **4.** $s \times 7 + 13 = 41$

5. **WRITE Math** ▸ Explain how the strategy *work backward* can be used to solve two-step equations.

Chapter 5 Review/Test

Check Vocabulary and Concepts

Choose the best term from the box.

1. The ? states that when the order of two factors is changed, the product is the same. (p. 118)

2. The ? states that the product of 0 and any number is 0. (p. 118)

3. The ? states that you can group factors in different ways and still get the same product. (p. 118)

Check Skills

Write an expression that matches the words. Tell what the expression represents. (pp. 122–125)

4. a number of toys, t, divided equally among 8 cats

5. several binders, b, that have 3 rings each

Follow the order of operations to find the value of each expression. (pp. 126–127)

6. $25 - 10 \div 2$

7. $11 + 1 \times (7 - 3)$

8. $3 \times (8 - 6) + 7$

9. $14 - (3 + 9) \div 6$

Solve the equation. (pp. 128–131)

10. $7 \times n = 56$

11. $d \div 6 = 4$

12. $w \times 6 = 30$

13. $p \div 6 = 7$

14. $k \div 4 = 2$

15. $35 \div m = 7$

16. $3 \times h \times 3 = 45$

17. $4 \times n \times 5 = 40$

Which of the numbers 1, 2, 6, and 8 make the inequality true? (pp. 136–137)

18. $a \geq 0$

19. $m < 6$

20. $r \leq 8$

21. $h - 3 \neq 5$

Find a rule. Write your rule as an equation. Use your rule to find the missing numbers. (pp. 138–139)

22.

Input, x	20	25	30	35	40
Output, y	4	5	6	▦	▦

23.

Input, n	3	4	5	▦	▦
Output, m	27	36	45	54	63

Check Problem Solving

Solve. (pp. 132–135)

24. The sum of two numbers is 17. Their product is 72. What are the numbers?

25. **WRITE Math** ▶ The product of two numbers is one less than their sum. Describe what you know about the numbers.

Unit Review/Test
Chapters 4–5

Multiple Choice

1. Which number makes the equation true?
   (p. 118)

   $$12 \times 4 = (12 \times 2) + (12 \times \blacksquare)$$

   A 1   **C** 3

   B 2   **D** 6

2. The table below shows taxi fares for trips outside the city.

Taxi Fares					
Distance (in km)	1	3	5	7	9
Fare	$2	$6	$10	$14	$\blacksquare$

   Which shows the taxi fare for a 9-kilometer trip? (p. 138)

   A $9   **C** $18

   B $15   **D** $27

3. A hotel has 5 floors. Each floor has 4 rooms. Each room has 2 beds. Which expression does **NOT** describe the total number of beds in the hotel? (p. 118)

   A $4 \times 2 \times 2$

   B $5 \times 2 \times 4$

   C $2 \times 4 \times 5$

   D $4 \times 5 \times 2$

4. Jamal weighs twice as much as his brother. If m represents Jamal's weight, which expression shows how much his brother weighs? (p. 122)

   A $m \times 2$ **C** $m - 2$

   B $m + 2$ **D** $m \div 2$

5. Nathan is going on a 5-day vacation. He needs 2 shirts for each day of his trip. How many shirts should Nathan pack?
   (p. 96)

   A 10   **C** 3

   B 7   **D** 2

6. The salespeople at Ultimate Used Cars sold 32 cars in 4 days. The same numbers of cars were sold each day. How many cars were sold each day?
   (p. 96)

   A 4   **C** 28

   B 8   **D** 36

7. What is the value of $64 \div t$ if $t = 8$?
   (p. 122)

   A 4   **C** 8

   B 6   **D** 10

8. Melissa is buying 4 dozen lemon tarts from a bakery. The table below shows the different discounts the bakery offers.

Bulk Discount Prices		
Discount 1	Discount 2	Discount 3
$11 per dozen	$1 per tart	$48 per 4 dozen

   Which discount gives Melissa the best price? (p. 102)

   A Discount 1

   B Discount 2

   C Discount 3

   D The discounts are the same

GO ONLINE. Technology Use *Online Assessment.*

9. Which expression best represents the arrangement of hearts shown below? (p. 92)

A $4 + 4 + 4 + 4$

B 4×4

C $3 + 3 + 3 + 3$

D 3×4

10. Which missing factor makes the equation true? (p. 108)

$$\blacksquare \times 5 = 21 + 9$$

A 10   **C** 5

B 6   **D** 3

11. Natasha is reading a book. The book is 99 pages long. How many pages must Natasha read each day to finish the book in 9 days? (p. 102)

A 8   **C** 10

B 9   **D** 11

12. Which number sentence is **NOT** in the same fact family as $6 \times 9 = \blacksquare$? (p. 94)

A $\blacksquare \div 9 = 6$

B $\blacksquare \div 6 = 9$

C $9 \times \blacksquare = 6$

D $9 \times 6 = \blacksquare$

Short Response

13. Write an expression to show that Evelyn spent $12 on a number of equally priced toys, t. (p. 122)

14. Write an inequality to match the words: the weight, w, is greater than 20. (p. 136)

15. Ben had softball practice at the same time every week for 9 weeks. He spent a total of 36 hours at practice. What number sentence can be used to find the number of hours Ben spent at softball practice each week? (p. 106)

16. The volleyball team is going to a restaurant for dinner. Each table at the restaurant can seat 4 people. There are 20 people on the team. Write and solve an equation to find how many tables are needed at the restaurant. (p. 128)

17. Mrs. Lin buys 11 boxes of party invitations. Each box has 12 invitations. How many invitations does Mrs. Lin buy in all? (p. 102)

Extended Response   WRITE Math ▸

18. **Explain** how to follow the order of operations to find the value of the expression. (p. 126)

$$8 + 28 \div 4$$

19. There are 3 times as many girls as boys in a ballet class. There are 12 girls in the class. **Explain** how to write an equation to find the number of boys in the ballet class. (p. 128)

20. **Explain** how to use mental math to find the product. (p. 118)

$$10 \times 5 \times 0$$

Money Around the World

Currency Exchange Rates

A cheeseburger might cost $2 in your town. In Mexico, it might cost 22 pesos! To buy a cheeseburger in Mexico, you can exhange your United States money for pesos.

The money, or currency, we use is made up of dollars and cents. Other countries use different currencies. The chart shows recent values for one dollar in other countries.

Currency Exchange Rates in January 2007

 ≈

One dollar is approximately equal to 8 Chinese *yuan*.

 ≈

One dollar is approximately equal to 11 Mexican *pesos*.

 ≈

One dollar is approximately equal to 7 South African *Rand*.

The symbol ≈ means "is approximately equal to."

FACT·ACTIVITY

Use the exchange rates above.

1. Is 5 dollars less than, approximately equal to, or greater than 72 pesos?
   Think: 1 dollar ≈ 11 pesos, so 5 dollars ≈ 5 × 11, or ▪ pesos.

2. Is 28 Chinese yuan less than, approximately equal to, or greater than 3 dollars?

3. Approximately how many dollars is 48 yuan worth?

4. Approximately how many dollars is 42 rand worth?

5. **Pose a Problem** Design your own currency, and define its exchange rate. Write a problem that requires you to exchange your currency for U.S. dollars. Have a classmate solve the problem.

The Mexican Peso

ALMANAC Fact

1 U.S. dollar ≈ 11 Mexican pesos
1 Norwegian Krone ≈
2 Mexican pesos
1 Polish zloty ≈ 4 Mexican pesos

When you travel to another country, you have to find out how much hotel rooms, food, and souvenirs cost in the other country's currency. Then you can decide how many U.S. dollars you need for your trip.

Just like United States bills, Mexican peso bills have portraits of famous leaders from history. Benito Pablo Juarez, whose picture is on the 20-peso bill, was president of Mexico in the 1860s and 1870s.

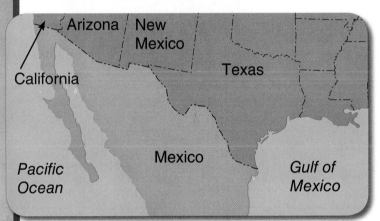

Arizona | New Mexico | Texas | California | Pacific Ocean | Mexico | Gulf of Mexico

FACT·ACTIVITY

Suppose you travel to Mexico. Plan the souvenirs you will buy.

▶ Decide which souvenirs you will buy and the number you will buy of each. Make a list.

▶ How many Mexican pesos will the souvenirs cost?

▶ Find the least number of U.S. dollars you will need to exchange. How many pesos will you have left over after you go shopping?

| Paper flower | Mini-vase | Bobbing turtle toy | Donkey piñata |

| 11 pesos | 44 pesos | 28 pesos | 100 pesos |

3 Time, Temperature, and Data

Math on Location

A DVD FROM
The Futures Channel

with
Chapter Projects

1

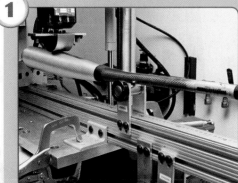

The data on how much of a bending load a bat takes is used to make a bar graph to compare bats.

2

A test measures speed of the bat, speed of the ball, and turn of the bat.

3

A batter hits balls thrown from a pitching machine. A radar gun measures the speed of the balls hit.

VOCABULARY POWER

TALK Math

What math do you see in the **Math on Location** photographs? What type of graph would be used to compare the maximum speed of each ball hit from the pitching machine?

READ Math

REVIEW VOCABULARY You learned the words below when you learned how to organize and analyze data. How do these words relate to **Math on Location**?

bar graph a graph that uses bars to show data

data information collected about people or things

pictograph a graph that uses pictures to show and compare information

tally table a table that uses tally marks to record data

WRITE Math

Copy and complete a semantic map like the one below. Use **Math on Location** and what you know about organizing and analyzing data to complete the map.

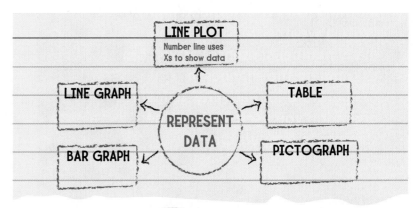

LINE PLOT
Number line uses
Xs to show data

LINE GRAPH

TABLE

REPRESENT DATA

BAR GRAPH

PICTOGRAPH

Technology
Multimedia Math Glossary link at
www.harcourtschool.com/hspmath

6 Time and Temperature

FAST FACT

The highest temperature ever recorded in the United States is 134°F. It was recorded in Death Valley, California. The lowest recorded temperature is ⁻80°F. It was recorded in northern Alaska.

Investigate

Temperatures usually rise from early morning lows to afternoon highs. Write a weather report. Use as many number sentences as you can to compare the changes in temperature for each city. Tell which operation you used to show the changes in temperature.

Average January Temperatures (in °F) for United States Cities		
City	High	Low
Charlotte, North Carolina	51	32
Cleveland, Ohio	33	19
Columbia, Missouri	37	18
Greenville, South Carolina	50	31
Louisville, Kentucky	41	25
Madison, Wisconsin	25	9
Springfield, Illinois	33	17

GO ONLINE

Technology
Student pages are available in the Student eBook.

Check your understanding of important skills needed for success in Chapter 6.

▶ **Use a Calendar**

For 1–4, use the calendar.

March						
Sun	Mon	Tue	Wed	Thu	Fri	Sat
						1
2	3	4	5	6	7	8
9	10	11	12	13	14	15
16	17	18	19	20	21	22
23	24	25	26	27	28	29
30	31					

1. What is the date of the third Thursday in March?

2. What day of the week is March 22?

3. List the dates of all the Mondays in March.

4. What date is 2 weeks after March 12?

▶ **Tell Time**

Write the time shown on the clock in numbers and words.

5.

6.

7.

8.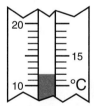

▶ **Measure Temperature**

Use the thermometer to find the temperature.

9.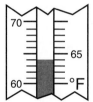

10.

11.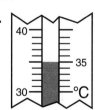

12.

VOCABULARY POWER

CHAPTER VOCABULARY

A.M.	negative
calendar	numbers
degree Celsius	P.M.
degree	positive
Fahrenheit	numbers
elapsed time	quarter
half hour	hour
hour	second
minute	time line

WARM-UP WORDS

elapsed time the amount of time that passes from the start of an activity to the end of that activity

negative numbers all the numbers to the left of zero on the number line; negative numbers are less than zero

second a small unit of time

Telling Time

OBJECTIVE: Estimate and tell time to the nearest minute and second.

Quick Review

What is another way to write 30 minutes?

_____

Vocabulary

second

Learn

PROBLEM Laci wants to see a movie. The movie starts at 2:10. The clock shows the time right now. Has the movie started yet?

Think: The time on the clock is 2:30, or 30 minutes after two. The movie started at 2:10, or 10 minutes after two.

So, the movie has already started.

The hour hand on a clock goes around the clockface twice each day to measure 24 hours. A.M. means "before noon." P.M. means "after noon." Did the movie start in the morning or afternoon?

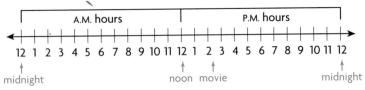

So, the movie started in the afternoon.

Units of Time
1 minute (min) = 60 seconds (sec)
1 quarter hour (hr) = 15 minutes
1 half hour = 30 minutes
1 hour = 60 minutes
1 day = 24 hours

Examples Estimate and measure time.

Ⓐ Nearest 5 minutes

Compare the location of the minute hand to the numbers on the clock.

Think: 1 is the 5-minute mark and 2 is the 10-minute mark. 3:07 is closer to 3:05 than to 3:10.

So, it is about 3:05.

Ⓑ Nearest minute

Write: 7:15 A.M.
Read: seven fifteen A.M., 15 minutes after seven in the morning, quarter after seven in the morning

Ⓒ Nearest second

A **second** is a small unit of time.

Write: 5:10:12
Read: 5:10 and 12 seconds, 10 minutes and 12 seconds after five

• What unit of time would you use to measure the length of a school day?

Guided Practice

1. Copy the clock face and draw the hands to show 46 minutes and 30 seconds after nine.

Write the time as shown on a digital clock.

2. 32 minutes after six ✓**3.** 47 minutes after twelve ✓**4.** 20 minutes before four

5. **TALK Math** Explain how telling time to the nearest second is different from telling time to the nearest minute on an analog clock.

Independent Practice (and Problem Solving)

Write the time as shown on a digital clock.

6. 24 minutes after three

7. 18 minutes before ten

8. quarter to five

Write two ways to read the time. Then estimate to the nearest 5 minutes.

9.  1:44 P.M.

10.  7:11 A.M.

11. 11:38 P.M.

12.

13.

14.

Tell whether to use seconds, minutes, hours, or days to measure the time.

15. to eat lunch

16. to run a 50-yd dash

17. to read a 400-page book

USE DATA For 18 and 20, use the watch.

18. The watch shows the time the movie ended. To the nearest 5 minutes, about what time was it? Include A.M. or P.M.

19. **FAST FACT** The silent movie *The Gold Rush* runs 96 minutes. To the nearest half hour, how long is that?

20. **WRITE Math** ▸ What's the Error? Alan says his watch shows the movie ended at 2:48 P.M. Explain Alan's error.

Mixed Review and Test Prep

21. Find a rule. Write your rule. (Grade 3)
3, 9, 27, 81

22. Jason tosses a number cube labeled 1 to 6. What is the probability that he tosses a 4? (Grade 3)

23. **Test Prep** Marta says the time is 8 minutes after two in the afternoon. Which time is it?

A 2:08 A.M. **C** 8:02 A.M.

B 2:08 P.M. **D** 8:02 P.M.

Extra Practice on page 172, Set A

Elapsed Time

OBJECTIVE: Calculate elapsed time using clocks and stopwatches.

Quick Review

Write the time shown on the clock in two ways.

4:30 P.M.

Vocabulary

elapsed time

Learn

PROBLEM From school, Darren and his dad are riding the bus to the mall to buy a new computer game. How long will the bus ride last?

The time that passes from the start of an activity to the end of that activity is **elapsed time**.

Bus Schedule

Bus Stop Location	Arrival Time
Avery School	3:00 P.M
Post Office	3:15 P.M.
Library	4:05 P.M.
Central Mall	4:35 P.M.

Example 1 Use a clock to find elapsed time.

You can use a clock to count forward from the starting time to the ending time.

Think: From 3:00 P.M. to 4:00 P.M., 1 full hour has passed.

Think: From 4:00 P.M. to 4:35 P.M., 35 minutes have passed.

1 hour + 35 minutes = 1 hour 35 minutes

So, the bus ride will last 1 hour 35 minutes.

ERROR ALERT

When you add times, remember to rename 60 minutes as 1 hour.

Example 2 Find the ending time.

Erin and her mother get on the bus at 4:35 P.M. Their ride home from Central Mall lasts 45 minutes. What time do they get home?

ONE WAY Count forward on a clock.

Count forward 5 minutes at a time.

ANOTHER WAY Use addition.

Add the hours and the minutes.

$$
\begin{array}{r}
4 \text{ hr } 35 \text{ min} \\
+ \quad 45 \text{ min} \\
\hline
4 \text{ hr } 80 \text{ min}
\end{array}
$$

Think: 60 min = 1 hr
80 min = 1 hr 20 min

4 hr + 1 hr + 20 min = 5 hr 20 min

So, Erin and her mother get home at 5:20 P.M.

Example 3 Find the starting time.

Dora and her son hiked for 35 minutes. They stopped for a snack at 4:15 P.M. When did they start hiking?

ONE WAY Count backward on a clock.

Count backward 5 minutes at a time.

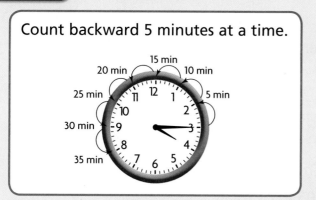

ANOTHER WAY Use subtraction.

$$\begin{array}{r} 4 \text{ hr } 15 \text{ min} \\ - \quad\quad 35 \text{ min} \end{array}$$

Think: 15 minutes is less than 35 minutes, so rename 4 hr 15 min as 3 hr 75 min, as follows: 1 hr = 60 min and 60 min + 15 min = 75 min.

$$\begin{array}{r} \overset{3}{\cancel{4}} \text{ hr } \overset{75}{\cancel{15}} \text{ min} \\ - \quad\quad 35 \text{ min} \\ \hline 3 \text{ hr } 40 \text{ min} \end{array}$$

So, Dora and her son started hiking at 3:40 P.M.

Activity Use a stopwatch to time and record everyday activities.

Materials ■ stopwatch

When you read time on most stopwatches, the first number names the minutes and the second number names the seconds. So, if the time shows 3:10, you read "three minutes, ten seconds."

In pairs, you will time each other to find out how long it takes to do everyday activities.

• How long does it take to write your name ten times?

Copy and complete the table. Use a stopwatch. You run the stopwatch while your partner completes the activity.

Name	Activity	Estimated Time	Elapsed Time
?	?	■	■

Step 1	**Step 2**	**Step 3**	**Step 4**
Estimate the time it will take to complete the activity. Record your estimate in the table.	You say, "GO!" Your partner begins writing. You push the Start/Stop button.	When finished, your partner says, "STOP!" You push the Start/Stop button.	You read the stopwatch readout and record the elapsed time in the table.

• Compare your estimated time with the actual elapsed time. Is your estimate reasonable? Explain.

• What are some other activities you could time with a stopwatch?

1. A television cartoon show begins at 10:30 A.M. and ends at 11:00 A.M. Find the elapsed time.

Find the elapsed time.

2. start: 8:10 A.M.
   end: 9:00 A.M.

3. start: 10:15 A.M.
   end: 12:15 P.M.

4. start: 6:15 P.M.
   end: 10:49 P.M.

✓5. start: 12:00 A.M.
   end: 3:07 P.M.

Find the end time.

6. start: 12:00 P.M.   11:45
   elapsed time:
   5 hr 45 min

7. start: 1:37 P.M.
   elapsed time:
   30 min

8. start: 7:12 A.M.
   elapsed time:
   3 hr 15 min

✓9. start: 3:07 A.M.
   elapsed time:
   7 hr 5 min

10. **TALK Math** It is 3:47 P.M. The game began at 2:05 P.M. **Explain** how to find how much time has passed since the game began.

Independent Practice and Problem Solving

Find the elapsed time.

11. start: 4:00 P.M.
    end: 11:30 P.M.

12. start: 9:15 P.M.
    end: 7:45 A.M.

13. start: 10:40 A.M.
    end: 2:10 P.M.

14. start: 7:30 P.M.
    end: 6:45 A.M.

Find the start time.

15. end: 11:50 P.M.
    elapsed time:
    1 hr 10 min

16. end: 9:45 A.M.
    elapsed time:
    2 hr 25 min

17. end: 10:15 P.M.
    elapsed time:
    1 hr 45 min

18. end: 8:30 A.M.
    elapsed time:
    9 hr

Algebra Copy and complete the tables.

	Start Time	End Time	Elapsed Time
19.	3:13 P.M.	3:45 P.M.	■
20.	■	11:40 A.M.	4 hr 30 min

	Start Time	End Time	Elapsed Time
21.	4:45 A.M.	■	8 hr 5 min
22.	■	3:00 A.M.	3 hr 15 min

USE DATA For 23–24, use the table.

23. Vincent timed the wait at each stop with a stopwatch. At which stop did the bus spend the least time?

24. The bus arrived at Avery School at 3:00 P.M. To the nearest second, what time did the bus leave the school?

25. **WRITE Math** Mary solves 1 problem every 3 minutes. If she starts at 11:05 A.M., can she solve 9 problems by 11:30 A.M.? **Explain.**

Time Spent at Bus Stops

Stop	Elapsed Time (min:sec)
Avery School	2:05
Central Mall	3:15
Library	1:34
Post Office	1:12

Learn About) Estimating Time

Use what you know about elapsed time to find how much time it will take to reach an object or place.

Darren got in line at the food court at 4:35 P.M. He is meeting his friend at 4:45 P.M. Five people are standing in front of Darren. It took the first person 3 minutes to receive food after ordering. If it takes each person the same amount of time, about how much time will pass before Darren places his food order? If Darren stays in line, will he be able to meet his friend on time?

ONE WAY Use repeated addition.

$$3 + 3 + 3 + 3 + 3 = 15$$

ANOTHER WAY Use multiplication.

$$3 \times 5 = 15$$

So, about 15 minutes will pass before Darren places his food order. He will not be able to meet his friend on time.

Try It

Copy and complete the chart.

	Starting Place	Number of People In Line	Estimated Time for Each Person in Line	Total Estimated Waiting Time
26.	Food Court Line	5 ahead of Michael	2 minutes	■
27.	Movie Line A	4 ahead of Erin	30 seconds	■
28.	Movie Line B	7 ahead of Billy	■	21 minutes
29.	Popcorn Line	■ ahead of Jane	50 seconds	5 minutes

Mixed Review and Test Prep

30. What is the missing number? (p. 66)

$$8 + (7 - 4) = ■ + 6$$

31. Test Prep The movie started at 6:52 P.M. and ended at 9:15 P.M. How long was the movie?

  A 2 hours 23 minutes

  B 2 hours 36 minutes

  C 3 hours 27 minutes

  D 3 hours 36 minutes

32. What is the time to the nearest 5 minutes? (p. 152)

  4:07:28 P.M.

33. Test Prep It is 4:25 P.M. What time did Brian's party start, if 3 hours and 10 minutes have passed since the guests arrived?

  A 2:40 P.M.   **C** 1:35 P.M.

  B 2:25 P.M.   **D** 1:15 P.M.

Elapsed Time on a Calendar

OBJECTIVE: Find elapsed time on a calendar.

Learn

PROBLEM On October 18, 1961, the New York Museum of Modern Art hung the painting *Le Bateau,* "The Sailboat," upside down. The mistake was not noticed until December 4, 1961. About how many weeks did the painting hang upside down?

◄ New York Museum of Modern Art

You can use a calendar to find elapsed time.

Example 1 Use a calendar to count.

To find the elapsed time, first count the weeks. Start with October 18, and count the weeks to November 29. Then count on the days to December 4.

October						
Sun	Mon	Tue	Wed	Thu	Fri	Sat
1	2	3	4	5	6	7
8	9	10	11	12	13	14
15	16	17	(18)	19	20	21
22	23	24	25	26	27	28
29	30	31				

November						
Sun	Mon	Tue	Wed	Thu	Fri	Sat
			1	2	3	4
5	6	7	8	9	10	11
12	13	14	15	16	17	18
19	20	21	22	23	24	25
26	27	28	29	30		

December						
Sun	Mon	Tue	Wed	Thu	Fri	Sat
					1	2
3	(4)	5	6	7	8	9
10	11	12	13	14	15	16
17	18	19	20	21	22	23
24	25	26	27	28	29	30
31						

Le Bateau hung upside down for 6 weeks 5 days.

So, *Le Bateau* hung upside down for about 7 weeks.

• Explain how to find the elapsed time in days.

Example 2 Use a calendar to solve.

Use the calendars above.

Ms. Vega is teaching an art history class about Henri Matisse. Her first class is on October 5. The class meets each Thursday for 9 weeks. On what day does the class end?

Think: Start on October 5. Count forward 8 more weeks.

So, the art history class ends on November 30.

▲ *Interior with a Phonograph,* by Henri Matisse

Guided Practice

For 1–3, use the calendars.

	January						
Sun	Mon	Tue	Wed	Thu	Fri	Sat
		1	2	3	4	5
6	7	8	9	10	11	12
13	14	15	16	17	18	19
20	21	22	23	24	25	26
27	28	29	30	31		

1. About how many weeks are there from January 1 to January 22?

2. Li went to the dentist on January 15. If today is February 29, how many weeks and days is it since she saw the dentist?

3. Frank finished building a model ship on February 26. If he worked on it for 8 weeks, when did he start the ship?

4. **TALK Math** Explain how you use a calendar to find elapsed time.

	February						
Sun	Mon	Tue	Wed	Thu	Fri	Sat
					1	2
3	4	5	6	7	8	9
10	11	12	13	14	15	16
17	18	19	20	21	22	23
24	25	26	27	28	29	

Independent Practice and Problem Solving

For 5–7, use the calendars above.

5. A store is having a sale on paints from January 7 to January 23. For how many days are paints on sale?

6. Presidents' Day was February 18. If Martin Luther King, Jr. Day was 4 weeks and 1 day earlier, when was it?

7. The moon will be full on January 8 and again 4 weeks and 2 days later. Name the date of the second full moon.

8. **Reasoning** Does this calendar show a leap year? **Explain** how you know.

USE DATA For 9–11, use the table and calendars above.

9. Which type of art will be shown for the greatest amount of time? Which will be shown for the least amount of time?

10. If the gallery doubles the number of days for its painting exhibit, what will be the last day of the exhibit?

11. How many days is the period of winter exhibits, from the first day of the painting exhibit to the last day of the pottery exhibit?

Art Gallery Winter Exhibits

Type of Art	Dates of Exhibit
Paintings	Jan 4 through Jan 20
Drawings	Jan 24 through Feb 3
Pottery	Feb 5 through Feb 14

12. **WRITE Math** Describe a pattern of the dates as you move down a calendar column for any day of the week.

Mixed Review and Test Prep

13. Is 5×6 greater than, less than, or equal to 3×10? (p. 118)

14. What kind of angles are formed by two perpendicular lines? (Grade 3)

15. **Test Prep** Use the calendars above. If today is February 15, how many days have passed since January 2?

   A 22 days   **C** 34 days

   B 26 days   **D** 44 days

Extra Practice on page 172, Set C

ALGEBRA

Change Units of Time

OBJECTIVE: Change units of time including years, months, days, hours, minutes, and seconds.

Learn

PROBLEM In the Antarctic, an adult male emperor penguin will keep a single egg warm for about 9 weeks until the egg hatches. About how many days will the penguin keep the egg warm?

To change weeks into days, you must know how these units are related. Then you can decide whether to multiply or divide.

Example 1 Use multiplication.

9 weeks = ■ days

Think: 1 week = 7 days

A week is longer than a day. When you change from longer units to shorter units, you need more of the shorter units, so multiply.

weeks		days in a week		total days
↓		↓		↓
9	×	7	=	63

So, the adult male emperor penguin will keep the egg warm for about 63 days.

- In Example 1, how can you use repeated addition to change from weeks to days?

Example 2 Use division.

How many years is 416 weeks?

416 weeks = ■ years

Think: 1 year = 52 weeks

A week is shorter than a year. When you change from shorter units to longer units, you need fewer of the longer units, so divide. You can divide 416 by 52 with a calculator.

So, 416 weeks equals 8 years.

- In Example 2, how can you use repeated subtraction to change weeks to years?

▲ The emperor is the world's largest penguin. It can weigh up to 88 pounds!

Units of Time
1 minute (min) = 60 seconds (sec)
1 hour (hr) = 60 minutes
1 day = 24 hours
1 week (wk) = 7 days
1 year (yr) = 12 months (mo), about 52 weeks, or 365 days
1 leap year = 366 days

Guided Practice

1. Copy and complete to change longer units to shorter units.

   Think: years × months in a year = total months

   2 years × ■ months in a year = ■ months

Complete. Tell whether you *multiply* or *divide*.

2. 3 weeks = ■ days   ✓ 3. 3 years = ■ days   ✓ 4. 120 hours = ■ days

5. [TALK Math] **Explain** how you remember whether to multiply or divide to change units.

Independent Practice and Problem Solving

Complete. Tell whether you *multiply* or *divide*.

6. 36 months = ■ years   7. 300 minutes = ■ hours   8. 3 days 6 hours = ■ hours

9. 360 seconds = ■ minutes   10. 4 minutes = ■ seconds   11. 2 years 24 days = ■ days

Compare. Write <, >, or = for each ●.

12. 3 weeks 2 days ● 1 month

13. 9 minutes 15 seconds ● 500 seconds

14. 152 weeks ● 2 years 48 weeks

15. 12 hours 11 minutes ● 750 minutes

USE DATA For 16–18, use the table.

16. Which two activities take about the same amount of time?

17. Male penguins keep the egg warm for about 63 days. How many weeks is 63 days?

18. **Pose a Problem** Look back at Problem 16. Write a similar problem by changing the event or activity.

19. [WRITE Math] ▸ **What's the Error?** Ann says 22 days is 4 weeks. Is she correct? **Explain.**

Emperor Penguin Facts	
Event or Activity	**Approximate Time**
Females make and lay eggs	2 months 1 week
Females keep egg warm	2 hours
Males keep egg warm	63 days
Females fish at sea	8 weeks
Males may go without food	4 months
Males fish at sea	24 days
Longest recorded dive for food	22 minutes

Mixed Review and Test Prep

20. Rewrite the expression using the Distributive Property and find the value: 5 × (6 + 6). (p. 122)

21. A class started at 1:20 P.M. and ended at 2:45 P.M. How long was the class? (p. 154)

22. **Test Prep** Mrs. Dorado has a 60-month car loan. How many years will it take Mrs. Dorado to repay the loan?

   A 2 years   **C** 7 years

   B 5 years   **D** 10 years

Extra Practice on page 172, Set D

Problem Solving Workshop
Skill: Sequence Information
OBJECTIVE: Solve problems using the skill *sequence information.*

Use the Skill

PROBLEM A time line shows dates or times and the order of events. Siena is making a time line about food inventions. The pop-up toaster is 27 years older than the microwave oven. What year was the pop-up toaster invented? Between which two dates should it be on the time line?

▲ Toaster

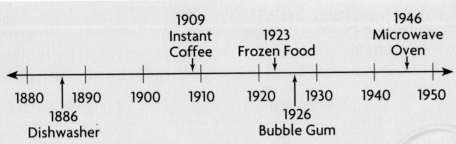

The time line shows when the microwave oven was invented.

Subtract 27 years from 1946 to find the year the pop-up toaster was invented. $1946 - 27 = 1919$

So, the pop-up toaster was invented in 1919. It should be between 1910 and 1920.

Remember
Years are whole numbers. So, you can add or subtract years the same way you add or subtract whole numbers.

▼ Dishwasher

Think and Discuss
Use the time line to sequence the information. Then solve the problem.

a. The paper drinking straw was invented 2 years after the dishwasher. The tin can was patented 22 years before the paper drinking straw. When was the tin can patented?

b. Order these inventions from earliest to latest.
   • Cornflakes™ were invented 22 years before bubble gum.
   • Cake mix was invented 3 years after the microwave oven.
   • Freeze-dried coffee was invented 29 years after instant coffee.

c. The air conditioner was invented 44 years before the microwave oven. The tea bag was invented 2 years after the air conditioner. Order the inventions from oldest to newest and tell what year each was invented.

▲ Frozen food

▼ Microwave

Guided Problem Solving

**Use a time line to sequence the information.
Then solve the problem.**

1. Montana became a state in 1889. Alaska became a state in 1959. New Mexico became a state 23 years after Montana. Idaho became a state 22 years before New Mexico. How many years before Alaska did New Mexico become a state?

   • Make a time line to sequence the information. Solve the problem.

2. **What if** New Mexico had become a state at the same time as Idaho? How many years before Alaska became a state would that have been?

3. Jo's class arrived at the science museum at 10:15 A.M. to study the invention of the airplane. The students had 3 hours 30 minutes in all at the museum. The class wanted 40 minutes for lunch and 25 minutes in the gift shop after lunch. What was the latest time they could stop for lunch? How long after they got to the museum would they need to stop for lunch?

Mixed Applications

4. Sarah has cooking lessons on Monday and Thursday. On Tuesday, she baby-sits her little sister. She has ballet after school on Wednesday and on Saturday. How many days pass from the time she baby-sits until her second cooking lesson?

5. The museum store sells books about inventions for $10 each. If you buy 2 books, you get $2 off the total price. If you buy 3 books, you get $5 off the total price. How can you buy 5 books and pay the least amount of money?

USE DATA For 6–7, use the train schedule.

6. If Greg takes the earliest train from Boyds to Rockville, will he have time to spend 2 hours in the science museum and meet a friend to see a movie before getting on a train to Union Station? **Explain.**

7. Which of the trips from Rockville to Union Station takes the longest time? How long?

8. Rae is driving to the museum. After 2 hours, she stops for 15 minutes. Then she drives for 30 minutes more. She arrives at the museum at 12:15 P.M. At what time did she leave for the museum?

Brunswick Line Train Schedule,
Monday through Friday

Train Number	100	200	300
City	Time (P.M.)		
Leaves BOYDS	5:51	7:02	8:09
Arrives ROCKVILLE	6:14	7:29	8:35
Arrives UNION STATION	6:45	8:05	9:12

9. **WRITE Math** Crayons were invented in 1903. They were sold in the United States in boxes of 8. If a carton held 100 boxes and each crate held 8 cartons, **explain** how to find how many crayons were in a crate.

Temperature

OBJECTIVE: Measure temperature and changes in temperature in degrees Fahrenheit and degrees Celsius.

Learn

Degrees Fahrenheit (°F) are customary units for measuring temperature. The United States uses the Fahrenheit scale. Water freezes at 32°F and boils at 212°F.

Read 32°F as "thirty-two degrees Fahrenheit."

Temperatures less than 0°F are negative temperatures. On a thermometer, negative temperatures are located below the zero. The record low temperature in Chicago, Illinois, was ⁻27°F.

Read ⁻27°F as "twenty-seven degrees below zero Fahrenheit."

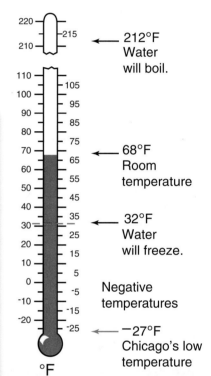

212°F
Water
will boil.

68°F
Room
temperature

32°F
Water
will freeze.

Negative
temperatures

−27°F
Chicago's low
temperature

°F

Example 1 Find the change in temperature.

If the temperature drops from a high of 19°F to a low of ⁻12°F, what is the change in temperature?

Step 1

Count the change in temperature from 19°F to 0°F. The change is 19°F.

Step 2

Count the change in temperature from 0°F to ⁻12°F. The change is 12°F.

Step 3

Add the two changes. 19° + 12° = 31°

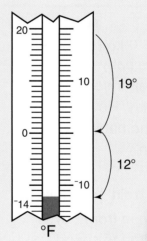

So, the temperature drops 31°F.

Example 2 Estimate the temperature.

Sometimes you do not need to know the exact temperature. You can estimate temperatures by rounding to the nearest 5 degrees.

Think: The temperature is closer to 80°F than to 85°F.

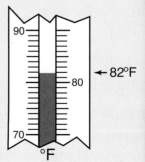

←82°F

So, the estimated temperature is about 80°F.

Degrees Celsius

Degrees Celsius (°C) are metric units for measuring temperature. Many countries use the Celsius scale. Water freezes at 0°C.

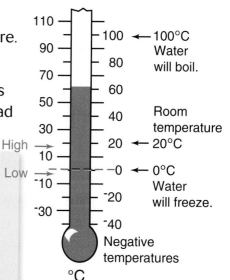

You can read temperatures in degrees Celsius the same way as in degrees Fahrenheit. Read 10°C as "ten degrees Celsius." Read ⁻5°C as "five degrees below zero Celsius."

Example 3 **Find the change in temperature.**

The temperature rose from a low of ⁻4°C to a high of 18°C. By how many degrees did the temperature rise?

Step 1

The change in temperature from ⁻4°C to 0°C is 4°C.

Step 2

The change in temperature from 0°C to 18°C is 18°C.

Step 3

Add the two changes. $4° + 18° = 22°$

So, the temperature rose 22°C.

- How do you find a drop in temperature from 80°C to 45°C?

- In Example 3, what does the scale on the thermometer represent?

Activity **Measure and compare temperatures.**

Materials ■ Fahrenheit and Celsius thermometers

- Estimate and measure the temperatures of a few places around your school in the morning in degrees Fahrenheit or degrees Celsius. Copy the table and record the places, times, estimated temperatures, and your measured temperatures.

Temperature Readings at School

Place	Time	Estimated Temperature (in °F or °C)	Measured Temperature (in °F or °C)	Change
_?_		■	■	■

- How do your estimated temperatures compare with your measured temperatures?

- Find the change in temperature. Estimate, measure, and record the temperatures in the afternoon. Measure the temperatures in the same places and with the same unit as your first measurement.

- Order the measured temperatures from coldest to warmest.

Guided Practice

1. Letter A shows a temperature of 4°C. What is the temperature that is 10 degrees warmer?

Use the thermometer to find the temperature shown by each letter.

2. B   ✓ 3. C   ✓ 4. D

5. **TALK Math** Explain how you can estimate the temperatures of hot soup and a cold drink using temperatures you already know.

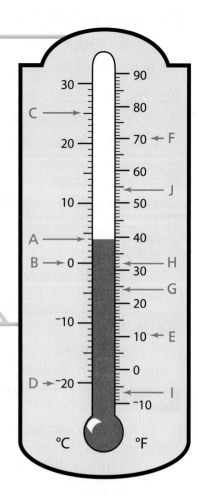

Independent Practice and Problem Solving

Use the thermometer to find the temperature shown by each letter.

6. E   7. F   8. G

9. H   10. I   11. J

Write each temperature. Then estimate to the nearest 5 degrees.

12.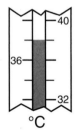
13.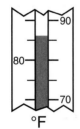
14.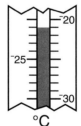
15.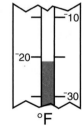

Use a thermometer to find the change in temperature.

16. 4°F to 12°F   17. 8°C to ⁻15°C   18. ⁻2°F to ⁻14°F

19. 32°F to 17°F   20. ⁻24°C to 3°C   21. ⁻47°F to ⁻32°F

Choose the better estimate.

22. ice cube: 32°F or 45°F   23. classroom: 20°C or 35°C   24. snow: ⁻5°C or 15°C

25. hot day: 65°F or 85°F   26. bedroom: 78°F or 92°F   27. hot cocoa: 20°C or 90°C

28. **Reasoning** Explain why zero degrees Fahrenheit is not the same temperature as zero degrees Celsius.

29. **WRITE Math** Write a paragraph to **describe** the temperatures in your area during spring, summer, fall, and winter.

Extra Practice on page 172, Set E

USE DATA For 30–32, use the table.

30. Order the cities from the greatest to least change in temperature.

31. Which city has a greater difference between its January and July temperatures, Fairbanks or Madison?

32. Draw a thermometer and show the January and July temperatures in Baltimore. Find the difference.

Average Monthly Temperatures in U.S. Cities		
City	January (in °F)	July (in °F)
Baltimore, MD	32	77
Fairbanks, AK	⁻10	62
Jackson, MS	45	81
Madison, WI	17	72

Learn About Comparing Temperatures

You can use thermometers to help you compare temperatures with the same units.

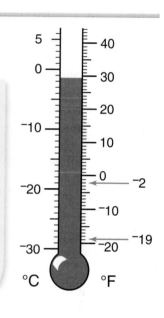

Example
In Pittsburgh, Pennsylvania, temperatures have reached lows of ⁻2°F and ⁻19°F. Which temperature is colder?

> On a Fahrenheit or Celsius thermometer, the greater or warmer temperature is closer to the top. The lesser or cooler temperature is closer to the bottom of the thermometer. The arrow for ⁻19°F is closer to the bottom of the thermometer.

So, ⁻19°F is colder than ⁻2°F.

Try It
Use a thermometer to compare the temperatures. Write < or >.

33. ⁻16°C ● ⁻11°C   34. ⁻10°F ● 10°F   35. ⁻15°C ● 2°C   36. ⁻1°F ● ⁻4°F

Mixed Review and Test Prep

37. Order from least to greatest:
5,032; 5,320; 5,203; 3,502. (p. 16)

38. Find the missing numbers.
65 days = ■ weeks ■ days (p. 160)

39. **Test Prep** The temperature rose from ⁻1°F to 5°F. What was the change in temperature?

A 3°F   **B** 4°F   **C** 5°F   **D** 6°F

40. **Test Prep** Which of the following is most likely to have a temperature of 25°C?

A Swimming pool   **C** Ice cube

B Refrigerator   **D** Hot cocoa

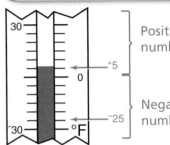

LESSON 7

Explore Negative Numbers

OBJECTIVE: Identify and name negative numbers by using a number line and counting techniques.

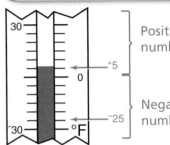

Quick Review

Order from least to greatest.

1. 25, 15, 35
2. 86, 84, 87
3. 1,556; 1,565; 1,555
4. 997, 996, 979
5. 1,763; 1,673; 1,765

Vocabulary

positive numbers

negative numbers

Learn

PROBLEM People in Fosston, Minnesota, enjoy outdoor winter sports such as skiing and snowmobiling. The normal low temperature in winter is 5°F. However, the coldest recorded temperature is ⁻25°F.

Look at the thermometer. **Positive numbers** are greater than 0, so they are above the 0 on a thermometer. **Negative numbers** are less than 0, so they are located below the 0. The number 0 is neither positive nor negative.

So, ⁺5 is a positive number and is read as "positive five," and ⁻25 is a negative number and is read as "negative twenty-five."

There are different ways to use negative and positive numbers.

Example 1

A Count up

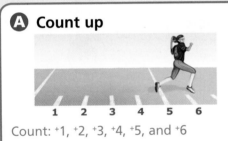

Count: ⁺1, ⁺2, ⁺3, ⁺4, ⁺5, and ⁺6

Positive number: ⁺6
Read: positive six

So, the quarterback gained 6 yards.

B Count back

Count: ⁻1, ⁻2, ⁻3, ⁻4, ⁻5, and ⁻6

Negative number: ⁻6
Read: negative six

So, the quarterback lost 6 yards.

Example 2

A Earn money

Pam earns $8 for weeding the neighbor's garden.
Positive number: ⁺8
Read: positive eight

So, Pam has $8 more in her pocket.

B Owe money

Paco pays his sister the $7 he owes her.
Negative number: ⁻7
Read: negative seven

So, now Paco has $7 less in his wallet.

▲ Usually, the air temperature must be less than 41°F, or 5°C, for snow to stay on the ground.

168

Compare and Order

Elevations are measured by their relationship to sea level. For example, our nation's capital in Washington, D.C., is 1 foot below sea level. Part of Japan is 13 feet below sea level. You can use the negative numbers ⁻1 and ⁻13 to represent these elevations. Locate these negative numbers on a number line.

Elevations Above and Below Sea Level		
Place	Location	Elevation (in feet)
Death Valley, CA	U.S.	⁻282
Dead Sea	Israel	⁻1,372
Hachiro-gata	Japan	⁻13
Mt. Arvin, MI	U.S.	1,979
Mt. McKinley, AK	U.S.	20,320
Mt. Everest	Nepal	29,035
Washington, D.C.	U.S.	⁻1

Example 3 Locate negative numbers on a number line.

On a number line, negative numbers are to the left of 0. Positive numbers are to the right of 0.

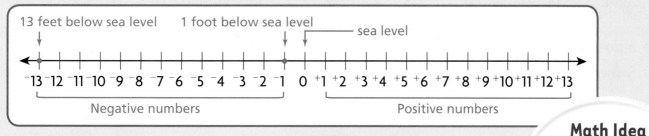

13 feet below sea level   1 foot below sea level   sea level

Negative numbers   Positive numbers

- How do you read the numbers representing the elevations listed in the table?

Example 4 Use a number line to compare the numbers.

⁻15   ⁻10   ⁻5   0   ⁺5   ⁺10   ⁺15

> **Math Idea**
> As you move to the left on a number line, the numbers decrease. As you move to the right, the numbers increase.

A Compare ⁺15 and ⁺5.
Since ⁺15 is to the right of ⁺5, ⁺15 > ⁺5.

B Compare ⁻2 and ⁻14.
Since ⁻2 is to the right of ⁻14, ⁻2 > ⁻14.

C Compare ⁻8 and ⁺10.
Since ⁻8 is to the left of ⁺10, ⁻8 < ⁺10.

- Order the numbers representing the elevations in the table above from least to greatest.

Guided Practice

1. Write the missing numbers from left to right on the number line.

⁻5 ▇ ⁻3 ▇ ⁻1 0 ⁺1 ▇ ⁺3 ▇ ⁺5

Name the number represented by each letter.

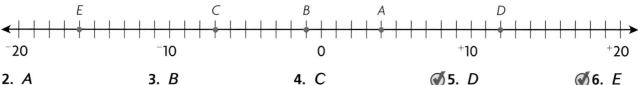

E   C   B   A   D

⁻20   ⁻10   0   ⁺10   ⁺20

2. A   3. B   4. C   ✓5. D   ✓6. E

7. **TALK Math** Explain how to use a number line to describe negative numbers.

Name the number represented by each letter.

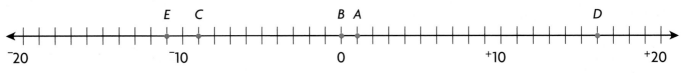

8. *A* 9. *B* 10. *C* 11. *D* 12. *E*

Draw a number line and graph the numbers. Compare using < or >.

13. $^+4$ and $^+7$ 14. $^-12$ and 0 15. $^+2$ and $^-2$ 16. $^-10$ and $^+10$ 17. $^-15$ and $^-18$

Write a positive or negative number to represent each situation.

18. Amy owes a friend $5.

19. Sunil earns $10.

20. Marvin added 12 cards to his collection.

21. Jacque dropped 7 pencils.

Algebra Write the missing numbers to complete a possible pattern.

22. $^+15, ^+12, ^+9, ^+6, ^+3,$ ■, ■, ■

23. $^+18, ^+14, ^+10, ^+6, ^+2,$ ■, ■, ■

USE DATA For 24–26, use the table.

24. Abby and her family played miniature golf. The player with the least score wins the game. Who won the game?

25. Order their total scores from least to greatest.

26. Which players had total scores that were greater than Buddy's?

27. **WRITE Math** Sense or Nonsense Lee says that since $^+10$ is greater than $^+7$, then $^-10$ is greater than $^-7$. **Explain** why you agree or disagree.

Foston Miniature Golf Score Card

Player	Hole 1	Hole 8	Hole 9	Total Score
Abby	+1	-2	+1	-9
Riley	-1	+2	-1	+6
Cassie	+1	+2	-2	+3
Buddy	+1	-1	-1	-3
Kelly	-1	-1	-1	+5

Mixed Review and Test Prep

28. The temperature rose from 45°F to 87°F. What was the change in temperature? (p. 164)

29. What is the value of ■? (p. 160)

    4 weeks 3 days = ■ days

30. **Test Prep** Order from least to greatest: $^-3, ^+6, ^-8,$ and $^+2$.

    A $^+2, ^-3, ^+6, ^-8$

    B $^-8, ^+6, ^-3, ^+2$

    C $^-3, ^+6, ^-8, ^+2$

    D $^-8, ^-3, ^+2, ^+6$

Technology Use Harcourt Mega Math, Fraction Action, *Number Line Mine*, Levels S, T.

Extra Practice on page 172, Set F

Race to the Finish

Reading Skill **Summarize**

The Kiawah Island Marathon is held on the 10-mile wide island in South Carolina. The race follows a route along the Atlantic Ocean. The map shows that the 26.2-mile course starts and finishes at the East Beach Conference Center. In December, when the marathon is held, the average temperature around Kiawah Island is about 53°F. The record low temperature for December is 14°F. What is the difference in temperatures between the average temperature and the record low temperature?

You can *summarize*, or restate in a shortened form, the given information to help you understand the problem.

Rewrite the paragraph in shortened form.

Summary: Kiawah Island Marathon is run on Kiawah Island in South Carolina. The island is 10 miles wide. The race is 26.2 miles long. The average temperature in December on Kiawah Island is 53°F, and the record low for December is 14°F.

Kiawah Island Marathon 26.2 miles

Atlantic Ocean

East Beach Conference Center

▲ Runners, walkers, and wheelchair athletes ages 18 to 75 compete in the Kiawah Island Marathon. The course record was 2 hours 21 minutes and 24 seconds, set by Terry Stanley in 1983.

Problem Solving Summarize to understand the problem.

1. Solve the problem above.

2. Mt. McKinley, Alaska, is 20,320 feet above sea level, Death Valley, California, is 282 feet below sea level, or ⁻282 feet, and Chicago, Illinois, is 580 feet above sea level. Order the elevations from lowest to highest.

Extra Practice

Set A Write the time as shown on a digital clock (pp. 152–153)

1. 21 minutes after six

2. 8 minutes before nine

3. quarter past eleven

4. 18 minutes before two

5. quarter to one

6. 3 minutes to five

Set B Find the elapsed time. (pp. 154–157)

1. start: 2:00 P.M.
end: 8:30 P.M.

2. start: 6:15 P.M.
end: 7:15 A.M.

3. start: 11:00 P.M.
end: 9:30 A.M.

4. start: 7:30 P.M.
end: 6:45 A.M.

5. Chris begins school at 9:15 A.M. He gets out at 3:45 P.M. How long is Chris at school?

Set C For 1–3, use the calendars. (pp. 158–159)

1. Melanie's birthday is 5 weeks and 2 days before June 30. On what day is Melanie's birthday?

2. Summer begins on June 21. How many days after May 29 is the first day of summer?

3. Flag Day is June 14. If today is May 17, how many weeks from today is Flag Day?

4. Sophie is planning a trip. She will leave on May 20 and return on June 4. What is the length of her trip in days?

May						
Sun	Mon	Tue	Wed	Thu	Fri	Sat
	1	2	3	4	5	6
7	8	9	10	11	12	13
14	15	16	17	18	19	20
21	22	23	24	25	26	27
28	29	30	31			

June						
Sun	Mon	Tue	Wed	Thu	Fri	Sat
			1	2	3	
4	5	6	7	8	9	10
11	12	13	14	15	16	17
18	19	20	21	22	23	24
25	26	27	28	29	30	

Set D Complete. Tell whether you *multiply* or *divide*. (pp. 160–161)

1. 5 years = ■ months

2. 96 hours = ■ days

3. 15 weeks = ■ days

4. 3 minutes 6 seconds = ■ seconds

5. 36 hours= ■ minutes

6. 1 day = ■ seconds

Set E Use a thermometer to find the change in temperature. (pp. 164–167)

1. 12°F and 21°F

2. 6°C and 26°C

3. 18°F and 27°F

4. ⁻1°F and 15°F

5. ⁻3°C and 9°C

6. ⁻1°C and ⁻20°C

Set F Draw a number line and graph the numbers. Compare using < or >. (pp. 168–171)

1. ⁺2 and ⁻8

2. ⁻4 and 0

3. ⁺3 and ⁻3

4. ⁻6 and ⁺6

5. ⁻9 and ⁻16

Technology
Use Harcourt Mega Math, The Number Games, *Tiny's Think Tank,* Levels D, E, P.

Time to Go

Get Ready!
2 teams

Get Set!
- Number cube labeled 1 to 6
- Time cards
- Two-color counters (1 for each team)

Play the Game!

■ Shuffle the time cards and place them facedown in a stack. Decide who will be red and who will be yellow.

■ Each team tosses the number cube once to get a starting time. For example, if the red team tosses a 3, they start at 3:00 P.M. The team tossing the highest starting time goes first. Then, the teams take turns.

■ A player picks the top card. This is the elapsed time from the team's starting time. The team finds the end time and records that time on a sheet of paper. If the end time is correct, place a counter on 1. Put the used cards in a discard pile.

■ For each turn, the time on the card must be added to the time from the team's previous turn. For each correct time, your team's counter moves ahead one space.

■ After all the cards have been used, shuffle them and place the cards facedown to use again.

■ The first team to reach 12 wins the round.

■ For round two, start on 12. Each team tosses the number cube once to get an ending time. A player picks the top card and counts back to find the correct starting time. The first team to reach 1 wins the game.

24-Hour Clock

Time Travel

There are different ways to tell time. The United States uses two 12-hour periods, A.M. and P.M., but many other countries use a system with one 24-hour period, called the 24-hour clock.

On a **24-hour clock**, the A.M. hours are from 0000 to 1200, and the P.M. hours are from 1200 to 2400 hours.

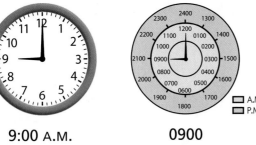

12-Hour Clock	24-Hour Clock
9:00 A.M.	0900
	Read: oh-nine hundred hours

 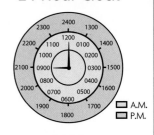

12-Hour Clock	24-Hour Clock
9:00 P.M.	2100
	Read: twenty-one hundred hours

What is 3:00 P.M. on a 24-hour clock?

To change a P.M. hour to time on a 24-hour clock, add 12 hours.

3:00 + 12:00 = 1500   **Read:** fifteen hundred hours

So, 3:00 P.M. on a 24-hour clock is 1500.

Examples

A **Find 0600 on a 12-hour clock.**
0600 is A.M. on a 12-hour clock.
0600 = 6:00
So, 0600 on a 12-hour clock is 6:00 A.M.

B **Find 2300 on a 12-hour clock.**
Subtract 1200, or 12 hours.
2300 − 1200 = 11:00
So, 2300 on a 12-hour clock is 11:00 P.M.

Try It

Write the time as shown on a 24-hour clock.

1. 1:00 P.M.   **2.** 1:00 A.M.   **3.** 8:00 P.M.   **4.** 11:00 A.M.

Write the time as shown on a 12-hour clock. Use A.M. or P.M.

5. 0900   **6.** 1800   **7.** 2200   **8.** 0500

9. **WRITE Math** ▸ Explain why A.M. and P.M. are not used on a 24-hour clock.

Chapter 6 Review/Test

Check Vocabulary and Concepts

Choose the best term from the box.

1. Water boils at 100 _?_. (p. 164)

2. _?_ are always less than zero. (p. 168)

3. Water freezes at 32 _?_. (p. 164)

Check Skills

Write the time as shown on a digital clock. (pp. 152–153)

4. 17 minutes after two

5. 26 minutes to twelve

6. quarter to nine

Write two ways to read the time. Then estimate to the nearest 5 minutes. (pp. 152–153)

7.  9:44 A.M.

8.  2:12 P.M.

9.

Find the elapsed time. (pp. 154–157)

10. start: 10:20 P.M.
    end: 12:30 P.M.

11. start: 8:15 A.M.
    end: 12:40 P.M.

12. start: 7:35 A.M.
    end: 10:09 A.M.

Complete. Tell whether you *multiply* or *divide*. (pp. 160–161)

13. 4 years = ■ months

14. 180 minutes = ■ hours

15. 6 weeks = ■ days

Use a thermometer to find the change in temperature. (pp. 164–167)

16. 6°F and 32°F

17. ⁻9°C and 12°C

18. ⁻18°F and ⁻37°F

19. 1°C and ⁻19°C

Draw a number line and graph the numbers. Compare using < or >. (pp. 168–171)

20. ⁺3 and ⁻4

21. ⁺12 and ⁺20

22. ⁻14 and ⁻23

23. ⁻31 and ⁻37

Check Problem Solving

Solve. (pp. 162–163)

24. Jay plans to fly from Newark to Miami on the 12:55 P.M. flight. How long is the flight?

25. **WRITE Math** ▶ Holly wants to get from Newark to Miami in the least time possible. Which flight should she take? **Explain** your answer.

Flight Schedule	
Leave Newark	**Arrive Miami**
6:35 A.M.	9:18 A.M.
12:55 P.M.	4:15 P.M.
3:50 P.M.	7:20 P.M.

Standardized Test Prep
Chapters 1–6

Number and Operations

1. What is the value of the digit 2 in 3,259,401? (p. 10)

   A 2,000   **C** 200,000

   B 20,000   **D** 2,000,000

2. The table shows the prices of Elena's favorite boxed sets of books at BB's Bookstore.

BB's Bookstore	
Boxed Set	**Price**
The Schoolhouse Mysteries	$13
Chad's Adventures	$35
Paper-Folding Fun	$27

Elena buys one of each boxed set. She pays with $100. How much change does she receive? (p. 42)

   A $75   **C** $40

   B $60   **D** $25

3. Theo earned $225 mowing lawns. He earned $324 painting fences. How much did Theo earn in all? (p. 42)

   A $549

   B $500

   C $100

   D $99

4. **WRITE Math** Each van can hold 7 children. **Explain** which operation you would use to find the total number of children in 8 vans. (p. 106)

Algebraic Reasoning

5. Which number makes the number sentence true? (p. 128)

$$108 \div \blacksquare = 9$$

   A 12   **C** 9

   B 11   **D** 8

6. Graham's Grocery sells tomatoes by the pound. There are 4 tomatoes in 1 pound. Which expression shows the number of tomatoes in 5 pounds? (p. 122)

   A 5×1 **C** 5×5

   B 1×4 **D** 5×4

7. Marina has 49 baseball cards. She sells some to a friend. Which expression can be used to find the number of baseball cards that Marina has left? (p. 66)

   A $49 + \blacksquare$

   B $49 - \blacksquare$

   C $49 \times \blacksquare$

   D $49 \div \blacksquare$

8. **WRITE Math** Write an inequality to represent the following statement.

The number of marbles, m, in the bag is at least 50.

Explain the symbol you used, and tell why you used it. (p. 136)

Measurement

9. The thermometer below shows the high temperature for one day in June. The low temperature for that day was 18°F lower than the high temperature. What was the low temperature? (p. 164)

   A 48°F

   B 66°F

   C 68°F

   D 108°F

10. Diego buys a large bag of apples at the farm market. There are 18 apples in the bag. Estimate the weight of the apples. (Grade 3)

    A 10 ounces

    B 1 pound

    C 18 ounces

    D 10 pounds

11. **WRITE Math** ▶ The clock below shows the time Jon's music lessons begin.

    His lessons last 85 minutes. At what time do his lessons end? **Explain** how you found your answer. (p. 154)

Data Analysis and Probability

Test Tip **Understand the problem.**

See Item 12. For each answer choice, you must compare two pieces of information from the pictograph. Compare the number of ☺s shown for each named sport.

12. Use the pictograph to determine which statement is true. (Grade 3)

School Sports	
Soccer	☺ ☺ ☺ ☺
Softball	☺ ☺ ☺ ☺ ☺ ☺
Lacrosse	☺ ☺
Football	☺ ☺ ☺

Key: Each ☺ = 3 students.

    A More students play soccer than softball.

    B More students play softball than lacrosse.

    C More students play lacrosse than football.

    D More students play football than soccer.

13. **WRITE Math** ▶ Sonya has 15 marbles of equal size in a bag. Ten of the marbles are red. She pulls one marble out of the bag without looking. **Explain** why she is more likely to pull a red marble than any other color. (Grade 3)

CHAPTER

7 Collect and Organize Data

FAST FACT

The tug of war was an Olympic sport from 1900 to 1920. In the 1904 Olympics, held in St. Louis, Missouri, U.S. teams won the first four places. First place went to the Milwaukee Athletic Club of Milwaukee, Wisconsin.

Investigate

Suppose your school is planning a field day. You survey your classmates. The table shows your results. Describe the data collected in the table. What question could you have asked to get these data?

Activity	Students
Three-Legged Race	⦀⦀ ⦀⦀ ‖‖
Water-Balloon Toss	⦀⦀ ‖‖
Sack Race	⦀⦀ ⦀⦀ ⦀⦀ ‖
Egg Relay	⦀⦀ ‖
Tug of War	⦀⦀ ⦀⦀ ⦀⦀ ⦀⦀ ⦀⦀ ‖
Bean-Bag Toss	⦀⦀ ⦀⦀ ‖

GO ONLINE

Technology
Student pages are available in the Student eBook.

**Check your understanding of important skills
needed for success in Chapter 7.**

▶ **Make and Use a Tally Table**

Use the data.

1. Use the data to make a tally table.

2. Which grade has the most students on the bus?

3. What is the total number of first- and second-grade students on the bus?

4. How many more third-grade than fourth-grade students are on the bus?

> The school bus from Tara's neighborhood carries 7 first-grade students, 12 second-grade students, 15 third-grade students, and 8 fourth-grade students.

▶ **Use Symbols in a Pictograph**

Use the pictograph.

5. How many cats are on the Horton farm?

6. How many more dogs than rabbits are there?

7. How many Guinea pigs and rabbits are there altogether?

8. How many pets are on the Horton farm?

Horton Farm Pets	
Dogs	🐾🐾
Cats	🐾🐾🐾🐾
Guinea Pigs	🐾🐾
Rabbits	🐾
Key: Each 🐾 = 2 animals.	

VOCABULARY POWER

CHAPTER VOCABULARY

categorical data	numerical
clump	data
frequency	range
interval	scale
line plot	survey
mean	Venn
median	diagram
mode	

WARM-UP WORDS

categorical data data that can be sorted into different groups

frequency the number of times an event occurs

numerical data data that can be counted or measured

LESSON 1

Collect and Organize Data

OBJECTIVE: Collect and organize data by conducting a survey and using a frequency table.

Learn

A **survey** is a method of gathering information. Follow these rules to take a survey:

- Decide on a question about which you want to gather data.

- Ask each person the question only one time.

- Use a tally mark to record each person's response.

Max took a survey by asking his classmates the question "What is your favorite subject in school?" He recorded their responses in a tally table.

Favorite Subject	
Subject	Tally
Reading	IIII
Math	IIII II
Science	IIII
Social Studies	IIII I

Since this set of data can be sorted into different groups, it is called **categorical data.** The groups in the table above are school subjects.

Quick Review

According to the tally table, who got the most votes?

Votes for Class President	
Student	Tally
Anna	IIII IIII
Dan	IIII II
Horatio	IIII III

Vocabulary

survey

categorical data

frequency

numerical data

Activity Take a survey and record the results in a tally table.

Step 1

Write a question for your survey. Make the question clear and simple.

Decide on the response choices.

Organize your question and response choices in a table like the sample survey to the right.

Step 2

Survey your classmates.
- Be sure each classmate gives only one response.
- Use a tally mark to record each response.

How Do You Get to School?	
Method	Tally
Bus	IIII
Car	I
Train	
Walk	
Other	

- Why do you ask each person the question only one time?

180

Frequency Tables

A frequency table helps you organize the data from a tally table. The **frequency** is the number of times a response occurs. In a frequency table, numbers are used instead of tally marks.

Jenna asked her classmates to pick their favorite tool for drawing pictures. First, she made a tally table to show the results of her survey. Then Jenna showed the same data in a frequency table.

The table below shows numerical data. **Numerical data** are data that are counted or measured.

Favorite Drawing Tool	
Drawing Tool	Tally
Color Pencil	III
Crayon	HHT III
Marker	HHT II

Favorite Drawing Tool	
Drawing Tool	Frequency
Color Pencil	3
Crayon	8
Marker	7

Time It Takes to Write Your Name				
Time (in seconds)	3	6	7	8
Frequency	7	3	7	2

- How are numerical data different from categorical data?

Guided Practice

1. Copy and complete the frequency table with the following data: eggs, toast, cereal, cereal, eggs, eggs, cereal, cereal, cereal.

Favorite Breakfast Food			
Food	Eggs	Cereal	Toast
Frequency			

For 2–3, use the Favorite Drawing Tool frequency table above. Tell whether each statement is true or false. Explain.

2. More students chose markers than crayons.

✓ 3. More students chose markers than color pencils.

For 4–7, use the Field Day Participants frequency table.

4. How many fourth-grade students have signed up?

5. If 2 sixth graders decide not to participate and 5 more fifth graders sign up, how many fifth and sixth graders will participate?

✓ 6. Each participant in Field Day receives a visor. Some students may sign up late and some students may be absent. Based on the data in the table, do you predict more or fewer than 300 visors will be needed? **Explain.**

7. [**TALK Math**] Explain how you can use a tally table to make a frequency table.

Field Day Participants	
Grade	Frequency (Number of Students)
K	45
1	42
2	54
3	58
4	41
5	55
6	50

Independent Practice and Problem Solving

For 8–10, use the Favorite Type of TV Show frequency table. Tell whether each statement is true or false. Explain.

8. More students chose comedies than mysteries as their favorite.

9. More students chose sports and comedy as their favorite than chose cartoons and mysteries.

10. Cartoons are the students' favorite choice to watch.

Students' Favorite Type of TV Show	
Type of Show	Frequency (Votes)
Comedy	8
Cartoons	9
Sports	7
Mysteries	6

For 11–14, use the Heights of Seedlings frequency table.

11. Describe the data set used to make this table.

12. How many more seedlings are 10 centimeters than 9 centimeters?

13. What is the height of the least number of seedlings?

14. **Reasoning** When the seedlings reach 8 centimeters they can be transplanted. How many seedlings can be transplanted? **Explain** your answer.

Heights of Seedlings	
Height (in centimeters)	Frequency (Seedlings)
7	2
8	3
9	6
10	8
11	4

Tell whether the data are *numerical* or *categorical*.

15. color of your eyes   16. test scores   17. favorite bird   18. student heights

Write a survey question and response choices. Survey your classmates. Record the responses in a frequency table. For 19–20, use the survey results to answer each question.

19. What conclusions can you make about the data?

20. How might the survey results change if you surveyed your teachers instead of your classmates?

For 21–24, use the Lessons for Wind Instruments bar graph.

21. Describe the data set used to make this graph.

22. How many more students take trumpet lessons than tuba lessons?

23. **Reasoning** Suppose 3 more students take flute lessons and 3 students stop taking tuba lessons. How will these data change the graph?

24. **WRITE Math** **What's the Error?** Sandra said that the graph shows that 5 students take flute lessons. **Explain** her mistake and how to correct it.

Learn About) Survey Results

Using the results of a survey is a good way to predict how people will respond to a decision. **Unbiased results** may occur when everyone has an equal chance to respond. **Biased results** may occur when only people with similar interests are asked to respond.

Emerson Elementary raised $400 from a bake sale. The money will be used for either a new basketball hoop or costumes for a play. Three students did surveys to find out which item most students want.

Try It

Use the survey results to answer the questions.

25. Whose results are biased? Whose are unbiased? **Explain.**

26. What other groups could be surveyed to obtain unbiased results?

Jared asked members of the drama club.

Which should the school buy?
Costumes ⅢⅢ ⅢⅢ
Basketball hoop ‖

Miko asked members of the basketball team.

Which should the school buy?
Costumes ⅢⅢ
Basketball hoop ⅢⅢ ⅢⅢ ‖

Sara asked the first 20 students who came to school on Monday.

Which should the school buy?
Costumes ⅢⅢ ⅢⅢ ‖‖‖
Basketball hoop ⅢⅢ ‖

Mixed Review and Test Prep

27. Use the order of operations to find the value of the expression. (p. 126)

$$12 - 3 \times 4$$

28. **Test Prep** How many people were surveyed?

Favorite Color			
Color	Red	Blue	Yellow
Votes	6	4	5

A 4

B 5

C 6

D 15

29. School starts at this time each morning. It ends at 2:45 P.M. Find the length of the school day. (p. 154)

30. **Test Prep** What question would you ask if you were doing a survey about favorite drinks?

Venn Diagrams

OBJECTIVE: Interpret and construct Venn diagrams to sort, describe, and classify data.

Learn

You can use Venn diagrams to sort information. A **Venn diagram** shows relationships among sets of things.

PROBLEM Every state has its own flag. Look at the state flags shown. What is one way these flags can be sorted?

Quick Review

Carl's scores on his math tests are 75, 80, 85, 97, 86, 99, 89, 79, 86, and 90. Sort and classify his scores by letter grades. Use A for 90 to 100, B for 80 to 89, and C for 70 to 79.

Vocabulary

Venn diagram

Example Make a Venn diagram.

Step 1

Decide how you will sort the flags. Some of the flags have symbols of **animals**, some have symbols of **people**, and some have **both**.

Step 2

Draw two overlapping ovals. Label each section with the description of each set. The data inside the area where the sets overlap are described by both labels.

State Flag Symbols
ANIMALS   PEOPLE

Step 3

Sort the state flag names.

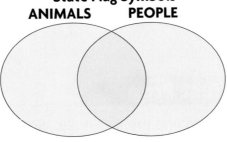

State Flag Symbols
ANIMALS   PEOPLE

Pennsylvania   New York
Illinois   New Jersey   Massachusetts

Write the states of the flags that have only animals in the section of the diagram labeled ANIMALS and the states that have only people in the section labeled PEOPLE. Write the states that have both animals and people in the section where the sets overlap.

So, one way to sort these flags is by their symbols.

• How can you check that your answer is correct?

• Suppose you sorted the flags by background color. Would the sets still overlap? Explain.

Pennsylvania

New York

ILLINOIS
Illinois

Massachusetts

New Jersey

Guided Practice

Copy the Venn diagrams. Place the numbers where they belong.

1.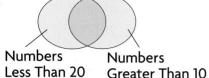

Numbers Less Than 20   Numbers Greater Than 10

2, 14, 33, 19, 5, 79, 21, 50, 6

2.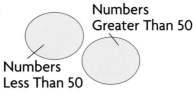

Numbers Greater Than 50

Numbers Less Than 50

1, 22, 53, 89, 49, 13, 57, 4, 32

3.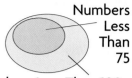

Numbers Less Than 75

Numbers Less Than 100

99, 24, 7, 63, 86, 24, 70, 12, 31

For 4–5, use the Venn diagram.

☑ 4. What label could you use for Section B?

☑ 5. Why are the numbers 6 and 12 sorted in the area where the sets overlap?

6. **TALK Math** **Explain** how a Venn diagram can help you understand relationships.

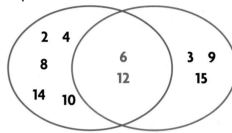

A Multiples of 2   B ___?___

2 4
8
14 10
6
12
3 9
15

Independent Practice and Problem Solving

For 7–8, use the Venn diagram.

7. Describe and label the data for Section B.

8. **Reasoning** Where would you sort the numbers 3, 175, and 2,001? Explain.

A Odd   B ___?___

5 7
9

4 12
18

For 9–10, use the table.

9. Copy and complete the table by surveying 10 classmates. Show the results in a Venn diagram.

10. **WRITE Math** **Explain** whether to use a Venn diagram with 2 overlapping ovals or 2 separate ovals for the table.

Toppings Liked on Pizza

Topping	Names of Students
Pepperoni Only	?
Sausage Only	?
Pepperoni and Sausage	?

Mixed Review and Test Prep

11. Dena drew two lines that will never cross. What kind of lines did she draw? (Grade 3)

12. At a football game, there were 64,856 fans. Round the number of fans to the nearest thousand. (p. 34)

13. **Test Prep** Look at the Venn diagram for Problem 7. Which number does **NOT** belong in Section A?

A 30   C 33

B 27   D 55

Extra Practice on page 196, Set B

Learn

The **mean** is the average of a set of numbers.

PROBLEM The Weather Watchers Club recorded the amount of rainfall to the nearest inch that Allegheny State Park typically gets during each of four warm months. What is the mean number of inches of rain over this period?

ONE WAY Use a model.

Materials ■ connecting cubes

Step 1	Step 2
Make stacks of cubes to model the number of inches of rain each month. 	Rearrange the stacks so that they are equal. The mean is the number of cubes in each equal stack.  4 cubes in each stack

Rainfall

Month	Amount (in inches)
April	3
May	4
June	5
July	4

So, the mean number of inches of rain is 4 inches.

You can find the mean by dividing the sum of a set of numbers by the number of addends.

ANOTHER WAY Use pencil and paper.

The table shows the number of miles hiked by students last weekend. Find the mean number of miles hiked.

Step 1	Step 2
Add all of the numbers in the data set. $2 + 2 + 2 + 6 + 8 = 20$	Divide the sum by the number of addends. The quotient is the mean. $20 \div 5 = 4$

ERROR ALERT

The frequency tells you how many times to list each number of miles hiked.

Miles Hiked

Miles	Frequency (Students)
2	3
6	1
8	1

So, the mean number of miles hiked is 4 miles.

• How can you use pencil and paper to find the mean in One Way?

Median and Mode

The **median** is the middle number in an ordered set of data. The **mode** is the number or item that occurs most often in a set of data.

Find the median and mode of the data.

Record High Temperatures in New Jersey							
Month	Aug	Sep	Oct	Nov	Dec	Jan	Feb
Temperature (in °F)	108	109	97	88	78	78	80

Activity

Materials ■ index cards

Step 1 **Find the median.**

Write the seven temperatures on index cards. Arrange the cards from least to greatest. Remove one card from each end. Keep doing this until only one number is left in the center. This number is the median, or middle number.

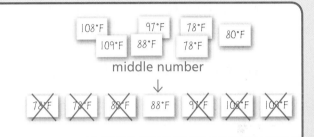

Step 2 **Find the mode.**

Sort the cards by numbers. The number that occurs most often is the mode. There may be more than one mode. If no number is repeated, there is no mode.

So, the median is 88°F and the mode is 78°F.

More Examples

A Median of an even number of data

Lowest Temperatures During 12 Days				
Temperature (in °F)	7	8	10	20
Frequency	1	5	5	1

Order the data from least to greatest.

~~7~~, ~~8~~, ~~8~~, ~~8~~, ~~8~~, 8, 10, ~~10~~, ~~10~~, ~~10~~, ~~10~~, ~~20~~

- There is an even number of data.
- Add the two middle numbers. 8 + 10 = 18
- Divide the sum by 2: 18 ÷ 2 = 9.

B Mode of categorical data

winter, fall, fall, spring, summer, winter, fall, summer, summer, fall, spring, summer, winter, summer, fall, fall

Organize the data in a table to find the mode.

Favorite Season			
Season	Winter	Spring	Summer	Fall
Frequency	3	2	5	6

Since fall has the most votes, it is the mode.

So, the median is 9°F.

- What is the mode of Example A?

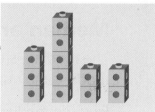

1. Tara used cubes to show the number of buds on each of 4 rose plants. What is the mean number of buds on each plant?

Find the mean, median, and mode.

2.

Snowfall						
Month	Nov	Dec	Jan	Feb	Mar	Apr
Inches	6	12	10	12	6	2

3.

Rainfall						
Month	Apr	May	Jun	Jul	Aug	Sep
Inches	8	7	5	9	4	3

✓ 4.

Books Read					
Month	Jan	Feb	Mar	Apr	May
Books	6	5	4	5	5

✓ 5.

Art Club				
Attendance	2	3	4	5
Frequency	4	3	2	1

6. **TALK Math** Describe what mean, median, and mode tell you about a set of numbers.

Independent Practice and Problem Solving

Find the mean, median, and mode.

7.

Computers in Each Computer Lab					
Lab	A	B	C	D	E
Computers	6	8	4	6	11

8.

Miles Biked					
Day	Mon	Tues	Wed	Thurs	Fri
Number of Miles	3	3	13	8	8

9.

Plants Sold				
Plant	Tomato	Pepper	Bean	Cucumber
Number	1	2	5	4

10.

Goals Scored per Game					
Goals	1	2	3	4	8
Frequency	1	4	1	1	1

For 11–12, use the graphs.

11. What is the difference between the medians for the animals adopted on Monday and on Friday?

12. **WRITE Math** What's the Question? The answer is 8.

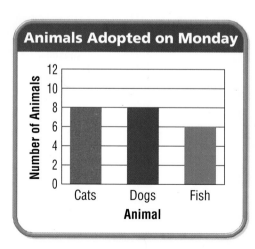

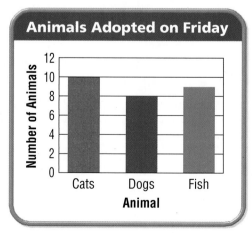

Comparing Sets of Data

These tables show the grades on a test taken by two classes. At lunch, the students talked about which class did better.

Mrs. Martel's Class						
Score	75	80	83	85	88	90
Frequency	2	5	4	3	3	2

Mr. Jensen's Class						
Score	77	80	83	87	88	91
Frequency	2	1	3	5	4	4

Compare the median scores of the classes.

Mrs. Martel's class: median = 83
Mr. Jensen's class: median = 87

Compare the modes of the two classes.

Mrs. Martel's class: mode = 80
Mr. Jensen's class: mode = 87

The median and mode for Mr. Jensen's class are greater than the median and mode for Mrs. Martel's class. So, Mr. Jensen's class did better on the test than Mrs. Martel's class.

Try It

13. Two groups of students were surveyed about how many days per week they have after-school activities. Find and compare the medians and modes for the two groups.

14. In which group do the students have fewer days per week with after-school activities?

Blue Group After-School Activities					
Days per Week	1	2	3	4	5
Students	2	4	6	3	2

Red Group After-School Activities					
Days per Week	1	2	3	4	5
Students	2	2	4	6	3

Mixed Review and Test Prep

15. Make a frequency table for these data. (p. 180)

Favorite Kind of Fruit Juice	
Fruit Juice	Tally
Apple	$\cancel{||||}\ ||$
Orange	$\cancel{||||}$
Pineapple	$\cancel{||||}\ \cancel{||||}$

16. **Test Prep** What is the mode for the following set of test scores?

75, 86, 72, 93, 85, 97, 80, 86

A 72   B 86   C 88   D 90

17. Find the missing factor. (p. 108)

$$7 \times \blacksquare = 56$$

18. **Test Prep** What is the mean for the data shown below?

Seashells Collected			
Type	Conch Shells	Angel Wings	Cat Paws
Number of Shells	12	5	7

LESSON 4 — Line Plots

OBJECTIVE: Use line plots to read and organize data.

Learn

PROBLEM The data show the number of shuttle missions that NASA launched each year between 1998 and 2002. During this period, in how many years did NASA launch 5 or more shuttles?

You can use a line plot to solve the problem. A **line plot** is a graph that shows the frequency of data along a number line.

> **NASA Shuttle Missions per Year, 1998–2002**
>
> 5, 3, 5, 6, 5

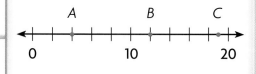

Activity **Materials** ▪ grid paper

Step 1	Step 2	Step 3
Order the data. Copy and complete the tally table.	Draw a number line from the least value of the data to the greatest.	Plot an X above the number line for each piece of data. Write a title for the line plot.

Step 1

NASA Shuttle Missions

Number per Year	Tally
3	|
5	|||
6	|

Step 2

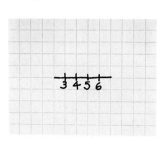

Step 3

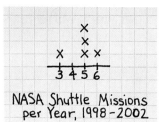

So, in 4 different years, NASA launched 5 or more shuttles per year.

The **range** is the difference between the greatest and least values in a set of data. So, the range for the mission data is 6 − 3, or 3.

Clumps show an area where there are many data values that are close together. The data show that most people have 0, 1, or 2 rocket models. The hole where there are no data means that no one has 5 models.

• Describe what conclusions you might draw about the median, range, and mode of the data by looking at the line plot.

• Describe what a line plot would look like where the data are spread out evenly.

```
        X  X
     X  X  X
     X  X  X
     X  X  X  X
     X  X  X  X  X        X
     +--+--+--+--+--+--+--+
     0  1  2  3  4  5  6
```
Number of Rocket Models

Quick Review

Write the numbers represented by each point on the number line.

```
            A          B        C
    +--+--+--+--+--+--+--+--+--+--+-->
    0          10          20
```

Vocabulary

line plot   **clump**   **range**

190

Guided Practice

1. Make a line plot to show the following data. Start by ordering the data. Then draw X's above the numbers on your number line to show the data.

> **Number of Rocket Models:**
> 2, 7, 3, 5, 1, 9, 7, 3, 2, 6, 2, 1, 7, 8

For 2–4, use the Tourist Time Survey data.

2. Make a tally table and line plot to show the data.

✓ 3. What is the range of the data?

✓ 4. How many hours did most tourists spend visiting the complex? How can you tell?

5. **TALK Math** Explain how you can use the shape of the data to draw conclusions about the tourists' visits.

> **Tourist Time Survey**
> Question: How many hours did you spend visiting Kennedy Space Center Visitor Complex?
> Responses: 2, 3, 4, 1, 2, 5, 1, 3, 2, 1, 2, 1, 3, 3, 2, 1, 0, 3, 4, 5, 1

Independent Practice and Problem Solving

For 6–8, use the Tourist Photo Survey data.

6. Make a tally table and line plot to show the data.

7. What is the range of the data?

8. **Reasoning** Describe the data using the words *hole* and *clump*.

> **Tourist Photo Survey**
> Question: How many pictures did you take while at Kennedy Space Center Visitor Complex?
> Responses: 10, 12, 12, 8, 4, 12, 10, 12, 10, 11, 11, 10, 10, 11, 12, 10, 10, 11, 10

For 9–11, use the line plot.

9. The line plot shows how many souvenirs Mimi bought at each price. How much money did Mimi spend on souvenirs in all?

10. Find the median, mode, and number of souvenirs bought.

11. **What if** Mimi bought 3 more items for $5 each? Would the range of the line plot change? **Explain.**

12. **WRITE Math** Explain how a line plot and a tally table are alike and how they are different.

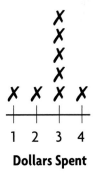

Dollars Spent

Mixed Review and Test Prep

13. Peter lives in a city with a population of 12,506. Write the number in word form. (p. 4)

14. How many days are in 9 weeks? (p. 160)

15. **Test Prep** Look at the line plot for Problems 9–11. What is the range of dollars spent?

   A $1   B $2   C $3   D $4

Technology
Use Harcourt Mega Math, The Number Games, *Arachnagraph*, Levels E, F.

Extra Practice on page 196, Set D

Choose a Reasonable Scale and Interval

OBJECTIVE: Choose a reasonable scale and interval for a set of data.

Quick Review

Make a frequency table for the following survey results.

Question: What is your favorite pet?

Responses: dog, dog, dog, cat, bird, dog, cat, hamster, cat, dog, hamster, dog, bird

Vocabulary

scale   interval

Learn

You can use different graphs to compare the same data.

A **scale** of a graph is a series of numbers placed at fixed, or equal, distances. The highest value on the scale should be greater than the greatest value of the data.

The **interval** of a graph is the difference between one number and the next on the scale of a graph.

Graph A

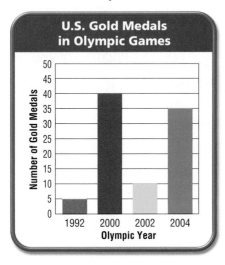

Graph B

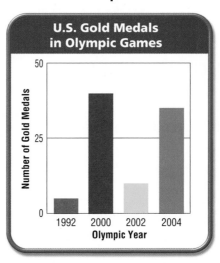

> **Math Idea**
> The interval should be small enough to show the data clearly, but large enough to fit all the data on the graph.

- Which graph makes it easier to compare the data? Why?
- Describe how the graphs are the same and how they are different.

Guided Practice

1. Would you use an interval of 1 to show the data in Graph A? **Explain.**

For 2–4, choose 5, 10, 25, or 100 as the most reasonable interval for each set of data. **Explain your choice.**

2. 25, 30, 20, 10, 15   ☑3. 200, 350, 100, 250, 500   ☑4. 25, 79, 50, 45, 90

5. **[TALK Math]** **Explain** how to decide what scale to use in graphs for the data in Problems 2, 3, and 4.

Independent Practice and Problem Solving

For 6–9, choose 5, 10, 25, or 100 as the most reasonable interval for each set of data. Explain your choice.

6. 45, 79, 30, 80, 21

7. 5, 16, 6, 15, 30

8. 80, 490, 920, 550, 150

9. 25, 75, 50, 100, 60

For 10–11, use the Favorite Winter Olympic Event graph.

10. What is a better interval to use to show these data?

11. **Reasoning** Why wouldn't 1 and 100 be reasonable intervals to use for the data shown in the graph?

For 12–14, use the Favorite Summer Olympic Event graph.

12. What are the scale and interval used in the graph?

13. About how many more votes did gymnastics get than basketball and diving combined?

14. **Pose a Problem** Use the information in the graph to write a problem. **Explain** how to find the answer to your problem.

15. **≡FAST FACT** The Winter Olympic Games were held in Lake Placid, New York, in 1932. They were held in Lake Placid again in 1980. How many years later was this?

16. **WRITE Math** ▶ **What's the Question?** Haley made a graph for the data in a problem. The answer is 0–100.

Favorite Winter Olympic Event

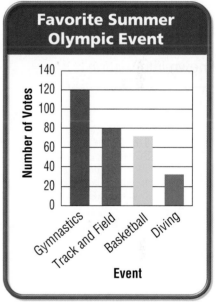

Favorite Summer Olympic Event

Mixed Review and Test Prep

17. Last year there were 2,104 students in Wallace Elementary school. During the summer 120 students moved away and 85 new students enrolled in the school. How many students attend the school now? (p. 48)

18. Alan, Tim, and Tara are in the band. Grace and Paul are in the chorus. Sophie is in the band and the chorus. Draw a Venn diagram to show this information. (p. 184)

19. **Test Prep** What is the scale for the graph below?

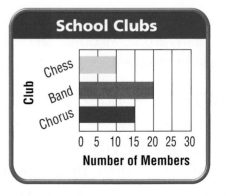

School Clubs

A 0–5 **B** 0–10 **C** 0–20 **D** 0–30

Extra Practice on page 196, Set E

Problem Solving Workshop
Skill: Make Generalizations

OBJECTIVE: Solve problems by using the skill *make generalizations*.

Use the Skill

PROBLEM A heart rate is the number of times the heart beats per minute. Grace has a resting heart rate of 85 beats per minute. Sara's resting heart rate is 77 beats per minute. Use the bar graph to find who is probably older, Grace or Sara.

A **generalization** is a conclusion based on given or known information. To help make a generalization, you can summarize data.

Identify the information in the bar graph.

Look at the graph. Write a paragraph identifying the known information.

> The heart rate at rest for newborns is about 140 beats per minute. For children, it is about 90 beats per minute. For adult females, it is about 80 beats per minute. For adult males, it is about 75 beats per minute. For adults over 65, it is about 65 beats per minute.

Look for patterns or connections in the information.

- The groups go from younger to older.
- The beats per minute decrease, or go from faster to slower.

Make a generalization and use it to make a prediction or draw a conclusion.

You can make the generalization that, as people get older, their resting heart rate slows down. Since $77 < 85$, Sara's heart rate is slower than Grace's.

So, Sara is probably older than Grace.

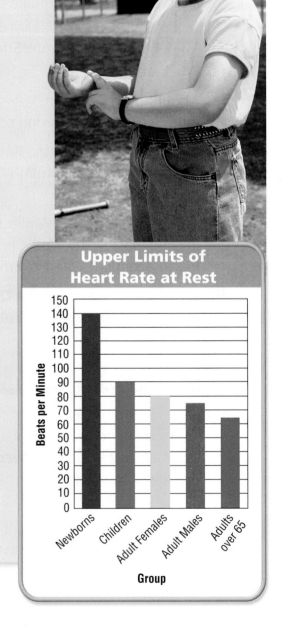

Upper Limits of Heart Rate at Rest

Think and Discuss

Make a generalization. Then solve the problem.

a. Jack and Mary are both 30 years old. Who probably has a faster heart rate, Jack or Mary?

For 1–3, use the table. Make a generalization. Then solve the problem.

1. When you exercise, your heart beats faster. The table shows maximum target heart rates for different ages. Copy and complete the chart with the data from the table.

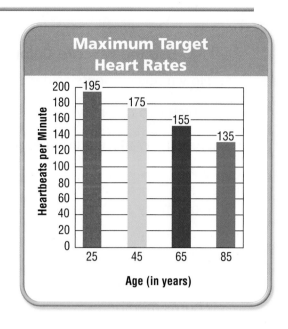

Maximum Target Heart Rates

Known Information	Patterns or Connections
The graph shows the maximum target heart rate for four groups of people. The maximum target heart rate for age ■ is ■. For age 45, it is ■. For age ■, it is 155; and for age ■, it is ■.	• The age groups go from younger to older, starting at ■ and going up every ■ years. • The beats per minute go from faster to slower, starting at ■ and going down by ■ beats per minute.

2. What might the target heart rate be for age 35?

3. Miyu is 25 years old. She does aerobics for a half hour and then measures her heart rate. If it is 180 beats per minute, should Miyu slow her exercising, or can she continue at the same pace? **Explain** your answer.

Mixed Applications

USE DATA For 4–6, use the table.

4. How many more calories does an 11-year-old male need than a 9-year-old female?

5. Beth and Travis are 12-year-old twins. Helena is 8 years old, and her sister Marta is 10 years old. List the names of the children in order from the one who needs the least calories to the one who needs the greatest calories. **Explain.**

6. Based on the data in the table, predict about how many calories a 15-year-old male might need.

Calories Needed by Active Children		
Age	Male	Female
8	2,000	1,800
9	2,000	1,800
10	2,200	2,000
11	2,200	2,000
12	2,400	2,200
13	2,400	2,200

7. **Algebra** Peter's dog weighs 24 pounds. His cat weighs n pounds. If his dog weighs 3 times as much as his cat, what is n?

8. **WRITE Math** On a hot, sunny day, bamboo can grow about an inch an hour. Ben's bamboo was 3 inches tall when he went to school. Now it is 11 inches tall. **Explain** how you can use a generalization to decide about how long Ben was gone.

Extra Practice

Set A Use the Favorite Color frequency table. (pp. 180–183)

1. How many students said orange was their favorite color?

2. Which two colors were chosen by the same number of students?

3. How many more students chose blue than orange?

4. Which color was chosen most often?

5. How many students were surveyed?

Favorite Color	
Color	Frequency (Number of Students)
Blue	36
Green	28
Orange	11
Purple	41
Red	28

Set B Use the Venn diagram. (pp. 184–185)

1. List the fourth-grade students who are chorus members.

2. List the fourth-grade students who are band members.

3. Why are some of the students' names in the area where the sets overlap?

Fourth-Grade Musicians

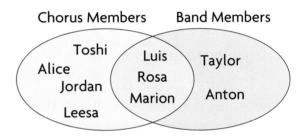

Set C Find the mean, median, and mode. (pp. 186–189)

1.

Neighborhood Pets				
Family	Walker	Chen	Damiano	Smith
Number of Pets	1	3	9	3

2.

Hours of Sleep Per Night					
Student	Andrew	Sheryl	Max	Shameka	Doria
Number of Hours	11	11	8	9	11

Set D Use the line plot. (pp. 190–191)

1. How many students have 4 letters in their first name?

2. How many more students have 7 letters in their first name than have 5 letters in their first name?

3. How many students were surveyed in all?

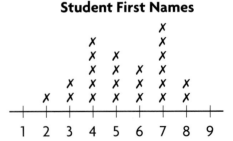

Set E Choose 5, 10, 25, or 100 as the most reasonable interval for each set of data. Explain your choice. (pp. 192–193)

1. 201, 450, 550, 600, 799

2. 19, 25, 15, 31, 20

3. 51, 20, 28, 90, 60

4. 75, 125, 50, 49

5. 300, 199, 420, 690

6. 9, 14, 30, 15, 45

Technology
Use Harcourt Mega Math, The Number Games, *ArachnaGraph*, Level E.

TECHNOLOGY ★ CONNECTION

Calculator: Find the Mean

Darla made phone calls each day after school. She made 3 calls on Monday, 6 calls on Tuesday, 5 calls on Wednesday, 6 calls on Thursday, and 5 calls on Friday. What was the mean number of calls she made each day?

You can use the Casio *fx-55* calculator to find the mean of a set of data.

You can find the mean of a set of numbers by dividing the sum of the numbers by the number of addends.

Step 1   Use the parentheses keys to find the sum of the set of numbers.

(3 + 6 + 5 + 6 + 5) =

$$= \quad 25.$$

Step 2   Divide the sum by the number of addends.

÷ 5 = $= \quad 5.$

So, the mean number of calls Darla made each day was 5.

Try It

Find the mean of each set of data.

1.

School Fire Drills			
Month	Mar	Apr	May	Jun
Drills	2	4	3	3

2.

Fish in Classroom Tanks			
Room	103	107	115	118
Fish	9	12	5	2

3.

Students' Steps (in inches)				
Student	Don	Elsie	Allie	Sam	Juan
Distance	15	21	17	18	19

4.

New Books Delivered		
Subject	Math	Science	English
Cartons	10	8	9

5. **Explore More**   **Explain** how you can tell whether the mean you have found is reasonable.

MATH POWER Stem-and-Leaf Plots

SCORE CARD

Henry kept track of the scores for each of his words when he played a word game.

Word Game Score							
13	15	19	31	24	33	27	22

Then he used a stem-and-leaf plot to show the data.

A **stem-and-leaf plot** shows groups of data arranged by place value.

Example Make a stem-and-leaf plot.

Step 1

Group the data by the tens digits.

10:   13 15 19

20:   24 27 22

30:   31 33

Step 2

Order the tens digits from least to greatest. Draw a line.

1 | Each tens digit is
2 | called a **stem**.
3 |

Step 3

Write each ones digit in order from least to greatest to the right of its tens digit.

1 | 3 5 9   Each ones
2 | 2 4 7   digit is called
3 | 1 3   a **leaf**.

Step 4

Include a title, labels, and a key.

Henry's Word Game Scores	
Stem	Leaves
1	3 5 9
2	2 4 7
3	1 3

2 | 4 = 24 points.

Try It
Use the table to make a stem-and-leaf plot.

1.

Number of Jumps							
10	22	12	11	20	25	31	26

2.

Number of Different Beads							
12	33	10	14	24	26	31	37

3. **WRITE Math** ▸ **Explain** how a stem-and-leaf plot uses place value.

Chapter 7 Review/Test

Check Vocabulary and Concepts

Choose the best term from the box.

1. The ? is the average of a set of numbers. (p. 186)

2. The ? is the difference between the greatest and the least values of a set of data. (p. 190)

VOCABULARY

range
median
mean

Check Skills

For 3–6, use the Favorite Music frequency table. (pp. 180–183, 192–193)

3. How many more students prefer rhythm and blues than classical music?

4. Which type of music is the most popular among the students surveyed?

5. How many students were included in the survey?

6. What interval would you choose if you were making a bar graph using these data? Why?

Favorite Music	
Type of Music	Frequency (Students)
Rock	23
Classical	7
Jazz	11
Hip-Hop	12
Rhythm and Blues	17

For 7–9, use the Venn diagram. (pp. 184–185)

7. What label could you use for section B?

8. Why are the numbers 12, 24, and 36 listed in the overlapping area of the Venn diagram?

9. In which section would you write the number 40?

Multiples of 4   B

28 8 16   12   18   30
20   4   24 36   6   42
    32

Gymnastics Team							
Age	8	9	10	11	12	13	14
Frequency (Team Members)	4	4	3	4	1	0	1

For 10–12, use the Gymnastics Team frequency table. (pp. 186–189, 190–191)

10. Make a line plot of the team members' ages.

11. Find the median and mode of the ages.

12. What is the range of the ages?

13. Write a set of data that has the same median and mode.

Check Problem Solving

Solve. (pp. 194–195)

14. Use the Gymnastics Team frequency table to make a generalization about the ages of the team members.

15. **WRITE Math** Explain how you know that all multiples of 12 are both multiples of 4 and multiples of 6.

Standardized Test Prep
Chapters 1–7

Algebraic Reasoning

1. Anna went to the mall with $51. She bought a sweater for $18 and a pair of jeans for $24. Which expression shows how much money Anna has left? (p. 66)

    A $51 - (18 - 24)$

    B $51 + (18 - 24)$

    C $51 - (18 + 24)$

    D $51 + (18 + 24)$

2. Jorge had some crayons. He gave 9 crayons to Juan and now has 8 left. Which equation could you use to find the number of crayons Jorge started with? (p. 70)

    A $9 - 8 = n$ C $9 + 8 = n$

    B $n + 8 = 9$ D $9 - n = 8$

3. Look at the table. Which equation is a rule for the table? (p. 78)

Input	n	13	14	15	16
Output	m	15	16	17	18

    A $m = n + 2$ C $m = n$

    B $m = n - 2$ D $n = m + 2$

4. **WRITE Math** ▸ An amusement park ride has the following sign.

    You may ride if $h > 48$.
    h = height in inches

    Explain the meaning of the inequality. (p. 136)

Data Analysis and Probability

5. If the mean number of students who play an instrument in fourth grade is 6, how many students in Room 204 play an instrument? (p. 186)

Fourth-Grade Musicians	
Room	Number of Students
201	8
202	7
203	4
204	?
205	8

    A 3   C 8

    B 4   D 9

6. Use the line plot below. How many baseball team members have at least 5 caps? (p. 190)

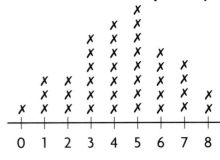

Baseball Team Cap Survey

Number of Caps

    A 8   C 17

    B 13   D 19

7. **WRITE Math** ▸ **Explain** how to find the median of a set of data if there is an even number of values. (p. 186)

Number and Operations

Test Tip **Eliminate choices.**

See Item 8. Latisha started with 57 cards and gave some away. So, she must have fewer than 57 cards now.

8. Latisha had 57 trading cards. She gave 19 to her sister. How many trading cards does Latisha have left? (p. 42)

   A 38   **C** 66

   B 42   **D** 76

9. David has 56 books. If he has placed them on 7 shelves with the same number of books on each shelf, how many books are on a shelf? (p. 98)

   A 8   **C** 10

   B 12   **D** 392

10. Phyllis and Mara play the piano. Phyllis has been taking lessons 4 years longer than Mara has. If Mara has been taking lessons for 3 years, for how long has Phyllis been taking lessons? (p. 32)

    A 4 years   **C** 6 years

    B 5 years   **D** 7 years

11. **WRITE Math** ▶ Find the missing numbers. **Describe** the relationship between the factors and the products. (p. 98)

$$4 \times 1 = \blacksquare \qquad 4 \times 4 = \blacksquare$$
$$4 \times 2 = \blacksquare \qquad 4 \times 8 = \blacksquare$$

Geometry

12. Which object has the same shape as a sphere? (Grade 3)

    A Box of cereal

    B Basketball

    C Can of orange juice

    D Number cube

13. Which figure appears to have exactly 2 lines of symmetry? (Grade 3)

    A ◯

    B ▭

    C ☐

    D ◺

14. Which two figures fit together to form a rectangle? (Grade 3)

    A

    B

    C

    D

15. **WRITE Math** ▶ **Explain** what a rectangle has to have in order for it to be a square. (Grade 3)

8 Interpret and Graph Data

≡FAST FACT

The five Great Lakes cover more than 94,000 square miles. They have about 6 quadrillion gallons of water. Their area and volume make them 5 of the world's 18 largest lakes.

Investigate

Suppose you wanted to compare data about the Great Lakes. What type of graph could you make to show the lengths of the lakes? What other information from the table could be shown in a graph? Make a graph that compares one type of data about the lakes.

The Great Lakes			
Lake	Length (in mi)	Average Depth (in ft)	Shoreline Length (in mi)
Superior	350	483	2,726
Michigan	307	279	1,638
Huron	206	195	3,827
Erie	241	62	871
Ontario	193	283	712

GO ONLINE

Technology
Student pages are available in the Student eBook.

Check your understanding of important skills
needed for success in Chapter 8.

▶ Classify Data

Write whether the data are categorical or numerical.

1. hours worked   **2.** hair colors   **3.** plant heights   **4.** types of dog

▶ Parts of a Graph

Use the bar graph.

5. What is the title of this graph?

6. What interval is used for the vertical scale?

7. What label would you place at the bottom?

8. What is the label for the vertical scale?

▶ Choose a Reasonable Interval

**Choose 5, 10, 25, or 100 as the most reasonable
interval for each set of data. Explain your choice.**

9. 22, 10, 15, 35, 24

10. 10, 27, 30, 70, 90

11. 115, 350, 480, 525, 600

12. 50, 150, 75, 400, 275

VOCABULARY POWER

CHAPTER VOCABULARY	
bar graph	ordered pair
circle graph	origin
coordinate grid	range
data	trends
double-bar	*x*-axis
graph	*x*-coordinate
function table	*y*-axis
line graph	*y*-coordinate

WARM-UP WORDS

bar graph a graph that uses bars to show data

circle graph a graph in the shape of a circle that shows data as a whole made up of different parts

coordinate grid a grid formed by a horizontal line called the *x*-axis and a vertical line called the *y*-axis

1 Bar Graphs

OBJECTIVE: Read and interpret bar graphs.

Learn

PROBLEM NASA has a school for astronauts. The bar graph shows how many students were in each class.

Use a **bar graph** to compare categorical data, or data about different groups. A bar graph can use vertical or horizontal bars to show data.

Example 1 Use a vertical bar graph.

How many students were in the 2004 class?

> Find the bar for the year 2004.
>
> Follow the top of the bar to the left to the scale. The number on the scale that matches the bar is 14.

So, the 2004 class had 14 students.

• How could you find how many students were in the 2000 class?

Example 2 Use a horizontal bar graph.

What is the range of the number of students in the classes?

> Find the greatest bar. Follow the end of the bar down to the scale.
>
> The greatest number of students is 25.
>
> Find the least bar. Follow the end of the bar down to the scale.
>
> The least number of students is 14.
>
> Subtract the least value from the greatest value to get the range.
>
> 25 − 14 = 11

So, the range of the number of students is 11.

• Write the data shown in the bar graph from least to greatest.

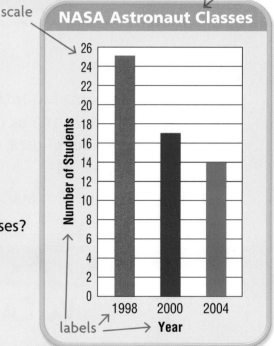

scale

title

NASA Astronaut Classes

Number of Students

labels → **Year**

1998 2000 2004

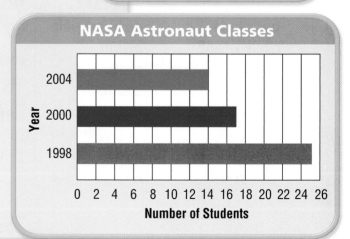

NASA Astronaut Classes

Year

2004

2000

1998

0 2 4 6 8 10 12 14 16 18 20 22 24 26

Number of Students

Guided Practice

For 1–4, use the Favorite Camp Choice graph.

1. Which camp do most students prefer? Find the tallest bar. This bar has the greatest value.

✓2. Which camp was chosen by the fewest students?

✓3. How many students chose space camp?

4. **TALK Math** How many more students chose space camp than sports camp? **Explain.**

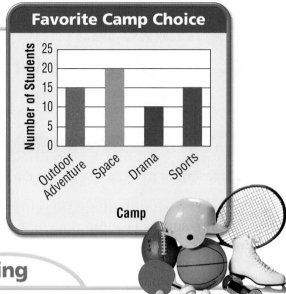

Favorite Camp Choice

Independent Practice and Problem Solving

For 5–8, use the Favorite Camp Choice bar graph above.

5. What is the range of votes for different camps?

6. Which two camps were chosen by the same number of students?

7. What interval is used on the scale?

8. What is the mode of the data?

For 9–11, use the Moons graph.

9. What is the median number of moons for the planets shown?

10. Which planet has more moons than Mars but fewer than Uranus?

11. **WRITE Math** ▸ **Sense or Nonsense** Jorge says that the interval for this bar graph is 34. Is Jorge correct? **Explain.**

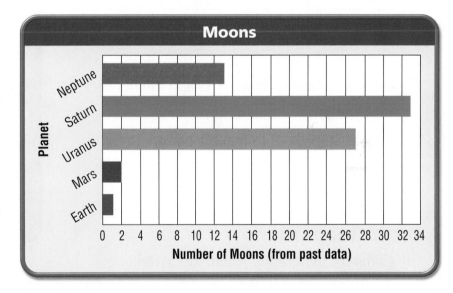

Moons

Mixed Review and Test Prep

12. What is the length of the line segment to the nearest inch? (Grade 3)

13. Write the missing factor. (p. 108)

$$\blacksquare \times (4 \times 2) = 64$$

14. **Test Prep** Look at the Moons graph. How many moons does Saturn have?

   A 1   **C** 33

   B 27   **D** 36

Extra Practice on page 232, Set A

2 Make Bar and Double-Bar Graphs

OBJECTIVE: Make and interpret bar graphs and double-bar graphs.

Investigate

Materials ■ bar-graph patterns ■ crayons or markers

Mrs. Lyon's fourth grade class took a survey of their favorite sports. Use the data in the table to make two bar graphs.

A Make a bar graph of the boys' favorite sports to watch. Decide on a title, labels, and a scale for the graph.

Favorite Sport to Watch

Sport	Boys	Girls
Football	17	5
Gymnastics	4	14
Ice Skating	6	12

B Draw a bar for each sport. Graph the number of boys who voted for each sport.

C Repeat Steps A–B to make a bar graph for the girls' favorite sport to watch. Use the same scale and interval as on the first graph.

Draw Conclusions

1. Compare the graphs you made. Write one difference the graphs show between the girls' and boys' votes for sports.

2. **Evaluation** Suppose the scales and intervals of the two bar graphs were different from each other. Would it be more or less difficult to compare how many girls and boys voted for football? Explain.

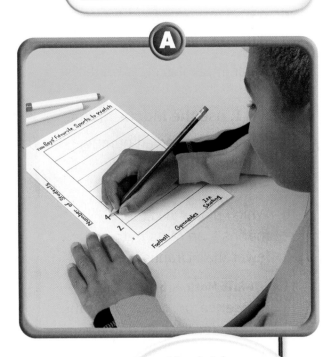

Math Idea

You can use a bar graph to show categorical data.

A **double-bar graph** is a graph used to compare similar types of data. This double-bar graph shows the same information as the two bar graphs you made on page 206.

Favorite Sport to Watch

Key: ■ Boys ■ Girls

Number of Students vs Sport (Football, Gymnastics, Ice Skating)

The key in the graph uses different colors to show the different data.

TALK Math

Which makes it easier to compare the data, the double-bar graph or the two single-bar graphs? Explain.

Practice

For 1–2, use the data in each table to make two bar graphs.
Then make a double-bar graph.

1.
Average High Temperature (in °F)			
City	Jan	Feb	Mar
Canton, Ohio	33	37	48
Detroit, Michigan	33	36	46

✓ 2.
Favorite Time of Day		
Time	Boys	Girls
Morning	6	8
Afternoon	20	17
Evening	33	31

For 3–6, use the double-bar graph.

✓ 3. Which city gets less rainfall from July through September?

4. Which city has a greater range of inches of rainfall during the three months? **Explain.**

5. How much more rain does Tampa get than Tucson in August?

6. **WRITE Math** ▶ Do you predict that Tucson or Tampa will have more rainfall in September next year? **Explain.**

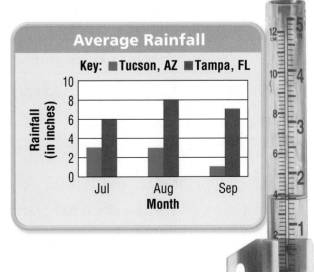

Average Rainfall

Key: ■ Tucson, AZ ■ Tampa, FL

Rainfall (in inches) vs Month (Jul, Aug, Sep)

Circle Graphs

OBJECTIVE: Read and interpret circle graphs.

Learn

Use a **circle graph** to show data as parts of a whole. You can use a circle graph to compare categorical data, or data about different groups.

PROBLEM Aisha took a survey of favorite summer activities. She recorded her data in a circle graph. Which activity got the most votes?

Favorite Summer Activity				
Activity	Hiking	Fishing	Visit Theme Park	Beach Activities
Votes	4	3	4	5

Example 1 Understand a circle graph.

Each color represents one category.

The circle represents the whole, or all the categories.

Favorite Summer Activity

Hiking · Beach Activities · Fishing · Theme Park

The number of equal sections shows the number of people Aisha surveyed.

Beach activities have the greatest amount shaded.

So, beach activities received the most votes.

Example 2 Interpret a circle graph.

Which type of pizza is least popular?

The smallest part of the circle is spinach.

So, the least popular pizza is spinach.

• Which type of pizza got $\frac{1}{2}$ of the votes?

• How is a circle graph like a bar graph? How is it different?

Favorite Pizza

Pepperoni 15 votes · Spinach 10 votes · Cheese 25 votes

For 1–4, use the Favorite Breakfast graph.

1. Did waffles, eggs, or cereal receive the most votes?

✓ 2. Which type of breakfast received the least number of votes?

✓ 3. Which type of breakfast received less than $\frac{1}{4}$ of the votes?

4. **TALK Math** What does the whole circle represent?

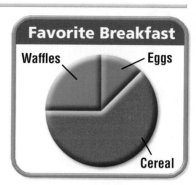

Favorite Breakfast

Independent Practice (and Problem Solving)

For 5–7, use the Favorite Fruit graph.

5. Which fruit received the greatest number of votes?

6. Which fruit received the least number of votes?

7. How many more people voted for oranges than pears?

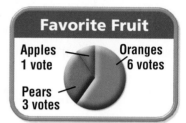

Favorite Fruit

Apples 1 vote — Oranges 6 votes — Pears 3 votes

For 8–9, use the Favorite Dog graph.

8. Which dog received the least number of votes?

9. Which dog received almost half the votes?

10. **Reasoning** Raymond's allowance is $10. He spends $5 for a movie ticket and $2 on snacks. He saves the rest. How would you show this in a circle graph?

11. **WRITE Math** ▸ **What's the Error?** Joey earns $1 on Monday, $4 on Wednesday, and $5 on Friday. He says Graph A matches the data. Describe Joey's error. Tell which graph matches the set of data.

Favorite Dog

Terrier — Poodle — Bulldog — Retriever

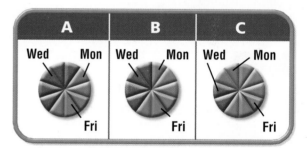

Mixed Review and Test Prep

12. What is the name of a polygon with exactly 4 sides? (Grade 3)

13. Make a bar graph using the data from the Favorite Fruit graph above. (p. 206)

14. **Test Prep** Look at the Favorite Dog graph above. Which dog received the most votes?

   A Retriever

   B Bulldog

   C Terrier

   D Poodle

Extra Practice on page 232, Set B

LESSON
4
ALGEBRA
Use a Coordinate Grid
OBJECTIVE: Identify, locate, and graph points on a
coordinate grid and describe paths.

Quick Review

Write the missing number
for each letter.

0 2 A 6 8 B 12 C D 18 E

1. *A*   2. *B*   3. *C*
4. *D*   5. *E*

Vocabulary

x-axis	ordered pair
y-axis	*x*-coordinate
coordinate grid	*y*-coordinate
origin	

Learn

A grid formed by a horizontal line called the **x-axis** and a
vertical line called the **y-axis** is a **coordinate grid**. The
point where the *x*-axis and the *y*-axis meet is the **origin**.

An **ordered pair** is a pair of numbers used to locate a
point on a coordinate grid. The **x-coordinate** tells how
many units to move horizontally, and the **y-coordinate**
tells how many units to move vertically.

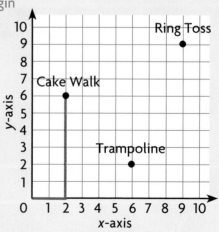

$$(3,4)$$

x-coordinate —↑ ↑— *y*-coordinate

PROBLEM The coordinate grid shows a map
of the activities at the school carnival. What
ordered pair gives the location of the trampoline?

Example 1 Find the ordered pair for the trampoline.

Step 1

Start at the point labeled Trampoline. Look down at
the *x*-axis. The point is 6 units to the right of the origin.
The *x*-coordinate is 6.

Step 2

Then look to the left at the *y*-axis. The point is 2 units up
from the origin. The *y*-coordinate is 2.

So, the trampoline is located at (6,2).

Example 2 What activity is located at (2,6)?

Step 1

Start at the origin. Count 2 units to the right.

Step 2

Then count 6 units up.

So, the cake walk is at (2,6).

• Describe how to go from the cake walk to the ring toss.

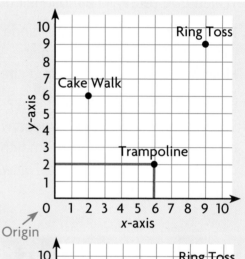

Example 3 Graph points.

A Graph a point at (0,3) to show the prize booth.

Start at the origin. Since the *x*-coordinate is 0, do not move right. Count 3 units up. Graph a point and label it.

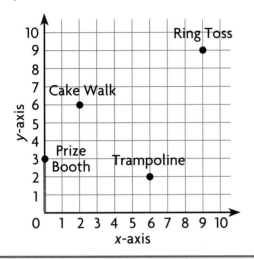

B Graph a point at (2,5) to show the snack stand.

Start at the origin. Count 2 units right. Count 5 units up. Graph a point and label it.

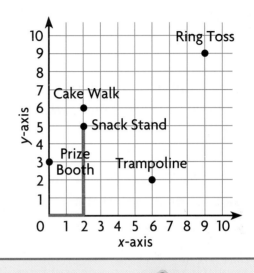

Example 4 Graph plane figures.

The fourth grade students are making a fenced area for parking their bikes. If the fence poles are placed at (8,0), (8,7), and (10,7), where should the fourth fence pole be located to form a rectangle?

ERROR ALERT

The first number is the number of units horizontally and the second number is the number of units vertically from the origin.

(1,3)
↑↑
horizontally vertically

Step 1

Graph the three points. Connect them with line segments.

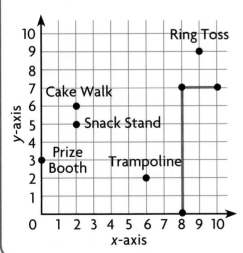

Step 2

Graph a point that will form a rectangle. Connect the line segments.

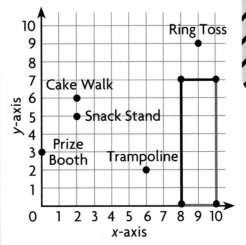

So, the fourth fence pole will be located at (10,0).

1. To graph the point (4,1), in which direction from the origin and how many units will you move first? What will you do next?

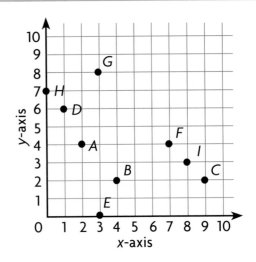

Write the point for each ordered pair on the coordinate grid.

2. (9,2)

3. (0,7)

 4. (2,4)

 5. (3,8)

6. **TALK Math** Explain how to move from point A to point C using *left*, *right*, *up*, or *down*.

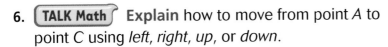

Independent Practice and Problem Solving

Write the point for each ordered pair on the coordinate grid above.

7. (7,4)

8. (1,6)

9. (4,2)

10. (3,0)

11. (8,3)

Use grid paper. Graph each point and label it using the ordered pair.

12. (5,5)

13. (0,10)

14. (5,10)

15. (0,5)

16. (2,3)

17. What polygon is formed by the points (5,5), (0,5), (0,10), and (5,10)?

18. What polygon is formed by the points (0,10), (5,10), and (0,5)?

For 19–22, use the map.

19. Emily is at the lemonade stand. She moves 4 units right and 3 units up. Then she moves 2 units left and 2 units down. Where is she now? Name the ordered pair.

20. Leo is at the spin art booth. He wants to go to the beanbag toss next. Describe a path he could take.

21. Which booth is located 1 unit right and 4 units down from the ticket booth?

22. There are flags at 4 of the booths. The flags are the vertices of a rectangle. What ordered pairs describe where the flags are located?

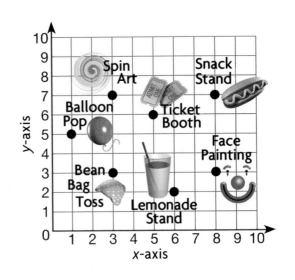

Technology
Use Harcourt Mega Math, The Number Games, *ArachnaGraph*, Level H.

23. Reasoning Explain how you know that the line segment joining (12,0) and (0,12) is not a horizontal line segment.

24. [WRITE Math] **What's the Question?** You start at the origin. You move 8 units right and then 5 units up.

Mixed Review and Test Prep

25. Make a double-bar graph for the data in the table. (p. 206)

Favorite Type of Music		
Type	**Girls**	**Boys**
Rock	10	14
Country	14	12
Jazz	6	4

26. What is the mean of the data? (p. 186)

10, 12, 14, 12, 5, 6, 4

27. Test Prep What is the origin on a coordinate grid?

A The *y*-axis

B The *x*-axis

C The point at (0,0)

D The scale

28. Test Prep How many units to the right of the origin is (2,3)?

Problem Solving [connects to] Music

The Romley High School marching band is learning a routine. The grid shows where each member should stand to form the letter F. The next letter they will form is a T.

1. Explain which band members must move to form the letter T. For each member that must move, describe the path he or she might take and give an ordered pair to show that member's new location. Use *north*, *south*, *east*, and *west* in your description.

2. Use grid paper to make a map like the one shown. Use a different formation for the band members. Describe how they could move to make a new formation. Use *forward*, *back*, *left*, and *right* and ordered pairs in your description.

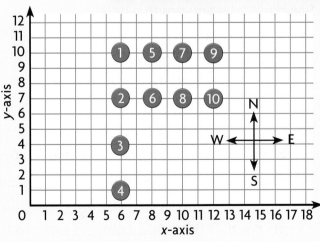

Line Graphs

OBJECTIVE: Read and interpret line graphs.

Quick Review

Graph each ordered pair on a coordinate grid.

1. (3,7)   2. (6,2)
3. (0,4)   4. (1,5)
5. (2,0)

Vocabulary

line graph   trends

Learn

A **line graph** uses line segments to show how data change over a period of time. Line graphs show numerical data.

PROBLEM For 4 weeks, Caroline kept track of the growth of a bean plant in her family's garden. How tall was the bean plant at Week 3?

Example 1 Find the height of the bean plant at Week 3.

Step 1

Find the grid line for Week 3. Follow that line up to the point (•).

Step 2

Follow the grid line to the scale on the left to locate the height at Week 3.

So, the bean plant was 11 inches tall at Week 3.

Math Idea
Points on a line graph can be read like an ordered pair.
(Week 1, 4 inches)

Each line segment shows the change in the bean plant's height each week.

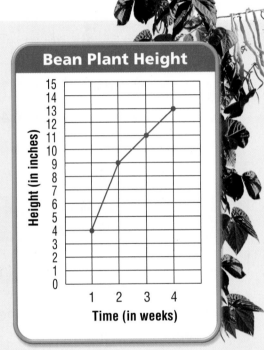

Bean Plant Height

Segments of a line graph where data increase, decrease, or stay the same over time are called **trends**.

Example 2 Describe trends.

Between which months did rainfall increase?
The line moves upward between April and July.

So, rainfall increased between April and July.

• Between which months did rainfall stay the same?

• Look at the trend between August and September. If the trend continues, do you predict rainfall will increase, decrease, or stay the same in October?

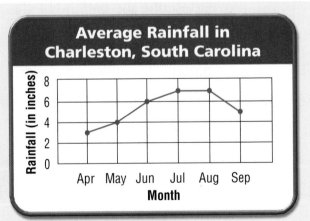

Average Rainfall in Charleston, South Carolina

Each line segment shows how the average rainfall varies between months.

Guided Practice

For 1–4, use the graph at the right.

1. Which day has the greatest data value? the least value? What is the range of the data?

2. What was the height of the water in the glass on Thursday?

3. Between which two days did the water level stay the same?

4. **TALK Math** Explain and describe what the line graph shows you about the water level over 5 days.

Height of Water in a Glass Outdoors

Independent Practice and Problem Solving

For 5–7, use the graph above.

5. Between which two days did the water level decrease the most?

6. By how many centimeters did the water level decrease during the 5 days?

7. Describe a trend in the data between Wednesday and Friday.

For 8–10, use the Weight of a Kitten graph.

8. What is the range in weight between birth and 4 weeks?

9. What is the median weight between birth and 4 weeks? the mean?

10. What trend in weight is shown by the graph?

11. **Pose a Problem** Look back at Problem 7. Write a similar problem by changing the days.

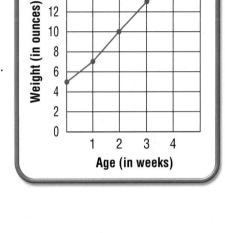

Weight of a Kitten

12. **WRITE Math** Explain and describe how you could use the Weight of a Kitten line graph to predict how much a kitten might weigh at 5 weeks.

Mixed Review and Test Prep

13. Write the missing factor. (p. 108)

$$34 + 14 = \blacksquare \times 6$$

14. Describe how to graph the point (4,9) on a coordinate grid. (p. 210)

15. **Test Prep** A horizontal line on a line graph shows the data are

   A increasing.   C staying the same.

   B decreasing.   D too large to graph.

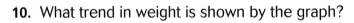

Extra Practice on page 233, Set D

6 Make Line Graphs

OBJECTIVE: Make line graphs.

Quick Review

How many more inches of snow fell during the fourth week than during the first?

Snowfall	
Week	Inches
1	2
2	4
3	1
4	5

Investigate

Materials ■ line-graph pattern or grid paper

Use the line-graph pattern to make a line graph to show the data in the table.

A Write a title for the graph. Choose a scale and interval for the data. Write the label and numbers in the scale along the left side of the graph. The last number on the scale should be greater than the greatest data value by as much as one interval.

Average Daily Temperature in Chicago, IL, January, 2006	
Day	Temperature (in Degrees Fahrenheit)
1	35
2	41
3	40
4	42
5	36
6	30
7	32

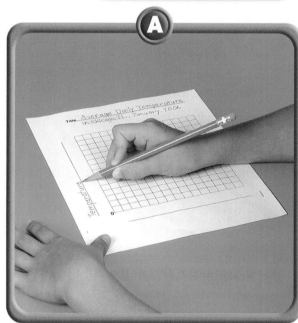

B Write the labels for the days along the bottom of the graph.

C Graph each point. Then draw line segments to connect the points from left to right.

Draw Conclusions

1. How did you choose the scale and interval for your graph?

2. Compare your graph with those of your classmates. Are there any differences in your graphs? Explain.

3. **Application** Think of some other kind of data that you could show in a line graph. Explain how you would make your graph.

Some line graphs show a rule. When a line graph shows a rule, you can extend the pattern to find information not shown on the graph.

The graph below shows the relationship between your distance from lightning and the number of seconds that pass until you hear thunder.

How far away is the lightning strike if thunder is heard 15 seconds later?

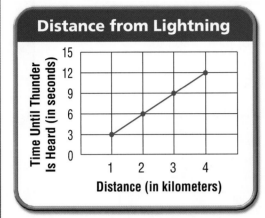

Distance from Lightning

Think: The rule is, divide the number of seconds by 3 to get the number of kilometers.

TALK Math

How do you know where to place each point on a line graph?

Continue a pattern on the line graph.
Divide 15 by 3 to get the distance in kilometers.

So, 15 seconds between lightning and thunder means lightning is 5 kilometers away.

Practice

For 1–2, use the data to make a line graph.

1.

Rainfall				
Month	Jun	Jul	Aug	Sep
Amount (in inches)	3	5	6	4

2.

Plant Growth				
End of Week	1	2	3	4
Height (in inches)	6	9	13	15

3. Use the data to make a line graph.
   How far will Aaron swim in 5 minutes if he continues at the same rate?

Aaron's Swim-a-Thon				
Time (in minutes)	1	2	3	4
Distance (in meters)	25	50	75	100

4. **WRITE Math** ▶ **Explain** how to use the data in a table to make a line graph.

Problem Solving Workshop
Strategy: Make a Graph

OBJECTIVE: Solve problems by using the strategy *make a graph.*

Learn the Strategy

Making a graph can help you organize and display data.
Different types of graphs show different types of information.

Make a bar graph or pictograph.

Ms. Fedders' class took a survey of the states they have visited.

Use a bar graph or pictograph to compare categorical data, or data about different groups.

States Visited	
State	**Number of Students**
Florida	11
California	10
New York	7
Nevada	6

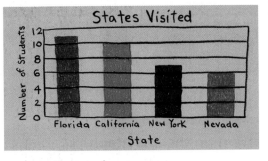

Make a line graph.

Taylor recorded the height of her tomato plant each week.

Use a line graph to show how data change over time.

Height of Tomato Plant	
Week	**Height (in inches)**
1	3
2	5
3	8
4	11

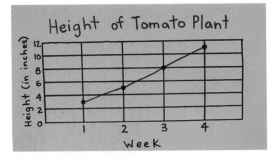

Make a line plot.

Shane recorded the number of library books each student in his class checked out.

Use a line plot to record data as they are collected or to show frequency of repeated amounts.

Library Books Checked Out						
Books	1	2	3	4	5	6
Number of Students	III	IIII	IIII	III	II	I

TALK Math

What type of data would you not display in a line plot?

Use the Strategy

PROBLEM The table shows about how many tourists from New Zealand came to California between February and June in 2004. What is the greatest monthly difference in the number of New Zealand tourists visiting California between February and June?

New Zealand Tourists in California (2004)	
Month	Number of Tourists
February	5,000
March	6,000
April	8,000
May	9,000
June	11,000

Read to Understand

- **What information is given?**
- **Is there information you will not use? If so, what?**

Plan

- **What strategy can you use to solve the problem?**
  You can make a graph to help you see the information clearly.

Solve

- **How can you use the strategy to solve the problem?**

  The data set includes different groups. Make a bar graph or pictograph to compare the number of New Zealand tourists visiting California each month.

  Reading Skill Classify and categorize the information you will use to solve the problem.

  Write a label for each row.

  Look at the numbers. Choose a key to tell how many each symbol stands for.

  February has the least number of symbols, and June has the most. June has 6 more symbols than February.

  So, the greatest difference is 6,000 tourists.

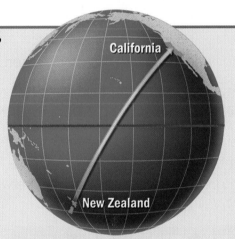

New Zealand Tourists in California (2004)	
February	🚶🚶🚶🚶🚶
March	🚶🚶🚶🚶🚶🚶
April	🚶🚶🚶🚶🚶🚶🚶🚶
May	🚶🚶🚶🚶🚶🚶🚶🚶🚶
June	🚶🚶🚶🚶🚶🚶🚶🚶🚶🚶🚶
Key: Each 🚶 = 1,000 tourists.	

Check

- **How can you check to see whether your solution is correct?**

1. The table shows the average number of visitors to Washington, D.C. each year from 2001 to 2004. Which two years had the greatest difference in the number of visitors?

   To compare information, you can use a bar graph or pictograph. Make a pictograph to compare the number of visitors each year.

   Decide on a symbol and a key for the pictograph.

   ### Washington, D.C. Visitors

2001	
2002	
2003	
2004	
Key: _?_	

   Washington, D.C. Visitors

Year	Visitors (in millions)
2001	18
2002	17
2003	17
2004	15

   Copy and complete the graph. Then solve the problem.

2. **What if** you add the data for 2000, when 19 million people visited Washington D.C.? Describe how the graph would change.

3. Manuel's class voted for their favorite places to visit. Make a double-bar graph to show the data. Then find which place had the greatest difference in votes between girls and boys.

Place Manuel's Class Would Like to Visit

Place	Girls	Boys
Lake	2	1
Ocean	4	2
National Park	2	7
Amusement Park	6	8

Problem Solving Strategy Practice

For 4–6, use the Exhibit Attendance table.
Make a graph to solve.

4. A museum is keeping track of the number of people who visit each exhibit. What is the range of the data?

5. What is the mode of the data? **Explain.**

6. **Reasoning** To save money, the museum is thinking of closing one exhibit. Which exhibit might it make sense to close? **Explain.**

7. **WRITE Math** Suppose the museum used another table to show the amount of money that was spent to set up each exhibit. Would it make more sense to use a circle graph or a line graph to display the data? **Explain.**

Exhibit Attendance

Exhibit	Number of People
Dinosaurs	90
Ancient Egypt	50
Titanic	45
Star Gallery	60
Machines	90

Mixed Strategy Practice

For 8–10, use the information in the map.

8. New York City is made up of 5 boroughs. Which borough is about twice the size of Manhattan?

9. The sum of the areas of two boroughs in New York City is 104 square miles. Which two boroughs are they?

10. **Pose a Problem** Look back at Problem 8. Write a similar problem about two different boroughs. Solve the problem.

11. Craig, Jim, and Pedro live in three different boroughs—Brooklyn, Queens, and Manhattan. Neither Craig nor Pedro lives in Brooklyn. Craig does not live in Queens. In which borough does each friend live?

12. Grace arrived at the museum at 9:15 A.M. It took 15 minutes to walk from her house to the train. She waited 10 minutes for the train. The train ride was 20 minutes. Then she walked 10 minutes from the train station to the museum. At what time did Grace leave her house to go to the museum?

13. **Open-Ended** Molly walks 3 blocks east to get from her house to her school in Brooklyn. Use grid paper to make a coordinate grid. Graph a point for Molly's house at (0,0). Then graph a point for her school. Decide on a point for the library so Molly's path from her house to school to the library and back home is a right triangle.

CHALLENGE YOURSELF

Central Park is in the center of the island of Manhattan. The park is a rectangle that is $2\frac{1}{2}$ miles long and $\frac{1}{2}$ mile wide. There are 26,000 trees and over 9,000 benches in Central Park.

14. If you were going to jog around Central Park, how many miles would you jog?

15. American elms make up 1,700 of the trees in Central Park. How many trees in the park are not American elms?

Choose a STRATEGY

Make a Table or Graph
Draw a Diagram or Picture
Make a Model or Act It Out
Make an Organized List
Find a Pattern
Predict and Test
Work Backward
Solve a Simpler Problem
Write an Equation
Use Logical Reasoning

The Size of the 5 Boroughs of New York City

Bronx: 44 square miles

Manhattan: 24 square miles

Queens: 112 square miles

Brooklyn: 82 square miles

Staten Island: 60 square miles

▲ New York City is broken into five different areas called *boroughs*.

Choose an Appropriate Graph

OBJECTIVE: Choose an appropriate graph.

Quick Review

Ronnie is making a pictograph to show the data below. What key should he use?

Favorite Car Color				
Color	Red	Blue	Green	Pink
Votes	5	10	5	20

Learn

The type of graph used to display data depends upon the type of information you want to show.

Examples

A

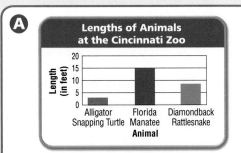

Use a bar graph or double-bar graph to show and compare data about different categories, or groups.

B

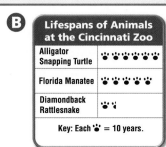

Use a pictograph to show and compare data about different categories, or groups.

C

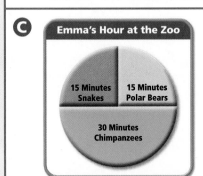

Use a circle graph to compare parts of a group to a whole group.

D

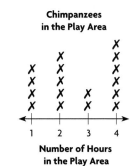

Use a line plot to show the frequency of the data along a number line.

E

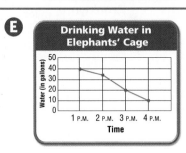

Use a line graph to show how data change over time.

Math Idea

Choosing the correct graph makes it easier to see trends, make predictions, and compare data to solve problems.

- Which types of graph or plot show categorical data? Which types show numerical data?

The Best Graph for the Data

Harrison and Kiyo made graphs to show the data in the table. Which is the better graph?

Sales on Sunday	
Item	**Number Sold**
Key Chains	3
Stuffed Animals	5
Toy Tractors	7
Inflatable Bats	8

A bar graph compares different groups of data. A bar graph is the better choice.

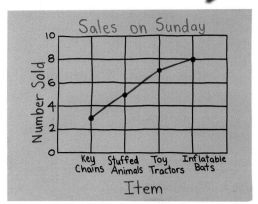

The data do not show changes over a period of time. So, a line graph is **not** the better way to show the data.

- **Reasoning** What other kind of graph could be used to show the data? Explain.

Guided Practice

1. To show how many days Ali worked 5 hours, would you use a line plot or a line graph? **Explain** your choice.

Hours Ali Worked						
Day	Mon	Tue	Wed	Thur	Fri	Sat
Hours Worked	5	5	6	7	8	5

For 2–7, choose and explain the best type of graph or plot for the data.

2. how Ana spent $5.00 at the zoo

3. the number of workers at each food booth

4. the temperature at the zoo between noon and 5 P.M.

5. how many classmates bought different numbers of drinks at the zoo

6. the number of inches of rain over 5 days

7. the number of people taking different types of transportation to the zoo

For 8, use the Hours Ali Worked table.

8. [TALK Math] **Explain** what kind of display would make it easiest to find the median hours Ali worked.

For 9–14, choose and explain the best type of graph or plot for the data.

9. height of a sunflower plant over time

10. how Jason spends 8 hours working

11. number of points scored at a basketball game by different players

12. number of people who scored different numbers of points at a hoop game

13.

Monday Lemonade Sales				
Size	Small	Medium	Large	X-Large
Number Sold	7	13	9	11

14.

Cars Washed by Students				
Students	4	6	3	1
Cars	1	2	4	5

For 15–16, use the line graph and bar graph.

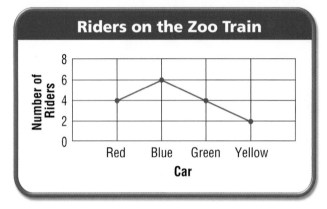

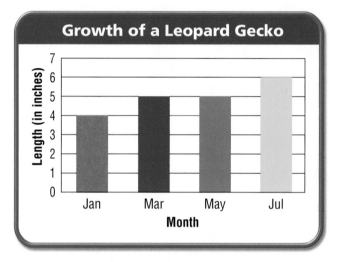

15. Why is a line graph not the best choice to show the riders on the zoo train?

16. Why is the bar graph not the best choice to show the growth of a gecko?

17. Collect data about the color of shoes in your class. Choose the best graph to display your data. Make the graph.

18. **WRITE Math** ▶ Write a type of data that you could show in a line graph. **Explain** why the data work in a line graph.

Mixed Review and Test Prep

19. What is the mean of the data shown in the table in Problem 13? (p. 186)

20. Last week, the zoo sold 698 tickets to the train ride. This week, the zoo sold 810 tickets to the train ride. About how many more tickets were sold this week? (p. 38)

21. **Test Prep** Which type of graph would best display daily high temperatures at the fair?

   A Bar graph

   B Circle graph

   C Line graph

   D Pictograph

Write a Conclusion

Some graphs show relationships, such as the relationship between time and distance. This graph shows the relationship between the distance Steven rode his bike and the time his trip took.

What does the graph show about the bike trip?

Read Deja's description of Steven's ride and her conclusions about the relationships in the graph.

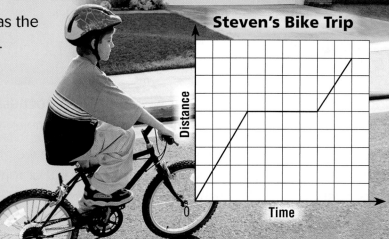

Steven's Bike Trip

The graph shows the relationship of distance and time during Steven's bike trip.

At the beginning of the ride, the line moves up. That means he is moving some distance. In the middle, the line is straight. That shows he is not moving any distance. He has stopped. Then the line moves up again. That means he is moving again.

The graph shows that Steven started to ride his bike, then stopped, maybe to talk to a friend, then began riding again.

Tips

To analyze a graph:

• Read the title and find out what the graph is about.

• Look at the labels to find out what relationship the graph shows.

• Describe and explain each change in the data.

• Write a conclusion to explain the action the data show.

Problem Solving Analyze and describe the data. Write a conclusion to explain the actions that the data show.

1. **Money in Ally's Savings Account**

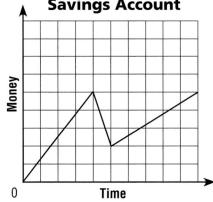

2. **Rita's 100-Meter Swimming Race**

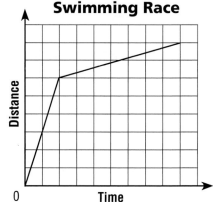

ALGEBRA

Graph Relationships

OBJECTIVE: Graph equations using a function table.

Learn

PROBLEM An elephant's molar weighs about 5 pounds. Elephants have 4 molars. How much do 4 elephant molars weigh?

You can write an equation using x and y to find the weight of 4 molars. Then you can make a function table and graph ordered pairs to show the relationship of x and y.

A **function table** is a table that matches each input value to an output value. The output values are determined by the function. Every input has exactly one output.

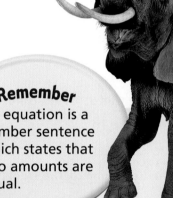

Example 1   Use a function table to graph an equation.

Step 1

Write an equation:

total weight = weight of each molar × number of molars
    ↓   ↓   ↓

y =   5   × x

You can also write this equation as $y = 5x$.

When you multiply a variable and a number, you don't need to write the multiplication sign. So, $5 \times x = 5x$.

Step 2

Make a function table for the equation. Think of this equation as a rule that says: to find y, multiply x by 5.

List values for x. Use the rule to find y.

Number of Molars, x	1	2	3	4
Total Weight in Pounds, y	5	10	15	20

Step 3

Write the ordered pairs for the data in the table.
(1,5), (2,10), (3,15), (4,20)

Step 4

Graph the ordered pairs.

So, 4 molars weigh 20 pounds.

Remember

An equation is a number sentence which states that two amounts are equal.

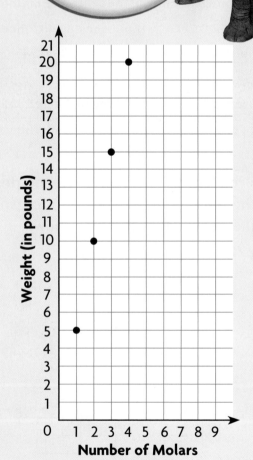

Graph Values from a Function Table

Example 2 Graph a division equation using a function table.
A Goliath beetle weighs about 3 ounces. How many Goliath
beetles weigh 12 ounces?

Step 1

Write an equation:

number of beetles = total number of ounces ÷ ounces for one beetle

$$y = x ÷ 3$$

Step 2

Make a function table for the equation. Think of this
equation as a rule that says: to find *y*, divide *x* by 3.

List values for *x*. Use the rule to find *y*.

Total Number of Ounces, *x*	3	6	9	12	15
Number of Beetles, *y*	1	2	3	4	5

Step 3

Write the ordered pairs. (3,1), (6,2), (9,3), (12,4), (15,5)

Step 4

Graph the ordered pairs.

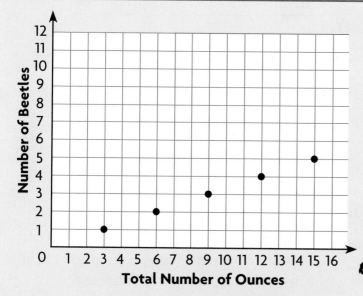

So, 4 Goliath beetles weigh 12 ounces.

- How many Goliath beetles weigh 15 ounces?

- Look at the graph for the equation $y = x ÷ 3$. What happens
  to *y* as *x* increases?

1. A function table has a rule of $y = x + 4$.

   If $x = 1$, then $y = 1 + 4$. If $x = 2$, then $y = \blacksquare + 4$.

   If $x = 3$, then $y = \blacksquare + 4$. If $x = 4$, then $y = \blacksquare + 4$.

Input, x	1	2	3	4
Output, y	5	6	7	8

Find a rule. Write your rule as an equation. Use the equation to find the missing numbers.

2.

Input, x	1	2	3	4	5	6	▦
Output, y	4	5	▦	7	8	▦	10

3.

Input, x	11	10	▦	8	7	6	▦
Output, y	6	▦	4	3	2	▦	0

✓ 4.

Yards, x	1	2	3	4	5	6	▦
Feet, y	3	▦	9	12	15	▦	21

✓ 5.

Pennies, x	10	20	▦	40	▦	60	▦
Dimes, y	1	▦	3	4	5	6	7

6. **TALK Math** **Explain** how to write ordered pairs from a function table.

Independent Practice and Problem Solving

Find a rule. Write your rule as an equation. Use the equation to find the missing numbers.

7.

Input, x	12	11	10	▦	8	7	6
Output, y	8	▦	6	5	4	3	▦

8.

Input, x	1	▦	3	▦	5	6	7
Output, y	9	10	▦	12	13	14	▦

9.

Cups, x	4	8	12	▦	20	24
Quarts, y	1	▦	3	4	5	▦

10.

Quarters, x	▦	2	3	4	▦	6
Nickels, y	5	10	▦	20	25	▦

Make a function table. Write the input/output values as ordered pairs. Graph the ordered pairs.

11. $y = 2x$ 12. $y = 4x$ 13. $y = 5x$ 14. $y = 6x$

For 15–16, write an equation and graph the function to solve.

15. Each book weighs 2 pounds. There are 7 books in a stack. How much does the stack of books weigh?

16. It takes 5 cups of flour to make a loaf of bread. How many cups of flour will Jacob need to make 6 loaves of bread?

17. **Reasoning** Tara graphed the points (1,3), (2,6), (3,9), (4,12). What equation could she have graphed?

18. **WRITE Math** **Explain** what happens to the value of y when the value of x changes in $y = 4x$.

Learn About

ALGEBRA
Using a Rule to Find Distance

You can find distance if you know the time traveled and the rate traveled during that time.

Example

Canoeists paddle an average of about 2 miles an hour. How far can a canoeist paddle in 6 hours?

You can show the relationship in a table.

Time in Hours, t	1	2	3	4	5	6
Distance in Miles, d	2	4	6	8	10	12

Notice that the distance a canoeist can paddle is equal to the rate of speed multiplied by the time, or distance = rate × time, or $d = rt$.

Use the rule to find the distance.

$d = 2 \times 6$
$d = 12$

So, a canoeist can paddle about 12 miles in 6 hours.

Try It

19. Mario bikes at 8 miles per hour. How many miles can he bike in 4 hours?

20. ≡**FAST FACT** On December 17, 1903, the Wright brothers flew the *Kitty Hawk* for 12 seconds at a rate of 10 feet per second. How far did the *Kitty Hawk* fly?

Mixed Review and Test Prep

21. How many minutes are in 2 hours 15 minutes? (p. 160)

22. What type of graph would be best to show the eye color of your classmates? (p. 222)

23. Test Prep Describe what happens to the value of y when the value of x increases in the equation $y = x \div 2$.

24. Test Prep Mia buys juice boxes for a picnic. Based on the information in the table, what should Mia do to find the number of juice boxes in 7 packages?

Packages, p	1	2	5	7
Juice Boxes, b	4	8	20	■

A Multiply 7 by 5.   **C** Divide 7 by 7.

B Multiply 7 by 4.   **D** Add 5 to 7.

Problem Solving Workshop
Skill: Identify Relationships

OBJECTIVE: Solve problems using the skill *identify relationships*.

Use the Skill

PROBLEM Marta wants to make a square garden in her backyard. She drew squares of different sizes to plan her garden. How is the length of a side of the garden related to the perimeter of the garden?

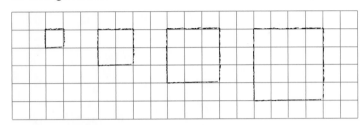

Remember

To find the perimeter, count the number of units around the figure.

You can use a function table to organize the data.

Length of a Side (in yards), *l*	1	2	3	4
Perimeter (in yards), *p*	4	8	12	16

$$1 \times 4 = 4 \quad 2 \times 4 = 8 \quad 3 \times 4 = 12 \quad 4 \times 4 = 16$$

You can identify the relationship by writing a rule for the function table.

Rule: Multiply *l* by 4 to find *p*.

So, the relationship is that the perimeter of a square is the length of a side multiplied by 4.

You can also show the information in a graph.

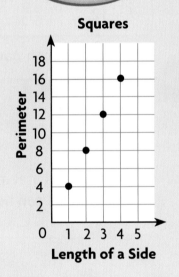

Squares

Think and Discuss

a. Make a function table for the ordered pairs shown on the graph at the right.

b. How is number of sides of a polygon related to the number of vertices?

c. Write an equation that shows the relationship between the number of sides and number of vertices of a polygon.

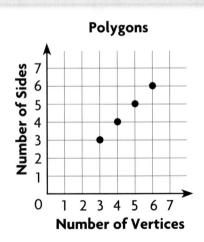

Polygons

Guided Problem Solving

1. Oscar is making a metal wind chime to hang in his garden. He uses four equilateral triangles. How is the perimeter of an equilateral triangle related to the length of one side of the triangle? Complete the function table and graph the ordered pairs to help solve.

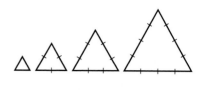

Each ⊢─⊣ = 1 inch.

Length of a Side (in inches), l	1	■	3	4
Perimeter (in inches), p	3	6	■	■

2. **What if** Oscar added another triangle that was 6 inches on each side? What would be the perimeter of that triangle?

3. Robin is fencing in a square garden that is 2 yards on each side. José is fencing in a square garden that is 4 yards on each side. How much more fencing does José need than Robin? Use the first graph on page 230.

Mixed Applications

4. Hilburn Gardens had 612 visitors on Monday. They had 423 visitors on Tuesday and 516 visitors on Wednesday. How many more visitors did they have on Monday than on Tuesday?

5. Rae is driving to the Missouri Botanical Garden in St. Louis. After 2 hours, she stops at a rest stop for 15 minutes. Then she drives 30 more minutes. She arrives at the garden at 12:15 P.M. At what time did she leave for the garden?

For 6–7, use the graph.

6. The graph shows the relationship between the lengths and widths of tiles sold at a garden shop. How is the width related to the length?

7. **WRITE Math** **What's the Error?** Erin says that a tile with a length of 5 inches will have a width of 5 inches. **Explain** why she is not correct.

8. Kirk plants marigolds around 6 trees in a park. He plants 12 marigolds around each tree. What operation does Kirk use to find how many marigolds he needs? How many marigolds does Kirk plant?

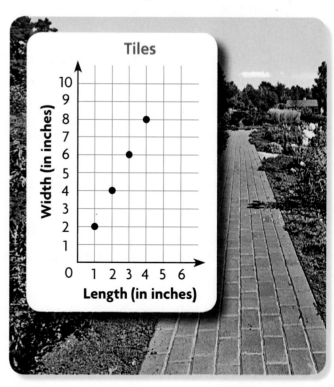

Extra Practice

Set A Use the Favorite Type of Movie bar graph. (pp. 204–205)

1. How many more students chose comedies than cartoons?

2. What is the range of the data?

3. Which types of movies were chosen by the same number of classmates?

4. What is the interval of the scale?

5. What is the mode of the data?

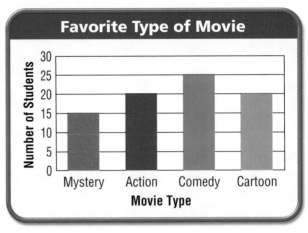

Set B Use the After-School Activity graph. (pp. 208–209)

1. In which after-school activity do the greatest number of students participate?

2. In which after-school activity do the least number of students participate?

3. In which activity do $\frac{1}{4}$ of the students participate?

4. Write an activity that is not the most popular or the least popular.

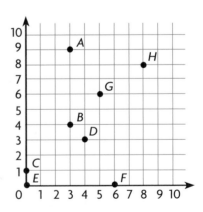

Set C Write the point for each ordered pair on the coordinate grid. (pp. 210–213)

1. (3,4)   2. (5,6)   3. (0,1)   4. (3,9)

5. (6,0)   6. (8,8)   7. (4,3)   8. (0,0)

Use grid paper. Graph each point and label it using the ordered pair.

9. (2,0)   10. (7,2)   11. (4,7)   12. (0,6)

13. (5,1)   14. (8,2)   15. (2,7)   16. (6,5)

Technology
Use Harcourt Mega Math, The Number Games, *Arachna Graph*, Levels B, C.

Set D Use the April Rain graph. (pp. 214–215)

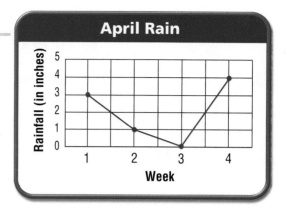

April Rain

1. Between which two weeks was there the greatest increase in the amount of rain?

2. By how many inches did the amount of rain decrease between Week 1 and Week 2?

3. During which week was there no rain?

4. What was the total rainfall for the 4 weeks?

5. What was the trend in rainfall between Week 1 and Week 3?

Set E Choose and explain the best type of graph or plot for the data. (pp. 222–225)

1.
Favorite Baseball Team			
Team	Yankees	Mets	Cubs	Reds
Votes	16	18	16	14

2.
Temperature on Monday			
Time	8:00	9:00	10:00	11:00
Temperature (in °F)	81	86	90	91

3. Ray tossed 2 number cubes 20 times. He recorded the sum for each toss.

4. types of sandwiches sold in the cafeteria for 1 week

5. the height of a sunflower plant during 12 weeks

6. how Jody spent her allowance last month

Set F Find a rule. Write your rule as an equation. Use the equation to find the missing numbers. (pp. 226–229)

1.
Input, x	4	■	9	10	12	15
Output, y	2	6	7	8	■	■

2.
Input, x	1	2	4	■	14	15
Output, y	7	■	10	12	20	■

3.
Dollars, x	1	2	4	6	■	10
Dimes, y	10	■	40	■	80	100

4.
Feet, x	1	2	■	■	8	■
Inches, y	12	24	48	72	■	108

Make a function table. Write the input/output values as ordered pairs. Graph the ordered pairs.

5. $y = x + 6$ 6. $y = 3x$ 7. $y = 7x$ 8. $y = x - 5$

9. Jason graphed the points (10,5), (12,6), (4,2), (14,7). What equation could he have graphed?

MATH POWER · Circle Graphs

Display Your Data

Janelle surveyed 100 students to find out their favorite winter activity. Then she showed the results of her survey in a bar graph.

You can use Janelle's bar graph to make a circle graph.

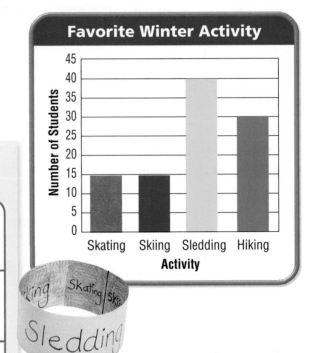

HANDS ON Activity

Materials ■ crayons ■ tape ■ ruler

Step 1

Trace the bars from the graph. Label each bar with the name of its activity.

Step 2

Cut out the bars. Tape them end-to-end to make a circle. The bars should not overlap.

Step 3

Place the circle on a sheet of paper, and trace around it. Mark the beginning and the end of each bar with a point on the circle.

Step 4

Mark the center of the circle you traced. Draw a radius from each of the points you marked.

Step 5

Label and color each section of the circle graph. Write the title for the graph.

Try It

Make a circle graph.

1.

Favorite Summer Activity			
Activity	Beach	Camping	Games
Votes	60	10	30

2. Conduct a survey of 10 classmates and use the data to make a circle graph with 3 or 4 categories.

3. [WRITE Math] **Explain** how a bar graph and a circle graph are alike and different.

Chapter 8 Review/Test

Check Vocabulary and Concepts

Choose the best term from the box.

VOCABULARY

origin
line graph
circle graph
function table

1. A __?__ is used to compare data as parts of a whole. (p. 208)

2. The point where the *x*-axis and the *y*-axis meet is the __?__. (p. 210)

3. A __?__ is a table that matches each input value to an output value. (p. 226)

Check Skills

For 4–6, use the bar graph at the right. (pp. 204–205)

4. On which days were the same number of tickets sold?

5. What is the interval of the scale?

6. How many tickets were sold during the week?

For 7–9, use the line graph at the right. (pp. 214–215, 222–225)

7. What was the trend from 3:00 to 5:00?

8. How much did the temperature increase between 1:00 and 3:00?

9. Why is a line graph an appropriate choice for these data?

Make a function table. Write the input/output values as ordered pairs. Graph the ordered pairs. (pp. 226–229)

10. $y = x$ 11. $y = 3x$ 12. $y = x + 3$ 13. $y = 2x - 2$

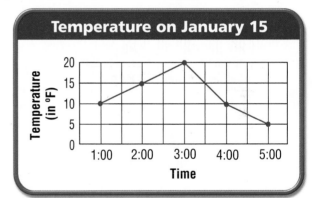
Talent Show Tickets — bar graph: Tickets Sold vs. Day (Mon, Tues, Wed, Thu, Fri)

Temperature on January 15 — line graph: Temperature (in °F) vs. Time (1:00–5:00)

Check Problem Solving

Solve. (pp. 218–221, 230–231)

Length of a Side (in inches), l	1	2	3	5	6	7	10
Perimeter (in inches), P	4	8	12	20	24	▪	▪

14. Jasmine is making ribbon borders for two square pillows. The red pillow is 10 inches on each side. The blue pillow is 7 inches on each side. How much more ribbon will she need for the red pillow? Use the table above to help.

15. **⟨WRITE Math⟩** ▸ **Explain** how you could make a graph to show how John spent $10 if he spent $3 on food, $4 on school supplies, and saved the rest.

Multiple Choice

1. Carrie took a survey of the color of students' shirts. Which data set matches the graph? (p. 204)

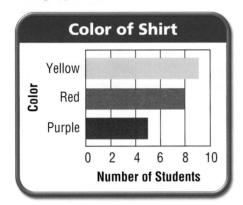

Color of Shirt

Color — Yellow, Red, Purple

Number of Students

A

Yellow	Red	Purple
卌 卌	卌	IIII

B

Yellow	Red	Purple
卌 IIII	卌 III	卌

C

Yellow	Red	Purple
IIII	II	卌

D

Yellow	Red	Purple
卌	卌 卌	III

2. Which is a way to read the time on the clock? (p. 152)

3:45 P.M.

A 45 minutes to 3

B Quarter to 3

C Quarter after 3

D Quarter to 4

3. How many minutes are in 2 hours? (p. 152)

A 10 minutes   **C** 70 minutes

B 60 minutes   **D** 120 minutes

4. When was the greatest increase in snowfall? (p. 214)

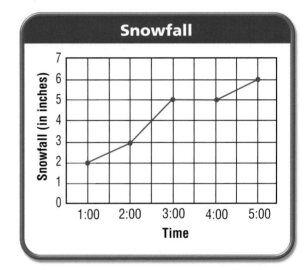

Snowfall

Snowfall (in inches)

Time

A From 1:00 to 2:00

B From 2:00 to 3:00

C From 3:00 to 4:00

D From 4:00 to 5:00

5. Which of the following inequalities is true? (p. 168)

A $^-2 > {}^-3$

B $^+4 < {}^-5$

C $0 < {}^-4$

D $^-6 > {}^+3$

GO Technology Use *Online Assessment.*
ONLINE

6. Zack and Marty are building a snow fort. What is a reasonable estimate of the outside temperature? (p. 164)

A $^-32°F$ **C** 70°F

B 25°F **D** 80°F

7. What is the ordered pair for point *F*? (p. 210)

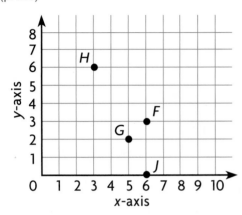

A (3,6) **C** (6,3)

B (5,2) **D** (8,4)

8. The graph below shows supplies needed for an art project.

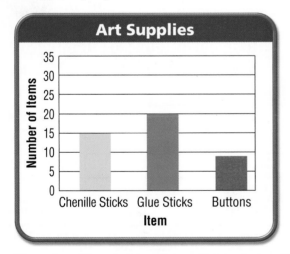

The chenille sticks will be divided equally among 5 students. How many chenille sticks will each student get? (p. 204)

A 3 **C** 5

B 4 **D** 10

Short Response

9. Make a function table for the equation $y = x + 3$. Use 1, 2, 5, 8, and 15 as values for *x*. (p. 226)

10. Dan is flying from Chicago to Dallas. The plane leaves at this time.

If the flight is 2 hours and ten mintues, when will he arrive in Dallas? (p. 154)

Extended Response ▤WRITE Math ▶

11. The line plot shows the number of matches won by all the team members.

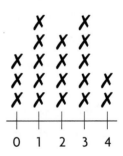

Tennis Team Matches Won

How many team members won at least 3 matches? **Explain.** (p. 190)

12. Use the data in the table to make a double-bar graph. (p. 206)

Summer Reading Contest			
Books Read	**June**	**July**	**August**
Red Team	20	15	35
Blue Team	25	20	20

Record High Temperatures

Hot Enough to Fry an Egg?

Although people joke about temperatures being hot enough to fry an egg on the sidewalk, it is really hard to do. Egg white begins to cook at 144°F, and yolk begins to cook at 149°F. Do you think a person could have fried an egg on the sidewalk on the date of the highest recorded temperature in the United States?

FACT · ACTIVITY

Use the table to answer the question.

1. Find the difference between the highest and lowest temperatures in the table. What is this number called?

2. The temperature 120°F occurs 4 times. What is this number called?

3. Is a bar graph with a scale from 0 to 200 with intervals of 100 a good way to display this data set? **Explain.**

4. Make a graph or line plot to display the data in the way you think is best. **Explain** why you chose that kind of display.

5. **WRITE Math** What do you notice about the dates of the record temperatures? **Explain** what this might mean.

Top 10 Record-High State Temperatures		
State	**Temperature (in °F)**	**Date**
Arizona	128	June 29, 1994
Arkansas	120	August 19, 1936
California	134	July 10, 1913
Kansas	121	July 24, 1936
Nevada	125	June 29, 1994
New Mexico	122	June 27, 1994
North Dakota	121	July 6, 1936
Oklahoma	120	June 27, 1994
South Dakota	120	July 5, 1936
Texas	120	June 28, 1994

Heat Waves

The hottest temperature ever recorded in the United States was 134°F, in Death Valley, California, on July 10, 1913.

Record temperatures of 100°F or higher are rare in the United States. More often, you will hear about heat waves. A *heat wave* means that the high temperature for the day, measured in the shade, is 90°F or greater for at least three days in a row.

Death Valley is the hottest and driest place in North America. About 2 inches of rain fall each year.

Temperatures (in °F) in August, 2005

Trenton, NJ	Chicago, IL	Buffalo, NY
Aug 1 86°	Aug 1 93°	Aug 1 85°
Aug 2 93°	Aug 2 91°	Aug 2 85°
Aug 3 95°	Aug 3 93°	Aug 3 87°
Aug 4 96°	Aug 4 90°	Aug 4 90°

FACT·ACTIVITY

Use the data on these two pages.

❶ Could the data above have been shown in line graphs? **Explain.**

❷ Which city's temperature varied the least between August 1 and August 2?

You are a science reporter in a city that has had a 7-day heat wave. Write a report to share with your class.

► Tell your audience about heat waves. Include a graph showing the temperature changes for the 7-day heat wave.

► Include some history and another display of data showing the highest recorded temperatures in some states.

► Find and include real data about the highest recorded temperature in your city or state.

4 Multiply by 1-Digit and 2-Digit Numbers

Math on Location

A DVD FROM
The Futures Channel

with
Chapter Projects

1

Meals are developed so astronauts have a balanced diet eating 4 pounds of food and drinking 10 cups of water each day.

2

Over 200 dishes, such as these scrambled eggs, are prepared through a process called freeze-drying.

3

The packages for a menu cycle of 10 days or longer are boxed for storage in the space module.

VOCABULARY POWER

TALK Math

What math do you see in the **Math on Location** photographs? How can you find how many pounds of food and how much water the astronauts have in 30 days?

READ Math

REVIEW VOCABULARY You learned the words below when you learned about multiplication facts. How do these words relate to **Math on Location**?

factor a number that is multiplied by another number to find a product

multiple the product of two counting numbers is a multiple of each of these numbers

product the answer to a multiplication problem

WRITE Math ▶

Copy and complete a word definition map like the one below. Use what you know about multiplication to answer the questions.

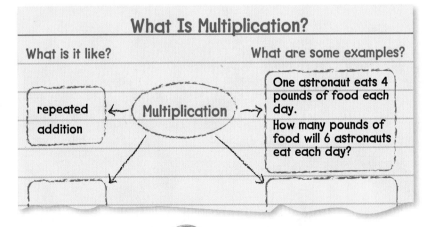

What Is Multiplication?

What is it like?

repeated addition ← Multiplication →

What are some examples?

One astronaut eats 4 pounds of food each day.
How many pounds of food will 6 astronauts eat each day?

Technology
Multimedia Math Glossary link at
www.harcourtschool.com/hspmath

9 Multiply by 1-Digit Numbers

≡ FAST FACT

A white rhino has two horns. The front horn is larger and measures 37 to 79 inches. The rear horn is smaller. It grows as long as 22 inches.

Investigate

In Africa, large and small animals often live side by side. Use the data for each animal. In what different ways can you use multiplication to compare their sizes?

Animal Heights and Weights		
Type of Animal	Average Height (in inches)	Average Weight (in pounds)
African Elephant	126	11,000
African Wild Dog	30	60
Antelope	72	2,000
Giraffe	192	2,500
Gorilla	66	400
White Rhino	72	5,000

GO ONLINE

Technology
Student pages are available in the Student eBook.

Check your understanding of important skills
needed for success in Chapter 9.

▶ **Regroup Tens and Ones**

Regroup. Write the missing numbers.

1.

3 tens 14 ones = ■ tens 4 ones

2.

5 tens 21 ones = ■ tens ■ one

3. 7 tens ■ ones = 8 tens 3 ones

4. ■ tens 28 ones = 6 tens 8 ones

▶ **Multiplication Facts**

Find the product.

5. 6×3 **6.** 4×4 **7.** 5×9 **8.** 6×2

9. 8×7 **10.** 9×8 **11.** 7×4 **12.** 0×5

▶ **Model Multiplication**

Write a multiplication sentence for the model.

13.   **14.**   **15.**

VOCABULARY POWER

CHAPTER VOCABULARY		WARM-UP WORDS
array	multiple	**compatible numbers** numbers that are easy to compute mentally
compatible numbers	partial product	**multiple** the product of two counting numbers is a multiple of each of those numbers
estimate	pattern	**partial product** a method of multiplying in which the ones, tens, hundreds, and so on are multiplied separately and then the products are added together
factor	product	
mental math	regroup	
	round	

MENTAL MATH
Multiplication Patterns

OBJECTIVE: Use a basic fact and a pattern to multiply mentally.

Learn

It is easy to multiply whole numbers mentally by multiples of 10, 100, and 1,000 if you know the basic facts.

PROBLEM Moe's Sun Fun rents 400 body boards each month. How many body boards do they rent in 6 months?

Example **Use mental math to multiply.** 6×400

Multplication can be thought of as repeated addition.

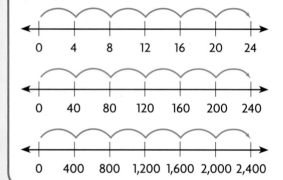

| 0 | 4 | 8 | 12 | 16 | 20 | 24 |

$6 \times 4 = 24 \leftarrow$ basic fact

| 0 | 40 | 80 | 120 | 160 | 200 | 240 |

$6 \times 40 = 240$

| 0 | 400 | 800 | 1,200 | 1,600 | 2,000 | 2,400 |

$6 \times 400 = 2,400$

So, Moe's Sun Fun rents 2,400 body boards in 6 months.

• What pattern do you see in the number sentences?

More Examples

A **Basic fact with a pattern**

$4 \times 7 = 28 \leftarrow$ basic fact
$4 \times 70 = 280$
$4 \times 700 = 2,800$
$4 \times 7,000 = 28,000$

B **Basic fact with a zero**

$8 \times 5 = 40 \leftarrow$ basic fact
$8 \times 50 = 400$
$8 \times 500 = 4,000$
$8 \times 5,000 = 40,000$

Math Idea
As the number of zeros in a factor increases, the number of zeros in the product increases.

Guided Practice

1. What basic multiplication fact does this picture represent? Use it to find 7×30 and $7 \times 3,000$.

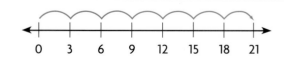

| 0 | 3 | 6 | 9 | 12 | 15 | 18 | 21 |

Use mental math to complete the pattern.

2. $4 \times 8 = 32$
$4 \times 80 = \blacksquare$
$4 \times 800 = \blacksquare$

3. $6 \times 2 = 12$
$6 \times 20 = \blacksquare$
$6 \times 200 = \blacksquare$

✓ **4.** $9 \times 6 = \blacksquare$
$9 \times 60 = \blacksquare$
$9 \times 600 = \blacksquare$

✓ **5.** $4 \times 5 = 20$
$4 \times \blacksquare = 200$
$4 \times 500 = \blacksquare$

6. **TALK Math** **Explain** how to use a basic fact and a pattern to find $9 \times 7,000$.

Independent Practice and Problem Solving

Use mental math to complete the pattern.

7. $3 \times 7 = 21$
$3 \times 70 = \blacksquare$
$3 \times 700 = \blacksquare$
$3 \times 7,000 = \blacksquare$

8. $10 \times 2 = \blacksquare$
$10 \times 20 = \blacksquare$
$10 \times 200 = \blacksquare$
$10 \times 2,000 = \blacksquare$

9. $3 \times 9 = 27$
$3 \times 90 = \blacksquare$
$3 \times \blacksquare = 2,700$
$3 \times 9,000 = \blacksquare$

10. $12 \times 5 = 60$
$12 \times \blacksquare = 600$
$12 \times 500 = \blacksquare$
$12 \times \blacksquare = 60,000$

Use patterns and mental math to find the product.

11. 9×700

12. $6 \times 8,000$

13. 7×700

14. $5 \times 9,000$

15. 5×40

16. 8×900

17. $9 \times 9,000$

18. $4 \times 3,000$

Algebra **Find the value of n.**

19. $9 \times 80 = n$

20. $5 \times n = 3,000$

21. $7 \times n = 56,000$

22. $n \times n = 100$

USE DATA For 23–24, use the table.

23. Make an input/output table to find the cost (c) to rent surfboards for different numbers of days (d). Write an equation to show a rule.

24. **WRITE Math** ▸ Gary rented snorkeling gear and swim fins for 2 weeks. Sue rented swim fins and a wetsuit for 9 days. Sue paid more than Gary. **Explain** why this happened.

Beach Rentals			
Item	Per Hour	Per Day	Per Week
Surfboard	$10	$20	$85
Skimboard	$5	$18	$60
Snorkeling Gear	$5	$18	$65
Swim Fins	$3	$8	$25
Wetsuit	$5	$15	$50

Mixed Review and Test Prep

25. Write 150,210 in word form. (p. 4)

26. A total of 88 students signed up to play soccer. Each team has 11 players. How many teams will there be? (p. 108)

27. **Test Prep** Which number is missing from this equation?
$$4 \times \blacksquare = 12,000$$
A 3
B 30
C 300
D 3,000

Extra Practice on page 262, Set A

MENTAL MATH

Estimate Products

OBJECTIVE: Estimate products by rounding factors or using compatible numbers and then finding the product mentally.

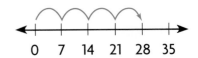
Learn

Sometimes you can solve a problem by finding an estimate.

PROBLEM An African elephant is the largest living land mammal. It uses its trunk to pick up objects that weigh up to 3 times as much as a 175-pound person. About how much weight can an African elephant pick up with its trunk?

ONE WAY Use rounding and mental math.

Estimate. 3 × 175

Step 1	Step 2
Round the greater factor to the nearest hundred. 3 × 175 ↓ 3 × 200	Use mental math. 3 × 2 = 6 ← basic fact 3 × 20 = 60 3 × 200 = 600

So, an African elephant can pick up about 600 pounds with its trunk.

ANOTHER WAY Use compatible numbers and mental math.

In one day, an African elephant eats 9 bags of food. Each bag weighs 57 pounds. How many pounds of food does the elephant eat?

Estimate. 9 × 57

Step 1	Step 2
Find compatible numbers. 9 × 57 ↓ 10 × 50	Use mental math. 10 × 5 = 50 ← basic fact 10 × 50 = 500

So, the African elephant eats about 500 pounds of food.

▲ An elephant can reach as high as 23 feet with its trunk.

More Examples Estimate the products.

A Compatible numbers	**B** Nearest thousand	**C** Nearest dollar
9 × 129 ↓ 10 × 130 = 1,300	5 × 7,441 ↓ 5 × 7,000 = 35,000	7 × $6.68 ↓ 7 × $7 = $49

• Describe how you could use a number line to estimate 4 × 52.

Guided Practice

Round the greater factor. Then use mental math to estimate the product.

1. 4×32 **2.** 7×98 **3.** 5×182 **4.** $3 \times \$4.15$ ✓**5.** 6×325

Estimate the product. Write the method.

6. 8×42 **7.** 2×67 **8.** 6×281 **9.** $9 \times 6{,}221$ ✓**10.** $7 \times \$7.59$

11. TALK Math Explain how you know whether an estimate of 560 is less than or greater than the exact product of 8 times 72.

Independent Practice and Problem Solving

Estimate the product. Write the method.

12. 4×37 **13.** 6×23 **14.** 5×630 **15.** $3 \times 1{,}914$

16. $4 \times \$9.78$ **17.** 9×38 **18.** 4×47 **19.** $9 \times \$8.81$

20. $\begin{array}{r} 89 \\ \times\ 3 \\ \hline \end{array}$ **21.** $\begin{array}{r} 709 \\ \times\ 4 \\ \hline \end{array}$ **22.** $\begin{array}{r} 2{,}509 \\ \times\ \ \ 7 \\ \hline \end{array}$ **23.** $\begin{array}{r} \$5.45 \\ \times\ \ \ 8 \\ \hline \end{array}$

USE DATA For 24–26, use the graph.

24. About how many more pounds of food do 5 monkeys eat in 6 weeks than 5 wallabies?

25. **Pose a Problem** Use the information in the graph to write a problem. Have a classmate solve the problem.

26. WRITE Math ▸ **What's the Error?** Tracy says that 8 lemurs eat about 160 pounds of food per week. Is she correct? **Explain.**

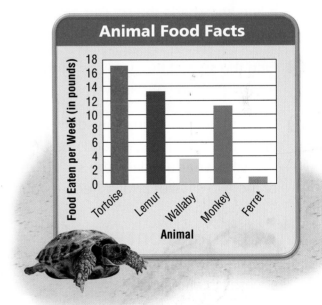

Animal Food Facts

Mixed Review and Test Prep

27. Which is less: $6 \times (2 \times 5)$ or $(9 \times 3) \times 7$?
(p. 122)

28. Find the median of 21, 23, 37, 15, 25, 24, 23, 32, and 31. (p. 186)

29. **Test Prep** Which number sentence would give the best estimate for 9×758?

A $9 \times 600 = \blacksquare$ **C** $9 \times 800 = \blacksquare$

B $9 \times 700 = \blacksquare$ **D** $9 \times 900 = \blacksquare$

Model 2-Digit by 1-Digit Multiplication

OBJECTIVE: Model multiplication by using arrays.

Quick Review

Estimate the product.

1. 3×81 2. 2×109
3. 9×79 4. 5×55
5. $7 \times 2,390$

Vocabulary

partial product

Investigate

Materials ■ centimeter grid paper ■ base-ten blocks

You can break apart numbers to make them easier to multiply.

A Draw a rectangular array on grid paper to find 6×18.

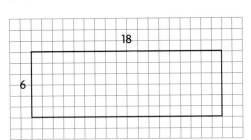

B Use the break-apart strategy to make two smaller arrays for products you know. Draw a line and shade the smaller arrays. Use two different colors.

C Find the sum of the products of the two smaller arrays. Record your answer.

D Draw the array again. Now, draw a line to break apart the array into tens and ones. Shade the two smaller arrays. Find the sum of the products of the two smaller arrays. Record your answer.

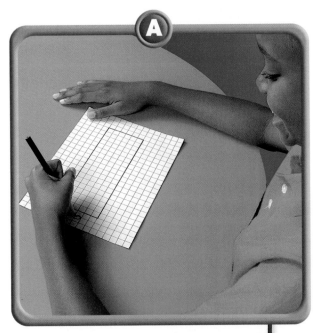

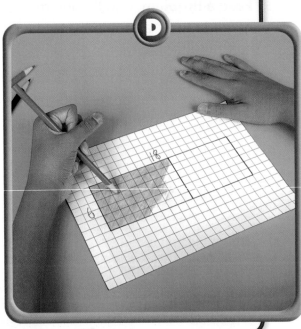

Draw Conclusions

1. Explain how you found the total number of squares in each array.

2. Compare your product with those of other classmates. What can you conclude? Explain.

3. **Evaluation** Which do you think is easier to find, the sum of 7×20 and 7×3 or the sum of 7×15 and 7×8? Explain.

Connect

You can solve the same problem by using base-ten blocks to show tens and ones.

Step 1	Step 2	Step 3
Make a model to find 6 × 18. Use tens and ones.	Break the model into tens and ones.	Add the tens and the ones to find the product.
6 rows of 1 ten 8 ones	(6 × 1 ten) (6 × 8 ones) (6 × 10) (6 × 8) 60 48	(6 × 10) + (6 × 8) 60 + 48 108

So, 6 × 18 = 108.

In Step 2, the model was broken into two parts. Each part shows a **partial product**. The partial products are 60 and 48.

TALK Math

How does breaking apart the model into tens and ones make finding the product easier?

Practice

Find the product.

1.

6 × 13 = ■

2.

5 × 18 = ■

✓3.

4 × 16 = ■

Use grid paper or base-ten blocks to model the product. Record your answer.

4. 2 × 21   **5.** 3 × 17   **6.** 7 × 15   **✓7.** 9 × 14

8. 4 × 19   **9.** 2 × 16   **10.** 9 × 19   **11.** 5 × 22

12. 7 × 13   **13.** 9 × 21   **14.** 6 × 23   **15.** 8 × 24

16. **WRITE Math ▸ Explain** how modeling partial products can be used to find the products of greater numbers.

Record 2-Digit by 1-Digit Multiplication

OBJECTIVE: Find products using partial products, place value, and regrouping.

Quick Review

Jim drew the model shown. Write a multiplication sentence the model represents.

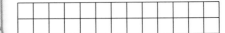

Learn

PROBLEM A roadrunner would rather run than fly. It can easily outrun a human. It can zip across the desert at speeds up to 22 feet per second. How far can a roadrunner run in 6 seconds?

ONE WAY Use partial products.

Multiply. 6×22 **Estimate.** $6 \times 20 = 120$

MODEL	THINK	RECORD
Step 1 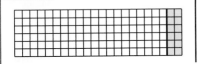	Multiply the ones.	$\begin{array}{r} 22 \\ \times\ 6 \\ \hline 12 \end{array}$ ← 6×2 ones = 12 ones
Step 2 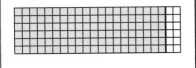	Multiply the tens.	$\begin{array}{r} 22 \\ \times\ 6 \\ \hline 12 \\ 120 \end{array}$ ← 6×2 tens = 12 tens
Step 3 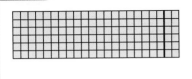	Add the partial products.	$\begin{array}{r} 22 \\ \times\ 6 \\ \hline 12 \\ +120 \\ \hline 132 \end{array}$

So, the roadrunner can run 132 feet in 6 seconds. Since 132 is close to the estimate of 120, it is reasonable.

Math Idea
You can use an estimate to see whether your answer is reasonable.

• **What if** a roadrunner ran 21 feet per second for 6 seconds? Would its total distance be greater than or less than 132 feet? Explain your reasoning.

ANOTHER WAY Use place value and regrouping.

Example 1 Use place value without regrouping.

How far can a roadrunner run in 3 seconds?

Multiply. 3×22 **Estimate.** $3 \times 20 = 60$

The multiplication sentence $3 \times 22 = 66$ can be expressed in different ways.

3 groups of 22 equal 66.

The product of 3 and 22 is 66.

3 times 22 equals 66.

MODEL	THINK	RECORD
Step 1	Multiply the ones. 3×2 ones = 6 ones	$\begin{array}{r} 22 \\ \times\ 3 \\ \hline 6 \end{array}$
Step 2	Multiply the tens. 3×2 tens = 6 tens	$\begin{array}{r} 22 \\ \times\ 3 \\ \hline 66 \end{array}$

So, a roadrunner can run 66 feet in 3 seconds. Since 66 is close to the estimate of 60, it is reasonable.

Example 2 Use place value and regrouping.

How far can a roadrunner run in 8 seconds?

Multiply. 8×22 **Estimate.** $8 \times 20 = 160$

MODEL	THINK	RECORD
Step 1	Multiply the ones. 8×2 ones = 16 ones. Regroup the 16 ones.	$\begin{array}{r} 1 \\ 22 \\ \times\ 8 \\ \hline 6 \end{array}$ Regroup 16 ones as 1 ten 6 ones.
Step 2	Multiply the tens. 8×2 tens = 16 tens. Add the regrouped ten. 16 tens + 1 ten = 17 tens. Regroup the 17 tens.	$\begin{array}{r} 1 \\ 22 \\ \times\ 8 \\ \hline 176 \end{array}$ Regroup 17 tens as 1 hundred 7 tens.

So, a roadrunner can run 176 feet in 8 seconds. Since 176 is close to the estimate of 160, it is reasonable.

Guided Practice

1. Make the model shown. Then use your model to find and record the product.

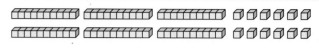

2×36

Estimate. Then record the product.

2.	3.	4.	5.	6.
42	32	$63	81	57
× 4	× 2	× 7	× 5	× 4

7. **TALK Math** **Explain** how to record your work to find 4×52.

Independent Practice and Problem Solving

Estimate. Then record the product.

8.	9.	10.	11.	12.
33	25¢	36	29	$94
× 2	× 3	× 8	× 6	× 5

Write each partial product. Then record the product.

13. 8×17 14. 6×42 15. 9×53 16. 3×67 17. 9×96

18. $2 \times 41¢$ 19. 9×62 20. 5×84 21. 7×49 22. 4×73

★ **Algebra** Write a rule. Find the missing numbers.

23.
Number of Pounds, p	2	3	4	5	6
Number of Ounces, o	32	48	64	■	■

24.
Number of Feet, f	1	2	3	4	5
Number of Inches, i	12	24	■	48	■

USE DATA For 25–27 use the table.

25. At the speeds shown, how much farther could a black-tailed jackrabbit run than a desert cottontail in 7 seconds?

26. A desert cottontail can run 88 feet in 4 seconds. How far can a black-tailed jackrabbit run in the same amount of time?

27. **≡FAST FACT** A black-tailed jackrabbit hops 5 to 10 feet at a time. It can reach speeds of 44 to 51 feet per second. How far can it hop in 5 seconds?

29. At the pet store, Mr. Wright bought 2 large bags of dry food at $15 each and 3 cases of canned dog food at $21 each. How much did Mr. Wright spend?

Animal Running Speeds	
Animal	**Speed (feet per second)**
Black-tailed Jackrabbit	51
Desert Cottontail	22

28. **Reasoning** The sum of two numbers is 31. The product of the two numbers is 150. What are the numbers?

30. **WRITE Math** 6×87 is more than 5×87. How much more? **Explain** how you know without multiplying.

Technology
Use Harcourt Mega Math, The Number Games, *Up, Up, and Array,* Level J.

Extra Practice on page 262, Set C

Learn About) MENTAL MATH
Multiplication

Using mental math can make multiplication easier.

Isabelle's Ice Cream Shop sells milkshakes. If it sells 79 milkshakes a week for 5 weeks, how many milk shakes will it sell in all?

Multiply. 5×79

Here are two ways to break apart numbers to make them easier to multiply.

ONE WAY Use addition.

Think: 79 is 70 plus 9.

$$5 \times 79 = 5 \times (70 + 9)$$
$$= (5 \times 70) + (5 \times 9)$$
$$= 350 + 45$$
$$= 395$$

ANOTHER WAY Use subtraction.

Think: 79 is 1 less than 80.

$$5 \times 79 = 5 \times (80 - 1)$$
$$= (5 \times 80) - (5 \times 1)$$
$$= 400 - 5$$
$$= 395$$

So, Isabelle's Ice Cream Shop will sell 395 milkshakes.

Try It

Use mental math to find the product.

31. 4×49 **32.** 5×24 **33.** 4×68 **34.** 8×45 **35.** 6×76

36. 5×99 **37.** 2×75 **38.** 6×29 **39.** 9×18 **40.** 3×39

41. 8×74 **42.** 6×36 **43.** 3×27 **44.** 4×73 **45.** 5×81

Mixed Review and Test Prep

46. A soccer tournament started at 10:30 A.M. and ended at 3:10 P.M. How long did the tournament last? (p. 154)

47. **Test Prep** Mr. Kara bought a book for $25 and 3 toys for $13 each. How much change did he get back from a $100 bill?

  A $26

  B $36

  C $46

  D $56

48. A room had 18 computers. Three were added, and then 6 were removed. Write an expression to show this situation. (p. 66)

49. **Test Prep** If the pattern in the number sentences below continues, could 65 be one of the products in this pattern? **Explain.**

$$2 \times 2 = 4$$
$$2 \times 2 \times 2 = 8$$
$$2 \times 2 \times 2 \times 2 = 16$$

5 Multiply 3-Digit and 4-Digit Numbers and Money

OBJECTIVE: Multiply 3-digit and 4-digit numbers and money by 1-digit numbers.

Learn

PROBLEM In 2005, an average of 615 visitors a week to Boston's National Historical Park participated in the Freedom Trail Tour, a tour highlighting historic sites. What is the average participation in this tour each month?

Example Multiply. 4×615 Estimate. $4 \times 600 = 2,400$

THINK | RECORD

Step 1

Multiply the ones. 4×5 ones $= 20$ ones
Regroup the 20 ones.

$$\begin{array}{r} \overset{2}{61}5 \\ \times\ \ 4 \\ \hline 0 \end{array}$$

Regroup 20 ones as 2 tens 0 ones.

Step 2

Multiply the tens. 4×1 ten $= 4$ tens
Add the regrouped tens.
4 tens $+$ 2 tens $=$ 6 tens

$$\begin{array}{r} \overset{2}{61}5 \\ \times\ \ 4 \\ \hline 60 \end{array}$$

Step 3

Multiply the hundreds.
4×6 hundreds $= 24$ hundreds

$$\begin{array}{r} \overset{2}{61}5 \\ \times\ \ 4 \\ \hline 2,460 \end{array}$$

Regroup 24 hundreds as 2 thousands 4 hundreds.

So, an average of 2,460 people participated in the tour each month. Since 2,460 is close to the estimate of 2,400, it is reasonable.

More Examples

A No regrouping

$$\begin{array}{r} 234 \\ \times\ \ 2 \\ \hline 468 \end{array}$$

B Regrouping

$$\begin{array}{r} \overset{4\,7}{359} \\ \times\ \ \ 8 \\ \hline 2,872 \end{array}$$

• In Example B, why does the product have four digits?

▲ The 3-mile-long tour highlights 16 sites, including the Old South Meeting House in historic Boston, Massachusetts.

Multiply 4-Digit Numbers and Money

Lily's family spent the day shopping at Faneuil Hall Marketplace in Boston. A shoe store in the marketplace sells an average of $3,345 worth of shoes each day. About how much will the shoe store sell in one week?

Example 2

Multiply. $7 \times \$3,345$ **Estimate.** $7 \times \$3,300 = \$23,100$

Step 1	Step 2	Step 3	Step 4
Multiply the ones.	Multiply the tens.	Multiply the hundreds.	Multiply the thousands.
$$\begin{array}{r} \overset{3}{\$3,345} \\ \times\ \ \ \ \ 7 \\ \hline 5 \end{array}$$	$$\begin{array}{r} \overset{33}{\$3,345} \\ \times\ \ \ \ \ 7 \\ \hline 15 \end{array}$$	$$\begin{array}{r} \overset{233}{\$3,345} \\ \times\ \ \ \ \ 7 \\ \hline 415 \end{array}$$	$$\begin{array}{r} \overset{233}{\$3,345} \\ \times\ \ \ \ \ 7 \\ \hline \$23,415 \end{array}$$

So, the shoe store will sell about $23,415 worth of shoes in one week.
Since $23,415 is close to the estimate of $23,100, it is reasonable.

More Examples

A Multiply dollars and cents.

$$\begin{array}{r} \$85.76 \\ \times\ \ \ \ 9 \\ \hline \end{array} \qquad \begin{array}{r} \overset{565}{8576} \\ \times\ \ \ \ 9 \\ \hline 77184 \end{array}$$

Multiply the same way you multiply whole numbers.

$$\begin{array}{r} \$85.76 \\ \times\ \ \ \ 9 \\ \hline \$771.84 \end{array}$$

Write the product in dollars and cents.

B Use a calculator.

$4 \times 9,823$ 4 ✕ 9 8 2 3 ▭   = 39'292.

Estimate to check. $4 \times 10,000 = 40,000$

Guided Practice

1. Copy each step of the problem at the right. Then tell what is happening in each step.

Step 1 $$\begin{array}{r} \overset{2}{274} \\ \times\ \ \ 6 \\ \hline 4 \end{array}$$ Step 2 $$\begin{array}{r} \overset{42}{274} \\ \times\ \ \ 6 \\ \hline 44 \end{array}$$ Step 3 $$\begin{array}{r} \overset{42}{274} \\ \times\ \ \ 6 \\ \hline 1,644 \end{array}$$

Estimate. Then find the product.

2. $$\begin{array}{r} 124 \\ \times\ \ 2 \\ \hline \end{array}$$

3. $$\begin{array}{r} 183 \\ \times\ \ 4 \\ \hline \end{array}$$

4. $$\begin{array}{r} 1,235 \\ \times\ \ \ \ 7 \\ \hline \end{array}$$

5. $$\begin{array}{r} \$2,853 \\ \times\ \ \ \ \ 6 \\ \hline \end{array}$$

✓6. $$\begin{array}{r} \$13.24 \\ \times\ \ \ \ \ 7 \\ \hline \end{array}$$

7. **TALK Math** Explain how many digits the product $4 \times 1,861$ will have.

Estimate. Then find the product.

8. 243 × 2	9. 714 × 1	10. 3,316 × 8	11. $2,519 × 7	12. $41.23 × 6

13. 6,214 × 4	14. 587 × 2	15. 1,368 × 9	16. 422 × 7	17. $17.57 × 5

18. 3 × 825   19. 5 × $24.81   20. 4 × $183   21. 8 × $91.42   22. 9 × 3,286

✦Algebra **Find the missing digits.**

23. 2■3 × ■ ——— ■86	24. ■3■ × 9 ——— 5,688	25. ■62 × 2 ——— 1,124	26. ■,4■8 × 2 ——— 6,■5■	27. 1,9■■ × 4 ——— ■,■72

Compare. Write <, >, or = for each ●.

28. 4 × 326 ● 3 × 467   29. 8 × $1.99 ● 5 × $3.21   30. 2 × 3,750 ● 3 × 2,500

31. 5 × $1,192 ● 4 × $2,315   32. 7 × 8,267 ● 5 × 9,834   33. 4 × 3,956 ● 2 × 7,962

Solve.

34. Emily bought 3 shirts for $11.99 each as souvenirs. She paid with a $50 bill. How much change did she receive?

35. **Reasoning** Can two different multiplication problems have the same estimated product? **Explain** your thinking.

36. How could you find 4 × 2,617 if the 4 button on your calculator is broken?

37. What number is 150 more than 5 times 489?

38. Tyrone bought 2 books that each cost $8.95 on his class field trip to the Charlestown Navy Yard. How much did he spend?

39. **WRITE Math** ▸ **Sense or Nonsense** Joe says the greatest possible 3-digit by 1-digit product is 111. Does Joe's statement make sense? **Explain.**

Mixed Review and Test Prep

40. What is 1,000 more than 42,921? (p. 48)

41. Rachel baked 3 batches of 36 cookies. How many cookies did she bake in all?
(p. 250)

42. **Test Prep** A music store sold 2,423 CDs in one month. If the CDs were on sale for $9 each, what were the total sales for the month? **Show** how you got your answer.

Use Graphic Aids

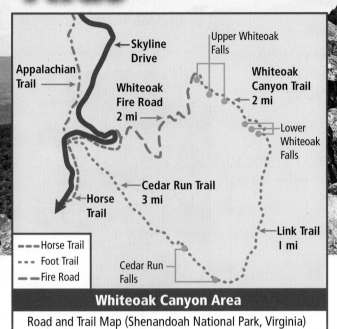

Whiteoak Canyon Area

Road and Trail Map (Shenandoah National Park, Virginia)

◀ Shenandoah National Park has over 500 miles of hiking trails, including 101 miles of the Appalachian Trail. There are also trails for horseback riding and bicycling.

Shenandoah National Park offers a variety of activities for active families. Daily exercise helps you think better, sleep better, and maintain a healthy weight. The table shows the number of calories a 75-pound person might burn in one hour.

Calories Burned Per Hour	
Activity	**Number of Calories**
Bicycling	288
Hiking	212
Horseback Riding	86
Rock Climbing	374

Problem Solving Use the graphic aids. Use the information to solve the problems.

1. Jason went horseback riding for 2 hours and went rock climbing for 3 hours. About how many calories did he burn?

2. Which activity burns more than 4 times as many calories as horseback riding?

3. On a camping trip, Jason and his parents hiked the Whiteoak Fire Road and the Cedar Run, Link, and Whiteoak Canyon trails each day for 4 days. How many miles did they hike in all?

4. **WRITE Math** ▸ Jason wants to compare the heights of waterfalls in the Whiteoak Canyon area. Which graphic aid would you use to show the heights: a table, a picture, a bar graph, or a map? **Explain** your answer.

Multiply with Zeros

OBJECTIVE: Multiply numbers with zeros by 1–digit numbers.

Learn

PROBLEM Carl has gone on the same trip for the last 5 years. The round-trip distance is 1,082 miles. What is the total number of miles his family has driven on this trip in the last 5 years?

Boston, MA
Hartford, CT
New York, NY
Hopedale, OH

Example

Multiply. 5 × 1,082   **Estimate.** 5 × 1,000 = 5,000

Step 1

Multiply the ones.
Regroup the ones.

$$\begin{array}{r} 1 \\ 1{,}082 \\ \times \quad 5 \\ \hline 0 \end{array}$$

Regroup 10 ones as 1 ten 0 ones.

Step 2

Multiply the tens.
Add the regrouped tens.
Regroup the tens.

$$\begin{array}{r} 41 \\ 1{,}082 \\ \times \quad 5 \\ \hline 10 \end{array}$$

Regroup 41 tens as 4 hundreds 1 ten.

Step 3

Multiply the hundreds.
Add the regrouped hundreds.

$$\begin{array}{r} 41 \\ 1{,}082 \\ \times \quad 5 \\ \hline 410 \end{array}$$

5 × 0 hundreds = 0 hundreds
0 hundreds + 4 hundreds =
4 hundreds

Step 4

Multiply the thousands.

$$\begin{array}{r} 41 \\ 1{,}082 \\ \times \quad 5 \\ \hline 5{,}410 \end{array}$$

ERROR ALERT

In Step 3, the 4 hundreds above the 0 hundreds have to be added after multiplying 5 by 0 hundreds.

So, Carl has driven 5,410 miles. Since 5,410 is close to the estimate of 5,000, it is reasonable.

More Examples

A Multiply a 4-digit number.

$$\begin{array}{r} 5 \\ 5{,}009 \\ \times \quad 6 \\ \hline 30{,}054 \end{array}$$

B Multiply dollars and cents.

$$\begin{array}{r} \$98.20 \\ \times \quad 4 \end{array} \rightarrow \begin{array}{r} 3 \\ 9820 \\ \times \quad 4 \\ \hline 39280 \end{array}$$ Multiply the same way you multiply whole numbers. $\rightarrow$ $$\begin{array}{r} \$98.20 \\ \times \quad 4 \\ \hline \$392.80 \end{array}$$ Write the product in dollars and cents.

1. Copy the problem at the right. Multiply the ones, then regroup. Multiply the tens, then regroup. Multiply the hundreds. Do you have to regroup? Then multiply the thousands. What is the product?

$$\begin{array}{r} 1{,}032 \\ \times \quad 6 \\ \hline \end{array}$$

Estimate. Then find the product.

2. $\begin{array}{r} 1{,}304 \\ \times \quad 3 \\ \hline \end{array}$

3. $\begin{array}{r} 4{,}002 \\ \times \quad 4 \\ \hline \end{array}$

4. $\begin{array}{r} \$53.50 \\ \times \quad 6 \\ \hline \end{array}$

✓5. $\begin{array}{r} \$10.20 \\ \times \quad 7 \\ \hline \end{array}$

✓6. $\begin{array}{r} \$4{,}046 \\ \times \quad 2 \\ \hline \end{array}$

7. **TALK Math** Explain how you can find $6 \times 2{,}430$.

Independent Practice and Problem Solving

Estimate. Then find the product.

8. $\begin{array}{r} 1{,}603 \\ \times \quad 3 \\ \hline \end{array}$

9. $\begin{array}{r} 2{,}019 \\ \times \quad 7 \\ \hline \end{array}$

10. $\begin{array}{r} \$50.06 \\ \times \quad 2 \\ \hline \end{array}$

11. $\begin{array}{r} 8{,}505 \\ \times \quad 4 \\ \hline \end{array}$

12. $\begin{array}{r} \$40.20 \\ \times \quad 6 \\ \hline \end{array}$

13. $1 \times 7{,}014$

14. $5 \times \$90.02$

15. $4 \times 2{,}806$

16. $3 \times 5{,}050$

17. $8 \times 8{,}109$

USE DATA For 18–19, use the picture.

18. Carl took the elevator from the lobby to the 86th floor and back 3 times. What is the total number of feet he traveled?

19. **≡FAST FACT** The Empire State Building is 1,454 feet tall. A builder wants to build a skyscraper that is 100 feet less than twice as tall as the Empire State Building. What will be the height of the skyscraper?

20. **WRITE Math** ▸ **What's the Question?** Don, Kay, and Jane each have 3 rolls of film. They can take 24 pictures with each roll. The answer is 216 pictures.

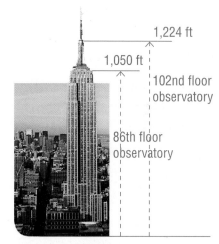

Empire State Building's
Height from Lobby

Mixed Review and Test Prep

21. Greg tosses a coin 5 times and gets tails each time. What is the probability of getting tails if he tosses again? (Grade 3)

22. Kim buys 4 packs of paper. Each pack has 512 sheets. About how many sheets does she buy in all? (p. 254)

23. **Test Prep** Liz bought 2 pairs of shoes for $48.05 each. How much did she spend?

A $96.30   C $95.30

B $96.10   D $95.10

Problem Solving Workshop
Skill: Evaluate Reasonableness

OBJECTIVE: Solve problems by using the skill *evaluate reasonableness*.

Use the Skill

PROBLEM The average person eats 160 bowls of cereal a year. How many bowls of cereal does a family of 4 eat in a year?

Start by choosing an operation. To find the answer to this question, you must multiply.

> You can use basic facts to find compatible numbers to estimate 4 × 160.
>
> **Think:** It is easy to multiply 4 × 120 and 4 × 200.
>
> 4 × 120 = 480   4 × 200 = 800

So, the answer is between 480 and 800.

> Find 4 × 160.
>
> $$\begin{array}{r} \overset{2}{1}60 \\ \times\ \ \ 4 \\ \hline 640 \end{array}$$
>
> Now decide whether your answer is reasonable.
>
> Since 640 is between 480 and 800, it is a reasonable answer.

So, a family of 4 eats 640 bowls of cereal a year.

- What other way could you check to see whether your answer is reasonable and makes sense?

TALK Math

How can you use estimation to evaluate the reasonableness of answers to 3-digit by 1-digit multiplication problems?

Think and Discuss

Solve the problem. Then evaluate the reasonableness of your answer. Explain.

a. Mark has 647 baseball cards. He sells 40 of them at a garage sale and gives 15 of them to a friend. How many cards does Mark have left?

b. Judi has 9 boxes of balloons. Each box has 125 balloons. How many balloons does Judi have in all?

c. Morgan's Greenhouse has plants arranged in 7 rows with 110 plants in each row. How many plants are there?

Solve the problem. Then evaluate the reasonableness of your answer.

1. More than 294 million people in the United States start the day with a bowl of cereal. How many bowls of cereal are eaten in the United States each week?

   First, decide which operation to use.

   Think: 7×294

   Next, solve the problem.

   Then, decide whether your answer is reasonable.

2. **What if** you were asked how many bowls of cereal people in the United States eat in 2 weeks? Would an answer of 6,174 million bowls be reasonable? Why or why not?

3. The Franklins have a breakfast budget. Each week, they spend $5 for cereal, $7 for bacon, $4 for bread, $2 for eggs, and $3 for juice. How much will they spend on breakfast in 4 weeks?

Mixed Applications

4. Each month, the Franklins record the total amount spent on breakfast. After 3 months, they've spent $252. Use this information to make a bar graph showing each monthly total for 6 months. **Explain** why your graph is reasonable.

5. Paul's father is a salesman. He drove 1,235 miles the second week, 987 miles the third week, and 845 miles the fourth week. During the four-week period, he drove a total of 3,742 miles. How far did he drive the first week?

6. Matt wants to fence a square corner of the yard for his dog. One side of the square is 41 feet long. How much fencing does Matt need?

7. The average high temperature in a Mojave Desert town is 108°F. The average low is 33°F. How many degrees warmer is the high temperature than the low temperature?

8. **WRITE Math** A group of 6 students each gave equal amounts to purchase a gift. The change from the purchase was $12. How much change should each student receive? **Explain**.

▲ The world's tallest thermometer is in Baker, California. Its height of 134 feet represents the highest temperature recorded (134°F) in that part of the Mojave Desert.

Extra Practice

Set A   Use mental math to complete the pattern. (pp. 244–245)

1. $6 \times 4 = 24$
$6 \times 40 = \blacksquare$
$6 \times 400 = \blacksquare$
$6 \times 4,000 = \blacksquare$

2. $5 \times 8 = \blacksquare$
$5 \times 80 = \blacksquare$
$5 \times 800 = \blacksquare$
$5 \times 8,000 = \blacksquare$

3. $9 \times 9 = 81$
$9 \times \blacksquare = 810$
$9 \times 900 = \blacksquare$
$9 \times \blacksquare = 81,000$

4. $7 \times \blacksquare = 42$
$7 \times 60 = \blacksquare$
$7 \times \blacksquare = 4,200$
$7 \times 6,000 = \blacksquare$

Set B   Estimate the product. Write the method. (pp. 246–247)

1. 3×56

2. $8 \times \$21$

3. 2×865

4. $5 \times \$6.89$

5. $7 \times 4,133$

6.
$$\begin{array}{r} \$59 \\ \times \ \ 4 \\ \hline \end{array}$$

7.
$$\begin{array}{r} 82 \\ \times \ \ 9 \\ \hline \end{array}$$

8.
$$\begin{array}{r} 876 \\ \times \ \ \ 8 \\ \hline \end{array}$$

9.
$$\begin{array}{r} \$5,236 \\ \times \ \ \ \ \ \ 6 \\ \hline \end{array}$$

10.
$$\begin{array}{r} 3,462 \\ \times \ \ \ \ \ 5 \\ \hline \end{array}$$

Set C   Estimate. Then record the product. (pp. 250–253)

1.
$$\begin{array}{r} 23 \\ \times \ \ 3 \\ \hline \end{array}$$

2.
$$\begin{array}{r} 91 \\ \times \ \ 3 \\ \hline \end{array}$$

3.
$$\begin{array}{r} 26 \\ \times \ \ 4 \\ \hline \end{array}$$

4.
$$\begin{array}{r} \$42 \\ \times \ \ 2 \\ \hline \end{array}$$

5.
$$\begin{array}{r} 83 \\ \times \ \ 9 \\ \hline \end{array}$$

6. $5 \times 17¢$

7. 2×31

8. $8 \times \$92$

9. $4 \times \$18$

10. 6×33

11. There are 9 floors in a building. Each floor on one side has 27 windows. How many windows are on that side of the building?

12. Mrs. Gomez drives a total of 74 miles each day to and from work. How many miles does she drive in 5 days?

Set D   Estimate. Then find the product. (pp. 254–257)

1.
$$\begin{array}{r} 232 \\ \times \ \ \ 3 \\ \hline \end{array}$$

2.
$$\begin{array}{r} 436 \\ \times \ \ \ 6 \\ \hline \end{array}$$

3.
$$\begin{array}{r} \$6.14 \\ \times \ \ \ \ \ 9 \\ \hline \end{array}$$

4.
$$\begin{array}{r} 5,857 \\ \times \ \ \ \ \ 2 \\ \hline \end{array}$$

5.
$$\begin{array}{r} \$3,746 \\ \times \ \ \ \ \ \ \ 7 \\ \hline \end{array}$$

6. $6 \times \$427$

7. $3 \times \$9.76$

8. $5 \times 7,794$

9. $8 \times 1,866$

10. $4 \times \$5,689$

Set E   Estimate. Then find the product. (pp. 258–259)

1.
$$\begin{array}{r} 6,036 \\ \times \ \ \ \ \ 7 \\ \hline \end{array}$$

2.
$$\begin{array}{r} 3,700 \\ \times \ \ \ \ \ 4 \\ \hline \end{array}$$

3.
$$\begin{array}{r} \$9,006 \\ \times \ \ \ \ \ \ 5 \\ \hline \end{array}$$

4.
$$\begin{array}{r} 3,408 \\ \times \ \ \ \ \ 9 \\ \hline \end{array}$$

5.
$$\begin{array}{r} \$40.06 \\ \times \ \ \ \ \ \ \ 3 \\ \hline \end{array}$$

6. $4 \times \$60.56$

7. $8 \times 5,007$

8. $9 \times 3,080$

9. $6 \times 4,500$

10. $7 \times \$6,078$

11. Julie bought 6 cans of paint for $10.25 each. How much did she pay for the paint?

12. Calvin is buying 3 boxes of blank CDs for $12.09 each. How much will he pay for the CDs?

CD ROM

Technology
Use Harcourt Mega Math, The Number Games, *Up, Up, and Array*, Level J

TECHNOLOGY ✦ CONNECTION

*i*Tools: Base-Ten Blocks

Juan can ride his bicycle at a rate of 16 miles per hour on flat roads.
How far could he ride at that same rate in 5 hours?

Step 1	Click on *Base-Ten Blocks*. Then select *Multiply* from the *Activities* menu.

Step 2	Click on the tens block. Then click 1 time in the workspace. Next, click the ones block and click 6 times in the workspace. If you make a mistake, click on the eraser. Notice that 1×16 appears at the bottom of the workspace.	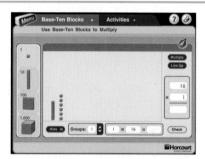
Step 3	Next, move your cursor to *Groups*, and click the up arrow until 5 appears. Each click adds a group of 16 blocks. Now the expression reads 5×16, and the workspace shows 5 groups of 16.	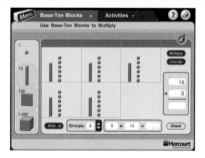

Step 4	Click on *Multiply*. Then click on *Regroup* until there are no more blocks to regroup.
Step 5	Type the answer. Then click on *Check* to verify your answer.

So, Juan could ride 80 miles in 5 hours.
Click on the broom to clear the workspace.

Try It

Follow the same steps to multiply.

1. $\begin{array}{r} 34 \\ \times\ 2 \\ \hline \end{array}$
2. 9×21
3. $\begin{array}{r} 88 \\ \times\ 3 \\ \hline \end{array}$
4. 4×56
5. $\begin{array}{r} 47 \\ \times\ 6 \\ \hline \end{array}$

6. **Explore More   Explain** how the *Base-Ten Blocks* activity above shows the relationship between multiplication and addition.

 Technology
*i*Tools are available online or on CD-ROM.

Distributive Property

Run for Fun

Each student in the Running Club plans to run for 35 minutes, 5 days a week. How many total minutes will each student run per week?

You can use mental math and the Distributive Property of Multiplication to find the product. The property states that multiplying a sum by a number is the same as multiplying each addend by the number and then adding the products.

Find 5×35.

$5 \times 35 = 5 \times (30 + 5)$ Think: $35 = 30 + 5$
$ = (5 \times 30) + (5 \times 5)$ Use the Distributive Property.
$ = 150 + 25$
$ = 175$

So, each student will run a total of 175 minutes per week.

Examples

A **Find 7×94.**

Think: $94 = 90 + 4$

$7 \times 94 = 7 \times (90 + 4)$
$ = (7 \times 90) + (7 \times 4)$
$ = 630 + 28$
$ = 658$

B **Find 3×132.**

Think: $132 = 100 + 30 + 2$

$3 \times 132 = 3 \times (100 + 30 + 2)$
$ = (3 \times 100) + (3 \times 30) + (3 \times 2)$
$ = 300 + 90 + 6$
$ = 396$

Try It

Use mental math and the Distributive Property to find the product.

1. 6×31 **2.** 4×92 **3.** 3×124 **4.** 5×318

5. 4×212 **6.** 5×240 **7.** $8 \times 2,005$ **8.** $6 \times 4,052$

9. Monica has dance class twice a week. Each class is 55 minutes long. How many minutes does Monica spend in class each week?

10. The Swim Club has 117 members. Each day, every member swims 4 laps to warm up. How many warm-up laps does the club swim each day?

11. 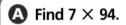 **WRITE Math** ▸ **Explain** why using the Distributive Property makes finding a product easier.

Chapter 9 Review/Test

Check Vocabulary and Concepts

Choose the best term from the box.

1. To find the product of a 2-digit number and a 1-digit number, you can multiply the ones, multiply the tens, and then add the __?__ together. (p. 248)

2. You can __?__ to find a number that is close to the exact amount. (p. 246)

Check Skills

Use mental math to complete the pattern. (pp. 244–245)

3. $2 \times 4 = 8$
   $2 \times 40 = \blacksquare$
   $2 \times 400 = \blacksquare$
   $2 \times 4,000 = \blacksquare$

4. $3 \times 6 = \blacksquare$
   $3 \times \blacksquare = 180$
   $3 \times 600 = \blacksquare$
   $3 \times \blacksquare = 18,000$

5. $10 \times 7 = \blacksquare$
   $10 \times 70 = \blacksquare$
   $10 \times \blacksquare = 7,000$
   $10 \times 7,000 = \blacksquare$

6. $8 \times 9 = \blacksquare$
   $8 \times \blacksquare = 720$
   $8 \times 900 = \blacksquare$
   $8 \times 9,000 = \blacksquare$

Estimate the product. Write the method. (pp. 246–247)

7. 8×26

8. 9×539

9. $4 \times 1,561$

10. $6 \times \$7.22$

11. $7 \times \$6.54$

12. 5×324

13. 8×476

14. $3 \times 2,799$

15. 4×721

16. 9×562

Estimate. Then find the product. (pp. 250–253, 254–257, 258–259)

17. $\begin{array}{r} 43 \\ \times\ 6 \\ \hline \end{array}$

18. $\begin{array}{r} 199 \\ \times\ 7 \\ \hline \end{array}$

19. $\begin{array}{r} 2,004 \\ \times\ 9 \\ \hline \end{array}$

20. $\begin{array}{r} 5,286 \\ \times\ 4 \\ \hline \end{array}$

21. $\begin{array}{r} \$8.40 \\ \times\ 7 \\ \hline \end{array}$

22. $\begin{array}{r} 56 \\ \times\ 3 \\ \hline \end{array}$

23. $\begin{array}{r} \$802 \\ \times\ 6 \\ \hline \end{array}$

24. $\begin{array}{r} 93 \\ \times\ 7 \\ \hline \end{array}$

25. $\begin{array}{r} \$24.04 \\ \times\ 8 \\ \hline \end{array}$

26. $\begin{array}{r} 96 \\ \times\ 4 \\ \hline \end{array}$

27. 4×84

28. 8×207

29. $9 \times \$638$

30. $4 \times \$5.65$

31. 6×38

Check Problem Solving

Solve. (pp. 260–261)

32. Jamie makes bead necklaces. She bought 6 bags of beads with 175 beads in each bag. Is it reasonable to say that Jamie bought about 1,000 beads? Why or why not?

33. **WRITE Math** Alex has a recipe for 3 dozen cookies. If he triples the recipe, he says he will have enough cookies for 100 people. **Explain** how Alex knows that his answer is reasonable.

Standardized Test Prep
Chapters 1–9

Number and Operations

1. In 2003, there were 45,033 beagles and 52,530 golden retrievers registered with the American Kennel Club. How many more golden retrievers were registered than beagles? (p. 54)

   A 7,497

   B 7,507

   C 17,507

   D 97,563

Test Tip **Eliminate choices.**

See Item 2. You can eliminate choices that do not have the digit 6 in the tens place. Then start at the left, and compare the digits in each place-value position until the digits differ.

2. Maggie drew the five cards with the numbers shown below.

       6 8 2 4 0

   If she uses each card only once, what is the greatest number possible with the digit 6 in the tens place? (p. 4)

   A 48,620

   B 82,460

   C 84,260

   D 86,420

3. **WRITE Math** ▶ **Explain** how to round 9,327 to the nearest thousand. (p. 34)

Algebraic Reasoning

4. The table below shows the cost of hot dogs at Hot Dog Haven.

Hot Dog Prices				
Number of Hot Dogs	1	2	3	4
Price	$2	$4	$6	$8

   Which expression shows how to find the cost of 14 hot dogs? (p. 66)

   A $14 - 2$

   B $14 + 2$

   C $14 \div 2$

   D 14×2

5. Tim sells potatoes by the bag. The table shows how many pounds are in each bag.

Potatoes				
Number of Bags	3	5	7	8
Number of Pounds	30	50	70	▪

   If Tim sells 8 bags of potatoes, how many pounds of potatoes is that? (p. 138)

   A 10

   B 80

   C 140

   D 160

6. **WRITE Math** ▶ **Explain** how you can use multiplication to find the number that makes this equation true. (p. 94)

   $$\blacksquare \div 12 = 12$$

Geometry

7. James drew the figures below.

Which statement is true? (Grade 3)

A They are all quadrilaterals.

B They all have the same perimeter.

C They all have the same area.

D They each have at least 2 lines of symmetry.

8. Which of these figures is a hexagon?
(Grade 3)

A

B

C

D

9. **WRITE Math** ▶ Karen is drawing a rectangle. She says that it has 2 right angles and 2 acute angles. Do you agree? **Explain** why or why not. (Grade 3)

Data Analysis and Probability

10. Elena made a bar graph to show the results of her marble experiment.

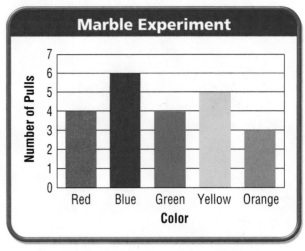

How many blue and yellow marbles did Elena pull? (p. 204)

A 9   **C** 11

B 10   **D** 22

11. Look at the spinner.

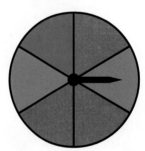

What is the probability of the pointer stopping on green? (Grade 3)

A 1 out of 4   **C** 2 out of 2

B 2 out of 4   **D** 2 out of 6

12. **WRITE Math** ▶ Pat is tossing a coin in the air. Predict how it will land. **Explain.**
(Grade 3)

10 Multiply by 2-Digit Numbers

 FAST FACT

Ellis Island, in New York Harbor, was the first stop for many European immigrants to the U.S. between 1892 and 1954. Today, Ellis Island is part of a national park. Part of the island is in New York, and part is in New Jersey.

Investigate

The sculpture in the photograph is called *American Flag of Faces*. If you look at it from one angle, you see faces of immigrants. From another angle, you see a flag. As you walk, it appears to change from faces to a flag and back again. The sculpture has 13 rows and 29 columns of blocks, with 2 photographs on each block. How can you break apart 13 × 29 to find the number of blocks on the sculpture?

- *American Flag of Faces* by Pablo Delano

  Height: 9 feet
  Width: 16 feet 6¾ inches
  Depth: 3 feet 2 inches

- The sculpture is made of clear plastic blocks. As a viewer moves, the flag appears to be waving.

GO ONLINE

Technology
Student pages are available in the Student eBook.

Check your understanding of important skills needed for success in Chapter 10.

▶ **Estimate Products**

Estimate the product.

1. 14
    × 7

2. 31
    × 6

3. 45
    × 5

4. 88
    × 3

5. 604
    ×   8

6. $555
    ×   3

7. $1.19
    ×   4

8. 2,353
    ×   9

▶ **Distributive Property**

Find the product.

9.

10.

11.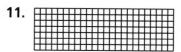

▶ **Multiply 2-, 3-, and 4-Digit Numbers by 1-Digit Numbers**

Estimate. Then find the product.

12. 29
     × 8

13. 726
     ×   4

14. 87
     × 5

15. 858
     ×   3

16. 2,317
     ×   5

17. $4,274
     ×   7

18. 3,706
     ×   9

19. $31.08
     ×   6

VOCABULARY POWER

CHAPTER VOCABULARY

addend
compatible numbers
Distributive Property
factor
multiple
partial product
product
round

WARM-UP WORDS

Distributive Property the property that states that multiplying a sum by a number is the same as multiplying each addend by the number and then adding the products

multiple the product of two counting numbers is a multiple of each of those numbers

partial product a method of multiplying in which the ones, tens, hundreds, and so on are multiplied separately and then the products are added together

MENTAL MATH

Multiplication Patterns

OBJECTIVE: Use a basic fact and a pattern to multiply mentally by multiples of 10, 100, and 1,000.

Learn

PROBLEM The actual length of an adult bumblebee is about 12 millimeters long. The photo shows part of the bee under a microscope at 10 times its actual size. What would the length of the bee appear to be at a magnification of 100 times its actual size?

Example 1 Multiply. 12×100

Use what you know about 1-digit multiplication to help you multiply by 2-digit numbers. The number lines show repeated addition.

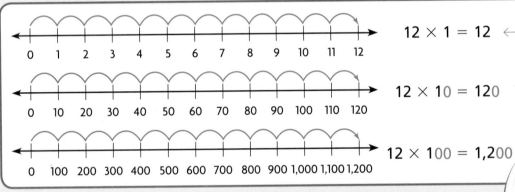

$12 \times 1 = 12$ ← basic fact

$12 \times 10 = 120$

$12 \times 100 = 1,200$

So, the bumblebee would appear to be 1,200 millimeters long.

• What pattern do you see in the number sentences?

Math Idea

The number of zeros in the factors should match the number of zeros in the product, unless the product of the basic fact has a zero.

More Examples

A Basic fact and a pattern

$6 \times 9 = 54$ ← basic fact
$60 \times 90 = 5,400$
$60 \times 900 = 54,000$

B Basic fact with a zero and a pattern

$10 \times 10 = 100$ ← basic fact
$10 \times 100 = 1,000$
$10 \times 1,000 = 10,000$

Guided Practice

1. What product does this number line show?
   Use it to find 12×20 and 12×200.

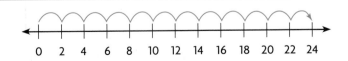

Use patterns and mental math to find the product.

2. 10×400 **3.** 11×60 **4.** 12×900 ✅**5.** $11 \times 1,000$ ✅**6.** $12 \times 6,000$

7. [TALK Math] **Explain** how to find $11 \times 4,000$ by using basic facts and patterns.

Independent Practice and Problem Solving

Use patterns and mental math to find the product.

8. 11×50 **9.** 10×20 **10.** 12×700 **11.** 12×600 **12.** $11 \times 8,000$

13. $30 \times 6,000$ **14.** 40×900 **15.** $10 \times 5,000$ **16.** 70×80 **17.** $20 \times 3,000$

⭐**Algebra** Copy and complete the tables by using mental math.

18. 1 roll = 50 dimes

Rolls	20	30	40	50	60
Dimes	1,000	▧	▧	▧	▧

19. 1 roll = 40 quarters

Rolls	20	30	40	50	60
Quarters	800	▧	▧	▧	▧

	×	6	70	800	9,000
20.	60	360	▧	▧	▧
21.	70	▧	4,900	▧	▧

	×	6	70	800	9,000
22.	80	▧	▧	64,000	▧
23.	90	▧	▧	▧	810,000

USE DATA For 24–25, use the table.

24. What if you wanted to magnify a carpenter bee 9,000 times? What would the length be?

25. If you magnified a termite 4,000 times and a wasp 3,000 times, which insect would appear longer? How much longer?

26. Reasoning How can you use what you know about 1-digit multiplication patterns to multiply by a 2-digit number?

Insect Lengths	
Insect	**Length (in mm)**
Carpenter Bee	19
Fire Ant	4
Termite	12
Wasp	15

27. [WRITE Math] **Explain** what the product of any factor times 100 always has.

Mixed Review and Test Prep

28. Which is greater, 5,006,719 or 5,017,691? (p. 12)

29. There are 64 paper cups in a box. How many cups are in 8 boxes? (p. 244)

30. Test Prep How many zeros are in the product $50 \times 10,000$?

A 4   **C** 6

B 5   **D** 7

(Extra Practice) on page 294, Set A

Multiply by Tens

OBJECTIVE: Multiply 2-digit numbers by multiples of ten using place value and mental math.

Learn

PROBLEM Animation for a computer-drawn cartoon requires about 15 frames per second. How many frames would need to be drawn for a 60-second cartoon?

ONE WAY Use place value.

Multiply. 15×60

THINK	RECORD
Step 1 Multiply by the ones. Place a zero in the ones place.	$\begin{array}{r} 15 \\ \times\ 60 \\ \hline 0 \end{array}$ ← 0 ones × 15 = 0 ones
Step 2 Multiply by the tens.	$\begin{array}{r} \overset{3}{1}5 \\ \times\ 60 \\ \hline 900 \end{array}$ ← 6 tens × 15 = 90 tens

So, 900 frames would need to be drawn for a 60-second cartoon.

ANOTHER WAY Use mental math.

Multiply. 16×40
You can use halving and doubling.

Step 1	Step 2
Find half of 16 and double 40. $16 \div 2 = 8$ and $40 \times 2 = 80$	Multiply. $8 \times 80 = 640$

So, $16 \times 40 = 640$.

- What is another way that you can use halving and doubling to multiply 16×40?

Math Idea
When you multiply a whole number by a multiple of ten, the digit in the ones place of the product is always zero.

Guided Practice

1. Multiply 18×20. Tell what method you chose. What is the first step to find the product? What is the second step?

Choose a method. Then find the product.

2. 15×10 **3.** 19×20 **4.** 34×40 ✓**5.** 78×60 ✓**6.** 90×18

7. [TALK Math] **Explain** which method of multiplying 2-digit numbers by multiples of ten you prefer, and give reasons why.

Independent Practice and Problem Solving

Choose a method. Then find the product.

8. 55×70 **9.** 64×30 **10.** 49×50 **11.** 88×20 **12.** 89×60

13. 20×27 **14.** 50×46 **15.** 30×68 **16.** 92×90 **17.** 40×77

⭐**Algebra** **Find the missing digit in the number.**

18. $64 \times 40 = 2{,}56\blacksquare$ **19.** $29 \times 50 = 1{,}\blacktriangle50$ **20.** $3\bigstar \times 47 = 1{,}410$

21. $\blacktriangle7 \times 90 = 5{,}130$ **22.** $20 \times \blacksquare9 = 1{,}980$ **23.** $20 \times 8\blacktriangle = 1{,}740$

USE DATA For 24–27, use the table.

24. How many frames did it take to produce 50 seconds of *Pinocchio*?

25. Are there more frames in 10 seconds of *The Flintstones* or 14 seconds of *The Enchanted Drawing*?

26. Write a multiplication problem that shows the total number of frames in 30 seconds of Little Nemo.

27. **Pose a Problem** Look back at Problem 24. Write a similar problem by changing the animated production and the number.

Animated Productions		
Title	Date Released	Frames per Second
The Enchanted Drawing©	1900	20
Little Nemo©	1911	16
Snow White and the Seven Dwarfs©	1937	24
Pinocchio©	1940	19
The Flintstones™	1960–1966	24

28. [WRITE Math] ▸ **What's the Error?** Tanya says that the product of a multiple of ten and a multiple of ten will always have only one zero. Is she correct? **Explain.**

Mixed Review and Test Prep

29. What might the next number in the pattern be? (p. 138)

$$3, 6, 12, 24, \blacksquare$$

30. If a pack of stickers costs $3, how much will Pam pay for 14 packs of stickers? (p. 250)

31. **Test Prep** Jade jogs 10 miles a week. How far will she have jogged in a year?

A 520 miles

B 530 miles

C 600 miles

D 620 miles

Extra Practice on page 294, Set B

MENTAL MATH
Estimate Products

OBJECTIVE: Estimate products by rounding factors or using compatible numbers and then finding the product mentally.

Learn

PROBLEM If the Smith family opens the door of their refrigerator 266 times in one week, about how many times is it opened during one year?

▼ The average number of times a refrigerator door is opened each day is 38 times.

ONE WAY Use rounding and mental math.

Estimate. 52 × 266.

Step 1	Step 2
Round each factor. 52 × 266 **Think:** There ↓ ↓ are 52 weeks 50 × 300 in a year.	Use mental math. 5 × 3 = 15 ← basic fact 50 × 30 = 1,500 50 × 300 = 15,000

So, the Smith family opens the refrigerator door about 15,000 times during one year.

• Will the actual number of times the refrigerator is opened in a year be greater than or less than 15,000? Explain.

ANOTHER WAY Use compatible numbers and mental math.

Compatible numbers are numbers that are easy to compute mentally.

Step 1	Step 2

52 × 266   **Think:** 50 × 30
 ↓   ↓   is easy to
 50 × 300   compute
 mentally.
	Multiply. If 5 × 3 = 15 and
	      50 × 30 = 1,500
	    Then 50 × 300 = 15,000

Remember

To round a number:
• Find the place to which you want to round. Look at the digit to its right.
• If the digit is less than 5, the digit in the rounding place stays the same.
• If the digit is 5 or greater, the digit in the rounding place increases by 1.
• Change all digits to the right of the rounding place to 0.

More Examples Estimate the products.

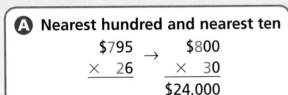

A Nearest hundred and nearest ten

$795 → $800
× 26   × 30
     $24,000

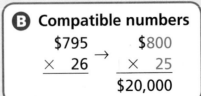

B Compatible numbers

$795 → $800
× 26   × 25
     $20,000

• Why are the products for rounding in Example A different from the products for compatible numbers in Example B?

Guided Practice

1. To estimate the product 62×28 by rounding, how would you round the factors? What would the estimated product be?

Estimate the product. Choose the method.

2. 96×34 　　**3.** $\$39 \times 26$ 　　**4.** 78×74 　　 ✓**5.** $\$23 \times 62$ 　　 ✓**6.** 41×178

7. ⟮ **TALK Math** ⟯ **Describe** how you know if your estimate will be greater than or less than the exact answer when you are estimating a product.

Independent Practice and Problem Solving

Estimate the product. Choose the method.

8. 54×73 　　**9.** 34×80 　　**10.** 67×23 　　**11.** $\$56 \times 27$ 　　**12.** 19×45

13. 61×318 　　**14.** 52×680 　　**15.** 26×448 　　**16.** 69×573 　　**17.** 24×393

18. 51×61 　　**19.** 28×31 　　**20.** $\$74 \times 85$ 　　**21.** 55×39 　　**22.** 81×94

USE DATA For 23, use the data on page 274.

23. Len has two refrigerators in his house. He opens each one the same amount as the Smith family. About how many times in a 2 week period are the refrigerator doors opened?

24. A new refrigerator costs about $97 per year to run. About how much will it have cost to run by the time it is 25 years old?

25. If Mel opens his refrigerator door 36 times every day, about how many times will it be opened in the month of March? Will the actual number of times be more than or less than the estimate? **Explain.**

26. ☰**FAST FACT** The average person in the United States eats about 23 quarts of ice cream each year. There are 27 students in Kay's class. About how many quarts of ice cream did Kay's class eat last year?

27. Reasoning What's the Question? I am thinking of two numbers that are multiples of ten. The answer is 2,800.

28. ⟮ **WRITE Math** ⟯ **Describe** how to estimate 19×123 using compatible numbers.

Mixed Review and Test Prep

29. Name the geometric figure that has exactly 3 angles. (Grade 3)

30. What is the product of 72 and 10? (p. 272)

31. Test Prep Choose the best estimate for the product 75×231.

　　A 24,000 　　　**C** 16,000

　　B 21,000 　　　**D** 1,600

⟮ Extra Practice ⟯ on page 294, Set C

Problem Solving Workshop
Strategy: Solve a Simpler Problem

OBJECTIVE: Solve problems by using the strategy *solve a simpler problem.*

Learn the Strategy

Solving a simpler problem can help you solve more difficult problems.

Break Apart

Ⓐ Factors

At the museum, an average of 89 visitors each hour view an exhibit. How many visitors will view the exhibit in a 7 hour period?

Break apart 89 into $80 + 9$. Multiply each addend by 7. Then add the partial products.

$$(7 \times 80) + (7 \times 9)$$
$$560 + 63$$
$$623$$

Ⓑ Addends

The baking contest at the county fair this year had 1,342 entries. Last year, there were 2,879 entries. How many entries have there been in the last two years?

Break apart the numbers by writing them in expanded form. Find the partial sums. Then add the partial sums.

$$1,000 + 300 + 40 + 2$$
$$+2,000 + 800 + 70 + 9$$
$$3,000 + 1,100 + 110 + 11 = 4,221$$

Find a pattern.

How many straws will be needed to make 5 hexagons that share a side?

Find the number of straws in the first figure. Then find the number of straws needed to construct each hexagon that follows.

+5   +5

TALK Math

What was done to make each problem simpler to solve?

Use the Strategy

PROBLEM During the month of February, people all over North America participate in the Great Backyard Bird Count. Here are results for the 2006 count of Bohemian waxwings in the Great Lakes region. Use the key. At least how many Bohemian waxwings were counted in all in locations that counted more than 16 of them?

Read to Understand

Reading Skill

- Use a graphic aid.
- What information is given in the map?
- What operation will you use?

Plan

- **What strategy can you use to solve the problem?**

  You can solve a simpler problem. One of the factors is 16. So you can use the Distributive Property to break apart 16 into factors that are easier to multiply and solve simpler problems.

Solve

- **How can you use the strategy to solve the problem?**

  Break apart 16 as 10 + 6. Multiply each addend by 21. Then add the partial products.

  $$16 \times 21 = (10 + 6) \times 21$$
  $$= (10 \times 21) + (6 \times 21)$$
  $$= 210 + 126$$
  $$= 336$$

  So, at least 336 Bohemian waxwings were counted in all in locations that counted more than 16 birds.

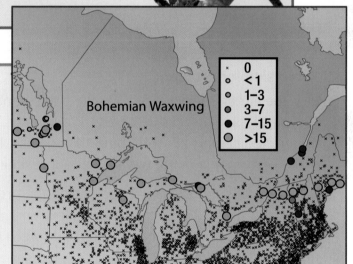

Bohemian Waxwing

×	0
○	<1
○	1–3
●	3–7
●	7–15
○	>15

Check

- **What other ways could you solve the problem?**
- **Look back at the problem. Does the answer make sense? Explain.**

1. In the state of Michigan, 172 participants in the Great Backyard Bird Count reported seeing about 30 mallards each. About how many mallards did they report in all?

   First, think about what you are asked to find.

   Think: 30×172

   Next, break apart one factor into numbers that are easy to multiply.

   $(30 \times 100) + (30 \times 70) + (30 \times 2)$

   Then, multiply and add the partial products.

2. **What if** the participants reported seeing 50 mallards each? How would your answer be different?

3. When Maggie goes on bird watching trips, she sees at least 45 birds. She has taken 12 bird watching trips a year over the past 16 years. How many birds has Maggie seen?

▲ Mallards are found in almost every state.

Problem Solving Strategy Practice

Solve a simpler problem.

4. In the Great Backyard Bird Count, participants in New Jersey reported seeing 353,992 birds. Participants in Delaware reported seeing 274,694 birds. Altogether, how many birds did participants in the two states report seeing?

5. Participants in Texas reported seeing the greatest number of birds, 497,122. Participants in New York reported seeing 264,620 birds. How many more birds were reported in Texas than in New York?

6. Nationwide, participants reported seeing 843,635 Canadian geese but only 207,324 American crows. How many more Canadian geese were seen than American crows?

7. Participants in New York sent in 222 checklists for wild turkeys. The total number of wild turkeys reported was about 18 times the number of checklists. About how many wild turkeys were reported?

8. **WRITE Math** Participants reported seeing 156,002 northern cardinals and 337,777 American goldfinches. How many northern cardinals and American goldfinches were reported altogether? **Explain.**

Mixed Strategy Practice

9. African ostrich eggs weigh 3 pounds each. Females lay up to 60 eggs in a group nest. How much could the eggs in the nest weigh?

10. According to legend, every year swallows arrive in San Juan Capistrano, California, on March 19 and leave on October 23. How long do the birds stay in San Juan Capistrano?

USE DATA For 11–17, use the information in the picture.

11. The wandering albatross has the largest wingspan of any bird. If it flies at its maximum speed for 10 hours, how far will it fly?

12. How much farther can a mallard fly in 2 hours than a house sparrow?

13. Which bird has a maximum length 8 times as long as a house sparrow?

14. **Pose a Problem** Look back at Problem 12. Write a similar problem by changing the types of birds and the number of hours they fly.

15. **Open-Ended** Write three different expressions that equal the maximum speed of the mallard. Use one or more operations.

CHALLENGE YOURSELF

The peregrine falcon is the fastest bird in the world. It can dive at a maximum speed of 217 miles per hour.

16. Write and solve a multiplication equation and an addition equation that shows the speed of the falcon and the speed of the carrion crow.

17. A peregrine falcon is 15 inches long. How can you compare the length of a falcon and the lengths of the birds pictured?

Choose a STRATEGY

Draw a Diagram or Picture
Make a Model or Act It Out
Make an Organized List
Find a Pattern
Make a Table or Graph
Predict and Test
Work Backward
Solve a Simpler Problem
Write an Equation
Use Logical Reasoning

◄ Carrion crow: maximum length is 20 inches and maximum speed is 31 miles per hour.

▲ House sparrow: maximum length is 6 inches and maximum speed is 31 miles per hour.

◄ Wandering albatross: maximum length is 48 inches and maximum speed is 34 miles per hour.

▲ Mallard: maximum length is 26 inches and maximum speed is 41 miles per hour.

5 Model 2-Digit by 2-Digit Multiplication

OBJECTIVE: Model multiplication using arrays.

Quick Review

Estimate the product.

1. 21 × 18
2. 59 × 28
3. 19 × 39
4. 27 × 52
5. 303 × 49

Learn

PROBLEM Matthew's family owns an apple orchard. The orchard has 17 rows of trees with 26 trees in each row. What is the total number of trees in the orchard?

You can make a model and break apart factors to make it easier to find the product.

 HANDS ON

Activity

Materials ■ grid paper ■ base-ten blocks ■ color pencils

Step 1	
Outline a rectangle that is 17 units long and 26 units wide. Think of the area as 17 × 26.	

Step 1

Outline a rectangle that is 17 units long and 26 units wide. Think of the area as 17 × 26.

Step 2

Break apart the model into smaller arrays to show factors that are easy to multiply.

Step 3

Find the number of squares in each of the smaller arrays. Add the partial products.

42 + 140 + 60 + 200 = 442

So, there are 442 trees in the orchard.

• **What if** the orchard plants 2 more rows with 26 trees in each? How many more trees would there be in the orchard?

Guided Practice

1. Copy and complete each step of the problem at the right. Then tell what is happening in each step.

Step 1 **Step 2** **Step 3**

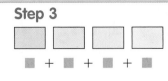

Use the model and partial products to solve.

2. 16×23

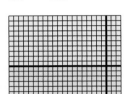

✓ **3.** 19×18

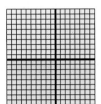

✓ **4.** 17×25

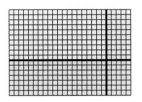

5. **TALK Math** **Explain** how breaking apart a model makes finding a product easier.

Independent Practice and Problem Solving

Use the model and partial products to solve.

6. 14×24

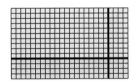

7. 17×22

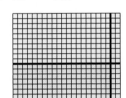

8. 16×28

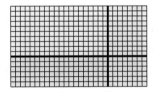

9. **≡FAST FACT** Each person in the United States eats an average of 65 fresh apples a year. How many apples do three families of 4 eat each year?

10. Apples harvested from an average tree can fill 20 bushel-sized boxes. If 1 row of Matthew's family orchard has 17 trees, how many boxes of apples can one row fill?

11. One tree uses the energy of 50 leaves to produce one apple. How many leaves does it take to produce 15 apples?

12. **WRITE Math** **Explain** how to find 37×28 by using a model.

Mixed Review and Test Prep

13. Name the faces of a square pyramid.
(Grade 3)

14. What is the best estimate for the product 44×278? (p. 274)

15. **Test Prep** What product is shown by the model?

Extra Practice on page 294, Set D

Record 2-Digit by 2-Digit Multiplication

OBJECTIVE: Find products by using partial products and place value.

Quick Review

1. 9×80
2. 2×67
3. 4×21
4. 7×15
5. 6×36

Learn

PROBLEM The amount of time it takes you to burn without sunscreen multiplied by the SPF number of your sunscreen tells you how long you can stay in the sun safely. Without sunscreen, Aaron will burn in about 15 minutes if the UV index is 8. If Aaron puts on lotion with SPF 45, how long can he stay in the sun?

ONE WAY Use arrays and partial products.

Multiply. 15×45 **Estimate.** $20 \times 40 = 800$

MODEL	THINK	RECORD
Step 1	Multiply the ones by the ones.	45 ×15 25 ← 5 × 5 ones = 25 ones
Step 2	Multiply the tens by the ones.	45 ×15 25 200 ← 5 × 4 tens = 20 tens
Step 3	Multiply the ones by the tens.	45 ×15 25 200 50 ← 10 × 5 ones = 50 ones
Step 4	Multiply the tens by the tens. Then add the partial products.	45 ×15 25 200 50 +400 ← 10 × 4 tens = 40 tens 675

▲ Sunscreen is labeled with a sun protection factor level, or SPF level. Checking the UV index, or the intensity of the sun for the day, can help you determine what level of sun protection you need.

ERROR ALERT

Line up partial products in the correct place value.

So, if Aaron puts on SPF 45, he can stay in the sun for 675 minutes. Since 675 is close to the estimate of 800, it is reasonable.

Example 1 Use place value.

Multiply. 32 × 31   **Estimate.** 30 × 30 = 900

Step 1	Step 2	Step 3
Think of 32 as 3 tens 2 ones. Multiply by 2 ones.	Multiply by 3 tens, or 30.	Add the partial products.
31 ×32 ――― 62 ← 2 × 31	31 ×32 ――― 62 930 ← 30 × 31	31 ×32 ――― 62 +930 ――― 992

So, 32 × 31 is 992. Since 992 is close to the estimate of 900, it is reasonable.

Example 2 Use place value with regrouping.

Multiply. 57 × 43   **Estimate.** 60 × 40 = 2,400

Step 1	Step 2	Step 3
Think of 57 as 5 tens 7 ones. Multiply by 7 ones.	Multiply by 5 tens, or 50.	Add the partial products.
2 43 ×57 ――― 301 ← 7 × 43	2̸¹ 43 ×57 ――― 301 2150 ← 50 × 43	2̸¹ 43 ×57 ――― 301 +2 150 ――― 2,451

So, 57 × 43 is 2,451. Since 2,451 is close to the estimate of 2,400, it is reasonable.

Guided Practice

1. Which product will you find first when you multiply 29 × 54 by using partial products? Which product will you find next? Find the product.

Estimate. Then choose either method to find the product.

2. 15 ×17	3. 21 ×19	4. 34 ×43	✓5. 76 ×31	✓6. 89 ×47

7. **TALK Math** **Explain** how you know in which place to begin when you multiply by 2-digit numbers.

Technology
Use Harcourt Mega Math, The Number Games, *Up, Up, and Array*, Level K.

Estimate. Then choose either method to find the product.

8. 36
  ×14

9. 63
  ×42

10. $82
  × 29

11. 71
  ×13

12. 57
  ×79

13. $75
  × 32

14. 80
  ×27

15. 55
  ×48

16. $25
  × 25

17. 41
  ×98

18. 19 × 41

19. $33 × 17

20. 28 × 39

21. 52 × 61

22. 82 × $65

USE DATA For 23–25, use the bar graph.

23. Last year, Sun Beach Parasail had 17 riders on each rainy day. How many riders in all parasailed last year on rainy days?

24. Sun Beach Parasail had 15 riders on each cold day. How many riders in all parasailed last year on cold days?

25. **Pose a Problem** Look back at Problem 24. Make the problem more open-ended.

26. Last week, Sheila planted 12 rows of seedlings with 15 seedlings in each row. This week, she planted 50 more seedlings. How many seedlings did she plant in all?

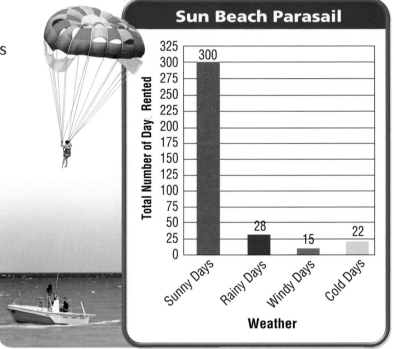

27. **Reasoning** Use the digits 1, 2, 3, and 5 to make two 2-digit numbers that will have the greatest product. Find the product.

28. **WRITE Math** ▶ Write a paragraph telling the method you like to use to multiply 2-digit numbers. **Describe** the method you like to use.

Mixed Review and Test Prep

29. Would you use a bar graph or a circle graph to show data as a whole made up of different parts? (p. 222)

30. A group of 25 students each jumped rope for 30 minutes. How many minutes in all did they jump rope? (p. 272)

31. **Test Prep** Dave bought 18 shrubs to plant in his garden. Each shrub cost $14. How much did the shrubs cost in all?

A $182

C $225

B $222

D $252

Extra Practice on page 295, Set E

Write to Explain

Writing an explanation helps you describe the steps you use to solve a problem.

David knows that the distance around the Earth is divided into 24 equal time zones—one zone for each hour of the day. Each time zone measures about 1,036 miles at the equator. David uses this information to solve this problem: What is the distance around the Earth at the equator?

Read David's explanation of how he used multiplication to find the answer.

Multiply the number of time zones by the measure of each time zone to find the answer.

$$24 \times 1,036$$

First, break apart 1,036 into $1,000 + 30 + 6$.

Then, multiply each addend by 24.

$$(24 \times 1,000) + (24 \times 30) + (24 \times 6)$$

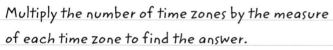

$$24,000 \quad + \quad 720 \quad + \quad 144$$

Finally, find the sum of $24,000 + 720 + 144$. The sum is 24,864. So, the distance around the Earth at the equator is about 24,864 miles.

Tips

- To write an explanation:
- First, identify the question.
- Then use time-order words, such as first, next, then, and finally to explain the steps in your answer.
- Use correct math vocabulary.
- Show all necessary computations.
- State your answer in the last sentence.

Problem Solving Explain how to solve each problem.

1. One degree of longitude is about 111 kilometers wide at the equator. What is the distance between two cities along the equator that are 12 degrees of longitude apart?

2. Each time zone spans 15 degrees of longitude. At the equator, each degree of longitude spans 60 nautical miles. How many nautical miles are in a time zone at the equator?

7 Multiply 2-Digit and 3-Digit Numbers and Money

OBJECTIVE: Multiply 2-digit and 3-digit numbers and money by 2-digit numbers.

Quick Review

1. 14×52
2. 22×37
3. 78×17
4. 91×16
5. 38×95

Learn

PROBLEM In 1914, Henry Ford streamlined the assembly line to make a Model T Ford car in 93 minutes. How many minutes did it take to make 105 Model Ts?

Example 1 Use place value.

Multiply. 93×105 **Estimate.** $90 \times 100 = 9,000$

THINK	RECORD
Multiply by the ones. Multiply by the tens. Add the partial products.	$\begin{array}{r} \overset{4}{\cancel{1}}05 \\ \times\ 93 \\ \hline 315 \\ +9450 \\ \hline 9,765 \end{array}$ ← 3×105 ← 90×105

▲ The first production Model T Ford was assembled at the Piquette Avenue Plant in Detroit on October 1, 1908.

So, it took 9,765 minutes to make 105 Model T Fords.

Multiply money the way you multiply whole numbers.

Math Idea
Use what you know about 1-digit multiplication to multiply a 2-digit number by 2-digit and 3-digit numbers.

Example 2 Multiply money amounts.

Multiply. $50 \times \$4.35$ **Estimate.** $50 \times \$5 = \$250$

Step 1	Step 2	Step 3
Multiply by the ones.	Multiply by the tens.	Then add the partial products. Place the decimal point to write the product in dollars and cents.
$\begin{array}{r} \$4.35 \\ \times\ 50 \\ \hline 0\,00 \end{array}$ ← 0×435 These zeros can be omitted.	$\begin{array}{r} \overset{1\,2}{\$4.35} \\ \times\ 50 \\ \hline 0\,00 \\ 217\,50 \end{array}$ ← 50×435	$\begin{array}{r} \$4.35 \\ \times\ 50 \\ \hline 0\,00 \\ +217\,50 \\ \hline \$217.50 \end{array}$

So, $50 \times \$4.35$ is $\$217.50$.

Different Ways to Multiply

You can use different ways to multiply and still get the correct answer. Both Shawn and Patty solved 67×436 correctly, but they used different ways.

Look at Shawn's paper.

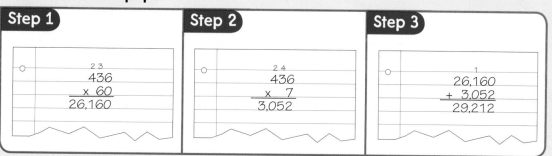

Step 1

$$
\begin{array}{r}
^{2\ 3} \\
436 \\
\times\ 60 \\
\hline
26{,}160
\end{array}
$$

Step 2

$$
\begin{array}{r}
^{2\ 4} \\
436 \\
\times\ 7 \\
\hline
3{,}052
\end{array}
$$

Step 3

$$
\begin{array}{r}
^{1} \\
26{,}160 \\
+\ 3{,}052 \\
\hline
29{,}212
\end{array}
$$

So, Shawn's answer is $67 \times 436 = 29{,}212$.

• What method did Shawn use to solve the problem?

Look at Patty's paper.

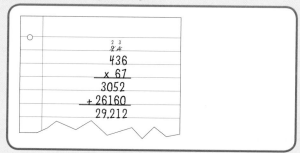

$$
\begin{array}{r}
^{2\ 3} \\
^{2\ 4} \\
436 \\
\times\ 67 \\
\hline
3052 \\
+\ 26160 \\
\hline
29{,}212
\end{array}
$$

So, Patty also found $67 \times 436 = 29{,}212$.

• What method did Patty use to solve the problem?

• **What if** the problem were $67 \times \$4.36$? What would the product be? Explain.

Guided Practice

1. What is the first partial product when you multiply 40×956? What numbers would you multiply next? Find the product.

Estimate. Then find the product.

2. $\begin{array}{r} 168 \\ \times\ 53 \\ \hline \end{array}$

3. $\begin{array}{r} 540 \\ \times\ 19 \\ \hline \end{array}$

4. $\begin{array}{r} 58 \\ \times 76 \\ \hline \end{array}$

✓5. $\begin{array}{r} \$3.99 \\ \times\ 30 \\ \hline \end{array}$

✓6. $\begin{array}{r} 901 \\ \times\ 27 \\ \hline \end{array}$

7. **TALK Math** Explain why you can omit the zeros of the first partial product when you multiply 20×348.

Independent Practice and Problem Solving

Estimate. Then find the product.

8. 308
    × 47

9. 92
    × 87

10. 627
    × 25

11. 145
    × 80

12. $2.59
    ×   13

13. 34 × 654

14. 17 × 429

15. 42 × $136

16. 62 × 427

17. 57 × $9.87

18. 55 × 668

19. 75 × $2.01

20. 92 × 547

21. 67 × 54

22. 73 × $6.81

REASONING Use each factor in the box only once.
Estimate the products to find the missing factors.

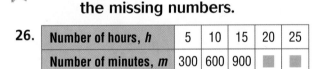

| 11 | 44 | 59 | 32 | 12 | 18 |

23. The product is between 100 and 150.

   ▨▨
   ×▨▨

24. The product is between 700 and 800.

   ▨▨
   ×▨▨

25. The product is between 1,500 and 2,000.

   ▨▨
   ×▨▨

⭐ **Algebra** Write a rule for the pattern. Use your rule to find the missing numbers.

26.
Number of hours, h	5	10	15	20	25
Number of minutes, m	300	600	900	▨	▨

27.
Number of years, y	12	14	16	18	20
Number of days, d	4,380	5,110	▨	6,570	▨

USE DATA For 28–30, use the pictures.

28. The hobby shop sold 34 radio remote 4WD monster trucks last year. How much did the truck bring in sales?

29. Less than $1,000 worth of off-road buggies were sold last year. What was the maximum number of this type of car sold?

30. Which costs more, 23 off-road buggies or 21 sports cars? How much more?

31. **Reasoning** Laura found 67 × 436 by multiplying and subtracting. Show how Laura found the product.

32. **⬛WRITE Math** ▸ **What's the Error?** Barry says the product of 80 and 729 is 5,832. Is he correct? **Explain.**

$135 ▼ Off-Road Buggy

$159 ▲ Sports Car

$85 ◀ Monster Truck

Extra Practice on page 295, Set F

33. Gary is driving from Philadelphia, Pennsylvania, to Minneapolis, Minnesota. The total distance is 1,168 miles. If Gary has already driven 729 miles, how much farther does he have to drive? (p. 50)

34. Explain how to estimate the product 29 × 681. Will the actual product be more than or less than the estimate? (p. 286)

35. Test Prep Last year, Rick ordered 45 pizzas for $9.99 each. How much did he spend on pizza in all?

A $449.55   **C** $450.00

B $449.65   **D** $459.55

36. Test Prep How many seconds are there in 12 hours? **Explain** how you found your answer.

Problem Solving connects to Science

Solar Power

The same amount of energy that it takes to operate a hair dryer can power a solar car for an entire day. Full size solar racers can run all day at about 40–50 milers per hour (mph) or as fast as 80 miles per hour for two hours if a battery pack is used.

College teams build solar cars and compete in the annual American Solar Challenge competition. In 2005, 10 teams competed in the 2,495-mile race from Austin, Texas, to Calgary, Alberta, Canada.

The table shows the first stages of the route and the mileage for each stage.

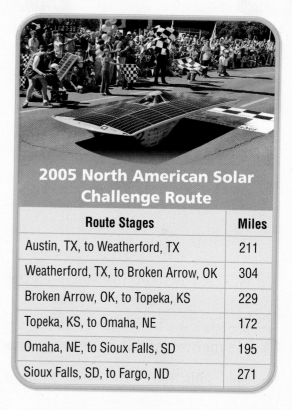

2005 North American Solar Challenge Route

Route Stages	Miles
Austin, TX, to Weatherford, TX	211
Weatherford, TX, to Broken Arrow, OK	304
Broken Arrow, OK, to Topeka, KS	229
Topeka, KS, to Omaha, NE	172
Omaha, NE, to Sioux Falls, SD	195
Sioux Falls, SD, to Fargo, ND	271

Use the information above to solve the problems.

1. If a team averaged 45 miles per hour for 6 hours for one of the stages, find which stage it might be. Explain how you know.

2. What is the total number of miles traveled by all cars during the first six stages of the race?

3. Challenge A hair dryer uses about 1,100 watts of energy to operate for an entire day. How many watts would it take to power a solar car for 1 week?

Choose a Method

OBJECTIVE: Choose paper and pencil, mental math, or a calculator to find the product.

Learn

PROBLEM Melanie is having a party at the Boston Children's Museum. She has invited 25 children. The cost per person is $11.60. How much will Melanie's party cost?

Example Use paper and pencil.

Multiply. 25 × $11.60   **Estimate.** 30 × $12 = $360

Step 1	Step 2	Step 3
Multiply by the ones.	Multiply by the tens.	Then add the partial products. Place the decimal point to write the product in dollars and cents.

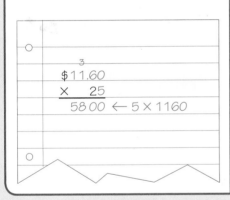

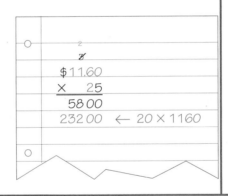

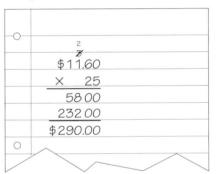

So, it will cost $290.00 for Melanie's party.

More Examples

A Use mental math.

Multiply. 20 × 6,025

Think: 20 × 6,000 = 120,000
and 20 × 25 = 500

120,000 + 500 = 120,500

B Use a calculator.

Multiply. 43 × 5,502

 5 5 0 2 × 4 3 =

 = 236586.

Estimate to check: 40 × 6,000 = 240,000

• Explain why using mental math is a good idea for finding 20 × 311.

• Would you use a calculator, paper and pencil, or mental math to find the product $37 × 469? Explain your choice.

1. Would you choose paper and pencil or mental math for 54 × $56.95? Explain?

Estimate. Then find the product. Write the method you used.

2. $33.33	3. 500	4. 598	✓5. 800	✓6. 325
× 22	× 50	× 76	× 30	× 24

7. **TALK Math** Explain why you chose the method you used to find the product for Problem 6.

Independent Practice and Problem Solving

Estimate. Then find the product. Write the method you used.

8. 444	9. 7,000	10. 707	11. 2,540	12. 999
× 20	× 60	× 70	× 44	× 33

13. 55 × 666   14. 75 × 2,000   15. 92 × 547   16. 67 × 5,243   17. 73 × $96.81

★**Algebra** Use a calculator to find the missing digit.

18. 44 × 234 = 10,■96   19. 2■ × 392 = 10,584   20. 19 × 5,■00 = 98,800

21. Thirteen of the children wanted to buy souvenir cups at the museum. Each cup costs $1.89. How much will the cups cost?

22. The museum sells dino balloons for $4.99 each. Seventeen of the children bought a balloon. Was the total spent more than or less than $85? How do you know?

23. The total cost for a weekend party for 25 children at the museum is $290. On weekdays, the total cost drops to $10.40 per person. What is the total cost of Melanie's museum party on a weekday?

24. **WRITE Math** What's the Error? Louisa says 40 × 321 is 1,284. Describe and correct her error.

Mixed Review and Test Prep

25. What might the missing number in the pattern be? (p. 78)

14, 21, 28, ■, 42

26. Tim ordered 30 binders for his office. Each binder cost $4.50. How much did the binders cost in all? (p. 286)

27. **Test Prep** Al sold shirts at a fundraiser. If he sold 68 shirts for $12.98 each, how much money did he raise?

A $882.64   C $80.98

B $181.72   D $55.02

Problem Solving Workshop
Skill: Multistep Problems

OBJECTIVE: Solve problems by using the skill *multistep problems*.

Use the Skill

PROBLEM The Chicago World's Fair of 1893 introduced the first Ferris wheel ever. It had 36 cars. Each car could carry 60 passengers. Today's London Eye observation wheel has 32 capsules. Each capsule can carry 25 passengers. How many more total passengers could the first Ferris wheel carry?

▲ The Ferris wheel at the Chicago World's Fair was 250 feet tall.

First, find the total number of passengers each wheel can hold.

	number of cars or capsules ↓	capacity of each car ↓		total capacity ↓
1893 Ferris wheel	36 ×	60	=	2,160
London Eye	32 ×	25	=	800

Then, find out how many more the 1893 Ferris wheel could carry.
Then subtract: 2,160 − 800 = 1,360

So, the 1893 Ferris wheel could carry 1,360 more passengers.

• Does your answer make sense? Explain how you know.

Think and Discuss

What steps would you take to solve the problem?
Solve the problem.

a. Gold braid comes in 15-foot rolls and costs $25 per foot. Silver braid comes in 31-foot rolls and costs $12 per foot. What is the total cost of one roll of each type of braid?

b. A bus travels the 1,377-mile trip from Miami to Chicago and then the 2,034 miles from Chicago to Los Angeles. How many miles will the bus travel if it makes 25 trips?

c. In one class, Mr. Thacker handed out 14 sheets of construction paper to each of the 20 students. He had 40 sheets of constuction paper left over. How many sheets of construction paper did he start with?

▲ The London Eye, in London, England, opened in 2000. It is 450 feet tall.

1. The Ferris wheel at the Chicago World's Fair of 1893 had 36 cars. Each car held 60 people who paid $0.50 each for a 20-minute ride. How much money did the Ferris wheel make in 8 hours if all the cars were filled all the time?

   First you need to know how many rides take place in 8 hours. Organize that information so it is clear.

Time	Number of Rides
20 minutes	1 ride
60 minutes, or 1 hour	3 rides
8 hours	24 rides

   What steps do you need to take to solve the problem? Solve the problem.

2. **What if** you wanted to know how much money the Ferris wheel would make in 24 hours if the cars were filled all the time? What would your answer be?

3. The Space Needle, built in 1962 for the Seattle World's Fair, is 605 feet tall. The Petronas Towers, an office building in Malaysia, has 88 stories. Each story is about 14 feet high. About how much taller is the Petronas Towers than the Space Needle?

Mixed Applications

USE DATA For 4–6, use the table.

4. Sal bought a magnolia and a mountain laurel. Both were 24 inches tall when he bought them. Which one will be taller in 5 years? How much taller?

5. How many inches taller than a full-grown mountain laurel at 180 inches is a 20-year-old holly?

6. If you plant an arborvitae that is 48 inches tall, how many inches tall will it be in 7 years?

7. Zora is training for a race. She ran 2 laps around the gym the first week, 4 laps the second week, 8 laps the third week, and 16 laps the fourth week. If the pattern continues, how many laps will she run in the fifth week?

8. **WRITE Math** A flight arrived in Atlanta from Dallas at 11:34 A.M. It then left Atlanta for Miami at 1:04 P.M. How long was the layover? **Explain.**

Popular Landscaping Trees

Tree	Average Yearly Growth (in inches)
Arborvitae	24 in.
Holly	12 in.
Magnolia	30 in.
Mountain Laurel	10 in.

Extra Practice

Set A Use patterns and mental math to find the product. (pp. 270–271)

1. 10×30 **2.** 11×400 **3.** 12×200 **4.** 11×700 **5.** $11 \times 6{,}000$

6. $40 \times 5{,}000$ **7.** 50×60 **8.** $12 \times 9{,}000$ **9.** 10×800 **10.** $70 \times 3{,}000$

11. The actual length of a wasp is 15 millimeters. How long would the wasp appear to be under a microscope at a magnification of 200 times its actual size?

Set B Choose a method. Then find the product. (pp. 272–273)

1. $\begin{array}{r} 14 \\ \times 60 \\ \hline \end{array}$ **2.** $\begin{array}{r} 28 \\ \times 30 \\ \hline \end{array}$ **3.** $\begin{array}{r} 36 \\ \times 50 \\ \hline \end{array}$ **4.** $\begin{array}{r} 47 \\ \times 80 \\ \hline \end{array}$ **5.** $\begin{array}{r} 56 \\ \times 70 \\ \hline \end{array}$

6. $\begin{array}{r} 77 \\ \times 30 \\ \hline \end{array}$ **7.** $\begin{array}{r} 49 \\ \times 40 \\ \hline \end{array}$ **8.** $\begin{array}{r} 67 \\ \times 30 \\ \hline \end{array}$ **9.** $\begin{array}{r} 89 \\ \times 50 \\ \hline \end{array}$ **10.** $\begin{array}{r} 38 \\ \times 90 \\ \hline \end{array}$

11. 20×63 **12.** 38×80 **13.** 50×25 **14.** 54×60 **15.** 36×40

16. Ms. Michaels has 30 packages of construction paper. Each package has 25 sheets of paper. How many sheets of paper does she have?

Set C Estimate the product. Choose the method. (pp. 274–275)

1. 63×24 **2.** 48×57 **3.** 32×21 **4.** 59×68 **5.** $\$37 \times 49$

6. 32×43 **7.** 458×61 **8.** 37×297 **9.** 378×29 **10.** 201×32

11. 33×56 **12.** $\$687 \times 29$ **13.** 799×33 **14.** 78×67 **15.** 607×48

16. A drawbridge opens 19 times each week. About how many times does the drawbridge open in one year?

Set D Use the model and partial products to solve. (pp. 280–281)

1. 15×21 **2.** 14×24 **3.** 18×23

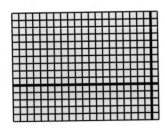 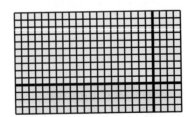 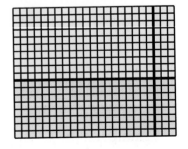

Technology
Use Harcourt Mega Math, The Number Games, *Up, Up, and Array,* Levels I, K.

Set E Estimate. Then choose either method to find the product. (pp. 282–285)

1.	29 ×74	2.	43 ×56	3.	63 ×45	4.	83 ×17	5.	37 ×64
6.	34 ×28	7.	73 ×35	8.	88 ×32	9.	49 ×51	10.	57 ×27

11. $78 × 54   12. 26 × 59   13. $66 × 17   14. 13 × 28   15. 94 × 41

16. Each page of a photo album holds 15 pictures. If there are 45 pages, how many pictures will the photo album hold?

Set F Estimate. Find the product. (pp. 286–289)

1.	253 × 44	2.	632 × 56	3.	731 × 35	4.	$4.37 × 62	5.	$7.57 × 84
6.	6,643 × 73	7.	2,511 × 14	8.	$3.29 × 56	9.	157 × 83	10.	808 × 25

11. $556 × 47   12. 713 × 89   13. 421 × 18   14. $6.54 × 32   15. 929 × 34

16. The library lends an average of 404 books a day. How many books are checked out in 2 weeks?

Set G Estimate. Then find the product. Write the method you used. (pp. 290–291)

1.	50 ×34	2.	95 ×67	3.	42 ×80	4.	14 ×26	5.	$8.99 × 42
6.	832 × 58	7.	6,492 × 15	8.	2,881 × 23	9.	4,261 × 51	10.	$5,698 × 33

11. 941 × 72   12. 1,975 × 17   13. 814 × 29   14. 658 × 46   15. 3,219 × 52

16. A soccer uniform costs $18.95. The team has 16 members. How much will be spent for the team's uniforms? If 2 new people join the team, what is the new total cost for the team uniforms?

TAKE A SEAT

There are 6 sections of seats in the Playhouse Theater. Each section has 15 groups of seats. Each group has 50 seats. How many seats are there in the auditorium?

You can use the Commutative and Associative Properties of Multiplication to make partial products that end in 0.

The Commutative Property of Multiplication states the order in which you multiply does not change the product. The Associative Property of Multiplication states the way in which you group the factors does not change the product.

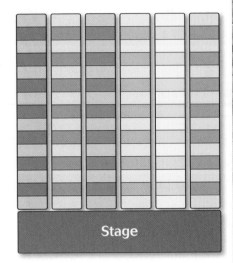

Stage

Multiply. $6 \times 15 \times 50$

$6 \times 15 \times 50 = 6 \times 50 \times 15$ ← Commutative Property
$= 300 \times 15$
$= 4,500$

So, the auditorium has 4,500 seats.

Examples Use mental math to find the product.

A **Associative Property**
$(14 \times 25) \times 8 = 14 \times (25 \times 8)$
$= 14 \times 200$
$= 2,800$

B **Commutative Property**
$3 \times 37 \times 10 = 3 \times 10 \times 37$
$= 30 \times 37$
$= 1,110$

Try It

Use mental math to find the product.

1. $3 \times 11 \times 30$
2. $5 \times (20 \times 35)$
3. $6 \times 32 \times 50$
4. $8 \times (25 \times 60)$

5. $(90 \times 4) \times 25$
6. $10 \times 12 \times 7$
7. $5 \times 40 \times 18$
8. $(21 \times 7) \times 80$

9. There are 13 members on the swim team. Each member swims 20 laps at practice. If they practice 5 days a week, how many laps does the team swim each week?

10. An apartment building has 8 floors. Each apartment has 12 windows, and there are 10 apartments on a floor. How many windows are there in the building?

11. **WRITE Math** ▸ **Explain** how using the properties makes it easier to multiply 3 factors mentally.

Chapter 10 Review/Test

Check Concepts

1. Explain how to use mental math to find the product: 12×50. (p. 270–271)

2. What is the pattern when multiplying a number by a multiple of ten? Give an example of the pattern. (p. 272–273)

3. Explain how to find the product by breaking apart a factor: 8×37. (p. 276–279)

Check Skills

Estimate the product. Choose the method. (pp. 274–275)

4. 36×47 5. 58×34 6. $\$76 \times 38$ 7. 92×24 8. 42×73

9. 405×28 10. 624×36 11. 18×763 12. $\$64 \times 26$ 13. 509×49

Find the product. (pp. 272–273, 280–281, 282–285, 286–289)

14. $\begin{array}{r} 44 \\ \times 60 \\ \hline \end{array}$
15. $\begin{array}{r} 62 \\ \times 70 \\ \hline \end{array}$
16. $\begin{array}{r} 57 \\ \times 80 \\ \hline \end{array}$
17. $\begin{array}{r} 36 \\ \times 50 \\ \hline \end{array}$
18. $\begin{array}{r} 92 \\ \times 35 \\ \hline \end{array}$

19. $\begin{array}{r} \$37 \\ \times 81 \\ \hline \end{array}$
20. $\begin{array}{r} 63 \\ \times 48 \\ \hline \end{array}$
21. $\begin{array}{r} \$241 \\ \times 25 \\ \hline \end{array}$
22. $\begin{array}{r} 73 \\ \times 49 \\ \hline \end{array}$
23. $\begin{array}{r} 508 \\ \times 27 \\ \hline \end{array}$

24. $\begin{array}{r} 2{,}315 \\ \times 39 \\ \hline \end{array}$
25. $\begin{array}{r} 87 \\ \times 44 \\ \hline \end{array}$
26. $\begin{array}{r} \$5.67 \\ \times 35 \\ \hline \end{array}$
27. $\begin{array}{r} 6{,}070 \\ \times 46 \\ \hline \end{array}$
28. $\begin{array}{r} \$2.89 \\ \times 28 \\ \hline \end{array}$

Check Problem Solving

Solve. (pp. 276–279, 292–293)

29. Allison's parents put $\$175$ each month into her college fund account. How much do they put in the account during 1 year?

30. George buys 20 dozen eggs for the Community Pancake Breakfast. How many eggs does he buy?

31. Sandy sold 35 adult tickets and 48 child tickets for the breakfast. An adult ticket costs $\$6.50$ and a child ticket costs $\$3.50$. How much did Sandy collect for the tickets?

32. Each level of a parking garage holds 110 cars. There are 5 garages with 6 levels in each garage. How many cars can be parked in all the garages?

33. **WRITE Math** ▶ List the steps needed to find the product 46×63.

Unit Review/Test
Chapters 9–10

Multiple Choice

1. Ben's family sold 2,000 toy cars this year at the flea market. They charged $4 for each car. How much money did they receive? (p. 244)

   A $800

   B $8,000

   C $80,000

   D $800,000

2. Sue buys 21 packages of hamburger buns for the school picnic. Each package has 8 buns. What is the best estimate of the number of buns Sue buys? (p. 246)

   A 160

   B 180

   C 200

   D 240

3. Monte watched 5 history videos for his history project. Each video was 75 minutes long. Which number sentence can be used to find the total number of minutes Monte spent watching the videos? (p. 250)

   A $75 - 5 = $ ▓

   B $5 + 75 = $ ▓

   C $5 \times 75 = $ ▓

   D $75 \div 5 = $ ▓

4. Carmen's Toy Shop ordered 18 boxes of yo-yos. There are 144 yo-yos in each box. How many yo-yos did the toy shop order? (p. 286)

   A 1,296

   B 2,262

   C 2,592

   D 2,800

5. Which pair of numbers best completes the equation? (p. 272)

   $\bigcirc \times 400 = \boxed{}$

   A $\bigcirc$ 60 and $\boxed{2,400}$

   B $\bigcirc$ 60 and $\boxed{24,000}$

   C $\bigcirc$ 6 and $\boxed{24,000}$

   D $\bigcirc$ 600 and $\boxed{24,000}$

6. There are 54 cases of baseballs in a warehouse. Each case contains 24 baseballs. Which is the best estimate of the number of baseballs in the warehouse? (p. 274)

   A 30   C 100

   B 70   D 1,000

GO ONLINE Technology Use *Online Assessment.*

7. The box office sold 79 tickets at $16.45 each for today's performance of the puppet show. How much money did the box office collect? (p. 286)

A $62.55

B $95.45

C $866.55

D $1,299.55

8. Lily's Laundromat has 20 washing machines. Each machine can wash about 50 loads of laundry each week. About how many loads of laundry can be washed each week at Lily's? (p. 272)

A 100

B 1,000

C 10,000

D 100,000

9. Mr. Sanders bought 2 oak trees and 3 birch trees for his landscape business.

Jackson's Nursery Tree Sale

Tree	Price
Maple	$175
Oak	$229
Birch	$155

Which expression can be used to find the total amount he spent? (p. 292)

A $(229 \times 3) \times (155 \times 2)$

B $(229 \times 2) \times (155 \times 3)$

C $(229 \times 3) + (155 \times 2)$

D $(229 \times 2) + (155 \times 3)$

Short Response

10. Photo Plus charges 29 cents to print a digital photo. How much will Sasha pay to have 8 digital photos printed? (p. 254)

11. One section of bleachers in a school gymnasium has 17 rows. Each row can seat 42 people. What is a good estimate of the number of people who can sit in that section? (p. 274)

12. Last year, Rosewood Middle School bought 15 new desks for every classroom. There are 23 classrooms. How many new desks did the school buy in all? (p. 282)

Extended Response WRITE Math ▶

13. Mr. Valdez earns $17 an hour. Yesterday he worked 8 hours. Did Mr. Valdez earn more than or less than $200? **Explain** how you can tell without calculating an exact answer. (p. 260)

14. The problem below shows part of the product 4×283. How many tens are shown in the product? What two digits are missing? **Explain** how to find them. (p. 254)

$$\begin{array}{r} 283 \\ \times\ \ 4 \\ \hline \blacksquare,\blacksquare 32 \end{array}$$

15. Use each of the digits 3, 5, 7, and 9 once to make a three-digit factor and a one-digit factor that will give the greatest product possible. **Explain** how you found your answer. (p. 254)

THE WORLD ALMANAC FOR KIDS

Space Travel

First Moon Landing

On February 20, 1962, John H. Glenn, Jr., became the first United States astronaut to orbit Earth. On July 20, 1969, *Apollo 11*'s lunar module, *Eagle,* landed on the moon in an area known as the Sea of Tranquility. Neil Armstrong became the first person to walk on the moon.

John H. Glenn, Jr.

Neil Armstrong

The Apollo lunar module was about 21 feet tall and 14 feet wide.

FACT·ACTIVITY

Use the data on this page.

1. About how many days passed between John Glenn's orbit of Earth and the first moon landing?

2. The *Apollo 11* astronauts collected about 49 pounds of soil and rock samples. About how many ounces was this?
   Think: 1 pound = 16 ounces

3. *Apollo 12* landed on the moon on November 18, 1969. About how many months after the *Apollo 11* moon landing was this? About how many days after?

4. **WRITE Math** Explain how you would find how many hours the *Apollo 11* mission took.

Suit Up for Space

The Apollo spacesuits were each one piece. Each member of the 3-person crew had 3 suits: a flight suit, a training suit, and a backup suit. The 2 backup astronauts had 2 suits each: a flight suit and a training suit.

Today's shuttle space suits are made in parts. The parts, such as a space helmet, can be made in different sizes.

Space helmets must provide oxygen for breathing, protection from extreme temperatures, and a visor to reflect harmful rays from the sun. Space helmets can include a slot for fruit and cereal snacks and adjustable blinders to block out the sun.

F A C T · A C T I V I T Y

Use the information about Apollo space suits.

❶ How many space suits were needed for one Apollo flight?

❷ How many would have been needed for 12 Apollo flights?

Use the diagram. Design, draw, and label your own space helmet for a mission to Mars.

► Will your helmet have visors and lights? How many of each?

► How many parts will be needed in all?

► Choose the number of astronauts to join you. What is the total number of helmet parts needed?

► Describe some extra items you would include in your own space helmet. How many parts will your helmet have? How many will you and your crew need in all?

► If NASA can send 4 missions like yours at the same time, what is the total number of helmet parts needed?

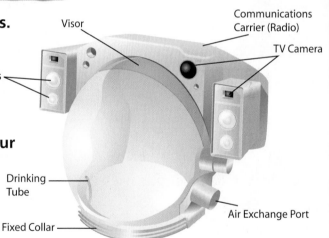

Visor · Communications Carrier (Radio) · TV Camera · Lights · Drinking Tube · Fixed Collar · Air Exchange Port

UNIT 5
Divide by 1-Digit and 2-Digit Divisors

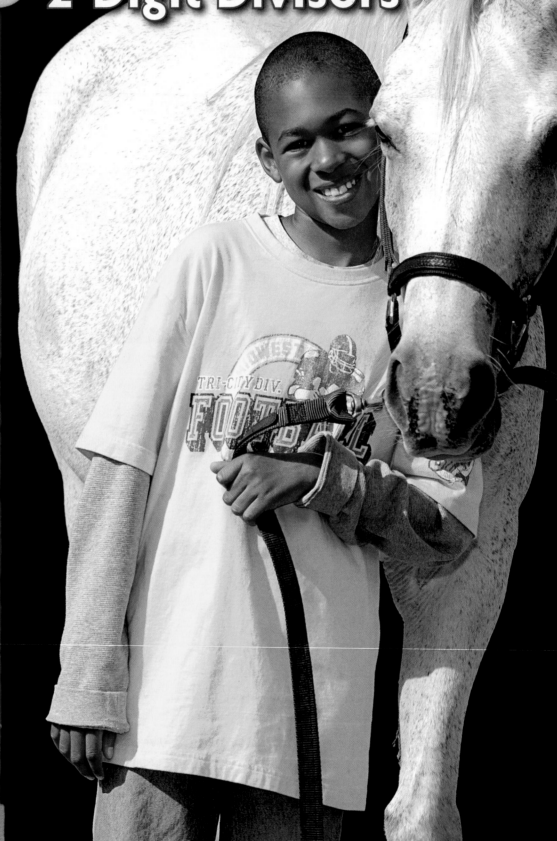

Math on Location

1

These actors live on a ranch near Hollywood. The fee paid to use them in movies pays for their hay.

2

The director of the movie has a budget of $250 to rent a stagecoach for 3 days.

3

The actors, both human and animal, are ready for this scene. Lights, camera, action!

VOCABULARY POWER

TALK Math

Look at the **Math on Location** photographs. How can you find how much it costs the director to rent a stagecoach for one day?

READ Math

REVIEW VOCABULARY You learned the words below when you learned about division facts. How do these words relate to **Math on Location**?

divide to separate into equal groups; the opposite operation of multiplication

factor a number that is multiplied by another to find a product

quotient the number, not including the remainder, that results from dividing.

WRITE Math

Copy and complete the word knowledge chart below. Mark the division words you know now with a check mark. Use a star to show the new words you know at the end of the unit.

Word	I Know	Sounds Familiar	Don't Know
divisor	✔		
dividend		✔	
quotient			
remainder			
compatible numbers			

11 Understand Division

Investigate

Visitors to Stanton Hall can see the home's original furniture. They also see unusual chandeliers and giant gold-framed mirrors. The table shows the number of people who visited Stanton Hall each day for four days. Use the data shown in the table. How many different equal-size groups of fewer than 10 people could have taken a tour? How could you use models to justify your answer?

FAST FACT

Stanton Hall was built in Natchez, Mississippi in 1857. The main hall on the ground floor is 72 feet long. The front and back rooms on one side open up to make one room that is as long as the main hall.

Visitors to Stanton Hall	
Day	Number of People
Monday	60
Tuesday	108
Wednesday	256
Thursday	240

GO ONLINE

Technology
Student pages are available in the student eBook.

Show What You Know

Check your understanding of important skills
needed for success in Chapter 11.

▶ 2-Digit Subtraction

Find the difference.

1.	47	2.	23	3.	76	4.	83	5.	54
	−26		−14		−34		−31		−39

6. $63 - 26$ 7. $39 - 17$ 8. $96 - 29$ 9. $31 - 20$ 10. $73 - 52$

▶ Model Division

Write the division fact that each picture represents.

11. 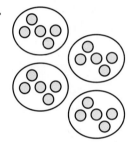   12. 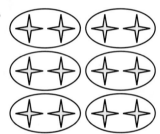   13.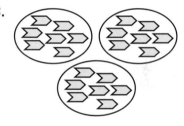

▶ Division Facts

Find the quotient.

14. $54 \div 6$ 15. $8\overline{)72}$ 16. $42 \div 6$ 17. $24 \div 3$ 18. $5\overline{)40}$

19. $6\overline{)18}$ 20. $27 \div 9$ 21. $8\overline{)32}$ 22. $4\overline{)28}$ 23. $63 \div 7$

VOCABULARY POWER

CHAPTER VOCABULARY	WARM-UP WORDS
compatible numbers	**dividend** the number that is to be divided in a division problem
dividend	
divisor	**divisor** the number that divides the dividend
estimate	
mental math	**remainder** the amount left over when a number cannot be divided equally
multiple	
quotient	
remainder	

Divide with Remainders

OBJECTIVE: Divide whole numbers that do not divide evenly.

Quick Review

1. $27 \div 9$ 2. 4×7
3. 3×8 4. $5\overline{)25}$
5. $3\overline{)12}$

Vocabulary

remainder

Learn

Sometimes a number cannot be divided evenly. The amount left over is called the **remainder**.

PROBLEM Three friends are playing a game of dominoes. There are 28 dominoes in the set. If each player receives the same number of dominoes, how many dominoes will each player get? How many dominoes will be left over?

Activity Make a model.

Materials ■ counters

Divide 28 by 3. Write $28 \div 3$ or $3\overline{)28}$.

Step 1	Step 2
Use 28 counters. 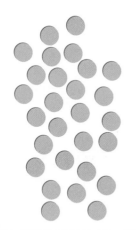	Draw 3 circles. Divide the 28 counters into 3 equal groups. The counter left over is the remainder. 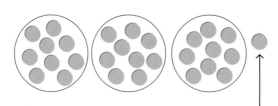 remainder

The quotient is 9 and the remainder is 1.

So, each player will get 9 dominoes. There will be 1 domino left over.

• Why does the remainder have to be less than the divisor?

ERROR ALERT

If the remainder is greater than the divisor, keep dividing the counters evenly until the remainder is less than the divisor.

Guided Practice

1. Use counters to model $17 \div 5$. Draw ■ circles. Place ■ counters in each circle. The quotient is ■. The remainder is ■.

Use counters to find the quotient and remainder.

2. $15 \div 6$ **3.** $26 \div 7$ **4.** $19 \div 4$ ✅ **5.** $24 \div 5$ ✅ **6.** $42 \div 5$

7. **TALK Math** **Explain** how you know when there will be a remainder in a division problem.

Independent Practice and Problem Solving

Use counters to find the quotient and remainder.

8. $18 \div 7$ **9.** $12 \div 5$ **10.** $21 \div 6$ **11.** $22 \div 4$ **12.** $56 \div 9$

Divide. You may wish to use counters or draw a picture to help.

13. $26 \div 3$ **14.** $37 \div 6$ **15.** $67 \div 9$ **16.** $3\overline{)47}$ **17.** $5\overline{)41}$

⭐**Algebra** **Find the missing value.**

18. $26 \div 4 = 6\ r\blacksquare$ **19.** $43 \div 8 = \blacksquare\ r3$ **20.** $\blacksquare \div 5 = 4\ r2$ **21.** $32 \div \blacksquare = 10\ r2$

USE DATA For 22–24, use the table.

22. Which set will have the greatest number of dominoes left over if 5 players equally divide the dominoes in each set?

23. Seven players divided a set of dominoes so that each had the same number. There were dominoes left over. Which set did they use? **Explain** your answer.

24. Some students are using a double twelve set. Each student has 11 dominoes. There are 3 dominoes left over. How many students are playing the game?

Domino Sets

Name of Set	Number of Dominoes
Double Six	28
Double Nine	55
Double Twelve	91

25. **WRITE Math** **What's the Error?** Frank says that the model represents $4\overline{)13}$. What is his error? Draw a correct model.

Mixed Review and Test Prep

26. What is the name of this figure? (Grade 3)

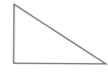

27. Chinese Checkers uses 10 marbles for each player. If there are 6 players, how many marbles do they need? (p. 98)

28. **Test Prep** Which problem does the model describe?

A $14 \div 2$ **C** $12 \div 4$

B $14 \div 3$ **D** $14 \div 4$

Extra Practice on page 324, Set A

2 Model 2-Digit by 1-Digit Division

OBJECTIVE: Model division by using base-ten blocks.

Investigate

Materials ■ base-ten blocks

The school lunchroom is serving 72 peaches in 3 bowls. Each bowl has the same number of peaches. How many peaches are in each bowl?

You can use base-ten blocks to find the number of objects in equal-size groups.

A Use base-ten blocks to model the 72 peaches. Show 72 as 7 tens 2 ones. Draw three circles.

B Place an equal number of tens into each group.

C If there are any tens left, regroup them as ones. Place an equal number of ones into each group.

D Count the number of tens and ones in each group to find the number of peaches in each bowl. Record your answer.

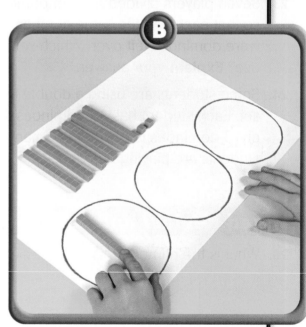

Draw Conclusions

1. Why did you draw 3 circles in Step A?

2. Why do you need to regroup in Step C?

3. How many peaches are in each bowl?

4. How can you check your answer?

5. **Synthesis** What if there are 96 peaches and 4 bowls? Describe how you can use base-ten blocks to find how many peaches will be in each bowl.

You can use base-ten blocks to model division with remainders.

Miguel's robot kit has 46 parts. He can build 4 matching robots with the parts. How many parts does Miguel need for each robot? How many parts will be left over?

Step 1

Show 46 as 4 tens 6 ones.

Step 2

Draw 4 circles. Place 1 ten in each circle.

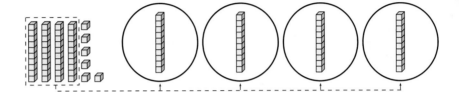

Step 3

Place 1 one in each circle. Count how many ones are left over.

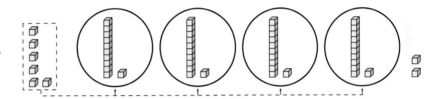

So, each robot needs 11 parts. There will be 2 parts left over.

TALK Math

Explain why the answer could not be 10 parts and 6 parts left over.

Practice

Use base-ten blocks to find the quotient and remainder.

1. $2\overline{)84}$
2. $96 \div 6$
3. $99 \div 8$
4. $5\overline{)67}$
5. $84 \div 3$
6. $2\overline{)52}$
7. $26 \div 4$
8. $5\overline{)81}$
9. $44 \div 3$
✓ 10. $7\overline{)84}$

Divide. You may wish to use base-ten blocks.

11. $52 \div 4$
12. $5\overline{)48}$
13. $87 \div 7$
14. $6\overline{)77}$
✓ 15. $97 \div 6$
16. $3\overline{)22}$
17. $3\overline{)72}$
18. $40 \div 6$
19. $23 \div 9$
20. $5\overline{)88}$

21. **WRITE Math** ▸ **Explain** how to model the quotient for $73 \div 5$.

Technology
Use Harcourt Mega Math, The Number Games, *Up, Up, and Array*, Level L.

Record 2-Digit by 1-Digit Division

OBJECTIVE: Divide 2-digit numbers by 1-digit numbers.

Learn

PROBLEM Raul, Jeremy, and Manuel have collected 53 baseball cards. They want to divide them equally. How many cards will each of the 3 boys get? How many cards will be left over?

ONE WAY Use long division.

Divide 53 by 3. Write $53 \div 3$ or $3\overline{)53}$.

	MODEL	THINK	RECORD	
Step 1		Divide the 5 tens. The difference, 2, must be less than the divisor.	$\begin{array}{r} 1 \\ 3\overline{)53} \\ -3 \\ \hline 2 \end{array}$	Divide. $5 \div 3$ Multiply. 3×1 Subtract. $5 - 3$ Compare. $2 < 3$
Step 2		Bring down the 3 ones. Regroup 2 tens 3 ones as 23 ones. Then divide the 23 ones. Write the remainder next to the quotient.	$\begin{array}{r} 17\ r2 \\ 3\overline{)53} \\ -3\downarrow \\ \hline 23 \\ -21 \\ \hline 2 \end{array}$	Divide. $23 \div 3$ Multiply. 3×7 Subtract. $23 - 21$ Compare. $2 < 3$
Step 3		To check, multiply the quotient by the divisor. Then add the remainder.	$\begin{array}{r} 17 \\ \times\ 3 \\ \hline 51 \\ +\ 2 \\ \hline 53 \end{array}$	quotient divisor remainder dividend

▲ In 1947 Jackie Robinson became the first African American to play on a major league baseball team.

Math Idea
The order of division is as follows:
Divide
Multiply
Subtract
Compare
Repeat this order until the division is complete.

So, each boy gets 17 cards with 2 left over.

• **What if** the remainder is equal to or greater than the divisor? What should you do?

• What conclusion can you make if you compare the quotient to the dividend when you divide whole numbers?

ANOTHER WAY Use partial quotients.

You can use partial quotients to divide.

Divide 53 by 3. Write $3\overline{)53}$.

Step 1

Make a list of multiples of 3.

$3 \times 2 = 6$

$3 \times 5 = 15$

$3 \times 10 = 30$

$3 \times 15 = 45$

Step 2

45 is close to 53, so use 15 as the first partial quotient. Subtract $53 - 45$.

$$
\begin{array}{r}
3\overline{)53} \\
-45 \\
\hline
8
\end{array}
\quad 15 \leftarrow
$$

Record partial quotients in a column.

Step 3

Repeat until the remainder is less than the divisor.

$$
\begin{array}{r}
3\overline{)53} \\
-45 \\
\hline
8 \\
-6 \\
\hline
2
\end{array}
\quad
\begin{array}{l}
15 \\
\\
2 \leftarrow \text{partial quotient}
\end{array}
$$

Step 4

Add the partial quotients.

$$
\begin{array}{r}
3\overline{)53} \\
-45 \\
\hline
8 \\
-6 \\
\hline
\text{remainder} \rightarrow 2
\end{array}
\quad
\begin{array}{l}
15 \\
\\
+2 \\
\hline
17 \leftarrow \text{quotient}
\end{array}
$$

So, $3\overline{)53} = 17$ r2.

• How can you use partial quotients to find $87 \div 5$?

More Examples

A Long division

$99 \div 4$

$$
\begin{array}{r}
24 \text{ r3} \\
4\overline{)99} \\
-8\downarrow \\
\hline
19 \\
-16 \\
\hline
3
\end{array}
$$

$99 \div 4 = 24$ r3

B Partial quotients

$65 \div 4$

Try $4 \times 10 = 40$.

$$
\begin{array}{r}
4\overline{)65} \\
-40 \\
\hline
25 \\
-24 \\
\hline
1
\end{array}
\quad
\begin{array}{l}
\leftarrow \quad 10 \ (4 \times 10) \\
\\
\leftarrow +6 \ (4 \times 6) \\
\hline
16
\end{array}
$$

$65 \div 4 = 16$ r1

Guided Practice

1. What is $49 \div 3$? Make a model to solve, and then record.

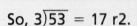

Choose a method. Then divide and record.

2. $4\overline{)59}$ 3. $2\overline{)68}$ 4. $3\overline{)76}$ ✓ 5. $5\overline{)85}$ ✓ 6. $8\overline{)93}$

7. **TALK Math** **Explain** how the long division and partial quotients methods are alike and how they are different.

Independent Practice and Problem Solving

Choose a method. Then divide and record.

8. $2\overline{)33}$ 9. $7\overline{)91}$ 10. $4\overline{)55}$ 11. $9\overline{)94}$ 12. $6\overline{)78}$

13. $93 \div 6$ 14. $64 \div 4$ 15. $77 \div 3$ 16. $82 \div 8$ 17. $90 \div 6$

18. $7\overline{)86}$ 19. $59 \div 4$ 20. $5\overline{)80}$ 21. $96 \div 3$ 22. $6\overline{)50}$

Use multiplication to check each answer.

23. $93 \div 2 = 46$ r1   24. $44 \div 5 = 8$ r4   25. $63 \div 3 = 21$ 26. $78 \div 7 = 11$ r1

⭐**Algebra** **Copy and complete each table.**

27.

Number of Feet	3	39	45	63	75
Number of Yards	1	13	▪	▪	▪

28.

Number of Days	7	77	84	91	98
Number of Weeks	1	11	▪	▪	▪

29. Fifty-six students signed up for baseball. The coach divided them into 4 equal teams. How many students are on each team?

30. Mr. Ro gave 81 golf tees to 7 golfers. Each golfer gets the same number of tees. How many did each get? How many are left over?

31. **≡FAST FACT** The highest scoring NFL game was November 27, 1966. The winning team scored 72 points! If touchdowns are worth 6 points, how many touchdowns could they have scored?

32. **WRITE Math** ▸ Write a set of directions to **describe** how to solve $47 \div 4$ using long division.

Mixed Review and Test Prep

33. If you make a bar graph of the number of days in each month of the year, which bars will be of equal height? (p. 206)

34. Kara cut 35 cakes into 16 slices each and she cut 7 cakes into 10 slices each. How many slices did she cut in all? (p. 282)

35. **Test Prep** Jared and his two brothers divided a package of 75 building blocks equally. How many blocks did each receive?

     A 23   **C** 72

     B 25   **D** 78

Soccer Games

 Reading Skill Draw Conclusions

There are 64 teams playing in the Women's NCAA Division I Soccer Tournament. The teams that win each round advance to the next round. The rounds are: first round, second round, third round, quarterfinals, semifinals, and championship. How many games will be played in the tournament?

You can draw conclusions from the data in a problem to help you solve it.

What I know: Two teams play against each other in each game. For each game in each round, there can be only one winner.

Conclusion: So, dividing the total number of teams by 2 will give you the number of games in each round. Repeat until only one game remains.

▲ The Penn State women's soccer team won their quarterfinal game in the 2005 NCAA Soccer Tournament.

Draw a diagram or make an organized list to keep track of the number of games played in each round. Add the total number of games in each round to find how many games are played in the Women's NCAA Division I Soccer Tournament.

Problem Solving Draw conclusions to solve the problem.

1. Solve the problem above.

2. If there were 32 teams playing in the tournament, how many games would be played in round 2?

3. **Explain** what conclusion you can draw about how many games the winning team will play to win the tournament.

Problem Solving Workshop
Strategy: Draw a Diagram

OBJECTIVE: Solve problems by using the strategy *draw a diagram.*

Learn the Strategy

Drawing a picture or a diagram can help you understand a problem and makes the solution visible. You can use different types of diagrams to show different problems.

Some diagrams can show groups.

Ahmed is making spaghetti sauce for a school fundraiser. He makes 25 cups of sauce. Each jar holds 5 cups of sauce.

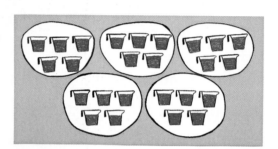

Some diagrams can show size.

Randy's model airplane is four times as long as Robin's. Together, the models are 25 inches long.

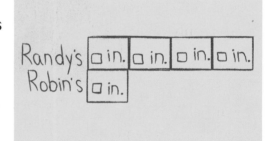

Some diagrams can show equal parts.

Greg and Wayne are planning to cut a 25-inch rope into 5 equal-size lengths.

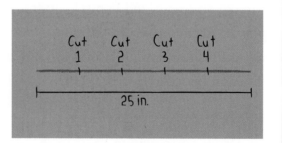

TALK Math

What is a question that can be answered by using each of the diagrams shown above?

To draw a diagram, carefully follow the information or action given in the problem. Keep the diagram simple. Label the parts to show what they represent.

Use the Strategy

PROBLEM Evan's dog weighs 5 times as much as Oxana's dog. Together the dogs weigh 96 pounds. How much does Evan's dog weigh?

Read to Understand

Plan

Solve

Check

Read to Understand

Reading Skill

- **Summarize what you are asked to find.**
- **What information will you use?**

Plan

- **What strategy can you use to solve the problem?**

  You can draw a diagram to help you solve the problem.

Solve

- **How can you use the strategy to solve the problem?**

  Draw a diagram that represents the relationship between the weights of the two dogs.

Evan's	■ lb	■ lb	■ lb	■ lb	■ lb
Oxana's	■ lb				

  } Total weight is 96 pounds.

  Divide 96 by 6 to find the value of each equal part.

  $96 \div 6 = 16$

  Each part is 16 pounds.
  Add five parts to find the weight of Evan's dog.

  $16 + 16 + 16 + 16 + 16 = 80$

  So, Evan's dog weighs 80 pounds.

Check

- **Is your answer reasonable? Explain.**
- **What other strategy could you use to solve the problem?**

Guided Problem Solving

Read to Understand

Plan

Solve

Check

1. Mia's dog weighs 4 times as much as her rabbit. Together the pets weigh 90 pounds. How much does Mia's dog weigh?

   First, draw a diagram to show the relationship between Mia's dog and rabbit.

   ? ▢ lb ▢ lb ▢ lb ▢ lb ⎫ Total weight
   ? ▢ lb   ⎬ is 90 pounds.

   Then, find the value of each equal part.

   Finally, add to find the dog's weight.

2. **What if** Mia's dog weighs 5 times as much as her rabbit. Together the pets weigh 60 pounds. How much does the dog weigh?

3. Ari runs a training school for pet actors. Last year he trained 3 times as many dogs as cats. If the total number of dogs and cats he trained last year is 84, how many cats did he train?

Problem Solving Strategy Practice

Draw a diagram to solve.

4. At a dog show, there are 4 times as many spaniels as other dogs. If there are a total of 60 dogs, how many are spaniels?

5. **WRITE Math** ▸ To get to a dog show, Mr. Luna first drives 7 miles west from his home and then 3 miles north. Next, he turns east and drives 11 miles to cross a bridge over the Mississippi River. Finally, he turns north and drives 4 miles to the dog show. How far north of Mr. Luna's home is the dog show? To solve the problem, Dara and Cliff drew diagrams. Which diagram is correct? **Explain.**

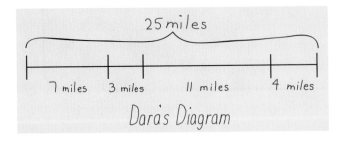

25 miles

7 miles   3 miles   11 miles   4 miles

Dara's Diagram

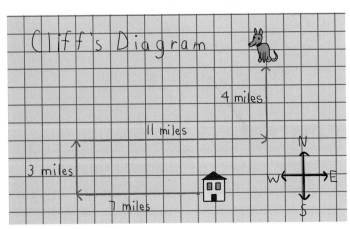

Cliff's Diagram

4 miles

11 miles

3 miles

7 miles

N · W · E · S

Mixed Strategy Practice

6. The Grant family paid $220 to attend a dog show for two days. Adult tickets were 3 times the cost of children's tickets. The Grants bought 3 adult tickets and 2 children's tickets. How much did they pay for each ticket?

7. Noah built a dog run that is 8 yards long and 6 yards wide. He placed posts at every corner and every yard along the length and width of the run. How many posts did he use?

USE DATA For 9 and 11, use the picture.

8. Petra walked four of the dogs in the picture. The second dog she walked was half as tall as the first, the third dog was 9 inches taller than the second, and the last dog was 8 inches taller than the third. The last dog she walked was the Irish setter. Which dog did Petra walk first?

9. Kari has pictures of a poodle, a beagle, a cocker spaniel, and a pug in a stack. The top picture is not a poodle and the last is not a spaniel. The beagle comes before the poodle and after the spaniel. Order the pictures from top to bottom.

10. **Pose a Problem** Look back at Problem 8. Write a similar problem by changing the types of dogs.

11. **Open-Ended** Pierre has three dogs. The tallest dog is 3 times as tall as the middle dog. The middle dog is 2 times as tall as the shortest dog. How tall could each dog be?

CHALLENGE YOURSELF

In 2004, there were about 150,000 Labrador retrievers registered by the American Kennel Club. There were also about 25,000 registered Chihuahuas.

12. The number of registered dachshunds was about 9,000 less than twice the number of registered Chihuahuas. How many dachshunds were registered?

13. The number of registered Labrador retrievers was about 15,000 more than 3 times the number of registered Yorkshire terriers. How many Yorkshire terriers were registered?

Choose a STRATEGY

Draw a Diagram or Picture
Make a Model or Act It Out
Make an Organized List
Find a Pattern
Make a Table or Graph
Predict and Test
Work Backward
Solve a Simpler Problem
Write an Equation
Use Logical Reasoning

Bichon Frise: 10 inches

Shar-Pei: 19 inches

Border Collie: 20 inches

Labrador Retriever: 24 inches

Irish Setter: 27 inches

MENTAL MATH

Division Patterns

OBJECTIVE: Use a basic fact and a pattern to divide mentally.

Learn

If you know basic facts, you can use them to divide multiples of 10, 100, or 1,000 mentally.

PROBLEM Trams take people to the top of the Gateway Arch in St. Louis, Missouri. If a tram makes 6 trips to the top, it can carry a total of 240 people. How many people fit in a tram?

Example Use a basic fact and a pattern.
Divide. $240 \div 6$

Think: 24 divided by 6 is 4

$24 \div 6 = 4 \leftarrow$ basic fact

$240 \div 6 = 40$

$2,400 \div 6 = 400$

So, 40 people will fit in a tram.

▲ On a clear day, you can see 30 miles in any direction from the top of the Gateway Arch.

More Examples

A Basic fact with a zero and a pattern

$30 \div 6 = 5 \leftarrow$ basic fact
$300 \div 6 = 50$
$3,000 \div 6 = 500$
$30,000 \div 6 = 5,000$

B Basic fact with a zero and a pattern

$40 \div 10 = 4 \leftarrow$ basic fact
$400 \div 10 = 40$
$4,000 \div 10 = 400$
$40,000 \div 10 = 4,000$

Math Idea

As the number of zeros in the dividend increases, so does the number of zeros in the quotient.

Guided Practice

1. What basic division fact can you use to find $90 \div 3$ and $9,000 \div 3$? Find $90 \div 3$ and $9,000 \div 3$.

Use mental math to complete the pattern.

2. $32 \div 8 = 4$
$320 \div 8 = \blacksquare$
$3,200 \div 8 = \blacksquare$

3. $28 \div 4 = \blacksquare$
$280 \div 4 = \blacksquare$
$2,800 \div 4 = \blacksquare$

✓4. $90 \div 9 = \blacksquare$
$900 \div 9 = \blacksquare$
$9,000 \div 9 = \blacksquare$

✓5. $64 \div 8 = \blacksquare$
$640 \div 8 = \blacksquare$
$6,400 \div 8 = \blacksquare$

6. [**TALK Math**] Explain how to use division facts you know to solve division problems with zeros at the end of the dividend.

Independent Practice and Problem Solving

Use mental math to complete the pattern.

7. $27 \div 9 = 3$
$270 \div 9 = \blacksquare$
$2,700 \div 9 = \blacksquare$
$27,000 \div 9 = \blacksquare$

8. $20 \div 5 = \blacksquare$
$200 \div 5 = \blacksquare$
$2,000 \div 5 = \blacksquare$
$20,000 \div 5 = \blacksquare$

9. $42 \div 7 = \blacksquare$
$\blacksquare \div 7 = 60$
$4,200 \div 7 = \blacksquare$
$\blacksquare \div 7 = 6,000$

10. $\blacksquare \div 3 = 2$
$60 \div 3 = \blacksquare$
$\blacksquare \div 3 = 200$
$6,000 \div 3 = \blacksquare$

Use mental math and patterns to find the quotient.

11. $120 \div 2$

12. $8,100 \div 9$

13. $400 \div 8$

14. $27,000 \div 3$

⭐**Algebra** **Find the value of *n*.**

15. $24,000 \div n = 3,000$ **16.** $6,300 \div n = 700$ **17.** $360 \div 6 = n$ **18.** $n \div 7 = 1,000$

USE DATA For 19–20, use the sign.

19. A camp paid $5,600 for a group of 15-year-olds to ride the tram. How many tickets did the camp buy?

20. Fae paid $280 for youth tickets and $90 for children's tickets. How many of each kind of ticket did she buy?

21. [**WRITE Math**] Explain why there is one more zero in the dividend than in the quotient when you find $40,000 \div 5$.

TRAM TICKETS

Type	Cost
Adults	$10
Youth 13–16	$7
Children 3–12	$3

Mixed Review and Test Prep

22. A theme park had 999 visitors on Saturday and 222 visitors on Sunday. How many visitors were there on both days? (p. 48)

23. A ball bounces half the height from which it is dropped. If the ball bounces 12 feet, from what height was it dropped? (p. 96)

24. **Test Prep** The zoo sold 210 tram tickets. The tram made 7 trips. If the tram was full each trip, how many people rode on the tram?

A 3
B 7
C 30
D 70

Extra Practice on page 324, Set C

MENTAL MATH
Estimate Quotients

OBJECTIVE: Estimate quotients by using rounding and compatible numbers, and then find the estimated quotient mentally.

Learn

PROBLEM A hummingbird beats its wings 6,240 times in 2 minutes. About how many times does it beat its wings in 1 minute?

Estimate. $6,240 \div 2$

ONE WAY Use rounding.

Step 1	Step 2
Round the dividend to the nearest thousand. $6,240 \div 2$ $\downarrow$ $6,000 \div 2$	Use mental math. $6 \div 2 = 3$ ← basic fact $60 \div 2 = 30$ $600 \div 2 = 300$ $6,000 \div 2 = 3,000$

So, a hummingbird beats its wings about 3,000 times in 1 minute.

▲ Hummingbirds visit more than 1,000 flowers a day!

ANOTHER WAY Use compatible numbers.

Step 1	Step 2
Find compatible numbers for 6,240 that can be divided evenly by 2. Think: $6 \div 2 = 3$ and $8 \div 2 = 4$ You can use 6,000 or 8,000 for 6,240.	Use mental math. $6,000 \div 2 = 3,000$ $8,000 \div 2 = 4,000$

So, a hummingbird beats its wings between 3,000 and 4,000 times in 1 minute.

More Examples Estimate using compatible numbers.

Ⓐ $558 \div 6$

Think: $54 \div 6 = 9$ and $60 \div 6 = 10$
You can use 540 or 600 for 558.
$540 \div 6 = 90$ and $600 \div 6 = 100$

So, both 90 and 100 are reasonable estimates.

Ⓑ $5,363 \div 9$

Think: $45 \div 9 = 5$ and $54 \div 9 = 6$
You can use 4,500 or 5,400 for 5,363.
$4,500 \div 9 = 500$ and $5,400 \div 9 = 600$

So, both 500 and 600 are reasonable estimates.

Guided Practice

1. Round the dividend to the nearest 100. Use mental math to estimate the quotient.

$263 \div 3$

Estimate the quotient.

2. $362 \div 4$ 3. $798 \div 2$ 4. $499 \div 7$ ✓5. $147 \div 3$ ✓6. $4,522 \div 9$

7. **TALK Math** Explain how you know whether your estimate is more than or less than the exact quotient.

Independent Practice and Problem Solving

Estimate the quotient.

8. $498 \div 5$ 9. $740 \div 7$ 10. $5,402 \div 6$ 11. $823 \div 9$ 12. $3,337 \div 3$

Estimate to compare. Write <, >, or = for each ●.

13. $613 \div 3$ ● $581 \div 2$ 14. $364 \div 4$ ● $117 \div 6$ 15. $2,718 \div 8$ ● $963 \div 2$

USE DATA For 16–19, use the table.

16. About how many times do a damselfly's wings beat in 1 minute?

17. About how many times do a scorpion fly's wings beat in 2 minutes?

18. About how many more times do an Aeschnid dragonfly's wings beat in 1 minute than a large white butterfly's wings?

19. **WRITE Math** What's the Question? The answer is about 700 beats in 1 minute.

Insect Wing Beats in 3 Minutes	
Insect	**Number of Wing Beats**
Aeschnid Dragonfly	6,840
Damselfly	2,880
Large White Butterfly	2,160
Scorpion Fly	5,040

Mixed Review and Test Prep

20. A teacher gave an equal number of pencils to 7 students. Write an expression to represent the situation. (p. 122)

21. In March, 18 schools signed up to do a bird count. Each school has 26 students counting birds. How many students are counting birds? (p. 282)

22. **Test Prep** A hummingbird's heart beats 3,782 times in 3 minutes. Which is the best estimate of the number of times its heart beats in 1 minute?

A 600   C 2,000

B 1,000   D 3,000

Extra Practice on page 324, Set D

7 Place the First Digit

OBJECTIVE: Place the first digit in a quotient by estimating or using place value.

Quick Review

Yen put 791 caps in 9 boxes. He put about the same number in each box. About how many caps were in each box?

Learn

PROBLEM Tamiqua has a bunch of 8 black-eyed susans. In all, she counts 168 petals on her flowers. If all the flowers have the same number of petals, how many petals are on one flower?

ONE WAY Use compatible numbers. Divide 168 by 8. Write $8\overline{)168}$.

Step 1	Step 2	Step 3
Use compatible numbers to estimate to place the first digit.	Divide the 16 tens.	Bring down the 8 ones. Divide the 8 ones.

Step 1

Think: $8\overline{)160}^{\,20}$ or $8\overline{)240}^{\,30}$

■ So, the first digit is
$8\overline{)168}$ in the tens place.

Step 2

$$\begin{array}{r} 2 \\ 8\overline{)168} \\ -16 \\ \hline 0 \end{array}$$

Divide. $8\overline{)16}$
Multiply. 8×2
Subtract. $16 - 16$
Compare. $0 < 8$

Step 3

$$\begin{array}{r} 21 \\ 8\overline{)168} \\ -16\downarrow \\ \hline 8 \\ -8 \\ \hline 0 \end{array}$$

Divide. $8\overline{)8}$
Multiply. 8×1
Subtract. $8 - 8$
Compare. $0 < 8$

So, there are 21 petals on one flower. Since 21 is between 20 and 30, the answer is reasonable.

ERROR ALERT

If you cannot divide the divisor into the first digit of the dividend, the quotient begins at the next place value to the right.

ANOTHER WAY Use place value. Divide 423 by 5. Write $5\overline{)423}$.

Step 1	Step 2	Step 3
Use place value to place the first digit. Look at the hundreds.	Divide 42 tens.	Bring down the 3 ones. Divide the 23 ones.

Step 1

$5\overline{)423}$ $4 < 5$, so look at the tens.

■
$5\overline{)423}$ $42 > 5$, so the first digit is in the tens place.

Step 2

$$\begin{array}{r} 8 \\ 5\overline{)423} \\ -40 \\ \hline 2 \end{array}$$

Divide. $5\overline{)42}$
Multiply. 5×8
Subtract. $42 - 40$
Compare. $2 < 5$

Step 3

$$\begin{array}{r} 84\ \text{r3} \\ 5\overline{)423} \\ -40\downarrow \\ \hline 23 \\ -20 \\ \hline 3 \end{array}$$

Divide. $5\overline{)23}$
Multiply. 5×4
Subtract. $23 - 20$
Compare. $3 < 5$

So, $5\overline{)423}$ is 84 r3.

Guided Practice

1. Use place value to place the first digit. Where should you place the first digit? Divide.

$4\overline{)459}$

Tell where to place the first digit. Then divide.

2. $7\overline{)228}$ **3.** $926 \div 4$ **4.** $777 \div 3$ ✓**5.** $6\overline{)126}$ ✓**6.** $889 \div 8$

7. **TALK Math** Explain why the first digit in the quotient $233 \div 3$ is in the tens place.

Independent Practice and Problem Solving

Tell where to place the first digit. Then divide.

8. $2\overline{)145}$ **9.** $455 \div 5$ **10.** $6\overline{)779}$ **11.** $132 \div 7$ **12.** $3\overline{)945}$

Divide.

13. $923 \div 8$ **14.** $2\overline{)184}$ **15.** $329 \div 5$ **16.** $4\overline{)696}$ **17.** $992 \div 6$

⭐**Algebra** Find the missing digit.

18. $426 \div 6 = 7\blacksquare$ **19.** $643 \div 7 = 9\blacksquare\ r6$ **20.** $664 \div 3 = \blacksquare21\ r1$

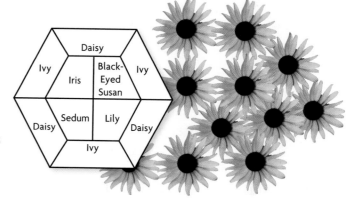

USE DATA For 21, use the garden plan.

21. If Ty has 125 daisy plants, how many plants will be left if he plants an equal number in each daisy section?

22. Lillie has a total of 56 flowers. She has 14 irises. The rest are ivy and sedum. She has twice as many ivy as sedums. How many sedum plants does she have?

23. **Reasoning** If the dividend is 3 digits and you place the first digit in the tens place, what does that tell you about the divisor?

24. **WRITE Math** Explain how you can determine the number of digits in the quotient $726 \div 9$ without dividing.

Mixed Review and Test Prep

25. How many days are in 5 weeks? (p. 160)

26. A shop has 652 coins in 7 cases. Each case has about the same number of coins. To the nearest hundred, about how many coins are in each case? (p. 320)

27. **Test Prep** In which place is the first digit in the quotient $497 \div 2$?

   A Thousands

   B Hundreds

   C Tens

   D Ones

Extra Practice on page 324, Set E

Extra Practice

Set A Use counters to find the quotient and remainder. (pp. 306–307)

1. $26 \div 8$ **2.** $22 \div 3$ **3.** $29 \div 6$ **4.** $38 \div 9$

Divide. You may wish to use counters or draw a picture to help.

5. $55 \div 7$ **6.** $5\overline{)58}$ **7.** $49 \div 6$ **8.** $4\overline{)51}$

9. Use the table at the right. Singh divides a bag of each brand of marbles into 6 equal-size groups. From which brand does he have the greatest number of marbles left over?

10. Use the table at the right. Marni makes 5 equal-size groups from a bag of each brand. From which brand will she have marbles left over?

Marbles	
Brand	**Marbles per Bag**
Kit's Cat's Eye	50
Smoothie	65
Clear as Glass	36

Set B Choose a method. Then divide and record. (pp. 310–313)

1. $88 \div 7$ **2.** $8\overline{)98}$ **3.** $65 \div 4$ **4.** $5\overline{)67}$ **5.** $79 \div 6$

6. $4\overline{)63}$ **7.** $57 \div 2$ **8.** $6\overline{)95}$ **9.** $76 \div 3$ **10.** $84 \div 5$

Set C Use mental math and patterns to find the quotient. (pp. 318–319)

1. $150 \div 3$ **2.** $4,500 \div 5$ **3.** $64,000 \div 8$ **4.** $4,900 \div 7$ **5.** $3,600 \div 4$

6. $2,400 \div 3$ **7.** $36,000 \div 9$ **8.** $630 \div 7$ **9.** $2,800 \div 4$ **10.** $5,600 \div 7$

11. Alan pays $320 for admission tickets to a theme park. If he buys 8 tickets, how much does he pay per ticket?

Set D Estimate the quotient. (pp. 320–321)

1. $299 \div 3$ **2.** $680 \div 5$ **3.** $5,402 \div 6$ **4.** $7,622 \div 8$ **5.** $4,211 \div 6$

6. $301 \div 5$ **7.** $549 \div 6$ **8.** $624 \div 7$ **9.** $333 \div 8$ **10.** $791 \div 8$

Set E Tell where to place the first digit. Then divide. (pp. 322–323)

1. $3\overline{)358}$ **2.** $949 \div 6$ **3.** $325 \div 4$ **4.** $7\overline{)653}$ **5.** $525 \div 4$

6. $8\overline{)971}$ **7.** $457 \div 3$ **8.** $621 \div 7$ **9.** $5\overline{)491}$ **10.** $918 \div 7$

Technology
Use Harcourt Mega Math, The Number Games, *Up, Up, and Array,* Levels L, M.

Divide All Five

Players
2 players

Materials
- 2-color counters
- Number cube labeled 1 to 6

35	27	64	81	90
76	50	28	41	52
49	43	39	56	4
18	82	70	60	12
65	32	26	24	80

How to Play

- The object is to cover 5 numbers in a row—across, down, or diagonally.

- Decide who will use yellow counters and who will use red counters.

- Players take turns. Toss the number cube. The player places his or her counter on the game board over any number that is divided evenly by the number tossed.

- If 1 is tossed, place a counter on any number still showing. If a number is tossed that does not divide evenly into one of the numbers still showing, the player ends his or her turn.

- The first player to cover five numbers in a row wins.

 **Short Division**

Maple Trees

The state tree of Wisconsin is the sugar maple. Sugar maple trees produce sap that is used for maple syrup.

A farmer sold 582 pints of maple syrup to 3 stores. Each store bought the same number of pints. How many pints of maple syrup did each store buy?

You can use short division to find the quotient. Short division uses mental math to solve problems. You write only the quotients and the remainders.

▲ One sugar maple tree produces about 20 gallons of sap in the spring, which makes 2 quarts of maple syrup.

Example
Divide. 582 ÷ 3   Estimate. 600 ÷ 3 = 200

Step 1	**Step 2**	**Step 3**
Divide the hundreds.	**Divide the tens.**	**Divide the ones.**
$$\begin{array}{r} 1 \\ 3\overline{)5} \\ -3 \\ \hline 2 \end{array}$$ Think: 5 hundreds divided by 3 ones is 1 hundred with a remainder of 2 tens.	$$\begin{array}{r} 9 \\ 3\overline{)28} \\ -27 \\ \hline 1 \end{array}$$ Think: 28 tens divided by 3 ones is 9 tens with a remainder of 1 ten.	$$\begin{array}{r} 4 \\ 3\overline{)12} \\ -12 \\ \hline 0 \end{array}$$ Think: 12 tens divided by 3 ones is 4 tens.
Write 1 in the quotient. Write 2 to make 28 in the tens place. $$\begin{array}{r} 1 \\ 3\overline{)5^28 2} \end{array}$$	Write 9 in the quotient. Write 1 to make 12 in the ones place. $$\begin{array}{r} 1\ 9 \\ 3\overline{)5^28^12} \end{array}$$	Write 4 in the quotient. $$\begin{array}{r} 1\ 9\ 4 \\ 3\overline{)5^28^12} \end{array}$$

So, each store bought 194 pints of maple syrup. 194 is close to 200, so the answer is reasonable.

More Examples

Ⓐ $$\begin{array}{r} 1\ 4\ 8 \\ 5\overline{)7^24^40} \end{array}$$ Ⓑ $$\begin{array}{r} 1\ 3\ 5 \\ 3\overline{)4^10^15} \end{array}$$ Ⓒ $$\begin{array}{r} 2\ 0\ 8 \\ 4\overline{)83^32} \end{array}$$

Try It
Use short division to find the quotient.

1. 534 ÷ 2   **2.** 784 ÷ 4   **3.** 810 ÷ 6   **4.** 816 ÷ 2

5. 531 ÷ 3   **6.** 903 ÷ 7   **7.** 952 ÷ 4   **8.** 746 ÷ 2

9. ▐WRITE Math▶ **Explain** how short division makes it easy to find 741 ÷ 3.

Chapter 11 Review/Test

Check Concepts

Use counters to find the quotient and remainder. (pp. 306–307)

1. $16 \div 3$
2. $37 \div 6$
3. $44 \div 8$
4. $23 \div 5$

Check Skills

Choose a method. Then divide and record. (pp. 310–313)

5. $65 \div 3$
6. $71 \div 5$
7. $4\overline{)72}$
8. $8\overline{)98}$

Use mental math and patterns to find the quotient. (pp. 318–319)

9. $150 \div 3$
10. $5,400 \div 9$
11. $360 \div 6$
12. $56,000 \div 8$
13. $4,900 \div 7$
14. $480 \div 6$
15. $7,200 \div 8$
16. $1,600 \div 4$

Estimate the quotient. (pp. 320–321)

17. $4,631 \div 9$
18. $63,999 \div 8$
19. $4,261 \div 5$
20. $349 \div 7$

Tell where to place the first digit. Then divide. (pp. 322–323)

21. $165 \div 4$
22. $342 \div 5$
23. $6\overline{)276}$
24. $736 \div 3$
25. $7\overline{)652}$
26. $8\overline{)672}$
27. $853 \div 7$
28. $261 \div 3$
29. $5\overline{)371}$
30. $861 \div 4$

Check Problem Solving

Solve. (pp. 314–317)

31. Pauline has 64 stuffed animals. She wants to put them on 3 shelves. If she puts the same number on each shelf, how many stuffed animals will be left over?

32. George is collecting leaves for a science project. He has 48 leaves. Each bag holds 6 leaves. How many bags does he need?

33. **WRITE Math** ▶ Sari weighs 8 times as much as her little brother. They weigh 108 pounds together. **Explain** how you can draw a diagram to find how much Sari weighs.

Standardized Test Prep
Chapters 1–11

Measurement

1. Ostriches lay eggs that hatch after about 42 days. How many weeks is 42 days? (p. 160)

A 5 weeks   **C** 7 weeks

B 6 weeks   **D** 8 weeks

2. Which of the following temperatures would be a comfortable room temperature? (p. 164)

A ⁻5°C   **C** 20°C

B 0°C   **D** 70°C

3. Labor Day is the first Monday in September. Betty starts school the day after Labor Day. The fair is 6 weeks and 3 days after the first day of school. What date is the fair? (p. 158)

September						
Sun	Mon	Tue	Wed	Thu	Fri	Sat
	1	2	3	4	5	6
7	8	9	10	11	12	13
14	15	16	17	18	19	20
21	22	23	24	25	26	27
28	29	30				

October						
Sun	Mon	Tue	Wed	Thu	Fri	Sat
			1	2	3	4
5	6	7	8	9	10	11
12	13	14	15	16	17	18
19	20	21	22	23	24	25
26	27	28	29	30	31	

A October 17   **C** October 10

B October 14   **D** October 7

4. **WRITE Math** ▸ Julio plans to take the train from his home in Flint, Michigan, to Chicago, Illinois. The train leaves Flint at 6:41 A.M. and arrives in Chicago at 11:14 A.M. **Explain** how to find the length of the train ride. (p. 154)

Number and Operations

5. In 2003, the population of New York City was 8,085,742. Round 8,085,742 to the nearest hundred thousand. (p. 34)

A 8,000,000   **C** 9,000,000

B 8,100,000   **D** 10,000,000

Test Tip **Check your work.**

See Item 6. If your answer does not match any of the choices, check your computation.

6. Movie tickets at Cinema City are $12 per person. How much money is collected for 252 tickets? (p. 286)

A $21   **C** $2,700

B $756   **D** $3,024

7. 5,603 − 2,497 (p. 48)

A 2,296   **C** 3,206

B 3,106   **D** 3,294

8. Toni is buying 4 bracelets at $5.09 each. How much does she pay in all? (p. 254)

A $20.36   **C** $23.36

B $23.06   **D** $24.16

9. **WRITE Math** ▸ Cyril has 75 pictures for his album. If he can fit 8 on each page, how many pages will he need? **Explain** your answer. (p. 306)

Data Analysis and Probability

10. Marta is setting up a monthly budget with different categories for her spending and savings. She is keeping a record of all the money she spends each month in each category. What type of graph could she use to show her expenses for the month? (p. 222)

A Circle graph

B Line plot

C Venn diagram

D Line graph

11. Yasir tossed a number cube labeled 1 to 6 twenty-five times. His results are shown in this line plot.

Number Cube Results

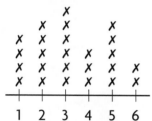

Number Tossed

How many times did Yasir toss a number greater than 4? (p. 190)

A 3

B 5

C 7

D 10

12. ⬛ **WRITE Math** ▶ **Explain** how to find the mean, median, and mode of this data set. (p. 186)

8, 6, 9, 3, 5, 10, 5, 18, 4, 12

Algebraic Reasoning

13. Follow the order of operations to find the value of the expression. (p. 126)

$$(16 + 8) \div 4 + 2 \times 3$$

A 60

B 24

C 12

D 1

14. Which number is represented by n? (p. 108)

$$3 \times n = 87$$

A 26

B 27

C 28

D 29

15. Emma wants to find the value of the expression $2 \times 7 \times 5$. To make the multiplication easier, she changes the order of the factors to $2 \times 5 \times 7$. What multiplication property is Emma using? (p. 118)

A Associative Property

B Identity Property

C Distributive Property

D Commutative Property

16. ⬛ **WRITE Math** ▶ **Explain** how adding the parentheses changes the value of the expression. (p. 126)

$$12 + 5 \times 3 - 21$$

$$(12 + 5) \times 3 - 21$$

12 Practice Division

Investigate

An octopus can fill its body with water. Then it can move fast by shooting out the water like a jet. An octopus can also move by using its arms to walk very slowly. Choose a number of centimeters an octopus might walk. How can you find the time it would take each octopus in the graph to walk that distance?

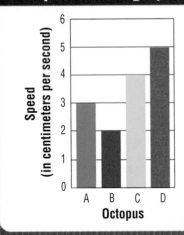

Octopus Walking Speed

FAST FACT

An octopus has eight arms and lives in the sea. The giant octopus is the largest. It can be 23 feet across. The California octopus is the smallest, less than an inch across.

GO ONLINE

Technology
Student pages are available in the Student eBook.

Show What You Know

Check your understanding of important skills
needed for success in Chapter 12.

▶ **Estimate Quotients**

Estimate the quotient.

1. $86 \div 3$ 2. $424 \div 7$ 3. $338 \div 8$ 4. $1,210 \div 4$

5. $2,605 \div 5$ 6. $1,420 \div 2$ 7. $4,316 \div 2$ 8. $275 \div 6$

▶ **2-Digit By 1-Digit Division**

Use the model to find the quotient and remainder.

9.

$25 \div 4 = \blacksquare$

10.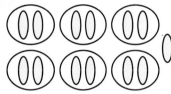

$13 \div 6 = \blacksquare$

11.

$17 \div 5 = \blacksquare$

12.

$33 \div 6 = \blacksquare$

▶ **Place Value Through Thousands**

Tell the value of the underlined digit.

13. 8,9<u>4</u>3   14. 9,08<u>2</u>   15. <u>1</u>,354   16. 3,<u>8</u>95

VOCABULARY POWER

CHAPTER VOCABULARY

compatible numbers
dividend
divisor
quotient
remainder

WARM-UP WORDS

dividend the number that is to be divided in a division problem

divisor the number that divides the dividend

quotient the number, not including the remainder, that results from dividing

Problem Solving Workshop
Skill: Interpret the Remainder

OBJECTIVE: Solve problems by using the skill *interpret the remainder.*

Use the Skill

PROBLEM There are 95 people with reservations for a guided raft trip on the Nenana River in Denali National Park in Alaska. Each raft holds 6 people. How many rafts are needed for the 95 people? How many rafts will be full? How many people will be in a raft that is not full?

When a division problem has a remainder, you interpret the remainder based on the situation and the question.

Divide. $95 \div 6$

A **Increase the quotient by 1.**

How many rafts are needed?

$$\begin{array}{r} 15\ r5 \\ 6)\overline{95} \\ -\ 6\downarrow \\ \hline 35 \\ -\ 30 \\ \hline 5 \end{array}$$

Think: Since 15 rafts only hold 90 people, one more raft is needed. So, drop the remainder, and increase the quotient by 1.

So, 16 rafts are needed.

B **Quotient stays the same. Drop the remainder.**

How many rafts will be full?
Think: A raft holds 6 people. Drop the remainder because 5 people do not fill a raft.

So, 15 rafts will be full.

C **Use the remainder as the answer.**

How many people will be in a raft that is not full?
Think: The remainder is the answer.

So, 5 people will be in a raft that is not full.

Think and Discuss

Solve the problem. Explain how you interpreted the remainder.

Another river guide company has rafts that hold 8 people. On Saturday, 99 people will take river trips.

  a. How many rafts are needed to take them on river trips?

  b. Will each raft be full? If not, how many people will be in the raft that is not full?

Solve. Write *a*, *b*, or *c*, to explain how to interpret the remainder.

   a. Increase the quotient by 1.

   b. Quotient stays the same. Drop the remainder.

   c. Use the remainder as the answer.

1. A group of 57 people is camping in Denali National Park. Each tent holds 5 people. How many tents are needed for all of the campers?

First, divide.

Think: 57 ÷ 5

Then, look back at the problem to see how to interpret the remainder.

2. **What if** you were asked how many tents will be full? How would your answer be different from your answer to Problem 1?

3. Guides lead groups of 9 people on biking tours in the park. There are 96 people who decided to go on the tours. How many people will be on a tour that is not full?

Mixed Applications

USE DATA For 4–6, use the table. On float trips, the guides take 6 passengers in each raft.

4. How many rafts are needed for the Saturday afternoon trips? Will all of the rafts on Saturday afternoon be full? **Explain.**

5. On which day were there more passengers? How many more passengers were there?

6. By the end of the week, the guides took 12 times as many people on float trips as were booked for the Sunday morning trips. How many people took float trips that week?

7. On Saturday morning, the temperature during the first trip was 63°F. The temperature during the first trip on Sunday was 7°F cooler. What was the temperature on Sunday?

8. **WRITE Math** ▶ A company signed up 67 people for float trips. If 8 people fit in a raft, how many rafts do they need? **Explain** whether you need an exact answer or estimate, and then solve.

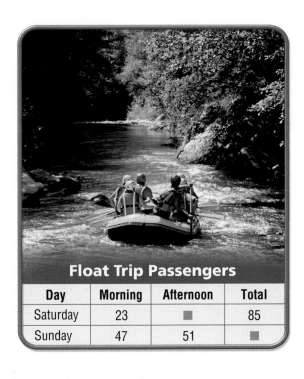

Float Trip Passengers

Day	Morning	Afternoon	Total
Saturday	23	■	85
Sunday	47	51	■

2 Divide 3-Digit Numbers and Money

OBJECTIVE: Divide 3-digit numbers and money by 1-digit numbers.

Learn

PROBLEM President Dwight D. Eisenhower liked vegetable soup so much, that he created his own recipe. One recipe makes about 193 ounces of soup. How many 8-ounce bowls can be filled by using 193 ounces of soup?

Example 1 Divide 193 by 8. Write $8\overline{)193}$.

Step 1

Estimate by rounding.
Think: 193 is about 190, and 8 is about 10.
$190 \div 10 = 19$

$8\overline{)193}$ Place the first digit in the tens place.

Step 2

Divide the 19 tens.

$$\begin{array}{r} 2 \\ 8\overline{)193} \\ -16 \\ \hline 3 \end{array}$$

Divide.
Multiply.
Subtract.
Compare.

Step 3

Bring down the 3 ones. Divide the 33 ones.

$$\begin{array}{r} 24 \text{ r}1 \\ 8\overline{)193} \\ -16\downarrow \\ \hline 33 \\ -32 \\ \hline 1 \end{array}$$

Divide.
Multiply.
Subtract.
Compare.

Step 4

To check, multiply the quotient by the divisor and add the remainder.

$$\begin{array}{r} 24 \\ \times\ \ 8 \\ \hline 192 \\ +\ \ 1 \\ \hline 193 \end{array}$$

quotient
divisor

remainder
dividend

So, 24 8-ounce bowls can be filled using 193 ounces. There will be 1 ounce left over.

Example 2 Divide 756 by 6. Write $6\overline{)756}$.

Step 1

Use division facts for 6 to find compatible numbers for 756.

$$\begin{array}{cc} 100 & 200 \end{array}$$
Think: $6\overline{)600}$ or $6\overline{)1,200}$

The quotient is between 100 and 200. So, place the first digit in the hundreds place.

Step 2

Divide the 7 hundreds.

$$\begin{array}{r} 1 \\ 6\overline{)756} \\ -6 \\ \hline 1 \end{array}$$

Divide.
Multiply.
Subtract.
Compare.

Step 3

Bring down the 5 tens. Divide the 15 tens.

$$\begin{array}{r} 12 \\ 6\overline{)756} \\ -6\downarrow \\ \hline 15 \\ -12 \\ \hline 3 \end{array}$$

Divide.
Multiply.
Subtract.
Compare.

Step 4

Bring down the 6 ones. Divide the 36 ones.

$$\begin{array}{r} 126 \\ 6\overline{)756} \\ -6 \\ \hline 15 \\ -12\downarrow \\ \hline 36 \\ -36 \\ \hline 0 \end{array}$$

Divide.
Multiply.
Subtract.
Compare.

So, $756 \div 6 = 126$. Since 126 is between 100 and 200, the answer is reasonable.

Divide Money

Divide money as you would divide whole numbers.

Example 3

At Ed's Electronics, 4 stereo speakers cost $168.
How much does 1 speaker cost?

Divide $168 by 4. Write $4\overline{)\$168}$.

Step 1	Step 2	Step 3	Step 4
Use place value to place the first digit. Look at the hundreds.	Divide the 16 tens.	Bring down the 8 ones. Divide the 8 ones.	Multiply to check.
$4\overline{)\$168}$ 1 < 4, so look at the tens. $\blacksquare$ 16 > 4, so use 16 tens. $4\overline{)\$168}$ Place the first digit in the tens place.	$\begin{array}{r}\$\ 4\\4\overline{)\$168}\\-16\\\hline 0\end{array}$ Divide. Multiply. Subtract. Compare.	$\begin{array}{r}\$\ 42\\4\overline{)\$168}\\-16\downarrow\\\hline 08\\-\ 8\\\hline 0\end{array}$ Divide. Multiply. Subtract. Compare.	$\begin{array}{r}\$42\\\times\ \ 4\\\hline \$168\end{array}$ quotient divisor dividend

So, one speaker costs $42.

- How do you know if the answer is reasonable?

Example 4

At the grocery store, 3 cans of green beans are on sale
for $2.59. What is the cost of 1 can of green beans?

Divide $2.59 by 3. Write $3\overline{)\$2.59}$.

$\begin{array}{r}\$0.86\ r1\\3\overline{)\$2.59}\\-2\,4\downarrow\\\hline 19\\-18\\\hline 1\end{array}$

Divide money as you divide whole numbers. Write the quotient in dollars and cents.

A store cannot charge parts of a cent. It increases a quotient to the next cent. $0.86 r1 is increased to $0.87.

So, the cost of 1 can of green beans is $0.87.

- **What if** the store sells 5 cans of green beans for $4.29? How much does 1 can cost?

Guided Practice

1. To find 456 ÷ 8, what two compatible numbers can you use for 456? Use these compatible numbers to estimate to place the first digit. Divide. In which place do you place the first digit of the quotient?

Divide and check.

2. 4)329   **3.** $7.23 ÷ 3   **4.** 7)655   ✓**5.** 924 ÷ 8   ✓**6.** 6)$5.82

7. **TALK Math** **Explain** how to place the first digit in Problem 5.

Independent Practice and Problem Solving

Divide and check.

8. 188 ÷ 2   **9.** 7)$8.26   **10.** 854 ÷ 6   **11.** 3)112   **12.** $7.98 ÷ 6

13. $332 ÷ 4   **14.** 5)725   **15.** 766 ÷ 8   **16.** 5)$845   **17.** 3)$9.48

18. 4)298   **19.** 2)$2.22   **20.** 9)$1.89   **21.** $1.24 ÷ 4   **22.** 292 ÷ 8

23. 2)483   **24.** 528 ÷ 7   **25.** 3)$4.83   **26.** 746 ÷ 5   **27.** 829 ÷ 9

⭐**Algebra** **Find the missing digit.**

28. ■7 / 5)485   **29.** 31 r1 / ■)125   **30.** 95 r4 / 6)■74   **31.** 35 r■ / 9)317

32. 45 r6 / 7)3■1   **33.** 229 r1 / ■)688   **34.** 49 r5 / 6)29■   **35.** ■1 r1 / 8)89

USE DATA For 36–40, use the table.

36. How much does 1 pound of cabbage cost at Krammer's?

37. How much does 1 pound of potatoes cost at Food Tiger?

38. How much do 3 pounds of carrots cost at Krammer's?

39. How much do 2 pounds of onions cost at Food Tiger?

40. **Pose a Problem** Look back at Problem 36. Exchange the known and unknown information. Then solve the problem.

41. **Reasoning** Which has the greater quotient, 654 ÷ 2 or 654 ÷ 3? **Explain** how you know.

42. **Explain** how to use compatible numbers to solve the problem 283 ÷ 9.

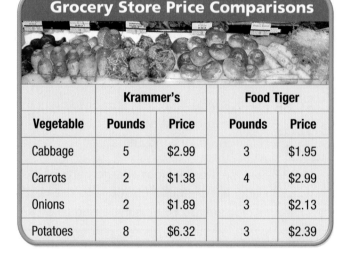

Grocery Store Price Comparisons

	Krammer's		Food Tiger	
Vegetable	Pounds	Price	Pounds	Price
Cabbage	5	$2.99	3	$1.95
Carrots	2	$1.38	4	$2.99
Onions	2	$1.89	3	$2.13
Potatoes	8	$6.32	3	$2.39

43. **WRITE Math** ▸ What's the Error? Describe the error, and then show the correct way to divide.

751
7)526
−49↓
  36
−35
   1

CD ROM **Technology** Use Harcourt Mega Math, The Number Games, *Buggy Bargains*, Level M.

44. Patty pulls a marble from a bag with 3 green marbles, 6 blue marbles, and 3 red marbles. All the marbles are the same size. Is she likely, unlikely, or equally likely to pull a blue marble as a red or green marble? (Grade 3)

45. Test Prep Three cans of tennis balls are on sale this week for $5.79. How much does one can of tennis balls cost?

46. There are 78 students going on a field trip. There will be 6 students in each van. How many vans are needed? (p. 310)

47. Test Prep Steven has 644 bottle caps. He divides his collection into 7 equal groups. How many are in each group?

A 91 r6   **C** 92 r6

B 92   **D** 916

Problem Solving connects to Science

Power plants convert other forms of energy into electricity so we can heat, cool, and light our homes, and use televisions and other household appliances. The table shows the estimated weekly use and cost for some household appliances.

Cost of using Some Household Appliances		
Appliance	**Estimated Weekly Use**	**Estimated Weekly Cost**
Dishwasher	7 loads	$1.26
Washing Machine	9 washes in hot wash/warm rinse with electric water heater	$7.11
Washing Machine	9 washes in warm wash/cold rinse with electric water heater	$2.61
Clothes Dryer	9 loads	$3.96
Refrigerator	7 days constant	$1.12

Use the table to solve the problems.

1. How much does it cost to run the dishwasher for one load?

2. How much does it cost to run the refrigerator for one day?

3. How much does it cost to do one load in the washing machine using hot wash/warm rinse?

4. How much does it cost to dry 8 loads of laundry in the clothes dryer?

5. Explain how you can find how much it costs to run the refrigerator for 3 days.

Zeros in Division

OBJECTIVE: Divide 3-digit numbers by 1-digit numbers when there are zeros in the quotient.

Learn

PROBLEM Mr. Bing collects 324 treasures for his backyard treasure hunt. He needs 3 treasures for each student who participates. How many students can participate?

Example

Divide 324 by 3. Write $3\overline{)324}$

Step 1	Step 2	Step 3	Step 4
Estimate to place the first digit in the quotient.	Divide the 3 hundreds.	Bring down the 2 tens. Divide the 2 tens.	Bring down the 4 ones. Divide the 24 ones.
Think: $\frac{100}{3\overline{)300}}$ or $\frac{200}{3\overline{)600}}$ $\blacksquare$ $3\overline{)324}$ So, place the first digit in the hundreds place.	$\begin{array}{r} 1 \\ 3\overline{)324} \\ -3 \\ \hline 0 \end{array}$	$\begin{array}{r} 10 \\ 3\overline{)324} \\ -3\downarrow \\ \hline 02 \\ -\ 0 \\ \hline 2 \end{array}$ The divisor 3 is greater than 2, so write a 0 in the quotient.	$\begin{array}{r} 108 \\ 3\overline{)324} \\ -3\ \mid \\ \hline 02\ \mid \\ -\ 0\downarrow \\ \hline 24 \\ -24 \\ \hline 0 \end{array}$

So, 108 students can participate in the backyard treasure hunt.

• **What if** Mr. Bing had 420 treasures? How many students could participate?

More Examples

A Divide with Zeros

$$\begin{array}{r} 102\ r1 \\ 4\overline{)409} \\ -4\downarrow\ \mid \\ \hline 00\ \mid \\ -\ 0\downarrow \\ \hline 09 \\ -\ 8 \\ \hline 1 \end{array}$$

CHECK

$$\begin{array}{r} 102 \\ \times\ \ 4 \\ \hline 408 \\ +\ \ 1 \\ \hline 409 \end{array}$$
quotient
divisor

remainder
dividend

B Divide Money

$$\begin{array}{r} \$104 \\ 5\overline{)\$520} \\ -5\downarrow\ \mid \\ \hline 02\ \mid \\ -\ 0\downarrow \\ \hline 20 \\ -20 \\ \hline 0 \end{array}$$

CHECK

$$\begin{array}{r} 2 \\ \$104 \\ \times\ \ 5 \\ \hline \$520 \end{array}$$
quotient
divisor
dividend

Correcting Quotients

The fourth-grade science classes displayed their treasures on tables for nature night. They put the same number of treasures on each table. There were 480 animal treasures on 6 tables. How many treasures were on each table?

Look at Ethan's paper. Ethan divided 480 by 6.

```
          Ethan

           8
       6)480
        -48
          0
```

- Describe Ethan's error. Find the correct number of treasures per table.

- Explain how basic facts and patterns could have helped Ethan find the correct answer.

Students who found plant and mineral treasures displayed 424 treasures on 4 tables. How many did they display on each table?

Look at Ava's paper. Ava divided 424 by 4.

```
         Ava

          16
      4)424
       -4
         24
        -24
          0
```

- Describe Ava's error. Find the correct number of treasures per table.

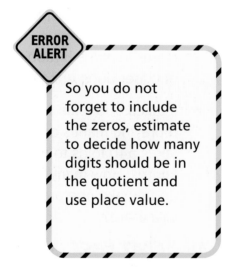

ERROR ALERT

So you do not forget to include the zeros, estimate to decide how many digits should be in the quotient and use place value.

Guided Practice

1. Copy the problem at the right. Estimate to place the first digit in the quotient. Divide the hundreds. Divide the tens. Do you need to write a zero in the quotient? Then divide the ones. What is the quotient?

$$2\overline{)210}$$

Write the number of digits in each quotient.

2. $360 \div 4$ 3. $714 \div 7$ 4. $3\overline{)420}$ 5. $8\overline{)960}$ ✓6. $400 \div 5$

Divide and check.

7. $5\overline{)305}$ 8. $803 \div 4$ 9. $6\overline{)840}$ 10. $901 \div 2$ ✓11. $9\overline{)927}$

12. **TALK Math** Think about the problem $216 \div 2$. **Explain** how you know there will be a 0 in the quotient.

Independent Practice and Problem Solving

Write the number of digits in each quotient.

13. $7\overline{)560}$ 14. $282 \div 4$ 15. $3\overline{)510}$ 16. $7\overline{)805}$ 17. $540 \div 6$

Divide and check.

18. $5\overline{)601}$ 19. $860 \div 2$ 20. $8\overline{)704}$ 21. $609 \div 3$ 22. $9\overline{)919}$

23. $283 \div 4$ 24. $763 \div 7$ 25. $870 \div 3$ 26. $6\overline{)724}$ 27. $407 \div 5$

28. $4\overline{)700}$ 29. $3\overline{)325}$ 30. $417 \div 2$ 31. $470 \div 4$ 32. $306 \div 3$

⭐ **Algebra** Find the missing value.

33. $701 \div 2 = \blacksquare$ 34. $\blacksquare \div 5 = 106\ r2$ 35. $901 \div 3 = \blacksquare\ r\blacksquare$ 36. $207 \div \blacksquare = 51\ r3$

37. Anna is making papier-mâché rabbits for a nature celebration. It takes 240 strips of paper to make 8 rabbits. How many strips of paper does Anna need per rabbit?

38. **Reasoning** The Science Center wants to display 110 science projects. Each display area holds 45 projects. Will all of the projects fit in the 2 areas? **Explain.**

39. It takes 606 folds for Brian to make 6 praying mantis origami figures. It takes 540 folds to make 6 Gila lizard figures. How many more folds does Brian do to make one praying mantis than one Gila lizard?

40. Jeri is painting cherry blossoms. She plans to make 5 blossoms. If she spends the same amount of time on each blossom, she should finish in 100 minutes. How long will it take to paint one cherry blossom?

41. **FAST FACT** Japanese legend says that folding a thousand paper cranes brings good health or peace. Mai made 864 origami cranes in 8 months. If she made the same number of cranes each month, how many cranes did she make in one month?

42. **WRITE Math** ▸ **What's the Question?** Jolie's forest fun book tells about different beaver lodges and gives the amount of time it takes a beaver to build one. The answer is 103 hours for each beaver lodge.

Learn About) Underestimates and Overestimates

When you estimate quotients, an underestimate gives you a quotient that is less than the actual quotient. An overestimate gives you a quotient that is more than the actual quotient.

Kari pays $105 for 3 DVDs on how to plant a garden. Estimate the cost of each DVD. Compare the estimate to the actual cost.

The actual cost of each DVD is $105 ÷ 3, or $35.

Examples

Underestimate.

Think: 90 is close to 105. 90 and 3 are
compatible numbers since $9 ÷ 3 = 3$.

$90 ÷ 3 = 30$ ← underestimate

So, the estimate of $30 is less than the actual cost of $35 since 90 is less than 105.

Overestimate.

Think: 120 is close to 105. 120 and 3 are compatible
numbers since $12 ÷ 3 = 4$.

$120 ÷ 3 = 40$ ← overestimate

So, the estimate of $40 is greater than the actual cost of $35 since 120 is greater than 105.

Try It

Tell whether the estimate is an underestimate or an overestimate. Then compare the estimate to the actual quotient.

43. A community center has 120 volunteers in 8 animal rescue teams. Each team has the same number of volunteers.

    Estimate: $160 ÷ 8 = 20$ volunteers per team

44. Justin sells 330 pinecone bird feeders at the flea market in 3 hours. He sells the same number each hour.

    Estimate: $300 ÷ 3 = 100$ feeders per hour

Mixed Review and Test Prep

45. Manny drew a figure on the board. It has 6 equal sides. What figure did he draw?
    (Grade 3)

46. **Test Prep** A total of 654 students will count turtle nests at 6 different sites. The same number of students will be at each site. How many students will be at one site?

    A 19   **B** 109   **C** 119   **D** 190

47. Write an expression that shows twice the number of stuffed animals. Let s represent the number of stuffed animals. (p. 122)

48. **Test Prep** There are 525 cans of soup on 5 shelves at the grocery store. The number of cans is divided evenly among the 5 shelves. How do you find the number of cans per shelf? **Explain.**

4 Choose a Method

OBJECTIVE: Choose paper and pencil, a calculator, or mental math to divide multidigit numbers.

Learn

PROBLEM There are about 2,580 different species of marine animals, birds, and fish in the Gulf of Maine. A photographic team took pictures of every species during a 6-month period. If they took the same number of pictures each month, about how many species did they photograph in 1 month?

Choose a method that works easily for the numbers given.

Example 1 Use paper and pencil.

Divide. $2,580 \div 6$

Step 1	Step 2	Step 3	Step 4
Estimate to place the first digit in the quotient. Think: $$\frac{400}{6)2,400} \text{ or } \frac{500}{6)3,000}$$ $\blacksquare$ So, place the $6)\overline{2,580}$ first digit in the hundreds place.	Divide the 25 hundreds. $$\begin{array}{r} 4 \\ 6)\overline{2,580} \\ -2\,4 \\ \hline 1 \end{array}$$	Bring down the 8 tens. Divide the 18 tens. $$\begin{array}{r} 43 \\ 6)\overline{2,580} \\ -2\,4\downarrow \\ \hline 18 \\ -18 \\ \hline 0 \end{array}$$	Bring down the 0 ones. Divide the 0 ones. $$\begin{array}{r} 430 \\ 6)\overline{2,580} \\ -2\,4 \\ \hline 18 \\ -18\downarrow \\ \hline 00 \\ -\,0 \\ \hline 0 \end{array}$$

So, the team photographed about 430 species in 1 month.

Example 2 Use a calculator.

Divide. $7,635 \div 4$.

Estimate to check. $8,000 \div 4 = 2,000$

So, $7,653 \div 4 = 1,908$ r3.

Example 3 Use mental math.

Divide. $1,824 \div 6$.

> Think: $1,824 = 1,800 + 24$
>
> $$\begin{array}{r} 1,800 \div 6 = 300 \\ 24 \div 6 = +4 \\ \hline 304 \end{array}$$

So, $1,824 \div 6 = 304$.

Math Idea

You can divide by using paper and pencil, by using a calculator, or by using mental math. Choose the method that works best with the numbers in the problem.

Guided Practice

1. Tell which problem would be easier to solve by using mental math. Then divide.

a. $6,440 \div 8$ **b.** $2,758 \div 5$

Divide. Write the method you used.

2. $5\overline{)1,780}$ **3.** $840 \div 6$ **4.** $4\overline{)3,285}$ ✓**5.** $8\overline{)\$26.08}$ ✓**6.** $2,198 \div 3$

7. **TALK Math** Explain how you chose the method you used to divide in Problem 2.

Independent Practice and Problem Solving

Divide. Write the method you used.

8. $7\overline{)203}$ **9.** $5\overline{)2,411}$ **10.** $9\overline{)1,881}$ **11.** $5\overline{)2,822}$ **12.** $7\overline{)2,051}$

13. $4\overline{)4,963}$ **14.** $6\overline{)2,226}$ **15.** $4\overline{)3,238}$ **16.** $6\overline{)2,077}$ **17.** $8\overline{)2,496}$

18. $5,728 \div 3$ **19.** $2,450 \div 6$ **20.** $370 \div 5$ **21.** $4,876 \div 8$ **22.** $2,240 \div 7$

⭐**Algebra** Find the dividend.

23. ■ $\div 4 = 392$ **24.** ■ $\div 7 = 506$ **25.** ■ $\div 6 = 416$ r1   **26.** ■ $\div 3 = 862$ r2

27. The same number of scientists from each of 9 nations worked to identify new fish. A total of 657 scientists worked on the project. How many scientists came from each nation? Which method did you use to solve the problem? Why?

28. Suppose 102 new fish are found in one 6-month period and 126 new fish are found in the next 6-month period. How many more new fish are found in each month of the second 6-month period than in the first, if the same number were found each month?

29. **WRITE Math** Tell the method you would use to find the quotients of $4,248 \div 6$ and $4,526 \div 6$. **Explain** your choice.

Mixed Review and Test Prep

30. Blair's team catalogs 850 fish. Bria's team catalogs 117 fewer fish. How many fish do they catalog in all? (p. 48)

31. Ron drives 618 miles in 3 days. He drives the same distance each day. How far does he drive each day? (p. 34)

32. **Test Prep** Mrs. Hansen donated $1,410 over a period of 6 months. She donated the same amount each month. How much did she donate each month?

A $225   **C** $236

B $235   **D** $325

Extra Practice on page 344, Set C

Extra Practice

Set A Divide and check. (pp. 334–337)

1. $254 \div 3$
2. $6)\overline{\$9.54}$
3. $656 \div 8$
4. $7)\overline{412}$
5. $\$4.52 \div 4$

6. $\$5.48 \div 2$
7. $3)\overline{814}$
8. $284 \div 9$
9. $4)\overline{\$7.56}$
10. $2)\overline{\$6.54}$

11. $621 \div 5$
12. $5)\overline{343}$
13. $971 \div 4$
14. $6)\overline{\$8.82}$
15. $381 \div 7$

16. Chelsea bought 4 pounds of apples for $5.96. How much did each pound of apples cost?

17. Stan counted 137 nickels in his coin bank. He made stacks of 5 nickels. How many stacks did he make? How many nickels were left?

Set B Write the number of digits in each quotient. (pp. 338–341)

1. $6)\overline{480}$
2. $600 \div 5$
3. $7)\overline{802}$
4. $3)\overline{240}$
5. $960 \div 7$

Divide and check.

6. $4)\overline{240}$
7. $918 \div 3$
8. $5)\overline{650}$
9. $609 \div 3$
10. $4)\overline{350}$

11. $641 \div 8$
12. $600 \div 4$
13. $903 \div 5$
14. $4)\overline{416}$
15. $914 \div 7$

16. $840 \div 6$
17. $9)\overline{938}$
18. $635 \div 7$
19. $2)\overline{721}$
20. $964 \div 8$

21. The fourth grade at Trails School took 9 buses on a field trip. If 360 people went on the field trip and each bus carried the same number of passengers, how many people rode on each bus?

Set C Divide. Write the method you used. (pp. 342–343)

1. $6)\overline{270}$
2. $4)\overline{2,303}$
3. $8)\overline{1,656}$
4. $7)\overline{361}$
5. $6)\overline{9,041}$

6. $3)\overline{4,952}$
7. $9)\overline{1,837}$
8. $5)\overline{4,517}$
9. $6)\overline{3,485}$
10. $9)\overline{8,632}$

11. $2,943 \div 4$
12. $3,671 \div 2$
13. $633 \div 9$
14. $3,619 \div 6$
15. $3,548 \div 9$

16. $5,628 \div 4$
17. $543 \div 6$
18. $2,519 \div 5$
19. $915 \div 7$
20. $3,926 \div 8$

21. Mr. Shaprio is giving his 1,782 baseball cards to his 3 grandchildren. If each grandchild receives the same number of cards, how many will each receive?

Technology
Use Harcourt Mega Math, The Number
Games, *Up, Up, and Array*, Levels L, N, O, P.

TECHNOLOGY ⭐ CONNECTION

Calculator: Remainders

Samira and Donald are playing a division game. They have to find the answers for the following problems: $321 \div 8 = \blacksquare$. $81 \div 2 = \blacksquare$, and $201 \div 5 = \blacksquare$. Samira says all three quotients are the same. Donald says they are not. Who is correct?

You can use the Casio *fx-55* calculator to prove who is correct.

Samira's Method	Donald's Method
Use the ÷R to divide.	Use the ÷ to divide.
Divide.	Divide.
a. [3] [2] [1] [÷R] [8] [=] =40 ^{R1}	**a.** [3] [2] [1] [÷] [8] [=] = 40.125
b. [8] [1] [÷R] [2] [=] =40 ^{R1}	**b.** [8] [1] [÷] [2] [=] = 40.5
c. [2] [0] [1] [÷R] [5] [=] =40 ^{R1}	**c.** [2] [0] [1] [÷] [5] [=] = 40.2

• Explain what you notice about the whole number part of Samira's and Donald's answers.

So, Samira and Donald are both correct.

Try It

Use ÷R and ÷ to find the answer in two ways.

1. $354 \div 5$
2. $722 \div 7$
3. $45 \div 6$
4. $99 \div 2$

5. $123 \div 4$
6. $22 \div 8$
7. $934 \div 3$
8. $434 \div 9$

9. **Explore More What's the Error?** Hector and Chula found the answers for $78 \div 7 = \blacksquare$ and $45 \div 4 = \blacksquare$. Chula said the answers are the same. Hector said they are not. Who made the error and what was it?

MENTAL MATH: Multiplication and Division

USE YOUR HEAD

You can use patterns and relationships to multiply and divide mentally.

If you know that $2 \times 7 = 14$, then you can find products using greater numbers.

$$2 \times 7 = 14$$
$$4 \times 7 = 28$$
$$8 \times 7 = 56$$
$$16 \times 7 = 112$$
$$32 \times 7 = 224$$

Look at the pattern for the first factor: 2, 4, 8, 16, 32. Each number is double the previous number. What happens to the product? Each product is doubled also.

If you know that $6 \div 3 = 2$, then you can find quotients using other dividends.

$$6 \div 3 = 2$$
$$12 \div 3 = 4$$
$$24 \div 3 = 8$$
$$48 \div 3 = 16$$
$$96 \div 3 = 32$$

The divisor stays the same, but the dividend changes. Look at the pattern for the dividend: 6, 12, 24, 48, 96. Each number is double the previous number. What happens to the quotient? Each quotient is doubled also.

You can use these patterns and the Distributive Property to find other products and quotients.

Examples

Ⓐ Find the product 48×7 mentally.
Use the Distributive Property.

$$48 \times 7 = (32 + 16) \times 7$$
$$= (32 \times 7) + (16 \times 7)$$
$$= 224 + 112$$
$$= 336$$

Ⓑ Find the quotient $108 \div 3$ mentally.
Use the Distributive Property.
$$108 \div 3 = (96 + 12) \div 3$$
$$= (96 \div 3) + (12 \div 3)$$
$$= 32 + 4$$
$$= 36$$

Try It

Complete.

1. $36 \times 7 = (\blacksquare + \blacksquare) \times 7 = (\blacksquare \times 7) + (\blacksquare \times 7) = \blacksquare + \blacksquare = \blacksquare$

2. $192 \div 3 = (\blacksquare + \blacksquare) \div 3 = (\blacksquare \div 3) + (\blacksquare \div 3) = \blacksquare + \blacksquare = \blacksquare$

3. $18 \times 5 = (\blacksquare + \blacksquare) \times 5 = (\blacksquare \times 5) + (\blacksquare \times 5) = \blacksquare + \blacksquare = \blacksquare$

4. $72 \div 3 = (\blacksquare + \blacksquare) \div 3 = (\blacksquare \div 3) + (\blacksquare \div 3) = \blacksquare + \blacksquare = \blacksquare$

5. **WRITE Math** ▸ **Explain** how you could use a pattern to find the product 128×7 mentally.

Chapter 12 Review/Test

Check Concepts

1. **Explain** how to find the number of digits in the quotient of a division problem. (p. 338)

2. **Explain** the error in this problem and find the correct quotient. (p. 334)

$$
\begin{array}{r}
15 \\
5)\overline{525} \\
-5 \\
\hline
025 \\
-25 \\
\hline
0
\end{array}
$$

Check Skills

Write the number of digits in each quotient. (pp. 338–341)

3. $4)\overline{302}$

4. $7)\overline{810}$

5. $3)\overline{1,008}$

6. $2)\overline{4,600}$

7. $9)\overline{1,023}$

Divide and check. (pp. 334–337, 338–341, 342–343)

8. $384 \div 4$

9. $6)\overline{252}$

10. $561 \div 6$

11. $801 \div 7$

12. $5)\overline{737}$

13. $246 \div 6$

14. $4)\overline{601}$

15. $920 \div 8$

16. $3)\overline{\$5.61}$

17. $367 \div 9$

18. $\$4.29 \div 3$

19. $3)\overline{928}$

20. $1,539 \div 5$

21. $5)\overline{\$6.45}$

22. $2)\overline{4,125}$

23. $6,305 \div 6$

24. $7)\overline{2,163}$

25. $7,261 \div 3$

26. $4)\overline{\$9.28}$

27. $9,104 \div 5$

Check Problem Solving

Solve. (pp. 332–333)

28. Taylor has 686 stamps. He wants to put 6 on each page of an album. How many pages will he need for his stamps?

29. There are 123 fourth-grade students in the school. How many groups of 5 students can be formed?

30. Scott has enough film to take 72 photos during his vacation. He wants to take the same number of photos of each of 5 monuments he will visit. How many photos should he take of each monument?

31. The fourth grade donated 526 tulip bulbs to be planted around the school. If they are going to plant the same number of bulbs in each of 8 flower beds, how many bulbs will be left over?

32. Each shipping box can hold 9 school jackets. How many boxes are needed to hold 70 jackets?

33. **WRITE Math** **Explain** how you interpreted the remainder differently in Problems 28 and 29.

Standardized Test Prep
Chapters 1–12

Measurement

1. An alarm clock is set for quarter to seven in the morning. At what time will the alarm go off? (p. 152)

    A 6:45 A.M.   C 6:45 P.M.

    B 7:15 A.M.   D 7:15 P.M.

2. On May 9, 1984, the Chicago White Sox and the Milwaukee Brewers played the longest Major League Baseball game ever played. It lasted 8 hours 6 minutes. If the game started at 4:55 P.M., what time did it end? (p. 154)

    A 11:03 P.M.

    B 12:01 P.M.

    C 12:51 P.M.

    D 1:01 A.M.

3. Look at the temperature on the thermometer. Three hours ago, it was 15°C cooler. What was the temperature 3 hours ago? (p. 164)

    A 8°C

    B 3°C

    C ⁻3°C

    D ⁻7°C

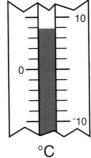
°C

4. **WRITE Math** ▸ Heika had her hair cut on May 20. Her next appointment is 5 weeks 3 days after that. **Explain** how you can use a calendar to find the date of her next appointment. (p. 158)

Number and Operations

5. $7\overline{)3,849}$ (p. 342)

    A 4,149 r6

    B 549 r6

    C 547

    D 507

Test Tip Choose the answer.

See Item 6. If your answer does not match any of the choices, check your computation. You could also reread the question to be sure you chose the correct operation.

6. Frank has 38 DVDs. He paid $12 for each of them. How much did he pay for all of his DVDs? (p. 286)

    A $50   C $114

    B $60   D $456

7. Ayesha has 6 one-dollar bills. She wants to exchange her bills for pennies. How many pennies will Ayesha receive? (p. 286)

    A 60   C 600

    B 100   D 6,000

8. **WRITE Math** ▸ Corey has 261 CDs. His CD storage cases hold 8 CDs each. How many storage cases does Corey need for all of his CDs? **Explain** how to interpret the remainder. (p. 332)

Data Analysis and Probability

9. How much longer does Janine swim each week than Lia? (p. 204)

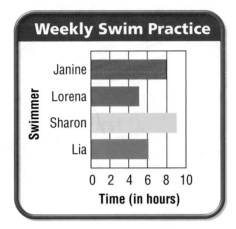

Weekly Swim Practice

A 2 hours   **C** 4 hours

B 3 hours   **D** 5 hours

10. Kelly kept track of the number of baskets scored by her class in a free-throw contest. She made a line plot to show the results.

Free-Throw Contest

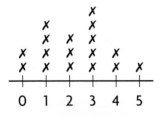

Baskets Scored

Find the median number of baskets scored. (p. 190)

A 0   **C** 3

B 2   **D** 4

11. ▌WRITE Math ▶ The principal counted the votes in the election for student council president. What type of graph could she make to show the results? (p. 222)
Explain.

Algebraic Reasoning

12. What number goes in the box to make this number sentence true? (p. 128)

$$(4 + 5) \times 8 = 9 \times \blacksquare$$

A 4   **C** 8

B 5   **D** 9

13. What is the value of the expression?
(p. 126)

$$(18 + 3) - (5 \times 3)$$

A 6

B 8

C 42

D 48

14. Daniel earns $12 for each car he washes. He earned $96 washing cars this week. Which equation shows how to find the number of cars, n, that he washed?
(p. 128)

A $96 \times 12 = n$

B $96 \div 12 = n$

C $96 - 12 = n$

D $12 + 96 = n$

15. ▌WRITE Math ▶ Find the missing numbers.

Input, x	1	2	▓	4	5
Output, y	4	8	12	▓	20

Explain the relationship between the ordered pairs. Write a rule for the table as an equation. (p. 138)

Record Division

OBJECTIVE: Record division by 2-digit divisors.

Learn

PROBLEM Jared's grandfather collected 258 Bicentennial quarters. He put an equal number of quarters in 11 display cases. How many quarters were in each case? How many quarters were left over?

◀ Bicentennial quarters were made betweeen 1975 and 1976.

Example Divide 258 by 11. Write $11\overline{)258}$.

MODEL	THINK	RECORD
Step 1 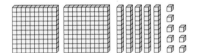	Estimate to place the first digit in the quotient. $$\begin{array}{cc} 25 & 26 \\ \text{Think: } 10\overline{)250} & \text{or } 10\overline{)260} \end{array}$$ So, place the first digit in the tens place.	$11\overline{)258}$
Step 2 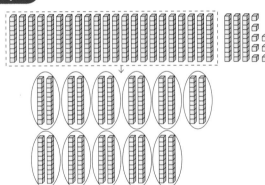	Regroup 2 hundreds 5 tens as 25 tens. Then, divide the 25 tens into 11 groups. There are 3 tens left over.	$$\begin{array}{r} 2 \\ 11\overline{)258} \\ -22 \\ \hline 3 \end{array}$$ Divide. $25 \div 11$ Multiply. 11×2 Subtract. $25 - 22$ Compare. $3 < 11$
Step 3 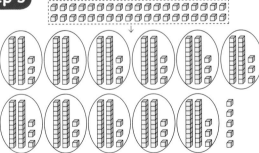	Regroup the 3 leftover tens as 30 ones. There are 38 ones altogether. Divide the 38 ones into 11 groups. There are 5 ones left over. Write the remainder next to the quotient.	$$\begin{array}{r} 23 \text{ r}5 \\ 11\overline{)258} \\ -22\downarrow \\ \hline 38 \\ -33 \\ \hline 5 \end{array}$$ Divide. $38 \div 11$ Multiply. 11×3 Subtract. $38 - 33$ Compare. $5 < 11$

So, there were 23 quarters in each case with 5 quarters left over.

• Explain why you regroup 3 tens as 30 ones in Step 3.

Data Analysis and Probability

9. How much longer does Janine swim each week than Lia? (p. 204)

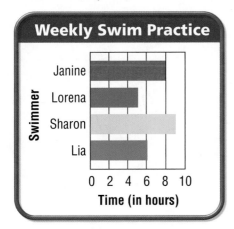

Weekly Swim Practice

A 2 hours   **C** 4 hours

B 3 hours   **D** 5 hours

10. Kelly kept track of the number of baskets scored by her class in a free-throw contest. She made a line plot to show the results.

Free-Throw Contest

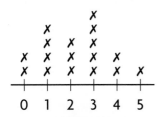

Baskets Scored

Find the median number of baskets scored. (p. 190)

A 0   **C** 3

B 2   **D** 4

11. **WRITE Math** The principal counted the votes in the election for student council president. What type of graph could she make to show the results? (p. 222) **Explain.**

Algebraic Reasoning

12. What number goes in the box to make this number sentence true? (p. 128)

$$(4 + 5) \times 8 = 9 \times \blacksquare$$

A 4   **C** 8

B 5   **D** 9

13. What is the value of the expression? (p. 126)

$$(18 + 3) - (5 \times 3)$$

A 6

B 8

C 42

D 48

14. Daniel earns $12 for each car he washes. He earned $96 washing cars this week. Which equation shows how to find the number of cars, n, that he washed? (p. 128)

A $96 \times 12 = n$

B $96 \div 12 = n$

C $96 - 12 = n$

D $12 + 96 = n$

15. **WRITE Math** Find the missing numbers.

Input, x	1	2	■	4	5
Output, y	4	8	12	■	20

Explain the relationship between the ordered pairs. Write a rule for the table as an equation. (p. 138)

13 Divide by 2-Digit Divisors

≡**FAST FACT**

Every day, the United States government prints 35,000,000 bills in Washington, D.C. The $100 bill is the denomination of greatest value printed today, and the $1 bill is the denomination of least value printed.

Investigate

Deb is a cashier at a toy store. At the end of each day, she counts the money in her cash register. Choose one of the days in the table, and list the numbers of $5 bills, $10 bills, and $20 bills she could have counted.

Deb's Report	
Day	**Total Counted**
Monday	$200
Tuesday	$350
Wednesday	$675
Thursday	$525
Friday	$865

GO ONLINE

Technology
Student pages are available in the Student eBook.

**Check your understanding of important skills
needed for success in Chapter 13.**

Estimate Quotients

Estimate using compatible numbers.

1. $355 \div 7$ 2. $244 \div 3$ 3. $481 \div 8$ 4. $121 \div 2$

5. $253 \div 5$ 6. $634 \div 9$ 7. $145 \div 3$ 8. $607 \div 4$

Place the First Digit

Tell where to place the first digit. Then divide.

9. $7\overline{)82}$ 10. $6\overline{)96}$ 11. $9\overline{)56}$ 12. $3\overline{)366}$

13. $2\overline{)615}$ 14. $8\overline{)256}$ 15. $3\overline{)197}$ 16. $4\overline{)304}$

2-Digit By 1-Digit Multiplication

Find the product.

17. $\begin{array}{r} 13 \\ \times\ 3 \\ \hline \end{array}$ 18. $\begin{array}{r} 18 \\ \times\ 4 \\ \hline \end{array}$ 19. $\begin{array}{r} 33 \\ \times\ 2 \\ \hline \end{array}$ 20. $\begin{array}{r} 26 \\ \times\ 5 \\ \hline \end{array}$

21. $\begin{array}{r} 47 \\ \times\ 6 \\ \hline \end{array}$ 22. $\begin{array}{r} 24 \\ \times\ 9 \\ \hline \end{array}$ 23. $\begin{array}{r} 16 \\ \times\ 7 \\ \hline \end{array}$ 24. $\begin{array}{r} 34 \\ \times\ 3 \\ \hline \end{array}$

25. $\begin{array}{r} 39 \\ \times\ 5 \\ \hline \end{array}$ 26. $\begin{array}{r} 65 \\ \times\ 8 \\ \hline \end{array}$ 27. $\begin{array}{r} 53 \\ \times\ 6 \\ \hline \end{array}$ 28. $\begin{array}{r} 89 \\ \times\ 2 \\ \hline \end{array}$

VOCABULARY POWER

CHAPTER VOCABULARY

compatible numbers
dividend
divisor
multiple
quotient
remainder

WARM-UP WORDS

compatible numbers numbers that are easy to compute mentally

multiple the product of two counting numbers is called a multiple of each of those numbers

remainder the amount left over when a number cannot be divided equally

Estimate Quotients

OBJECTIVE: Estimate quotients by using compatible numbers and patterns, and then find the estimated quotient mentally.

Quick Review

Quick Review

1. $40 \div 2$
2. $2,400 \div 6$
3. $270 \div 90$
4. $4,900 \div 7$
5. $12,000 \div 3,000$

Learn

PROBLEM When it swims near the surface, an adult humpback whale's heart beats 273 times in 45 minutes. About how many times does the whale's heart beat in one minute?

You can find a reasonable estimate to solve the problem.

Example 1 Estimate. $273 \div 45$

Step 1	**Step 2**
Find compatible numbers.	Use mental math.
$273 \div 45$	$30 \div 5 = 6$ ← basic fact
$\downarrow \quad \downarrow$	$300 \div 50 = 6$
$300 \div 50$	

Remember

Compatible numbers are numbers that are easy to compute mentally.

So, a whale's heart beats about 6 times in one minute.

Example 2 Estimate. $7,234 \div 38$

Step 1	**Step 2**
Find compatible numbers.	Use a basic fact and a pattern of multiples of 10.
$7,234 \div 38$	$8 \div 4 = 2$ ← basic fact
$\downarrow \quad \downarrow$	$80 \div 40 = 2$
$8,000 \div 40$	$800 \div 40 = 20$
	$8,000 \div 40 = 200$

▲ Humpback whales can be 45 feet long and weigh 40 tons.

So, a reasonable estimate for $7,234 \div 38$ is 200.

Guided Practice

1. Estimate $378 \div 76$.

$378 \div 76$
$\downarrow \quad \downarrow$
$350 \div \blacksquare \quad \rightarrow \quad 350 \div \blacksquare = \blacksquare$

Write the compatible numbers you would use to estimate
the quotient. Then estimate.

2. $636 \div 82$ **3.** $33\overline{)1,989}$ **4.** $443 \div 86$ ✓**5.** $23\overline{)188}$ ✓**6.** $3,600 \div 37$

7. [**TALK Math**] **Explain** how to use a basic fact and a
pattern to find $2,700 \div 90$.

Independent Practice and Problem Solving

Write the compatible numbers you would use to estimate
the quotient. Then estimate.

8. $63\overline{)431}$ **9.** $918 \div 27$ **10.** $42\overline{)1,625}$ **11.** $463 \div 81$ **12.** $92\overline{)6,250}$

13. $2,710 \div 35$ **14.** $259 \div 32$ **15.** $76\overline{)288}$ **16.** $16\overline{)1,179}$ **17.** $5,249 \div 49$

18. $3,519 \div 18$ **19.** $626 \div 23$ **20.** $39\overline{)366}$ **21.** $34\overline{)9,275}$ **22.** $52\overline{)4,759}$

USE DATA For 23–26, use the table.

23. About how many times does a horse's heart
beat in one minute?

24. About how many more times does a giraffe's
heart beat in one minute than an elephant's
heart?

25. About how many times does a large dog's
heart beat in 60 minutes?

26. **Pose a Problem** Look at Problem 24. Write a
similar problem, but change the animals.

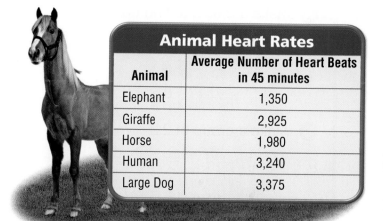

Animal Heart Rates	
Animal	Average Number of Heart Beats in 45 minutes
Elephant	1,350
Giraffe	2,925
Horse	1,980
Human	3,240
Large Dog	3,375

27. Kenzie has 101 inches of ribbon. She wants
to make 19 bookmarks. About how much
ribbon will she use for each bookmark?

28. Carter's school earned $3,852 from a
fundraiser. If 18 students were in the
fundraiser, about how much money did
each student earn?

29. [**WRITE Math**] **Explain** how to use compatible
numbers to estimate $249 \div 12$.

Mixed Review and Test Prep

30. How many days are there in 4 weeks?
(p. 160)

31. Barbara ran 6 miles on Saturday and
ran again on Thursday. She ran 15 miles
in all. How many miles did she run on
Thursday? (p. 70)

32. **Test Prep** What is the best estimate of
$798 \div 42$?

A 10   **C** 30

B 20   **D** 40

(Extra Practice) on page 364, Set A

2 Model Division by 2-Digit Divisors

OBJECTIVE: Model division by 2-digit divisors by using base-ten blocks.

Investigate

Materials ■ base-ten blocks

Mrs. Vondrake is making a stained glass window. She has 68 pieces of glass. For each window, she needs 21 pieces of glass. How many stained glass windows can she make? How many pieces of glass will be left over?

You can use base-ten blocks to divide a 2-digit dividend by a 2-digit divisor.

A Make a model to find $68 \div 21$. Show 68 as 6 tens 8 ones.

B Make a group of 21.

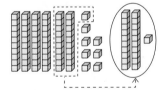

C Continue making groups of 21.

D Count the number of equal groups. Count how many are left over. Record your answer.

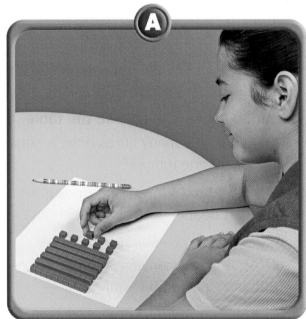

Draw Conclusions

1. How many stained glass windows can she make? How many pieces of glass will be left over?

2. Why did you make groups of 21?

3. How do you know how many groups to make? What do the leftover blocks represent?

4. **Synthesis** How can you use base-ten blocks to find $46 \div 18$? How many groups of the divisor can you make? How many blocks will be left over?

Connect

You can draw a picture to help you solve a division problem.

Divide. $116 \div 52$

Step 1

Draw a picture to show 116.

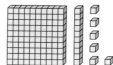

Step 2

Estimate $116 \div 52$.

Think: $100 \div 50 = 2$

So, try to make 2 groups of 52. You need to regroup 1 hundred as 10 tens.

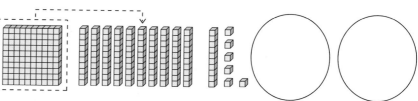

Step 3

Make 2 groups of 52. Count how many are left over.

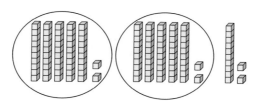

So, $116 \div 52 = 2$ r12.

TALK Math

Explain why you regroup 1 hundred as 10 tens in Step 2.

Practice

Use base-ten blocks to divide.

1. $38 \div 11$
2. $76 \div 33$
3. $49 \div 23$
4. $96 \div 44$
✓5. $99 \div 31$

Draw a picture to divide.

6. $106 \div 21$
7. $126 \div 42$
8. $156 \div 51$
9. $169 \div 32$
✓10. $187 \div 61$

Divide. You may use base-ten blocks or draw a picture.

11. $88 \div 27$
12. $35 \overline{)109}$
13. $123 \div 41$
14. $\$91 \div 13$
15. $27 \overline{)117}$
16. $\$216 \div 36$
17. $52 \overline{)268}$
18. $226 \div 45$
19. $27 \overline{)191}$
20. $\$368 \div 46$

21. **WRITE Math ▸ Reasoning** There are 5 groups with 2 tens blocks and 5 ones blocks in each group. What division equation can you write to tell the size of each group?

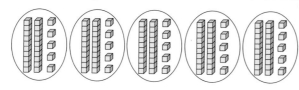

Technology

CD ROM Use Harcourt Mega Math, The Number Games, *Up, Up, and Array*, Level Q.

Record Division

OBJECTIVE: Record division by 2-digit divisors.

Learn

PROBLEM Jared's grandfather collected 258 Bicentennial quarters. He put an equal number of quarters in 11 display cases. How many quarters were in each case? How many quarters were left over?

◀ Bicentennial quarters were made betweeen 1975 and 1976.

Example Divide 258 by 11. Write $11\overline{)258}$.

MODEL	THINK	RECORD
Step 1 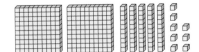	Estimate to place the first digit in the quotient. Think: $\overset{25}{10\overline{)250}}$ or $\overset{26}{10\overline{)260}}$ So, place the first digit in the tens place.	$11\overline{)258}$
Step 2 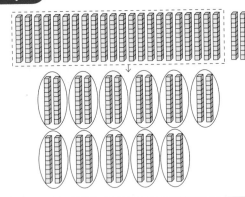	Regroup 2 hundreds 5 tens as 25 tens. Then, divide the 25 tens into 11 groups. There are 3 tens left over.	$\begin{array}{r} 2 \\ 11\overline{)258} \\ -22 \\ \hline 3 \end{array}$ Divide. $25 \div 11$ Multiply. 11×2 Subtract. $25 - 22$ Compare. $3 < 11$
Step 3 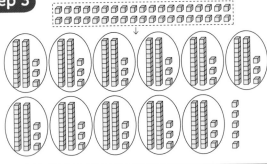	Regroup the 3 leftover tens as 30 ones. There are 38 ones altogether. Divide the 38 ones into 11 groups. There are 5 ones left over. Write the remainder next to the quotient.	$\begin{array}{r} 23 \text{ r}5 \\ 11\overline{)258} \\ -22\downarrow \\ \hline 38 \\ -33 \\ \hline 5 \end{array}$ Divide. $38 \div 11$ Multiply. 11×3 Subtract. $38 - 33$ Compare. $5 < 11$

So, there were 23 quarters in each case with 5 quarters left over.

• Explain why you regroup 3 tens as 30 ones in Step 3.

1. Copy and complete.

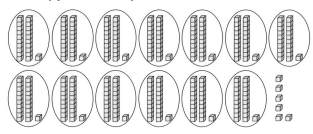

$$\begin{array}{r} 2\blacksquare \text{ r}\blacksquare \\ 13\overline{)279} \\ -26\downarrow \\ \hline \blacksquare9 \\ -13 \\ \hline \blacksquare \end{array}$$

2 tens in each group

26 tens used
How many are left?

13 ones used
How many are left over?

Divide and record.

2. $13\overline{)312}$ **3.** $781 \div 19$ **4.** $26\overline{)294}$ ✓**5.** $688 \div 22$ ✓**6.** $35\overline{)841}$

7. **TALK Math** **Explain** why it is helpful to estimate before you divide.

Independent Practice and Problem Solving

Divide and record.

8. $493 \div 12$ **9.** $23\overline{)483}$ **10.** $887 \div 73$ **11.** $92\overline{)424}$ **12.** $895 \div 48$

13. $64 \div 16$ **14.** $856 \div 25$ **15.** $38\overline{)162}$ **16.** $73 \div 28$ **17.** $19\overline{)847}$

★**Algebra** Find the missing number.

18. $613 \div 27 = 22 \text{ r}\blacksquare$ **19.** $\blacksquare \div 14 = 63$ **20.** $346 \div 18 = \blacksquare \text{ r}4$ **21.** $\blacksquare \div 42 = 7$

22. Ken had 537 pennies. He put them into piles of 25. How many piles did he make? How many pennies were left over?

23. Conner had $4.42 in pennies. He put the pennies in stacks of 11. How many pennies were left over?

24. **≡FAST FACT** The diameter of a dime is about 18 millimeters. How many dimes would be in a row of dimes that is 918 millimeters long?

25. Ms. Ramos has 152 photos. She puts 12 photos on each page of her album. How many are on each page? How many are left over?

26. **Reasoning** Which has a greater quotient, $16\overline{)528}$ or $12\overline{)528}$? Tell how you know.

27. **WRITE Math** ▶ **What's the Question?** Emma bought 12 T-shirts for $168. The answer is $14.

Mixed Review and Test Prep

28. Which is greater: 5,439 or 5,493? (p. 12)

29. There are 384 seats in a theater with 24 seats in each row. How many rows of seats are there? (p. 356)

30. **Test Prep** Marci's class made 336 stars. They want to put them in 48 boxes. **Explain** how to use division to find how many stars will be put in each box.

4 Adjusting Quotients

OBJECTIVE: Adjust the quotient when the estimated digit is too high or too low.

Quick Review

1. $108 \div 9$
2. $187 \div 6$
3. $26\overline{)643}$
4. $18\overline{)216}$
5. $12\overline{)187}$

Learn

PROBLEM Keiko and his family drive 172 miles from Toledo, Ohio, to Circleville, Ohio, to visit his grandmother. Because of bad weather, they average only 43 miles per hour. How long will it take to drive to Circleville?

Toledo

OHIO

Circleville

Example 1 Divide 172 by 43. Write $43\overline{)172}$.

Step 1	Step 2	Step 3
Use compatible numbers to estimate to place the first digit in the quotient. $172 \div 43$ ↓ ↓ $200 \div 40 = 5$	Try the estimate, 5. $43 \times 5 = 215$ $\begin{array}{r} 5 \\ 43\overline{)172} \\ -215 \end{array}$ Since 215 > 172, the estimated digit is too high.	Adjust. Try 4. $43 \times 4 = 172$ $\begin{array}{r} 4 \\ 43\overline{)172} \\ -172 \\ \hline 0 \end{array}$

So, it will take 4 hours to drive to Circleville.

ERROR ALERT

Your estimated digit in the quotient may be too high or too low.

• **What if** it was 344 miles from Toledo to Circleville? How long will it take?

Example 2 Divide 224 by 35. Write $35\overline{)224}$.

Step 1	Step 2	Step 3
Use compatible numbers to estimate to place the first digit in the quotient. $224 \div 35$ ↓ ↓ $200 \div 40 = 5$	Try the estimate, 5. $35 \times 5 = 175$ $\begin{array}{r} 5 \\ 35\overline{)224} \\ -175 \\ \hline 49 \end{array}$ Since 49 > 35, the estimated digit is too low.	Adjust. Try 6. $35 \times 6 = 210$ $\begin{array}{r} 6\ r14 \\ 35\overline{)224} \\ -210 \\ \hline 14 \quad 14 < 35 \end{array}$

So, $224 \div 35 = 6$ r14.

• How do you know when the first estimated digit in a quotient is too high or too low?

Example 3 Divide 1,737 by 25. Write $25\overline{)1,737}$.
Estimate. $1,500 \div 30 = 50$

Step 1	Step 2	Step 3	Step 4
Try the estimate, 50. So, place the first digit, 5, in the tens place.	Adjust. Try 6 in the tens place.	Bring down the 7 ones. Then divide 237 ones. Estimate the next digit in the quotient. Think $240 \div 30 = 8$. **Try 8.**	Adjust. Try 9 in the ones place.

Step 1:
$$\begin{array}{r} 5 \\ 25\overline{)1,737} \\ -125 \\ \hline 48 \end{array}$$
Since $48 > 25$, the estimated digit is too low.

Step 2:
$$\begin{array}{r} 6 \\ 25\overline{)1,737} \\ -150 \\ \hline 23 \end{array}$$
$23 < 25$

Step 3:
$$\begin{array}{r} 68 \\ 25\overline{)1,737} \\ -150\downarrow \\ \hline 237 \\ -200 \\ \hline 37 \end{array}$$
Since $37 > 25$, the estimated digit is too low.

Step 4:
$$\begin{array}{r} 69\ r12 \\ 25\overline{)1,737} \\ -150\downarrow \\ \hline 237 \\ -225 \\ \hline 12 \end{array}$$
$12 < 25$

So, $1,737 \div 25$ is 69 r12.

Example 4 Divide $5,253 \div 75$. Write $75\overline{)5,253}$.
Estimate. $5,600 \div 70 = 80$

Step 1	Step 2	Step 3
Try the estimate, 80. So, place the first digit, 8, in the tens place.	Adjust. Try 7 in the tens place.	Bring down the 3 ones. Divide the 3 ones.

Step 1:
$$\begin{array}{r} 8 \\ 75\overline{)5,253} \\ -600 \end{array}$$
Since $600 > 525$, the estimated digit is too high.

Step 2:
$$\begin{array}{r} 7 \\ 75\overline{)5,253} \\ -525 \\ \hline 0 \end{array}$$
$0 < 75$

Step 3:
$$\begin{array}{r} 70\ r3 \\ 75\overline{)5,253} \\ -525\downarrow \\ \hline 03 \end{array}$$
Since 3 is less than 75, write a zero in the quotient.

So, $5,253 \div 75$ is 70 r3.

Guided Practice

1. Divide 616 by 22. Estimate. $600 \div 20 = 30$
   Try 3 in the tens place. Adjust, if needed. Then divide.
$$\begin{array}{r} 3 \\ 22\overline{)616} \\ -66 \end{array}$$

Adjust the estimated digit in the quotient, if needed. Then divide.

2. $26\overline{)208}$ with 7

3. $23\overline{)217}$ with 1

4. $18\overline{)613}$ with 3

5. $45\overline{)210}$ with 3

6. $37\overline{)1,582}$ with 5

Divide.

7. $17\overline{)423}$

8. $25\overline{)752}$

9. $12\overline{)720}$

10. $32\overline{)2,432}$

11. $58\overline{)5,336}$

12. **TALK Math** **Explain** how you might adjust the estimated digit in the quotient if it is too low.

Independent Practice and Problem Solving

Adjust the estimated digit in the quotient, if needed. Then divide.

13. $63\overline{)548}$ quotient 9	14. $26\overline{)220}$ quotient 7	15. $98\overline{)1,971}$ quotient 2	16. $33\overline{)913}$ quotient 3	17. $36\overline{)1,571}$ quotient 4
18. $17\overline{)425}$ quotient 2	19. $46\overline{)318}$ quotient 5	20. $55\overline{)956}$ quotient 2	21. $74\overline{)2,490}$ quotient 3	22. $12\overline{)256}$ quotient 2
23. $37\overline{)3,596}$ quotient 9	24. $69\overline{)552}$ quotient 7	25. $82\overline{)3,857}$ quotient 5	26. $31\overline{)2,970}$ quotient 8	27. $25\overline{)211}$ quotient 8

Divide.

28. $42\overline{)294}$	29. $53\overline{)2,120}$	30. $73\overline{)225}$	31. $67\overline{)3,489}$	32. $49\overline{)2,452}$
33. $36\overline{)1,420}$	34. $51\overline{)537}$	35. $13\overline{)222}$	36. $84\overline{)5,286}$	37. $23\overline{)1,725}$
38. $62\overline{)462}$	39. $18\overline{)1,710}$	40. $53\overline{)314}$	41. $97\overline{)291}$	42. $88\overline{)4,360}$
43. $44\overline{)232}$	44. $65\overline{)4,815}$	45. $27\overline{)1,438}$	46. $77\overline{)250}$	47. $42\overline{)378}$

⭐ **Algebra** **Find the value of n.**

48. $924 \div 33 = n$ 49. $n \div 31 = 11$ 50. $924 \div 84 = n$ 51. $360 \div n = 24$

USE DATA **For 52–54, use the map.**

52. Riley drives from Brookville to Hammond. If it takes him 6 hours, how many miles per hour does he average?

53. On a trip from Brookville to Milltown and back to Brookville, Joel uses 15 gallons of gas. How many miles per gallon does his car travel?

54. Mia's car travels 23 miles per gallon of gas. How many gallons does she need to drive from Hammond to Milltown?

55. **Explain** how to adjust a quotient.

56. **WRITE Math** **What's the Error?** Gina estimated the first digit in the quotient of $2,183 \div 42$ as 4. She adjusted the quotient by writing 3. **Describe** her error and tell what she should have written.

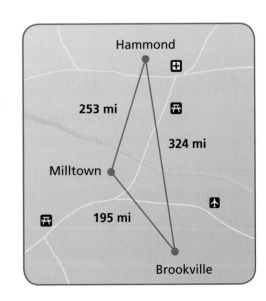

Learn About) Partial Quotients

You can divide using partial quotients.

Helena and her younger brother packed 185 toys into 14 boxes. Each box had the same number of toys. How many toys were in each box? How many toys were left over?

Example
Divide 185 by 14. Write $14\overline{)185}$.

Step 1

Make a list of multiples of 14.

$14 \times 1 = 14$
$14 \times 2 = 28$
$14 \times 10 = 140$

Step 2

140 is close to 185, so use 10 as the first partial quotient.

$$14\overline{)185}$$
$$-140 \quad 10 \leftarrow \text{Record partial quotients}$$
$$45 \qquad\qquad \text{in a column.}$$

Step 3

Repeat until the remainder is less than the divisor.

$$14\overline{)185}$$
$$-140 \quad 10$$
$$45$$
$$-28 \quad 2$$
$$17$$
$$-14 \quad 1$$
$$3$$

Step 4

Add the partial quotients.

$$14\overline{)185}$$
$$-140 \quad 10$$
$$45$$
$$-28 \quad 2$$
$$17$$
$$-14 \quad +1$$
$$\text{remainder} \rightarrow 3 \quad 13 \leftarrow \text{quotient}$$

So, there were 13 toys in each box. There were 3 toys left over.

Try It

Use partial quotients to divide.

57. $25\overline{)372}$ **58.** $16\overline{)134}$ **59.** $37\overline{)2,572}$ **60.** $56\overline{)4,256}$ **61.** $73\overline{)3,440}$

Mixed Review and Test Prep

62. Henry had $6 to spend. He spent $1 on gum, $3 on a book, and $2 on pencils. How would you show this in a circle graph? (p. 208)

63. Brianna's soccer practice starts at 4:15 P.M. and ends at 5:10 P.M. How long is soccer practice? (p. 154)

64. Test Prep Rachel bought some bags of beads to make jewelry. Each bag has 21 beads. She bought 336 beads in all. How many bags of beads did she buy?

A 11 r7   C 16 r2

B 16   D 128

Problem Solving Workshop
Skill: Too Much/Too Little Information

OBJECTIVE: Solve problems using the skill *too much/too little information.*

Use the Skill

PROBLEM Madison saved the money she made raking lawns. She bought a portable music player for $159. She put 528 songs on the player. If Madison listens to 16 songs on the player each day, how many days can she listen without repeating a song?

- **Read the problem. Decide what the problem asks you to find.**
  The problem asks you to find the number of days Madison can listen to the songs without repeating a song.

- **Decide what information you need to solve the problem.**
  You need to know the total number of songs on the player and the number of songs Madison listens to each day.

- **Read the problem again carefully. Decide if there is too much information or not enough information to solve the problem.**
  There is too much information. You do not need to know the cost of the portable music player or how she made the money.

- **Solve the problem, if possible.**

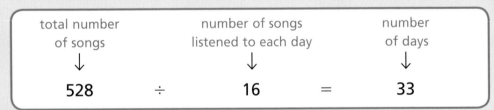

total number of songs		number of songs listened to each day		number of days
↓		↓		↓
528	÷	16	=	33

So, Madison can listen for 33 days without repeating a song.

Math Idea
Sometimes you have too much or too little information to solve a problem. If there is too much, you have to decide what to use. If there is too little, you can't solve the problem.

Think and Discuss

Decide if the problem has too much or too little information. Then, solve if possible. If there is too little information, identify the missing information.

a. Celia listened to 70 minutes of songs last week. She listened for 140 minutes today on a car trip. About how many minutes is each song?

b. Celia downloaded 406 songs. She listened to 7 songs a day for 23 days. How many songs did she listen to in all?

Guided Problem Solving

Decide if the problem has too much or too little information. Then, solve if possible. If there is too little information, identify the missing information.

1. Kaitlyn made a stack of her favorite CDs. Seven of the CDs have 13 songs, 4 of the CDs have 10 songs, and 5 of the CDs have 11 songs. How many CDs does she have in all?

   First, decide what the problem asks you to find.

   Then, decide what information you need.

   Finally, solve the problem, if possible.

✓ 2. **What if** it takes Kaitlyn 52 minutes to listen to a CD? About how long is each song?

✓ 3. A radio station plays 49 minutes of music each hour. The rest of the hour, commercials are played. In 2 hours, the station played 32 songs. How many minutes of commercials does the station play in 3 hours?

Mixed Applications

4. Alice practiced the violin each day for 42 weeks last year. She learned 12 songs. How many hours did she practice last year? Do you have too much or too little information to solve the problem? **Explain.** Then, solve the problem, if possible.

5. Chelsea, Lin, George, and Rosa are in line for a movie. Lin is ahead of Chelsea. Chelsea is second. Rosa is not last. Who is third?

USE DATA For 6–7, use the sign.

6. **WRITE Math** ▸ Juan has $50. Does he have enough to buy one of each type of CD on sale? **Explain** whether you need an exact answer or estimate, and then solve.

Last Chance
CD SALE

Top 10...............$13
Books on CD....$14
Soundtracks.....$11

7. How much more do two soundtrack CDs cost than one Top 10 CD?

8. Fourth grade students are going to a concert on buses. Each bus seats 70 passengers. How many buses do they need if 237 students and adults attend the concert? **Explain.**

9. **Pose a Problem** Write a problem that has too much information.

Extra Practice

Set A Write the compatible numbers you would use to estimate the quotient. Then estimate. (pp. 352–353)

1. $41\overline{)823}$
2. $756 \div 24$
3. $35\overline{)1,859}$
4. $353 \div 36$
5. $62\overline{)1,892}$

6. $323 \div 29$
7. $31\overline{)2,887}$
8. $851 \div 19$
9. $71\overline{)8,002}$
10. $908 \div 15$

11. Ashleigh has 609 square feet of fabric. She wants to make 15 tablecloths that are the same size. About how many square feet will each tablecloth be?

12. A fourth-grade teacher is renting a bus for a field trip. The cost of the bus is $2,597. The bus holds 53 people. Estimate the cost per person.

Set B Divide and record. (pp. 356–357)

1. $72 \div 36$
2. $18\overline{)576}$
3. $678 \div 42$
4. $53\overline{)651}$
5. $977 \div 62$

6. $951 \div 38$
7. $578 \div 17$
8. $59\overline{)486}$
9. $96 \div 14$
10. $29\overline{)927}$

11. Morton has 523 nickels. He puts the nickels into rolls of 40. How many rolls does he make? How many nickels are left over?

12. Rhonda has 218 quarters. She puts them in stacks of 25. How many stacks does she make? How many quarters are left over?

Set C Adjust the estimated digit in the quotient if needed. Then divide. (pp. 358–361)

1. $17\overline{)398}$ — 3
2. $16\overline{)147}$ — 9
3. $27\overline{)898}$ — 2
4. $52\overline{)678}$ — 1
5. $15\overline{)877}$ — 7

6. $42\overline{)327}$ — 8
7. $73\overline{)1,428}$ — 2
8. $98\overline{)175}$ — 1
9. $21\overline{)1,113}$ — 4
10. $62\overline{)3,259}$ — 5

Divide.

11. $28\overline{)771}$
12. $17\overline{)984}$
13. $109 \div 23$
14. $39\overline{)516}$
15. $468 \div 17$

16. $46\overline{)3,174}$
17. $29\overline{)2,043}$
18. $25\overline{)243}$
19. $71\overline{)4,331}$
20. $23\overline{)410}$

21. Spencer's family is driving from Columbus, Ohio, to Flint, Michigan, a distance of about 300 miles. They plan to drive an average of 50 miles per hour. About how long will it take them to drive from Columbus to Flint?

22. Natasha lives in Dover, Delaware. She is taking a train to Jacksonville, Florida, to visit her aunt. The distance from Dover to Jacksonville is about 745 miles. The train averages about 62 miles per hour. About how long is the train ride?

CD ROM Technology
Use Harcourt Mega Math, The Number Games, *Up, Up, and Array*, Level Q.

Remainder or Not?

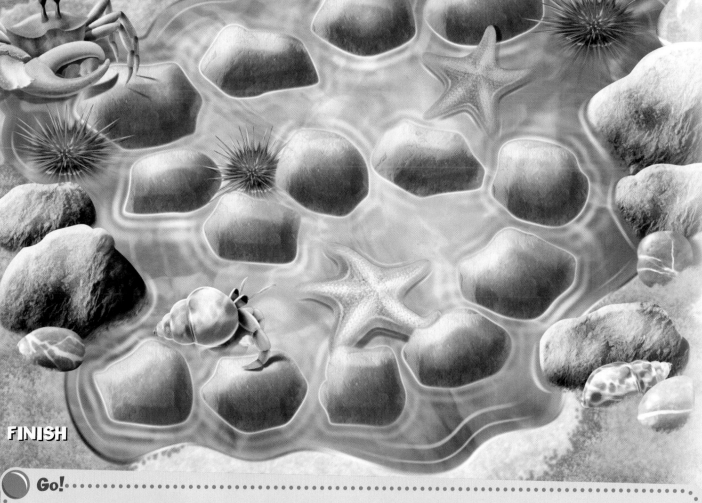

On Your Mark!
2, 3, or 4 players

Get Set!
- Divisor and dividend cards
- 2 coins

START

FINISH

Go!

■ Place the divisor cards and dividend cards facedown in two stacks.

■ Each player selects a different coin and places the coin on START.

■ Take turns. The first player chooses one card from each stack. The player uses mental math to find the quotient.

■ If a problem has a remainder, the player moves one space. If there is no remainder, the player does not move.

■ The other player should check the quotient before play continues.

■ The first player to reach FINISH wins.

Use Number Sense

Catch That Cookie Crook!

Serena Super Sleuth has been tracking a cookie crook all over the city. She finally had all of the clues she needed to crack the case, but she accidentally wrote the numbers in disappearing ink! Can you help her put the digits in the right places so she can catch the crook?

Use what you know about multiplication and estimation to find the missing numbers to make a correct division sentence. Then match each letter to its place in the sentence at the bottom of the page.

1. Quotient: 2   **Digits:** 1, 1, 7, 5, 4

▢▢▢ ÷ ▢▢ = **2**

    M

Think: The dividend is about 2 times the divisor.

2. Quotient: 5   **Digits:** 5, 0, 0, 7, 3

▢▢▢ ÷ ▢▢ = **5**

     H

3. Quotient: 3   **Quotient:** 7, 2, 8, 6, 2

▢▢▢ ÷ ▢▢ = **3**

   T

4. Quotient: 4   **Digits:** 1, 6, 3, 4, 9

▢▢▢ ÷ ▢▢ = **4**

  A

5. Quotient: 8   **Digits:** 7, 2, 9, 3, 6

▢▢▢ ÷ ▢▢ = **8**

   O

6. Quotient: 6   **Digits:** 5, 4, 3, 8, 8

▢▢▢ ÷ ▢▢ = **6**

   C

7. Quotient: 7   **Digits:** 7, 8, 5, 2, 4

▢▢▢ ÷ ▢▢ = **7**

 S

So, the crook hid the cookies in his

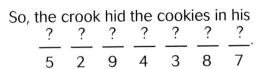

$$\frac{?}{5}\ \frac{?}{2}\ \frac{?}{9}\ \frac{?}{4}\ \frac{?}{3}\ \frac{?}{8}\ \frac{?}{7}.$$

8. **WRITE Math** ▶ **Explain** how estimation helped you make correct division sentences.

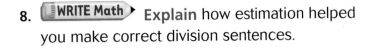

Chapter 13 Review/Test

Check Concepts

1. **Explain** how to use compatible numbers to estimate the first digit in a quotient. (p. 352)

2. **Explain** how to model $188 \div 17$. (p. 354)

3. Do you need to adjust the estimated digit in the quotient? $24\overline{)984}$ with 3 above. **Explain.** (p. 358)

Check Skills

Write the compatible numbers you would use to estimate the quotient. Then estimate. (pp. 352–353)

4. $28\overline{)851}$

5. $573 \div 68$

6. $58\overline{)2,396}$

7. $779 \div 37$

Divide. (pp. 354–355, 356–357, 358–361)

8. $13\overline{)78}$

9. $152 \div 19$

10. $24\overline{)432}$

11. $489 \div 23$

12. $587 \div 38$

13. $691 \div 34$

14. $975 \div 25$

15. $33\overline{)2,874}$

16. $51\overline{)1,824}$

17. $901 \div 37$

18. $28\overline{)651}$

19. $700 \div 19$

Adjust the estimated digit in the quotient, if needed. Then divide. (pp. 358–361)

20. $19\overline{)424}$ with 1 above

21. $16\overline{)490}$ with 3 above

22. $35\overline{)3,225}$ with 9 above

23. $16\overline{)93}$ with 8 above

Check Problem Solving

Solve. (pp. 362–363)

24. Alyssa's family drives 275 miles from Burlington, Vermont, to Hackensack, New Jersey, to visit friends each summer. If they drive an average of 55 miles per hour, how long does the trip take?

25. **WRITE Math** ▶ Joseph works out and listens to music at the gym for about 90 minutes each day. He uses the treadmill and lifts weights. How many songs does he listen to each day? **Explain** what information is missing to solve this problem.

Standardized Test Prep
Chapters 1–13

Number and Operations

1. What is the place value of the underlined digit? (p. 10)

$$4,\underline{6}38,291$$

- **A** Hundreds
- **B** Thousands
- **C** Ten thousands
- **D** Hundred thousands

Test Tip | **Understand the problem.**

See Item 2. The answer is a lesser number because you are putting the total number of cards into piles. You must divide to find the answer.

2. Dominique has 336 baseball cards. She puts them in piles of 24 cards. How many piles are there? (p. 356)

- **A** 13
- **C** 24
- **B** 14
- **D** 8,064

3. Which number is represented by point *A* on the number line? (p. 168)

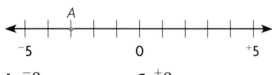

- **A** ⁻3
- **C** ⁺2
- **B** ⁻2
- **D** ⁺3

4. ▌WRITE Math ▶ Sanjay is saving for a DVD player. He has been saving $7.50 for 12 weeks. The DVD player costs $95. Does Sanjay have enough money for the DVD player? **Explain** your answer. (p. 286)

Measurement

5. Josh looks at the thermometer and reads the temperature as 30°F. What could Josh be doing? (p. 164)

- **A** Playing in the snow
- **B** Swimming in the lake
- **C** Building a sand castle at the beach
- **D** Sitting in a classroom

6. Election Day is the first Tuesday in November. New Year's Eve is the last day in December. About how many weeks away from New Year's Eve is Election Day? (p. 158)

November						
Sun	Mon	Tue	Wed	Thu	Fri	Sat
						1
2	3	4	5	6	7	8
9	10	11	12	13	14	15
16	17	18	19	20	21	22
23	24	25	26	27	28	29
30						

December						
Sun	Mon	Tue	Wed	Thu	Fri	Sat
	1	2	3	4	5	6
7	8	9	10	11	12	13
14	15	16	17	18	19	20
21	22	23	24	25	26	27
28	29	30	31			

- **A** 4 weeks
- **C** 8 weeks
- **B** 6 weeks
- **D** 10 weeks

7. What time is shown on the clock? (p. 152)

- **A** Quarter to 2
- **B** Quarter to 3
- **C** Quarter after 2
- **D** 15 minutes before 2

8. ▌WRITE Math ▶ Alexa went to a movie that started at 7:45 P.M. and ended at 9:35 P.M. How long was the movie? **Explain** how you found your answer. (p. 154)

Algebraic Reasoning

9. Which number sentence is related to ■ × 5 = 45? (p. 94)

A ■ × 45 = 5

B 5 ÷ ■ = 45

C 5 ÷ 45 = ■

D 45 ÷ 5 = ■

10. Which equation describes the data in the table? (p. 138)

Input, n	16	32	48	64
Output, m	2	4	6	8

A $m \div 8 = n$ **C** $8 \div m = n$

B $2 \times n = m$ **D** $n \div 8 = m$

11. Which equation is represented on the graph? (p. 226)

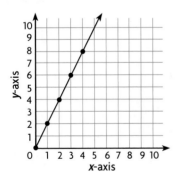

A $y = x$ **C** $y = 3x$

B $y = 2x$ **D** $y = 4x$

12. **WRITE Math** ▸ **Explain** how you would use the order of operations to find the value. How would the value change if the parentheses in the expression were removed? (p. 126)

$$36 \div (6 + 3)$$

Data Analysis and Probability

13. Find the mean and the median of this set of data. (p. 186)

$$9, 3, 6, 3, 4$$

A Mean 3; median 4

B Mean 4; median 3

C Mean 5; median 4

D Mean 6; median 3

14. The graph shows the number of books read by students in a weekly reading contest. About how many books did the boys read altogether? (p. 206)

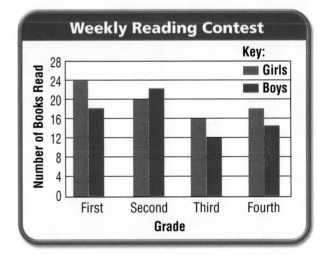

A 66   **C** 78

B 72   **D** 144

15. **WRITE Math** ▸ Male Great Danes grow to be from 30 to 34 inches tall. Female Great Danes are usually from 28 to 32 inches tall. What whole-number heights can both males and females reach? **Explain** how you could use a Venn diagram to show these data. (p. 184)

14 Number Theory and Patterns

Investigate

Knitting is taught in many schools today. Knit and purl are names of knitting stitches. The first row of this panel was started by making 2 knit stitches and then 2 purl stitches. This pattern was repeated over and over to complete the first row. Make another knitting pattern similar to this one for a panel. Then have a classmate describe and extend the pattern.

FAST FACT

There are 150 yards of cotton yarn and 219 yards of wool yarn inside a baseball. If you stretched out the yarn, it would be longer than 3 football fields.

GO ONLINE

Technology
Student pages are available in the Student eBook.

Show What You Know

Check your understanding of important skills
needed for success in Chapter 14.

▶ **Arrays**

Use the array to find the product.

1. ■ ■ ■ ■ ■
■ ■ ■ ■ ■
■ ■ ■ ■ ■

2. ■ ■ ■ ■ ■ ■ ■
■ ■ ■ ■ ■ ■ ■

3.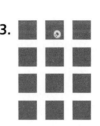

■ rows of ■ = ■   ■ rows of ■ = ■   ■ rows of ■ = ■
■ × ■ = ■   ■ × ■ = ■   ■ × ■ = ■

▶ **Multiplication Facts**

Find the product.

4.   8
     ×6

5.   11
     × 4

6.   2
     ×8

7.   9
     ×5

8.   3
     ×7

9.   5
     ×6

10.   12
      × 5

11.   7
      ×7

▶ **Number Patterns**

Write a rule for each pattern. Then find the missing numbers.

12. 3, 6, 9, 12, ■, ■, ■   **13.** 42, 36, 30, 24, ■, ■, ■

14. 18, 27, 36, 45, ■, ■, ■   **15.** 36, 32, 28, 24, ■, ■, ■

VOCABULARY POWER

CHAPTER VOCABULARY	
array	multiple
composite	pattern
number	pattern
divisible	unit
even	prime
factor	number
	product

WARM-UP WORDS

composite number a whole number greater than 1 that has more than two factors

divisible capable of being divided so that the quotient is a counting number and the remainder is zero

prime number a whole number greater than 1 that has only two factors: 1 and itself

Factors and Multiples

OBJECTIVE: Find factors and multiples using arrays and number lines.

Learn

A factor is a number multiplied by another number to find a product. Every whole number greater than 1 has at least two factors, that number and 1.

$$18 = 1 \times 18 \qquad 7 = 7 \times 1 \qquad 342 = 1 \times 342$$

↑ ↑

factor factor

Many numbers can be broken into factors in different ways.

$$16 = 1 \times 16 \qquad 16 = 4 \times 4 \qquad 16 = 2 \times 8$$

HANDS ON

Activity Materials ■ square tiles ■ grid paper

Make arrays to show all the factors of 24.

• Use all 24 tiles to make an array. Record the array on grid paper. Write the factors shown by the array.

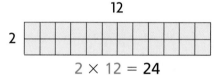

12

2

$2 \times 12 = 24$
Factors: 2, 12

• Make as many different arrays as you can with 24 tiles. Record the arrays on grid paper and write the factors shown.

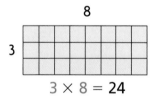

8

3

$3 \times 8 = 24$
Factors: 3, 8

6

4

$4 \times 6 = 24$
Factors: 4, 6

24

1

$1 \times 24 = 24$
Factors: 1, 24

So, the factors of 24 listed from least to greatest are 1, 2, 3, 4, 6, 8, 12, and 24.

• Can you arrange the tiles in each array another way and show the same factors? Explain.

ERROR ALERT

Don't forget to list 1 and the number itself as factors.

Find Multiples

To find multiples of any counting number, skip-count or multiply by the counting numbers 1, 2, 3, and so on.

PROBLEM Rachel has a new charm bracelet with 18 links. She put a charm on each link that is a multiple of 3. Which links have charms?

> **Math Idea**
> A multiple of a counting number is any product that has that number as a factor. The number of multiples a number has is endless.

ONE WAY **Make a model.**

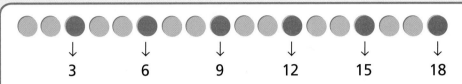

↓ ↓ ↓ ↓ ↓ ↓
3   6   9   12   15   18

The numbers of the red counters are all multiples of 3.

So, the 3rd, 6th, 9th, 12th, 15th, and 18th links have charms.

• **What if** the bracelet had 27 links? Which other links would have charms?

ANOTHER WAY **Multiply and make a list.**

Find the first six multiples of 4.

$1 \times 4 = 4$ $2 \times 4 = 8$ $3 \times 4 = 12$ $4 \times 4 = 16$ $5 \times 4 = 20$ $6 \times 4 = 24$

So, the first six multiples of 4 are 4, 8, 12, 16, 20, and 24.

• Explain how you know that 30 is a multiple of 5.

• Can a number that is a multiple of 3 have 5 as a factor? Explain.

Guided Practice

1. Use the arrays to name the factors of 12.

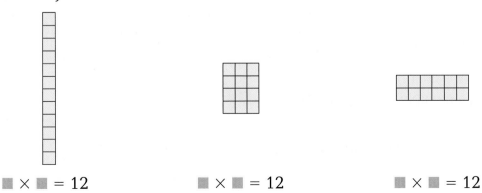

■ × ■ = 12   ■ × ■ = 12   ■ × ■ = 12

The factors of 12 are 1, ■, 3, ■, 6, and ■.

Use arrays to find all the factors of each product.

2. 20   **3.** 5   **4.** 49   **5.** 28   ✓**6.** 25

List the first twelve multiples of each number.

7. 6   **8.** 2   **9.** 11   **10.** 4   ✓**11.** 8

12. [TALK Math] **Explain** how the numbers 3 and 12 are related. Use the words *factor* and *multiple* in your explanation.

Independent Practice and Problem Solving

Use arrays to find all the factors of each product.

13. 30   **14.** 42   **15.** 9   **16.** 50   **17.** 33

18. 64   **19.** 21   **20.** 75   **21.** 18   **22.** 17

List the first twelve multiples of each number.

23. 9   **24.** 1   **25.** 7   **26.** 10   **27.** 12

28. 3   **29.** 8   **30.** 5   **31.** 2   **32.** 6

Is 6 a factor of each number? Write *yes* or *no*.

33. 6   **34.** 16   **35.** 48   **36.** 24   **37.** 18

Is 36 a multiple of each number? Write *yes* or *no*.

38. 8   **39.** 9   **40.** 18   **41.** 36   **42.** 5

⭐**Algebra** Skip-count to find the missing multiple.

43. 4, 8, ■, 16   **44.** 7, 14, 21, ■   **45.** 5, ■, 15, 20   **46.** 20, 40, 60, ■

USE DATA For 47–48, copy and complete the Venn diagram. Then use it to solve the problems.

47. What multiples of 4 are not factors of 48?

48. What factors of 48 are also multiples of 4?

49. Kia paid $40 for two charms. The price of each charm was a multiple of $4. What are the possible prices for the charms?

50. [WRITE Math] ▶ **What's the Question?** The answer is 1, 2, 3, 6, 9, and 18.

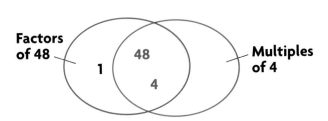

374   Extra Practice on page 390, Set A

Learn About Common Multiples

S	M	T	W	T	F	S
1	2	3	4	5	6	7
8	9	10	11	12	13	14
15	16	17	18	19	20	21
22	23	24	25	26	27	28
29	30					

Starting June 1, an ice-cream truck visits Sasha's street every 3 days and Brad's street every 5 days. What are the first 2 days the truck visits both streets on the same day?

The days the ice-cream truck visits both streets on the same day are common multiples of 3 and 5.

A **common multiple** is a multiple of two or more numbers. You can use a number line to find common multiples.

Example Use a number line.

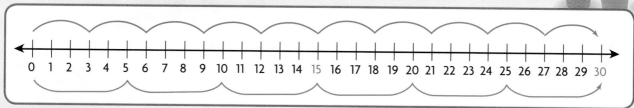

So, the first 2 days the truck visits both streets are June 15 and 30.

Try It

List the first six multiples of each. Find the common multiples.

51. 2 and 4

52. 9 and 12

53. 4 and 8

54. 3 and 4

55. 3 and 6

56. 2 and 5

57. 3 and 9

58. 5 and 10

Mixed Review and Test Prep

59. Find a rule. Write your rule as an equation. Use the equation to extend your pattern.
(p. 78)

Input	x	50	61	108	123	177
Output	y	47	58	105	■	■

60. Evan has 93 action figures. How many shelves will he need if he puts 31 action figures on each shelf? (p. 356)

61. Test Prep What multiple of 7 is a factor of 7?

62. Test Prep Ana is arranging 9 photos on a bulletin board. She wants to put the photos in equal rows. In what ways can she arrange the photos?

A Rows of 1, 3, or 6

B Rows of 1, 2, or 9

C Rows of 1, 3, or 9

D Rows of 3, 6, or 9

OBJECTIVE: Use divisibility rules for 2, 5, 10, and 25.

Learn

A number is **divisible** by another number when the quotient is a counting number and the remainder is zero.

PROBLEM The Knitting Club knitted 135 squares. They are sewing the squares together to make blankets for a hospital. Can they make 5 equal-sized blankets?

HANDS ON

ONE WAY   **Divide.   Materials** ■ base-ten blocks

Use base-ten blocks to find if 135 is divisible by 5. Model 135.

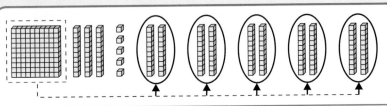

Divide the hundred into 5 equal groups. No hundreds are left.

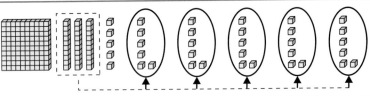

Divide the tens into 5 equal groups. No tens are left.

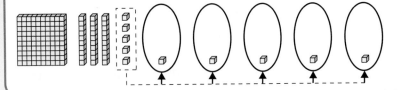

Divide the ones into 5 equal groups. No ones are left.

So, 135 is divisible by 5. They can make 5 equal-sized blankets.

ANOTHER WAY   **Use divisibility rules.**

Is 860 divisible by 2? by 25?

> 860   0 is an even number.
> So, 860 is divisible by 2.
>
> 860   60 is not 00, 25, 50, or 75.
> So, 860 is not divisible by 25.

Number	Divisibility Rule
2	The last digit must be even.
5	The last digit must be 0 or 5.
10	The last digit must be 0.
25	The last two digits must be 00, 25, 50, or 75.

• Are all numbers that are divisible by 5 also divisible by 10? Explain.

1. Is 775 divisible by 2, 5, 10, or 25?

The last digit in 775 is an odd number, so 775 is not divisible by ■.

The last digit in 775 is 5, so 775 is divisible by ■.

The last digit in 775 is not 0, so 775 is not divisible by ■.

The last two digits in 775 are ■, so 775 is divisible by ■.

Tell whether the number is divisible by 2, 5, 10, or 25.

2. 78   **3.** 90   **4.** 355   ✓**5.** 480   ✓**6.** 675

7. TALK Math **Explain** whether all odd numbers are divisible by 5.

Independent Practice and Problem Solving

Tell whether the number is divisible by 2, 5, 10, or 25.

8. 515   **9.** 698   **10.** 290   **11.** 325   **12.** 800

13. 67   **14.** 500   **15.** 235   **16.** 850   **17.** 212

Write *true* or *false* for each statement. Explain.

18. All numbers that are divisible by 5 are also divisible by 25.

19. All numbers that are divisible by 10 are also divisible by 2.

20. Reasoning Lisa knitted 15 squares a day for 7 days. Could she sew together squares to make 5 equal-sized blankets? **Explain.**

21. Pose a Problem Change the numbers in Problem 20 to write a new problem. The total number of squares should be a 3-digit number. Have a classmate solve.

22. WRITE Math ▶ **Explain** how you can use the model to find if 124 is divisible by 2.

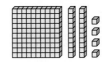

Mixed Review and Test Prep

23. What is the perimeter of a square with a side length of 3 centimeters? (Grade 3)

24. Sierra saved the same amount of money each month for a year. At the end of the year, she had $84. How much did she save each month? (p. 102)

25. Test Prep Which number is divisible by 2 and 25?

A 505   **C** 825

B 660   **D** 900

3 Prime and Composite Numbers

OBJECTIVE: Identify whether a number is prime or composite by using arrays.

Quick Review

1. $3 \times \blacksquare = 27$
2. $\blacksquare \times 4 = 20$
3. $8 \times \blacksquare = 48$
4. $\blacksquare \times 7 = 42$
5. $\blacksquare \times 5 = 10$

Vocabulary

prime number

composite number

Learn

PROBLEM Linda has 7 postcards. She wants to arrange them in equal rows on her bulletin board. How many ways can Linda arrange the postcards?

Activity 1

Materials ■ square tiles

Make all the arrays you can with 7 square tiles to show all the factors of 7.

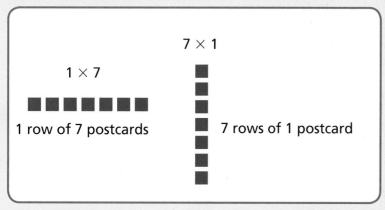

7×1

1×7

1 row of 7 postcards

7 rows of 1 postcard

So, Linda can arrange 7 postcards in exactly two ways.

The number 7 has only two factors, 1 and 7. A whole number greater than 1 that has only two factors, 1 and itself, is a **prime number**. So, 7 is a prime number.

• Is 9 a prime number? Explain.

• Name a number between 10 and 20 that is prime.

Math Idea

The number 1 is neither prime nor composite because it has only one factor, 1.

Activity 2

Materials ■ square tiles

Make all the arrays you can with 6 square tiles
to show all the factors of 6.

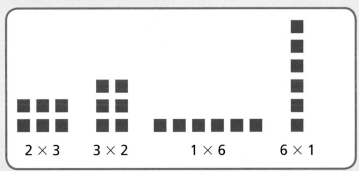

2 × 3   3 × 2   1 × 6   6 × 1

The factors of 6 are 1, 2, 3, and 6. A whole number greater
than 1 that has more than two factors is a **composite number**.
So, 6 is a composite number.

Every whole number greater than 1 is either prime or composite.
You can tell whether a number is prime or composite by making
all the arrays you can for that number.

Activity 3

Materials ■ square tiles

- Use square tiles to make all
  the arrays you can for the
  numbers 2 through 11.
- Record the arrays and
  factors in a table. Write *prime*
  or *composite* for each number.
- How can you tell whether a
  number is prime or composite
  by looking at the Factors column
  of the table?

Number	Arrays	Factors	Prime or Composite?
2		1, 2	prime
3		1, 3	prime
4		1, 2, 4	composite
5			

Guided Practice

1. Use the arrays to find the factors of 12. Is 12 *prime* or *composite*?

   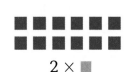

1 × ■   ■ × 4   2 × ■

Make arrays to find the factors. Write *prime* or *composite* for each number.

2. 14 **3.** 17 **4.** 36 ✓**5.** 39 ✓**6.** 43

7. [TALK Math] **Explain** how prime and composite numbers are alike. Explain how they are different.

Independent Practice and Problem Solving

Make arrays to find the factors. Write *prime* or *composite* for each number.

8. 21 **9.** 16 **10.** 23 **11.** 32 **12.** 13

13. 19 **14.** 44 **15.** 28 **16.** 30 **17.** 34

Write *prime* or *composite* for each number.

18. 99 **19.** 48 **20.** 67 **21.** 81 **22.** 71

23. 50 **24.** 65 **25.** 15 **26.** 83 **27.** 31

28. 22 **29.** 97 **30.** 70 **31.** 35 **32.** 29

USE DATA For 33–34, use the picture of stamps.

33. What other ways might the stamps be arranged in equal rows?

34. Is 25 prime or composite? **Explain.**

35. ≡*FAST FACT* A collection of 18,500 historic postcards is stored in the library at the University of Maryland. How can divisibility rules help you decide if 18,500 is a prime or composite number?

36. [WRITE Math] ▶ **What's the Error?** Marco listed the first five prime numbers as 2, 3, 7, 11, and 13. Describe his error. Write the correct answer.

Mixed Review and Test Prep

37. Ann is buying five cards. The prices are $2.00, $1.25, $1.50, $2.00, and $1.80. What is the median price? (p. 186)

38. Jackson has a 486-page book. If he reads 54 pages a day, how many days will it take to read the book? (p. 360)

39. Test Prep Which of the following is a composite number?

A 1 **C** 33

B 31 **D** 43

Technology
Use Harcourt Mega Math, Ice Station Exploration, *Arctic Algebra*, Level O.

Justify an Answer

Sometimes you need to provide an argument to justify an answer. Look at the question to identify the important words. Words such as all and only are key words to help you develop your argument.

Lisa was asked the question, "Are all multiples of the prime number 7 composite?" She answered "No," and wrote this argument to defend her answer.

All multiples of the prime number 7 are not composite numbers.
First, I found some multiples of 7.

$1 \times 7 = 7$ $2 \times 7 = 14$ $3 \times 7 = 21$

Then, I noticed that the first multiple of 7 is 7. The number 7 is a prime number because it has only two factors, 1 and 7.

So, because I found one example of a multiple of 7 that is not a composite number, my answer is correct.

Tips

- First, state your answer.
- Next, show several examples and decide whether each example supports your answer.
- Write an explanation about how each example relates to your answer.
- Write a statement that summarizes the reason for your answer.

Problem Solving Make mathematical arguments to justify the answer.

1. Are all odd numbers prime?

2. Are all the factors of 4 also factors of 12?

3. Are all multiples of the prime number 5 prime?

4. Why is 2 the only prime number that is even?

4 Number Patterns

OBJECTIVE: Identify, describe, extend, and make patterns.

Quick Review

Find the missing number.

1. $5 \times \blacksquare = 15$
2. $7 + \blacksquare = 13$
3. $12 \div \blacksquare = 3$
4. $50 - \blacksquare = 40$
5. $830 + \blacksquare = 930$

Learn

PROBLEM Morgan counts as he juggles three balls. He tosses the red ball on the count of 3, 6, 9, and 12. What numbers will he count for the next two tosses of the red ball?

Example 1

Find a rule. Then find the next two numbers in your pattern.

3, 6, 9, 12, ■, ■

Step 1

Think: What rule changes 3 to 6?

Try multiply by 2 because $2 \times 3 = 6$.

Test: $2 \times 6 \neq 9$

Try add 3 because $3 + 3 = 6$.

Test: $6 + 3 = 9$ $9 + 3 = 12$

The rule add 3 works.

Step 2

Use the rule to find the next two numbers in the pattern.

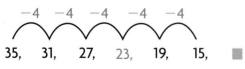

```
    +3   +3   +3    +3    +3
   ⌒    ⌒    ⌒     ⌒     ⌒
3,   6,   9,   12,   15,   18
```

So, he will count 15, 18 for the next two tosses of the red ball.

If a number pattern increases, try addition or multiplication. If it decreases, try subtraction or division.

Example 2

Find a rule. Then find the missing numbers in your pattern.

35, 31, 27, ■, 19, 15, ■

Step 1

Write a rule for the pattern.

Try subtract 4.

```
    -4   -4   -4    -4    -4
   ⌒    ⌒    ⌒     ⌒     ⌒
35,  31,  27,  23,  19,  15,   ■
```

The rule subtract 4 works.

Step 2

Use the rule to find the missing numbers in your pattern.

```
                 -4            -4
                ⌒            ⌒
35,  31,  27,  23,  19,  15,   11
```

So, the missing numbers are 23 and 11.

• Look at this pattern: 1, 2, 4, ■. If the missing number is 8, what is a rule for your pattern? If the missing number is 7, what is a rule for your pattern?

Find and Make Patterns

The rules for some patterns have more than one operation. When numbers in a pattern increase **and** decrease, try two operations.

Math Idea

You can use the strategy *find a possible pattern* to help. Compare each number with the next.

Example 3 Use two operations.

Find a rule. Then find the next two numbers in your pattern.
5, 1, 10, 2, 20, 4, 40, ■, ■

Step 1

Write a rule for the pattern.
Try divide by 5, multiply by 10.

$$\div 5 \quad \times 10 \quad \div 5 \quad \times 10 \quad \div 5 \quad \times 10$$
5,   1,   10,   2,   20,   4,   40

The rule divide by 5, multiply by 10 works.

Step 2

Use your rule to find the missing numbers.
$40 \div 5 = 8$ $10 \times 8 = 80$

So, the next two numbers in the pattern are 8 and 80.

Example 4 Use a calculator.

Use the rule *add 13, multiply by 4* to make a pattern.
Start with 1. Find the next three numbers in the pattern.

Step 1

Enter the first operation. Press:

◄ *Op1*

Step 2

Enter the second operation. Press:

◄ *Op1 Op2*

Step 3

Find the second number in the pattern. Press:

Op1 Op2
1 + 13
1   14

Step 4

Find the third number in the pattern. Press:

Op1 Op2
14 X 4
1   56

Step 5

Find the fourth number in the pattern. Press:

Op1 Op2
56 + 13
1   69

So, the next three numbers in the pattern are 14, 56, and 69.

- **What if** you start with 2? What would be the fourth number in the pattern?

Guided Practice

1. What are the next two numbers in the pattern?

$$-2 \quad -2 \quad -2$$

58, 56, 54, 52, ▣, ▣

Find a rule. Then find the next two numbers in your pattern.

✓**2.** 18, 28, 38, 48, ▣, ▣

✓**3.** 4, 7, 5, 8, 6, 9, 7, ▣, ▣

4. (TALK Math) **Describe** how to find missing numbers in a number pattern.

Independent Practice and Problem Solving

Find a rule. Then find the next two numbers in your pattern.

5. 775, 675, 575, 475, ▣, ▣

6. 160, 80, 40, 20, ▣, ▣

7. 47, 52, 51, 56, 55, 60, 59, ▣, ▣

8. 99, 95, 98, 94, 97, 93, 96, ▣, ▣

⭐**Algebra** **Find a rule. Then find the missing numbers in your pattern.**

9. 2, 4, ▣, 16, 32, 64

10. 46, 40, ▣, 28, 22, ▣, 10

11. ▣, 130, 145, 160, 175, ▣

Use the rule to make a number pattern. Write the first four numbers in the pattern.

12. Rule: Divide by 2. Start with 24.

13. Rule: Subtract 8. Start with 72.

14. Rule: Add 3, subtract 2. Start with 16.

15. Jordan is juggling 3 balls. He starts by keeping 1 ball in his hand and tossing 2 balls into the air. The diagram shows how many balls are in the air and in his hand with each toss. How many balls will be in the air and in his hand with the next toss?

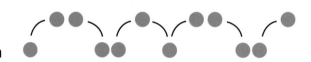

16. Carolyn counts as she juggles 4 balls. She tosses the red ball on the count of 4, 8, 12, and 16. What numbers will she count when she tosses the next two red balls?

17. **Pose a Problem** Make a number pattern. Write the first six numbers. Have a classmate copy your pattern, write a rule for the pattern, and use that rule to find the next three numbers.

18. **Reasoning** Look at the following number pattern: 2, 4, 8, ▣. What is a rule for the pattern if the missing number is 14? What is a rule for the pattern if the missing number is 16?

19. (WRITE Math) ▸ **Explain** how you can tell by looking at a pattern that a rule for the pattern might have two operations.

(**Extra Practice** on page 390, Set D)

CD ROM **Technology**
Use Harcourt Mega Math, The Number Games, *Tiny's Think Tank*, Level K.

Learn About) ALGEBRA **Fibonacci Numbers**

Fibonacci, a mathematician from Italy, discovered the following number pattern about 800 years ago.

1, 1, 2, 3, 5, 8, 13, . . .

What might the next two numbers in the pattern be?

▲ Fibonacci numbers are found by counting petals on a daisy or spirals on a pinecone.

Step 1	**Step 2**
Write a rule for the pattern. 0 + 1 1 + 1 1 + 2 2 + 3 3 + 5 5 + 8 1, 1, 2, 3, 5, 8, 13, ■, ■ **Rule:** Start at 1. Find the sum of the two previous whole numbers.	Use the rule to find the next two numbers in the pattern. 8 + 13 = 21 13 + 21 = 34

So, the next two numbers in the pattern are 21 and 34.

Try It

20. Is 144 a Fibonacci number? **Explain** your answer.

21. Choose a number. Use it to make a pattern similar to the Fibonacci pattern. Describe your pattern.

Mixed Review and Test Prep

22. Sophie had 20 oranges. She put an equal number of oranges in 5 bags. How many oranges were in 2 bags? (p. 96)

23. The table shows populations for different states. Which state in the table has the least population? (p. 16)

2003 State Populations	
State	**Number of People**
California	33,484,453
Illinois	12,653,544
Texas	22,118,509

24. **Test Prep** Which of the following describes a rule for this pattern?

5, 9, 7, 11, 9, 13, 11

A Add 2.

B Multiply by 2.

C Add 4, subtract 2.

D Add 2, multiply by 2.

25. **Test Prep** What might the next two numbers in this pattern be?

24, 21, 18, 15, ■ , ■

Problem Solving Workshop
Strategy: Find a Pattern

OBJECTIVE: Solve problems by using the strategy *find a pattern*.

Learn the Strategy

Patterns can be found everywhere in the real world. You can use math to talk about patterns in nature, architecture, music, dance, art, and language. You can use patterns to solve problems.

Geometric patterns can be based on color, size, shape, position, or number of figures.

What might be the next floor tile to be put down?

The last tiles were two rhombuses. So, the next tile might be an octagon.

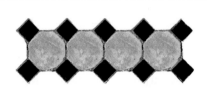

Pattern unit:

Number patterns can increase, decrease, repeat, or stop.

What is the date of the third Wednesday in May?

Rule: Start at 3. Add 7. 3, 10, 17, 24, 31
So, the third Wednesday in May is the 17th.

May						
Sun	Mon	Tue	Wed	Thu	Fri	Sat
		1	2	③	4	5	6
7	8	9	⑩	11	12	13
14	15	16	17	18	19	20
21	22	23	㉔	25	26	27
28	29	30	㉛			

Some visual patterns can be described using numbers.

Erin is building a model of a skyscraper with square tiles. She will build one more array for the base of the skyscraper. How many squares might be in the base if the pattern continues?

Rule: Increase the number of rows and columns of tiles by 1.

So, the base will be a 5-by-5 array, with 25 tiles.

Design	Number of Tiles
	1
	4
	9
	16

TALK Math
How can finding a rule help you predict what comes next?

Use the Strategy

PROBLEM Claire's family is putting a wall with the stair-step pattern shown in their bathroom. If they want the wall to be 5 cubes tall, how many cubes will they need?

Read to Understand
Plan
Solve
Check

Read to Understand

- **What information is given?**

Plan

- **What strategy can you use to solve the problem?**
  You can find a pattern to solve the problem.

Solve

Reading Skill

- **How can you use the strategy and graphic aids to solve the problem?**
  Write a rule for the pattern.

Design	Pattern Description	Number of Cubes
■	1-cube base, 0 on top	1
	2-cube base, 1 on top	3
	3-cube base, then 2, then 1 on top	6
	4-cube base, then 3, then 2, then 1 on top	10

Rule: For each new design, the base has 1 more cube than the design before.

Use the rule to find the number of cubes in a wall that is 5 cubes tall.

So, a wall that is 5 cubes tall has 15 cubes.

Check

- **Look at the Number of Cubes column. What is a number pattern for the number of cubes in each figure?**

Guided Problem Solving

Read to Understand

Plan

Solve

Check

1. Parker is building a model of a ziggurat wall with blocks. How many blocks might he place in the next row?

   Write a rule for the pattern.

   Rule: Subtract ■ from the previous row.

   Use the rule to find the number of blocks in the next row.

   $9 - ■ = ■$

▲ A ziggurat is a kind of ancient temple.

9 blocks
11 blocks
13 blocks
15 blocks

2. **What if** Parker continued the pattern? Could the pattern continue without end? **Explain.**

3. The table shows the number of windows on each floor of a skyscraper. How many windows might be on the tenth floor?

Floor	1	2	3	4	5	6	7	8	9
Number of Windows	4	8	6	10	8	12	10	14	12

Problem Solving Strategy Practice

Find a pattern to solve.

4. Draw a pattern unit for the two center rings of the tree grate. This photograph shows one fourth of the tree grate. How many large trapezoids might be in the center ring of the whole grate?

5. Many brick columns use this pattern. Write a number pattern that describes the lengths of the bricks in each row.

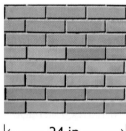

|← 24 in. →|

6. The mailboxes in Hannah's apartment building are in an array. Some of the numbers have fallen off the mailboxes. Look for a pattern in the rows. Look for a pattern in the columns. What might be the missing numbers?

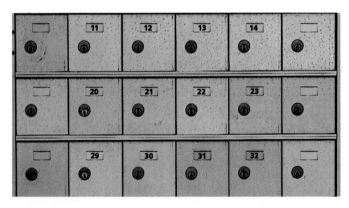

Height: 1,483 ft
Petronas Tower
Kuala Lumpur
Malaysia

Height: 986 ft
Eiffel Tower
Paris
France

Height: 1,046 ft
Chrysler
Building
New York City

Height: 1,250 ft
Empire State
Building
New York City

Choose a
STRATEGY

Draw a Diagram or Picture
Make a Model or Act It Out
Make an Organized List
Find a Pattern
Make a Table or Graph
Predict and Test
Work Backward
Solve a Simpler Problem
Write an Equation
Use Logical Reasoning

Mixed Strategy Practice

USE DATA For 7–10, use the information in the picture.

7. Two buildings have a difference in height of 60 feet. Which are the two buildings?

8. The U.S. Bank Tower in Los Angeles is x feet taller than the Eiffel Tower. The U.S. Bank Tower is 1,018 feet tall. What is x?

9. **Pose a Problem** Look back at Problem 7. Write a similar problem by changing the difference in height.

10. **WRITE Math** One mile is 5,280 feet. Estimate to find whether all four skyscrapers put together would be about one mile high. **Explain** how you estimated.

11. **Open-Ended** Use grid paper to draw a picture of a skyscraper. Include a numerical pattern in your drawing. For example, the number of windows on each floor might increase by 3. Write a rule for your pattern.

CHALLENGE YOURSELF
The Eiffel Tower, at 986 feet tall, was the tallest building in the world when it was built in 1889 for the Paris World's Fair. It takes 50 tons of paint to cover the Eiffel Tower.

12. Before the Eiffel Tower was completed, the Washington Monument was the world's tallest building. The Washington Monument stands 185 yards tall. Is the Eiffel Tower about 3 times taller than the Washington Monument? **Explain.**

13. The Eiffel Tower is painted every 7 years. How many tons of paint were used between the year the Eiffel Tower opened and 2008?

Extra Practice

Set A **Use arrays to find all the factors of each product.** (pp. 372–375)

1. 24
2. 35
3. 41
4. 56
5. 32

List the first twelve multiples of each number.

6. 7
7. 3
8. 12
9. 11
10. 5

11. Emma bought some key chains. If she paid $24 for the key chains, and each one cost the same amount, how many could she have bought?

Set B **Tell whether the number is divisible by 2, 5, 10, or 25.** (pp. 376–377)

1. 55
2. 94
3. 333
4. 405
5. 675

6. 85
7. 110
8. 270
9. 585
10. 704

Set C **Write *prime* or *composite* for each number.** (pp. 378–381)

1. 33
2. 17
3. 40
4. 43
5. 72

6. 56
7. 21
8. 18
9. 19
10. 37

11. In August, Cade has piano lessons every third day. His first lesson is on August 3. On what dates in August are his other lessons? Which lesson date is a prime number?

Set D **Find a rule. Then find the next two numbers in your pattern.** (pp. 382–385)

1. 38, 41, 44, 47, 50, ■, ■
2. 211, 216, 221, 226, 231, ■, ■
3. 986, 886, 786, 686, 586, ■, ■
4. 29, 36, 33, 40, 37, 44, 41, ■, ■
5. 59, 54, 56, 51, 53, 48, 50, ■, ■
6. 15, 3, 15, 3, 15, 3, ■, ■

Find a rule. Then find the missing numbers in your pattern.

7. 5, ■, 13, 17, 21, ■
8. 45, ■, 35, 30, 25, ■
9. 22, 24, ■, 28, 30, ■
10. 7, ■, 21, 28, ■, 42

11. Shawna is passing out programs in the auditorium. She places the first program on the second chair and then puts a program on every third chair. On which chair does she place the fifth program?

Technology
Use Harcourt Mega Math, Ice Station Exploration, *Arctic Algebra*, Level M.

PRACTICE GAME

Factor Farm

On Your Mark!
2 to 3 players

Get Set!
- Number cards (2–10)
- 2-color counters

21	35	18	16	6
32	40	12	10	3
20	4	9	27	8
39	28	5	15	22
2	25	14	7	36

Go!

- Shuffle the number cards and place them facedown in a stack.
- Draw a number card from the stack. If the number is a factor of one of the numbers on your grid, put a counter on that number.
- You may put a counter on only one number for each number card drawn.
- The first player to place counters on 5 numbers in a horizontal, vertical, or diagonal line wins.

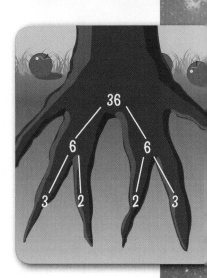

MATH POWER — Find Prime Factors

THE ROOT OF THE PROBLEM

Every composite number can be written as the product of prime numbers. A factor that is a prime number is a **prime factor**. You can use a **factor tree** to find the prime factors of a composite number.

What are the prime factors of 36? Choose any two factors of 36, and continue factoring until only prime factors are left.

ONE WAY Use 6 × 6.

```
        36
       /  \
      6  ×  6   ← composite, so
     /\    /\      factor again
   2×3 × 2×3   ← prime
```

36 = 2 × 3 × 2 × 3

ANOTHER WAY Use 4 × 9.

```
        36
       /  \
      4  ×  9   ← composite, so
     /\    /\      factor again
   2×2 × 3×3   ← prime
```

36 = 2 × 2 × 3 × 3

List the factors from least to greatest.

So, 36 = 2 × 2 × 3 × 3.

Examples

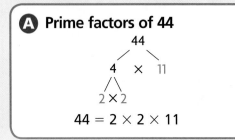

A Prime factors of 44

```
        44
       /  \
      4  ×  11
     /\
   2×2
```

44 = 2 × 2 × 11

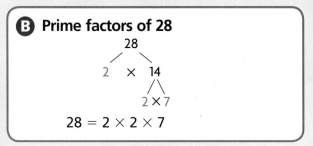

B Prime factors of 28

```
        28
       /  \
      2  ×  14
            /\
          2×7
```

28 = 2 × 2 × 7

- Does it matter which two factors you use in the first branch of a factor tree? Explain.

Try It
Use a factor tree to find the prime factors.

1. 10	**2.** 24	**3.** 18	**4.** 50	**5.** 16
6. 30	**7.** 12	**8.** 27	**9.** 33	**10.** 48

11. ⬛WRITE Math ▸ **Explain** how you know when a factor tree is complete.

Chapter 14 Review/Test

Check Vocabulary and Concepts

Choose the best term from the box.

VOCABULARY

composite number
divisible
prime number

1. A whole number greater than 1 that has only two factors, 1 and itself, is called a ___?___ . (p. 378)

2. The factors of 100 are 1, 2, 4, 5, 10, 20, 25, 50, and 100, so 100 is called a ___?___ . (p. 378)

Check Skills

Use arrays to find all the factors of each product. (pp. 372–375)

3. 36   4. 45   5. 24   6. 42   7. 27

Tell whether the number is divisible by 2, 5, 10, or 25. (pp. 376–377)

8. 80   9. 98   10. 275   11. 300   12. 625

Write *prime* or *composite* for each number. (pp. 378–381)

13. 25   14. 53   15. 39   16. 41   17. 26

Find a rule. Then find the next two numbers in your pattern. (pp. 382–385)

18. 34, 38, 42, 46, 50, ■, ■   19. 89, 84, 79, 74, 69, ■, ■

20. 56, 66, 63, 73, 70, ■, ■   21. 24, 6, 24, 6, 24, 6, ■, ■

Find a rule. Then find the missing numbers in your pattern. (pp. 382–385)

22. 17, ■, 23, 26, 29, ■   23. 78, ■, 56, 45, 34, ■

Check Problem Solving

Solve. (pp. 386–389)

24. Andy went jogging on Monday, and then again every other day after that. On what day did he go jogging for the tenth time?

25. **WRITE Math** ▶ The table shows the number of stickers on each page of Rosie's notebook. Write a rule to describe her pattern. **Explain** how you found her pattern.

Page Number	1	2	3	4	5	6
Number of Stickers	3	6	9	12	15	18

Unit Review/Test
Chapters 11–14

Multiple Choice

1. Estimate the quotient. (p. 320)

   $$952 \div 5$$

   A 100

   B 200

   C 300

   D 400

2. If a pack of 52 cards is divided equally among 4 people, how many cards does each person get? (p. 310)

   A 6

   B 8

   C 12

   D 13

3. Which number is a factor of 10? (p. 372)

   A 30

   B 20

   C 15

   D 5

4. Ming has $99. He decides to spend an equal amount of money on music, books, and computer games. How much will he spend on music? (p. 310)

   A $297

   B $102

   C $66

   D $33

5. Which number is divisible by 2 and 5? (p. 376)

   A 150

   B 152

   C 155

   D 158

6. Which pair of numbers completes the equation? (p. 356)

   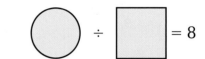

   A 80 and 11

   B 92 and 12

   C 96 and 12

   D 98 and 11

7. Which statement is true? (p. 372)

   A 1 is a factor of only odd numbers.

   B 1 is not a factor of any number.

   C 1 is a factor of every number.

   D 1 is a factor of only 0.

GO ONLINE Technology Use *Online Assessment.*

8. Mr. Rodrigues has 126 stickers for the students in his class. If there are 9 students in the class, how many stickers does each student receive? (p. 334)

   A 12

   B 13

   C 14

   D 15

9. The number 1,423 is a prime number. Which number is a factor of 1,423?
   (p. 378)

   A 1

   B 2

   C 3

   D 4

10. Neena has 97 cents. What is the greatest number of nickels she could have? (p. 310)

    A 20

    B 19

    C 18

    D 17

11. Which number is a multiple of 4? (p. 372)

    A 6

    B 10

    C 18

    D 24

Short Response

12. Write a rule to describe this pattern. (p. 382)

    1, 6, 11, 16, 21, 26

13. Make arrays to find all the factors of 32.
    (p. 372)

14. The table shows the number of students in the summer basketball league.

Summer Basketball League	
Grade	Number of Students
Third	84
Fourth	99
Fifth	72

    Each team has 9 students. How many teams of fourth graders are there? (p. 310)

Extended Response WRITE Math ▶

15. **Explain** how you know that 13 is a prime number. (p. 378)

16. **Explain** the difference between a factor and a multiple. (p. 372)

17. Dwayne has 43 books. If each storage box holds 9 books, how many boxes does he need to store all of his books? **Explain** your answer. (p. 332)

18. **Explain** how you know that all even numbers greater than 2 are composite.
    (p. 378)

THE WORLD ALMANAC FOR KIDS

Amazing Collectibles

World-Record Collections

Are you a collector? Millions of people have hobbies that involve collectibles. Some people collect model cars, dolls, or stamps. Others collect more unusual items, such as potato-chip bags or gum wrappers. It is amazing how many unusual items one person can collect!

Amazing Collections

Type of Collection	Number
Banana Labels	6,583
Colored Vinyl Records	1,180
Handmade Walking Canes	639
Model Cars	3,711
Retired Traffic Signs	600

FACT·ACTIVITY

Use the Amazing Collections table to answer the questions.

1. If the walking-cane collector took 9 years to collect the canes and collected the same number each year, how many were collected each year?

2. If the collector of banana labels places them in a scrapbook with 30 on each page, how many pages will be filled? How many labels will go on another page?

3. The collector of retired traffic signs might find 15 a year. At this rate, how many years will it take to collect 600 signs?

4. A collector finds 4 colored vinyl records per month. Estimate how many years it will take to collect the number of records listed in the table.

5. **Pose a Problem** Write a division problem about the model car collection.

What Do You Collect?

There is no limit to what you can collect! Many adult collectors began collecting when they were children. Kids all over the world collect objects that are interesting to them.

Bottle Caps

Penguins

Stamps

FACT·ACTIVITY

Think of something you would like to collect. Answer the questions about planning your collection.

► What do you want to collect? How many items would you like to have in your collection?

► Where will you keep the items? Will you arrange them in equal groups, such as 10 figurines per shelf or 16 stamps per page? Will there be items left over?

► Write division sentences to show how your collection might be arranged in equal groups. Try a few different ways to arrange them.

6 Fractions and Decimals

Math on Location

A DVD FROM
The Futures Channel

with
Chapter Projects

1

1¼" ALLEN HEAD

Customers choose the components of a skateboard by their size and color.

2

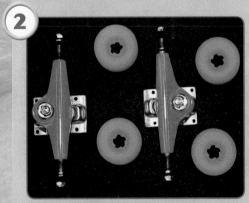

A skateboard is made up of a deck, grip tape, 2 trucks, 4 wheels, and 8 bearings.

3

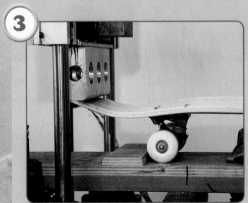

The deck is 7 layers of $\frac{1}{16}$-inch maple veneer. Its strengh is tested by measuring the amount of flex to a fraction of an inch.

VOCABULARY POWER

TALK Math

What math is used in making a skateboard? Look at the green, pink, red, clear, and white wheels in the **Math on Location** photographs. How could you represent what fraction of the wheels are each color?

READ Math

REVIEW VOCABULARY You learned the words below when you first learned about fractions. How do these words relate to **Math on Location**?

denominator the part of a fraction below the bar, that tells how many equal parts are in the whole or in the group

equivalent fractions two or more fractions that name the same amount

fraction a number that names part of a whole or part of a group

WRITE Math

Copy and complete the chart below, using what you know about fractions. Use your own words to write the definition. Write as many facts, examples, and nonexamples as you can think of.

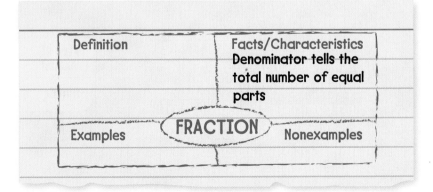

Definition	Facts/Characteristics
	Denominator tells the total number of equal parts
Examples	FRACTION	Nonexamples

Technology
Multimedia Math Glossary link at
www.harcourtschool.com/hspmath

15 Understand Fractions and Mixed Numbers

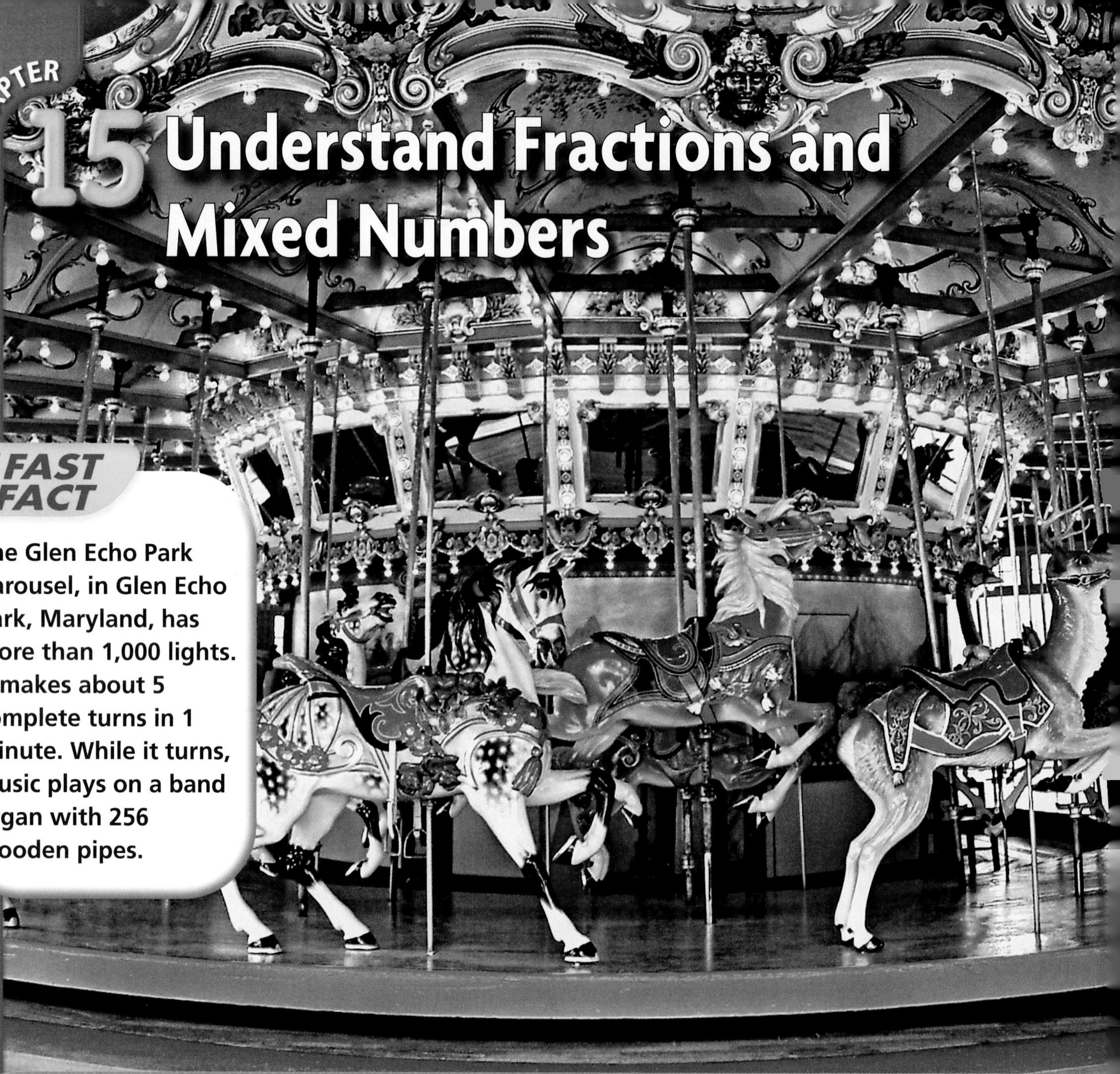

FAST FACT

The Glen Echo Park Carousel, in Glen Echo Park, Maryland, has more than 1,000 lights. It makes about 5 complete turns in 1 minute. While it turns, music plays on a band organ with 256 wooden pipes.

Investigate

Use the animals on the carousel. Using fractions, compare the number of each type of animal. Then compare the number of each type of animal to the total number of animals on the carousel. Write as many fractions as you can.

Glen Echo Park Carousel						
Type of Animal	Horse	Rabbit	Ostrich	Giraffe	Deer	Lion	Tiger
Number	40	4	4	1	1	1	1

GO ONLINE

Technology
Student pages are available in the Student eBook.

Check your understanding of important skills
needed for success in Chapter 15.

▶ **Parts of a Whole**

Write a fraction for each shaded part.

1.   2. 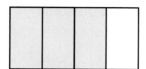   3.   4.

▶ **Parts of a Group**

Write a fraction for each shaded part.

5. 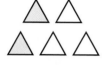   6. 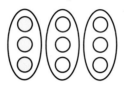   7. 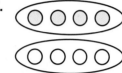   8.

▶ **Locate Numbers on a Number Line**

Write the number that names the point.

9.    10.    11.

VOCABULARY POWER

CHAPTER VOCABULARY

denominator   numerator
equivalent   simplest
  fractions   form
fourths   thirds
fraction   whole
group
halves
mixed number

WARM-UP WORDS

denominator the number below the bar in a fraction that tells how many equal parts are in the whole or in the group

fraction a number that names part of a whole or part of a group

numerator the number above the bar in a fraction that tells how many parts of the whole or group are being considered

Read and Write Fractions

OBJECTIVE: Read and write fractions.

Learn

PROBLEM For lunch Ben had an orange with 8 equal sections. He ate 2 of the sections. What fraction represents the amount of orange Ben ate?

A **fraction** is a number that names part of a whole or part of a group.

Example 1 Name part of a whole.

The number of sections Ben ate were part of the total number of sections in the orange.

number of parts Ben ate → 2 ← numerator
total equal parts → 8 ← denominator

Read: two eighths
two out of eight
two divided by eight

Write: $\frac{2}{8}$

So, Ben ate $\frac{2}{8}$ of the orange.

Example 2 Count equal parts of a whole.

You can count equal parts, such as eighths, to make one whole.

$\frac{1}{8}$ $\frac{2}{8}$ $\frac{3}{8}$ $\frac{4}{8}$ $\frac{5}{8}$ $\frac{6}{8}$ $\frac{7}{8}$ $\frac{8}{8}$

$\frac{8}{8}$ = one whole, or 1

Each equal part of the whole is $\frac{1}{8}$. The fraction $\frac{1}{8}$ is a unit fraction.

A **unit fraction** has a numerator of 1.

• In Example 1, how can you find the fraction of the orange that Ben did not eat by counting equal parts?

Quick Review

Name the number each letter represents.

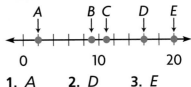

0   10   20

1. A 2. D 3. E
4. C 5. B

Vocabulary

fraction   denominator
numerator   unit fraction

Example 3 Show division.

ONE WAY Use a model.

Ben's 4 sisters share 3 waffles equally.
How much waffle will each sister get?

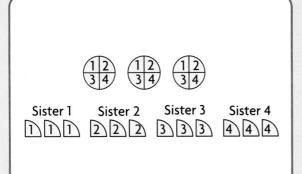

Sister 1   Sister 2   Sister 3   Sister 4

So, each sister will get $\frac{3}{4}$ of a waffle.

ANOTHER WAY Use a number line.

Emma's 3 brothers share a box of cereal equally.
What fraction of the cereal will each brother get?

A number line can be used to represent one whole. The line can be divided into any number of equal parts.

This number line is divided into three equal parts, or thirds.

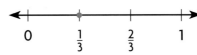

0      $\frac{1}{3}$ $\frac{2}{3}$ 1

The point shows the location of $\frac{1}{3}$.

So, each brother will get $\frac{1}{3}$ of the box of cereal.

• In Example 3, what do the numerator and the denominator in $\frac{3}{4}$ represent?

Example 4 Name part of a group.

Kelly baked 12 muffins in one pan. She gave 5 of the muffins to her neighbor. What fraction of the muffins did Kelly give away?

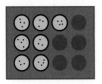

number given away → $\frac{5}{12}$ ← numerator
total number in the group →   ← denominator

Read: five twelfths   **Write:** $\frac{5}{12}$
five out of twelve
five divided by twelve

So, $\frac{5}{12}$ of the muffins were given away.

Guided Practice

1. Sam drew a square with four equal parts. He shaded $\frac{3}{4}$ of the square. Which square could he have drawn?

   A   B   C

Write a fraction for the shaded part. Write a fraction for the unshaded part.

2.

3.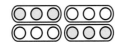

4.

5.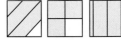

6. TALK Math Explain what a fraction can represent.

Independent Practice and Problem Solving

Write a fraction for the shaded part. Write a fraction for the unshaded part.

7.

8.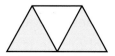

9.

10.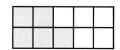

Draw a picture and shade part of it to show the fraction. Write a fraction in word form for the unshaded part.

11. $\frac{7}{8}$

12. $\frac{5}{9}$

13. $\frac{12}{12}$

14. $\frac{8}{10}$

Write the fraction for each.

15. one seventh

16. six out of six

17. three divided by four

18. two thirds

Write the fraction that names the point.

19.

20.

21.

⭐**Algebra** Write the missing fraction.

22. $\frac{1}{8}, \frac{2}{8}, \blacksquare, \frac{4}{8}, \frac{5}{8}$

23. $\frac{5}{12}, \frac{6}{12}, \frac{7}{12}, \frac{8}{12}, \blacksquare$

24. $\frac{7}{16}, \frac{6}{16}, \frac{5}{16}, \blacksquare, \frac{3}{16}$

USE DATA For 25–27, use the picture.

25. What fraction of the items on the tray is fruit?

26. What fraction of the items on the tray is neither muffins nor apples?

27. Write the total number of items on the tray as a fraction.

28. Mike bought 15 apples, 5 bananas, and 10 pears for a party. What fraction of the fruit Mike bought is pears?

29. **WRITE Math** **Explain** how you can model the same fraction three different ways. Then give examples of your explanation.

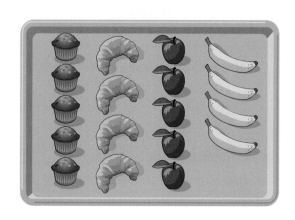

Technology
Use Harcourt Mega Math, Fraction
Action, *Fraction Flare Up*, Levels B, C.

Learn About) Finding a Fraction of a Group

You can find a fraction of a group or a collection, even if the
denominator of the fraction is not the same as the number in the group.

Examples

A Find $\frac{2}{3}$ of 6.

Draw 6 objects.

The denominator is 3. Make 3 equal
groups.

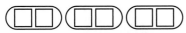

Then shade 2 groups. Count the
total objects shaded.

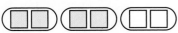

So, $\frac{2}{3}$ of 6 is 4.

B Find $\frac{3}{4}$ of 16.

Draw 16 objects.

The denominator is 4.
Make 4 equal groups.

Then shade 3 groups.
Count the total
objects shaded.

So, $\frac{3}{4}$ of 16 is 12.

Try It

Draw a picture to solve.

30. $\frac{1}{2}$ of 6   **31.** $\frac{1}{4}$ of 8   **32.** $\frac{2}{3}$ of 15   **33.** $\frac{5}{6}$ of 12   **34.** $\frac{3}{8}$ of 24

Mixed Review and Test Prep

35. A meeting room needs 35 chairs set up
in 7 equal rows. Write a division sentence
to show how many chairs will be in each
row. (p.128)

36. Test Prep Five friends share 3 small pizzas
equally. How much of the pizzas will each
friend get?

A $\frac{1}{5}$ **B** $\frac{1}{3}$ **C** $\frac{2}{5}$ **D** $\frac{3}{5}$

37. Kim is buying candles to put on a cake.
The candles come in boxes of 6. How
many boxes does she need to buy in
order to have 10 candles on the cake?
(p. 98)

38. Test Prep Eli has 10 tiles. Of these tiles,
$\frac{1}{10}$ are blue, $\frac{3}{10}$ are yellow, and the rest
are green. What fraction of the tiles are
green? **Explain.**

Model Equivalent Fractions

OBJECTIVE: Model equivalent fractions.

Learn

PROBLEM As of 2005, there were 10 giant pandas in zoos in the United States and Mexico. The National Zoo, in Washington, D.C., had 2 of these pandas. What fraction of the pandas is this?

$\frac{2}{10}$ ← National Zoo pandas
$\quad$ ← total pandas

$\frac{1}{5}$ ← National Zoo pandas
$\quad$ ← total pandas

So, $\frac{2}{10}$, or $\frac{1}{5}$ of the giant pandas are at the National Zoo. $\frac{2}{10}$ and $\frac{1}{5}$ are **equivalent fractions** because they name the same amount.

Activity Find equivalent fractions for $\frac{2}{3}$.

Materials ■ fraction bars ■ number lines

ONE WAY Use fraction bars.

Step 1

Line up two $\frac{1}{3}$ bars for thirds with the bar for 1 to show $\frac{2}{3}$.

Step 2

Line up other bars of the same type to show the same amount as $\frac{2}{3}$.

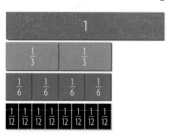

ANOTHER WAY Use number lines.

Draw a number line divided into thirds, one below it divided into sixths, and another divided into twelfths.

Locate $\frac{2}{3}$ on the top number line, $\frac{4}{6}$ on the second number line, and $\frac{8}{12}$ on the third number line.

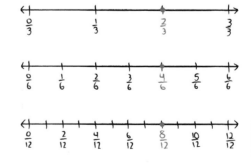

Fractions that line up with $\frac{2}{3}$ are equivalent to $\frac{2}{3}$.

Remember
There are many ways to write 1 as a fraction. In every case, the numerator and denominator are the same.

So, $\frac{4}{6}$ and $\frac{8}{12}$ are equivalent to $\frac{2}{3}$.

Multiply or Divide

You can multiply both the numerator and denominator of a fraction by any number except zero to find equivalent fractions.

If the numerator and denominator have a common factor, you can also divide both by that factor to find an equivalent fraction.

Find fractions that are equivalent to $\frac{4}{16}$.

ONE WAY Multiply the numerator and the denominator by the same number.

Try 2. $\frac{4}{16} = \frac{4 \times 2}{16 \times 2} = \frac{8}{32}$

So, $\frac{8}{32}$ is equivalent to $\frac{4}{16}$.

ANOTHER WAY Divide the numerator and the denominator by the same number.

Try 4. $\frac{4}{16} = \frac{4 \div 4}{16 \div 4} = \frac{1}{4}$

So, $\frac{1}{4}$ is equivalent to $\frac{4}{16}$.

You can also find equivalent fractions for whole numbers.

$1 = \frac{1}{1} = \frac{1 \times 10}{1 \times 10} = \frac{10}{10}$

So, $\frac{10}{10}$ is equivalent to 1.

$4 = \frac{4}{1} = \frac{4 \times 3}{1 \times 3} = \frac{12}{3}$

So, $\frac{12}{3}$ is equivalent to 4.

A fraction is in **simplest form** when the only number that can be divided into the numerator and the denominator evenly is 1.

ONE WAY Use a model.

Find the simplest form of $\frac{8}{10}$.

Line up eight $\frac{1}{10}$ bars with the bar for 1 to show $\frac{8}{10}$.

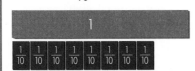

Then line up other bars of the same type with denominators smaller than 10 to show the same amount as $\frac{8}{10}$.

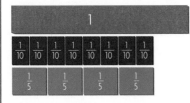

Fifths are the largest fraction pieces that are equal to tenths.

So, the simplest form of $\frac{8}{10}$ is $\frac{4}{5}$.

ANOTHER WAY Divide.

Find the simplest form of $\frac{36}{48}$.

Try 6. Divide the numerator and denominator by 6.

$\frac{36}{48} = \frac{36 \div 6}{48 \div 6} = \frac{6}{8}$

Next, try 2. Divide the numerator and denominator by 2.

$\frac{6}{8} = \frac{6 \div 2}{8 \div 2} = \frac{3}{4}$

Now the only number that can be divided into the numerator and denominator of $\frac{3}{4}$ is 1.

So, the simplest form of $\frac{36}{48}$ is $\frac{3}{4}$.

1. What two equivalent fractions are shown by these models? Which fraction is in simplest form?

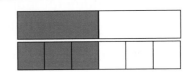

Write two equivalent fractions for each model.

2.

✅ 3. $\frac{1}{4}$

✅ 4.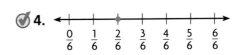

5. **TALK Math** Explain why equivalent fractions are equal. Use fraction bars.

Independent Practice and Problem Solving

Write two equivalent fractions for each model.

6.

7.

8.

Write two equivalent fractions for each.

9. $\frac{1}{4}$　　10. $\frac{12}{16}$　　11. $\frac{3}{5}$　　12. $\frac{7}{8}$　　13. $\frac{4}{12}$　　14. $\frac{9}{9}$

Tell whether the fractions are equivalent. Write = or ≠.

15. $\frac{3}{4}, \frac{8}{10}$　　16. $\frac{2}{18}, \frac{1}{9}$　　17. $\frac{4}{12}, \frac{1}{3}$　　18. $\frac{9}{12}, \frac{4}{6}$　　19. $\frac{10}{25}, \frac{3}{5}$　　20. $\frac{8}{16}, \frac{1}{2}$

Tell whether the fraction is in simplest form. If not, write it in simplest form.

21. $\frac{12}{18}$　　22. $\frac{12}{20}$　　23. $\frac{8}{15}$　　24. $\frac{8}{8}$　　25. $\frac{11}{12}$　　26. $\frac{15}{25}$

⭐**Algebra** Find the missing numerator or denominator.

27. $\frac{3}{5} = \frac{\blacksquare}{15}$　　28. $\frac{10}{16} = \frac{5}{\blacksquare}$　　29. $\frac{4}{4} = \frac{\blacksquare}{8}$　　30. $\frac{7}{14} = \frac{\blacksquare}{2}$　　31. $\frac{6}{9} = \frac{24}{\blacksquare}$　　32. $\frac{5}{6} = \frac{20}{\blacksquare}$

33. **Reasoning** What is one way that you know that a fraction is in simplest form without dividing the numerator and denominator? **Explain.**

34. **WRITE Math** ▶ **What's the Question?** If you multiply the numerator and denominator by 4, you get $\frac{12}{24}$.

Technology
Use Harcourt Mega Math, Fraction Action, *Fraction Flare Up*, Levels D, E.

Learn About) Ratios

The charge to park a car at the city zoo is $3 per car. You can use a ratio to compare the charge to the number of cars.

A **ratio** compares two amounts.

Example

A ratio can be shown as a picture.

Read: $3 per car

The ratio can be written three ways.

Write: 3:1 $\frac{3}{1}$ 3 to 1 **Read:** three to one

This relationship can also be expressed as $3, 1 car.

The ratio of the charge to park to the number of cars will be equivalent to 3:1 no matter the amount of money collected or number of cars parked.

Try It

Draw a picture and write a ratio to compare the cost to park and the number of cars.

35. 2 cars **36.** $15 **37.** 6 cars **38.** $24 **39.** 7 cars

40. The parking attendant collects $3 for each car. Write the relationship if the attendant collects $36.

Mixed Review and Test Prep

41. Nina has 6 cousins. All but one of her cousins are boys. What fraction of her cousins are boys? (p. 402)

42. The sum of 2 sides of a square is 12 centimeters. How long is each side? (Grade 3)

43. Test Prep Explain why $\frac{6}{9}$ is not equivalent to $\frac{9}{12}$.

44. Test Prep Which fraction is equivalent to $\frac{4}{5}$?

A $\frac{8}{10}$

B $\frac{13}{15}$

C $\frac{16}{25}$

D $\frac{20}{35}$

Compare and Order Fractions

OBJECTIVE: Compare and order fractions.

Quick Review

Find the missing numerator or denominator.

1. $\frac{1}{2} = \frac{4}{\blacksquare}$ 2. $\frac{6}{12} = \frac{\blacksquare}{6}$

3. $\frac{1}{3} = \frac{\blacksquare}{12}$ 4. $\frac{1}{16} = \frac{2}{\blacksquare}$

5. $\frac{6}{8} = \frac{3}{\blacksquare}$

Learn

PROBLEM On the Midway Carousel, located at Cedar Point Amusement Park in Sandusky, Ohio, $\frac{1}{5}$ of the horses are standing horses and $\frac{4}{5}$ of the horses are jumping horses. Which type of horse is there a greater fraction of?

Activity 1

Materials ■ two-color counters ■ fraction bars

A Compare fractions with like denominators.

Compare $\frac{1}{5}$ and $\frac{4}{5}$ using counters.
Model $\frac{1}{5}$ and $\frac{4}{5}$.

$\frac{1}{5}$  $\frac{4}{5}$

Compare the number of yellow counters: $1 < 4$, so $\frac{1}{5} < \frac{4}{5}$.
When you compare fractions with like denominators, only compare the numerators.

So, the jumping type of horse is a greater fraction of the horses on the carousel.

B Compare fractions with unlike denominators.

ERROR ALERT

When you compare two fractions, make sure the wholes are the same size.

ONE WAY Compare $\frac{7}{12}$ and $\frac{2}{3}$ using fraction bars.

Line up seven $\frac{1}{12}$ bars and two $\frac{1}{3}$ bars with the bar for 1.

Compare the two rows of fraction bars.

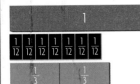

The longer row represents the greater fraction.

So, $\frac{7}{12} < \frac{2}{3}$, or $\frac{2}{3} > \frac{7}{12}$.

ANOTHER WAY Compare $\frac{3}{4}$ and $\frac{5}{8}$ using number lines.

Draw a number line divided into fourths and one below it divided into eighths. Locate $\frac{3}{4}$ on the top number line and $\frac{5}{8}$ on the other.

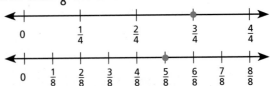

The fraction farther to the right is the greater fraction.

So, $\frac{3}{4} > \frac{5}{8}$, or $\frac{5}{8} < \frac{3}{4}$.

Activity 2 Order Fractions.

Materials ■ fraction bars

ONE WAY Order $\frac{1}{2}$, $\frac{3}{10}$, and $\frac{3}{5}$ from greatest to least using fraction bars.

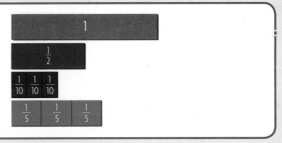

Line up one $\frac{1}{2}$ bar, three $\frac{1}{10}$ bars, and three $\frac{1}{5}$ bars with the bar for 1.

Compare the rows of fraction bars.

The longest row represents the greatest fraction.

So, the order from greatest to least is $\frac{3}{5}$, $\frac{1}{2}$, $\frac{3}{10}$.

ANOTHER WAY Order $\frac{1}{3}$, $\frac{5}{6}$, and $\frac{7}{9}$ from least to greatest using number lines.

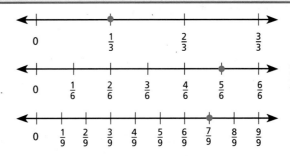

Draw a number line divided into thirds, one divided into sixths, and another one divided into ninths.

Place $\frac{1}{3}$ on the top number line, $\frac{5}{6}$ on the second number line, and $\frac{7}{9}$ on the third number line.

$\frac{1}{3}$ is farthest to the left, so it is the least of these fractions.

$\frac{5}{6}$ is farthest to the right, so it is the greatest of these fractions.

So, the order from least to greatest is $\frac{1}{3}$, $\frac{7}{9}$, $\frac{5}{6}$.

You can use the symbols <, >, =, and ≠ to compare and order fractions.

• Write the fractions in One Way from least to greatest using symbols.

• How can you use equivalent fractions to order the fractions in Another Way from greatest to least?

Guided Practice

1. The model at the right shows $\frac{2}{8}$ and $\frac{4}{8}$. Which model has more yellow counters? Which fraction is greater?

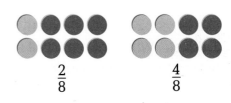

$\frac{2}{8}$ $\frac{4}{8}$

Compare. Write <, >, or = for each ●.

2. $\frac{2}{6}$ ● $\frac{3}{6}$

3. $\frac{3}{4}$ ● $\frac{1}{2}$

✓4. $\frac{1}{4}$ ● $\frac{5}{8}$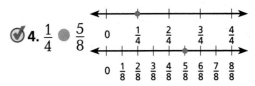

Order the fractions from least to greatest.

5. $\frac{10}{12}, \frac{1}{2}, \frac{2}{3}$

6. $\frac{1}{6}, \frac{3}{8}, \frac{3}{4}$

 7. $\frac{4}{6}, \frac{1}{3}, \frac{9}{12}$

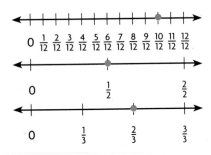

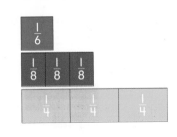

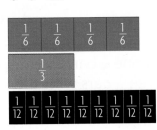

8. **TALK Math** Explain how you would use fraction bars or number lines to compare $\frac{5}{6}$ and $\frac{2}{3}$.

Independent Practice and Problem Solving

Compare. Write <, >, or = for each ●.

9. $\frac{3}{8}$ ● $\frac{6}{8}$ ●●●●○ ●●●● ○○○○ ●●●○

10. $\frac{1}{6}$ ● $\frac{1}{5}$

11. $\frac{4}{10}$ ● $\frac{2}{4}$

Order the fractions from least to greatest.

12. $\frac{1}{2}, \frac{1}{8}, \frac{1}{4}$

13. $\frac{8}{16}, \frac{1}{5}, \frac{3}{10}$

14. $\frac{5}{6}, \frac{2}{3}, \frac{1}{2}$

15. $\frac{3}{5}, \frac{2}{4}, \frac{8}{12}$

Order the fractions from greatest to least.

16. $\frac{2}{4}, \frac{8}{10}, \frac{3}{12}$

17. $\frac{1}{6}, \frac{1}{8}, \frac{1}{2}$

18. $\frac{2}{6}, \frac{9}{9}, \frac{1}{12}$

19. $\frac{2}{3}, \frac{2}{4}, \frac{2}{5}$

USE DATA For 20–22, use the information in the picture.

20. Elle buys 12 tickets so she can go on each ride once. What fraction of her tickets will she use for each ride?

21. Pete buys 10 tickets. Then he rides the roller coaster and Ferris wheel. Ken buys 8 tickets and rides the tilt-a-whirl. Who has used the greater fraction of his tickets?

22. Elle buys 12 tickets, Pete buys 10 tickets, and Ken buys 8 tickets. Which of them will use the greatest fraction of tickets to ride the roller coaster?

23. **FAST FACT** A turtle lives an average of 100 years. An elephant can live $\frac{2}{5}$ as long and a parrot can live $\frac{3}{4}$ as long. List the animals in order from the longest life span to the shortest.

24. **WRITE Math** Explain the difference between comparing fractions with like denominators and comparing fractions with unlike denominators.

Benchmark Fractions

You can use benchmarks of 0, $\frac{1}{2}$, or 1 to judge the size of fractions.

Example 1 Find benchmarks for $\frac{1}{8}$, $\frac{5}{8}$, and $\frac{7}{8}$.

If the numerator is much less than half the denominator, the fraction is close to 0.	If the numerator is about half the denominator, the fraction is close to $\frac{1}{2}$.	If the numerator is much more than half the denominator, the fraction is close to 1.
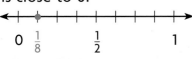		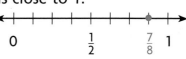

So, $\frac{1}{8}$ is close to 0.   So, $\frac{5}{8}$ is close to $\frac{1}{2}$.   So, $\frac{7}{8}$ is close to 1.

Example 2 Compare $\frac{3}{4}$ and $\frac{1}{6}$.

$\frac{1}{6} < \frac{1}{2}$ because 1 is less than half of 6.

$\frac{3}{4} > \frac{1}{2}$ because 3 is greater than half of 4.

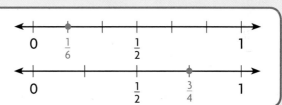

So, $\frac{3}{4} > \frac{1}{6}$.

Try It

Write whether the fraction is closest to 0, $\frac{1}{2}$, or 1.
Use the number line.

25. $\frac{8}{10}$ **26.** $\frac{6}{10}$ **27.** $\frac{2}{10}$ **28.** $\frac{9}{10}$ **29.** $\frac{4}{10}$

Use benchmarks to compare. Write $<$, $>$, or $=$ for each ●.

30. $\frac{2}{3}$ ● $\frac{5}{6}$ **31.** $\frac{1}{5}$ ● 0 **32.** $\frac{4}{10}$ ● $\frac{6}{8}$ **33.** $\frac{3}{8}$ ● $\frac{3}{4}$ **34.** $\frac{11}{12}$ ● $\frac{4}{9}$

Mixed Review and Test Prep

35. There are 4 red marbles and 2 green marbles of the same size in a bag. If you pull a marble without looking, is it *more likely* or *less likely* you will pull red? (Grade 3)

36. There are 24 juice boxes in a carton. Trent buys 6 cartons. How many juice boxes does he buy? (p. 98)

37. Test Prep Which makes this true?

$$\frac{3}{4} > \frac{\blacksquare}{8}$$

A 3   **B** 6   **C** 7   **D** 8

38. Test Prep Esteban jogged for $\frac{2}{3}$ hour. He swam for $\frac{5}{6}$ hour. Which activity took longer? **Explain.**

Read and Write Mixed Numbers

OBJECTIVE: Read and write mixed numbers and express fractions greater than one as mixed numbers.

Quick Review

Order from least to greatest.

1. $\frac{1}{4}, \frac{1}{2}, \frac{1}{8}$ 2. $\frac{1}{8}, \frac{5}{8}, \frac{3}{8}$

3. $\frac{2}{3}, \frac{2}{10}, \frac{2}{5}$ 4. $\frac{4}{6}, \frac{5}{6}, \frac{1}{6}$

5. $\frac{7}{12}, \frac{5}{9}, \frac{2}{3}$

Vocabulary

mixed number

Learn

PROBLEM Carlos made a large candle from one and two-thirds cups of wax. Write a mixed number for the number of cups of wax.

A **mixed number** is made up of a whole number and a fraction.

The picture shows one and two-thirds cups of wax.

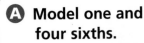

Read: one and two thirds

Write: $1\frac{2}{3}$

 Activity 1 Use pattern blocks.

Materials ■ pattern blocks

A Model one and four sixths.

$1 + \frac{4}{6} = 1\frac{4}{6}$, or $1\frac{2}{3}$

B Model two and one half.

$2 + \frac{1}{2} = 2\frac{1}{2}$

C Model one and one third.

$1 + \frac{1}{3} = 1\frac{1}{3}$

• Look at Example A. How many sixths make two wholes?

You can locate mixed numbers on a number line.

 Activity 2 Use a number line.

Draw a number line to locate $1\frac{4}{5}$ and $3\frac{2}{5}$.

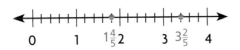

First, divide the number line into four equal parts. Label the whole numbers.

Then, mark five equal parts between each whole number. Each part represents one fifth.

Locate and label $1\frac{4}{5}$ and $3\frac{2}{5}$.

Rename Fractions and Mixed Numbers

Sometimes the numerator of a fraction is greater than the denominator. These fractions have a value greater than 1. They can be renamed as mixed numbers.

ONE WAY Use fraction bars.

Rename $1\frac{3}{8}$ as a fraction.
Use fraction bars to rename the mixed number as a fraction. Model $1\frac{3}{8}$.

Place $\frac{1}{8}$ bars under the bars for $1\frac{3}{8}$.

The total number of $\frac{1}{8}$ bars is the numerator of the fraction. The numerator of the fraction is 11.

So, $1\frac{3}{8}$ renamed as a fraction is $\frac{11}{8}$.

ANOTHER WAY Use division.

Rename $\frac{11}{3}$ as a mixed number.

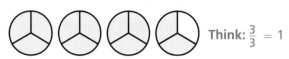 Think: $\frac{3}{3} = 1$

Since $\frac{11}{3}$ means $11 \div 3$, you can use division to rename a fraction greater than 1 as a mixed number.

$$\text{denominator} \rightarrow 3\overline{)11}^{\ 3\ r2} \leftarrow \text{numerator}$$
$$\underline{-9}$$
$$2 \leftarrow \text{number of thirds left over}$$

Write the quotient as the whole number part. Then write the remainder as the numerator and the divisor as the denominator.

So, $\frac{11}{3}$ renamed as a mixed number is $3\frac{2}{3}$.

A fraction greater than 1 is sometimes called an *improper fraction*.

So, $\frac{11}{8}$ and $\frac{7}{5}$ are examples of improper fractions.

- How can you use multiplication to rename a mixed number as a fraction?

- What does a mixed number represent?

Guided Practice

1. Copy and complete to name the mixed number shown by the picture.

$1 + \dfrac{\blacksquare}{3} = \blacksquare$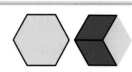

Write a mixed number for each picture in standard and word form.

2. 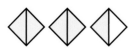　　　3. 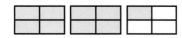　　　✓ 4.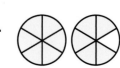

Rename each fraction as a mixed number and each mixed number as a fraction. You may wish to draw a picture.

5. $\frac{15}{2}$ 6. $2\frac{3}{4}$ 7. $\frac{12}{7}$ 8. $9\frac{1}{3}$ 9. $5\frac{5}{6}$ ✓ 10. $\frac{26}{8}$

11. **TALK Math** Explain how to model $3\frac{1}{6}$.

Independent Practice and Problem Solving

Write a mixed number for each picture in standard and word form.

12.    13. 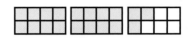   14.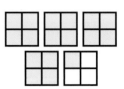

Use the number line to write the letter each mixed number or fraction represents.

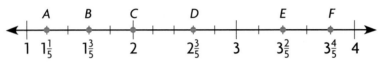

15. $\frac{6}{5}$ 16. $2\frac{3}{5}$ 17. $\frac{8}{5}$ 18. $3\frac{2}{5}$ 19. $\frac{19}{5}$ 20. $\frac{10}{5}$

Rename each fraction as a mixed number and each mixed number as a fraction. You may wish to draw a picture.

21. $\frac{13}{5}$ 22. $1\frac{1}{6}$ 23. $\frac{21}{4}$ 24. $2\frac{1}{2}$ 25. $\frac{13}{6}$ 26. $\frac{19}{3}$

27. $6\frac{2}{9}$ 28. $\frac{17}{8}$ 29. $7\frac{2}{7}$ 30. $\frac{35}{6}$ 31. $\frac{28}{12}$ 32. $5\frac{3}{4}$

33. Jodi cut a piece of ribbon $3\frac{3}{8}$ inches long. Draw a number line and locate and label $3\frac{3}{8}$.

34. Miguel takes a craft class that lasts $2\frac{1}{2}$ hours. Draw a picture to represent the length of the class.

35. Madeleine buys six and a half dozen candles. Write the number of dozens she bought as a mixed number and a fraction.

36. **WRITE Math** **Sense or Nonsense** Jack thinks $4\frac{1}{3} = \frac{13}{3}$. Is he correct? You may use models or draw a picture. **Explain.**

37. **Reasoning** Adam needs 1 cup of wax to make a pear-shaped candle. Is this more than or less than $\frac{15}{8}$ cups, the amount of wax needed to make an apple-shaped candle? **Explain.**

CD ROM **Technology** Use Harcourt Mega Math, Fraction Action, *Number Line Mine*, Levels F, H, J.

Locating Mixed Numbers on a Ruler

A ruler is a type of number line. You can locate mixed numbers on a ruler.

Example

The longest marks on the ruler below show whole numbers. All the marks, including the shortest marks, show eighths. Notice that some eighths marks are longer than others. These marks show quarters and halves.

Locate $3\frac{7}{8}$ on the ruler.

Draw a line segment $3\frac{7}{8}$ inches long.

Start at the left edge of the ruler. Draw the line segment to reach $3\frac{7}{8}$ inches.

$3\frac{7}{8}$
↓

From 3, count seven $\frac{1}{8}$-inch marks to the right of the 3-inch mark to reach $3\frac{7}{8}$ inches.

Try It

Use a ruler. Draw a line segment for each length.

38. $2\frac{3}{8}$ inches
39. $4\frac{1}{8}$ inches
40. $1\frac{3}{4}$ inches
41. $3\frac{1}{2}$ inches
42. $5\frac{1}{4}$ inches

Mixed Review and Test Prep

43. Show tickets cost $18 for adults and $13 for children. What is the cost for 2 adults and 3 children? (p. 292)

44. Ahmed drank $\frac{1}{2}$ cup of milk for breakfast and $\frac{2}{3}$ cup of milk for lunch. Did he drink more milk for breakfast or for lunch? (p. 410)

45. **Test Prep** Stephanie made bread using $\frac{7}{4}$ cups of flour. Which shows $\frac{7}{4}$ as a mixed number?

    A $1\frac{1}{4}$

    B $1\frac{3}{4}$

    C $1\frac{4}{7}$

    D $4\frac{1}{3}$

46. **Test Prep** Drew's class ate $4\frac{5}{8}$ pizzas at their pizza party. Draw a picture to show the mixed number. **Explain** how you drew your picture.

5 Compare and Order Mixed Numbers

OBJECTIVE: Compare and order mixed numbers.

Learn

PROBLEM Amanda had many after school activities last week. The table shows the amount of time she spent doing each activity. Did she spend more time working on her science project or at soccer practice?

Amanda's After School Activities Last Week	
Activity	Time (in hours)
Homework	$2\frac{2}{3}$
Piano Lessons and Practice	$2\frac{1}{4}$
Science Project	$1\frac{2}{3}$
Soccer Practice	$1\frac{1}{3}$

HANDS ON

Activity 1

Materials ■ fraction bars

A **Compare mixed numbers with like denominators.**

Compare $1\frac{2}{3}$ and $1\frac{1}{3}$ using fraction bars.

Model $1\frac{2}{3}$, then line up the bars for $1\frac{1}{3}$ below it.

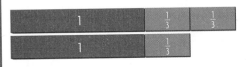

Compare the two rows of fraction bars. The longer row represents the greater mixed number.

$1\frac{2}{3} > 1\frac{1}{3}$, so Amanda spent more time on her science project than at soccer practice.

- When you compare $1\frac{2}{3}$ and $1\frac{1}{3}$, why do you have to compare only the fraction parts?

B **Compare mixed numbers with unlike denominators.**

Did Amanda spend less time doing homework or at piano lessons and practice?

Compare $2\frac{2}{3}$ and $2\frac{1}{4}$ using number lines.

Draw a number line, and divide it into thirds between each whole number. Locate $2\frac{2}{3}$.

Draw another number line, and divide it into fourths between each whole number. Locate $2\frac{1}{4}$.

The mixed number farther to the right is the greater number.

$2\frac{2}{3} > 2\frac{1}{4}$, so Amanda spent less time at piano lessons and practice.

Activity 2 Compare and order mixed numbers.

ONE WAY Use drawings.

Compare and then order $2\frac{1}{2}$, $1\frac{1}{6}$, and $1\frac{3}{4}$ from greatest to least.

Draw pictures for $2\frac{1}{2}$, $1\frac{1}{6}$, and $1\frac{3}{4}$.

$2\frac{1}{2}$ $\qquad$ $1\frac{1}{6}$ $\qquad$ $1\frac{3}{4}$

First, compare the whole numbers. Since $2 > 1$, $2\frac{1}{2}$ is the greatest.

Then compare the other two fractions by finding equivalent fractions.

$1\frac{1}{6} = 1\frac{2}{12}$ $\qquad$ $1\frac{3}{4} = 1\frac{9}{12}$

Since, $2 < 9$, $1\frac{3}{4}$ is greater than $1\frac{1}{6}$.

So, the order from greatest to least is $2\frac{1}{2}$, $1\frac{3}{4}$, $1\frac{1}{6}$.

ANOTHER WAY Use a number line.

> **Math Idea**
> To order mixed numbers, compare the whole number parts first. Then compare the fraction parts.

Order $\frac{5}{2}$, $2\frac{3}{4}$, and $2\frac{3}{8}$ from least to greatest using a number line.

Find equivalent fractions. $\frac{5}{2} = 2\frac{1}{2} = 2\frac{4}{8}$ $\qquad$ $2\frac{3}{4} = 2\frac{6}{8}$

Draw a number line showing 2 and 3 with the distance between them divided into eighths. Place each mixed number on the number line.

The mixed number farthest to the right is the greatest number.
The mixed number farthest to the left is the least number.

So, the order from least to greatest is $2\frac{3}{8}$, $\frac{5}{2}$, $2\frac{3}{4}$.

Guided Practice

1. Use the number line. Is $3\frac{4}{5}$ greater than or less than $3\frac{2}{5}$?

Compare the mixed numbers. Use $<$, $>$, or $=$ for each ●.

2.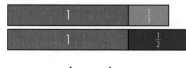

$1\frac{1}{3} ● 1\frac{1}{2}$

3.

$1\frac{3}{4} ● 1\frac{3}{8}$

4.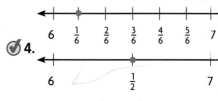

$6\frac{1}{6} ● 6\frac{1}{2}$

Order the mixed numbers from greatest to least.

5. $4\frac{1}{6}$, $3\frac{2}{3}$, $4\frac{3}{4}$

6. $5\frac{1}{4}$, $6\frac{3}{8}$, $5\frac{1}{12}$

7. $3\frac{3}{4}$, $3\frac{2}{5}$, $3\frac{1}{2}$

✓8. $1\frac{7}{9}$, $1\frac{1}{2}$, $1\frac{12}{18}$

9. **TALK Math** Explain how you would compare the mixed numbers $4\frac{5}{12}$ and $2\frac{7}{8}$.

Independent Practice and Problem Solving

Compare the mixed numbers. Write <, >, or = for each ●.

10.

$1\frac{3}{4}$ ● $1\frac{2}{5}$

11.

$1\frac{1}{8}$ ● $1\frac{1}{3}$

12.

$4\frac{2}{3}$ ● $4\frac{1}{3}$

Order the mixed numbers from least to greatest.

13. $8\frac{3}{4}$, $7\frac{3}{10}$, $8\frac{1}{2}$

14. $3\frac{1}{2}$, $3\frac{2}{3}$, $2\frac{4}{16}$

15. $4\frac{2}{6}$, $4\frac{2}{3}$, $4\frac{2}{12}$

16. $5\frac{2}{5}$, $5\frac{6}{10}$, $5\frac{2}{7}$

Algebra Find the missing numerator or denominator.

17. $1\frac{1}{4} < 1\frac{1}{\blacksquare} < 1\frac{1}{2}$

18. $2\frac{5}{6} > 2\frac{\blacksquare}{5} > 2\frac{1}{3}$

19. $4\frac{\blacksquare}{6} < 4\frac{2}{5} < 4\frac{3}{4}$

20. $2\frac{1}{5} < 2\frac{3}{10} < 2\frac{\blacksquare}{2}$

USE DATA For 21–23, use the table.

21. Which activity takes Amanda the most time? the least time?

22. Which activity does Amanda spend $\frac{11}{4}$ hours doing? Which activity does she spend almost as much time doing?

How Amanda Spends Her Day			
Activity	Free Time	Homework	Sleep
Time (in hours)	$2\frac{3}{4}$	$2\frac{2}{3}$	$9\frac{1}{4}$

23. **Pose a Problem** Use the information in the table to write a problem involving ordering mixed numbers. Have a classmate solve the problem.

24. **WRITE Math** What's the Error? Amy says that $3\frac{1}{2}$ is less than $\frac{13}{4}$ because a denominator of 2 is less than a denominator of 4. Describe her error.

Mixed Review and Test Prep

25. Find the missing numerator in the equivalent fraction. (p. 406)

$$\frac{\blacksquare}{3} = \frac{8}{12}$$

26. Julia hiked $\frac{14}{3}$ miles. Write $\frac{14}{3}$ as a mixed number. (p. 415)

27. **Test Prep** The lengths of four movies are shown. Which movie is the longest?

A $1\frac{7}{8}$ hours   **C** $2\frac{2}{5}$ hours

B $2\frac{2}{3}$ hours   **D** $2\frac{1}{2}$ hours

Extra Practice on page 424, Set E

Write Number Riddles

Ms. Owens asked her students to write a riddle about fractions and mixed numbers. She told them to explain how they used what they knew about fractions and mixed numbers to write a riddle that had only one answer.

Elena's group wrote this riddle and explanation.

> I am a mixed number between 1 and 2.
>
> My fraction part is greater than $\frac{1}{2}$.
>
> My denominator is 8 and my numerator is an even number.
>
> What number am I?

First, we drew a number line and located a mixed number on it.

1          $1\frac{6}{8}$ 2

Our first clue tells about the whole number part of the answer to our riddle.

Next, we decided to give clues about the numerator and denominator in our riddle.

Finally, we checked our riddle.
$\frac{5}{8}, \frac{6}{8}, \frac{7}{8}$ are greater than $\frac{1}{2}$. 6 is the only even numerator. The answer is $1\frac{6}{8}$.

Tips

- Use a drawing or model to understand what is being asked.
- You may want to use comparisons in the riddle.
- Include clues about the numerator and the denominator of a fraction.
- Put the clues together to write the riddle.
- Solve your riddle to check that there are enough clues. Make sure the clues make sense and there is only one correct answer.

Problem Solving Write a number riddle for each answer given.

1. a fraction less than $\frac{1}{2}$

2. a fraction greater than $\frac{1}{2}$

3. a mixed number between 2 and 3

4. any fraction or mixed number written in simplest form

Problem Solving Workshop
Skill: Sequence Information

OBJECTIVE: Solve problems by using the skill *sequence information*.

Use the Skill

PROBLEM Cats can spend $\frac{2}{3}$ of a day sleeping. Cows can spend $\frac{1}{4}$ of a day sleeping. Dogs can sleep for $\frac{1}{2}$ of a day. Lions can sleep for $\frac{5}{6}$ of a day. Which animal can spend the greatest amount of time sleeping? Which can spend the least?

To solve the problem, you can sequence the information. One way to sequence information is to put it in order on a number line.

Step 1

Find equivalent fractions with a denominator of 12.

$$\frac{2 \times 4}{3 \times 4} = \frac{8}{12} \qquad \frac{1 \times 3}{4 \times 3} = \frac{3}{12} \qquad \frac{1 \times 6}{2 \times 6} = \frac{6}{12} \qquad \frac{5 \times 2}{6 \times 2} = \frac{10}{12}$$

Step 2

Use a number line to sequence the equivalent fractions. Draw a number line and divide it into twelfths. Locate each of the equivalent fractions on the number line.

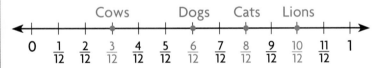

The order from greatest to least is $\frac{10}{12}, \frac{8}{12}, \frac{6}{12}, \frac{3}{12}$.

So, lions can spend the greatest amount of time sleeping and cows can spend the least amount of time sleeping.

▲ Different animals have different sleeping patterns.

Think and Discuss

Sequence the information to solve.

a. Jan bought $1\frac{1}{3}$ yards of ribbon, Monica bought $1\frac{1}{4}$ yards, and Sheila bought $1\frac{1}{8}$ yards. Which girl bought the most ribbon?

b. Mike, Scott, and David used a total of 10 stamps. Scott used $\frac{1}{2}$ of the total, and David used $\frac{1}{5}$. Who used the least number of stamps?

Sequence information to solve.

1. Newborn babies spend $\frac{2}{3}$ of a day sleeping. School-age children sleep for $\frac{5}{12}$ of a day. Adults sleep for $\frac{1}{4}$ of a day. Which age group spends the least time sleeping? Which spends the greatest time?

   First, find equivalent fractions.
   Then, use a number line to sequence the equivalent fractions.

   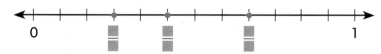

   Finally, find the age group for the least and greatest fractions.

2. **What if** one piece of data is added to the number line? Add the following information to the number line: Teenagers sleep for $\frac{1}{3}$ of a day.

3. Gloria gives her youngest cat $1\frac{1}{2}$ cups of food. She gives the oldest cat $\frac{7}{8}$ cup of food and the second-oldest cat $1\frac{3}{4}$ cups of food. Draw a number line to represent the amounts of food. Which cat gets the most food?

Mixed Applications

4. After school, Abby ran $\frac{2}{3}$ mile, Kyle ran $\frac{1}{2}$ mile, and Matt ran $\frac{3}{4}$ mile. Order the distances from least to greatest.

5. Jose and his friend made cookies. They each ate 2 cookies. Jose took 10 cookies to school and gave 6 to his neighbor. What fraction of the cookies did Jose take to school?

6. Bart spent $\frac{8}{6}$ hours at his friend's house. Dana spent $\frac{5}{4}$ hours at her friend's house. Who stayed longer?

7. Lisa bought 2 rolls of film. Each roll holds 24 pictures. If Lisa has $\frac{1}{3}$ of a roll left, how many pictures did she take?

8. **Open-Ended** Viv, Troy, and Ming check out library books. Each reads half a book but a different number of pages. For each student, write a fraction that could show the number of pages read and the number of pages in the book.

9. **WRITE Math** Find a pattern in this set of fractions. **Describe** your pattern.

$$\frac{1}{2}, \frac{1}{4}, \frac{1}{8}, \frac{1}{16}$$

Extra Practice

Set A Write a fraction for the shaded part.
Write a fraction for the unshaded part. (pp. 402–405)

1.
2.
3.
4.

Set B Find two equivalent fractions for each. (pp. 406–409)

1. $\frac{3}{4}$
2. $\frac{2}{10}$
3. $\frac{8}{12}$
4. $\frac{5}{8}$
5. $\frac{3}{9}$
6. $\frac{5}{5}$

7. Pam baked 20 cupcakes. She took 15 of them to school.
   Write the fraction of cupcakes she took to school in simplest form.

Set C Compare. Write <, >, or = for each ●. (pp. 410–413)

1. $\frac{4}{5}$ ● $\frac{2}{5}$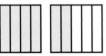
2. $\frac{3}{8}$ ● $\frac{3}{4}$
3. $\frac{5}{9}$ ● $\frac{1}{6}$

Order the fractions from least to greatest.

4. $\frac{3}{4}, \frac{6}{12}, \frac{2}{3}$
5. $\frac{1}{3}, \frac{1}{8}, \frac{1}{6}$
6. $\frac{7}{8}, \frac{1}{2}, \frac{12}{12}$
7. $\frac{3}{5}, \frac{9}{10}, \frac{1}{2}$

Set D Write a mixed number for each picture
in standard and word form. (pp. 414–417)

1.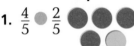
2.
3.
4.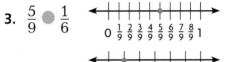

Rename each fraction as a mixed number and each mixed
number as a fraction. You may wish to draw a picture.

5. $\frac{9}{5}$
6. $1\frac{2}{3}$
7. $\frac{7}{3}$
8. $3\frac{1}{4}$
9. $\frac{12}{5}$
10. $4\frac{1}{10}$

Set E Compare the mixed numbers. Write <, >, or = for each ●. (pp. 418–421)

1.

$1\frac{1}{3}$ ● $1\frac{1}{2}$

2.

$3\frac{1}{4}$ ● $3\frac{3}{4}$

3.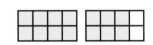

$1\frac{3}{6}$ ● $1\frac{5}{8}$

Technology
Use Harcourt Mega Math, Fraction Action,
Fraction Flare Up, Levels B, C, D, E, F.

TECHNOLOGY ★ CONNECTION

iTools: Fractions

Kelly's cookie recipe calls for $\frac{3}{4}$ cup brown sugar and $\frac{2}{3}$ cup powdered sugar. Does the recipe call for more brown sugar or more powdered sugar?

Step 1 Click on *Fractions*. Select *Compare* from the *Activities* menu.	
Step 2 Click on the fraction bar for $\frac{1}{4}$. Then click in the top workspace 3 times. Notice that $\frac{3}{4}$ appears at the bottom of the screen. If you make a mistake, click on the eraser.	
Step 3 Click on the fraction bar for $\frac{1}{3}$. Then click in the bottom workspace 2 times. Notice that $\frac{2}{3}$ appears at the bottom of the screen.	**Step 4** Click on the "?". Choose $>$, $=$, or $<$ to make a true comparison. Then click on *Check*.

$\frac{3}{4} > \frac{2}{3}$, so the recipe calls for more brown sugar than powdered sugar.

Try It

1. Click on the tab for *Fraction Circles* at the bottom of the left column. Do fraction circles make it easier to compare the fractions? **Explain.**

Click on the broom to clear the workspace.

Follow the same steps to compare fractions. Write <, >, or = for each ●.

2. $\frac{3}{6}$ ● $\frac{4}{6}$ 3. $\frac{4}{10}$ ● $\frac{1}{3}$ 4. $\frac{3}{5}$ ● $\frac{5}{8}$ 5. $\frac{4}{6}$ ● $\frac{8}{12}$

6. **Explore More** **Explain** how you decided whether to use <, >, or = when comparing the fractions above.

GO ONLINE **Technology** *iTools* are available online or on CD-ROM.

Explore Ratios and Proportions

At the Vet

A veterinarian examines 2 cats for every 5 dogs. How many cats will she examine if she examines 20 dogs?

A **ratio** is a comparison of two amounts. You can use a ratio to compare amounts in three ways.

Comparison	Type of Ratio	Ratio
Cats to dogs	Part to part	**Write:** 2 to 5 2:5 $\frac{2}{5}$ **Read:** two to five
Dogs to pets	Part to whole	**Write:** 5 to 7 5:7 $\frac{5}{7}$ **Read:** five to seven
Pets to cats	Whole to part	**Write:** 7 to 2 7:2 $\frac{7}{2}$ **Read:** seven to two

A **proportion** is an equation that shows two ratios are equal. You can write a proportion by finding equivalent ratios.

Examples

A Find an equivalent ratio for $\frac{2}{5}$ that has a denominator of 20.

$\frac{2 \times 4}{5 \times 4} = \frac{8}{20}$ The new ratio of cats examined to dogs examined is $\frac{8}{20}$.

$\frac{2}{5}$ and $\frac{8}{20}$ are equivalent ratios. They form the proportion, $\frac{2}{5} = \frac{8}{20}$.

So, the veterinarian will examine 8 cats if she examines 20 dogs.

B Find two ratios that are equivalent to 3:8.

$\frac{3 \times 2}{8 \times 2} = \frac{6}{16}$ $\frac{3 \times 3}{8 \times 3} = \frac{9}{24}$

Think: Write the ratio as a fraction. Then multiply the numerator and denominator by the same number.

So, 3:8 = 6:16 = 9:24.

Try It

Write two equivalent ratios for each. Then write the equivalent ratios as a proportion.

1. 1:3   2. 2:3   3. 4 to 5   4. $\frac{6}{4}$ 5. $\frac{3}{7}$ 6. 8 to 9

7. **WRITE Math** Explain how you can write a proportion when you have a ratio.

Chapter 15 Review/Test

Check Vocabulary and Concepts

Choose the best term from the box.

> **VOCABULARY**
>
> equivalent fractions
> fraction
> mixed number
> simplest form

1. A __?__ is made up of a whole number and a fraction. (p. 414)

2. Two or more fractions that name the same amount are __?__. (p. 406)

3. A __?__ is a number that names part of a whole or part of a group. (p. 402)

Check Skills

Write the fraction or mixed number for each picture. (pp. 402–405, 414–417)

4.
5.
6.
7.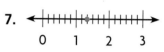

Tell whether the fraction is in simplest form. If not, write it in simplest form. (pp. 406–409)

8. $\dfrac{2}{12}$

9. $\dfrac{15}{20}$

10. $\dfrac{6}{9}$

11. $\dfrac{9}{16}$

Compare. Write $<$, $>$, or $=$ for each ●. (pp. 410–413, 418–421)

12. $\dfrac{2}{3}$ ● $\dfrac{9}{12}$

13. $4\dfrac{1}{3}$ ● $4\dfrac{1}{4}$

14. $\dfrac{9}{10}$ ● $\dfrac{3}{5}$

15. $2\dfrac{2}{6}$ ● $2\dfrac{3}{9}$

Order the fractions or mixed numbers from greatest to least. (pp. 410–413, 418–421)

16. $\dfrac{7}{8}, \dfrac{12}{12}, \dfrac{3}{4}$

17. $2\dfrac{2}{3}, 2\dfrac{1}{6}, 2\dfrac{5}{12}$

18. $\dfrac{1}{7}, \dfrac{1}{9}, \dfrac{1}{3}$

19. $1\dfrac{2}{3}, 1\dfrac{3}{4}, 1\dfrac{5}{6}$

Rename each fraction as a mixed number and each mixed number as a fraction. (pp. 414–417)

20. $4\dfrac{1}{4}$

21. $\dfrac{17}{5}$

22. $2\dfrac{7}{8}$

23. $\dfrac{14}{9}$

Check Problem Solving

Solve. (pp. 422–423)

24. Reggie has a set of measuring cups. Three of the sizes are $\frac{1}{2}$, $\frac{1}{4}$ and $\frac{1}{3}$ cup. Which measuring cup holds the greatest amount?

25. **WRITE Math** Meg ran $3\frac{1}{2}$ laps, Jill ran $3\frac{3}{8}$ laps, and Randy ran $3\frac{1}{4}$ laps around a track. **Explain** how to use a number line to find who ran the greatest distance.

Standardized Test Prep
Chapters 1–15

Number and Operations

1. Marisol is making bead necklaces. She uses 25 beads in each necklace. How many beads does she need to make 36 necklaces? (p. 282)

   A 61

   B 90

   C 610

   D 900

Test Tip **Look for important words.**

In Item 2, an important word is *prime*. Determine which number is prime.

2. Robert says his age is a prime number. Which is Robert's age? (p. 378)

   A 19

   B 20

   C 21

   D 22

3. Rachel bought 9 CDs. Each CD cost the same amount. She spent $126 in all. How much did each CD cost? (p. 334)

   A $14

   B $15

   C $17

   D $1,134

4. **WRITE Math** ▶ **Explain** how to use an array to find 12×26. (p. 280)

Measurement

5. The table shows the schedule of four bus routes. Which bus route lasts 2 hours 15 minutes? (p. 154)

Bus Route Schedule		
Bus Number	**Leave**	**Arrive**
1	9:20 A.M.	11:25 A.M.
2	11:30 A.M.	1:45 P.M.
3	2:05 P.M.	4:25 P.M.
4	5:50 P.M.	8:00 P.M.

   A Bus 1   **C** Bus 3

   B Bus 2   **D** Bus 4

6. The temperature at 8:00 A.M. was ⁻2°F. It rose 5° by noon. What was the temperature at noon? (p. 168)

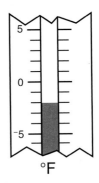

   A ⁻7°F

   B ⁻3°F

   C 3°F

   D 7°F

7. **WRITE Math** ▶ **Explain** how to find the elapsed time for Bus 1 in the bus route schedule above. (p. 154)

Algebraic Reasoning

8. The table shows how much Liam earns for mowing lawns.

Liam's Lawn Mowing

Number of lawns	1	2	3	4
Money earned	$5	$10	$15	$20

How much will Liam earn if he mows 7 lawns? (p. 138)

A $11

B $24

C $28

D $35

9. Kim is 4 years younger than her brother Jim. If Kim's age is *k* years, which expression best discribes Jim's age? (p. 66)

A $k + 4$ **C** $4 - k$

B $k - 4$ **D** $k \times 4$

10. Look at the equation below.

$$6 \times \blacksquare = 9 \times 6$$

Which number should go in the box to make the equation true? (p. 118)

A 3

B 9

C 15

D 54

11. ▌WRITE Math▶ **Explain** how to use the order of operations to evaluate $56 - 8 \times 5$. (p. 126)

Probability and Statistics

12. The bar graph shows the number of medals won on field day by the students in each fourth-grade class.

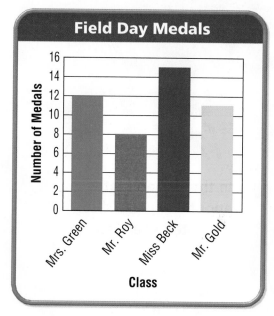

How many more medals were won by the students in Mr. Gold's class than by the students in Mr. Roy's class? (p. 204)

A 1   **C** 4

B 3   **D** 8

13. What kind of graph would be best to show your height each year since birth? (p. 222)

A Line plot

B Pictograph

C Circle graph

D Line graph

14. ▌WRITE Math▶ **Explain** how to find the median of the following set of data. (p. 186)

6, 7, 10, 8, 6, 5, 9

16 Add and Subtract Fractions and Mixed Numbers

FAST FACT

In the United States, about 350 pizza slices are eaten every second of every day. That many slices would cover more than 75 football fields!

Investigate

After visiting a pizza farm, students were asked how much pizza they would like for lunch. Each small pizza is divided into eighths. Their responses are shown on the line plot at the right. Use the data in the line plot to write a word problem that can be solved with the number sentence $\frac{2}{8} + \frac{2}{8} + \frac{2}{8} = \frac{6}{8}$.

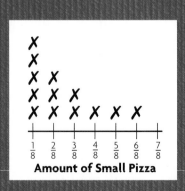

Amount of Small Pizza

GO ONLINE

Technology
Student pages are available in the student eBook.

Check your understanding of important
skills needed for success in Chapter 16.

▶ **Model Fractions and Mixed Numbers**

Write a fraction or mixed number for the shaded part of each picture.

1.

2.

3.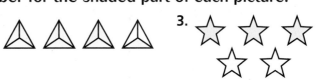

▶ **Equivalent Fractions**

Write two equivalent fractions for the shaded part of each picture.

4.

5.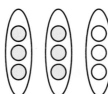

6.

▶ **Simplest Form**

Tell whether each fraction is in simplest
form. If it is not, write it in simplest form.

7. $\dfrac{8}{12}$　　8. $\dfrac{8}{10}$　　9. $\dfrac{3}{8}$　　10. $\dfrac{10}{12}$　　11. $\dfrac{12}{3}$　　12. $\dfrac{6}{12}$

VOCABULARY POWER

CHAPTER VOCABULARY

denominator　mixed
equation　　　number
equivalent　　simplest
　fractions　　　form
fraction　　　unlike
like fractions　　fractions
numerator　　variable

WARM-UP WORDS

equivalent fractions two or more fractions that
name the same amount

like fractions fractions with the same denominator

unlike fractions fractions with different denominators

1 Model Addition

OBJECTIVE: Use models to add like fractions.

Quick Review

Jamie drew the model shown. What fraction of the model is shaded?

Investigate

Materials ■ pattern blocks

You can use pattern blocks to explore adding like fractions. **Like fractions** are fractions with the same denominator.

A The yellow hexagon represents 1 whole. Use a fraction to describe the value of each pattern block shown.

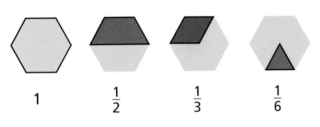

| 1 | $\frac{1}{2}$ | $\frac{1}{3}$ | $\frac{1}{6}$ |

B The model shows $\frac{1}{3}$.

Show how to model $\frac{1}{3} + \frac{1}{3}$. Then, record the sum.

C Model $\frac{4}{6} + \frac{2}{6}$. Record the sum.

Draw Conclusions

1. Explain how the pattern blocks show the numerator of the sum in Step B.

2. Compare your model in Step B with those of other classmates. What can you conclude? Explain.

3. What rule could you write to add fractions with like denominators?

4. **Formulation** Explain how you could use pattern blocks to find $\frac{1}{6} + \frac{3}{6}$.

Vocabulary

like fractions

You can use drawings to add fractions.

Step 1

Draw a number line and divide it into 8 equal parts. Model the fraction $\frac{1}{8}$ by shading 1 part of the line green.

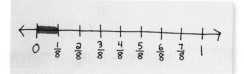

Step 2

Add the fraction $\frac{5}{8}$ by shading 5 more parts of the line red.

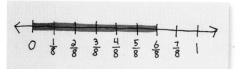

Step 3

Add the fractions. Since there are 8 equal parts, the denominator stays the same. Add the numerators and record the sum over the denominator.

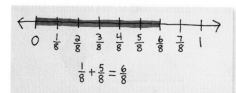

So, $\frac{1}{8} + \frac{5}{8} = \frac{6}{8}$.

To add like fractions, add the numerators. Use the same denominator as in the like fractions.

TALK Math

How does using a number line help you add like fractions?

Practice

Find the sum.

1.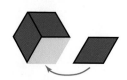

$\frac{2}{3} + \frac{1}{3}$

2.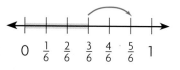

$\frac{3}{6} + \frac{2}{6}$

✓ 3.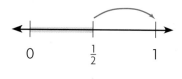

$\frac{1}{2} + \frac{1}{2}$

Model the sum. Record your answer.

4. $\frac{4}{6} + \frac{1}{6}$

5. $\frac{1}{4} + \frac{3}{4}$

6. $\frac{1}{8} + \frac{3}{8}$

✓ 7. $\frac{5}{12} + \frac{2}{12}$

8. $\frac{4}{10} + \frac{3}{10}$

9. $\frac{5}{6} + \frac{1}{6}$

10. $\frac{4}{12} + \frac{9}{12}$

11. $\frac{2}{5} + \frac{1}{5}$

12. **WRITE Math** Would you use pattern blocks or a number line to find $\frac{2}{9} + \frac{5}{9}$? **Explain** your choice.

CD ROM **Technology**
Use Harcourt Mega Math, Ice Station Exploration, *Arctic Algebra*, Level G.

2 Model Subtraction

OBJECTIVE: Use models to subtract like fractions.

Quick Review

Ryan modeled the fraction shown with pattern blocks. Write the fraction.

Investigate

Materials ■ pattern blocks

You can use pattern blocks to explore subtracting like fractions.

A The yellow hexagon represents 1 whole. Use fractions to describe the pattern blocks shown.

1     $\frac{1}{2}$ $\frac{1}{3}$ $\frac{1}{6}$

B Use a take away model. Place 5 triangle pattern blocks on the hexagon. Take away 3 of the 5 blocks. What do you notice? What is $\frac{5}{6} - \frac{3}{6}$?

C Use a compare model. Place 5 triangle pattern blocks on a hexagon. Then use 3 triangle blocks to cover 3 of the first group of the triangle blocks. Compare the groups of blocks. What do you notice? What is $\frac{5}{6} - \frac{3}{6}$?

Draw Conclusions

1. Explain how you used the pattern blocks to subtract in part B.

2. Explain how you used the pattern blocks to subtract in part C.

3. What rule could you write to subtract fractions with like denominators?

4. **Synthesis** How does subtraction of fractions compare to addition of fractions?

You can solve $\frac{7}{10} - \frac{3}{10}$ using a number line.

Step 1

Draw a number line divided into 10 equal parts. Model the fraction $\frac{7}{10}$ by shading 7 parts of the line green.

Step 2

To subtract on a number line, move left. To subtract $\frac{3}{10}$ from $\frac{7}{10}$, start at $\frac{7}{10}$ and move 3 parts to the left.

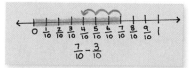

Step 3

Record your answer. Since there are 10 equal parts, the denominator stays the same. Subtract the numerators and record the difference over the denominator.

$$\frac{7}{10} - \frac{3}{10} = \frac{4}{10}$$

So, $\frac{7}{10} - \frac{3}{10} = \frac{4}{10}$.

TALK Math

What other ways could you find the difference?

Practice

Find the difference.

1.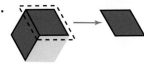

$$\frac{2}{3} - \frac{1}{3}$$

2.

$$\frac{5}{6} - \frac{1}{6}$$

✓3.

$$\frac{1}{2} - \frac{1}{2}$$

Model the difference. Record your answer.

4. $\frac{3}{4} - \frac{2}{4}$

5. $\frac{11}{12} - \frac{5}{12}$

6. $\frac{5}{8} - \frac{3}{8}$

✓7. $\frac{2}{3} - \frac{1}{3}$

8. $\frac{9}{10} - \frac{3}{10}$

9. $\frac{3}{6} - \frac{1}{6}$

10. $\frac{7}{12} - \frac{5}{12}$

11. $\frac{7}{8} - \frac{4}{8}$

12. **WRITE Math** Explain how to find $\frac{5}{12} - \frac{1}{12}$ by using a number line.

 Technology
ROM
Use Harcourt Mega Math, Ice Station Exploration, *Arctic Algebra,* Level G.

Record Addition and Subtraction

OBJECTIVE: Model and record addition and subtraction of fractions with like denominators.

Learn

PROBLEM Rory's herb garden is in a window box. He divided it into 4 equal parts. He used 1 part for mint, 1 part for basil, and 2 parts for thyme. What part of Rory's garden is either basil or mint?

Example 1 Use fraction bars. Add. $\frac{1}{4} + \frac{1}{4}$

MODEL	THINK	RECORD
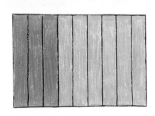	Count the $\frac{1}{4}$ fraction bars. There are two $\frac{1}{4}$ fraction bars.	$\frac{1}{4} + \frac{1}{4} = \frac{2}{4}$ Write the sum in simplest form. $\frac{2}{4} = \frac{1}{2}$

So, $\frac{2}{4}$, or $\frac{1}{2}$, of Rory's garden is either basil or mint.

Example 2 Use drawings. Add. $\frac{3}{9} + \frac{6}{9}$

MODEL	THINK	RECORD
	Count the number of dark green sections and the number of light green sections. There are 3 dark green sections and 6 light green sections.	$\frac{3}{9} + \frac{6}{9} = \frac{9}{9}$ Write the sum as a whole number. $\frac{9}{9} = 1$

So, $\frac{3}{9} + \frac{6}{9} = \frac{9}{9}$, or 1.

Example 3 Use paper and pencil. Add. $\frac{2}{5} + \frac{4}{5}$

THINK	RECORD
The denominators are the same. Add the numerators.	$\frac{2}{5} + \frac{4}{5} = \frac{6}{5}$ Write the sum as a mixed number. $\frac{6}{5} = \frac{5}{5} + \frac{1}{5} = 1\frac{1}{5}$

So, $\frac{2}{5} + \frac{4}{5} = \frac{6}{5}$, or $1\frac{1}{5}$.

Subtract Like Fractions

Tia's garden is divided into 10 equal sections. $\frac{7}{10}$ of her garden has various leafy herbs, and $\frac{3}{10}$ of her garden has chives. How much more of her garden is leafy herbs than chives?

Example 4 Compare. Subtract. $\frac{7}{10} - \frac{3}{10}$

MODEL	THINK	RECORD
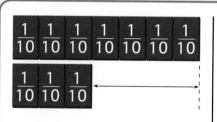	Compare the rows of $\frac{1}{10}$ bars. Find the difference. The difference is four $\frac{1}{10}$ bars.	$\frac{7}{10} - \frac{3}{10} = \frac{4}{10}$ Write the answer in simplest form. $\frac{4}{10} = \frac{2}{5}$

So, $\frac{4}{10}$, or $\frac{2}{5}$, more of Tia's garden space has leafy herbs than chives.

Example 5 Take away. Subtract. $\frac{5}{8} - \frac{3}{8}$

MODEL	THINK	RECORD
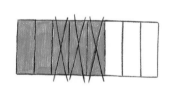	Cross out 3 of the shaded parts. There are 2 shaded parts not crossed off.	$\frac{5}{8} - \frac{3}{8} = \frac{2}{8}$ Write the answer in simplest form. $\frac{2}{8} = \frac{1}{4}$

So, $\frac{5}{8} - \frac{3}{8} = \frac{2}{8}$, or $\frac{1}{4}$.

- Find the difference in the numerators of $\frac{5}{8} - \frac{3}{8}$. How does this compare to the numerator of the difference, $\frac{2}{8}$, found in Example 5?

Example 6 Use paper and pencil. Subtract. $\frac{5}{6} - \frac{2}{6}$

THINK	RECORD
The denominators are the same. Subtract the numerators.	$\frac{5}{6} - \frac{2}{6} = \frac{3}{6}$ Write the answer in simplest form. $\frac{3}{6} = \frac{1}{2}$

So, $\frac{5}{6} - \frac{2}{6} = \frac{3}{6}$, or $\frac{1}{2}$.

Guided Practice

1. Make the model shown. Then use your model to find and record the sum.

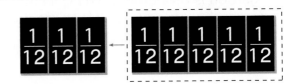

Find and record the sum or difference.

2. $\frac{5}{8} + \frac{2}{8}$

3. $\frac{9}{10} - \frac{2}{10}$

✓ 4. $\frac{4}{6} + \frac{3}{6}$

✓ 5. $\frac{3}{4} - \frac{1}{4}$

6. **TALK Math** **Explain** why the denominator does not change when you add or subtract like fractions.

Independent Practice and Problem Solving

Find and record the sum or difference.

7. $\frac{5}{8}$
   $-\frac{4}{8}$

8. $\frac{8}{10}$
   $-\frac{3}{10}$

9. $\frac{27}{100}$
   $+\frac{48}{100}$

10. $\frac{5}{8}$
    $+\frac{5}{8}$

11. $\frac{5}{10} + \frac{7}{10}$

12. $\frac{7}{12} - \frac{6}{12}$

13. $\frac{3}{4} + \frac{1}{4}$

14. $\frac{7}{100} - \frac{2}{100}$

Compare. Write <, >, or = for each ●.

15. $\frac{2}{3} + \frac{2}{3}$ ● 1

16. $\frac{1}{2}$ ● $\frac{7}{8} - \frac{3}{8}$

17. $\frac{1}{5} + \frac{2}{5}$ ● $\frac{4}{5}$

18. $\frac{2}{3}$ ● $\frac{11}{12} - \frac{1}{12}$

★ **Algebra** Find the value of n.

19. $\frac{5}{9} + \frac{2}{n} = \frac{7}{9}$

20. $\frac{n}{7} - \frac{2}{7} = \frac{4}{7}$

21. $\frac{n}{5} - \frac{1}{5} = \frac{3}{5}$

22. $\frac{3}{n} + \frac{9}{n} = 1$

USE DATA For 23–24, use the graph.

23. How much taller is the dill plant than the marjoram plant?

24. If the basil plant grows another $\frac{7}{8}$ inch by the end of next week, how tall will it be?

25. The height of the mint plant at two weeks measured $\frac{4}{8}$ inch. If the plant continues to grow at this rate, how tall will the plant be at 4 weeks?

26. **Pose a Problem** Look back at Problem 25. Write a similar problem by changing the numbers.

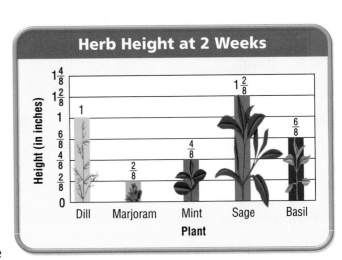

27. Ron has 3 equal-sized jars. One has $\frac{2}{8}$ cup paint, one has $\frac{4}{8}$ cup paint, and the other has $\frac{6}{8}$ cup paint. Which jar has the least amount of paint?

28. **What's the Error?** Ken wrote $\frac{1}{5} + \frac{2}{5} = \frac{3}{10}$. Dora wrote $\frac{1}{5} + \frac{2}{5} = \frac{3}{5}$. Who is correct? **Explain** your reasoning.

Mixed Review and Test Prep

29. The sides of a triangle are 5 meters, 8 meters, and 9 meters long. What is the perimeter of the triangle? (Grade 3)

30. **Test Prep** Andy bought $\frac{3}{8}$ pound of ham and $\frac{7}{8}$ pound of roast beef. How much more of roast beef than ham did he buy?

  A $\frac{3}{8}$ pound   **C** $\frac{7}{8}$ pound

  B $\frac{1}{2}$ pound   **D** $1\frac{1}{4}$ pounds

31. What mixed number does the model show? (p. 414)

32. **Test Prep** Sam jogged $\frac{5}{8}$ mile in the morning and $\frac{6}{8}$ mile in the afternoon. How far did he jog in all?

Problem Solving [connects to] Social Studies

Regions of the United States

The map shows the five regions of the United States. Of the 50 states, what part makes up the Northeast and the Middle West?

Find the fraction of states that make up the Northeast: $\frac{11}{50}$

Find the fraction of states that make up the Middle West: $\frac{12}{50}$

Add to find the total part: $\frac{11}{50} + \frac{12}{50} = \frac{23}{50}$

So, $\frac{23}{50}$ of the states make up the Northeast and the Middle West.

Solve.

1. How much greater is the fraction of states in the Southeast than in the Southwest?

2. **Reasoning** Do a greater fraction of the states have coastline along the Pacific Ocean or the Atlantic Ocean? **Explain.**

Problem Solving Workshop
Strategy: Write an Equation

OBJECTIVE: Solve problems using the strategy *write an equation.*

Learn the Strategy

Writing an equation can help you understand how the facts in a problem are related. Remember that an equation is a number sentence that shows that two quantities are equal.

Write an addition equation.

Greg walks $\frac{5}{8}$ mile to the store from his home. Then he continues in the same direction and walks to the library. The library is $\frac{7}{8}$ mile from his home. How far is it from the store to the library?

Let *b* represent the distance from the store to the library.

$$\frac{5}{8} + b = \frac{7}{8}$$

Write a subtraction equation.

Raven had 5 yards of fabric. She used some of the fabric to make a banner. She has 2 yards left. How much fabric did Raven use to make the banner?

Let *f* represent the amount of fabric she used to make the banner.

$$5 - f = 2$$

Write a multiplication equation.

Len's class has set up seats for the play. There are 7 seats in each row. There are 56 seats in all. How many rows of seats are there?

Let *s* represent the number of rows of seats.

$$s \times 7 = 56$$

Write a division equation.

Mrs. Hall has 24 stickers. She gives the same number of stickers to each of 8 students. How many stickers does each student receive?

Let *t* represent the number of stickers each student receives.

$$24 \div 8 = t$$

To write an equation, choose a variable to represent an unknown quantity. Then choose the operation that relates the unknown quantity to the known quantities.

TALK Math

What are some questions that you can ask yourself to help choose the correct operation?

Use the Strategy

PROBLEM During her dance class, Maria spends $\frac{3}{6}$ of the class on ballet. The rest of the class is spent on tap. The class lasts 1 hour. What fraction of the class is spent on tap?

Read to Understand

Reading Skill
- Identify the details in the problem.
- What details will you use?

Plan

- **What strategy can you use to solve the problem?**
  You can write an equation. An equation can show how the information in the problem is related.

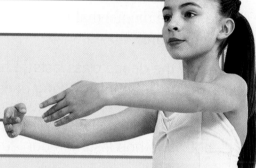

Solve

- **How can you use the strategy to solve the problem?**
  Choose a variable to represent the unknown time. Tell what the variable represents. Let x represent the time Maria spends on tap during her dance class. Choose the operation you will use.

Write an equation.

fraction of an hour spent on ballet		fraction of an hour spent on tap		total length of class
↓		↓		↓
$\frac{3}{6}$	$+$	x	$=$	$\frac{6}{6}$

Use mental math to solve the equation.

$\frac{3}{6} + x = \frac{6}{6}$ **Think:** $\frac{3}{6}$ plus what fraction equals $\frac{6}{6}$?

$x = \frac{3}{6}$, or $\frac{1}{2}$

So, $\frac{3}{6}$, or $\frac{1}{2}$, of the class is spent on tap.

Check

- **How can you check your answer?**
- **What other ways can you solve the problem? Explain.**

Guided Problem Solving

1. Monday's dance class lasts for $\frac{3}{4}$ hour and consists of ballet and jazz. The first part of the class is ballet. After ballet, jazz lasts for $\frac{1}{4}$ hour. How long does ballet last?

   First, choose a variable. Tell what the variable represents.

   Then, choose the operation and then write an equation.

   Finally, use mental math to solve the equation.

   Let b represent the fraction of the hour spent on ballet.

   $$b + \frac{1}{4} = \frac{3}{4}$$
   $$b = \blacksquare$$

2. **What if** the dance class lasts $\frac{11}{12}$ hour, and the jazz part of the class lasts $\frac{4}{12}$ hour. How long does ballet last?

3. Jen takes a dance class of hip-hop and jazz. The class lasts $\frac{9}{10}$ hour. Hip-hop lasts $\frac{4}{10}$ hour. Which part lasts longer?

Problem Solving Strategy Practice

Write an equation to solve.

4. Camille bought $\frac{7}{8}$ foot of elastic for her ballet slippers. She used some elastic for her slippers and had $\frac{5}{8}$ foot of elastic left. How much elastic did she use for her slippers?

5. In Wednesday's class, $\frac{3}{5}$ of the students are boys. What fraction of the students are girls?

USE DATA For 6–8, use the table.

6. At Level C, students dance to a CD for $\frac{2}{6}$ hour. A pianist plays for the rest of the class. How long does the pianist play?

7. Meg is in Level A. She takes two classes a week. How many hours does she spend in class each week?

8. **WRITE Math** At Level B, students take tap for $\frac{3}{10}$ hour, jazz for $\frac{3}{10}$ hour, and hip-hop for the rest of the class. **Explain** how to write and solve an equation to find how long the students take hip-hop in the class.

Academy Dance Classes	
Level	Class Length (in hours)
A	$\frac{11}{12}$
B	$\frac{9}{10}$
C	$\frac{5}{6}$

Mixed Strategy Practice

USE DATA For 9–12, use the circle graph.

9. **Reasoning** Beth takes 4 hours of ballet each week. How many hours does she spend taking jazz?

10. Does Beth spend more time taking ballet and tap or ballet and jazz each week? How much more time?

11. **Pose a Problem** Look back at Problem 10. Write a similar problem comparing the types of dance lessons that Beth takes.

12. **Open-Ended** Write three different equations that can be solved by using the circle graph. Use at least one addition equation and one subtraction equation. Ask a question that can be answered by solving one of your equations.

13. Nate, Sean, and Jonah take chorus, drama, and band. Jonah and Sean do not like drama best. Jonah's favorite is not band. What is each boy's favorite type of class?

14. **Reasoning** Gavin spends 90 minutes each week taking violin lessons. How many hours each week does he spend taking violin lessons? Express your answer as a mixed number.

Choose a
STRATEGY

Draw a Diagram or Picture

Make a Model or Act It Out

Make an Organized List

Find a Pattern

Make a Table or Graph

Predict and Test

Work Backward

Solve a Simpler Problem

Write an Equation

Use Logical Reasoning

Beth's Weekly Dance Lessons for 8 Hours of Classes

CHALLENGE YOURSELF

Lara is a member of a community orchestra. One half of its members play string instruments, $\frac{1}{6}$ of its members play brass instruments, $\frac{2}{12}$ of its members play woodwind instruments, and $\frac{1}{6}$ of its members play percussion instruments.

15. What part of the orchestra do the string, woodwind, and brass sections make up? How does this compare to the whole orchestra?

16. Next year, the conductor expects only $\frac{1}{3}$ of the members to play string instruments. How would the fraction of the members in each of the other sections need to change in order to make one whole?

Add and Subtract Mixed Numbers

OBJECTIVE: Add and subtract mixed numbers with like denominators.

Learn

PROBLEM Keoni and Jack are making puppets for the library puppet show. The thigh of each puppet is $1\frac{1}{4}$ inches longer than the forearm. How long is the thigh if the forearm is $3\frac{2}{4}$ inches long?

Example 1 Add. $1\frac{1}{4} + 3\frac{2}{4}$

MODEL	THINK	RECORD
Step 1 Draw a picture for each mixed number. Add the fractions first. 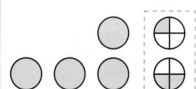	Count the number of fourths shaded.	$\begin{array}{r} 1\frac{1}{4} \\ + 3\frac{2}{4} \\ \hline \frac{3}{4} \end{array}$
Step 2 Then add the whole numbers. 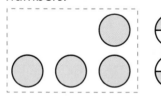	Count the number of whole circles shaded.	$\begin{array}{r} 1\frac{1}{4} \\ + 3\frac{2}{4} \\ \hline 4\frac{3}{4} \end{array}$

So, the thigh is $4\frac{3}{4}$ inches long.

ERROR ALERT

Remember to add the additional whole number if the fractional part of a sum is greater than 1.

More Examples

Ⓐ Like Fractions

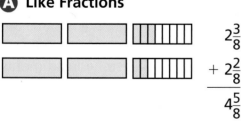

$\begin{array}{r} 2\frac{3}{8} \\ + 2\frac{2}{8} \\ \hline 4\frac{5}{8} \end{array}$

Ⓑ Like Fractions

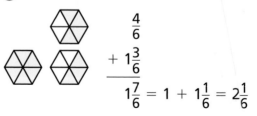

$\begin{array}{r} \frac{4}{6} \\ + 1\frac{3}{6} \\ \hline 1\frac{7}{6} = 1 + 1\frac{1}{6} = 2\frac{1}{6} \end{array}$

Subtract Mixed Numbers

Subtracting mixed numbers is similar to adding mixed numbers.

The body of an eagle puppet is $1\frac{1}{3}$ feet shorter than its wingspan. The wingspan of the puppet is $3\frac{2}{3}$ feet long. How long is the puppet's body?

$3\frac{2}{3}$ feet

Example 2 **Subtract.** $3\frac{2}{3} - 1\frac{1}{3}$

MODEL	THINK	RECORD

Step 1

Draw a model for the first mixed number. Subtract the fractions first. 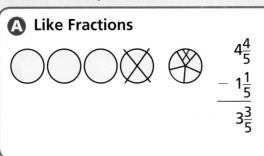	Cross off 1 of the shaded parts.	$3\frac{2}{3}$ $-\ 1\frac{1}{3}$ $\overline{\quad\frac{1}{3}}$

Step 2

Then subtract the whole numbers.	Cross off 1 whole.	$3\frac{2}{3}$ $-\ 1\frac{1}{3}$ $\overline{\quad2\frac{1}{3}}$

So, the puppet's body is $2\frac{1}{3}$ feet long.

More Examples

A **Like Fractions**

$4\frac{4}{5}$
$-\ 1\frac{1}{5}$
$\overline{\quad3\frac{3}{5}}$

B **Like Fractions**

$3\frac{3}{7}$
$-\ 3\frac{1}{7}$
$\overline{\quad\frac{2}{7}}$

- How do models help you add or subtract mixed numbers?

Guided Practice

1. Use the model. Subtract. $2\frac{7}{10} - 1\frac{4}{10}$

Model and record the sum or difference.

2. $1\frac{3}{4}$
$+2\frac{1}{4}$

3. $4\frac{5}{8}$
$-3\frac{1}{8}$

4. $2\frac{1}{3}$
$+2\frac{1}{3}$

5. $5\frac{3}{4}$
$-1\frac{2}{4}$

✓6. $3\frac{1}{6}$
$+1\frac{3}{6}$

✓7. $1\frac{4}{5}$
$-\frac{2}{5}$

8. **TALK Math** Explain how to use models to find $3\frac{2}{12} + 1\frac{4}{12}$.

Independent Practice and Problem Solving

Model and record the sum or difference.

9. $3\frac{4}{10}$
$+2\frac{3}{10}$

10. $6\frac{3}{5}$
$-2\frac{1}{5}$

11. $2\frac{7}{12}$
$+2\frac{3}{12}$

12. $5\frac{5}{8}$
$-3\frac{1}{8}$

13. $\frac{2}{5}$
$+1\frac{3}{5}$

14. $3\frac{6}{8}$
$-2\frac{5}{8}$

15. $3\frac{9}{12} - 1\frac{5}{12}$

16. $4\frac{5}{6} + \frac{2}{6}$

17. $3\frac{1}{2} + 1\frac{1}{2}$

18. $4\frac{2}{3} - 4\frac{1}{3}$

⭐**Algebra** Find the value of n.

19. $5\frac{n}{4} + 2\frac{1}{4} = 7\frac{3}{4}$

20. $2\frac{n}{6} + 1\frac{1}{6} = 3\frac{5}{6}$

21. $3\frac{1}{8} + 1\frac{n}{8} = 4\frac{6}{8}$

22. $4 - n = 3\frac{2}{5}$

USE DATA For 23–24 and 28, use the table.

23. A $3\frac{3}{4}$-inch rod is used to extend the length of a rod puppet. How long is the puppet with the extension?

24. Order the types of puppets from longest to shortest. How much longer is the longest puppet than the shortest puppet?

25. Pablo stores hand puppets in boxes of 18 and marionettes in boxes of 15. He has 4 boxes filled with hand puppets and 3 boxes filled with marionettes. How many hand puppets and marionettes does he have in all?

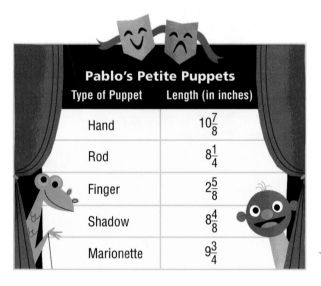

Pablo's Petite Puppets	
Type of Puppet	Length (in inches)
Hand	$10\frac{7}{8}$
Rod	$8\frac{1}{4}$
Finger	$2\frac{5}{8}$
Shadow	$8\frac{4}{8}$
Marionette	$9\frac{3}{4}$

26. **Reasoning** Nilda needs $1\frac{3}{4}$ cups of milk for one recipe and $2\frac{3}{4}$ cups of milk for another recipe. Will Nilda have enough milk if she buys a quart? **Explain.**

27. **☰FAST FACT** The first puppet show in Boston, Massachusetts was in 1768. In 2008, how many years ago was this?

28. **WRITE Math** ‣ **What's the Question?** Compare the lengths of two of Pablo's puppets. The answer is this puppet is $1\frac{1}{2}$ inches longer.

Extra Practice on page 450, Set B

Learn About — Estimating Fraction Sums and Differences

Rounding fractions to 0, $\frac{1}{2}$, or 1 can help you estimate fraction sums and differences. Rounding mixed numbers to the nearest whole number can help you estimate mixed number sums and differences.

Examples

Estimate. $\frac{1}{8} + \frac{5}{6}$

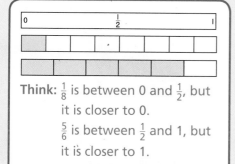

Think: $\frac{1}{8}$ is between 0 and $\frac{1}{2}$, but it is closer to 0.

$\frac{5}{6}$ is between $\frac{1}{2}$ and 1, but it is closer to 1.

$0 + 1 = 1$

So, $\frac{1}{8} + \frac{5}{6}$ is about 1.

Estimate. $4\frac{9}{10} - 1\frac{3}{5}$

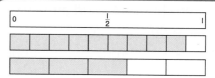

Think: $\frac{9}{10}$ is between $\frac{1}{2}$ and 1, but it is closer to 1. So, $4\frac{9}{10}$ is close to 5.

$\frac{3}{5}$ is between $\frac{1}{2}$ and 1, but it is closer to $\frac{1}{2}$. So, $1\frac{3}{5}$ is close to $1\frac{1}{2}$.

$5 - 1\frac{1}{2} = 3\frac{1}{2}$

So, $4\frac{9}{10} - 1\frac{3}{5}$ is about $3\frac{1}{2}$.

Try It

Use models to estimate the sum or difference. Then find the actual sum or difference and compare it to the estimate to determine whether your answer is reasonable.

29. $\frac{5}{12} + \frac{2}{5}$ **30.** $\frac{5}{8} + \frac{5}{6}$ **31.** $\frac{7}{8} - \frac{1}{5}$ **32.** $3\frac{11}{12} - 1\frac{3}{8}$ **33.** $2\frac{1}{4} + 4\frac{1}{10}$

Mixed Review and Test Prep

34. A bag contains 50 dimes. A coin is pulled from the bag. Is it certain or impossible the coin drawn is a penny?

(Grade 3)

35. Test Prep Kylie painted for $1\frac{4}{6}$ hours in the morning and $1\frac{5}{6}$ hours after lunch. How long did she paint altogether?

A $\frac{1}{6}$ hour   **C** $2\frac{1}{2}$ hours

B $2\frac{1}{6}$ hours   **D** $3\frac{1}{2}$ hours

36. Trish and Devon shared a pizza. Each ate $\frac{2}{6}$ of the pizza. How much of the pizza did they eat in all? (p. 436)

37. Test Prep Toby has hiked $2\frac{1}{4}$ miles. The trail to the lake is $2\frac{3}{4}$ miles long. How much farther does Toby have to hike to reach the lake? **Explain.**

6 Model Addition and Subtraction of Unlike Fractions

OBJECTIVE: Add and subtract fractions with unlike denominators.

Quick Review

1. $\frac{1}{4} + \frac{1}{4}$ 2. $\frac{3}{6} + \frac{1}{6}$

3. $\frac{2}{8} + \frac{5}{8}$ 4. $\frac{2}{3} - \frac{1}{3}$

5. $\frac{7}{10} - \frac{3}{10}$

Vocabulary

unlike fractions

Investigate

Materials ■ pattern blocks ■ fraction bars

You can use pattern blocks to add and subtract fractions with unlike denominators.
Unlike fractions have different denominators.

A Use the values shown for the pattern blocks.

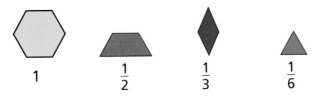

1          $\frac{1}{2}$ $\frac{1}{3}$ $\frac{1}{6}$

B Use pattern blocks to model and find $\frac{1}{2} + \frac{1}{3}$. First, find like denominators by looking for a block you can use to model both fractions. Record the equivalent fractions.

$\frac{1}{2} = \frac{3}{6}$ $\frac{1}{3} = \frac{2}{6}$

C Model and then add the equivalent fractions. Record the sum.

D Now use the pattern blocks to model and find $\frac{1}{2} - \frac{1}{6}$. First, find like denominators by modeling equivalent fractions. Then subtract. Record the difference.

Draw Conclusions

1. Explain how you found like denominators so you could add or subtract the fractions.

2. Why is it helpful to find like denominators to add or subtract fractions?

3. **Contrast** How does adding unlike fractions contrast with adding like fractions?

You can also use fraction bars to add or subtract unlike fractions.
Find $\frac{3}{5} - \frac{1}{2}$.

Step 1

Place three $\frac{1}{5}$ fraction bars under the bar for 1. Then place one $\frac{1}{2}$ fraction bar under the three $\frac{1}{5}$ bars.

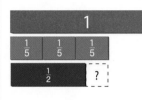

Step 2

Find like fraction bars that are equivalent to $\frac{3}{5}$ and $\frac{1}{2}$.

$$\frac{3}{5} = \frac{6}{10} \qquad \frac{1}{2} = \frac{5}{10}$$

Step 3

Compare the rows of bars. Find the number of $\frac{1}{10}$ bars that fit exactly under the difference $\frac{3}{5} - \frac{1}{2}$.

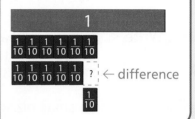
← difference

So, $\frac{3}{5} - \frac{1}{2} = \frac{1}{10}$.

In Step 2, you must find equivalent fractions with the same denominator to model the difference.

TALK Math

How would you use fraction bars to find $\frac{3}{5} + \frac{1}{2}$?

Practice

Model the sum or difference. Draw a picture of your model.

1. $\frac{1}{4} + \frac{1}{8}$
2. $\frac{1}{2} + \frac{1}{6}$
3. $\frac{7}{12} + \frac{1}{4}$
4. $\frac{2}{3} + \frac{1}{6}$

5. $\frac{1}{2} - \frac{1}{4}$
6. $\frac{7}{12} - \frac{1}{3}$
7. $\frac{2}{3} - \frac{1}{2}$
8. $\frac{7}{10} - \frac{2}{5}$

Find the sum or difference.

9. $\frac{1}{3} + \frac{1}{6}$
10. $\frac{3}{4} + \frac{1}{2}$
11. $\frac{1}{2} + \frac{5}{12}$
12. $\frac{9}{10} - \frac{3}{5}$

13. $\frac{1}{2} - \frac{3}{8}$
14. $\frac{3}{4} - \frac{3}{8}$
15. $\frac{7}{8} - \frac{1}{2}$
16. $\frac{2}{3} + \frac{1}{2}$

17. **WRITE Math** How would you find $\frac{4}{6} - \frac{1}{3}$? **Explain** how to use equivalent fractions to find the difference.

Extra Practice

1. $\dfrac{3}{5}$
   $+\dfrac{1}{5}$

2. $\dfrac{7}{8}$
   $-\dfrac{4}{8}$

3. $\dfrac{7}{10}$
   $+\dfrac{4}{10}$

4. $\dfrac{3}{4}$
   $-\dfrac{1}{4}$

5. $\dfrac{12}{100}$
   $+\dfrac{19}{100}$

6. $\dfrac{5}{6}$
   $-\dfrac{2}{6}$

7. $\dfrac{3}{8}$
   $+\dfrac{2}{8}$

8. $\dfrac{9}{12}$
   $-\dfrac{6}{12}$

Compare. Write $<$, $>$, or $=$ for each ●.

9. $\dfrac{8}{10} + \dfrac{3}{10}$ ● 1

10. $\dfrac{2}{3} - \dfrac{1}{3}$ ● $\dfrac{1}{2}$

11. $\dfrac{5}{8} + \dfrac{3}{8}$ ● $\dfrac{7}{8}$

12. $\dfrac{11}{12} - \dfrac{5}{12}$ ● $\dfrac{1}{2}$

13. Lisa brings home a small pizza for dinner. The pizza is divided into 12 equal slices. If Lisa eats 3 slices and her sister eats 4 slices, what part of the pizza do Lisa and her sister eat?

14. Hunter buys $\dfrac{2}{3}$ pound of Swiss cheese and the same amount of mozzarella cheese. How many pounds of cheese does he buy in all?

Set B Model and record the sum or difference. (pp. 444–447)

1. $3\dfrac{1}{4}$
   $+1\dfrac{3}{4}$

2. $6\dfrac{5}{8}$
   $-2\dfrac{3}{8}$

3. $9\dfrac{7}{10}$
   $-1\dfrac{4}{10}$

4. $3\dfrac{5}{6}$
   $+2\dfrac{1}{6}$

5. $4\dfrac{5}{12}$
   $+3\dfrac{2}{12}$

6. $2\dfrac{3}{4}$
   $-1\dfrac{1}{4}$

7. $2\dfrac{3}{5}$
   $+ \dfrac{4}{5}$

8. $6\dfrac{2}{3}$
   $-4\dfrac{1}{3}$

9. $2\dfrac{3}{5} + 4\dfrac{1}{5}$

10. $3\dfrac{6}{7} + 4\dfrac{1}{7}$

11. $6\dfrac{3}{5} - 2\dfrac{2}{5}$

12. $10 - 9\dfrac{1}{3}$

13. Barb baby-sat for $2\dfrac{1}{2}$ hours yesterday and $1\dfrac{1}{2}$ hours today. How many hours did she baby-sit?

14. Grant volunteered $3\dfrac{3}{4}$ hours this week and $1\dfrac{1}{4}$ hours last week. How many more hours did he volunteer this week than last?

Technology
Use Harcourt Mega Math, Ice Station
Exploration, *Arctic Algebra*, Levels F, G.

Race to One

On Your Mark!
2 players

Get Set!
- 2 sets of fraction bars
- Number cube labeled $\frac{1}{2}$, $\frac{1}{3}$, $\frac{1}{4}$, $\frac{1}{6}$, $\frac{1}{8}$, and $\frac{1}{12}$

What if...

1. on his first turn, player A tosses $\frac{1}{3}$?

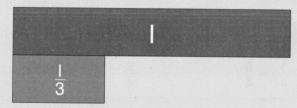

2. on his next turn, player A tosses $\frac{1}{6}$?

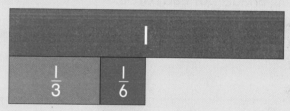

3. player A then trades $\frac{1}{6}$ and $\frac{1}{3}$ for $\frac{1}{2}$?

Think: $\frac{1}{3} + \frac{1}{6} = \frac{2}{6} + \frac{1}{6} = \frac{3}{6} = \frac{1}{2}$

4. player B already has $\frac{1}{3}$ and $\frac{1}{4}$ and tosses $\frac{1}{2}$?

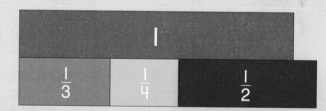

Go!

- Each player takes a bar for 1 and tosses the number cube. The player with the lesser fraction goes first.

- The first player tosses the number cube and lines up the matching fraction bar with the bar for 1.

- Players take turns tossing the number cube and adding fraction bars along the the bar for 1.

- If a player tosses a fraction resulting in a sum greater than 1, the player loses a turn and removes that piece.

- Players can trade fraction bars for an equivalent bar at any time.

- The first player to exactly match the bar for 1 wins the round.

Multiply Fractions by Whole Numbers

Pizza Party

A customer ordered 3 small pizzas from a pizzeria. The pizzeria's dough recipe calls for $\frac{3}{4}$ cup flour for each batch. How many cups of flour are used to make this order?

You can multiply to find the answer.

Example 1 Multiply. $3 \times \frac{3}{4}$

Step 1	**Step 2**	**Step 3**
Draw 3 circles divided into fourths. Shade $\frac{3}{4}$ of each circle.	Write an addition sentence to find the total number of fourths shaded.	Write the answer as a mixed number.
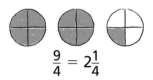	$\frac{3}{4} + \frac{3}{4} + \frac{3}{4} = \frac{9}{4}$	$\frac{9}{4} = 2\frac{1}{4}$

So, $3 \times \frac{3}{4} = \frac{9}{4}$, or $2\frac{1}{4}$.

Example 2 Multiply. $4 \times \frac{2}{6}$

Step 1	**Step 2**	**Step 3**
Draw 4 groups of $\frac{2}{6}$.	Write an addition sentence to find the total number of sixths shaded.	Write the answer as a mixed number.
	$\frac{2}{6} + \frac{2}{6} + \frac{2}{6} + \frac{2}{6} = \frac{8}{6}$	$\frac{8}{6} = 1\frac{2}{6}$, or $1\frac{1}{3}$

So, $4 \times \frac{2}{6} = \frac{8}{6}$, or $1\frac{2}{6}$, or $1\frac{1}{3}$.

Try It
Find the product.

1. $2 \times \frac{2}{3}$

2. $4 \times \frac{1}{2}$

3. $5 \times \frac{7}{8}$

4. $3 \times \frac{5}{6}$

5. 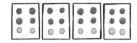 **Explain** how to draw a model to find $6 \times \frac{3}{10}$.

Chapter 16 Review/Test

Check Vocabulary and Concepts

Choose the best term from the box.

1. Fractions with the same denominator are called __?__ . (p. 432)

2. The fractions $\frac{2}{3}$ and $\frac{1}{4}$ are called __?__ . (p. 448)

Check Skills

Model the sum or difference. Record your answer. (pp. 432–433, 434–435)

3. $\frac{2}{5} + \frac{3}{5}$

4. $\frac{3}{6} - \frac{1}{6}$

5. $\frac{5}{8} + \frac{1}{8}$

6. $\frac{7}{12} - \frac{3}{12}$

Find and record the sum or difference. (pp. 436–439, 444–447, 448–449)

7. $\begin{array}{r} \frac{2}{6} \\ + \frac{1}{6} \\ \hline \end{array}$

8. $\begin{array}{r} \frac{2}{3} \\ - \frac{1}{3} \\ \hline \end{array}$

9. $\begin{array}{r} \frac{7}{10} \\ + \frac{9}{10} \\ \hline \end{array}$

10. $\begin{array}{r} \frac{37}{100} \\ - \frac{26}{100} \\ \hline \end{array}$

11. $\begin{array}{r} 3\frac{1}{8} \\ + 1\frac{4}{8} \\ \hline \end{array}$

12. $\begin{array}{r} \frac{5}{6} \\ - \frac{2}{3} \\ \hline \end{array}$

13. $\begin{array}{r} 2\frac{4}{9} \\ + 7\frac{4}{9} \\ \hline \end{array}$

14. $\begin{array}{r} \frac{2}{3} \\ - \frac{1}{2} \\ \hline \end{array}$

15. $\begin{array}{r} \frac{1}{4} \\ + \frac{1}{2} \\ \hline \end{array}$

16. $\begin{array}{r} 6\frac{3}{7} \\ - 5\frac{1}{7} \\ \hline \end{array}$

17. $\begin{array}{r} \frac{2}{10} \\ + \frac{1}{2} \\ \hline \end{array}$

18. $\begin{array}{r} 3\frac{11}{12} \\ + 7\frac{1}{12} \\ \hline \end{array}$

Check Problem Solving

Solve. (pp. 440–443)

19. Allison practices piano for $\frac{1}{3}$ hour on Monday. She practices for $\frac{1}{2}$ hour on Tuesday. How long does she practice piano during the 2 days?

20. **WRITE Math** Mia and Brady picked strawberries to sell at a fruit stand. Brady picked $1\frac{1}{3}$ quarts. Together, they picked $4\frac{2}{3}$ quarts. How many quarts did Mia pick? **Explain** how you know.

Standardized Test Prep
Chapters 1–16

Number and Operations

Test Tip Get the information you need.

See Item 1. You need to know the number of weeks in a year. Multiply that information by the amount saved per week.

1. Karen plans to save $28 each week for a year. How much will she have saved by the end of the year? (p. 282)

   A $80   C $1,456

   B $336   D $2,800

2. The table below shows attendance numbers for the science museum during a holiday weekend.

Science Museum Visitors			
Friday	Saturday	Sunday	Monday
928	864	952	896

   The museum was open for 8 hours on Saturday. How many people, on average, visited each hour? (p. 334)

   A 18   C 116

   B 108   D 119

3. Roberto's cat weighed $6\frac{3}{4}$ pounds last year. Then the cat gained $1\frac{1}{2}$ pounds. How much does the cat weigh now? (p. 444)

   A $5\frac{1}{4}$ pounds   C $7\frac{3}{4}$ pounds

   B $7\frac{1}{4}$ pounds   D $8\frac{1}{4}$ pounds

4. **WRITE Math** ▶ Explain how to use compatible numbers to estimate $432 \div 7$. (p. 320)

Measurement

5. Mario rode his bike to the lake. The clock on the left shows the time he started his bike ride. The clock on the right shows the time he arrived at the lake. How long was the bike ride? (p. 154)

   A 35 minutes

   B 1 hour 35 minutes

   C 2 hours 35 minutes

   D 3 hours 35 minutes

6. Vera checked the temperature on her porch at 3:00 P.M. It was 52°F. She checked the temperature again at 8:00 P.M. The temperature had dropped 15°F. What was the temperature at 8:00 P.M.? (p. 164)

   A 37°F

   B 47°F

   C 52°F

   D 67°F

7. **WRITE Math** ▶ Explain how to decide whether 10°F or 60°F is a more reasonable temperature for a very cold winter day. (p. 164)

Probability and Statistics

8. Use the bar graph.

Who read twice as many books as Randy? (p. 204)

A Kayla

B Randy

C Pablo

D Madison

9. Which event is equally as likely to happen as tossing an even number on a number cube labeled 1 to 6? (Grade 3)

A Tossing a 2

B Tossing a 6

C Tossing an odd number

D Tossing a multiple of 3

10. **WRITE Math** ▶ Would you use a bar graph, a circle graph, or a line graph to show the results of the election for student council president? **Explain.** (p. 222)

Geometry and Spatial Reasoning

11. Which figure appears to have exactly two lines of symmetry? (Grade 3)

A

B

C

D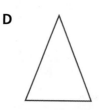

12. Which figure always has no equal sides? (Grade 3)

A Right triangle

B Scalene triangle

C Equilateral triangle

D Isosceles triangle

13. **WRITE Math** ▶ Describe a rectangular prism. **Explain** what a rectangular prism must have to be a cube. (Grade 3)

17 Understand Decimals and Place Value

Investigate

The top five senior women's all-around scores at the 2004 U.S. Gymnastic Championships are shown on the scoreboard. Suppose you are reporting the scores in the school newspaper. What can you write about the outcome of the meet?

All-Around Scores

Terin Humphry	75.45
Allyse Ishino	75.15
Courtney Kupets	76.45
Courtney McCool	75.3
Carly Patterson	76.45

≡ FAST FACT

The 2004 U.S. Gymnastic Championships took place at the Gaylord Entertainment Center in Nashville, Tennessee. About 200 of America's best gymnasts competed.

GO ONLINE
Technology
Student pages are available in the Student eBook.

Check your understanding of important skills
needed for success in Chapter 17.

▶ Model Fractions and Mixed Numbers

Write the fraction or the mixed number for the shaded part.

1.   2. 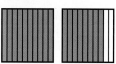   3.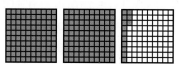

▶ Fractions with Denominators of 10 and 100

Write a fraction for each. You may wish to draw a picture.

4. six tenths   **5.** eight hundredths   **6.** thirty-three hundredths

Complete to show equivalent fractions. You may wish to draw a picture.

7. $\frac{1}{10} = \frac{\blacksquare}{100}$ **8.** $\frac{4}{10} = \frac{\blacksquare}{100}$ **9.** $\frac{8}{10} = \frac{\blacksquare}{100}$

▶ Money Notation

Name the amount shown.

10.   11.

Write a decimal for the money amount.

12. five dollars and twenty-eight cents   **13.** twelve dollars and five cents

VOCABULARY POWER

CHAPTER VOCABULARY

decimal	mixed number
decimal point	not equal to (≠)
equal to (=)	tenth
fraction	thousandth
hundredth	

WARM-UP WORDS

decimal a number with one or more digits to the right of the decimal point

decimal point a symbol used to separate dollars from cents in money amounts and to separate the ones and the tenths places in a decimal

thousandth one of one thousand equal parts

Relate Fractions and Decimals

OBJECTIVE: Model, read, and write fractions as decimals.

Learn

PROBLEM Ty is reading a 100-page book about metamorphic rocks. He has read $\frac{7}{10}$ of the book. Only 1 page in the book has a picture. What decimal part of the book has Ty read? What decimal part has pictures?

A **decimal** is a number with one or more digits to the right of the **decimal point.**

ONE WAY Use models.

A Use decimal models.

Shade the model to show 1.   Shade $\frac{7}{10}$ of the model.   Shade $\frac{1}{100}$ of the model.

Fraction	**Decimal**	**Fraction**	**Decimal**	**Fraction**	**Decimal**
Read: one	**Read:** one	**Read:** seven tenths	**Read:** seven tenths	**Read:** one hundredth	**Read:** one hundredth
Write: $\frac{1}{1}$	**Write:** 1.0	**Write:** $\frac{7}{10}$	**Write:** 0.7	**Write:** $\frac{1}{100}$	**Write:** 0.01

So, Ty has read 0.7 of the book, and 0.01 of the book has pictures.

B Use money.

1 dollar   10 dimes = 1 dollar   100 pennies = 1 dollar

                    1 dime = $\frac{1}{10}$, or 0.1, of a dollar   1 penny = $\frac{1}{100}$, or 0.01 of a dollar

$1.00 $0.10 $0.01

C Decimals, like whole numbers can be written in standard form, word form, and expanded form.

Ones	.	Tenths	Hundredths
0	.	2	8

0 × 1	.	2 × 0.1	8 × 0.01
0	.	0.2	0.08

Standard Form	Word Form	Expanded Form
0.6	six tenths	0.6
0.28	twenty-eight hundredths	0.2 + 0.08
$0.14	fourteen cents	$0.10 + $0.04

> **ERROR ALERT**
>
> Always place the decimal point between the ones digit and the tenths digit.
>
> decimal point
> ↓
> 0.1
> ↑
>
> A zero is used to show there are no ones.

A number line divided into 100 equal parts can be used to model fractions and decimals. You can also write a fraction that has a denominator other than 10 or 100 as a decimal.

Examples

D Use a number line.

Locate the point 0.75. What fraction names this point on the number line?

$$\frac{75}{100}$$

$\frac{0}{100}$ $\frac{10}{100}$ $\frac{20}{100}$ $\frac{30}{100}$ $\frac{40}{100}$ $\frac{50}{100}$ $\frac{60}{100}$ $\frac{70}{100}$ $\frac{80}{100}$ $\frac{90}{100}$ $\frac{100}{100}$

0 0.1 0.2 0.3 0.4 0.5 0.6 0.7 | 0.8 0.9 1
0.75

So, 0.75 names the same amount as $\frac{75}{100}$ and $\frac{3}{4}$.

E Use a model.

First write the fraction using a denominator of 10 or 100.

What decimal shows the amount as $\frac{1}{5}$?

$\frac{1}{5} = \frac{1 \times 2}{5 \times 2} = \frac{2}{10}$, or 0.2

So, 0.2 shows the same amount as $\frac{1}{5}$.

Guided Practice

1. Copy the model and shade to show $\frac{8}{10}$. Write the amount as a decimal.

Write the fraction and decimal shown by each model.

2.

3.

  4. $\frac{0}{10}$ $\frac{5}{10}$ $\frac{10}{10}$

0   0.5   1

 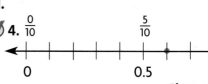

Write each fraction as a decimal. You may draw a picture.

5. $\frac{2}{10}$ **6.** $\frac{80}{100}$ **7.** $\frac{3}{5}$ **8.** $\frac{2}{4}$ ✓ **9.** $\frac{5}{100}$

10. TALK Math **Explain** how the models that represent one whole, one tenth, and one hundredth are related.

Independent Practice and Problem Solving

Write the fraction and decimal shown by each model.

11.   **12.**    **13.**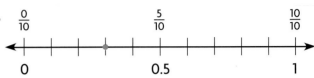

Write each fraction as a decimal. You may draw a picture.

14. $\frac{9}{10}$ **15.** $\frac{3}{4}$ **16.** $\frac{4}{10}$ **17.** $\frac{42}{100}$ **18.** $\frac{4}{5}$

Write the amount as a fraction of a dollar, as a decimal, and as a money amount.

19. 8 dimes   **20.** 3 dimes, 5 pennies   **21.** 6 pennies   **22.** 1 dollar, 2 dimes, 6 pennies

⭐ **Algebra** Copy and complete.

23. 6 tenths + 2 hundredths = 0.■2   **24.** 0 tenths + ■ hundredths = 0.04

25. $0.58 = ■ dimes + ■ pennies   **26.** 0.04 = ■ tenths + ■ hundredths

USE DATA For 27–28, use the table.

27. Write a decimal to show what part of the rocks listed in the table are igneous.

28. Sedimentary rocks make up 0.3 of Ramon's collection. Write this decimal as a fraction and in word form.

29. Josh paid for three books with two $20 bills. He received $1 in change. Each book was the same price. How much did each book cost?

30. WRITE Math **Explain** how to use a model to write the fraction $\frac{12}{100}$ as a decimal.

Classifying Rocks	
Name	**Type**
Basalt	Igneous
Rhyolite	Igneous
Granite	Igneous
Peridotite	Igneous
Shale	Sedimentary
Limestone	Sedimentary
Sandstone	Sedimentary
Gness	Metamorphic
Slate	Metamorphic
Scoria	Igneous

Changing Fractions and Decimals on a Calculator

Ken says that 0.45 of the rocks in his collection are igneous rocks.
What fraction of Ken's collection contains igneous rocks?

You can use a calculator to change a decimal to an equivalent
fraction and a fraction to an equivalent decimal.

Ⓐ Use F↔D to find what fraction
of Ken's rocks are igneous.

Change 0.45 to a fraction.

So, Ken's collection contains $\frac{9}{20}$
igneous rocks.

Ⓑ To change a fraction to an
equivalent decimal, you can
divide. Write the fraction as a
division problem. Use the ÷ key.

Change $\frac{4}{5}$ to a decimal.

So, $\frac{4}{5}$ is equivalent to 0.8.

Try It

For each decimal, write an equivalent fraction. For each fraction,
write an equivalent decimal. You may use a calculator.

31. 0.4

32. $\frac{4}{100}$

33. 0.65

34. $\frac{70}{100}$

35. $\frac{3}{4}$

36. 0.32

37. $\frac{2}{5}$

38. 0.78

Mixed Review and Test Prep

39. The students in the Culture club each
bought tickets to 7 shows during the
year. Each ticket cost $8. If there are 37
students in the club, how much did they
spend in all on show tickets? (p. 290)

40. Bob used 7 eggs from a carton of 12.
He used the expression $12 - n$ to find the
number of eggs he has left. If n represents
the number of eggs he used, how many
eggs does Bob have left? (p. 64)

41. Test Prep Hal walks 0.5 mile to school.
Anya walks $\frac{1}{2}$ mile to the same school.
Hal says he has to walk farther than Anya.
Explain how to determine if Hal is correct.

42. Test Prep Which shows the fraction $\frac{8}{10}$ in
decimal form?

A 0.08

B 0.8

C 0.810

D 8.1

Decimals to Thousandths

OBJECTIVE: Read and write fractions as decimals to the thousandths place.

Learn

PROBLEM Argentine ants are about 0.316 centimeter long. How can you read and write this decimal number?

Thousandths are smaller parts than hundredths. If one hundredth is divided into ten equal parts, each part represents one **thousandth**.

▲ Ants can lift 20 times their own body weight.

ONE WAY Use models.

Use the models below to read and write fractions as decimals through thousandths.

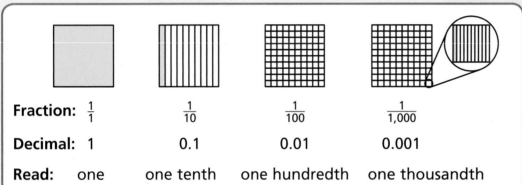

Fraction: $\frac{1}{1}$	$\frac{1}{10}$	$\frac{1}{100}$	$\frac{1}{1,000}$
Decimal: 1	0.1	0.01	0.001
Read: one	one tenth	one hundredth	one thousandth

The decimal, 0.316, has three decimal places.

Read: three hundred sixteen thousandths

Write: 0.316

• What pattern do you see in the decimal models for 0.1, 0.01, and 0.001?

ANOTHER WAY Use place value.

You can use a place-value chart to help you understand thousandths. Decimals, like whole numbers, can be written in standard form, word form, and expanded form.

Ones	.	Tenths	Hundredths	Thousandths		Standard Form	Word Form	Expanded Form
0	.	5	2	4		0.524	five hundred twenty-four thousandths	0.5 + 0.02 + 0.004
0	.	0	3	5		0.035	thirty-five thousandths	0.03 + 0.005
0	.	0	0	6		0.006	six thousandths	0.006

• What is the value of the digit 2 in 0.012?

1. How many thousandths are in one hundredth? How many thousandths are in one?

Write each decimal as a fraction.

2. 0.586   3. 0.425   4. 0.012   ✓5. 0.303   ✓6. 0.007

7. **TALK Math** Explain how the value of each digit 2 in the decimal 0.222 is related.

Independent Practice and Problem Solving

Write each decimal as a fraction.

8. 0.102   9. 0.078   10. 0.721   11. 0.606   12. 0.014

Write each fraction as a decimal.

13. $\frac{4}{1,000}$ 14. $\frac{61}{1,000}$ 15. $\frac{445}{1,000}$ 16. $\frac{312}{1,000}$ 17. $\frac{17}{1,000}$

Write the decimal in two other ways.

18. 0.621   19. 0.056   20. 0.013

21. 0.087   22. 0.03 + 0.005   23. 0.8 + 0.09 + 0.005

USE DATA For 24–25, use the table.

24. The length of which ant has the digit 5 in the thousandths place?

25. What is the length of the cornfield ant written as a fraction in simplest form?

26. Matt studied for his science test from 4:30 P.M. to 5:45 P.M. Then he studied again from 7:15 P.M. to 9:00 P.M. How many hours did he study altogether?

27. **WRITE Math** Explain how to change a fraction with a denominator of 1,000 to a decimal.

Ant Lengths	
Type of Ant	Length (in cm)
Carpenter	0.635
Thief	0.079
Cornfield	0.25
Pharaoh	0.159

Mixed Review and Test Prep

28. Find the missing number in the following number sentence. (p. 66)

    $(47 + 54) + 23 = \blacksquare + (54 + 47)$

29. Write the fraction $\frac{4}{100}$ in decimal form. (p. 458)

30. **Test Prep** Which decimal is equivalent to $\frac{18}{1,000}$?

    A 18   C 1.8

    B 0.18   D 0.018

3 Equivalent Decimals

OBJECTIVE: Find equivalent decimals.

Quick Review

Write each fraction as a decimal.

1. $\frac{4}{10}$ 2. $\frac{40}{100}$

3. $\frac{4}{100}$ 4. $\frac{60}{100}$

5. $\frac{6}{10}$

Vocabulary

equivalent decimals

Investigate

Materials ■ tenths and hundredths models

Equivalent decimals are decimals that name the same number.

Use tenths and hundredths models to find equivalent decimals.

Are 0.3 and 0.30 equivalent decimals?

A Shade 0.3 of the tenths model and 0.30 of the hundredths model.

0.3   0.30

B Fold the tenths model to show 0.3 and the hundredths model to show 0.30.

C Compare the folded parts of the models for both decimals. What can you conclude?

D Repeat the steps to find whether 0.5 and 0.60 are equivalent. What can you conclude?

Draw Conclusions

1. How do you write 0.3 and 0.30 as fractions?

2. How much did you fold in each of the models?

3. How can you tell when a tenths decimal and a hundredths decimal are equivalent?

4. **Application** Is 0.03 equivalent to 0.3? Explain.

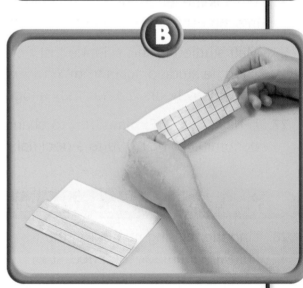

You can use money amounts to model tenths and hundredths.

Example 1

Draw a dime to model 1 tenth.

1 dime $= \frac{1}{10} = \frac{10}{100} = 0.10$ of $1.00

Draw dimes to model 10 tenths.

10 dimes $= \frac{10}{10} = \frac{100}{100} = \$1.00$

Example 2

Draw dimes to model 4 tenths.

4 dimes $= \frac{4}{10} = \frac{40}{100} = 0.40$ of $1.00

Draw pennies to model 4 tenths.

40 pennies $= \frac{40}{100} = 0.40$ of $1.00

TALK Math

How can you use pennies to show $0.60? How can you use dimes to show the same amount?

Practice

Use a tenths model and a hundredths model. Are the two decimals equivalent? Write = or ≠.

1. 0.4 and 0.44

2. 0.50 and 0.5

✓ 3. 0.71 and 0.17

4. 0.20 and 0.2

5. 0.60 and 0.06

6. 0.57 and 0.75

Write an equivalent decimal for each. You may use decimal models.

7. 0.4

8. 0.3

9. 0.70

✓ 10. 0.20

11. 0.90

12. 0.1

13. $\frac{1}{2}$

14. $\frac{1}{4}$

Algebra Write an equivalent decimal. Use the models to help.

15.

0.1 + 0.05 = ■

16.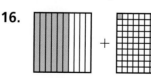

■ + ■ = 0.61

17. **WRITE Math** ▶ **Explain** why models can help you find if two decimals are equivalent.

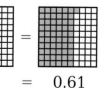

Technology
Use Harcourt Mega Math, Fraction Action, *Number Line Mine,* Levels P, Q.

4 Relate Mixed Numbers and Decimals

OBJECTIVE: Model, read, and write mixed numbers as decimals.

Quick Review

Marni bought 1.7 pounds of cheese. Write a fraction for the amount of cheese that Marni bought.

Learn

PROBLEM Many pocket-sized toy cars are about two and six tenths inches long. How can you write this length as a mixed number and as a decimal?

Activity 1 Use a model.

Materials ■ tenths models

Use models to write and read mixed numbers as decimals.

Shade the whole number and the fraction of the mixed number.

Mixed Number: $2\frac{6}{10}$

Decimal: 2.6

Read: two and six tenths

So, you can write the length as $2\frac{6}{10}$, or 2.6, inches.

Examples

A Write and read the value of the model as a mixed number and as a decimal.

Mixed Number: $1\frac{27}{100}$

Decimal: 1.27

Read: one and twenty-seven hundredths

B Write and read the value of the model as a mixed number and as a decimal.

Mixed Number: $2\frac{4}{100}$

Decimal: 2.04

Read: two and four hundredths

• What model other than the one used in Activity 1 could you use to show 2.6?

Activity 2 Use a number line.

Materials ■ number line

Find the decimal equivalent for $1\frac{25}{100}$.

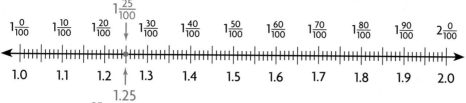

First, locate $1\frac{25}{100}$ on the number line.

Next, name the decimal that names this point.

Locate and label three other points on your number line.

Name the decimal and the mixed number that names each point.

Example 1 Use place value.

Decimals, like whole numbers, can be written in standard form, word form, and expanded form.

Ones	.	Tenths	Hundredths	Thousandths
2	.	7		
3	.	6	5	
5	.	0	0	2

Standard Form	Word Form	Expanded Form
2.7	two and seven tenths	$2 + 0.7$
3.65	three and sixty-five hundreths	$3 + 0.6 + 0.05$
5.002	five and two thousandths	$5 + 0.002$

Example 2 Use models to show mixed numbers and decimals that are equivalent.

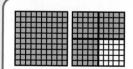 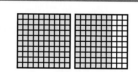 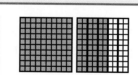

$1.75 = 1\frac{75}{100} = 1\frac{3}{4} = \frac{7}{4}$ | $1.70 = 1\frac{70}{100} = 1\frac{7}{10} = \frac{17}{10}$ | $1.60 = 1\frac{60}{100} = 1\frac{6}{10} = 1\frac{3}{5}$

Guided Practice

1. Look at the model at the right. What whole number part is modeled? What fraction is modeled? Write the mixed number as a decimal.

Write an equivalent mixed number and a decimal for each model.

2.

 3.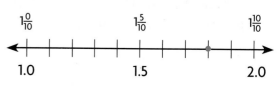

Write an equivalent mixed number or a decimal for each.
Then write the word form. You may use a model.

4. $1\frac{8}{10}$ **5.** 3.1 **6.** $1\frac{57}{100}$ **7.** 4.05 **8.** $2\frac{3}{4}$

9. [TALK Math] **Explain** how a decimal equivalent for a mixed number is like a decimal equivalent for a fraction and how it is different.

Independent Practice and Problem Solving

Write an equivalent mixed number and a decimal for each model.

10.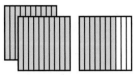

11.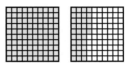

12.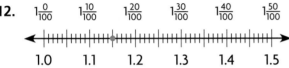
$1\frac{0}{100}$ $1\frac{10}{100}$ $1\frac{20}{100}$ $1\frac{30}{100}$ $1\frac{40}{100}$ $1\frac{50}{100}$

1.0   1.1   1.2   1.3   1.4   1.5

13.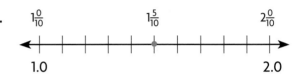
$1\frac{0}{10}$ $1\frac{5}{10}$ $2\frac{0}{10}$

1.0   2.0

Write an equivalent mixed number or a decimal for each.
Then write the word form. You may use a model.

14. 2.3 **15.** $7\frac{1}{2}$ **16.** 3.45 **17.** $3\frac{3}{4}$ **18.** 4.01

Algebra Write the missing number for each ▪.

19. $7.16 = 7 + ▪ + 0.06$ **20.** $1.58 = 1 + 0.5 + ▪$ **21.** $4.02 = ▪ + 0.02$

22. Nate is thinking of some decimals between 1 and 2. What might they be? Give at least 15 answers.

23. Reasoning Sense or Nonsense Tara said her temperature was 10.15 when she was sick. Does this make sense? **Explain.**

24. ≡**FAST FACT** The smallest camera is only 1.65 centimeters thick. Write this measure as a mixed number.

25. [WRITE Math] ▸ **What's the Question?** The answer is one and six hundredths.

Mixed Review and Test Prep

26. Mark's bedroom is a square. If it is 12 feet long, what is the perimeter of the bedroom? (Grade 3)

27. In simplest form, what is an equivalent fraction for the decimal 0.50? (p. 464)

28. Test Prep Which mixed number is equivalent to 2.05?

A $2\frac{1}{5}$ **C** $2\frac{5}{100}$

B $2\frac{5}{10}$ **D** $2\frac{1}{500}$

  (Extra Practice on page 476, Set C)

CD ROM **Technology**
Use Harcourt Mega Math, Fraction Action, *Fraction Flare Up*, Level N.

Tiny Robots

Reading Skill **Identify the Details**

When you think of robots, you usually think of those metal robots you see in the movies. But there is a very small robot, the world's smallest robot, called Monsieur Microbot. It is less than 1 centimeter tall, has a mass of 1.5 grams, and is made up of about 97 watch parts. What mixed number can you write for the mass of this robot?

In order to solve this problem, you must identify the details. Then choose only the details you need to answer the question.

▲ This light-sensitive robot was built in Japan in 1992.

Make a list of the details you are given in the problem.	smallest robot in the world a mass of 1.5 grams 97 watch parts
↓	
Think about what you are asked to find.	Write a mixed number for the mass of the robot.
↓	
Choose the details you need to solve the problem.	Write a mixed number for 1.5 grams.

Problem Solving **Identify the details to understand the problem.**

1. Solve the problem above.

2. The world's smallest submarine is 2.95 meters long, 1.14 meters wide, and 1.42 meters high. What mixed number can you write for the length of this submarine?

LESSON 5
Compare and Order Decimals

OBJECTIVE: Compare and order decimals.

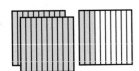
Learn

PROBLEM Grant Elementary School had a track and field day in May. In the long jump competition, Rachel jumped 2.3 meters. Tamara jumped 2.6 meters. Who jumped farther?

Use models, number lines, or place value to compare and order decimals.

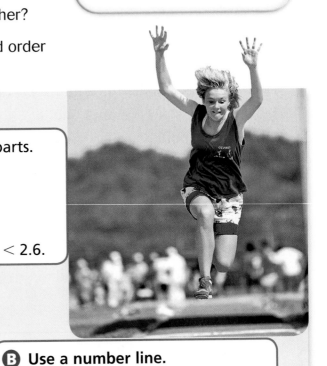

 Use models.

Model 2.3 and 2.6. Compare the number of shaded parts.

Since the model for 2.3 has 3 fewer shaded parts, 2.3 < 2.6.

So, Tamara jumped farther.

 **OTHER WAYS**

A Use money.

Compare $0.10 and $0.04.

$0.10 = 0.1 of a dollar $0.04 = 0.04 of a dollar

So, 0.1 > 0.04.

B Use a number line.

Compare 1.23 and 1.15.

```
1.15 ⌐        ⌐ 1.23
◄─┼┼┼┼┼┼┼┼┼┼┼┼┼┼┼┼┼┼┼┼┼┼┼┼┼┼►
 1.0  1.1  1.2  1.3  1.4  1.5
```

Since 1.23 is to the right of 1.15, 1.23 is greater than 1.15.

So, 1.23 > 1.15.

C Use place value.

Compare 8.05 and 8.1.

Think: 8.1 and 8.10 are equivalent decimals. Line up the decimal points. Compare digits beginning with the greatest place value.

Ones	.	Tenths	Hundredths
8	.	0	5
8	.	1	0

8 = 8   0 < 1   5 > 0

Since 0 < 1, 8.05 < 8.1.

So, 8.05 < 8.1.

470

Order Decimals

ONE WAY Use a number line.

Order $6.50, $6.32, and $6.75 from greatest to least.

Locate each decimal on the number line

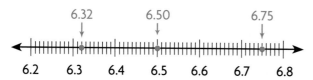

6.32   6.50   6.75

6.2   6.3   6.4   6.5   6.6   6.7   6.8

Think: The decimal farthest to the right is the greatest. The decimal farthest to the left is the least.

ERROR ALERT

Remember to compare digits with the same place value. Begin comparing digits in the greatest place-value position.

So, the order from greatest to least is $6.75, $6.50, $6.32.

ANOTHER WAY Use place value.

Order 71.52, 70.097, and 71.59 from least to greatest.

Step 1	Step 2	Step 3	Step 4
Line up the decimal points. **Think:** Compare the digits in the greatest place. 71.52 ↓ 70.097 7 = 7 ↓ 71.59 There are the same number of tens.	Then compare the ones. 71.52 ↓ 70.097 0 < 1 ↓ 71.59 Since 0 < 1, 70.097 is the least.	Compare the tenths. 71.52 ↓ 5 = 5 71.59 There are the same number of tenths.	Compare the hundredths. 71.52 ↓ 2 < 9 71.59 So, the order from least to greatest is 70.097, 71.52, 71.59.

• How would you change the order to show the decimals from greatest to least?

Guided Practice

1. Compare these decimal models. Write your answer using < or >.

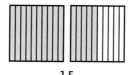

1.5   1.65

Compare. Write <, >, or = for each ●.

2. $0.70 ● $0.75   3. 0.40 ● 0.4   4. 1.3 ● 2   5. 2.20 ● 2.015   ✓ 6. $1.64 ● $1.46

 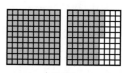

Use the number line to order the decimals from least to greatest.

2.0 2.1 2.2 2.3 2.4 2.5 2.6 2.7 2.8 2.9 3.0

7. 2.11, 2.2, 2.01, 2.1   **8.** 2.32, 2.23, 2.3, 2.2   ✓**9.** $2.90, $2.09, $2.50, $2.55

10. **TALK Math** Explain two different methods you can use to compare and order decimals.

Independent Practice and Problem Solving

Compare. Write <, >, or = for each ●.

11. 2.3 ● 2   **12.** 0.9 ● 0.90   **13.** $0.50 ● $1.05   **14.** 53.20 ● 53.18

15. $2.14 ● $2.41   **16.** 0.047 ● 0.740   **17.** 1.20 ● 1.198   **18.** 93.45 ● 92.85

Use the number line above to order the decimals from least to greatest.

19. 2.31, 2.3, 2.03, 2.13   **20.** 2.8, 2.09, 2.5, 2.55   **21.** $2.40, $2.04, $2.38, $2.44

22. 2.79, 2.7, 2.07, 2.9   **23.** 2.6, 2.61, 2.06, 2.16   **24.** $2.15, $2.50, $3.00, $2.25

Order the decimals from greatest to least.

25. $31.41, $34.14, $31.14   **26.** 7.03, 7.3, 6.98, 6.89   **27.** $42.15, $41.89, $41.09

28. 1.247, 0.968, 1.044, 0.096   **29.** 5.5, 5.55, 5.005, 5.015   **30.** $0.95, $0.80, $1.00, $1.95

Algebra **Tell whether each number sentence is** *true* **or** *false.*
If the number sentence is false, write the correct number sentence.

31. 5.3 < 5.30   **32.** 20.085 > 20.009   **33.** $1.65 < $1.06   **34.** 89.08 < 89.111

USE DATA For 35–38, use the table.

35. Who swam the fastest? Who swam the slowest?

36. List the top three swimmer's times in order from fastest to slowest.

37. What is Nadine Smara's time written as a mixed number?

38. **Pose a Problem** Write a problem involving comparing or ordering decimals using the data in the table.

39. Order the following numbers from least to greatest: 2.4, $1\frac{1}{2}$, 1.05, $2\frac{9}{100}$.

2005 AAU Junior Olympics 50-Meter Girls 10 & Under Freestyle Results	
Swimmer	**Final Time (in sec)**
Trey Ross	32.52
Nadine Smara	33.43
Danielle Dugas	32.08
Gabrielle Westcamp	33.59

Extra Practice on page 476, Set D

40. Which of the following numbers has the same value as the digit 2 in the number 146.27?

20, 2, 0.2, 0.02

41. Reasoning List all of the possible digits that make the statement true.

$2.57 < 2.\blacksquare8 < 2.89$

42. Three girls jumped the following distances in the long jump: 2.6 meters, 2.65 meters, 2.58 meters. Lara's distance is less than Alli's and Alli's is greater than Kate's. How far did each girl jump?

43. **WRITE Math** ▸ **What's the Error?** Erin says that $4.5 < 4.49$ because the last digit in 4.5 is less than the last digit in 4.49. Describe her error. Find the correct answer.

Mixed Review and Test Prep

44. Copy and complete the Venn diagram. Write the numbers 3, 5, 2, 13, and 9 in the appropriate section. (p.190)

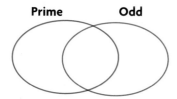

Prime   Odd

45. Peter ran a 50-yard dash in 5.65 seconds. How can you write this time as a mixed number? (p. 466)

46. **Test Prep** Which number sentence is correct?

A $3.5 > 3.09$

B $12.008 > 12.2$

C $6.3 = 6.03$

D $4.704 < 4.09$

47. **Test Prep** Order the decimals from least to greatest.

4.5, 4.75, 4.058, 4.15

Problem Solving connects to Science

The line graph shows the average monthly rainfall in International Falls, Minnesota, from January to May.

1. Which months have an average rainfall that is greater than 0.6 inch and less than 0.9 inch?

2. If you list the inches of average rainfall for each of the months in order from greatest to least, which amount is second on the list? Which month has this amount of rainfall?

3. In which months is the average rainfall greater than 0.8 inch?

Average Monthly Rainfall in International Falls, MN

Problem Solving Workshop
Skill: Draw Conclusions

OBJECTIVE: Solve problems by using the skill *draw conclusions*.

Read to Understand
Plan
Solve
Check

Use the Skill

PROBLEM The newspaper ads show the cost of basketball trading cards at three different sporting goods stores. Which store has the lowest price for a box of cards?

You can draw conclusions to help you solve the problem. To draw conclusions, combine the facts from the problem with what you know from your own experience.

Facts from the Problem	What You Know
Angelo's Sports: $6.95 per box Sports Palace: $6.59 per box Town Sports: $5.95 per box	• Bills and coins can be used to model decimals. • You can order decimals by comparing the place value of each digit, beginning with the greatest place value. • The best price is the lowest price.

To draw a conclusion about the lowest price, use models and place value to order the money amounts. Then choose the lowest price.

Materials ▪ play money

Ones	.	Tenths	Hundredths
6	.	9	5
6	.	5	9
5	.	9	5

Order of prices from least to greatest: $5.95, $6.59, $6.95.
So, Town Sports has the lowest price for a box of cards.

Angelo's Sports
Hottest new basketball stars **$6.95** per box of cards

TOWN SPORTS
Basketball trading cards
$5.95 per box of cards

SPORTS PALACE
The basketball players you want.
1 box of cards **$6.59**

Think and Discuss

Tell which facts from the problem and what information you know can be used to draw conclusions. Solve the problem.

a. Ted can run a mile in 7.25 minutes. Rick runs it in 7.05 minutes, and Leroy runs it in 7.5 minutes. Who can run the fastest mile?

b. A store sells 3 types of gym bags. One costs $13.98, another sells for $13.89, and the other costs $13.90. Which bag costs the most?

Guided Problem Solving

1. The ads to the right show the price of a new best-selling book at three different bookstores. Which bookstore has the best price for the book?

   Copy and complete the chart.

Facts from the Problem	What You Know
Bob's Bookstore: ■	• __?__ can be used to model decimals.
Books Are Us: ■	• You can order decimals by __?__.
Books on Broadway: ■	• The best price is the __?__ price.

   How can you use the information in the chart to draw a conclusion?

2. **What if** Open Page Bookstore sells the same book for $19.80? Then which store has the best price?

3. Megan lives 2.4 miles from Bob's Bookstore. Josh lives 2.15 miles away, and Sam lives 2.09 miles away. Who lives closest to Bob's Bookstore?

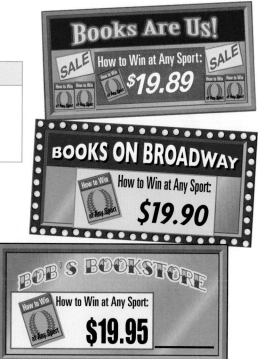

Mixed Applications

USE DATA For 4–5, use the map.

4. Who walks farther to school, Morgan or Dan? **Explain.**

5. Greg lives 2.8 miles from the mall. Warren lives 2.54 miles from the mall. Use the map and this information to list the four students in order from nearest to farthest distance from the mall.

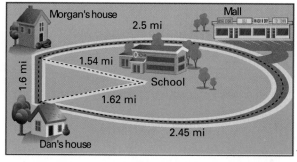

6. A basketball jersey at a sporting goods store costs $45. Sharif paid for the jersey with three $20 bills. How much change did he get back? Do you need an estimate or an exact answer?

7. The school needs 150 boxes of juice to give to the students going to the baseball game. If the juice comes in packages of 4 boxes, how many packages must the school buy?

8. **WRITE Math** ▸ Ezra jogged 125 miles in 3 weeks of training. He jogged 32 miles during the first week and 39 miles during the second week. **Explain** how to choose the more reasonable answer for the number of miles he jogged during the third week: 54 miles or 34 miles.

9. Hannah ran the 50-yard dash in 8.23 seconds. Tarika ran the dash in 7.95 seconds, and Rita ran the dash in 8.2 seconds. Who ran the dash the fastest?

Extra Practice

Set A Write the fraction and decimal shown by each model (pp. 458–461)

1.

2.

3.
$$\frac{0}{10} \qquad \frac{5}{10} \qquad \frac{10}{10}$$

0   0.5   1

Write each fraction as a decimal. You may draw a picture.

4. $\frac{9}{10}$ **5.** $\frac{17}{100}$ **6.** $\frac{7}{10}$ **7.** $\frac{5}{100}$ **8.** $\frac{14}{100}$

Write the amount as a fraction of a dollar, a decimal, and a money amount.

9. 3 quarters   **10.** 2 dimes, 2 pennies   **11.** 1 quarter, 1 nickel

Set B Write each decimal as a fraction (pp. 462–463)

1. 0.236   **2.** 0.689   **3.** 0.404   **4.** 0.001   **5.** 0.049

Write each fraction as a decimal. (pp. 462–463)

6. $\frac{7}{1,000}$ **7.** $\frac{377}{1,000}$ **8.** $\frac{27}{1,000}$ **9.** $\frac{37}{1,000}$ **10.** $\frac{352}{1,000}$

Set C Write an equivalent mixed number and a decimal for each model. (pp. 466–469)

1.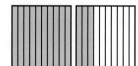

2.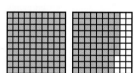

3.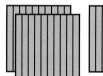

Write an equivalent mixed number or a decimal for each. Then write the word form. You may use a model.

4. $2\frac{9}{10}$ **5.** 3.17   **6.** $4\frac{9}{100}$ **7.** $3\frac{1}{10}$ **8.** 6.5

9. Morris runs 2.25 miles each day. Write the distance as a mixed number.

Set D Compare. Write <, >, or = for each ●. (pp. 470–473)

1. 2.05 ● 2.5   **2.** $65.99 ● $66.00   **3.** 3.4 ● 3.40   **4.** 7.01 ● 7.001

Order the decimals from least to greatest.

5. $2.53, $3.25, $2.35, $2.50   **6.** 18.6, 18.06, 17.98, 19.87   **7.** 3.3, 3.33, 3.003, 3.031

8. A paper wasp is 0.5 inch long, a bald-faced hornet is 0.75 inch long, and a yellow jacket is 0.625 inch long. Order the lengths of the insects from greatest to least.

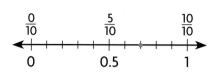

Technology
Use Harcourt Mega Math, Fraction Action, *Number Line Mine*, Levels P, Q, R.

ORDER, PLEASE!

Get Ready!
2 or 3 players and a dealer

Get Set!
Set of index cards with these decimal numbers: 0.1–0.9, 0.15–0.25, 0.01–0.09

Play the Game!

- The object of the game is to have 5 decimal cards in order from least to greatest.

- The dealer shuffles the cards and places 5 cards faceup in front of each player and places the remaining cards facedown in a stack. The cards should remain in this order throughout the game.

- At each turn, a player chooses one card to replace, and places it in the discard stack. The dealer gives the player a new card from the top of the stack to be placed in the same spot as the card that was just given to the dealer.

- A player who thinks all 5 of his or her cards are in order from least to greatest calls out "Order!"

- If the cards are in order, that player wins.

- When all the cards in the stack have been used, the dealer shuffles the cards in the discard stack, places them facedown, and starts a new stack.

- Whoever loses becomes the dealer for the next round.

An Apple a Day

The Produce Place sold 100 apples, bananas, and peaches. One-half of the fruit sold was apples. What percent is this of the total fruit sold?

Percent (%) means "per hundred." You can write a percent as a fraction and as a decimal.

$100\% = \frac{100}{100}$, or $\frac{1}{1} = 1$ $50\% = \frac{50}{100}$, or $\frac{1}{2} = 0.50$ $25\% = \frac{25}{100}$, or $\frac{1}{4} = 0.25$

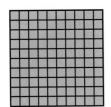   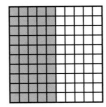   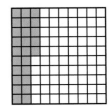

Think: 100 out of 100 squares are shaded.   **Think:** 50 out of 100 squares are shaded.   **Think:** 25 out of 100 squares are shaded.

So, 50% of the fruit sold was apples.

You also can find the percent of a number.

Examples

A **Find 25% of 24 oranges.**

Think: $25\% = \frac{25}{100} = \frac{1}{4}$

So, 25% of 24 is $\frac{1}{4}$ of 24.

Divide 24 into 4 equal groups.

Circle $\frac{1}{4}$ of them.

So, 25% of 24 oranges is 6 oranges.

B **Find 40% of 20 watermelons.**

Think: $40\% = \frac{40}{100} = \frac{4}{10} = \frac{2}{5}$

So, 40% of 20 is $\frac{2}{5}$ of 20.

Divide 20 into 5 equal groups.

Circle $\frac{2}{5}$ of them.

So, 40% of 20 watermelons is 8 watermelons.

Try It

Find the percent of each number. You may wish to draw a model.

1. 50% of 20 eggplants

2. 25% of 36 onions

3. 20% of 40 peppers

4. 100% of 60 tomatoes

5. **WRITE Math** ▸ **Explain** how you can use a hundredths model to show the decimal and percent equivalents of $\frac{38}{100}$.

Chapter 17 Review/Test

Check Vocabulary and Concepts

Choose the best term from the box.

1. The _?_ separates the ones place and the tenths place. (p. 462)

2. One hundredth can be broken into ten equal parts. These ten equal parts are called _?_. (p. 462)

Check Skills

Write each fraction or mixed number as a decimal. You may draw a picure. (pp. 462–463, 466–469)

3. $\frac{9}{10}$

4. $\frac{17}{100}$

5. $\frac{9}{100}$

6. $\frac{124}{1,000}$

7. $\frac{37}{1,000}$

8. $5\frac{6}{10}$

9. $3\frac{5}{100}$

10. $6\frac{1}{1,000}$

11. $2\frac{81}{1,000}$

12. $9\frac{31}{100}$

Write the amount as a fraction of a dollar, as a decimal, and as a money amount. (pp. 462–463)

13. 1 dime

14. 1 quarter, 1 dime

15. 2 pennies

16. 4 dimes, 1 penny

Write an equivalent decimal for each. You may use decimal models. (pp. 464–465)

17. 0.9

18. 0.20

19. $\frac{1}{4}$

20. $\frac{1}{2}$

Compare. Write <, >, or = for each ●. (pp. 464–465, pp. 470–473)

21. 4.6 ● 4.06

22. $73.70 ● $74.00

23. 4.40 ● 4.4

24. 56.8 ● 56.08

Order the decimals from greatest to least. (pp. 470–473)

25. 8.06, 8.4, 7.89, 8.89

26. 1.35, 0.89, 1.05, 0.09

27. $4.20, $4.16, $4.41

28. $90.78, $97.08, $98.70

29. 15.24, 14.25, 15.44

30. 30.16, 36.01, 31.61

Check Problem Solving

Solve. (pp. 474–475)

31. Kate swam the 50-meter freestyle race in 30.05 seconds. Which of the girls listed in the table beat Kate in the race?

32. Of the results listed in the table, who swam the fastest?

33. **WRITE Math** ▶ If Kate and the four girls listed in the table were the only ones in the race, who came in fifth place? **Explain** how you know.

50–Meter Freestyle Results	
Swimmer	**Time (in seconds)**
Larisa	31.02
Michelle	30.2
Sara	30.52
Rebecca	30.01

GO ONLINE Technology Use *Online Assessment.*

Standardized Test Prep
Chapters 1–17

Number and Operations

1. Which of the following does **NOT** show equivalent amounts? (p. 458)

   A 0.75 and $\frac{3}{4}$

   B 0.6 and $\frac{3}{5}$

   C 0.3 and $\frac{3}{10}$

   D 0.08 and $\frac{8}{10}$

2. On the number line below, what number does point *P* represent? (p. 414)

   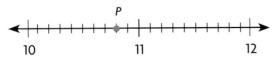

   A $10\frac{2}{10}$

   B $10\frac{8}{10}$

   C $11\frac{2}{10}$

   D $11\frac{8}{10}$

3. What decimal is represented in expanded form below? (p. 462)

   $$0.3 + 0.08 + 0.005$$

   A 0.583

   B 0.538

   C 0.385

   D 0.358

4. **WRITE Math** ▸ Use $<$, $>$, or $=$ to compare.

   $$0.65 \bullet \frac{3}{4}$$

   Explain how you know. (p. 470)

Measurement

5. Stephen practiced his guitar for $3\frac{1}{2}$ hours. For how many minutes did he practice? (p. 160)

   A 210 minutes

   B 240 minutes

   C 300 minutes

   D 360 minutes

 Test Tip **Check your work.**

See Item 6. Do you know the number of days in 2 weeks? You can use addition to check your answer.

6. Sonja is going on a two-week vacation. She leaves home on July 5. On what date will Sonja return?

   (p. 158)

July						
Sun	Mon	Tue	Wed	Thu	Fri	Sat
		1	2	3	4	5
6	7	8	9	10	11	12
13	14	15	16	17	18	19
20	21	22	23	24	25	26
27	28	29	30	31		

   A July 19

   B July 21

   C July 24

   D July 26

7. **WRITE Math** ▸ A loaf of bread has 32 slices. Each slice weighs 1 ounce. How many pounds does the loaf weigh? **Explain** your answer. (Grade 3)

Algebraic Reasoning

8. Which of the following is a composite number? (p. 378)

  A 5

  B 11

  C 15

  D 17

9. Nan bought 4 books at the book fair. She spent $48. Each book cost the same amount. Let c represent the cost of each book. Which equation below can be used to find the cost of each book. (p. 128)

  A $48 - c = 4$

  B $4 \times c = 48$

  C $c \div 4 = 48$

  D $4 \times 48 = c$

10. What might the next 3 numbers in the pattern be? (p. 382)

$$23, 28, 33, 38$$

  A 43, 53, 63

  B 43, 53, 58

  C 48, 53, 55

  D 43, 48, 53

11. **WRITE Math** ▶ Find the value of each expression. Are the values the same? **Explain** why or why not. (p. 126)

$$(4 + 9) \times 2 - 15$$
$$4 + 9 \times 2 - 15$$

Geometry

12. A basketball is the shape of which of these solid figures? (Grade 3)

  A Cone

  B Cylinder

  C Sphere

  D Rectangular prism

13. Which figure is **NOT** a quadrilateral? (Grade 3)

A   **C**

B   **D**

14. In which figure is the blue line a line of symmetry? (Grade 3)

A    **C**

B   **D**

15. **WRITE Math** ▶ Mitch drew an obtuse scalene triangle. **Describe** what you know about the sides and angles of his triangle. (Grade 3)

18 Add and Subtract Decimals and Money

Investigate

After visiting the zoo, you stop at the gift shop. Suppose you have $20.00 to spend. What is the greatest number of different items you can buy without going over your budget? How much money will you have left?

GIFT SHOP

Animal Puzzle	$ 8.25
Small Stuffed Zebra	$ 5.00
Medium Stuffed Zebra	$ 9.00
Large Stuffed Zebra	$13.25
Stuffed Frog	$10.75
Zoo Pen	$ 2.50
Animal Calendar	$11.95
T-shirt	$ 9.99
Pencil Case	$ 3.50

FAST FACT

More than 20,000 local people helped build the Brevard Zoo in Melbourne, Florida, in 1992. The zoo now has more than 550 animals from 156 different species.

GO ONLINE

Technology
Student pages are available in the student eBook.

Show What You Know

Check your understanding of important skills
needed for success in Chapter 18.

▶ **Count Bills and Coins**

Write the amount.

1.

2.

3.

▶ **Model Decimals**

Write the decimal for the shaded part.

4. [grid model]   5. [grid model]   6. [grid model]

7. [grid model]   8. [grid model]   9. [grid model]

▶ **Decimal Place Value**

Write the value of the underlined digit in each decimal.

10. 0.2<u>3</u>   11. 0.<u>5</u>7   12. 0.1<u>4</u>   13. 0.6<u>3</u>

14. 0.3<u>8</u>   15. 0.<u>9</u>4   16. 0.<u>4</u>6   17. 0.8<u>7</u>

VOCABULARY POWER

CHAPTER VOCABULARY

decimal
decimal point
digit
estimate
hundredth
round
tenth
thousandth

WARM-UP WORDS

decimal a number with one or more digits to the right of the decimal point

digit any one of the ten symbols 0, 1, 2, 3, 4, 5, 6, 7, 8, or 9 used to write numbers

round to replace a number with another number that tells about how many or how much

Round Decimals

OBJECTIVE: Round decimals.

Learn

PROBLEM The amount of wool cut from one sheep is called a fleece. In the United States the average weight of one fleece is 8.2 pounds. What is this weight to the nearest pound?

ONE WAY Use a number line.

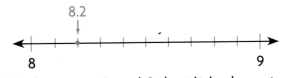

8.2 is between 8 and 9, but it is closer to 8.

So, the weight of a fleece to the nearest pound is 8 pounds.

ANOTHER WAY Use place value.

A **Round to the nearest whole number.**

32.89

Look at the tenths place.
Since 8 > 5, the digit 2 increases by 1.

So, 32.89 rounded to the nearest whole number is 33.

B **Round to the nearest tenth.**

6.73

Look at the hundredths place.
Since 3 < 5, the digit 7 stays the same.

So, 6.73 rounded to the nearest tenth is 6.7.

C **Round to the nearest dollar.**

$23.49

Look at the tenths place.
Since 4 < 5, the digit 3 stays the same.

So, $23.49 rounded to the nearest dollar is $23.

D **Round to the nearest hundredth.**

12.065

Look at the thousandths place.
Since 5 = 5, the digit 6 increases by 1.

So, 12.065 rounded to the nearest hundredth is 12.07.

Remember
To round a number you can:
- Find the place to which you want to round.
- Look at the digit to its right.
- If that digit is less than 5, the digit in the rounding place stays the same.
- If that digit is 5 or greater, the digit in the rounding place increases by 1.

- **What if** you round 32.89 in Example 1 to the nearest tenth? Explain how you would round 32.89 to the nearest tenth.

Guided Practice

1. In which numbers is the digit in the tenths place 5 or greater? Which numbers will round to 15 when rounded to the nearest whole number?

   14.9 15.23
   15.5 14.498

Round each number to the nearest tenth and each money amount to the nearest dollar.

2. 45.67 3. 8.23 4. $19.35 ✓5. 5.55 ✓6. $48.92

7. **TALK Math** Explain how to use a number line to round 7.33 to the nearest tenth.

Independent Practice and Problem Solving

Round each number to the nearest tenth and each money amount to the nearest dollar.

8. 4.56 9. 5.87 10. 12.97 11. 123.08 12. 645.55

13. $3.57 14. $9.98 15. $32.12 16. $87.55 17. $123.68

Round each number to the nearest hundredth.

18. 6.789 19. 5.246 20. 15.801 21. 32.719 22. 57.899

USE DATA For 23–24, use the map.

23. For each state shown, round the weight per fleece to the nearest whole number. Then make a bar graph for the data.

24. Order the states shown according to the lightest weight per fleece to the heaviest.

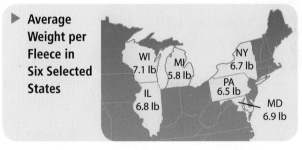

▶ Average Weight per Fleece in Six Selected States

WI 7.1 lb
MI 5.8 lb
NY 6.7 lb
PA 6.5 lb
IL 6.8 lb
MD 6.9 lb

25. **Reasoning** For what digits will 3.9■ rounded to the nearest tenth be 4.0? **Explain.**

26. **WRITE Math** ▶ What's the Question? A skein of wool, or wool wrapped in a loose coil, costs $3.75. The answer is $4.

Mixed Review and Test Prep

27. Nine students are sorting 72 books into equal piles. Write and solve a multiplication equation to find the number of piles. (p. 128)

28. Tara is 60.5 inches tall. Jeremy is 60.71 inches tall. Who is taller? (p. 470)

29. **Test Prep** Jack drove 25.68 miles to work. Which shows the distance he drove rounded to the nearest tenth?

   A 25.6 miles   **C** 26 miles

   B 25.7 miles   **D** 26.7 miles

Extra Practice on page 500, Set A

Estimate Decimal Sums and Differences

OBJECTIVE: Estimate decimal sums and differences.

Learn

PROBLEM A record-breaking 26.9 inches of snow fell in New York City on February 12, 2006. On the same day in Boston, Massachusetts, 17.5 inches of snow fell. How much more snow fell in New York City?

You can use a variety of estimation strategies to estimate sums and differences of decimals.

ONE WAY Use front-end estimation.

Estimate. 26.9 − 17.5

26.9	Subtract the front digits of each number.
−17.5	Write zeros for the other digits.
10.0	

So, about 10 more inches of snow fell in New York City.

ANOTHER WAY Use rounding.

▲ A commuter jumps over a pile of snow the day after the 2006 storm in New York City.

A **Estimate.** 1.79 + 1.36

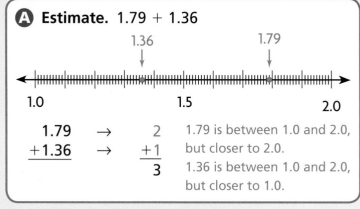

1.79	→	2	1.79 is between 1.0 and 2.0, but closer to 2.0.
+1.36	→	+1	1.36 is between 1.0 and 2.0, but closer to 1.0.
		3	

B **Estimate.** 42.6 + 57.3 + 28.0

42.6	→	40	Line up the decimal points.
57.3	→	60	
+28.0	→	+30	Round to the nearest ten.
		130	

So, 42.6 + 57.3 + 28.0 is about 130.

So, 1.79 + 1.36 is about 3.

• Can front-end estimation and rounding give you the same estimate? Explain and give an example.

Guided Practice

1. Round each addend to the nearest whole number. Add both rounded numbers. What is the estimated sum?

$$34.56 \rightarrow 3\blacksquare$$
$$+25.19 \rightarrow 2\blacksquare$$
$$\blacksquare\blacksquare$$

Estimate the sum or difference.

2. $48.781 - 23.928$ **3.** $6.9 + 5.8$ **4.** $\$91.24 - \$39.87$ **5.** $4.0 + 8.9 + 1.4$

6. **TALK Math** Explain how you can tell if 127.79 is a reasonable answer for $29.38 + 98.41$.

Independent Practice and Problem Solving

Estimate the sum or difference.

7. $3.8 - 2.5$ **8.** $5.68 - 2.19$ **9.** $\$72.94 + \$49.57$ **10.** $8.92 + 6.58$

11. $65.543 + 32.098$ **12.** $\$56.18 - \$12.83$ **13.** $12.6 + 32.8 + 49.5$ **14.** $65.126 - 21.781$

Estimate to compare. Write $<$, $>$, or $=$ for each ●.

15. $56.12 - 14.78$ ● $17.03 + 13.98$ **16.** $45.89 + 42.70$ ● $87.01 - 10.90$

17. $10.741 - 6.003$ ● $13.75 - 7.55$ **18.** $41.63 + 34.20$ ● $86.10 - 9.07$

USE DATA For 19–20, use the table.

19. About how much more does it snow during the first two months of winter in Buffalo than during the last two months of winter?

20. The average snowfall in Buffalo for April is 3.2 inches. About how much less is this than the average snowfall in March?

21. **WRITE Math** Explain how to find if a total of 46.2 inches of snow is reasonable for the following months: Month 1, 8.5 inches; Month 2, 15.4 inches; Month 3, 22.3 inches.

Average Snowfall Buffalo, New York

Month	Snowfall (in inches)
December	24.3
January	24.0
February	17.7
March	12.5

Mixed Review and Test Prep

22. Jan leaves her house for school at 7:45 A.M. School starts 45 minutes later. What time does school start? (p. 154)

23. A new sweater costs $28.99. How much is this rounded to the nearest dollar?
(p. 484)

24. **Test Prep** The Peters family drove 78.75 miles on their vacation on Monday and 59.25 miles on Tuesday. About how many more miles did they drive on Monday than on Tuesday? **Explain.**

Extra Practice on page 500, Set B

3 Model Addition

OBJECTIVE: Model addition of decimals.

Investigate

Materials ■ decimal models ■ color pencils

Use decimal models to find 0.34 + 0.66.

A Shade 34 squares on a decimal model red to represent 0.34.

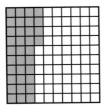

B Shade 66 squares on the same decimal model blue to represent 0.66.

C Make three more models with addends whose sum is 1.00.

Draw Conclusions

1. What is the sum of 0.34 and 0.66?

2. How did the decimal models help you find the sum?

3. What are two decimals you could add by using tenths models?

4. **Synthesis** If you add two decimals that are both less than 0.5, will the sum be less than or greater than 1.0?

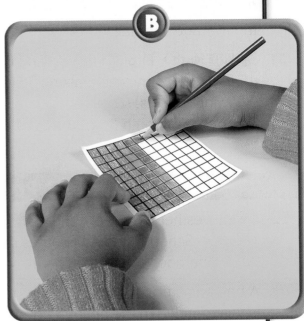

You can draw a picture to help you add decimals.

Add. 0.5 + 0.8

Step 1

Shade 5 columns red.

Step 2

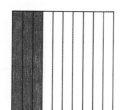

Shade 8 columns blue.
Count the total number
of columns shaded.

So, 0.5 + 0.8 = 1.3.

TALK Math

How would you model
the sum of 1.42 and 0.36?

Practice

Use models to find the sum.

1. 0.45
   +0.89

2. 0.9
   +0.7

3. 0.92
   +0.47

✓ 4. 1.6
   +1.0

5. 3.71 + 0.54

6. 1.05 + 0.98

7. 2.75 + 0.84

✓ 8. 2.3 + 0.59

Algebra Use the models to find the missing addend.

9.

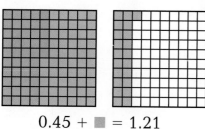

0.45 + ■ = 1.21

10.

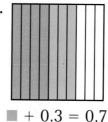

■ + 0.3 = 0.7

11. **WRITE Math** Summarize how you can use
decimal models to find the sum of any two decimals.

Technology
Use Harcourt Mega Math, Fraction Action,
Number Line Mine, Levels P, Q.

4 Model Subtraction

OBJECTIVE: Model subtraction of decimals.

Investigate

Materials ■ decimal models ■ color pencils

Use decimal models to find 0.8 − 0.5.

A Shade 8 columns on a decimal model red to represent 0.8.

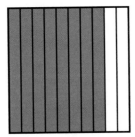

B Cut out 5 shaded columns from the shaded model.

C Make three models to show subtracting a decimal from 1.0.

D Use decimal models to find 0.81 − 0.46.

Draw Conclusions

1. What is the difference between 0.8 and 0.5?

2. How did the decimal model help you find the difference?

3. What are two decimals you could find the difference between by using tenth models?

4. **Synthesis** If two decimals are both less than 1.0, what can you say about the difference between them?

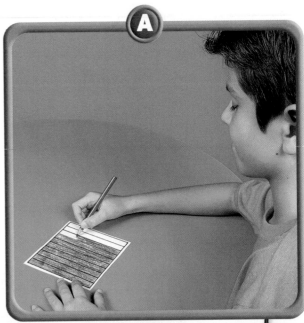

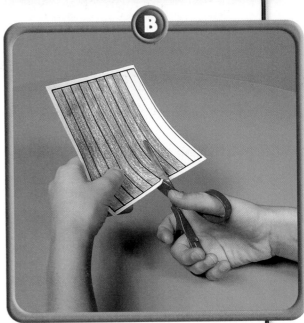

You can draw a picture to help you subtract decimals.

Subtract. 0.75 − 0.29

Step 1

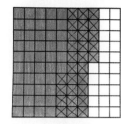

Shade 75 squares red.

Step 2

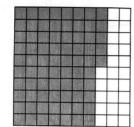

Draw Xs on 29 squares of the shaded part. Then, count the shaded squares that do not have Xs.

So, 0.75 − 0.29 = 0.46.

TALK Math

How would you use models to find the difference of any two decimals?

Practice

Use models to find the difference.

1.   0.56
   −0.32

2.   0.8
   −0.2

3.   0.72
   −0.37

✓4.   1.1
   −0.4

5. 2.71 − 1.34

6. 0.62 − 0.18

7. 4.05 − 1.61

✓8. 1.3 − 0.52

⭐**Algebra** **Use the models to find the missing number.**

9.

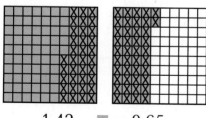

1.42 − ■ = 0.65

10.

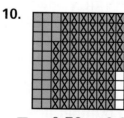

■ − 0.73 = 0.23

11. **WRITE Math** ▶ **Explain** how you can use models to find 0.6 − 0.45.

Technology
Use Harcourt Mega Math, Fraction Action, *Number Line Mine*, Levels P, Q.

OBJECTIVE: Record addition and subtraction of decimal and money amounts.

Learn

PROBLEM Each year, the average American eats about 3.36 pounds of peanut butter and about 2.21 pounds of fruit spread, per person. How many pounds of peanut butter and fruit spread does each person eat per year?

Example 1 **Add.** $3.36 + 2.21$ **Estimate.** $3 + 2 = 5$

MODEL	THINK	RECORD
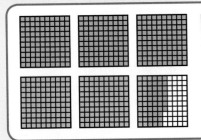	Count the number of squares in the partially shaded models. Then count the number of models that are completely shaded.	$\begin{array}{r} 3.36 \\ + 2.21 \\ \hline 5.57 \end{array}$

So, each person eats about 5.57 pounds of peanut butter and fruit spread per year. Since the sum 5.57 is close to the estimate of 5, it is reasonable.

Math Idea
You can add decimals the same way you add whole numbers if you line up the decimal points first.

Example 2

Subtract. $3.36 - 2.21$ **Estimate.** $3 - 2 = 1$

MODEL	THINK	RECORD
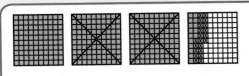	Cross out 21 squares on the partially shaded model and 2 completely shaded models. Count the number of squares not crossed out to find what is left.	$\begin{array}{r} 3.36 \\ - 2.21 \\ \hline 1.15 \end{array}$

So, $3.36 - 2.21 = 1.15$.

Example 3 Count up on a number line.

Subtract. $2.5 - 0.7$ **Estimate.** $3 - 1 = 2$

Count up from 0.7 to 2.5. Add the amounts you counted up by: $0.3 + 1.0 + 0.5 = 1.8$.

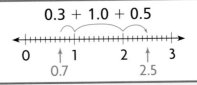

So, $2.5 - 0.7 = 1.8$.

Use Equivalent Decimals

Sometimes one number has more decimal places after the decimal point than the other. Write equivalent decimals with the same number of decimal places before adding or subtracting.

Allan buys a 2.5-pound jar of peanut butter. He has 0.75 pound left in another jar. How much peanut butter does he have in all?

Example **Add.** 2.5 + 0.75   **Estimate.** 3 + 1 = 4

Step 1

Line up the decimal points. Place a zero to the right of the last digit after the decimal point so each number has the same number of digits after the decimal point.

$$2.50$$
$$+0.75$$

Step 2

Add as you do with whole numbers. Place the decimal point in the sum.

$$\overset{1}{2}.50$$
$$+0.75$$
$$\overline{3.25}$$

> **Math Idea**
> You can add decimals the same way you add whole numbers if you line up the decimal points first.

So, Allan has 3.25 pounds of peanut butter. Since 3.25 is close to the estimate of 4, it is reasonable.

More Examples

A Use equivalent decimals to subtract.

5.8 − 2.94   Estimate. 6 − 3 = 3

$$\overset{17}{\cancel{4}}\,\overset{}{\cancel{7}}10$$
$$\cancel{5}.8\cancel{0}$$
$$-\,2.94$$
$$\overline{2.86}$$

Place a zero to the right of the digit 8 in 5.8.

B Add money amounts.

$12.00 + $34.98

Estimate. $12 + $35 = $47

$$\$12.00$$
$$+\ \$34.98$$
$$\overline{\$46.98}$$

C Subtract money amounts.

$52.07 − $11.45

Estimate. $52 − $11 = $41

$$\overset{1\ 10}{\$5\cancel{2}.\cancel{0}7}$$
$$-\ 11.45$$
$$\overline{\$40.62}$$

D Use a calculator.

3.46 + 6.09 + 4.26

| 3 | . | 4 | 6 | **+** | 6 | . | 0 | 9 | **+** |

| 4 | . | 2 | 6 | Enter **=** | 3.46 + 6.09
+ 4.26 = 13.81 |

Estimate to check. 3 + 6 + 4 = 13

Guided Practice

1. Which of the choices shows how to record what is shown in the model?

   a. 1.00 − 0.67   **b.** 0.10 + 0.67   **c.** 1.00 + 0.67

 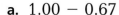

Estimate. Then record the sum or difference.

2. 4.8
      +2.4

3. 35.83
      −12.18

✓**4.** $23.44
       +$19.85

✓**5.** 67.1
       − 9.98

6. **TALK Math** **Explain** how using equivalent decimals can help you add and subtract.

Independent Practice and Problem Solving

Estimate. Then record the sum or difference.

7. 6.5
      +3.9

8. 71.82
      −52.39

9. $42.13
       +$81.32

10. $31.50
        −$19.17

11. $2.03 + $27.89   **12.** 8.75 − 6.43   **13.** 3.5 + 42.32   **14.** 12.64 − 5

Compare. Write <, >, or = for each ●.

15. $1.00 + $1.10 ● $1.00 + $0.40   **16.** 57.1 − 25.09 ● 3.4 + 32.75

⭐**Algebra** **Find the missing decimals. The sums are given at the end of each row and bottom of each column.**

17.

21.5	0.64	▨	33.83
▨	17.16	65.2	85.34
58.7	▨	9.34	70.24
83.18	20	86.23	▨

18.

19.

20.

21.

▨	14.5	6.03	24.33
7.56	▨	74.68	99.89
61.98	10.01	▨	93.29
73.34	42.16	102.01	▨

22.

23.

24.

USE DATA For 25–27, use the nutrition label.

25. How many grams of fat in 2 tablespoons of this peanut butter are not saturated fat, polyunsaturated fat, or monounsaturated fat?

26. Write an equation to show how many more grams of sugar than grams of dietary fiber are in 2 tablespoons of peanut butter. Then solve.

27. **Pose a Problem** Write a problem that uses the nutrition label.

28. **≡FAST FACT** The world's largest peanut butter and jelly sandwich measured 2.44 meters long by 2.44 meters wide. It was made on September 7, 2002, in Oklahoma City, OK. Do you need an estimate or an exact answer to determine whether the sandwich was longer than 2.03 meters? **Explain.**

29. **WRITE Math** **Explain** how adding and subtracting decimals is like adding and subtracting whole numbers. Then tell how it is different.

Nutrition Facts
Serving Size 2 tbsp (32.0g)

Amount Per Serving

Calories	190
Calories from Fat	147

% Daily Value*

Total Fat 16.3g	**25**%
Saturated Fat 3.6g	**18**%
Polyunsaturated Fat 4.4g	
Monounsaturated Fat 7.8g	
Cholesterol 0mg	**0**%
Sodium 5mg	**0**%
Total Carbohydrates 6.2g	**2**%
Dietary Fiber 1.9g	**8**%
Sugars 2.5g	
Protein 8.1g	

Vitamin A 0%
Vitamin C 0%
Calcium 1%
Iron 3%
Nutritional Units 5
* Based on a 2000 calorie diet

Learn About) **Estimating Decimal Sums and Differences**

Rounding decimals to 0, 0.5, or 1.0 can help you estimate decimal sums and differences.

Examples

Estimate. 0.46 + 0.85 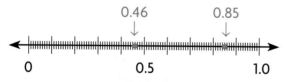 **Think:** 0.46 is between 0 and 0.5, but it is closer to 0.5. 0.85 is between 0.5 and 1.0, but it is closer to 1.0. **0.5 + 1.0 = 1.5**	**Estimate.** 0.75 − 0.11 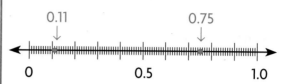 **Think:** 0.75 is between 0.5 and 1.0, but it is closer to 1.0. 0.11 is between 0 and 0.5, but it is closer to 0. **1.0 − 0 = 1.0**

So, 0.46 + 0.85 is about 1.5. So, 0.75 − 0.11 is about 1.0.

Try It

Use a number line to estimate the sum or difference. Then find the actual sum or difference and compare it to your estimate to determine whether your estimate is reasonable.

30. 0.22 + 0.54 **31.** 0.68 − 0.43 **32.** 0.55 + 0.33 **33.** 0.87 − 0.31 **34.** 0.09 + 0.73

Mixed Review and Test Prep

35. What scale and interval would you use to make a bar graph for the following data set? (p. 192)

        10, 25, 15, 20

36. Morgan jogs 13.75 miles each week. How far is this rounded to the nearest whole number? (p. 484)

37. Test Prep Alda is 62.5 inches tall. Her younger brother is 3.75 inches shorter than she is. How tall is Alda's younger brother?

38. Test Prep Dale bought a pair of sneakers on sale for $33.95. This was $12.95 less than the original price. Which shows the original price for the sneakers?

  A $46.80   **C** $22.00

  B $46.90   **D** $21.00

Make Change

OBJECTIVE: Make change and count money.

Quick Review

1. $2.56 + $5.03
2. $32.45 + $12.89 + $4
3. $5 + $6.79
4. $7.12 − $0.87
5. $13 − $11.76

Learn

PROBLEM Tamara bought a sandwich at the snack bar. She paid with a $10 bill. How much change should she receive?

BEACH SNACK BAR

FOOD ITEM	PRICE
Salad	$1.75
Sandwich	$3.39
Yogurt	$0.99
Fruit Cup	$1.45

ONE WAY Count on to make change.

Step 1

Start with the cost of the sandwich. Then, count on with coins and bills to the amount Tamara paid.

$3.39

$3.40 → $3.50 → $3.75 → $4.00 → $5.00 → $10.00

Step 2

Count the coins and bills: 1 penny, 1 dime, 2 quarters, 1 $1 bill, and 1 $5 bill equal $6.61.

So, Tamara receives $6.61 in change.

Math Idea
To make change, count on from the amount owed to the amount paid.

ANOTHER WAY Subtract.

Step 1

Subtract to make change.

$20.00	amount paid
−$17.49	amount owed
$2.51	change received

Step 2

Count on to find the amount of change. Start with the bills.

$1.00 → $2.00 → $2.25 → $2.50 → $2.51

Guided Practice

1. Explain how to count on from $3.18 to $5 using the following coins and bills.

$3.18

Make change. List the bills and coins.

2. Cost: $12.49
   Paid with:

3. Cost: $6.57
   Paid with:

4. Cost: $3.34
   Paid with:

5. (TALK Math) **Explain** how you can subtract decimals to make change.

Independent Practice and Problem Solving

Make change. List the bills and coins.

6. Cost: $1.54
Paid with:

7. Cost: $8.77
Paid with:

8. Cost: $42.39
Paid with:

USE DATA For 9–10, use the picture.

9. Curt, Debby, and Amelia each paid for the items they bought with a $10 bill. How much change should each person receive?

Curt bought a shovel and a pail.
Debby bought flippers.
Amelia bought goggles and a beach ball.

10. Arturo bought one of each of the items on the shelf for his trip to the beach. When he got to the register, he found the sand pail was on sale for $0.50 less than the price on the tag. He gave the cashier $25. How much change should he receive?

11. Reasoning Evan has two $2 Australian coins. He wants to have one of every type of coin as a souvenir. Australian coins include $2, $1, 50¢, 20¢, 10¢, and 5¢. Which coins can he trade for one of the $2 coins so that he has one or more of every type of coin?

12. Reasoning Tyrone bought a sandwich that cost $3.58. He handed the cashier $4.08. What should his change be? Why did he pay with $4.08 instead of $4.00?

13. (WRITE Math) **What's the Error?** Jess buys a toy for $3.63. She pays for it with a $5 bill and 63¢. Her change is three $1 bills. Describe the clerk's error.

Mixed Review and Test Prep

14. There are 12 rows of seats in a movie theater. There are 180 people in the seats. If the same number of people are sitting in each row, how many people are in each row? (p. 356)

15. Serena bought a pen for $2.89 and a pencil for $1.79. Nelson bought a pen and pencil set for $5. Who paid more? How much more? (p. 492)

16. Test Prep Sid paid for a $29.75 pair of shoes and received $10.25 in change. Which of the following amounts did Sid give the cashier for the shoes?

A Two $20 bills

B One $10 bill and one $20 bill

C One $20 bill and 3 quarters

D One $20 bill, one $5 bill, four $1 bills, and 3 quarters

Extra Practice on page 500, Set D

Problem Solving Workshop
Strategy: Compare Strategies

OBJECTIVE: Compare different strategies to solve problems.

Use the Strategy

PROBLEM The vending machine at the community center takes exact change only, including bills and coins. Anthony wants to buy a bottle of water that costs $1.50. He has a $1 bill, 2 quarters, 2 dimes, and 3 nickels. What are all the different ways that Anthony can pay for the bottle of water?

Read to Understand

Reading Skill

- Visualize the types of coins available.
- Is there information you will not use? If so, what?

Plan

- **What strategy can you use to solve the problem?**
  You can make a table or you can predict and test.

Solve

- **How can you use each strategy to solve the problem?**

Make a Table

Start with the greatest values of bill and coins.

$1 Bills	Quarters	Dimes	Nickels	Total
1	2			1 $1, 2 Q
1	1	2	1	1 $1, 1 Q, 2 D, 1 N
1	1	1	3	1 $1, 1 Q, 1 D, 3 N

Predict and Test

Make an organized list to record your prediction. To test your prediction, add to check the total.

So, Anthony can pay for the water in three different ways: one $1 bill, 2 quarters or one $1 bill, 1 quarter, 2 dimes, and 1 nickel or one $1 bill, 1 quarter, 1 dime, and 3 nickels.

1 $1 and 1 Q = $1 + $0.25 = $1.25
1 $1 and 2 Q = $1 + $0.50 = $1.50
1 $1, 1 Q, 1 D, and 1 N = $1 + $0.25 + $0.10 + $0.05 = $1.40
1 $1, 1 Q, 2 D, and + N = $1 + $0.25 + $0.20 + $0.05 = $1.50
1 $1, 1 Q, 1 D, and 3 N = $1 + $0.25 + $0.10 + $0.15 = $1.50
1 $1, 2 Q, 2 D, and 3 N = $1 + $0.50 + $0.20 + $0.15 = $1.85

Check

- **Which strategy was more helpful, Make a Table or Predict and Test? Explain.**

Guided Problem Solving

Choose a
STRATEGY

Draw a Diagram or Picture

Make a Model or Act It Out

Make an Organized List

Find a Pattern

Make a Table or Graph

Predict and Test

Work Backward

Solve a Simpler Problem

Write an Equation

Use Logical Reasoning

1. Sara wants to buy a can of apple juice from the vending machine. She needs exactly $2.30. She has two $1 bills, 5 quarters, 2 dimes, and 2 nickels. What are all the different ways that Sara can pay for the juice?

   First, decide whether to make a table or predict and test which bills and coins to use.

   Predict and Test
   2 $1, 1 Q, and 1 D = $2.00 + $0.25 + $0.10 = $2.35
   2 $1, 1 Q, and 1 N = $2.00 + $0.25 + $0.05 = ■
   1 $1, 5 Q, and 1 N = $1.00 + ■ + $0.05 = ■
   1 $1, 4 Q, 2 D, and 2 ■ = ■

   Copy and complete the boxes to predict and test the different possible combinations to make $2.30.

2. **What if** Sara wants to buy grape juice that costs $1.85? What are all the different ways she can make exactly $1.85 with the bills and coins she has? Solve and explain the strategy you used.

3. The vending machine has 10 drinks left. Some are juice and some are water. There are more cans of juice left than bottles of water. What possible combinations of water and juice could be left in the machine?

Mixed Strategy Practice

USE DATA For 4–5, use the table.

4. The community center has a swimming pool. Henry paid the entrance fee with 8 coins. Do you need an estimate or an exact answer? What coins did Henry use? **Explain.**

5. How many different ways can you pay the exact amount for a towel if you have the following bills and coins?

COMMUNITY CENTER POOL	
Item	Price
Entrance Fee	$1.50
Bathing Cap	$2.75
Towel	$5.55

6. Kay is swimming in the lap lane 12 feet behind Lee and 6 feet in front of Mindy. Mindy is swimming an equal distance between Lee and Alan. How far is the first swimmer from the last?

Extra Practice

Set A Round each number to the nearest tenth and each money amount to the nearest dollar. (pp. 484–485)

1. 5.48
2. 42.07
3. 412.11
4. $56.72
5. 5.16

6. $8.08
7. 4.53
8. 5.82
9. $65.61
10. $248.92

Round each number to the nearest hundredth.

11. 5.909
12. 5.418
13. 25.892
14. 23.178
15. 413.073

Set B Estimate the sum or difference. (pp. 486–487)

1. $6.5 - 3.4$
2. $9.31 - 5.26$
3. $58.36 + 29.99
4. $9.87 + 6.54$

5. $25.709 + 54.011$
6. $47.09 - 21.99
7. $23.5 + 21.9 + 63.7$
8. $72.748 - 38.094$

9. Domingo had $19.11. He bought a book for $16.09. About how much money does Domingo have left?

10. Gabriella had $24.75. Her mother gave her $13.06. About how much money does Gabriella have now?

Set C Estimate. Then record the sum or difference (pp. 492–495)

1. 8.6
   $+1.8$

2. 73.91
   -19.68

3. $33.42
   $+$72.46$

4. $53.28
   $-$27.34$

5. $36.66 + 23.51$
6. $9.25 - 5.11
7. $52.78 + 4.91$
8. $10.55 - 6$

9. Nathan has $5.83 in his bank. He has $6.41 in his pocket. Estimate how much Nathan has to the nearest dollar.

10. Isabelle had $15.85. She spent $5.41 on a necklace. Estimate how much Isabelle has left to the nearest dollar.

Set D Make change. List the bills and coins. (pp. 496–497)

1. Cost: $0.25
   Paid with:

2. Cost: $7.59
   Paid with:

3. Cost: $18.01
   Paid with:

4. Tess bought a set of luggage for $96.95. She paid with a $100 bill. How much change did she receive?

Decimal Train

START

Pack your bags!
2 or more players

Buy your ticket!
Decimal cards

All aboard!

■ Shuffle the decimal cards. Place them facedown in a stack. Players will take turns.

■ The first player takes the top two decimal cards. Place one card on the engine and one card on the first car of the train. Find the sum of the two decimals. If the sum is correct, a player receives 1 point, and the cards stay on the train. If the sum is incorrect, the player receives no points, and the cards go to the bottom of the stack.

■ After two cards are on the train, each player will choose one card from the stack and add it to the train. Each new decimal is added to the sum of all the previous decimals. Keep a running total. Do not forget to return a card to the stack if a sum is incorrect. Keep track of your scores, too.

■ Repeat until the train is full of cards.

■ The player with the most points wins.

FINISH

Decimal Points

You can use models to multiply and divide decimals by whole numbers.

Examples

A **Find 2 × 0.7.**

Use tenths models. Shade 0.7, or 7 tenths, two times. Count the shaded tenths. There are 14 tenths, or 1 whole and 4 tenths.

So, 2 × 0.7 = 1.4.

B **Find 3 × $0.29.**

Use a hundredths model. Shade 0.29, or 29 hundredths, three times. Count the shaded hundredths.

There are 87 shaded hundredths.

So, 3 × $0.29 = $0.87.

C **Find 0.8 ÷ 4.**

Use a tenths model. Shade 0.8, or 8 tenths. Cut 8 tenths from the model.

Divide the tenths into 4 equal groups. Each group has 2 tenths.

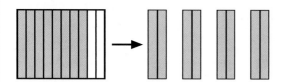

So, $0.8 ÷ 4 = $0.2.

D **Find $0.24 ÷ 3.**

Use a hundredths model. Shade 0.24, or 24 hundredths. Cut 24 hundredths from the model. Divide the hundredths into 3 equal groups. Each group has 8 hundredths.

So, $0.24 ÷ 3 = $0.08.

Try It

Find the product or quotient. You may wish to make a model.

1. 5 × $0.24
2. 4 × 0.8
3. 1.6 ÷ 4
4. $0.42 ÷ 6

5. Theresa is buying 7 pencils for $0.19 each. How much does she pay in all?

6. Marcus is buying 3 identical erasers for $1.17. How much does one eraser cost?

7. **WRITE Math** ▸ **Explain** how to use models to multiply and divide decimals by whole numbers.

Chapter 18 Review/Test

Check Concepts

1. Explain how to round 7.645 to the nearest whole number. (pp. 484–485)

2. Explain how you can use hundredths models to find the sum of $0.15 + 0.81$. (pp. 488–489)

3. Summarize how you can draw a picture to help you subtract 0.63 and 0.36. (pp. 490–491)

Check Skills

Round each number to the nearest tenth and each money amount to the nearest dollar. (pp. 484–485)

4. 34.91   5. $12.49   6. 7.53   7. $199.98   8. 439.17

Estimate the sum or difference. (pp. 486–487)

9. $4.2 - 1.9$ 10. $\$44.29 + \$36.71$ 11. $\$11.94 - \$7.22$ 12. $10.6 + 9.4 + 13.7$

Estimate. Then record the sum or difference. (pp. 492–495)

13. $\begin{array}{r} 3.9 \\ +5.7 \\ \hline \end{array}$

14. $\begin{array}{r} 14.65 \\ -\ 8.77 \\ \hline \end{array}$

15. $\begin{array}{r} 26.88 \\ +11.74 \\ \hline \end{array}$

16. $\begin{array}{r} \$46.83 \\ -\$38.27 \\ \hline \end{array}$

17. $\begin{array}{r} 45.38 \\ -26.97 \\ \hline \end{array}$

18. $\begin{array}{r} 85.91 \\ +23.05 \\ \hline \end{array}$

19. $\begin{array}{r} \$27.51 \\ +\$36.99 \\ \hline \end{array}$

20. $\begin{array}{r} 57.12 \\ -38.09 \\ \hline \end{array}$

Make change. List the bills and coins. (pp. 496–497)

21. Cost: $3.26
    Paid with:

22. Cost: $2.64
    Paid with:

23. Cost: $18.45
    Paid with:

Check Problem Solving

Solve. (pp. 498–499)

24. Dante wants to buy a baseball. He has two $1 bills, 5 quarters, 3 dimes, and 4 nickels. What are all the different ways Dante can pay for the baseball?

25. **WRITE Math** Emma bought a baseball bat and chalk. **Explain** why Emma gave the cashier $20.08, and tell how much change Emma should receive.

$29.99
$1.75
$16.09
$2.99

Multiple Choice

1. The model is shaded to represent $1\frac{4}{10}$.

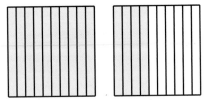

Which decimal does the model represent? (p. 466)

A 1.6

B 1.4

C 1.0

D 0.4

2. What number on the number line does point *P* best represent? (p. 414)

A $1\frac{1}{5}$

B $1\frac{1}{2}$

C $1\frac{3}{5}$

D $1\frac{4}{6}$

3. Laura was 21.65 inches long when she was born. How many inches was this, rounded to the nearest inch? (p. 484)

A 22 inches

B 21.7 inches

C 21 inches

D 20 inches

4. Molly lives 0.97 mile from the library. Karen lives 0.83 mile from the library. How much farther from the library does Molly live? (p. 490)

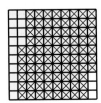

A 0.07 mile

B 0.14 mile

C 0.70 mile

D 1.4 miles

5. Hiro bought one set of notebooks and one folder. He paid with a $5 bill. How much change did he receive? (p. 496)

School Supplies	
Item	**Price**
Set of Notebooks	$3.79
Package of Pencils	$1.29
Folder	$0.49

A $9.28

B $4.28

C $1.28

D $0.72

6. A recipe for chocolate cake calls for $1\frac{1}{4}$ cups of milk. Which decimal is equivalent to $1\frac{1}{4}$? (p. 466)

A 1.14   **C** 1.4

B 1.25   **D** 1.5

GO ONLINE Technology Use *Online Assessment.*

7. The table shows how much of each type of cheese Mindy bought.

Cheese Tray	
Cheese	**Weight (in pounds)**
American	$\frac{3}{8}$
Swiss	$\frac{4}{8}$
Muenster	$\frac{7}{8}$
Cheddar	$\frac{1}{8}$

How much cheese did Mindy buy in all? (p. 438)

A $1\frac{3}{8}$ pounds

B $1\frac{5}{8}$ pounds

C $1\frac{7}{8}$ pounds

D 2 pounds

8. Which of these equations is **NOT** represented by the model? (p. 490)

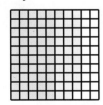

A $0.51 + 0.28 = 0.79$

B $0.79 - 0.28 = 0.51$

C $0.28 + 0.79 = 0.51$

D $0.79 - 0.51 = 0.28$

9. Look at the number line.

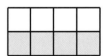

Which inequality is true? (p. 470)

A $1.54 < 1.5$ **C** $1.29 < 1.19$

B $1.4 < 1.40$ **D** $1.03 < 1.3$

Short Response

10. Nathan's soup recipe calls for $2\frac{3}{4}$ cups of tomato sauce. He has $2\frac{2}{3}$ cups of tomato sauce. Make a model to show whether Nathan has enough tomato sauce for the recipe. (p. 418)

11. Roeisha is 41 inches tall. There are 12 inches in a foot.

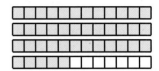

How many feet tall is she? Write your answer as a mixed number. (p. 414)

12. Write two fractions that are equivalent to $\frac{4}{8}$. (p. 406)

13. Enrique ran $1\frac{1}{4}$ miles on Monday morning and again on Tuesday morning. How many miles did he run altogether? (p. 444)

Extended Response ⟦WRITE Math⟩

14. Matthew added 3.196 and 2.04. He got a sum of 5.2. Is he correct? **Explain.** (p. 492)

15. Tonya says that 3.30 is greater than 3.3. Do you agree? **Explain** your thinking. (p. 464)

16. Explain how to use a model to find the missing number. (p. 490)

$$0.42 - \blacksquare = 0.29$$

Cool Kites

Kites on the Job

Did you know that a kite helped the town of Niagara Falls, New York, build a bridge more than 150 years ago?

Tall cliffs, high winds, and dangerous currents stopped engineers from stretching the first bridge cables from one side of the river to the other. A 10-year old boy had the idea of flying a kite across. It worked! When the winds died down, the kite fell to the other side. Then engineers sent heavier cables across the kite line to build the bridge.

F A C T · A C T I V I T Y

A kite train is two or more kites flown together in a line. Kite trains have been used to pull boats across water or go-carts across sand. Most of the time, people fly kite trains just for fun.

Use the kite train photographs.

❶ **WRITE Math** A student says that 3 kites in each kite train are red, so $\frac{3}{5} = \frac{3}{9}$. Is the student correct? **Explain** why or why not. Draw a diagram to support your answer.

❷ What fraction of the 5-kite train is yellow? Draw and color a kite train with 10 kites that shows the equivalent fraction.

ALMANAC Fact

In 1847, 10-year-old Homan Walsh was paid $10 to fly a kite across the Niagara River.

Design a Kite

The earliest known kites had simple flat shapes, like squares, rectangles, and diamonds, but kites can be made in other shapes. In the early 1900s, Orville and Wilbur Wright studied box-shaped kites to help them design the first airplane. Kites can even be made in fun shapes, like birds or dragons.

Sled kite

Box kite

Diamond kite

FACT·ACTIVITY

Design your own flat kite. The dimensions of kites vary in size depending on their shape.

► What shape will your kite be? What will its dimensions (length and width) be? Make at least one dimension be a mixed number.

► Draw a diagram of your kite. Label its dimensions.

► Write a number sentence about the dimensions of your kite.

► Write a number sentence to compare the dimensions of your kite to those of a classmate's kite.

► **WRITE Math** ► Think about the types of jobs kites have done. **Describe** a job your kite alone or in a kite train might be able to do. Then research and make a list of other ways kites can help people.

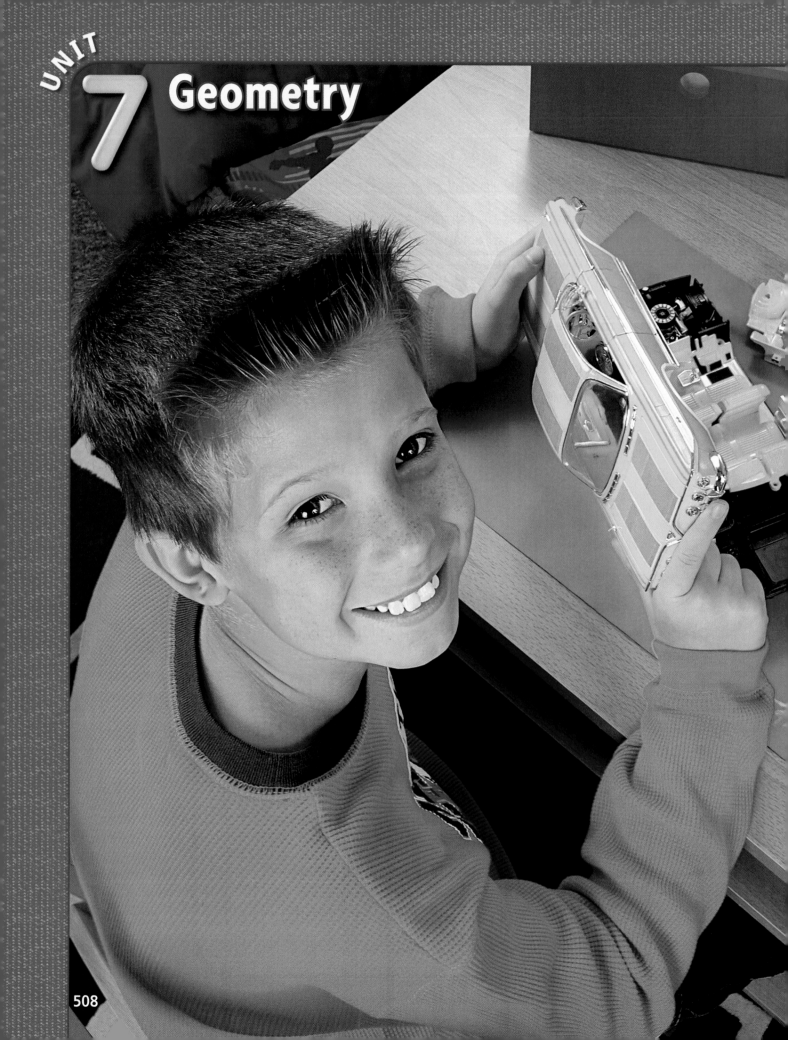

Math on Location

A DVD FROM
The Futures Channel

with
Chapter Projects

1

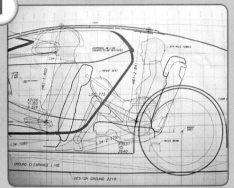

Designers and engineers use points, lines, angles, and plane figures in concept drawings.

2

The drawing is made into a 3-dimensional clay model to test its resistance to air.

3

A top-view drawing shows the symmetry in the car's design.

VOCABULARY POWER

TALK Math

What math do you see in the **Math on Location** photographs? What geometric words can you use to talk about car designs?

READ Math

REVIEW VOCABULARY You learned the words below when you learned about geometry. How do these words relate to **Math on Location**?

angle a figure formed by two rays or line segments that share an endpoint

circle a closed figure made up of points that are the same distance from the center

polygon a closed plane figure formed by three or more straight sides that are line segments

WRITE Math

Copy and complete the degrees-of-meaning grid below for geometric figures. Use what you know about geometry to complete the table.

General	Less General	Specific	More Specific
polygon			
solid figure			

Technology
Multimedia Math Glossary link at
www.harcourtschool.com/hspmath

19 Lines, Rays, Angles, and Plane Figures

The Modern Art Museum of Fort Worth is in Fort Worth, Texas. Its 2,600 pieces of art include paintings, sculptures, drawings, and photographs.

Investigate

Homage to Victory Boogie Woogie No. 2, by Leon Polk Smith, hangs in the Modern Art Museum of Fort Worth. What geometric figures do you see in the painting? Draw a picture by combining two or more of those figures.

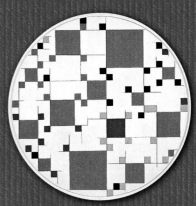

GO ONLINE

Technology
Student pages are available in the Student eBook.

Check your understanding of important skills needed for success in Chapter 19.

▶ **Identify Geometric Figures**

Write the name of each figure.

1. •

2. •——•

3. (angle with arrows)

4. •——→

5. (square)

6. (rectangle)

7. (triangle)

8. (circle)

▶ **Types of Lines**

Describe the lines. Write *parallel* or *intersecting*.

9. (two parallel lines with arrows)

10. (two intersecting lines)

11. (two intersecting lines)

12. (two parallel diagonal lines)

▶ **Sides and Angles**

Write the number of sides and angles in each figure.

13. (right triangle)

14. (pentagon)

15. (rectangle)

16. (octagon)

17. (parallelogram)

18. (triangle)

19. (hexagon)

20. (trapezoid)

VOCABULARY POWER

CHAPTER VOCABULARY

center
chord
circle
decagon
degree (°)
dimension
endpoint
equilateral triangle

obtuse triangle
one-dimensional
plane
protractor
quadrilateral
radius
regular polygon
Venn diagram

WARM-UP WORDS

parallelogram a quadrilateral whose opposite sides are parallel and equal, or congruent

right triangle a triangle with one right angle

two-dimensional is a measure in two directions, such as length and width

Points, Lines, and Rays

OBJECTIVE: Identify, describe, and draw points, lines, line segments, rays, and planes.

Quick Review

Draw a line segment.

Vocabulary

point	plane
line segment	dimension
endpoint	one-dimensional
line	two-dimensional
ray	

Learn

The vocabulary of geometry helps describe plane and solid figures you see both in nature and in the things people make. You can use the following geometric ideas and terms to describe the world around you.

TERM AND DEFINITION	DRAW IT	READ IT	WRITE IT	EXAMPLE
A **point** names an exact location in space.	A •	point A	point A	
A **line segment** is part of a line. It has two **endpoints**, the points at either end of a line segment, and all of the points between them.	D———E	line segment DE or line segment ED	$\overline{DE}$ or $\overline{ED}$	
A **line** is a straight path of points that continues without end in both directions with no endpoints.	B———C	line BC or line CB	$\overleftrightarrow{BC}$ or $\overleftrightarrow{CB}$	
A **ray** is part of a line that has one endpoint and continues without end in one direction.	F———G→	ray FG	$\overrightarrow{FG}$	EXIT →
A **plane** is a flat surface that continues without end in all directions.	K M L	plane KLM	plane KLM	

A plane is named by at least three points that are in the plane and do not form a straight line.

Dimension is a measurement along a straight line of length, width, or height of a figure. **One-dimensional** is a measure in only one direction, such as length. **Two-dimensional** is a measure in two directions, such as length and width. A rectangle is an example of a two-dimensional figure. Its dimensions are length and width.

1. Name the figure at the right. **Think:** It has 2 endpoints.

A •———————• B

Name a geometric term that represents the object.

2. tip of a tack   **3.** train track rail   ✓ **4.** flagpole   ✓ **5.** laser beam

6. [TALK Math] **Describe** how points, lines, line segments, and rays are alike and different.

Independent Practice and Problem Solving

Name a geometric term that represents the object.

7. one-way arrow   **8.** tip of a marker   **9.** parking lot   **10.** edge of a desk

Name an everyday object that represents the term.

11. line   **12.** line segment   **13.** ray   **14.** plane

Draw and label an example of each.

15. line *XY*   **16.** point *H*   **17.** ray *MN*   **18.** plane *PQR*

USE DATA For 19–20, use the photograph.

19. What geometric term describes where 2 walls and a floor meet?

20. What features on the building show line segments?

21. **Reasoning** Draw four points. What is the greatest number of line segments you can draw by connecting the points?

22. Write all the names for this ray.

23. [WRITE Math] **Explain** how you know which path is the shortest distance between point C and point D.

   a.   **b.**

Mixed Review and Test Prep

24. Use a basic fact and a pattern to find 12 × 700. (p. 270)

25. Jake bought a bowling ball on sale for $56.79. To the nearest dollar, how much did it cost? (p. 484)

26. **Test Prep** Which geometric term describes the yellow line in the photograph above?

   A Plane   **C** Line

   B Line segment   **D** Ray

Measure and Classify Angles

OBJECTIVE: Measure, classify, and draw right, acute, obtuse, and straight angles.

Learn

Two rays or line segments with the same endpoint form an **angle**. The shared endpoint is called a **vertex**. Angles are measured in **degrees (°)** using a **protractor**. A protractor is a tool that is marked from 0° to 180°.

DRAW IT	READ IT	WRITE IT
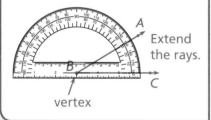	angle *ABC* angle *CBA* angle *B*	∠*ABC* ∠*CBA* ∠*B*

NOTE: The vertex is always the middle letter or the single letter that names the angle.

PROBLEM In the Commodore Barry Bridge, angles are formed where the steel supports meet. The angle marked in red has the same measure as ∠*ABC* above. What is the measure of ∠*ABC*?

▲ **The Commodore Barry Bridge** spans the Delaware River between Chester, Pennsylvania, and Bridgeport, New Jersey.

HANDS ON

Activity Use a protractor to measure ∠*ABC*.

Materials ■ protractor

Trace and label ∠*ABC* on your paper. Extend $\overrightarrow{BA}$ and $\overrightarrow{BC}$.

Step 1	**Step 2**	**Step 3**
Place the center point of the protractor on the vertex of the angle.	Line up the center point and the 0° mark with $\overrightarrow{BC}$.	Read the measure of angle where $\overrightarrow{BA}$ passes through the scale. Use the scale that makes sense for the angle size.

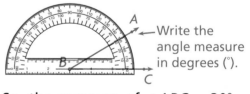

So, the measure of ∠*ABC* = 30°.

• Trace each angle and extend the rays. Then measure the angle.

a.   b.   c.

Quick Review

Write the name of each figure.

1. • 2. ⟶

3. ⟷ 4. •—•

5.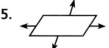

Vocabulary

angle	right angle
vertex	acute angle
degree (°)	straight angle
protractor	obtuse angle

Classify Angles

An angle can be classified according to the size of the opening between its rays. The measure of ∠B is 90°. A **right angle** measures 90°. A right angle forms a square corner.

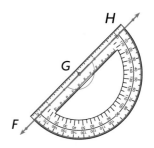

This mark means "right angle" and represents 90°.

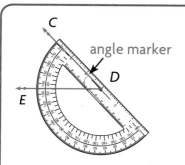

angle marker

The measure of ∠D is 45°.

An **acute angle** measures greater than 0° and less than 90°.

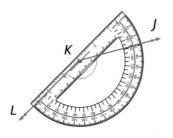

The measure of ∠K is 150°.

An **obtuse angle** measures greater than 90° and less than 180°.

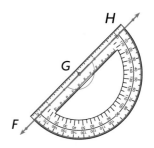

The measure of ∠G is 180°.

A **straight angle** measures 180°. A straight angle forms a line.

- Name some objects in your classroom that have right angles.

- Where can you find right, acute, straight, and obtuse angles in the Commodore Barry Bridge photograph on page 514? You may trace the angle and use a protractor.

- Do you always need a protractor to find out if an angle is right, acute, straight, or obtuse? Explain.

HANDS ON

Activity Make and use a right angle.

Materials ■ paper

To estimate the size of an angle, you can compare it to a right angle. Fold the paper twice evenly to make what appears to be a 90° angle.

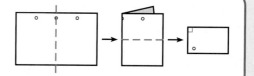

Name each angle below. Then use the right angle you made to classify the following as greater than or less than a right angle. Estimate their measure. Then use a protractor to measure each angle and check your estimate.

a.

b.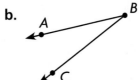

c.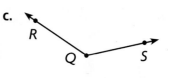

1. Compare the angle to a right angle. Is it greater than or less than a right angle? Is it greater than or less than 90°? Classify the angle.

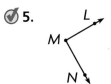

Trace each angle. Use a protractor to measure the angle. Then write *acute, right, straight,* **or** *obtuse.*

2.

3.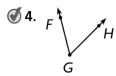

✓ **4.**

✓ **5.**

6. **TALK Math** Explain how a straight, a right, an acute, and an obtuse angle are formed.

Independent Practice (and Problem Solving)

Trace each angle. Use a protractor to measure the angle. The write *acute, right, straight,* **or** *obtuse.*

7.

8.

9.

10.

Draw and label an example of each angle. Identify and name the points and rays of each angle.

11. right angle *ABC*   **12.** obtuse angle *DEF*   **13.** straight angle *JKL*   **14.** acute angle *MNO*

Write the letter of the phrase that best describes each angle.

15.

16.

17.

18.

15.
a. less than 45°
b. greater than 90°

16.
a. less than 180°
b. less than 90°

17.
a. less than 45°
b. equal to 180°

18.
a. greater than 90°
b. equal to 0°

Classify each angle. Write *right, acute, obtuse,* **or** *straight.*

19.

20.

21.

22.

Extra Practice on page 534, Set B

 Technology ——
Use Harcourt Mega Math, Ice Station
ROM Exploration, *Polar Planes,* Level B.

USE DATA For 23–24, use the picture of the bridge.

23. Classify angle *B*.

24. Which angle appears to be an obtuse angle?

25. Name an obtuse angle, a right angle, a straight angle, and an acute angle in Figure X. Classify each angle.

26. **WRITE Math** Explain how you know the names of the rays that form an angle.

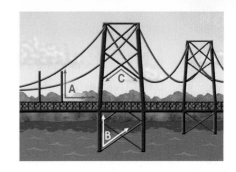

Figure X

Mixed Review and Test Prep

27. Tell the time as shown on the digital clock two different ways. (p. 152)

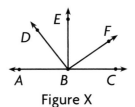

28. **Test Prep** Which word describes an angle that has a measure of 145°?

   A Acute   **C** Straight

   B Right   **D** Obtuse

29. **Explain** how a line and a ray are different. (p. 512)

30. **Test Prep** What is the best estimate of the measure of the angle below?

   A Between 10° and 30°

   B Between 30° and 45°

   C Between 45° and 70°

   D Between 70° and 90°

Problem Solving [connects to] Science

Constellations

Astronomers study the stars and other objects in space. Cepheus is a constellation of stars named after an ancient mythological Greek king. Cepheus is visible in the northern sky all year long.

Trace the constellation. Then answer the questions.

1. How many line segments are contained in this drawing of Cepheus?

2. How many points are in the constellation?

3. How would you classify ∠*B* and ∠*D*?

4. Which angles appear to be right angles?

5. Which angle is an acute angle?

Line Relationships

OBJECTIVE: Identify, describe, and draw intersecting, parallel, and perpendicular lines.

Quick Review

Name the angle that forms a square corner.

_____

Vocabulary

intersecting lines

parallel lines

perpendicular lines

Learn

PROBLEM Participants march in the Independence Day parade in Montclair, New Jersey. Use the terms below to identify and describe examples of each type of line on the parade route map.

TERM AND DEFINITION	DRAW IT	READ IT	WRITE IT
Lines that cross each other at exactly one point are **intersecting lines**. They form four angles.	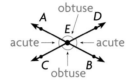	Line *AB* intersects line *CD* at point *E*.	$\overleftrightarrow{AB}$ intersects $\overleftrightarrow{CD}$ at point *E*.
Lines in the same plane that never intersect and are always the same distance apart are **parallel lines**.		Line *FG* is parallel to line *HJ*.	$\overleftrightarrow{FG} \parallel \overleftrightarrow{HJ}$ The symbol ‖ means "is parallel to."
Lines that intersect to form four right angles are **perpendicular lines**.		Line *KL* is perpendicular to line *MN*.	$\overleftrightarrow{KL} \perp \overleftrightarrow{MN}$ The symbol ⊥ means "is perpendicular to."

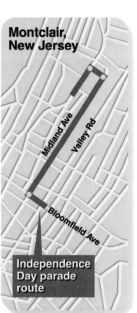

Montclair, New Jersey

▲ The red line shows the Independence Day parade route.

• Identify and describe the relationship between Midland Avenue and Valley Road.

Activity   Materials ■ paper ■ straightedge

Fold paper to make intersecting, parallel, and perpendicular lines.

• As shown in the diagram at the right, fold the paper in half twice so that the vertical edges meet. Which term best identifies the three crease lines after you unfold the paper?

• Now fold the paper in half the other way. When you open the paper, describe how the crease lines appear. Which terms best identify the crease lines?

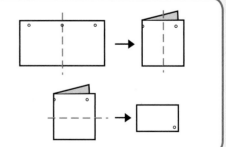

• Use grid paper to draw and label a pair of parallel lines, a pair of intersecting lines, and a pair of perpendicular lines.

1. How do you know if two lines are parallel? How do you know if two lines are perpendicular?

Name any line relationships you see in each figure.
Write *intersecting*, *parallel*, or *perpendicular*.

2.

3.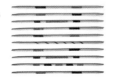

⊘ 4.

⊘ 5.

6. **TALK Math** How does the symbol ∥ help you remember its meaning?

Independent Practice and Problem Solving

Name any line relationships you see in each figure.
Write *intersecting*, *parallel*, or *perpendicular*.

7.

8.

9.

10.

USE DATA For 11–13, use the map.

11. Name a street that appears to be parallel to S 17th Street.

12. Name a street that appears to be parallel to Vernon Street and intersects S 17th Street. Classify the angle.

13. What street intersects both S 17th Street and S 19th Street and appears to be perpendicular to them? Classify the angles.

14. **WRITE Math** ▶ **What's the Error?** Trina says that all intersecting lines are perpendicular lines. **Explain** her error.

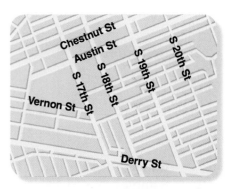

Mixed Review and Test Prep

15. A bag has 8 green and 6 red marbles of the same size. Are you more likely, less likely, or equally likely to draw a red marble than a green marble from the bag? (Grade 3)

16. What geometric term describes an edge of a photograph? (p. 512)

   A Line   C Line Segment

   B Ray   D Point

17. **Test Prep** Which best describes perpendicular lines?

   A They never meet.

   B They form 4 right angles.

   C They form 1 acute angle.

   D They form 1 obtuse angle.

LESSON 4

Polygons

OBJECTIVE: Identify, classify, and describe polygons and determine whether polygons are regular or not regular.

Quick Review

Write the number of sides each figure has.

1. 2.

3. 4.

5.

Learn

A **polygon** is a closed plane figure formed by three or more straight sides that are line segments, which intersect at the endpoints. Polygons are named by the number of sides, angles, or vertices they have.

PROBLEM Name the polygons you see in this painting by artist Paul Klee.

Vocabulary

polygon	hexagon
triangle	octagon
quadrilateral	decagon
pentagon	regular polygon

triangle	quadrilateral	pentagon
3 sides 3 angles 3 vertices	4 sides 4 angles 4 vertices	5 sides 5 angles 5 vertices

hexagon	octagon	decagon
6 sides 6 angles 6 vertices	8 sides 8 angles 8 vertices	10 sides 10 angles 10 vertices

So, you can see triangles, quadrilaterals, a pentagon, and a hexagon in the painting.

• Can a polygon have a different number of sides than angles?

• Do any of the figures with curved paths in Klee's painting form polygons? Explain your answer.

• **What if** you cut a hexagon into 2 polygons? What 2 polygons could be formed?

▲ Paul Klee, a Swiss painter who lived from 1879 to 1940, is considered one of the most original painters of modern art.

Example Decide if each figure is a polygon.

Polygon	Not a Polygon	Not a Polygon	Not a Polygon

Closed plane figure with 5 sides and 5 angles	Sides intersect, but not at the endpoints.	Line segments do not connect.	A curved path is not a line segment.
So, it is a polygon.	So, it is not a polygon.	So, it is not a polygon.	So, it is not a polygon.

- How can you tell what kind of polygon a figure is?
- Find an example of a polygon in the classroom. Describe the polygon.

A **regular polygon** has all sides equal in length and all angles equal in measure.

Regular Polygons	Not Regular Polygons
	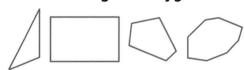
All sides have equal length. All angles have equal measure.	Not all the sides have equal length. Not all the angles have equal measure.

- Describe a regular hexagon.
- **What if** a hexagon had all sides equal? Would it be regular?

Activity Materials ▪ dot paper ▪ ruler

Draw a regular quadrilateral.

Step 1
Mark four points that are all the same distance apart.

Step 2
Connect the four points to form a regular quadrilateral.

Draw a quadrilateral that is not regular.

Step 1
Mark four points that are not the same distance apart.

Step 2
Connect the four points to form a quadrilateral that is not regular.

- How are the two quadrilaterals alike? How are they different?
- What is another name for a regular quadrilateral?

Guided Practice

1. Does the figure have straight sides? Is it a closed figure? Is the figure a polygon?

Name the polygon. Tell if it appears to be *regular* or *not regular*.

2.    3.   ✔ 4.    ✔ 5.

6. **TALK Math** **Explain** how you would draw a regular polygon with five sides and five angles on dot paper.

Independent Practice *and Problem Solving*

Name the polygon. Tell if it appears to be *regular* or *not regular*.

7.   8.   9.   10.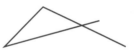

Tell if each figure is a polygon. Write *yes* or *no*. Explain.

11.    12.    13.   14.

Use dot paper to draw each polygon.

15. a triangle that is not regular

16. an octagon that is not regular

17. a hexagon that is not regular

18. a regular quadrilateral

19. Choose the figure that does not belong. **Explain.**

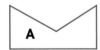 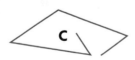

A   B   C   D

USE DATA For 20–21, use the painting.

20. **Reasoning** Is the guitar in the center of Picasso's painting a polygon? **Explain** your thinking.

21. What polygons do you see in the painting?

22. **WRITE Math** **What's the Question?** Samir drew a picture with 2 triangles, 3 quadrilaterals, and 4 pentagons. The answer is 38.

▲ Pablo Picasso's *Mandolin and Guitar*

CD ROM **Technology**
Use Harcourt Mega Math, Ice Station Exploration, *Polar Planes*, Level D.

23. Enrico bought a barbecue grill for $139 and a vacuum cleaner for $229. How much did Enrico spend to the nearest hundred dollars? (p. 34)

24. Test Prep Which is a five-sided polygon?

A Triangle

B Pentagon

C Octagon

D Hexagon

25. Trace the angle. Use a protractor to measure the angle. Then write *acute*, *obtuse*, or *right* to describe the angle. (p. 514)

26. Test Prep A stop sign has eight sides of equal length and eight angles of equal measure. What is the name of the shape of a stop sign?

Problem Solving [connects to] **Art**

Geometry

Architecture is the art and science of designing and building structures. Architects want to build structures that are pleasing to the eye. Architect I. M. Pei faced challenges when he designed the award winning East Wing of the National Gallery of Art on land shaped like a triangle.

Mr. Pei moved to the United States from Shanghai, China, to study architecture when he was 18. His designs won the Pritzker Prize in 1983. Mr. Pei works in the abstract form with stone, concrete, glass, and steel.

▲ I. M. Pei

1. Name the polygons you see in the aerial view of the East and West wings of the National Gallery.

2. How many sides does the polygon at the front of the photograph of the East Wing have?

▶ An aerial view of the East and West Wings

▶ The National Gallery of Art is located in Washington, D.C. This is a view of the East Wing.

Classify Triangles

OBJECTIVE: Classify triangles by the lengths of their sides and the measures of their angles.

Learn

PROBLEM Objects shaped like triangles are often found in nature. One example is the leaf of a cottonwood tree. What type of triangle does this cottonwood leaf appear to be?

Example Classify triangles.

Classify by the lengths of their sides.	**Classify by the measures of their angles.**
An **equilateral triangle** has 3 equal sides. 2 cm / 2 cm / 2 cm	A **right triangle** has 1 right angle.
An **isosceles triangle** has 2 equal sides. 3 cm / 3 cm / 2 cm	An **acute triangle** has 3 acute angles.
A **scalene triangle** has no equal sides. 4 cm / 2 cm / 3 cm	An **obtuse triangle** has 1 obtuse angle.

▲ The leaf of a cottonwood tree appears to be shaped like a triangle.

Math Idea

An equilateral triangle has 3 equal angles. An isosceles triangle has 2 equal angles. A scalene triangle has no equal angles.

So, the cottonwood leaf appears to look like an equilateral triangle and an acute triangle. You may use the corner of a piece of paper to check.

• Is the equilateral triangle above also a regular triangle?

• Which of the two sides of a right triangle are perpendicular?

Guided Practice

1. How many sides of the triangle are equal? Classify each of the angles in the triangle.

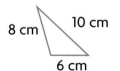

8 cm 10 cm 6 cm

Classify each triangle. Write *isosceles, scalene,* or *equilateral.*
Then write *right, acute,* or *obtuse.*

2. 3 in. ⟍ 5 in.
4 in.

☑ **3.** 9 ft ⟍ 6 ft
7 ft

☑ **4.** 9 yd △ 9 yd
9 yd

5. (TALK Math) **Explain** the difference between a right, an acute,
and an obtuse triangle.

Independent Practice (and Problem Solving)

Classify each triangle. Write *isosceles, scalene,* or *equilateral.*
Then write *right, acute,* or *obtuse.*

6. 10 ft △ 10 ft
17 ft

7. 5 in. ◺ 13 in.
12 in.

8. 3 in. ▷ 3 in.
3 in.

Classify each triangle by the lengths of its sides.

9. 4 in., 4 in., 4 in.

10. 30 cm, 40 cm, 50 cm

11. 3 ft, 7 ft, 7 ft

Measure the angles of each triangle using a protractor. Then
classify each triangle by the measures of its angles.

12.

13.

14.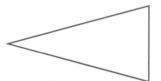

USE DATA For 15, use the photograph.

15. ≣**FAST FACT** The American crocodile's head appears to
be shaped like a triangle. Classify the shape of the head by
the lengths of its sides. Write *isosceles, scalene,* or *equilateral.*

16. Draw 2 equilateral triangles that share a side. What polygon is
formed? Is it a regular polygon?

17. (WRITE Math) ▸ **Explain** how a triangle can be isosceles and obtuse.

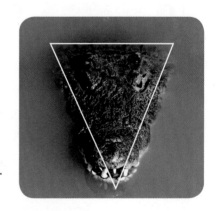

Mixed Review and Test Prep

18. Find the missing factor. (p. 108)

$$\blacksquare \times 3 = 18$$

19. What kind of polygon has exactly 8 sides?

(p. 520)

20. **Test Prep** Which kind of triangle has
3 equal sides?

A Right

C Isosceles

B Scalene

D Equilateral

(Extra Practice) on page 535, Set E

Classify Quadrilaterals

OBJECTIVE: Identify, classify, and describe quadrilaterals.

Quick Review

Draw a quadrilateral.

Vocabulary

parallelogram

rhombus

trapezoid

Learn

Architects use quadrilaterals when designing buildings.
A quadrilateral is a polygon with 4 sides and 4 angles.
There are many kinds of quadrilaterals. They can be classified
by their features.

HANDS ON

Activity Exploring quadrilaterals.

Materials ■ geoboard ■ rubber bands ■ dot paper

Copy each quadrilateral on a geoboard. Use dot paper to
record your work.

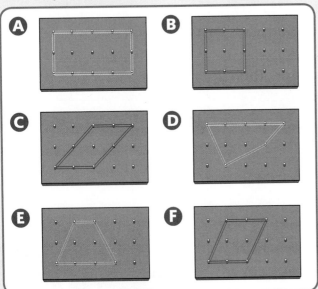

▲ PPG Place in downtown Pittsburgh,
Pennsylvania has at least two special
types of quadrilaterals.

- Which quadrilaterals have 2 pairs of parallel sides?
  Which of these do you see in the photograph?

- Which quadrilaterals have 4 right angles?
  Which of these do you see in the photograph?

- Which quadrilaterals have 2 pairs of opposite sides
  that are equal? Which of these do you see in the photograph?

- Which quadrilateral has only 1 pair of parallel sides?
  Do you see this quadrilateral in the photograph?

- Which quadrilateral has no parallel sides? Do you see this
  quadrilateral in the photograph?

Special Quadrilaterals

There are five special types of quadrilaterals: **parallelogram**, square, rectangle, **rhombus**, and **trapezoid**. Each has different features, and some can be classified in more than one way. Use the diagram to help you identify each type of quadrilateral.

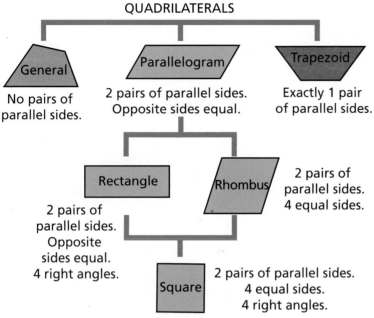

QUADRILATERALS

General — No pairs of parallel sides.

Parallelogram — 2 pairs of parallel sides. Opposite sides equal.

Trapezoid — Exactly 1 pair of parallel sides.

Rectangle — 2 pairs of parallel sides. Opposite sides equal. 4 right angles.

Rhombus — 2 pairs of parallel sides. 4 equal sides.

Square — 2 pairs of parallel sides. 4 equal sides. 4 right angles.

▲ *Geometrico* by Mario Carreno

- Which quadrilaterals are parallelograms? not parallelograms?

- Is a square a rhombus? a rectangle? Explain.

Guided Practice

1. Which are rectangles? Which is a trapezoid? Which are parallelograms?

   A   B   C

Classify each figure in as many of the following ways as possible. Write *quadrilateral, parallelogram, rhombus, rectangle, square,* **or** *trapezoid.*

2.

3.

4.

✓ 5.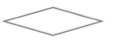

Draw an example of each quadrilateral.

6. It has 2 pairs of equal and parallel sides.

7. It has 4 right angles.

✓ 8. It has no parallel sides.

9. **TALK Math** **Explain** how squares, rectangles, parallelograms, and trapezoids are alike and how they are different.

Classify each figure in as many of the following ways as possible. Write *quadrilateral, parallelogram, rhombus, rectangle, square,* or *trapezoid.*

10.  **11.**   **12.**   **13.**

Draw an example of each quadrilateral.

14. It has exactly 1 pair of parallel sides.

15. It has 4 equal sides.

16. It has 2 pairs of parallel sides.

Write the letters of the figures that answer the questions.

17. Which are parallelograms?

18. Which are rectangles?

19. Which are quadrilaterals?

USE DATA For 20–21, use the photograph.

20. What are the different ways to classify the quadrilateral shown on the side of the building?

21. **Pose a Problem** Write a problem about a quadrilateral in the photograph. Give at least three clues that will help identify the quadrilateral.

22. **Reasoning** Is a square also a parallelogram? **Explain.**

23. Draw three equilateral triangles. Arrange them so they form one quadrilateral. Classify the quadrilateral.

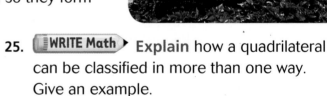

24. I have 4 sides and 4 angles. At least one of my angles is acute. What figure could I be?

25. **WRITE Math** **Explain** how a quadrilateral can be classified in more than one way. Give an example.

Mixed Review and Test Prep

25. Which line is perpendicular to $\overleftrightarrow{AB}$? (p. 518)

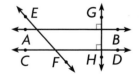

26. Is a book about 8 inches wide or 8 feet wide? (Grade 3)

27. **Test Prep** Which is the best description for the figures?

A Quadrilaterals   **C** Trapezoids

B Parallelograms   **D** Rectangles

 Technology
Use Harcourt Mega Math, Ice Station Exploration, *Polar Planes,* Level G.

Building Models

Reading Skill **Classify and Categorize**

Students made a model of the window outlined in the photograph of the first United States Post Office. First, they built a quadrilateral frame with 2 pairs of parallel sides and 4 right angles. The opposite sides of the frame are equal. Then, the students cut out a quadrilateral that has exactly 1 pair of parallel sides for the top of the window frame. Last, they cut out quadrilaterals with 2 pairs of parallel sides, 4 right angles, and 4 equal sides for window panes. How many types of quadrilaterals were made by the students for their model?

▲ The first post office in the United States is located in Philadelphia, Pennsylvania. It was founded by Benjamin Franklin.

Using the reading strategy classify and categorize can help you organize and understand information in math problems. Use the table to classify and categorize the quadrilaterals the students made for their model.

Quadrilaterals			Not Quadrilaterals
No parallel sides	1 pair of parallel sides	2 pairs of parallel sides	
General			

Problem Solving Classify and categorize to understand the problem.

1. Solve the problem above.

2. The students will make the window panes for their model. What type of quadrilateral will be used best for the windowpanes?

Circles

OBJECTIVE: Identify, draw, and label parts of a circle.

Quick Review

1. 2×11 2. $14 \div 2$
3. 15×2 4. $10 \div 2$
5. $26 \div 2$

Vocabulary

circle   center   chord
diameter   radius   compass

Learn

PROBLEM A hurricane is a large tropical cyclone with winds that spin around the storm's "eye". The spinning winds of a hurricane form a shape that appears to look like a circle. Around what geometric point do the winds spin?

Example Identify parts of a circle.

A **circle** is a closed figure made up of points that are the same distance from the **center**. A circle can be named by its center, which is labeled with a capital letter. Other parts of a circle:

center

Circle *P*

◀ A tropical cyclone is called a hurricane if winds are greater than 74 miles per hour.

A **chord** is a line segment that has its endpoints on the circle.	A **diameter** is a chord that passes through the center.	A **radius** is a line segment with one endpoint at the center of the circle and the other endpoint on the circle.
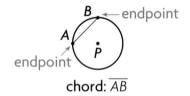 chord: $\overline{AB}$	diameter: $\overline{CD}$	radius: $\overline{PK}$ The radius of a circle is half the length of the diameter.

So, the winds spin around the geometric point called the center, or eye, of the hurricane.

A **compass** is a tool used to construct circles.

Activity Materials ■ compass ■ ruler

Step 1	**Step 2**	**Step 3**
Draw a point to be the center of the circle. Label it with the letter *P*.	Set the compass to the length of the radius you want.	Hold the compass point at point *P*, and move the compass to make the circle.

1. A circle has a diameter of 12 inches. How would you find the length of the radius?

Construct circle *J* with a 5-centimeter radius. Label each of the following.

2. radius: $\overline{JA}$ ✓ 3. chord: $\overline{EF}$ ✓ 4. diameter: $\overline{BC}$

5. **TALK Math** Explain why a diameter can be a chord.

Independent Practice and Problem Solving

Construct circle *L* with a 2-inch radius. Label each of the following.

6. radius: $\overline{LN}$ 7. diameter: $\overline{XY}$ 8. chord: $\overline{ST}$

For 9–12, use the drawing of circle *Z* and a centimeter ruler. Copy and complete each table.

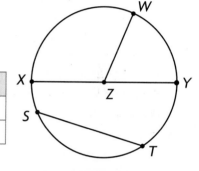

Name	Part of Circle	Length in cm
9. $\overline{ZY}$	?	■
10. $\overline{ZW}$	?	■

Name	Part of Circle	Length in cm
11. $\overline{ST}$	?	■
12. $\overline{XY}$	?	■

USE DATA For 13–15, use the diagram.

13. **≡FAST FACT** The strength of a hurricane is measured by its size and by the force of its winds. What is the radius of Hurricane A in miles?

14. What is the diameter of Hurricane B in miles?

15. How much greater is the diameter of Hurricane B than the diameter of Hurricane A?

16. **WRITE Math** Explain why a circle can have more than one radius.

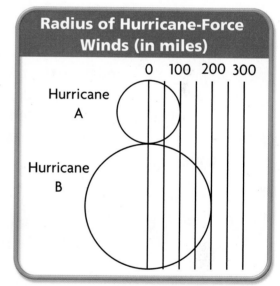

Radius of Hurricane-Force Winds (in miles)

Mixed Review and Test Prep

17. Make a bar graph that compares the diameters of the hurricanes in the diagram above. (p. 206)

18. The sides of a triangle are 8 cm, 6 cm, and 8 cm. Is the triangle isosceles, scalene, or equilateral? (p. 524)

19. **Test Prep** What is the length of the radius of a circle with a diameter of 22 inches?

   A 11 inches   **C** 22 inches

   B 12 inches   **D** 44 inches

Problem Solving Workshop
Strategy: Compare Strategies

OBJECTIVE: Compare different strategies to solve problems.

Use the Strategy

PROBLEM Jack's parents bought a new pool. The pool has at least one right angle and two equal sides. Which figure looks like their pool?

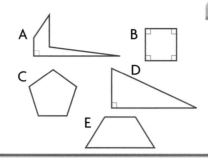

Read to Understand

Reading Skill

- Classify and categorize the plane figures.
- What information is given?

Plan

- What strategy can you use to solve the problem?

  You can use logical reasoning or make a table.

Solve

- How will you solve the problem?

Use Logical Reasoning

Make a Venn diagram with two overlapping ovals. Label one oval *2 or More Equal Sides* and the other oval *At Least 1 Right Angle*. Sort the figures. In the area where the two ovals intersect, write the letter of the figure that fits both categories.

Swimming Pool Diagrams

2 or More Equal Sides — C, E, (B), A, D — At Least 1 Right Angle

Make a Table

Make a table that has columns for each figure and possibility. Then fill in rows and circle the figure with the correct number of both angles and sides.

Figure	A	B	C	D	E
2 or More Equal Sides	X	✓	✓	X	✓
At Least 1 Right Angle	✓	✓	X	✓	X

So, Figure B looks like Jack's pool because it has at least one right angle and two equal sides.

Check

- How do you know your answer is correct?
- Compare strategies. Which one is easier for you? Explain.

Guided Problem Solving

1. Which of the swimming pool diagrams below has at least one set of parallel sides and at least one acute angle?

A   B   C   D   E

First, choose a strategy.

Next, draw and label a Venn diagram with overlapping ovals. Label one oval "At Least 1 Set of Parallel Sides" and the other oval "At Least 1 Acute Angle."

Then, use the diagram to classify and categorize the figures to help you organize and understand the information.

2. **What if** you were asked to find the swimming pool diagrams that had at least two sets of parallel sides and at least one obtuse angle? What would your answer be?

3. George wants to design a swimming pool that has at least two sets of parallel sides and and at least two sets of equal sides. Which of the swimming pool diagrams above would appear to look like George's design?

Mixed Strategy Practice

4. Jack's aunt bought a new pool that was shaped like a diamond with two obtuse angles. Classify her pool in as many ways as possible.

USE DATA For 5, use the picture.

5. Jack and his sisters Rika and Daria combined their money to buy a snorkel kit to use in the new pool. The amounts they gave are shown in the picture. Jack gave more than Daria, and Rika gave more than Jack. How much did each person pay?

6. Rika throws 6 coins with a total value of $0.40 into the swimming pool. She has only two different kinds of coins. What coins did Rika throw to the bottom of the pool?

7. *Swimmer* magazine costs $3 per issue at the newsstand. Daria will save $21 if she buys a 12-issue subscription. How much does a 12-issue subscription to the magazine cost?

8. **WRITE Math** ▸ Make a list of everything you know about a rhombus and a square. **Compare** how your two lists are alike and different.

Choose a STRATEGY

Make a Table or Graph
Use Logical Reasoning
Draw a Diagram or Picture
Make a Model or Act It Out
Make an Organized List
Find a Pattern
Predict and Test
Work Backward
Solve a Simpler Problem
Write an Equation

Extra Practice

Set A **Name a geometric term that represents the object.** (pp. 512–513)

1. fishing pole
2. the tip of a pen
3. table top
4. edge of ruler

Draw and label an example of each.

5. ray *AB*
6. plane *CDE*
7. line *NM*
8. point *P*

9. Which geometric term is a straight path of points that continues without end in both directions with no endpoints?

Set B **Trace each angle. Use a protractor to measure the angle. Then write** *acute, right, straight,* **or** *obtuse.* (pp. 514–517)

1.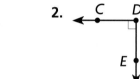
2.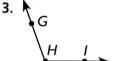
3.
4.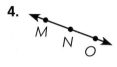

Draw and label an example of each angle. Identify and name the points and rays of each angle.

5. right angle *HJW*
6. straight angle *CMG*
7. acute angle *RST*
8. obtuse angle *XYZ*

Set C **Name any line relationship you see in each figure. Write** *intersecting, parallel,* **or** *perpendicular.* (pp. 518–519)

1.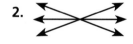
2.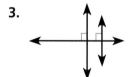
3.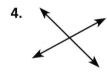
4.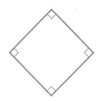

Set D **Name the polygon. Tell if it appears to be** *regular* **or** *not regular.* (pp. 520–523)

1.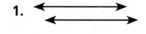
2.
3.
4.

Tell if each figure is a polygon. Write *yes* **or** *no.* **Explain.**

5.
6.
7.
8.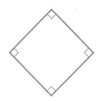

CD ROM **Technology**
Use Harcourt Mega Math, Ice Station
Exploration, *Polar Planes,* Levels A, B, D, F, G.

Set E Classify each triangle. Write *isosceles*, *scalene*, or *equilateral*. Then write *right*, *acute*, or *obtuse*. (pp. 524–525)

1.

8 ft 8 ft
8 ft

2.
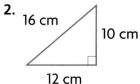
16 cm 10 cm
12 cm

3.

6 in.
5 in.
4 in.

4.

7 in.
5 in.
5 in.

Classify each triangle by the lengths of its sides. Write *isosceles*, *scalene*, or *equilateral*.

5. 6 m, 8 m, 9 m   **6.** 8 ft, 8 ft, 8 ft   **7.** 9 in., 9 in., 13 in.   **8.** 7 cm, 24 cm, 25 cm

Set F Classify each figure in as many of the following ways as possible. Write *quadrilateral, parallelogram, rhombus, rectangle, square,* or *trapezoid.* (pp. 526–529)

1.
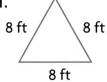

2.

3.

4.

5. I have 4 sides and 4 angles. At least one of my angles is acute. What figures could I be?

Set G Use the drawing of circle Y and a centimeter ruler. Copy and complete the table. (pp. 530–531)

	Name	Part of circle	Length in cm
1.	$\overline{AB}$	?	▪
2.	$\overline{YA}$	?	▪
3.	$\overline{YE}$	?	▪
4.	$\overline{DE}$	?	▪

5. A carousel has a diameter of 50 feet. What is the length of the carousel's radius?

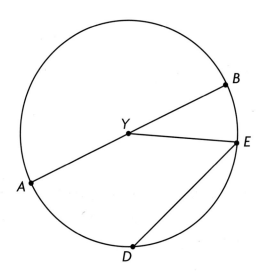

MATH POWER — Use Visual Thinking

Look Closely

Kevin made this figure on his geoboard. How many triangles are in his figure?

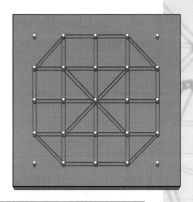

To find the number of triangles in the figure, look for triangles that are made of one part, two parts, three parts, or four parts. Organize the information in a table to keep track of each type of triangle.

  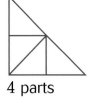

1 part   2 parts   4 parts

Triangles	
Parts	Number
One Part	12
Two Parts	4
Three Parts	0
Four Parts	4

Number of triangles: $12 + 4 + 0 + 4 = 20$
So, the figure has 20 triangles.

Examples

What other polygons do you see in the figure? Do you see rectangles? trapezoids? pentagons? other polygons? You can find each of these polygons in the figure.

A How many squares are in the figure?

Think: Two triangles make a square.

Squares: $12 + 5 = 17$

Squares				
Parts	1	2	3	4
Number	12	0	0	5

B How many rectangles that are not squares are in the figure?

Rectangles: $16 + 8 + 4 + 4 + 2 = 34$

Rectangles that are not squares.						
Parts	2	3	4	5	6	7	8
Number	16	8	4	0	4	0	2

Try It

Copy and complete the table. Find the number of polygons in each figure.

1.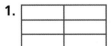

Parts	1	2	3	4	5	6
Rectangles	■	■	■	■	■	■

2.

Parts	1	2	3
Triangles	■	■	■

3. **WRITE Math** Explain how a table can help you keep track of the number of polygons in a figure.

Chapter 19 Review/Test

Check Vocabulary and Concepts

Choose the best term from the box.

1. A(n) __?__ is a polygon with 8 sides. (p. 520)

2. A __?__ is a line segment with one endpoint at the center of a circle and the other endpoint on the circle. (p. 530)

Check Skills

Trace each angle. Use a protractor to measure the angle. Then write *acute, right, straight,* or *obtuse.* (pp. 514–517)

3.

4.

5.

6.

Name any relationships you see in each figure. Write *intersecting, parallel,* or *perpendicular.* (pp. 518–519)

7.

8.

9.

10.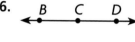

Classify each figure in as many ways as possible. (pp. 524–525, 526–529)

11.

12.

13.

14.

15.

16.

17.

18.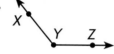

Check Problem Solving

Solve. (pp. 532–533)

19. Sort these polygons into a Venn diagram showing Regular Polygons and Quadrilaterals.

20. **WRITE Math** ▸ **Explain** how to draw a Venn diagram showing 6 types of quadrilaterals sorted into two groups, one with *2 pairs of parallel sides* and one with *fewer than 2 pairs of parallel sides.*

Standardized Test Prep
Chapters 1–19

Number and Operation

1. What fraction is best represented by point R on the number line? (p. 402)

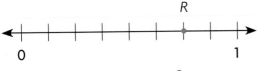

R

0   1

A $\frac{3}{8}$ C $\frac{6}{8}$

B $\frac{5}{8}$ D $\frac{7}{8}$

2. The Arts Center has 28 rows of seats. There are 16 seats in each row. How many seats are in the Art Center?

(p. 282)

A 448   C 280

B 160   D 44

3. The table shows the changes in the population of a city during 10 years.

City Population	
Year	Population
1995	8,200,312
2000	8,259,417
2005	8,402,011

What is the best estimate of the population in 2000 to the nearest hundred thousand? (p. 34)

A 8,000,000   C 8,300,000

B 8,200,000   D 8,400,000

4. **WRITE Math** Explain how you could use a pattern to divide 20,000 by 5. (p. 318)

Algebraic Reasoning

5. Which number makes the number sentence true? (p. 128)

$$2 \times 6 = t \times 6$$

A 2   C 8

B 6   D 10

6. Jack has two grocery bags of equal weight. Bag 1 has 4 large cans, and Bag 2 has 3 small cans and 3 large cans. If he adds one large can to each bag, which bag will weigh more? (p. 118)

A Bag 1

B Bag 2

C They will both weigh the same.

D Not enough information given

7. Look at the equation.

$$x + y = 45$$

If $x = 9$, what is y? (p. 70)

A 5

B 11

C 34

D 36

8. **WRITE Math** Mariah bought three kittens. She paid the same price for each kitten. **Explain** how to write an expression to show the total amount Mariah paid for the kittens. (p. 122)

Geometry

9. What geometric term best describes a mirror? (p. 512)

A Plane

B Ray

C Line

D Point

10. Rosa graphed ordered pairs representing the equation $y = x - 4$. She connected them with a straight line. Which ordered pair lies on that line? (p. 226)

A $(8,5)$ **C** $(5,8)$

B $(7,3)$ **D** $(3,7)$

11. Identify a radius of circle T. (p. 530)

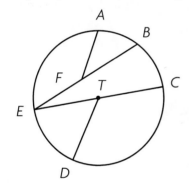

A $\overline{AF}$ **C** $\overline{CE}$

B $\overline{BE}$ **D** $\overline{DT}$

12. ▌WRITE Math ▶ Look at this figure.

Is it a polygon? **Explain** how you know. (p. 520)

Data Analysis and Probability

Test Tip

Get the information you need.

See Item 13. Look at the answer choices to see what information is needed from the graph. You need to know how many students prefer magazines and how many prefer fiction.

13. Leonardo surveyed 32 of his classmates to find what they preferred to read. The bar graph shows his findings.

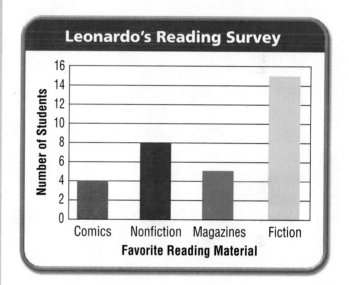

Which statement is true? (p. 204)

A 15 students prefer magazines.

B 8 students prefer magazines.

C 15 students prefer fiction.

D 8 students prefer fiction.

14. ▌WRITE Math ▶ **Explain** the differences between a line plot and a line graph. Give an example of data you could use to make a line plot and an example of data you could use to make a line graph. (p. 520)

20 Motion Geometry

Investigate

Which flowers have symmetry? Study and describe the symmetry in each flower shown. Draw a flower that has one line of symmetry and one that has more than one line of symmetry. Explain how your two flowers are alike and how they are different.

Blue violet

Black-Eyed Susan

FAST FACT

The Minnesota state flower is the showy lady's slipper. It is a pink-and-white orchid. They are hard to find. But in one year, 1,922 of the plants were counted in a one-mile stretch called the Wildflower Mile.

GO ONLINE

Technology
Student pages are available in the Student eBook.

Check your understanding of important skills
needed for success in Chapter 20.

▶ Compare Figures

Tell whether the two figures appear to be
the same shape and size. Write *yes* or *no*.

1.
2.
3.
4.

▶ Slides, Flips, and Turns

Tell which type of motion was used to move each figure. Write *slide*, *flip*, or *turn*.

5.
6.
7.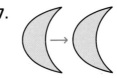
8.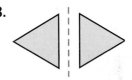

▶ Identify Symmetric Figures

Tell whether the blue line appears to be a line of symmetry. Write *yes* or *no*.

9.
10.
11.
12.

VOCABULARY POWER

CHAPTER VOCABULARY

angle	reflection
clockwise	rotation
congruent	rotational symmetry
counterclockwise	similar
degree	slide
flip	tessellation
line symmetry	transformation
pattern	translation
pattern unit	turn

WARM-UP WORDS

congruent having the same size and shape

rotational symmetry what a figure has if it can be turned around a center point and still look the same in at least two positions

similar having the same shape but possibly different in size

transformation the movement of a figure by a translation, reflection, or rotation

Congruent and Similar Figures

OBJECTIVE: Identify congruent and similar figures.

Quick Review

Identify the figure.

1.   2.

3.   4.

5.

Learn

PROBLEM **Congruent** figures have the same shape and size. Which pairs contain congruent figures?

   A   B   C   D   E

Pair	Shape	Size	Congruent?
A	Same	Same	Yes
B	Same	Different	No
C	Same	Same	Yes
D	Different	Different	No
E	Different	Different	No

So, pair A and pair C contain congruent figures.

• Are the two turtle designs congruent? Are the two train designs congruent? Explain your answer.

Vocabulary

congruent   similar

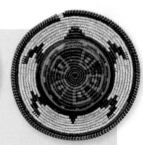

▲ Basket weaving designs: Turtle, Train

Activity 1 Explore congruent figures.

Materials ■ dot paper ■ scissors ■ ruler

Step 1

Copy the figures on dot paper.

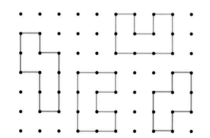

Step 2

Cut out one of each pair of figures and move it in any way to check for congruency.

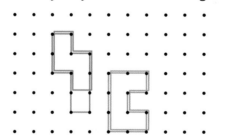

• Which pair of figures is congruent? Describe the movements you used to decide.

Figures that are the same size and shape but have a different orientation are still congruent.

Similar Figures

Similar figures are figures that have the same shape but are possibly different in size. Which pairs contain figures that are similar?

| A | B | C | D |

Pair	A	B	C	D
Shape	Same	Same	Different	Same
Size	Different	Different	Different	Different
Similar?	Yes	Yes	No	Yes

• What similar figures do you see in the painting? Explain.

Painting by ▶ Expressionist Wassily Kandinsky

Math Idea
Two congruent figures are always similar.

Activity 2 Explore congruent and similar figures.

Materials ■ 2 congruent paper squares ■ ruler ■ scissors

Step 1
Label one square *A*. Cut the other square in half as shown.

Step 2
Label one new piece *B*. Cut the other piece in half as shown.

Step 3
Label one new piece *C*. Cut the other piece in half. Label the two new pieces *D* and *E*.

Step 4
Look at *A*, *B*, *C*, *D*, and *E*. Which are congruent? Which are similar?

• Name six pairs of pieces that are neither congruent nor similar.

• How can you draw two figures that are congruent? Similar? Describe how you know.

Guided Practice

1. Do the figures have the same shape? Are they similar? Do they have the same size? Are they congruent?

Tell whether the two figures are *congruent and similar*, *similar*, or *neither*.

2.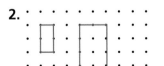

3.

✓ 4.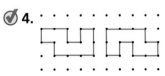

✓ 5.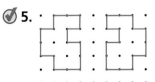

6. **TALK Math** Identify and describe two objects in your classroom that are congruent and two objects in your classroom that are similar. **Explain** how you know they are congruent or similar.

Independent Practice and Problem Solving

Tell whether the two figures are *congruent and similar, similar,* or *neither*.

7.    8.    9.    10.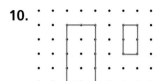

11. On dot paper, draw figures A, B, and C. Which pairs of figures are congruent? Similar but not congruent?

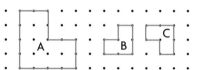

USE DATA For 12–13, use the coordinate grid.

12. Are triangles A and C congruent? Are triangles B and D similar but not congruent? Give the coordinates of these triangles.

13. On a coordinate grid, draw a triangle that is congruent to triangle A and a triangle that is similar but not congruent to triangle A.

14. Two triangles are congruent. The sides of one are 3 cm, 4 cm, and 5 cm. Two sides of the other triangle are 3 cm and 5 cm. What is the measure of the third side?

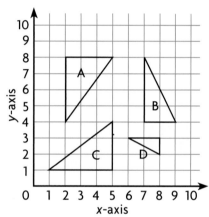

15. **Open–Ended** If you use two congruent figures to make a rectangle, what might the figures be?

16. **WRITE Math** ▶ Draw two figures on dot paper that are congruent. **Explain** why all congruent figures are similar.

Mixed Review and Test Prep

17. On Sunday, Matt ran 1.45 miles. Mindy ran 1.54 miles. Who ran farther? (p. 470)

18. **Test Prep** Which two figures below appear to be congruent?

A

B

C

D

19. What is the name of the triangle that has two congruent sides? (p. 524)

20. **Test Prep** Draw a square that is similar to this one. Then **explain** why all squares are similar.

Technology
Use Harcourt Mega Math, Ice Station
Exploration, *Polar Planes,* Levels H, I.

Write to Explain

Sometimes you are asked to explain how you solved a problem. Writing an explanation helps you think through the steps you used to find the solution.

Trent drew a pattern of similar rectangles for an art project. He asked Yolanda to draw the next-smaller rectangle and name the ordered pairs that form the vertices of the rectangle. Yolanda wrote this explanation of her solution.

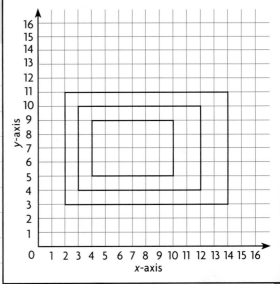

First, I looked at Trent's pattern of rectangles to figure out how the rectangles in his drawing are related. I read the question to find out that I need to name the ordered pairs that form the vertices of the next-smaller rectangle.

Next, I found this pattern in the positions of each vertex of the rectangles:

Top left moves 1 unit right, 1 unit down. Bottom left moves 1 unit right, 1 unit up. Top right moves 2 units left, 1 unit down. Bottom right moves 2 units left, 1 unit up.

Then, I used this pattern to draw a rectangle and to identify the ordered pair of each vertex.

The ordered pairs for each vertex of the next-smaller rectangle are—(5,6), (5,8), (8,6), and (8,8).

Tips

To write an explanation:

- Tell what information you are given and what you are asked to find.
- Use sequence words such as *first*, *next*, and *then* as you write each step you took.
- Write a sentence that clearly states the solution to the problem.

Problem Solving Explain how to solve each problem.

1. **Explain** how to find the ordered pairs that form the vertices for the next-larger rectangle. What are the ordered pairs of the next-larger rectangle?

2. **Explain** how to find the ordered pairs of a 4 unit by 2 unit rectangle centered in the smallest rectangle. What are the ordered pairs for this rectangle?

Turns and Symmetry

OBJECTIVE: Relate angle measures to $\frac{1}{4}$, $\frac{1}{2}$, $\frac{3}{4}$, and full turn and identify line and rotational symmetry in geometric figures.

Learn

Turning ray $\overrightarrow{AB}$ around the circle makes angles of different sizes. A complete turn around the circle is 360°.

Ray $\overrightarrow{AB}$ can be turned **clockwise**, the direction the clock hands move, or **counterclockwise**, the direction opposite from the way clock hands move.

clockwise

counterclockwise

Quick Review

Lea wants a set of two congruent squares for a design. Which squares appear to be congruent?

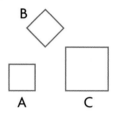

Vocabulary

clockwise

counterclockwise

line symmetry

rotational symmetry

Activity 1 Use turns of geostrips to show different angles.

Materials ■ 2 strips of paper ■ paper fastener

Step 1	Step 2	Step 3	Step 4
Turn the geostrip to form a 90° angle.	Now turn the geostrip $\frac{1}{4}$ turn more to make a 180° angle.	Turn the geostrip another $\frac{1}{4}$ turn to make a 270° angle.	Turn the geostrip another $\frac{1}{4}$ turn. When the strips meet, they make a 360° angle.
This is a $\frac{1}{4}$, or quarter, or 90-degree turn around a point.	This is a $\frac{1}{2}$, or half, or 180-degree turn around a center point.	This is a $\frac{3}{4}$, or three-quarter, or 270-degree turn around a point.	This is a full, or 360-degree turn around a center point.

- How many quarter turns are in a complete turn? Identify and describe each turn.

- **What if** you opened the geostrip in Step 1 to form a 90° counterclockwise turn? What is another way to name the measure and direction of the angle?

Symmetry

A figure can have line symmetry, rotational symmetry, both, or neither. Figures that have **line symmetry** can be folded along a line so that the two parts match exactly. Figures that have **rotational symmetry** can be turned about a center point and still look the same in at least two positions.

▲ The pinwheel has rotational symmetry. It looks the same at each $\frac{1}{4}$ turn.

▲ This beetle has line symmetry.

 HANDS ON

Activity 2 Check for line symmetry.

Materials ■ pattern blocks ■ tracing paper ■ scissors

- Trace and cut out each of the pattern blocks.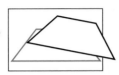

- Fold each tracing in half so that one half matches the other exactly. Find all the possible folds.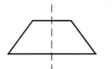

- Tell whether there are no lines of symmetry, 1 line of symmetry, or more than 1 line of symmetry for each pattern block.

ERROR ALERT

To avoid errors, you may use a mirror to check for symmetry.

 HANDS ON

Activity 3 Check for rotational symmetry.

Materials ■ pattern blocks ■ tracing paper

- Trace each pattern block. Place the tracing on top of the pattern block. Put an X at the top of the tracing.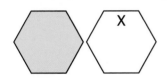

- Keeping the center points together, turn the tracing to see if it matches exactly in another position.

- Record the number of times the figure matches in another position until the X appears at the top of the tracing. If the figure matches in more than one position, the figure has rotational symmetry.

- Which pattern blocks have rotational symmetry? Draw a figure that does not have rotational symmetry.

Examples Identify the types of symmetry.

Ⓐ Rotational	Ⓑ  Both line and rotational	Ⓒ  None	Ⓓ 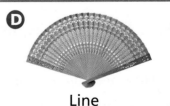 Line

- Describe the symmetry shown in Examples A–D.

Guided Practice

1. Copy and complete the design on dot paper. Does your completed figure have line symmetry? Does it have rotational symmetry?

Tell whether the figure appears to have *line symmetry*, *rotational symmetry*, *both*, or *neither*.

2.

3.

✓ 4.

✓ 5.

6. **TALK Math** **Explain** how you can show a turn.

Independent Practice and Problem Solving

Tell whether the figure appears to have *line symmetry*, *rotational symmetry*, *both*, or *neither*.

7.

8.

9.

10.

Trace each figure. Then draw the line or lines of symmetry.

11.

12.

13.

14.

Draw a figure that has the following. Draw the line or lines of symmetry.

15. 0 lines of symmetry

16. 1 line of symmetry

17. 2 lines of symmetry

Tell whether the rays on the circle show a $\frac{1}{4}$, $\frac{1}{2}$, $\frac{3}{4}$, or full turn.

18.

19.

20.

21.

USE DATA For 22–24, use the chart.

22. Which letters appear to have only one line of symmetry?

23. How many letters appear to have no lines of symmetry?

24. Which letters appear to have more than one line of symmetry?

A	F	S
B	H	T
C	I	U
D	J	V
E	L	W

Extra Practice on page 562, Set B

25. Jack put up the flag on his mailbox. Describe the turn.

26. Reasoning Trace the figure. Then show how you can change the figure so that it has at least one line of symmetry.

27. **WRITE Math** ▸ **What's the Error?** Casey says that all regular polygons have line symmetry but none have rotational symmetry. Describe and correct her error.

28. Give an example of a figure with at least two lines of symmetry. Then write a set of directions how to find and draw the lines of symmetry in your figure.

Mixed Review and Test Prep

29. What is the value of *y*? (p. 128)

$$42 \div y = 6$$

30. What type of line segments meet at a square corner? (p. 518)

31. Test Prep Which best describes the symmetry in the word WOW?

A Line   **C** Both

B Rotational   **D** None

32. Test Prep The rays on the circle show the turn Jeremy made on his skateboard. Describe the turn.

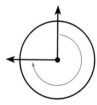

Problem Solving [connects to] Art

Kirigami

Materials ■ paper ■ scissors

Kirigami is the art of folding paper and then cutting it to make ornamental objects or designs. This design was made by folding paper once.

Fold a sheet of paper in half and then in half again on the first fold. Cut out a hole in whatever shape you wish along the fold.

Use what you know about symmetry to predict what the design will look like.

Then open the paper. Was your prediction right?

Predict what the figure will look like when the paper is unfolded. Check by folding, cutting, and then unfolding the paper.

1.

2.

3.

4.

Transformations

OBJECTIVE: Identify, predict, and describe the results of transformations.

Quick Review

Do the figures appear congruent? Write *yes* or *no*.

1. 2.

3. 4.

5.

Vocabulary

transformation   rotation

translation   reflection

Learn

PROBLEM The space shuttle turns 180 degrees after liftoff and looks as if it is flying upside down. Before entering orbit, the space shuttle turns again to a right-side-up position. How can you describe this movement?

A **transformation** is the movement of a figure by a translation, reflection, or rotation.

TERM	DEFINITION	EXAMPLE
Translation	A translation, or a slide, moves a figure to a new position along a straight line.	
Rotation	A rotation, or a turn, moves a figure around a point.	
Reflection	A reflection, or a flip, flips a figure over a line.	

So, the space shuttle rotates 180 degrees when it moves from upside-down to right-side-up.

▲ The space shuttle rotates shortly after liftoff.

Activity 1 Draw examples of transformations.

Materials ■ pattern block ■ dot paper

Step 1	Step 2	Step 3	Step 4
Trace the pattern block.	Slide the block in any direction and trace it.	Trace another pattern block. Turn the block clockwise 90° and trace it.	Flip the block over a vertical line and trace it.
original	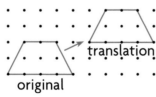 translation original	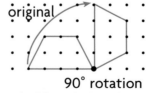 original 90° rotation	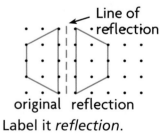 Line of reflection original reflection
Label it *original*.	Label it *translation*.	Label it *90° rotation*.	Label it *reflection*.

• How is a counterclockwise rotation different from a clockwise rotation?

• Predict how the rotated figure would look if the point of rotation were in the center of the original figure.

Activity 2 Check for congruence.

Work with a partner to determine whether two figures are congruent.
Materials ■ pattern blocks ■ scissors

Step 1

Fold a sheet of paper in half. Place a pattern block along the unfolded edge, and trace it. Then cut out the figure from both layers of the paper.

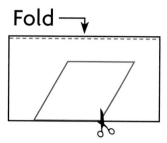

Fold

Step 2

Lay out the two figures on the table randomly.
Your partner predicts the transformations that must be used to move one figure until it fits exactly on top of the other.

Step 3

When you and your partner complete the activity, test the prediction by transforming the figure using translations, reflections, and rotations until it fits on top of the other figure.

Step 4

Describe the transformations used to determine whether the two figures are congruent.

Math Idea

After a translation, a rotation, and a reflection, the size and shape of a figure remain the same. So, the original figure and the transformed figure are congruent.

• Are the two figures congruent? Describe how you know.

• Is there another way to move the figure so that it fits exactly on top of the other?

• Can you change the order in which you do the transformations and move the figure so that it fits exactly on top of the other? Explain.

Guided Practice

1. Is the transformed figure a translation, rotation, or reflection?

Tell how each figure was moved. Write *translation*, *rotation*, or *reflection*.

2.

3.

4.

✓ 5.

Copy each figure on dot paper. Then draw figures to show
a translation, a rotation, and a reflection of each.

6. 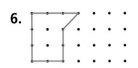   7. 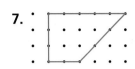   8. 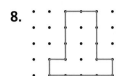   ✓ 9.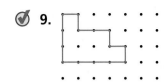

10. **TALK Math** Compare and contrast the transformations in
Problem 8.

Independent Practice and Problem Solving

Tell how each figure was moved. Write *translation*, *rotation*,
or *reflection*.

11.    12.    13.    14.

Copy each figure on dot paper. Then draw figures to show
a translation, a rotation, and a reflection of each.

15. 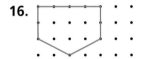   16. 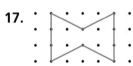   17.    18.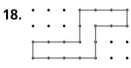

For 19–21, copy the figure at the right on dot paper. Write the
letter of the figure that shows how it will look after each move.   original

19. translation   20. reflection   21. rotation

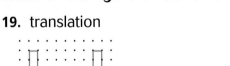

  a   b   a   b   a   b

22. Tell what moves were made to transform
each figure into its next position.

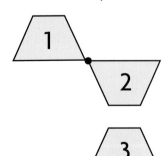

23. Which describe the drawing?

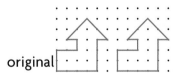

original

  a. The figures are congruent.

  b. The figures show a reflection.

  c. The figures show a translation.

  d. The figures show a rotation.

552   Extra Practice on page 562, Set C

USE DATA For 24–26, use the diagram.

24. What type of transformation describes the change in position from A to B?

25. Trace D and draw its reflection.

26. Redraw the diagram so that B is a translation of A, and D is a 180° rotation of C.

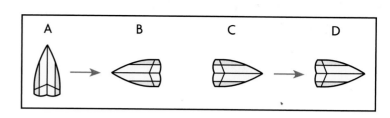

27. **Reasoning** Name a figure that would look the same after a translation, a rotation, and a reflection. Draw an example.

28. [WRITE Math] Draw a figure that has been translated and a figure that has been rotated. Then compare and contrast the two figures.

Mixed Review and Test Prep

29. Which polygon has exactly 5 sides and 5 angles? (p. 520)

30. How many lines of symmetry does an equilateral triangle have? (p. 546)

31. **Test Prep** Which describes a rotation?

   A Slide along a straight line

   B A turn around a point

   C A flip over a line

   D A reflection

32. **Test Prep** If you reflect the regular hexagon shown below and then rotate it 180° clockwise, how will the transformed hexagon compare to the original?

Problem Solving connects to Art

VISUAL THINKING

Jigsaw puzzles are put together by translating and rotating the pieces. These four puzzle pieces form a picture.

Solve and make puzzles.

Materials ■ tracing paper ■ scissors

1. Trace the puzzle pieces and arrange them as shown. Then predict and test how each piece needs to be moved to form a picture from the four pieces. What is the picture?

2. Design your own puzzle. Transform the squares, and exchange the puzzle with a classmate to solve. **Describe** the transformations you used.

Problem Solving Workshop
Strategy: Act It Out

OBJECTIVE: Solve the problem by using the problem solving strategy *act it out.*

Learn the Strategy

Acting out a problem can help you understand what it is about and find a reasonable solution. You can act it out by role-playing or using a model.

Act it out with your classmates.

Jim, Mark, and Hannah are finalists in a spelling bee. Before the last round starts, they will all shake hands once. How many handshakes are there in all?

Act it out by using models.

A Betty bought a camping kit for $96, lanterns for $49, and a cabin tent for $222. If Betty had $500 to spend on her camping trip, how much does she have left after buying her camping supplies?

B Amy draws a parallelogram on dot paper for her computer animation. Her art teacher asks her to rotate the original figure 90° clockwise and then draw its vertical reflection in the last frame. Describe how Amy's geometric figures are alike and different after she does this.

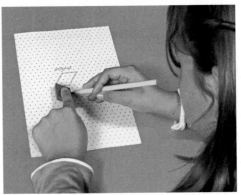

TALK Math

Explain how you decide which way to use the *act it out* strategy.

Use the Strategy

PROBLEM Andy used pattern blocks to make a butterfly. How can you prove his design has line symmetry?

Read to Understand

Reading Skill

- **Visualize what you are asked to find.**
- **What information is given?**

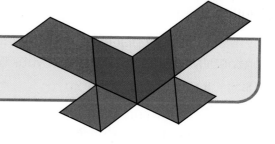

Plan

- **What strategy can you use to solve the problem?**

  You can act it out.

Solve

- **How can you use the strategy to solve the problem?**

  Copy the design, using pattern blocks. Use a mirror to act it out. Place the mirror where you think the line of symmetry is, and look into the mirror.

  Compare the reflection in the mirror to the side of the butterfly that is behind the mirror. If they are the same, the figure has line symmetry.

  So, Andy's butterfly has line symmetry.

Check

- **What other strategies could you use to solve the problem?**
- **How can you check your results?**

1. Cassie made a butterfly, using different pattern blocks. Does her butterfly have line symmetry?

   First, act it out by using pattern blocks to make a butterfly design.

   Then, act it out by placing a mirror vertically and horizontally across the middle of your butterfly design to see if it has line symmetry.

Cassie's Butterfly Design

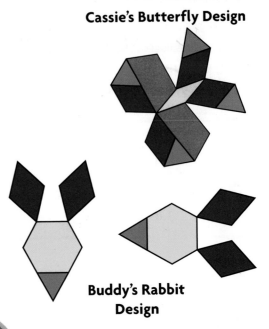

2. **What if** Cassie wants to use the strategy *act it out* to determine whether her design has more than 1 line of symmetry? Does her butterfly have more than 1 line of symmetry? **Explain** how you know.

3. Buddy used pattern blocks to make the two rabbits shown at the right. Are the rabbits congruent? **Explain** how you know.

Buddy's Rabbit Design

Problem Solving Strategy Practice

Act it out to solve.

4. Cody biked 2 miles north from the Lancaster Quilt & Textile Museum in Lancaster, Pennsylvania. Then he biked 6 miles east and 3 miles north. On the following day, he biked 4 miles east and then 5 miles south. How far is it directly back to the museum?

For 5–8, use the tangram puzzle pieces.

5. Trace and cut out all 7 tangram puzzle pieces shown in the grid on the right. Use some or all of the tangram puzzle pieces to design a figure that has line symmetry.

6. Make another figure using the tangram puzzle pieces. Then trace its reflection. Does the design have line symmetry?

7. **WRITE Math** Make a new design. Trace your design and label it *original*. Translate your design up, down, left, right or diagonally. Trace the design and label it *translation*. Are your two designs congruent? **Explain.**

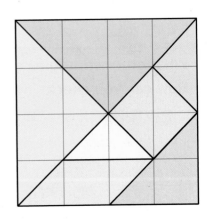

8. Use your tangram puzzle pieces to make another design. Does your design have symmetry? If so, what kind?

Mixed Strategy Practice

9. Missy uses one hexagonal, two rectangular, and four triangular pieces of fabric to make one bug design for a quilt. If she uses 70 pieces in all to make bug designs, how many of each shape does she use?

10. Grady is making a tablecloth by piecing together red, white, and blue fabric squares in a pattern. Colors in the first row are red, white, blue, red, and white. Colors in the second row are blue, red, white, blue, and red. These two rows repeat for a total of 8 rows. How many squares of each color does he use?

USE DATA For 11–14, use the toy quilt designs.

11. Lu is making a quilt that is 20 squares wide and has 24 rows. The border of the quilt is made by using each toy design equally as often. Each square can hold one design. How many of each design does she have?

12. Starting in the first square of her quilt, Lu lined up her toy designs in this order: plane, car, firetruck, helicopter, crane, and wagon. Using this repeating pattern, which design will Lu place in the fifteenth square?

13. **Pose a Problem** Look back at Problem 11. Write a similar problem by changing the size of the quilt.

14. **Open-Ended** Lu plans a quilt that has 90 squares around the border. She uses at least two toy designs and the same number of each along the border. What are 4 ways she can do this? **Explain.**

CHALLENGE YOURSELF

A store sells quilt patterns for $8, squares for $9, $12, and $15, and designs for $6 each.

15. Hannah spends $92 at the store. She buys 1 pattern, 4 identical squares, and 6 designs. What is the cost of each square?

16. Lu buys a total of 6 squares for $69. She buys 3 for one price, 2 for a different price, and 1 for another different price. How many of each price of square does Lu buy?

Choose a
STRATEGY

Draw a Diagram or Picture

Make a Model or Act It Out

Make an Organized List

Find a Pattern

Make a Table or Graph

Predict and Test

Work Backward

Solve a Simpler Problem

Write an Equation

Use Logical Reasoning

5 Tessellations

OBJECTIVE: Identify and describe figures that tessellate and make tessellations.

Investigate

Materials ■ tagboard ■ construction paper ■ ruler ■ scissors

A repeating pattern of closed figures that covers a surface with no gaps and no overlaps is called a **tessellation**.

Tessellations can be found in nature, art, and architecture patterns.

Test figures to see whether they tessellate.

A Using tagboard, draw and cut out a pattern for a triangle.

B Trace the triangle onto construction paper and cut out about 20 triangles.

C Use the triangles to try to design a tessellation.

D Repeat steps A through C, using a pentagon.

Draw Conclusions

1. Did your triangle tessellate? Explain how you know.

2. What transformations did you use to make your tessellation?

3. How many figures do you need to put together to prove that a figure will tessellate?

4. Did your pentagon tessellate? Explain how you know.

5. **Evaluation** Compare your classmates' pentagons. What is the difference between the figures that did tessellate and those that did not tessellate?

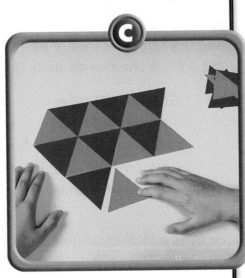

Connect

You can make a design by tessellating more than one figure.

 square parallelogram equilateral triangle

Materials ■ pattern blocks ■ colored pencils or markers

Step 1
Choose two pattern blocks that will tessellate.

Step 2
Trace several copies of each figure. Make a tessellation.

Step 3
Color it to make a pleasing design.

 hexagon rhombus trapezoid

- Do the beige parallelogram and yellow hexagon pattern blocks tessellate? Explain.

- What combinations of pattern blocks will not tessellate?

- Describe the figures in the tessellation by M. C. Escher. Other than shape, what does Escher use to complete the pattern?

▲ *Tessellation* by M. C. Escher

TALK Math
Do circles tessellate? Explain your answer.

Practice

Trace and cut out several of each figure. Tell whether the figure will tessellate. Write *yes* or *no*.

1.

2.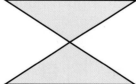

✔ 3.

4.

5.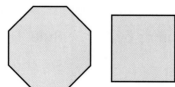

6.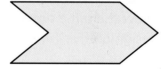

7.

8.

✔ 9.

10. **WRITE Math** ▶ **Explain** how you know if a pattern of figures forms a tessellation.

Geometric Patterns

OBJECTIVE: Identify, describe, extend, and make geometric patterns.

Learn

PROBLEM Geometric patterns are often used as ornaments on buildings. They can be based on color, size, shape, position, and number of figures.

In geometric patterns, the pattern unit is repeated over and over. In this Victorian pattern, the unit is a leaf inside a border. The rule for this pattern is rotate 180°, and then repeat.

Example **Look for a possible pattern. Write a rule.**

Color rule: yellow, orange, blue
Size rule: small, large

So, the color rule is yellow, orange, blue, and the size rule is small, large.

 Activity **Materials** ■ 1-inch squares of tracing paper ■ color pencils

Step 1

Draw the same simple design on five 1-inch squares of paper.

Step 2

Use transformations to form a repeating pattern with the squares.

• What is a rule for this pattern?

• Where will the orange rectangle be in the eighth figure?

More Examples

A Write a rule for the pattern. Copy the pattern and draw the next figure.

Rule: Increase the number of columns by 1.

So, the next figure is ▪▪▪▪▪ .

B Write a rule for the pattern. Draw the missing figure.

Rule: Decrease the number of sides by 1.

So, the missing figure is ⬠.

• Describe the sixth figure of the pattern in Example A.

1. Use the rule *repeat orange square, turn red trapezoid 90° clockwise* to make a repeating pattern. Then trace each figure, and color the figures to match the pattern you made.

Find a possible pattern. Then copy and draw the next two figures in your pattern.

2.  3. 4.

5. **TALK Math** Make a pattern that uses a rectangle and a dot. Write a rule for your pattern.

Independent Practice and Problem Solving

Find a possible pattern. Then copy and draw the next two figures in your pattern.

6. 7. 8.

Write a possible pattern. Then draw the missing figure in your pattern.

9.  10. 11.

USE DATA For 12–13, use the quilt.

12. Does a rule for the pattern appear to include color? **Explain.**

13. Compare and contrast the patterns you see in the bottom two rows of the quilt.

14. **≡FAST FACT** Frieze patterns repeat in one direction. Describe the translations, reflections, or rotations in this frieze pattern.

Frieze Pattern

15. **WRITE Math** Make your own pattern. **Explain** the rule you used to make your pattern.

Mixed Review and Test Prep

16. Make a bar graph showing Ari has 2 dogs, 3 cats, 5 birds, and 7 fish. (Grade 3)

17. Do equilateral triangles tessellate? Draw a picture to explain. (p. 558)

18. **Test Prep** Look at Problem 9. What will be the tenth figure in the pattern?

A

C

B

D

Extra Practice

Set A Tell whether the two figures are *congruent and similar, similar,* or *neither.* (pp. 542–545)

1.

2.

3.

4.

Set B Tell whether the figure appears to have *line symmetry, rotational symmetry, both,* or *neither.*

1.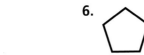

2.

3.

4.

Trace each figure. Then draw the line or lines of symmetry. (pp. 546–549)

5.

6.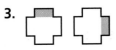

7.

8.

Set C Tell how each figure was moved. Write *translation, rotation,* or *reflection.* (pp. 550–553)

1. **2.** **3.** **4.**

5. Tell what moves were made to transform each figure into its next position.

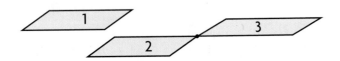

6. Which describes the drawing?

    a. The figures appear to be congruent.
    b. The figures show a reflection.
    c. The figures show a translation.
    d. The figures show a rotation.

Set D Write a rule for the pattern. Then draw the missing figure in your pattern. (pp. 560–561)

1. , ?

2. , ?

3. , ?

 Technology
ROM Use Harcourt Mega Math, Ice Station Exploration, *Polar Planes,* Levels H, I, J, K, M, N, O, T.

TECHNOLOGY ★ CONNECTION

iTools: Geometry

A bee honeycomb is an example of a tessellation made with regular hexagons.

You can make your own honeycomb tessellation.

Step 1	Click on *Geometry*. Then select *Tessellations* from the *Activities* menu. Next click on the *Computer Tessellation* tab.
Step 2	Click on the hexagon. You can use the buttons to the right of the workspace to reshape, resize, or move the figure. Click on one of the buttons then on the hexagon to make the change.
Step 3	Click on *Tessellate*. Watch the hexagon to cover the workspace without gaps or overlaps.

Click on the broom to clear the workspace for a new drawing. Click on ⑦ for more help.

Try It

Follow the same steps to make a tessellation.

1. Make a tessellation with a polygon that is not regular. Select a hexagon. Then click on the hand and drag a side or vertex of the hexagon. Another side or vertex will also move in the same direction.

2. Click on the *Tessellation* tab to make a tessellation by combining two or more plane figures. Drag a plane figure next to another plane figure. The edges will snap together to form a new plane figure.

3. **Explore More** **Describe** the transformations you used to make your own tessellation in Problem 2.

Technology
iTools are available online or on CD-ROM.

MATH POWER · Tangrams

PUZZLE PIECES

Tangrams are originally from China and have been a popular puzzle for almost 200 years. You can make a tangram by following these steps.

Example Materials ■ large square sheet of unlined paper ■ scissors

Step 1 Use a large square sheet of unlined paper. Fold the paper on the diagonal. Cut along the fold to make two congruent isosceles right triangles.

Step 2 Fold one triangle in half. Cut along the fold to make two congruent isosceles right triangles.

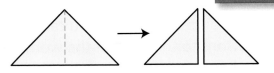

Step 3 Fold the other triangle from the vertex to the midpoint of the opposite side. Cut along the fold to make a triangle and a trapezoid.

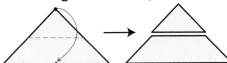

Step 4 Fold the trapezoid as shown. Cut along the fold to make a right triangle and a quadrilateral.

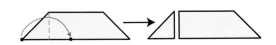

Step 5 Fold the quadrilateral as shown. Cut along the fold to make a square and a quadrilateral.

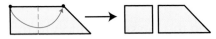

Step 6 Fold the quadrilateral as shown. Cut along the fold to make a right triangle and a parallelogram.

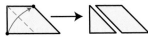

You will have seven tangram pieces with which to make figures.

Try It
Use all of the tangram pieces to make the picture.

1.

2.

3.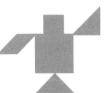

4.

5. **WRITE Math** Explain in a set of instructions how to make a different figure or picture by using the tangram pieces. Use the terms *translate, reflect,* and *rotate.*

Chapter 20 Review/Test

Check Vocabulary and Concepts

Choose the best term from the box.

1. <u>?</u> figures have the same shape and size. (p. 542)

2. A repeating pattern of closed figures that covers a surface with no gaps and no overlays is called a <u>?</u>. (p. 546)

VOCABULARY

congruent

line symmetry

tessellation

Check Skills

Tell whether the two figures are *congruent and similar, similar,* or *neither.* (pp. 542–545)

3.

4.

5.

6.

Tell whether the figure appears to have *line symmetry, rotational symmetry, both,* or *neither.* (pp. 546–549)

7.

8.

9.

10.

Tell whether the rays on the circle show a $\frac{1}{4}$, $\frac{1}{2}$, $\frac{3}{4}$, or full turn. (pp. 546–549)

11.

12.

13.

14.

Tell how each figure was moved. Write *translation, rotation,* or *reflection.* (pp. 550–553)

15. 16. 17. 18.

Check Problem Solving

Solve. (pp. 554–557)

19. Write a rule for the pattern. Draw the next three figures in your pattern.

20. **WRITE Math** ▸ Draw the lines of symmetry for each regular polygon. Count the lines for each figure. **Explain** how to find the number of lines of symmetry in any regular polygon.

Standardized Test Prep
Chapters 1–20

Geometry

1. How many lines of symmetry does this figure appear to have? (p. 544)

- **A** 5
- **B** 4
- **C** 3
- **D** 2

2. Which two figures appear to be congruent?

A

B

C

D

3. WRITE Math ▸ Gina draws the following triangles. (p. 524)

Explain two ways she can classify each triangle.

Number and Operations

Test Tip Eliminate choices.

See Item 4. To order from least to greatest, the smallest fraction must be written first. Since $\frac{1}{4}$ is the smallest fraction, *A* and *C* are eliminated.

4. Which list shows the fractions in order from least to greatest? (p. 410)

- **A** $\frac{3}{4}, \frac{7}{8}, \frac{1}{2}, \frac{1}{4}$
- **B** $\frac{1}{4}, \frac{1}{2}, \frac{3}{4}, \frac{7}{8}$
- **C** $\frac{7}{8}, \frac{3}{4}, \frac{1}{2}, \frac{1}{4}$
- **D** $\frac{1}{4}, \frac{1}{2}, \frac{7}{8}, \frac{3}{4}$

5. Which decimal is equivalent to $\frac{9}{10}$? (p. 458)

- **A** 0.10
- **C** 0.9
- **B** 0.25
- **D** 0.910

6. Jack is making a batch of cookies. The recipe says to start with $1\frac{1}{4}$ cups of flour. Later in the recipe, he uses another $\frac{1}{2}$ cup of flour. How much flour does Jack use? (p. 444)

- **A** $\frac{3}{4}$ cup
- **C** $1\frac{1}{2}$ cups
- **B** $1\frac{1}{4}$ cups
- **D** $1\frac{3}{4}$ cups

7. WRITE Math ▸ The sheriff's office bought 95 bike helmets to hand out on Bike Safety Day. They paid $19.95 each. Estimate the total cost. **Explain** the strategy you used to estimate.

Algebraic Reasoning

8. Look at the problem below.

$$\blacksquare = \blacktriangle + 6$$

If $\blacktriangle = 9$, what is $\blacksquare$? (p. 70)

A 27   **C** 15

B 18   **D** 3

9. Nina invited some friends to her house. There was $\frac{7}{8}$ of a pizza in the refrigerator. Nina and her friends ate $\frac{4}{8}$ of the pizza. Which equation shows how to find the part of the pizza that was left? (p. 440)

A $\frac{7}{8} - \frac{4}{8} = n$

B $n - \frac{4}{8} = \frac{7}{8}$

C $\frac{4}{8} - n = \frac{7}{8}$

D $\frac{7}{8} + \frac{4}{8} = n$

10. What is the value of the expression below? (p. 126)

$$(15 + 8) - (2 \times 9)$$

A 189

B 37

C 7

D 5

11. **WRITE Math** ▶ Make a function table for the equation.

$$y = 2x + 1$$

Graph the ordered pairs. **Explain** how x and y are related. (p. 226)

Data Analysis and Probability

12. Hazel took a survey about the number of times students bought lunch in the cafeteria last week. The results of her survey are shown in the line plot.

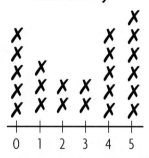

Lunch Survey

Lunches in Cafeteria

Find the median of the data above.

(p. 186)

A 1   **C** 3

B 2   **D** 4

13. **WRITE Math** ▶ Look at the line graph.

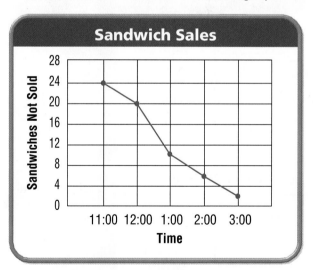

The Band Boosters' goal was to sell at least 20 sandwiches. Did they meet their goal? **Explain** how you know. (p. 214)

21 Solid Figures

Investigate

Design your own 3-layer cake. Choose different solid geometric figures for each layer. Draw the front and side views of your cake.

Types of Solid Figures

rectangular prism	triangular prism
square pyramid	cone
triangular pyramid	cylinder

FAST FACT

In 2005, Las Vegas, Nevada, celebrated the city's centennial by making the world's largest cake. The cake was 102 feet long and weighed 130,000 pounds.

GO ONLINE

Technology
Student pages are available in the Student eBook.

Show What You Know

Check your understanding of important skills needed for success in Chapter 21.

▶ Identify Plane Figures
Name each plane figure.

1.

2.

3.

4.

5.

6.

7.

8.

▶ Identify Solid Figures
Name each solid figure.

9.

10.

11.

12.

13.

14.

15.

16. (sphere)

VOCABULARY POWER

CHAPTER VOCABULARY

base	rectangular prism
cone	rectangular pyramid
cube	sphere
cylinder	square pyramid
diagonal	three-dimensional
edge	triangular prism
face	triangular pyramid
net	two-dimensional
	vertex

WARM-UP WORDS

edge the line segment where two faces of a solid figure meet

face a polygon that is a flat surface of a solid figure

three-dimensional measured in three directions, such as length, width, and height

vertex the point where three or more edges meet in a solid figure; the top point of a cone

1 Faces, Edges, and Vertices

OBJECTIVE: Identify, classify, describe, and make solid figures.

Vocabulary

edge	three-dimensional
face	triangular prism
vertex	triangular pyramid
base	rectangular pyramid

Learn

Everywhere you look, you see solid figures—in buildings, in sculptures, and in everyday objects. Solid figures have length, width, and height, so they are **three-dimensional** figures.

The line segment where two faces meet is an **edge**.

A polygon that is a flat surface is a **face**.

The point at which three or more edges meet is a **vertex**. The plural of *vertex* is *vertices*.

Math Idea
Solid figures can be classified by the shape and the number of their bases, faces, vertices, and edges.

Prisms and pyramids are named by the polygons that form their **bases**.

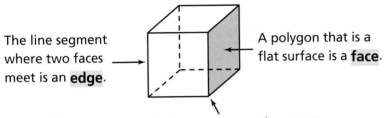

| cube, square prism | rectangular prism | **triangular prism** | square pyramid | **rectangular pyramid** | **triangular pyramid** |

Prisms have two congruent and parallel bases.

Pyramids have one base.

• Look at the photograph on page 571. What solid figure do you see? Look carefully at the faces of the rectangular pyramid below.

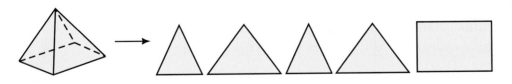

The faces are triangles and a rectangle. Name the plane figures found in the faces of the other solid figures above.

Some solid figures have curved surfaces. A cylinder has two circular bases. A cone has one circular base.

cylinder   cone   sphere

▲ The Mapparium, in Boston, Massachusetts, is a 3-story-tall stained-glass globe that has a diameter of 30 feet.

Activity

Materials ■ straws ■ modeling clay or fastener material

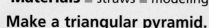
▶ **Grande Louvre, Paris, France**

A Make a triangular pyramid.

Step 1 First, make a triangle. 	**Step 2** Add a straw to 1 vertex. Then add a lump of clay to the other end of that straw. 
Step 3 Add 2 more straws at the other 2 vertices. 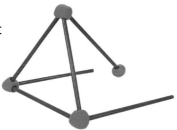	**Step 4** Join the ends of the three new straws. 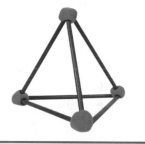

- **What if** you wanted to make a square pyramid? How many straws would you need? How many edges does a square pyramid have? How many vertices? How many faces?

B Make a cube.

Step 1 First, make a square. 	**Step 2** Add a straw to each vertex so that it is perpendicular to the other straws. Add a lump of clay on the other end of each new straw. 	**Step 3** To join the new straws, add 4 more straws to complete the cube. 

- How many straws did you use to make the cube? How many edges does a cube have? How many vertices? How many faces?

- Look at the edges of the cube at the right. Trace and extend $\overline{AB}$ and $\overline{DC}$ to make lines. Trace and extend $\overline{EH}$ and $\overline{HG}$ to make lines. Which pair of lines appear to be parallel? Which pair of lines appear to be perpendicular?

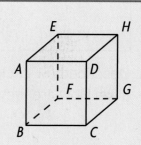

1. What is the base of the solid figure at the right? Are the faces rectangles or triangles? Name the solid figure.

Name a solid figure that is described.

2. 6 faces   3. 4 vertices   ✔ 4. 8 edges   ✔ 5. one circular base

6. **TALK Math** Describe how cubes and rectangular prisms are alike. How are they different?

Independent Practice and Problem Solving

Name a solid figure that is described.

7. 5 faces   8. all triangular faces

9. two circular bases   10. more than 5 vertices

Which solid figure or figures do you see in each?

11.    12.    13.    14.

For 15–18, copy and complete the table.

	Figure	Name	Name of Faces and Number of Each	Number of Faces	Number of Edges	Number of Vertices
15.		Cube	▣	▣	▣	▣
16.		Triangular Prism	▣	▣	▣	▣
17.		Triangular Pyramid	▣	▣	▣	▣
18.		Square Pyramid	▣	▣	▣	▣

19. Describe how circles and spheres are alike. How are they different?

20. Describe how squares and cubes are alike. How are they different?

Technology
Use Harcourt Mega Math, Ice Station Exploration, *Frozen Solids*, Levels C, D, E.

Extra Practice on page 590, Set A

For 21–22, look at the edges of the prism.

21. Name a pair of parallel line segments.

22. Name a pair of perpendicular line segments.

23. Which solid figure has more edges—a triangular prism or a triangular pyramid? How many more?

24. **Reasoning** If you remove a label from a soup can and look at the label, what plane figure do you see?

25. **Reasoning** Are all rectangular pyramids square pyramids? **Explain** your thinking.

26. **WRITE Math** ▸ What's the Question? The answer is 2 triangular faces and 3 rectangular faces.

Learn About **Rotational Symmetry**

A three-dimensional figure with rotational symmetry can be rotated about one or more lines. This line is called the axis of symmetry. As the figure rotates around the axis of symmetry, it fits into the same position but has a different orientation.

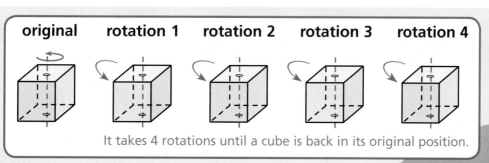

| original | rotation 1 | rotation 2 | rotation 3 | rotation 4 |

It takes 4 rotations until a cube is back in its original position.

Try It

Tell how many rotations it takes to return the figure to its original position.

27.

28.

29.

30.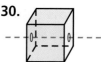

Mixed Review and Test Prep

31. Use the table on page 572. Make a pictograph that shows the number of faces for each solid figure. (p. 218)

32. Which letter appears to have a line of symmetry? (p. 546)

    A   N   R   S

33. **Test Prep** Which of the following figures has no faces or straight edges?

  A Cube   **C** Triangular prism

  B Sphere   **D** Rectangular pyramid

Draw Figures

OBJECTIVE: Describe and draw plane and solid figures.

Learn

PROBLEM The 1914 Toy of the Year, Tinkertoy®, was based on a right triangle made of sticks and spools. The base of a small triangle could become the side of a bigger triangle, and a three-dimensional figure could be made. How can you draw a picture of a right triangle?

You can use dot paper to draw plane figures.

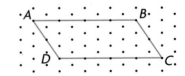

Activity 1 Draw a right triangle.

Materials ■ square dot paper ■ straightedge

Think: The triangle must have one right angle.

Step 1	Step 2	Step 3
Draw a line segment 4 units long.	From one endpoint, draw another line segment perpendicular and 3 units long.	Connect the endpoints. Then label the vertices.

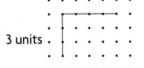

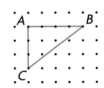

Activity 2 Draw a parallelogram.

Materials ■ isometric dot paper ■ straightedge

Think: A parallelogram has 2 pairs of parallel sides with opposite sides congruent.

Step 1	Step 2	Step 3
Draw a line segment 4 units long.	From one endpoint, draw a slanted line segment 2 units long.	Draw lines parallel to and congruent to the line segments already drawn. Then label the vertices.

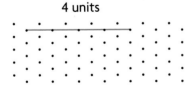

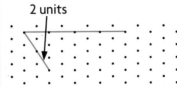

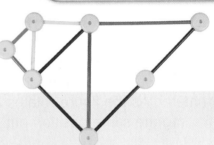

• Identify and name the vertices and line segments of the triangle and of the parallelogram.

Draw Solid Figures

Thomas likes to record in his sketchbook each new object he builds with his toys. How can he use dot paper to draw a picture of a rectangular prism?

Activity 3 Draw a rectangular prism.

Materials ■ square dot paper ■ straightedge

Think: A rectangular prism has 6 faces, 12 edges, and 8 vertices.

Step 1		**Step 2**	
Draw a square with sides of 3 units. 3 units		Draw slanted line segments from 3 vertices, as shown.	
Step 3		**Step 4**	
Connect the endpoints of the slanted line segments.		Draw dashed line segments to show the faces that are hidden. Then label the vertices.	

- Identify and name two pairs of parallel and perpendicular line segments in the rectangular prism.

Activity 4 Draw a triangular pyramid.

Materials ■ isometric dot paper ■ straightedge

Think: A triangular pyramid has 4 faces, 6 edges, and 4 vertices.

Step 1		**Step 2**	
Draw a triangle, as shown.		Draw dashed line segments to show the faces that are hidden. Then label the vertices.	

- How many edges can be seen in the rectangular prism? in the pyramid?
  How many edges are hidden in the rectangular prism? in the pyramid?

- Identify and name the vertices, edges, and faces in the triangular pyramid.

Guided Practice

1. How many sides does a square have? How many line segments are needed to draw a square? How many edges does a cube have? How many line segments are needed to draw a cube?

For 2–5, use the pictures.

2. What plane figure does the game board look like?

3. Use dot paper to draw the game board.

4. What solid figure does the number cube look like?

5. Use dot paper to draw the number cube.

6. **TALK Math** **Explain** how to draw a square pyramid.

Independent Practice and Problem Solving

Copy each figure on dot paper. Draw the missing line segments so that each figure matches its label.

7. rectangle

8. hexagon

9. pentagon

For 10–13, use dot paper to draw each figure. Label the vertices. Identify and name any parallel and perpendicular line segments you see in each figure.

10. a figure with eight sides that are each 2 units long

11. a trapezoid that has one right angle and whose longest side has a length of 6 units

12. a rectangular prism that has at least one edge with a length of 4 units

13. a triangular pyramid whose base has one right angle

For 14–17, use the table.

14. What solid figure does the game player look like?

15. Use dot paper to draw the video game player.

16. What solid figure does the tent look like?

17. Use dot paper to draw the model tent.

Toy	Vertices	Edges	Faces
Video Game Player	8	12	6 rectangles
Model Tent	5	8	4 triangles, 1 rectangle

18. **Reasoning** A model railroad car is shaped like a rectangular prism. Its length is greater than its height and width. Is this model a cube? **Explain.**

19. **WRITE Math** Mitch drew 2 squares and 2 pentagons. Courtney drew a triangle, a square, and an octagon. Who drew more line segments? **Explain.**

Learn About Spatial Relationships

Perspective is a technique used in drawing to make three-dimensional objects on a flat surface appear to have depth and distance. Perspective imitates the way people see things in real life, with objects appearing nearer or farther away. For example, you know that railroad tracks are always the same distance apart. However, in a photograph of railroad tracks, perspective makes the tracks seem to get closer together and then disappear in the distance.

• In the drawing below, which building appears to be the farthest away?

Try It

For 20–23, use the block.

20. If you were standing directly to the left of the block, would you see the letter B?

   Front View ▲

21. If you were standing directly to the right of the block, would you see the letter A?

22. If the block were on a shelf shorter than you and you were standing directly in front of the block, what letters would you see?

23. If the block were on a shelf taller than you, would you see the letter C?

For 24–26, use the drawing below.

24. Which building is to the right of the car?

25. Which building appears to be the closest?

26. **WRITE Math** ▸ **Describe** the location of Building B. Include words like *left*, *right*, *farthest*, or *closest* in your description.

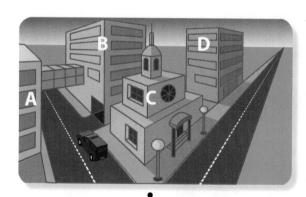

You are here.

Mixed Review and Test Prep

27. The container for Tinkertoy was designed to be mailed easily. What solid figure describes this container? (p. 570)

28. A school has 24 classrooms. Each room has 12 gray desks and 15 black desks. How many desks are there in all? (p. 282)

29. **Test Prep** Use dot paper to draw a triangular prism that has at least one edge with a length of 2 units and another edge with a length of 4 units. Label each vertex.

30. **Test Prep** How many line segments do you need to draw a square pyramid?

   A 5   **C** 8

   B 6   **D** 12

Patterns for Solid Figures

OBJECTIVE: Identify solid figures by their nets and make patterns to draw solid figures.

Learn

PROBLEM A **net** is a two-dimensional pattern that can be folded to make a three-dimensional figure. How can you make a net for the box shown?

You can cut apart a three-dimensional box to make a two-dimensional pattern.

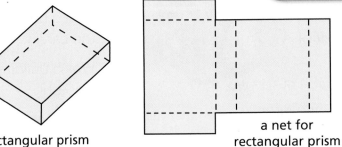

rectangular prism

a net for rectangular prism

Activity Make a net.

Materials ■ empty container, such as a cereal box ■ scissors ■ tape

Step 1

Cut along some of the edges until the box is flat. Be sure that each face is connected to another face by at least one edge.

Step 2

Trace the flat shape on a sheet of paper. This shape is a net of the box.

Step 3

Cut out the net. Fold it into a three-dimensional box. Use tape to hold it together.

• Compare your net with those of your classmates. What can you conclude?

Guided Practice

1. What shapes make up the net of a rectangular prism? How many of them are there?

Draw a net that can be cut to make a model of each solid figure.

2.   **3.**   ✓**4.**   ✓**5.**

6. **TALK Math** **Explain** how the nets for a cube and a rectangular prism are alike. How they are different?

Independent Practice and Problem Solving

Draw a net that can be cut to make a model of each solid figure.

7.   **8.**   **9.**   **10.**

Would the net make a cube? Write *yes* or *no*.

11.   **12.**   **13.**   **14.**

For 15–17, use the patterns.

15. Which patterns can you use to make a cylinder?

16. Identify the solid figure you can make with pattern B.

17. Which pattern can you use to make a triangular pyramid?

a.   b.   c.

18. **Reasoning** Look at the net at the right. When the net is folded, which face will be parallel to face *A*? Which faces will be perpendicular to face *B*?

19. **WRITE Math** ▸ **What's the Error?** Eric said the net at the right can be folded to make a triangular prism. Describe Eric's mistake. Then draw a net he could use to make a triangular prism.

Mixed Review and Test Prep

20. Aiko drew the shape below. How many lines of symmetry does this shape appear to have? (p. 546)

21. Bob and 3 of his friends each rented skates. They spent $20 total. Write an equation to show the cost to rent a pair of skates. (p. 128)

22. **Test Prep** What solid figure can you make from the net shown?

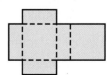

Extra Practice on page 590, Set C

 LESSON

4 Different Views of Solid Figures

OBJECTIVE: Identify and describe solid figures from different perspectives.

Quick Review

Antonio cuts out a net with 5 faces and tapes it together to make a triangular prism. What shapes are the faces?

Learn

PROBLEM Objects look different when viewed from different directions. If you draw the front view of the Capitol Records building, what shape would you draw?

HANDS ON

Activity **Draw different views.**

Materials ■ solid wooden cylinder

- Look at the top of the cylinder. Draw the top view.
- Look at the front of the cylinder. Draw the front view.
- Look at the side of the cylinder. Draw the side view.

So, you would draw a rectangle.

▲ The Capitol Records building in Hollywood, California, is shaped like a cylinder.

You can identify solid figures by the way they look from different views.

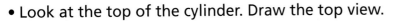

Examples **Use different views to identify each solid figure.**

A   top view   front view   side view

The top view shows that the base is a triangle and that the faces come together at a point.

The front and side views show the solid figure looks like a triangle.

So, this solid figure is a triangular pyramid.

B   top view   front view   side view

The top view shows that the base is a circle and that the top comes to a point.

The front and side views show the solid figure looks like a triangle.

So, this solid figure is a cone.

- Which solid figure looks like a circle from any direction?
- How are the views of a rectangular prism and a cylinder alike? How are they different?
- **Reasoning** What plane figure could be used to describe the shadow of a building that is shaped like a rectangular prism?

ERROR ALERT

You cannot always identify a solid figure from just one view or two views.

1. All of the faces of a rectangular prism are rectangles. What is the top view of a rectangular prism? The front view? The side view?

Name the solid figure that has the following views.

✓2.   top view   front view   side view   ✓3.   top view   front view   side view

4. **TALK Math** Choose an object in your classroom. Draw the top, front, and side views.

Independent Practice and Problem Solving

Name the solid figure that has the following views.

5.   top view   front view   side view   6.   top view   front view   side view

Draw the top, front, and side views of each solid figure.

7.    8.   9.    10.

For 11–12, use the different views.

11. What solid figures have a rectangle as one of the views?

12. What solid figures have a triangle as one of the views?

13. **Pose a Problem** Look back at Problem 11. Write a similar problem by giving clues to identify a solid figure.

14. **WRITE Math** Explain how you can identify whether a prism is a triangular prism, a rectangular prism, or a cube by its views.

Mixed Review and Test Prep

15. How many faces does a cube have? (p. 570)

16. There were $5\frac{1}{2}$ cups of milk left in a carton. Sue used $2\frac{1}{2}$ cups to make a cake and drank $\frac{1}{2}$ cup. How much milk is left in the carton now? (p. 444)

17. **Test Prep** Which figure is the top view of a cylinder?

   A Circle   **C** Square

   B Rectangle   **D** Triangle

Problem Solving Workshop
Strategy: Make a Model

OBJECTIVE: Solve problems by using the strategy *make a model.*

Learn the Strategy

It can be difficult to understand what is being described in a problem. Sometimes you can use a model to show the actions in a problem.

A model can show the actions in a problem.

Amy baked 16 brownies. She took half of them to school for the bake sale. She gave Jamie half of what was left. She wants to know how many brownies are left.

Action 1  ← Amy baked 16 brownies.

Action 2 ← She took half to school.

Action 3

↑ She gave Jamie half of what was left.   ↑ Brownies left.

A model can show a situation before and after a change.

Tyrell built a prism that was 3 cubes long, 3 cubes wide, and 3 cubes high. Then he removed 6 cubes. What might his model look like now?

3 cubes   3 cubes

3 cubes

Before   **After**

A model can show the relationships in a problem.

Susan wants to know how many cubes she will need to make the next cube in this pattern.

1   **2**   **3**

When making a model, reread the problem to make sure that your model shows each part of the problem.

TALK Math

How is the strategy *make a model* like the strategy *act it out*? How are they different?

Use the Strategy

PROBLEM After John studied the buildings of architect Moshe Safdie, he used cubes to design a building. He drew a top view, a front view, and a side view of his building. How many cubes will John need to build his model?

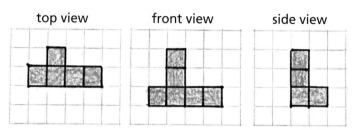

top view   front view   side view

▲ Moshe Safdie designed these buildings for Expo 67, the 1967 World's Fair in Montreal, Canada. They were made from 354 stacked cubes.

Read to Understand

- **What are you asked to find?**
- **What information is given? Is there information you will not use? If so, what?**

Plan

- **What strategy can you use to solve the problem?**

 You can make a model to help you visualize the details in the problem.

Solve

- **How can you use the strategy to solve the problem?**

  You can use cubes to make a model of the building.

  First, build the top view. The model shows 5 cubes.

  Next, stack cubes to match the front view. The model now shows 7 cubes.

  Finally, decide whether the model matches the side view. If necessary, make any changes. Since the side view matches, no changes are needed.

  So, John will need 7 cubes to build his model.

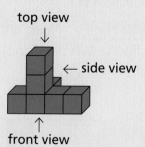

top view
← side view
↑ front view

Check

- **How can you check your model?**
- **What other strategy could you use to solve the problem?**

Guided Problem Solving

1. Antoine made the model shown at the right by using 9 cubes. Draw a top view, a front view, and a side view on grid paper.

   First, draw the top view.

   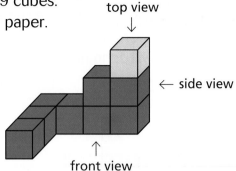

   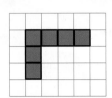

   Next, look at the figure from the front, and draw what you see.

   Finally, look at the figure from the side, and draw the side view.

2. **What if** the yellow cube were removed? Which of the three views would change? Draw each new view on grid paper, and label the view.

3. Alicia used the fewest possible cubes to make a building, whose views are shown at the right. How many cubes did she use?

   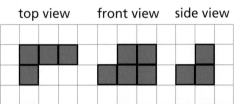

Problem Solving Strategy Practice

Make a model to solve.

4. Sandra has 40 cubes. She uses half of them to make a building. She gives Jeffrey half of what is not used so that he can make a building. If Jeffrey uses 8 cubes in his building, how many of the 40 cubes are still not used?

5. Riko has 60 cubes. She builds a staircase beginning with 1 cube, then 3, then 6, then 10, and so on. When she has made the largest possible staircase, how many cubes will she have left over?

6. **WRITE Math** ▸ Micah and Natalie each drew the front view of this figure. Whose drawing is correct? **Explain.**

   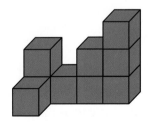

   Micah   **Natalie**

   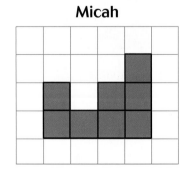

Mixed Strategy Practice

7. Ellie wants to sort the objects on the table according to their shape. Make an organized list of how she can sort the objects.

Choose a STRATEGY

Draw a Diagram or Picture
Make a Model or Act It Out
Make an Organized List
Find a Pattern
Make a Table or Graph
Predict and Test
Work Backward
Solve a Simpler Problem
Write an Equation
Use Logical Reasoning

USE DATA For 8–10, use the cube in the picture.

8. **What if** Rubik had designed a puzzle that was 6 cubes long, 6 cubes wide, and 6 cubes high? How many small squares would it have on one face?

9. The center of Rubik's puzzle is missing one small cube. How many small cubes make up the puzzle?

10. ☰**FAST FACT** When Rubik was designing his puzzle, he first used colored paper squares to cover each small square on the outside of the big cube. How many small paper squares did he need?

11. **Pose a Problem** Write a problem about a model made with 10 cubes.

12. **Open-Ended** Suppose you have 40 cubes. How could you make a pattern with some or all of the cubes? Describe the pattern.

▼ Erno Rubik invented one of the best-selling puzzles in history in 1974. The small cubes can be arranged in more than 43,000,000,000,000,000,000, or 43 quintillion, different ways. Only 1 of the ways is correct.

CHALLENGE YOURSELF
Use the figure at the right. There are no hidden cubes in the figure. Do not make a model to solve.

13. How many more cubes would be needed to change the model into a cube that has 16 small squares on each face? **Explain.**

14. Suppose you change the figure into a prism 2 cubes long, 2 cubes wide, and 2 cubes high. Would you need to add cubes or take cubes away? How many?

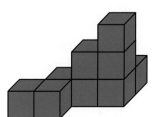

Combine and Divide Figures

OBJECTIVE: Predict the results of combining and dividing plane figures and solid figures.

Learn

Architects, artists, craftspeople, and designers combine and divide figures when designing buildings, sculptures, furniture, baskets, games, topiaries, and other things. You can combine and divide plane figures and solid figures to make other figures.

Activity Combine and divide plane figures.
Materials ■ pattern blocks ■ tracing paper ■ color paper

A Combine pattern blocks to make quadrilaterals.

• In what other ways can you combine pattern blocks to make quadrilaterals?

• Classify in as many ways as possible each quadrilateral you made. Are any of your quadrilaterals congruent? Explain.

• What other figures do you think you can make? Test your prediction.

B Place a sheet of tracing paper over a sheet of color paper so that they overlap.

• What figure did your overlap make?

• In what other ways can you overlap the sheets to make a triangle? A square? A rectangle? A trapezoid?

• What other figures do you think you can make? Test your prediction.

C A **diagonal** is a line segment that connects two vertices of a polygon that are not next to each other. Draw a quadrilateral. Then divide it by drawing diagonals.
diagonal

• Describe the figures you made out of the quadrilateral by dividing it with diagonals. Are any of your figures congruent? Explain.

▼ *Unfoldings,* a painting by Jae Hahn

Activity Combine and divide solid figures.

Materials ■ wooden solid figures ■ modeling clay ■ thin string

A Combine solid figures to make other solid figures.

- In what other ways can you combine a cube and a rectangular prism?
- In what ways can you combine two cubes and a square pyramid?

B Make a model of a rectangular prism with the modeling clay. Use the string to cut the rectangular prism in half as shown.

When a solid figure is cut straight through, other solid figures are formed.

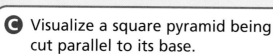

- What solid figures did you make?
- **What if** you were to cut one of the new figures diagonally? What solid figures would you make?

C Visualize a square pyramid being cut parallel to its base.

- Name the solid figure formed by the top portion. Name the faces of the bottom portion.
- Describe how you could combine and divide solid figures to make models of the buildings shown in the photographs.

▲ Rock and Roll Hall of Fame and Museum, in Cleveland, Ohio

▲ Hirshhorn Museum and Sculpture Garden, in Washington, D.C.

▲ Taking away one or more edges from a cube made each of the 122 forms in Sol LeWitt's sculpture *Incomplete Open Cubes.*

Chapter 21   587   GO ON

1. Name the quadrilateral made by these two pattern blocks. What pattern blocks were used? What other pattern blocks could be combined to make this quadrilateral?

Draw a picture to show the new figure.

2. Divide a rectangle to make two triangles.

3. Combine two rectangles to make a square.

4. **TALK Math** If you cut off the corner of a cube, what solid figure is cut off? **Explain** how you know.

Independent Practice (and Problem Solving

Draw a picture to show the new figure.

5. Divide a rectangle to make two trapezoids.

6. Combine two right triangles to make a triangle.

7. Combine two triangles to make a parallelogram.

8. Divide a triangle to make a triangle and a trapezoid.

What figures do you see in each?

9.

10.

11.

12.

For 13–15, use the picture.

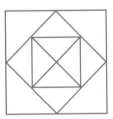

13. How many squares are in the picture?

14. How many right triangles are in the picture?

15. How many rectangles are in the picture?

16. What figures are made if you overlap a triangular sheet of tracing paper and a rectangular sheet of color paper?

17. Draw a pentagon. Then draw a diagonal to make two new polygons. How many sides do the new polygons have?

18. What solid figures can you combine to make a solid figure that looks like a table? **Describe** how you could combine them to build the table.

19. **WRITE Math** **Sense or Nonsense** Sonya said that if you cut a rectangle into two equal parts, you will always get two congruent rectangles. Does Sonya's statement make sense? **Explain.**

20. How many edges does a triangular prism have? (p. 570)

21. Test Prep If the regular hexagon is divided on the dashed line, what are the new figures?

   A Hexagons   **C** Parallelograms

   B Pentagons   **D** Trapezoids

22. Write a rule for the pattern. Use your rule to find the next two numbers. (p. 382)

   37, 42, 38, 43, 39, 44, 40, ■, ■

23. Test Prep Use pattern blocks to combine two equilateral triangles. What figure did you make? Add a third equilateral triangle to your figure. What figure do you have now?

Problem Solving [connects to] Art

Tessellations

You can make a new tessellation design by dividing one or more figures and combining one or more other figures.

▲ *Metamorphosis II*
by M.C. Escher

Make a stair-step design from a tessellation of hexagons.

Materials ■ tessellation pattern ■ tracing paper

Step 1

Lightly trace the hexagon pattern. Divide each hexagon into a rectangle and two triangles.

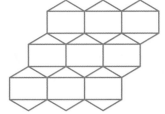

Step 2

Combine two triangles into one parallelogram by erasing a line segment between the triangles. Darken the lines to make the stair steps.

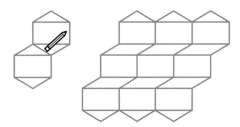

1. Make your own design that uses a tessellation of hexagons. **Describe** how you made your design.

2. Make your own design that uses a tessellation of equilateral triangles. **Describe** how you made your design.

Extra Practice

Set A Name a solid figure that is described. (pp. 570–573)

1. 6 congruent faces   **2.** 4 triangular faces   **3.** one circular base   **4.** 12 edges

Which solid figure or figures do you see in each?

5.    **6.**    **7.**    **8.**

Set B Copy each figure on dot paper. Draw the missing line segments so that each figure matches its label. (pp. 574–577)

1. parallelogram   **2.** octagon   **3.** trapezoid

For 4–5, use the table.

4. What solid figure does the cake box look like?

5. Use dot paper to draw the cake box.

Item	Vertices	Edges	Faces
Cake Box	8	12	6 squares

Set C Draw a net that can be cut to make a model of the solid figure shown. (pp. 578–579)

1.   **2.**    **3.**   **4.**

Set D Draw the top, front, and side views of each solid figure. (pp. 580–581)

1.   **2.**   **3.**   **4.**

Set E Draw a picture to show the new figure. (pp. 586–589)

1. Divide a right triangle to make a right triangle and a trapezoid.

2. Divide a rectangle to make a square and a rectangle.

3. Trace a pattern block trapezoid. Divide it to make two right triangles and a square.

 Technology
Use Harcourt Mega Math Ice Station Exploration, *Frozen Solids*, Levels A, B, C, D, E, F, G, H, M.

Build the View

Builders!
2 teams, at least 2 players on each team

Building Blocks!
- Index cards (15)
- Centimeter cubes (15 for each team)
- Two-color counters

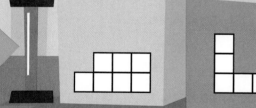
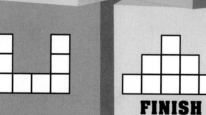

FINISH

Build!

- Shuffle the cards. Place them facedown in a stack.

- Begin with the space labeled START. Teams take turns drawing the top card. Teams use cubes to build a figure that has the view shown on the space and can be described by the view on the card.

- If both teams agree that the figure is correct, the team places a counter on that space. If the figure does not have that

view, the other team draws the next view card and tries to build a figure. If neither team can build a figure with that view, the space is out of play.

- Move to the next space on the board. The team draws the top card and continues to play.

- Play ends with the space labeled FINISH. The team with the greater number of counters on the board wins.

 **Patterns in Prisms and Pyramids**

Faces, Vertices, and Edges

Leonhard Euler was a Swiss mathematician who lived in the 1700s. He discovered that the numbers of faces, vertices, and edges in prisms and in pyramids are related.

Prisms	Pyramids
sides = number of sides on the base	sides = number of sides on the base
sides + 2 = faces	sides + 1 = faces
sides × 2 = vertices	sides + 1 = vertices
sides × 3 = edges	sides × 2 = edges

▲ **Leonhard Euler** (1707–1783)

Examples

A Find the number of faces, vertices, and edges of a cube.

A cube has 4 sides on the base.

4 + 2 = 6 faces

4 × 2 = 8 vertices

4 × 3 = 12 edges

So, a cube has 6 faces, 8 vertices, and 12 edges.

B Find the number of faces, vertices, and edges of a square pyramid.

A square pyramid has 4 sides on the base.

4 + 1 = 5 faces

4 + 1 = 5 vertices

4 × 2 = 8 edges

So, a square pyramid has 5 faces, 5 vertices, and 8 edges.

Try It

Tell how many faces, vertices, and edges each figure has.

1. rectangular pyramid
2. rectangular prism
3. triangular pyramid
4. triangular prism

5. **Challenge** If you read that a prism had 8 faces, 8 vertices, and 12 edges, how would you know that the information is incorrect?

6. **WRITE Math** Explain how to find the number of edges on any pyramid or prism if you know the number of sides on the base.

Chapter 21 Review/Test

Check Vocabulary and Concepts

Choose the best term from the box.

VOCABULARY

rectangular pyramid
triangular pyramid
triangular prism

1. A _?_ has triangular bases and rectangular faces. (p. 570)

2. A _?_ has a rectangular base and triangular faces. (p. 570)

Check Skills

Which solid figure or figures do you see in each? (pp. 570–573, 586–589)

3.

4.

5.

6.

Copy each figure on dot paper. Draw the missing line segments so that each figure matches its label. (pp. 574–577)

7. isosceles triangle 8. square 9. parallelogram 10. trapezoid

Draw the top, front, and side views of each solid figure. Then draw a net that can be cut to make a model of each figure. (pp. 578–579, 580–581)

11.   12. 13.   14.

Draw a picture to show the new figure. (pp. 586–589)

15. Divide a square to make 2 trapezoids. 16. Combine 2 triangles to make a square.

17. Combine 3 triangles to make a trapezoid. 18. Divide a rhombus to make 2 triangles.

Check Problem Solving

For 19–20, use the picture to solve. (pp. 582–585)

19. Melanie used 8 cubes to build this figure. Draw the top view, front view, and side view.

20. **WRITE Math** Explain how the views would change if the yellow cube were removed.

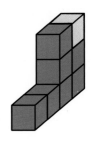

Unit Review/Test
Chapters 19–21

Multiple Choice

1. Which of the following appears to be an acute angle? (p. 514)

A **C**

B **D**

2. The figure below is an example of what type of quadrilateral? (p. 526)

A Rectangle

B Square

C Parallelogram

D Trapezoid

3. Nila built a rectangular prism with centimeter cubes. Which view could be represented below? (p. 580)

A Top view

B Front view

C Side view

D None of the views

4. Which pair of lines appears to be perpendicular? (p. 518)

A

B

C

D

5. How many lines of symmetry does the figure appear to have? (p. 546)

A 1

B 2

C 3

D 4

6. Look at the net for the solid figure.

Which solid figure will it form? (p. 578)

A **B**

C **D**

 Technology Use *Online Assessment.*

7. Which of the following triangles is an equilateral triangle? (p. 524)

A

B

C

D

8. Elvis carved the model below from a bar of soap. How many edges does this figure have? (p. 570)

A 6   C 10

B 8   D 12

9. Jan drew a circle and measured the length of the radius. How can she find the length of the diameter of the circle? (p. 530)

A Add 2 to the length of the radius.

B Double the length of the radius.

C Triple the length of the radius.

D Divide the length of the radius by 2.

10. A $\frac{1}{4}$ turn is equal to a turn of how many degrees? (p. 546)

A 90°

B 270°

C 180°

D 360°

Short Response

11. Classify this figure in as many ways as possible. (p. 526)

12. What single transformation is shown by these figures? (p. 550)

13. What is the measure of a right angle? (p. 514)

14. Draw a circle. Draw and label a diameter and radius. (p. 530)

15. Look at the map. Which streets appear to be parallel to each other? (p. 518)

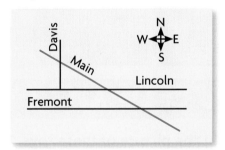

Extended Response WRITE Math ▶

16. Explain why it is **NOT** possible to draw an equilateral scalene triangle. (p. 524)

17. Explain the differences between a triangular pyramid and a triangular prism. Draw an example of each. (p. 570)

18. Are all circles congruent? Are all circles similar? **Explain** how you know. (p. 542)

19. Write a rule for the pattern. Then draw the next two figures in your pattern. (p. 560)

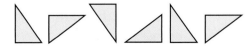

THE WORLD ALMANAC FOR KIDS

Looking at Toys

Symmetric Toys

Have you ever made a heart by drawing half of it on a folded piece of paper and then cutting it out? If so, you have made a symmetric figure. Many old and new toys and games have symmetry. They may have line symmetry, rotational symmetry, both, or neither.

Mr. Potato Head, invented in 1952, was the first toy for sale on TV. Its nose, ears, and eyes could be stuck onto a real potato.

  The game of dominoes began hundreds of years ago in China. These dominoes have both line symmetry and rotational symmetry.

FACT·ACTIVITY

Look at the picture of these toys. Tell whether each toy has *line symmetry*, *rotational symmetry*, *both*, or *neither*.

1 Boomerang

2 Electronic game

3 Dot cube

Each picture shows part of a toy. Copy and complete each picture to show line symmetry.

4 Robot

5 Football

6 Guitar

7 **WRITE Math** Describe a toy or game not pictured here that has symmetry. **Explain** how you know.

Game Boards

ALMANAC Fact

People have been using boomerangs for 10,000 years. Non-returning varieties were used in ancient Egypt. The returning variety came from early native people in Australia.

Number cubes have been found in ancient Egyptian tombs.

Chess and backgammon are games that have been played all over the world for centuries. Backgammon is one of the oldest games in recorded history. Early versions were played in Mesopotamia thousands of years ago. Chess was developed in India in the sixth century. Both are games of strategy for two people. Plane figures and solid figures were used in the design of these board games.

FACT·ACTIVITY

Suppose a large toy company asks you to design a new board game.

1 Draw the game board. Decide what plane figures you want to use. Then color your design.

► Name the plane figures you used.

► Describe how you combined or transformed the plane figures to make your game board.

► Does your design show a tessellating pattern? **Explain.**

► Does your game board show symmetry? **Explain.**

2 Draw one of your game pieces. Show the front and top views.

8 Measurement and Probability

Math on Location

A DVD FROM
The Futures Channel

with
Chapter Projects

1

Different woods are cut to exact lengths, widths, and depths and glued together to form the guitar's body.

2

Custom guitars have different shapes. Each surface has a different length and width or area.

3

Choices of shape, wood, finish, number of strings and electronics result in many different guitars.

VOCABULARY POWER

TALK Math

What math is used in the **Math on Location** photographs? How could you find the length of each string on a guitar? What units would you use to measure the length? Why?

READ Math

REVIEW VOCABULARY You learned the words below when you learned about measurement. How do these words relate to **Math on Location**?

centimeter a metric unit for measuring length or distance; 100 centimeters = 1 meter

foot a customary unit used for measuring length or distance; 1 foot = 12 inches

perimeter the distance around a figure

WRITE Math

Copy and complete the word association tree below. Use what you know about measurement to complete the tree.

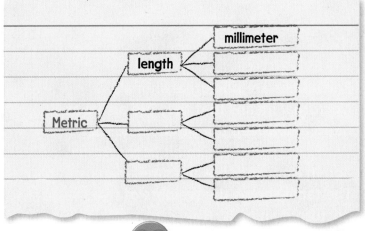

Word association tree: Metric branches to length, which branches to millimeter and an empty box; Metric also branches to two empty boxes each leading to more empty boxes.

GO ONLINE Technology
Multimedia Math Glossary link at
www.harcourtschool.com/hspmath

22 Customary and Metric Measurement

An adult Indian crested porcupine is about 2 to $2\frac{1}{2}$ feet long. To frighten away other animals, a porcupine fans out its spines and rattle its quills.

Investigate

Porcupines are nocturnal animals. *Nocturnal* means that they are active at night and asleep during the day. The World of Darkness exhibit at the Bronx Zoo in New York has noctural animals. The table shows the weights of five nocturnal animals. How can you compare the weights?

Estimated Weights of Some Nocturnal Animals

Animal	Newborn Weight	Adult Weight
Coyote	8 ounces	480 ounces
Red Fox	3 ounces	12 pounds
Indian Crested Porcupine	12 ounces	35 pounds
Raccoon	4 ounces	320 ounces
Skunk	1 ounce	6 pounds

Technology
Student pages are available in the Student eBook.

Check your understanding of important skills
needed for success in Chapter 22.

▶ **Measure Length**

Measure the length of each to the nearest $\frac{1}{2}$ inch.

1.

2.

Measure the length of each to the nearest centimeter.

3.

4.

▶ **Multiply and Divide**

Find the product or quotient.

5. $38 \times 3 = $ ■   **6.** $76 \div 4 = $ ■   **7.** $12 \times 9 = $ ■   **8.** $27 \div 3 = $ ■

9. $80 \div 16 = $ ■   **10.** $42 \div 2 = $ ■   **11.** $36 \div 12 = $ ■   **12.** $7 \times 16 = $ ■

▶ **Multiplication and Division Patterns**

Use a pattern to find each product or quotient.

13. 4×10
4×100
$4 \times 1,000$

14. $50 \div 10$
$500 \div 10$
$5,000 \div 10$

15. 7×10
7×100
$7 \times 1,000$

16. $90 \div 10$
$900 \div 10$
$9,000 \div 10$

VOCABULARY POWER

CHAPTER VOCABULARY

centigram (cg)	centimeter (cm)
foot (ft)	decimeter (dm)
linear units	fluid ounce (fl oz)
mile (mi)	gallon (gal)
millimeter (mm)	kilometer (km)
milliliter (mL)	liter (L)
ounce (oz)	mass
pound (lb)	milligram (mg)
ton (T)	meter (m)
yard (yd)	pint (pt)

WARM-UP WORDS

linear units units that measure length, width, height, or distance

mass the amount of matter in an object

ounce a customary unit for measuring weight; 16 ounces = 1 pound

Measure Fractional Parts

OBJECTIVE: Estimate and measure length to the nearest whole, $\frac{1}{2}$, $\frac{1}{4}$, and $\frac{1}{8}$ inch.

Learn

Units of measure used to measure length, width, height, or distance are called **linear units**. The customary units of length include **inch (in.)**, **foot (ft)**, **yard (yd)**, and **mile (mi)**.

You can use a common object or event to help you visualize the size of each unit.

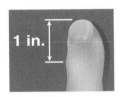

The length of your thumb from the tip to the knuckle is about 1 inch.

The length of a license plate is about 1 foot.

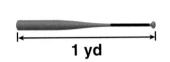

The length of a baseball bat is about 1 yard.

The distance you can walk in 20 minutes is about 1 mile.

• What unit would you use to measure the length of a driveway? Explain.

You can use an inch ruler to measure to the nearest inch.

Activity 1 **Materials** ■ paper clips ■ inch ruler ■ desk

Length				
	Paper Clips		**Inches**	
Object	**Estimate**	**Actual**	**Estimate**	**Actual**
desk	■	■	■	■

• Look at the length of a paper clip. Use that length to estimate the width of your desk in paper clips. Record your estimate in a table like the one shown.

• Measure your desk. Use a paper clip as your unit. Count the number of paper clips you used. Record the measurement to the nearest paper clip in the table.

• A small paper clip measures about 1 inch long. Use the paper clip to estimate the length of the top of your desk in inches. Then measure the length of your desk to the nearest inch. Record your measurement in the table.

• How does your estimate compare to the actual measurement you found by using the ruler?

Fractions in Measurements

Sometimes the length of an object is not a whole unit. For example, the length of a paper clip is more than 1 inch but less than 2 inches.

You can use an inch ruler to measure objects to the nearest $\frac{1}{2}$, $\frac{1}{4}$, and $\frac{1}{8}$ inch. Measuring to the nearest fractional unit is like rounding a number.

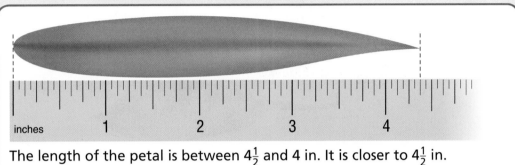

Example 1 Measure to the nearest $\frac{1}{2}$ inch.

The length of the petal is between $4\frac{1}{2}$ and 4 in. It is closer to $4\frac{1}{2}$ in.

So, to the nearest $\frac{1}{2}$ inch, the petal's length is about $4\frac{1}{2}$ in.

Example 2 Measure to the nearest $\frac{1}{4}$ inch.

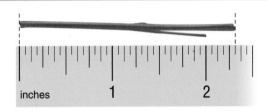

The length of the twig is closer to $2\frac{1}{4}$ in. than $2\frac{2}{4}$ in. So, to the nearest $\frac{1}{4}$ in., the twig's length is about $2\frac{1}{4}$ in.

Example 3 Measure to the nearest $\frac{1}{8}$ inch.

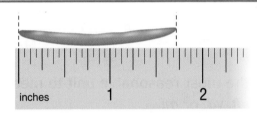

The length of the peapod is closer to $1\frac{6}{8}$ in. than $1\frac{5}{8}$ in. So, to the nearest $\frac{1}{8}$ in., the peapod's length is about $1\frac{6}{8}$ in., or $1\frac{3}{4}$ in.

Activity 2 Materials ■ 5 classroom objects ■ inch ruler ■ yardstick

- Make a table like the one shown. Estimate the length of 5 classroom objects to the nearest yard, foot, and inch. Record your estimates in the table.

- Use a ruler to measure the length of each object to the nearest yard, foot, $\frac{1}{2}$, $\frac{1}{4}$, and $\frac{1}{8}$ inch. Record your measurements.

Length of Objects

Object	Estimate	\multicolumn{6}{c}{Actual Measurements to the nearest:}
		yd	ft	1 in.	$\frac{1}{2}$ in.	$\frac{1}{4}$ in.	$\frac{1}{8}$ in.
?	■	■	■	■	■	■	■

- What is the order of the objects from shortest to longest?

- Is a measurement ever exact? Explain?

1. What is the length of the leaf to the nearest $\frac{1}{4}$ inch?

Choose the most reasonable unit to measure.
Write *in., ft, yd,* **or** *mi.*

2. the length of a dog

3. the height of an oak tree

☑ **4.** the length of a dollar bill

Estimate to the nearest inch. Then measure to the nearest $\frac{1}{2}$ inch.

5.

☑ **6.**

7. ⎡**TALK Math**⎤ Toby measured the length of a ribbon to the nearest $\frac{1}{2}$ inch. Nellie measured the length of the ribbon to the nearest $\frac{1}{8}$ inch. Whose measurement is more accurate? **Explain.**

Independent Practice and Problem Solving

Choose the most reasonable unit to measure.
Write *in., ft, yd,* **or** *mi.*

8. the width of a cell phone

9. the distance between states

10. the length of a football field

Estimate to the nearest $\frac{1}{2}$ inch. Then measure to the nearest $\frac{1}{8}$ inch.

11.

12.

13.

14.

Order the measurements from least to greatest.

15. 2 in., $1\frac{7}{8}$ in., $2\frac{1}{4}$ in., $2\frac{3}{8}$ in.

16. $5\frac{1}{2}$ in., $4\frac{3}{4}$ in., 5 in., $5\frac{1}{4}$ in.

17. $8\frac{5}{8}$ in., $8\frac{1}{4}$ in., 8 in., $8\frac{1}{2}$ in.

Use a ruler. Draw a line for each length.

18. $2\frac{1}{4}$ in.

19. $5\frac{5}{8}$ in.

20. 6 in.

21. $3\frac{1}{2}$ in.

22. $4\frac{3}{4}$ in.

23. $7\frac{7}{8}$ in.

USE DATA For 24–26, use the graph.

24. **Reasoning** Lydia measured each plant in inches. Which measurements are more accurate, Lydia's or the measurement given? **Explain.**

25. For which plant would it be most reasonable to measure the height in yards? **Explain.**

26. **WRITE Math** ▸ **Sense or Nonsense** Thomas has a plant that is about the height of 6 license plates placed end to end. He thinks his plant is the same size as the cosmo plant. Is he right? **Explain.**

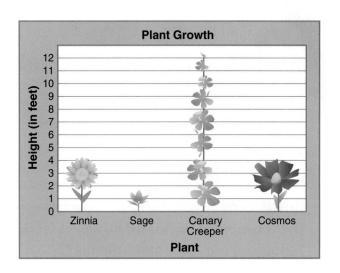

Plant Growth

Learn About Choosing the Appropriate Tool and Unit

It is important to use the right tool and know what unit to use when you are measuring.

An *odometer*, *trundle wheel*, or *pedometer* can be used to measure distances greater than 1 yard.

| odometer | trundle wheel | pedometer |

Tools and Units

Length	
• ruler	• inch
• odometer	• foot
• yardstick	• yard
• measuring wheel	• mile
• pedometer	

Weight	
• spring scale	• ounce
	• pound
	• ton

Capacity	
• measuring cup	• cup
• 1-pint, 1-quart, 1-gallon containers	• pint
	• quart
	• gallon

Try It

Tell what tool and unit you would use to measure each.

27. distance across the U.S.

28. capacity of a pitcher

29. length of a pen

30. weight of a cell phone

Mixed Review and Test Prep

31. How many edges, faces, and vertices does a rectangular prism have? (p. 570)

32. **Test Prep** What is the length of the yarn to the nearest $\frac{1}{8}$ inch?

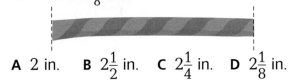

A 2 in. **B** $2\frac{1}{2}$ in. **C** $2\frac{1}{4}$ in. **D** $2\frac{1}{8}$ in.

33. Myra spent $14.66 on soil and $12.75 on plants. She pays with $40. How much change will she receive? (p. 496)

34. **Test Prep** Yao's art project included a button $2\frac{3}{4}$ in. wide, a strip of paper 3 in. long, and a piece of yarn $2\frac{7}{8}$ in. long. Order the size of the materials from greatest to least.

ALGEBRA
Change Customary Linear Units

OBJECTIVE: Change linear units by multiplying or dividing.

Learn

PROBLEM Myra needs 3 feet of fabric to make a hat for her costume. She has 40 inches of fabric. Does Myra have enough material to make the hat?

You can use multiplication and division to change from one customary unit of measure to another.

Customary Units of Length
1 foot (ft) = 12 inches (in.)
1 yard (yd) = 3 feet, or 36 inches
1 mile (mi) = 5,280 feet, or 1,760 yards

Example 1 Use multiplication.

3 feet = ■ inches

Think: 1 foot = 12 inches, so multiply the number of feet by 12.

feet	inches in 1 foot	total inches
↓	↓	↓
3	× 12	= 36

36 inches is less than 40 inches.

So, Myra has enough fabric to make the hat.

Example 2 Use division.

11,379 feet = ■ yards

Think: 1 yard = 3 feet, so divide the number of feet by 3.

$11379 \div 3 = 3793$

So, 11,379 feet equal 3,793 yards.

Example 3 Use an equation.

Use the equation $y = f \div 3$ to complete the table.

Feet, f	Yards, y
27	■
33	■
36	■

$y = f \div 3$

$y = 27 \div 3$, so $y = 9$.

$y = 33 \div 3$, so $y = 11$.

$y = 36 \div 3$, so $y = 12$.

Feet, f	Yards, y
27	9
33	11
36	12

Math Idea
To change from a larger unit to a smaller unit, you need more of them, so multiply.
To change from a smaller unit to a larger unit, you need fewer of them, so divide.

Guided Practice

1. Use the equation $i = f \times 12$. Copy and complete the table to find the number of inches in 5, 7, and 9 feet?

Feet, f	5	7	9
Inches, i	■	■	■

Complete. Tell whether you _multiply_ or _divide_.

2. 15,840 ft = ■ mi

3. 7 yd = ■ in.

4. 12 ft = ■ in.

5. 48 ft = ■ yd

6. **TALK Math** Explain how you know whether to multiply or divide to change from one unit to another.

Independent Practice and Problem Solving

Complete. Tell whether you _multiply_ or _divide_.

7. 34 ft = ■ in.

8. 132 in. = ■ ft

9. 23 yd = ■ ft

10. 1,200 ft = ■ yd

Compare. Write <, >, or = for each ●.

11. 30 in. ● 4 ft

12. 72 ft ● 24 yd

13. 200 in. ● 5 yd

14. 6 ft ● 72 in.

Algebra Write an equation you can use to complete each table. Copy and complete each table.

15.
Yards, y	4	5	6	7	8
Feet, f	12	15	■	■	■

16.
Inches, i	36	72	108	144	180
Yards, y	■	2	■	■	5

USE DATA For 17–19, use the pictures.

17. Kenny has 11 feet of fabric to make the cape. Does he have enough fabric to make two capes? **Explain.**

18. The jacket is made from red velvet. How many inches of red velvet are needed?

19. **WRITE Math** **What's the Error?** Zanta has 6 yards of pants fabric. She thinks she has enough fabric to make 4 pairs of pants. Is she correct? **Explain.**

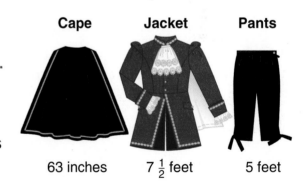

Cape — 63 inches   Jacket — $7\frac{1}{2}$ feet   Pants — 5 feet

Mixed Review and Test Prep

20. Jake wants to make a bar graph using this data: green–20, red–12, blue–8. Which color will have the longest bar? (p. 206)

21. **Test Prep** Stephen is 48 inches tall. How many feet tall is he?

22. How long is the ribbon to the nearest $\frac{1}{8}$ inch? (p. 602)

Weight

OBJECTIVE: Estimate and measure the weights of objects and change units of weight.

Learn

Weight is how heavy an object is. Customary units of weight include **ounce (oz)**, **pound (lb)**, and **ton (T)**.

Common objects can be used as benchmarks for customary units of weight.

5 new pencils weigh about 1 ounce.

4 sticks of butter weigh about 1 pound.

A small car weighs about 1 ton.

HANDS ON

Activity 1

Materials ■ spring scale ■ classroom objects

- Make a table like the one shown. Estimate the weight of 5 classroom objects in ounces or pounds. Record your estimates in the table.

- Now weigh each object using the spring scale. Record the actual weight in the table.

Weight			
Object	**Unit (oz/lb)**	**Estimate**	**Actual**
dictionary	lb	3 lb	■
?	■	■	■

- Are your estimates reasonable? Explain how you know.

- Compare one of the objects you weighed to the weight of 5 new pencils. What can you conclude?

Customary Units of Weight
1 pound (lb) = 16 ounces (oz)
1 ton (T) = 2,000 pounds

You can use multiplication and division to change units of weight.

Example 1 Use multiplication.

How many ounces equal 6 pounds?

6 pounds = ■ ounces

pounds	ounces in 1 pound	ounces
↓	↓	↓
6 ×	16 =	96

So, 6 pounds equal 96 ounces.

Example 2 Use division.

How many tons equal 8,000 pounds?

8,000 pounds = ■ tons

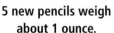

⟨8⟩⟨0⟩⟨0⟩⟨0⟩ ⟨÷⟩ ⟨2⟩⟨0⟩⟨0⟩⟨0⟩ ⟨Enter⟩

$8000 \div 2000 = 4$

So, 8,000 pounds equal 4 tons.

Guided Practice

1. An adult elephant weighs about 17,500 pounds. Does this baby elephant weigh about 200 ounces, 200 pounds, or 200 tons?

Complete. Tell whether you *multiply* or *divide*.

2. ■ lb = 56 T

✓ 3. 128 oz = ■ lb

✓ 4. 7 lb = ■ oz

5. **TALK Math** Which number of units is greater, the weight of a baby giraffe in ounces or the weight of the giraffe in pounds? **Explain.**

Independent Practice (and Problem Solving)

Choose the more reasonable measurement.

6.

9 oz or 9 lb

7.

2 lb or 2 T

8.

6 oz or 6 lb

Complete. Tell whether you *multiply* or *divide*.

9. 5 lb = ■ oz

10. ■ lb = 192 oz

11. 6,000 lb = ■ T

12. 11 T = ■ lb

13. 4 lb = ■ oz

14. ■ lb = 160 oz

USE DATA For 15–18, use the table.

15. How many pounds of monkey biscuits are used by the zoo each year?

16. Order the amounts in the table from least to greatest.

17. **WRITE Math** The weight of three apples is about 1 pound. About how many apples does the zoo use per year? **Explain.**

18. **≡FAST FACT** An Australian Gippsland earthworm can weigh up to 24 ounces. About how many of these earthworms could the zoo use per year?

Food Used Each Year at the St. Louis Zoo	
Food Type	Amount
Apples	21 T
Earthworms	120 lb
Monkey Biscuits	6 T

Mixed Review and Test Prep

19. Sean's dog is 36 inches tall. How many feet tall is the dog? (p. 606)

20. Diane packs 9 books in each of 8 boxes. How many books did she pack in all? (p. 98)

21. **Test Prep** Jeff buys 25 pounds of dog food. How many ounces is that?

   A 300 ounces   C 850 ounces

   B 400 ounces   D 50,000 ounces

Extra Practice on page 626, Set C

Customary Capacity

OBJECTIVE: Estimate and measure the capacity of containers and change units of capacity.

Learn

Capacity is the amount a container can hold when filled. Customary units of capacity include **teaspoon (tsp)**, **tablespoon (tbsp)**, **cup (c)**, **pint (pt)**, **quart (qt)**, **gallon (gal)**, and **fluid ounce (fl oz)**.

Commonly used containers can be used as benchmarks for customary units of capacity.

1 teaspoon   1 tablespoon   1 cup = 8 fluid ounces   1 pint   1 quart   1 gallon

HANDS ON

Activity 1

Materials ■ 1-cup, 1-pint, 1-quart, and 1-gallon containers ■ water

- A coffee cup holds about 1 cup. Estimate the number of cups in a pint, a quart, and a gallon. Record your estimates.
- Use the 1-cup measure to fill each container. Record the actual number of cups.
- Compare your estimates with the actual measurements. Are your estimates reasonable? Explain.

- Did you need more cups or quarts to fill the gallon container? Explain.

Capacity

Container	Estimate (cups)	Actual (cups)
Pint	■	■
Quart	■	■
Gallon	■	■

Customary Units for Measuring Liquids

1 tablespoon (tbsp) = 3 teaspoons (tsp)
1 cup (c) = 8 fluid ounces (fl oz)
1 pint (pt) = 2 cups
1 quart (qt) = 2 pints
1 gallon (gal) = 4 quarts

You can multiply or divide to change units of capacity.

Example 1 Use multiplication.

5 pints = ■ cups

pints		cups in 1 pint		cups
↓		↓		↓
5	×	2	=	10

So, 5 pints equal 10 cups.

Example 2 Use division.

16 quarts = ■ gallons

quarts		quarts in 1 gallon		gallons
↓		↓		↓
16	÷	4	=	4

So, 16 quarts equal 4 gallons.

- **What if** you wanted to fill a bathtub with water? Which would be better to use, a bucket or a paper cup? Explain.

Guided Practice

1. Does this pitcher of iced tea hold 3 gallons, 3 quarts, 3 pints, or 3 cups?

Copy and complete each table. Change the units.

2.

Teaspoon, t	9	12	36
Tablespoon, s	▣	▣	▣

✓ **3.**

Gallons, g	5	▣	8
Pints, p	▣	56	▣

✓ **4.**

Cups, c	28	40	▣
Quarts, q	▣	▣	16

5. **TALK Math** Which is greater, the number of cups or the number of quarts needed to fill a pitcher? **Explain.**

Independent Practice and Problem Solving

Choose the more reasonable unit of capacity.

6.

gallon or cup

7.

quart or cup

8.

pint or tablespoon

Copy and complete each table. Change the units.

9.

Cups, c	10	16	20
Pints, p	▣	▣	▣

10.

Gallons, g	▣	9	▣
Quarts, q	20	▣	48

11.

Cups, c	48	▣	▣
Gallons, g	▣	4	9

USE DATA For 12–13, and 15 use the recipe.

12. How many total fluid ounces of orange juice and water are used in the recipe?

13. Leah doubles the recipe. Does she need more or less than 1 quart of apricot nectar? **Explain.**

APRICOT ORANGE TEA
$2\frac{1}{2}$ cups apricot nectar
1 cup orange juice
1 cup water
1 tablespoon sugar
4 lemon slices
12 whole cloves
2 teaspoons instant tea
1 teaspoon ground cinnamon sugar
Makes four 1-cup servings.

14. **Reasoning** Could 2 different containers have the same capacity? **Explain.**

15. **WRITE Math** ▶ What's the Question? Vinny makes 4 times the recipe. The answer is 1 gallon.

Mixed Review and Test Prep

16. Mr. Jansen bought 16 packs of tea. Each pack has 10 bags. How much tea does he have? (p. 292)

17. Linda baked 2 pounds of scones. How many ounces of scones did Linda bake? (p. 608)

18. **Test Prep** Abigail makes 3 gallons of lemonade. How many pints of lemonade does she make? **Explain.**

Extra Practice on page 626, Set D

Problem Solving Workshop
Strategy: Compare Strategies

OBJECTIVE: Compare different strategies to solve problems.

Use the Strategy

PROBLEM Rosanna has a fishbowl that holds 4 quarts of water. She plans to use a pint container to fill the bowl. How many pints of water will Rosanna need to fill her fishbowl?

Read to Understand

Reading Skill

- **Identify the details.**
- **What are you asked to find?**

Plan

- **What strategy can you use to solve the problem?**

  Sometimes you can use more than one strategy to solve a problem. You can *draw a diagram* or *make a table* to help you solve this problem.

Solve

- **How can you use the strategies to solve the problem?**

Draw a Diagram	*Make a Table*
Show how to find the total number of pints.	Show the relationship between quarts and pints.
4 quarts = ■ pints	Use this information to complete the table.
Think: 1 quart = 2 pints	**Think:** 1 quart = 2 pints

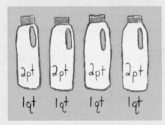

$4 \times 2 = 8$

Quart, q	1	2	3	4
Pint, p	2	4	6	8

So, Rosanna needs 8 pints of water.

Check

- **How can you check your answer?**
- **What other ways could you solve the problem?**

Guided Problem Solving

Choose a strategy to solve. Explain your choice.

1. Tim has a fish tank that is 3 feet long. How many inches long is the tank?

   First, decide if you should draw a diagram or make a table.

   Think: 1 foot = 12 inches

   Then, make a table.

Feet, *f*	1	2	3
Inches, *i*	12	▉	▉

   Finally, use the table to show many inches are in 3 feet.

2. **What if** Tim had a tank that was 5 feet long? How many inches long is the tank?

3. **≡FAST FACT** An angler is a person who fishes for fun. Mia is an angler. Mia caught a fish that weighed 6 pounds. How many ounces did the fish weigh?

Choose a STRATEGY

Draw a Diagram or Picture

Make a Model or Act It Out

Make an Organized List

Find a Pattern

Make a Table or Graph

Predict and Test

Work Backward

Solve a Simpler Problem

Write an Equation

Use Logical Reasoning

Mixed Strategy Practice

USE DATA, For 4–6 and 8, use the picture.

4. How many ounces does the white bass weigh?

5. **Pose a Problem** Use the information in the table to write a problem changing inches to feet.

6. How much longer is the blue catfish than the Walleye?

7. Ian is going fishing with his dad. He can either fish in the ocean or a lake. He can choose to use shrimp, worms, or minnows for bait. How many different fishing choices does Ian have? **Explain.**

8. **⌨WRITE Math** ▶ Lilly's favorite fish is shown in the picture. She catches a different fish that weighs 3 pounds more than half the weight of her favorite fish. The fish she caught weighs 11 pounds. Which fish is Lilly's favorite? **Explain.**

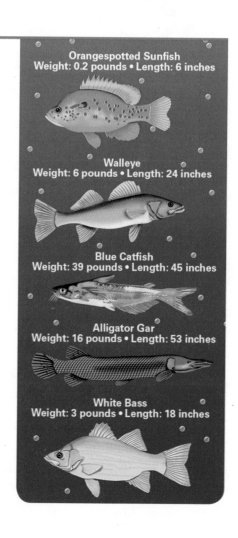

Orangespotted Sunfish
Weight: 0.2 pounds • Length: 6 inches

Walleye
Weight: 6 pounds • Length: 24 inches

Blue Catfish
Weight: 39 pounds • Length: 45 inches

Alligator Gar
Weight: 16 pounds • Length: 53 inches

White Bass
Weight: 3 pounds • Length: 18 inches

Quick Review

Round to the nearest whole number.

1. 5.7   2. 10.9
3. 0.7   4. 8.3
5. 3.4

Vocabulary

millimeter (mm)

meter (m)

centimeter (cm)

kilometer (km)

decimeter (dm)

Learn

PROBLEM Is the wingspan of a dragonfly about 10 millimeters, 10 centimeters, or 10 meters?

Length can be measured using metric units of measure. The metric units of length include **millimeter (mm)**, **centimeter (cm)**, **decimeter (dm)**, **meter (m)**, and **kilometer (km)**. You can use benchmark measurements to relate metric and customary units. One inch is about $2\frac{1}{2}$ centimeters. One meter is a little longer than 1 yard. One mile is a little longer than $1\frac{1}{2}$ kilometers.

Common objects can be used as benchmarks for metric units of length.

The thickness of a dime is about 1 millimeter.

The width of your index finger is about 1 centimeter.

The width of an adult's hand is about 1 decimeter.

The width of a door is about 1 meter.

It takes about 10 minutes to walk 1 kilometer.

So, the wingspan of a dragonfly is about 10 centimeters.

- Which metric unit of length would you use to measure your driveway? Explain.

Activity 1

Materials ■ 5 classroom objects ■ centimeter ruler ■ meterstick

- Estimate the lengths of 5 objects in your classroom. Record your work in a table like the one shown.

- Choose the unit you would use to measure each object. Write *mm*, *cm*, *dm*, or *m* in the table. Then measure each object to the nearest millimeter, centimeter, decimeter, or meter.

- Order the objects in the table from shortest to longest.

Length			
Objects	Unit	Estimate	Actual Measurement
desk	dm	■	■
?	■	■	■

Measure Longer Lengths with Different Units

You can also measure longer lengths.

Activity 2 Materials ■ centimeter ruler ■ meterstick

- Estimate the length of your classroom. Decide which tool and which unit you should use. Measure the length of your classroom.

- Compare your results with a classmate. Are the measurements of your classroom the same? If not, why not?

Using different metric units to measure the length of an object can help you understand how the units are related.

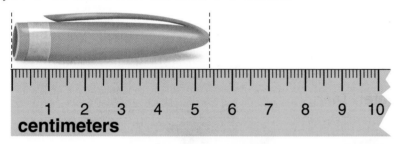

Math Idea
In the metric system, fractional widths are usually written by using decimals.
$6\frac{1}{2}$ cm = 6.5 cm

The right edge of the pen cap is closest to the 54 millimeter mark. So, the pen cap is 54 millimeters long to the nearest millimeter.

The right edge of the pen cap is closest to the 5.5 centimeter mark. So, the pen cap is 5.5 centimeters long to the nearest half centimeter.

The right edge of the pen cap is closest to the 1 decimeter mark. So, to the nearest decimeter, the pen cap is 1 decimeter long.

Guided Practice

1. What is the length of this yarn to the nearest half centimeter and to the nearest millimeter?

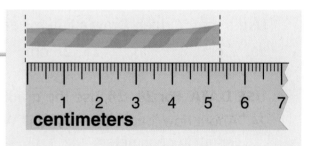

Choose the most reasonable unit of measure. Write *mm, cm, dm, m,* or *km.*

2.

☑ 3.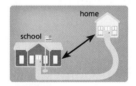

☑ 4.

☑ 5. **TALK Math** Mia measured the length of her insect house to the nearest half centimeter. Kyle measured the length of his insect house to the nearest millimeter. Whose measurement is more exact? **Explain.**

Choose the most reasonable unit of measure. Write *mm*, *cm*, *dm*, *m*, or *km*.

6.

7.

8.

Estimate the nearest centimeter. Then measure to the nearest half centimeter. Write the answer as a decimal.

9.

10.

11.

12.

Estimate to the nearest half centimeter. Then measure to the nearest millimeter.

13.

14.

15.

16.

Compare. Write <, >, or = for each ●.

17. 4 m ● 4 cm

18. 10 km ● 10 m

19. 25 cm ● 25 dm

Use a metric ruler. Draw a line for each length.

20. 7 cm

21. 25 cm

22. 16 cm

23. 56 cm

USE DATA For 24–26, use the graph.

24. About how long is the ladybug? Write the length in centimeters.

25. **Reasoning** How many millimeters longer is the checkerspot butterfly than the honeybee? **Explain.**

26. **WRITE Math** For which insect can the length be written as a whole number using three different units? Write each of the lengths. **Explain.**

Lengths of State Insects

Insect:
- Checkerspot Butterfly
- Ladybug
- Honeybee
- Monarch Butterfly

Length (in cm): 0 1 2 3 4 5 6 7 8 9 10 11

Technology —
Use Harcourt Mega Math, Ice Station Exploration, *Linear Lab*, Level I.

Learn About) Using a Map Scale

A map gives information about a place. A map scale shows how distances on a map compare to actual distances. Maps use scales to show distance. Scales represent the actual distances between places on the map.

The map at the right shows Michoacán, Mexico, where the famous Sierra Chincua Butterfly Preserve is located. More than 100 million monarch butterflies migrate to the preserve every fall from up to 4,800 kilometers away.

The scale on this map is 1 centimeter = 50 kilometers. This means that every 1 centimeter shown on the map represents 50 kilometers of actual distance.

On the map, the distance from Morelia to the Butterfly Preserve is about 2 centimeters. $2 \times 50 = 100$. So, the actual distance is about 100 kilometers.

▼ The monarch butterfly is the state insect of Illinois, Minnesota, and Texas.

Try It

Use your ruler and the scale to find each actual distance.

27. Lazaro Cardenas to Butterfly Preserve

28. Butterfly Preserve to Cololo

29. Morelia to Los Reyes

30. Tizupan to Morelia

Mixed Review and Test Prep

31. A monarch butterfly can migrate more than 2,500 miles. How many yards is that? (p. 606)

32. Test Prep What is the length of the inchworm to the nearest half centimeter?

   A 2.0 centimeters

   B 2.5 centimeters

   C 3.0 centimeters

   D 3.5 centimeters

33. Joan's art class started at 5:45 P.M. and ended at 8:30 P.M. How long was the class? (p. 154)

34. Test Prep What is the most reasonable unit of measure that can be used to measure the length of a pen?

   A Millimeter

   B Centimeter

   C Meter

   D Kilometer

ALGEBRA

Change Metric Linear Units

OBJECTIVE: Change metric linear units by multiplying or dividing.

Learn

PROBLEM A rabbit digs a burrow 15 decimeters below the ground. How many centimeters deep is the burrow?

You can multiply or divide by 10, 100, or 1,000 to change metric units.

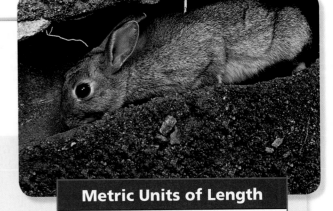

Example 1 Use multiplication.

A decimeter is larger than a centimeter. To change larger units to smaller units, you need more of the smaller units, so multiply by 10.

Metric Units of Length
1 centimeter (cm) = 10 millimeters (mm)
1 decimeter (dm) = 10 centimeters
1 meter = 10 decimeters
1 meter (m) = 1,000 millimeters
1 kilometers (km) = 1,000 meters

15 decimeters = ■ centimeters

depth of burrow in decimeters	centimeters in 1 decimeter	depth of burrow in centimeters
↓	↓	↓
15	× 10	= 150

So, the rabbit burrow is 150 centimeters deep.

To change smaller units to larger units, you need fewer of the larger units, so divide by 10, 100, or 1,000.

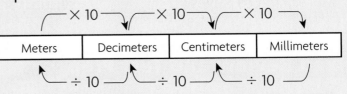

Example 2 Use division.

A Use a calculator.

5,000 mm = ■ m
Since a millimeter is a smaller unit than a meter, divide.

$5000 \div 1000 = 5$

So, 5,000 millimeters equal 5 meters.

B Use a basic fact and a pattern.

4,000 m = ■ km
Since a meter is a smaller unit than a kilometer, divide.

$$4 \div 1 = 4 \quad \leftarrow \text{basic fact}$$
$$40 \div 10 = 4$$
$$400 \div 100 = 4$$
$$4,000 \div 1,000 = 4$$

So, 4,000 meters equal 4 kilometers.

• Draw a picture to show how many centimeters are in 20 millimeters.

Guided Practice

1. Complete to find the number of meters in 89 kilometers.

$$89 \times 1,000 = \blacksquare$$

Complete. Tell whether you _multiply_ or _divide_.

2. 90 cm = ■ mm   ✅ **3.** 7 km = ■ m   ✅ **4.** 566 mm = ■ dm

5. [TALK Math] Which has the greater number of units, a measurement given in decimeters or the same measurement given in millimeters? **Explain.**

Independent Practice and Problem Solving

Complete. Tell whether you _multiply_ or _divide_.

6. 7 m = ■ mm   **7.** 57 km = ■ m   **8.** ■ cm = 6,100 mm

9. ■ mm = 24 cm   **10.** 7 dm = ■ cm   **11.** 4,500 mm = ■ dm

Write the correct unit.

12. 9,000 ■ = 9 m   **13.** 16 m = 160 ■   **14.** 7,030 cm = 703 ■

15. 11 km = 11,000 ■   **16.** 90 ■ = 900 mm   **17.** 800 cm = 8 ■

⭐ **Algebra** Compare. Write <, >, or = for each ●.

18. 60 cm ● 600 mm   **19.** 5,600 m ● 6 km   **20.** 78 dm ● 700 cm

21. 8,400 mm ● 8 m   **22.** 1,800 cm ● 180 dm   **23.** 25 cm ● 100 mm

24. Julianna has a baby rabbit. A rabbit's teeth can grow as much as 4 millimeters each week. How many centimeters long could her baby rabbit's teeth be after 5 weeks?

25. [WRITE Math] ▸ In 1997, the world record height for a jumping rabbit was 99.5 centimeters. In 2002, a new world record was set 5 millimeters higher. What is the new world record in meters? **Explain.**

Mixed Review and Test Prep

26. Jake pulls a marble from a bag that contains 3 green marbles and 2 red marbles. How likely is it for him to pull a green marble? (Grade 3)

27. Alex's rabbit weighs 9 pounds. How many ounces does the rabbit weigh? (p. 608)

28. Test Prep Fred's rabbit has ears that are 709 millimeters long. How many decimeters long are his rabbit's ears?

  A 0.709 decimeter   **C** 70.9 decimeters

  B 7.09 decimeters   **D** 7,090 decimeters

Extra Practice on page 627, Set F

Mass

OBJECTIVE: Estimate and measure the mass of objects and change units of mass.

Learn

Matter is what all objects are made of. **Mass** is the amount of matter an object contains. It is measured with a balance. Metric units of mass include **milligram (mg)**, **centigram (cg)**, **gram (g)** and **kilogram (kg)**. One kilogram is a little more than 2 pounds. One ounce is about 28 grams. Mass and weight are not the same thing. Weight is a measure of the gravitational force acting on an object. It is measured with a scale.

Common objects can be used as benchmarks for metric units of mass.

The mass of a toothpick is about 1 milligram.

The mass of 10 toothpicks is about 1 centigram.

The mass of a dollar bill is about 1 gram.

The mass of a baseball bat is about 1 kilogram.

Activity 1

Materials ■ balance ■ gram and kilogram masses ■ objects

- Make a table like the one shown. Estimate the mass of 5 objects in grams or kilograms. Record your estimates.
- Find the mass of each object using the balance and gram and kilogram masses. Record the actual mass.

Mass of Objects			
Object	Unit (g/kg)	Estimate	Actual
scissors	g	50 g	■
?	■	■	■

Units of Mass
1 kilogram (kg) = 1,000 grams (g)

- Are your estimates reasonable? Explain how you know.
- List the objects in your table in order from least mass to greatest mass.

You can use multiplication and division to change units of mass.

Example 1 Use multiplication.

9 kilograms = ■ grams

Think: There are 1,000 grams in 1 kilogram.

9 kg = 9 × 1,000 = 9,000 g

Example 2 Use division.

32,000 grams = ■ kilograms

Think: There are 1,000 grams in 1 kilogram.

32000 ÷ 1000 = 32

So, 9 kilograms equal 9,000 grams.   So, 32,000 grams equal 32 kilograms.

Guided Practice

1. What is the most reasonable measurement for the cereal box, 2,000 milligrams, 200 grams, or 20 kilograms?

Complete. Tell whether you *multiply* or *divide*.

2. 2,000 g = ■ kg

✓ 3. ■ kg = 10,000 g

✓ 4. 3 kg = ■ g

5. ⌈TALK Math⌉ Which unit of metric mass can you use to measure the mass of a hockey puck? **Explain.**

Independent Practice and Problem Solving

Choose the more reasonable measurement.

6.

14 g or 14 kg

7.

5,000 kg or 500 g

8.

1 kg or 10 g

Complete. Tell whether you *multiply* or *divide*.

9. 8 kg = ■ g

10. 7,000 g = ■ kg

11. 16 kg = ■ g

12. 5,000 g = ■ kg

13. ■ kg = 9,000 g

14. ■ g = 119 kg

USE DATA For 15–17, use the picture.

15. What is the order of the sports balls from greatest mass to least mass?

16. A baseball has a mass of about 145 grams. Kelly has 2 basketballs and 2 baseballs in her gym bag. Is the mass of the balls in her bag more or less than 2 kg? **Explain.**

17. ⌈WRITE Math⌉ ▶ About how many tennis balls have a total mass of 1 kilogram? **Explain** your answer.

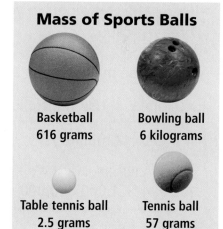

Mass of Sports Balls

Basketball
616 grams

Bowling ball
6 kilograms

Table tennis ball
2.5 grams

Tennis ball
57 grams

Mixed Review and Test Prep

18. Bowling shoes cost $39.99 a pair. How much do 4 pairs of bowling shoes cost? (p. 254)

19. The diameter of a basketball is 75 centimeters. How many millimeters is this? (p. 618)

20. **Test Prep** Linda buys 2 kilograms of popcorn. How many grams of popcorn did Linda buy?

A 2 grams

C 2,000 grams

B 1,000 grams

D 20,000 grams

⌈Extra Practice⌉ on page 627, Set G

Metric Capacity

OBJECTIVE: Estimate and measure the capacity of containers and change units of capacity.

Learn

Capacity is the amount of liquid a container can hold. Metric units of capacity are a **liter (L)** and a **milliliter (mL)**. One liter is a little more than 1 quart. Commonly used containers can be used as benchmarks for metric units of capacity.

A dropper holds about 1 milliliter.

This water bottle holds 1 liter.

Activity **Materials** ■ 1-liter container ■ metric measuring cup ■ dropper ■ large and small containers

• Make a table like the one shown. Estimate the capacities of 5 containers in milliliters or liters. Record your estimates.

• Select the 1-liter container, measuring cup, or dropper and find the capacity of each container. Record the actual capacity.

Capacity			
Object	Unit (mL/L)	Estimate	Actual
spoon	mL	5	■
?	■	■	■

• Are your estimates reasonable? Explain how you know.

• Order the containers in your table from least capacity to greatest capacity.

You can use multiplication and division to change units of mass.

Units of Capacity

1 liter (L) = 1,000 milliliters (mL)

Example 1 Use multiplication.

4 liters = ■ milliliters

Think: There are 1,000 milliliters in 1 liter.

$4 L = 4 \times 1,000 = 4,000$ milliliters

So, 4 liters equal 4,000 milliliters.

Example 2 Use division.

93,000 milliliters = ■ liters

Think: There are 1,000 milliliters in 1 liter.

9 3 0 0 0 ÷

1 0 0 0 Enter $93000 \div 1000 = 93$

So, 93,000 milliliters equal 4 liters.

Guided Practice

1. Does this bottle of maple syrup hold about 250 mL or 250 L?

Complete. Tell whether you *multiply* or *divide*.

2. 10 L = ▪ mL
☑ 3. 12,000 mL = ▪ L
☑ 4. 3L = ▪ mL

5. **TALK Math** Which number of units is greater, the capacity of a container given in liters or milliliters? **Explain.**

Independent Practice and Problem Solving

Choose the most reasonable measurement. Write *a, b,* or *c.*

6.
a. 2 L
b. 20 mL
c. 5 mL

7.
a. 5 mL
b. 15 mL
c. 10 L

8.
a. 1 mL
b. 100 mL
c. 100 L

Complete. Tell whether you *multiply* or *divide*.

9. 13 L = ▪ mL

10. ▪ L = 9,000 mL

11. 2 L = ▪ mL

Estimate and tell whether each object has a capacity of *about a liter, less than a liter,* or *more than a liter.*

12.

13.

14.

USE DATA For 15–18, use the table.

15. You can save money by driving vehicles that use less fuel per 100 kilometers. Which car helps you save the most money? **Explain.**

16. Write the vehicles in order from greatest fuel used per 100 kilometers to least fuel used.

17. **Reasoning** Kim drives 300 kilometers in a smart car. Does she use more or less than 10 liters of fuel? **Explain.**

Fuel Usage	
Vehicle	Amount Used (per 100 km)
Traditional Car	9,000 mL
Smart Car	4 L
Bus	64 L

18. **WRITE Math** Jerry's minivan uses 12 liters of fuel for every 100 kilometers of driving. Which vehicles cost more than Jerry's minivan to use? **Explain.**

Mixed Review and Test Prep

19. Write the next number in the pattern. (p. 382)

    21, 18, 15, 12, ▪

20. Is the mass of a large car about 3,000 kilograms or 3,000 grams? (p. 620)

21. **Test Prep** Tabitha put 50 liters of gas in her car. How many milliliters is this?

    A 500 milliliters   C 50,000 milliliters

    B 5,000 milliliters D 500,000 milliliters

Extra Practice on page 627, Set H

LESSON 10

Problem Solving Workshop
Strategy: Make a Table

OBJECTIVE: Solve problems by using the strategy *make a table*.

Use the Strategy

PROBLEM Connor is buying a hat. He needs to know the distance around his head to buy the right size. He knows that he is 135 centimeters tall. How can he use this information to find his hat size?

Read to Understand

- **What information is given?**
- **What are you asked to find?**

Plan

- **What strategy can you use to solve the problem?**

  You can *make a table* to help you solve this problem.

Solve

- **How can you use the strategy to solve the problem?**

  Materials ■ string ■ centimeter ruler or metric tape measure

  Measure your height and the distance around your head in centimeters. Then measure the head size and height of three other classmates. Record your work in the table.

Measurements (in cm)				
Head size	■	■	■	■
Height	■	■	■	■

  Look for a pattern in each classmate's head size and height.

   Generalize.

  Think: Each person's height is about 3 times their head size.

  Connor's height is 135 centimeters and 135 ÷ 3 is 45.

  So, Connor's hat size is about 45 centimeters.

Check

- **How can you check your answer?**

Guided Problem Solving

1. Mia knows the length of her foot is 21 centimeters. How can she use this measurement to find the length of her forearm?

   First, measure the length of your forearm and foot and the forearm and foot of at least three other classmates.

   Then, record the measurements in a table.

   Finally, look for patterns between the length of each person's foot and the length of their forearm.

2. **What if** Katie's forearm is 2 decimeters long. How many centimeters long is her foot?

3. Juan is making keychains to sell at a craft fair. He plans to sell them for $4 each. How much money will he make if he sells 14 keychains?

Choose a
STRATEGY

Draw a Diagram or Picture
Make a Model or Act It Out
Make an Organized List
Find a Pattern
Make a Table or Graph
Predict and Test
Work Backward
Solve a Simpler Problem
Write an Equation
Use Logical Reasoning

Mixed Strategy Practice

4. **≡FAST FACT** The length of a person's arm span is about the same as the height of the person. Perry is 60 inches tall. How many feet long is his arm span?

5. **Pose a Problem** Look back at Problem 4. Write a similar problem by changing the units.

6. The 42-ton mechanical elephant in the picture was part of a French theater group's performance in London, England, in 2006. How many pounds did the elephant weigh?

7. A 18-foot tall girl marionette was also part the French theater group's performance. About how many times taller is the girl marionette than a 6-foot tall person?

8. It costs Elizabeth 12 cents a minute to make a call on her cell phone. How much will a 10-minute call cost?

9. **WRITE Math** Bea is making a puppet with her dad. She can make either a cat or dog puppet. She can choose to use gray, brown, white, or spotted fur. How many different puppet choices does Bea have? **Explain.**

Extra Practice

Set A Choose the most reasonable unit
to measure. Write *in.*, *ft*, *yd*, or *mi*. (pp. 602–605)

1. the distance to Hawaii

2. the height of a tree

3. the length of your hand

Estimate to the nearest $\frac{1}{2}$ inch. Then measure to the nearest $\frac{1}{8}$ inch.

4.

5.

Set B Complete. Tell whether you *multiply* or *divide*. (pp. 606–607)

1. 3 mi = ■ yd

2. 2 yd = ■ in.

3. ■ yd = 372 ft

Write an equation you can use to complete each table. Copy and
complete each table.

4.

Feet, *f*	6	9	12	15	18
Yards, *y*	■	3	■	5	■

5.

Inches, *i*	60	72	84	96	108
Feet, *f*	5	■	7	■	■

Set C Choose the more reasonable estimate (pp. 608–609)

1.

6 T or 6 lb

2.

8 lb or 8 oz

3.

10 oz or 10 lb

Compete. Tell whether you *multiply* or *divide*.

4. ■ lb = 48 oz

5. 6 T = ■ lb

6. ■ lb = 80 oz

Set D Copy and complete each table. Change the units. (pp. 610–611)

1.

Pints, *p*	16	■	56
Gallons, *g*	■	5	■

2.

Tablespoons, *s*	■	■	12
Teaspoons, *t*	18	27	■

3.

Quarts, *q*	5	■	■
Cups, *c*	■	32	40

4. A recipe for 8 quarts of punch calls for
20 cups of ginger ale, and the rest juice.
Is a gallon or a cup a more reasonable
unit of capacity to use for the juice?

5. Zach needs 32 pints of water to fill his
aquarium. How many gallons does he
need?

Technology
Use Harcourt Mega Math, The Number
Games, *Tiny's Think Tank*, Levels M, N, O.

Set E Choose the most reasonable unit of measure.
Write *mm, cm, dm, m,* or *km*. (pp. 614–617)

1.

2.

3.

Estimate to the nearest half centimeter. Then measure to the nearest millimeter.

4.

5.

6.

Set F Complete. Tell whether you *multiply* or *divide*. (pp. 618–619)

1. 6 m = ▇ cm

2. 45 cm = ▇ mm

3. 500 mm = ▇ dm

Write the correct unit.

4. 6 m = 6,000 ▇

5. 50 cm = 5 ▇

6. 7,000 m = 7 ▇

Set G Choose the more reasonable estimate. (pp. 620–621)

1.

4 g or 4 kg

2.

36 kg or 36 g

3.

5 kg or 50 kg

Complete. Tell whether you *multiply* or *divide*.

4. 11 kg = ▇ g

5. 4,000 g = ▇ kg

6. ▇ g = 15 kg

Set H Choose the more reasonable measurement. Write *a, b,* or *c*. (pp. 622–623)

1.
a. 20 L
b. 200 L
c. 200 mL

2.
a. 120 mL
b. 12 L
c. 12 mL

3.
a. 40 mL
b. 40 L
c. 4 L

Complete. Tell whether you *multiply* or *divide*.

4. 5 L = ▇ mL

5. ▇ L = 14,000 mL

6. 1 L = ▇ mL

Measure Length, Weight, and Capacity

Something Fishy

You can measure an object in more than one way.

Yuri wants to buy a fish tank at the pet store. He needs information about the length, weight, and capacity of the tank.

Example 1 Find length.

The length of the tank is 24 inches long. How many feet is this?

$$24 \text{ in.} = \blacksquare \text{ ft}$$

Think: 12 in. = 1 ft

$24 \div 12 = 2$

24 in. = 2 ft

So, the tank is 2 feet long.

Example 2 Find weight.

The weight of the tank, when filled, is 225 pounds. How many ounces is this?

$$225 \text{ lb} = \blacksquare \text{ oz}$$

Think: 1 lb = 16 oz

$225 \times 16 = 3,600$

225 lb = 3,600 oz

So, the tank, when filled, weighs 3,600 ounces.

Example 3 Find capacity.

The capacity of the tank is 20 gallons. How many quarts does the tank hold?

$$20 \text{ gal} = \blacksquare \text{ qt}$$

Think: 1 gal = 4 qt

$20 \times 4 = 80$

20 gal = 80 qt

So, the tank holds 80 quarts.

Try It

Use metric and customary measurements to solve.

1. Kevin's fish tank, when filled, has a mass of 5,000 grams. What is the mass of the tank in kilograms?

2. Hallie's small fish tank holds 5 gallons of water. What is the capacity of the tank in pints?

3. **WRITE Math** ▶ A koi is a type of fish that is kept in many aquariums. A koi can grow to be 90 centimeters long. Is that greater than, less than, or equal to 1 meter? **Explain.**

Chapter 22 Review/Test

Check Vocabulary and Concepts

Choose the best term from the box.

VOCABULARY
- capacity
- centimeter
- meter
- yard

1. A __?__ is a customary unit equal to 3 feet. (p. 602)
2. __?__ is the amount of liquid a container can hold. (p. 610)
3. A metric unit that is about the width of your finger is called a __?__ . (p. 614)

Check Skills

Choose the most reasonable unit to measure. Write *in.*, *ft*, *yd*, or *mi*. (pp. 602–605)

4. length of your arm
5. distance to Paris
6. width of your shoe

Estimate to the nearest $\frac{1}{2}$ inch. Then measure to the nearest $\frac{1}{8}$ inch.

7. 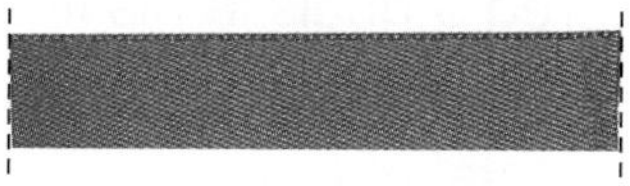
8. 
9. 

Complete. Tell whether you *multiply* or *divide*. (pp. 606–607, 608–609, 618–619, 620–621, 622–623)

10. ■ lb = 112 oz
11. ■ mi = 5,280 yd
12. 6,000 lb = ■ T
13. 23 ft = ■ in.
14. ■ m = 6 km
15. 4,000 mL = ■ L
16. 11,000 g = ■ kg
17. ■ mm = 13 dm

Choose the most reasonable unit to measure. Write *mm*, *cm*, *dm*, *m*, or *km*. (pp. 614–617)

18. width of your pencil
19. height of a door
20. length of a classroom

Estimate to the nearest centimeter. Then measure to the nearest half centimeter and nearest millimeter. (pp. 614–617)

21. 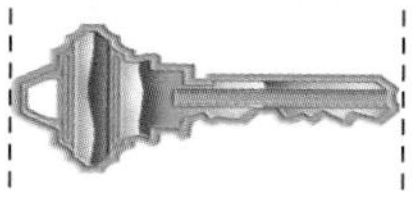
22. 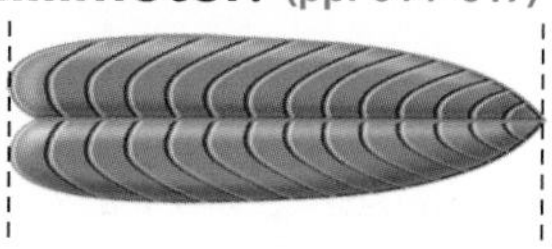
23. 

Check Problem Solving

Solve. (pp. 612–613, 624–625)

24. Trails Elementary serves 6 gallons of milk at lunch every day. The milk is served in half-pint cartons. How many cartons are served each day?
25. **WRITE Math** Michael drew a line 75 millimeters long. Susan's line was 7 centimeters long, and Ed's was 1 decimeter long. **Explain** how you can order the lengths from least to greatest.

GO ONLINE Technology Use *Online Assessment.*

Standardized Test Prep
Chapters 1–22

Number and Operations

1. Janet read $\frac{3}{4}$ of a book. Which fraction is equivalent to $\frac{3}{4}$? (p. 406)

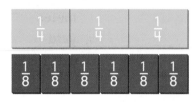

A $\frac{2}{8}$ C $\frac{6}{8}$

B $\frac{5}{8}$ D $\frac{7}{8}$

Test Tip Eliminate choices.

See Item 2. The ones place is the same for all answer choices, so check your subtraction of the tens and hundreds places.

2. There were 3,548 visitors at the science museum in 2006. In 2007, there were 3,397 visitors. How many more people visited the science museum in 2006? (p. 48)

A 141

B 251

C 241

D 151

3. **WRITE Math** Leo planted a total of 40 flower seeds. He planted the same number of seeds for 5 different types of flowers. How many seeds were there for each type of flower? **Explain** how you know. (p. 310)

Algebraic Reasoning

4. Which equation can be used to show the relationship in the table below? (p. 128)

Inches, i	12	24	36	48
Feet, f	1	2	3	4

A $f \times 12 = i$

B $f + 12 = i$

C $f \div 12 = i$

D $f - 12 = i$

5. Mitchell scored 3 goals in his first game and 2 goals in his second game. He scored a total of 8 goals in his first three games. Let g represent the goals in the third game. Which equation represents this situation? (p. 70)

A $3 + 2 = g + 8$

B $g + 3 = 2 + 8$

C $3 + 2 + 8 = g$

D $3 + 2 + g = 8$

6. Emily can ride her bike b miles in one hour. Which expression can be used to find how many miles she can ride in 5 hours? (p. 66)

A $b - 5$ C $5 \div b$

B $b + 5$ D $5 \times b$

7. **WRITE Math** How can you use addition to check that $6,374 - 1,443 = 4,931$? **Explain** how you know. (p. 32)

Measurement

8. Order the lengths from least to greatest. (p. 602)

3 inches, $1\frac{3}{4}$ inches, $2\frac{1}{2}$ inches, $3\frac{1}{8}$ inches

A 3 in., $3\frac{1}{8}$ in., $2\frac{1}{2}$ in., $1\frac{3}{4}$ in.

B $3\frac{1}{8}$ in., 3 in., $1\frac{3}{4}$ in., $2\frac{1}{2}$ in.

C $2\frac{1}{2}$ in., $1\frac{3}{4}$ in., $3\frac{1}{8}$ in., 3 in.

D $1\frac{3}{4}$ in., $2\frac{1}{2}$ in., 3 in., $3\frac{1}{8}$ in.

9. Which tool would be most appropriate to use to measure the height of a plant? (p. 614)

A    **C**

B    **D**

10. ⌐WRITE Math⌐ Does a swimming pool have a capacity of *about a liter, less than a liter*, or *more than a liter*? (p. 622)

Probability and Statistics

11. This table shows the results of spinning a pointer on a spinner 20 times. Which color is most likely to be spun next? (Grade 3)

Color Spinner Tally Results	
Color	Tally
Red	|||
Orange	卌 |||
Blue	||||
Green	卌

A Red   **C** Blue

B Orange   **D** Green

12. Cherie has 3 pairs of pants and 5 shirts. How many combinations of pants and shirts can she wear? (Grade 3)

A 10   **C** 15

B 12   **D** 20

13. Jim has a penny and a nickel in his pocket. If he reaches into his pocket and pulls out a coin without looking, what is the probability that the coin will be a penny? (Grade 3)

A 0   **C** 2 out of 2

B 1 out of 2   **D** 1

14. ⌐WRITE Math⌐ What are the possible outcomes for pulling a marble of equal size out of this bag? **Explain** how you know. (Grade 3)

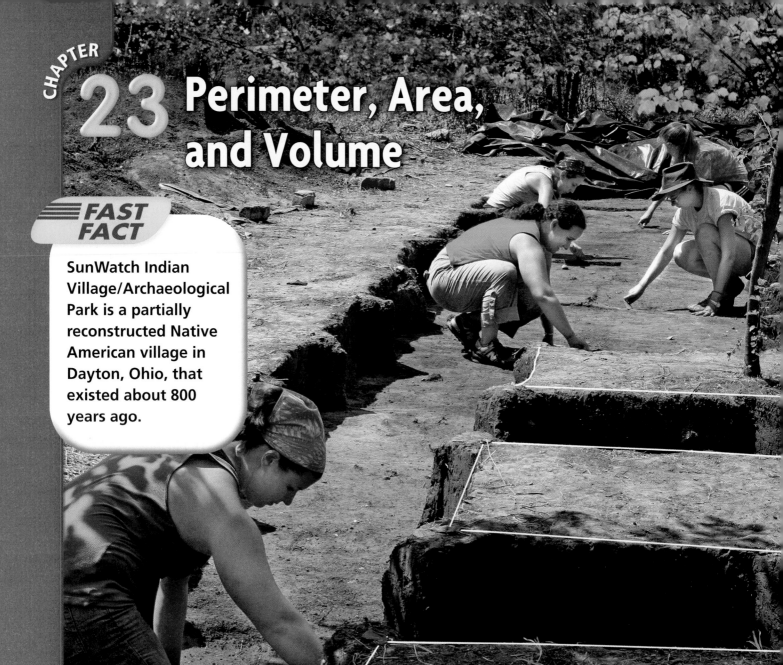

23 Perimeter, Area, and Volume

≣ FAST FACT

SunWatch Indian Village/Archaeological Park is a partially reconstructed Native American village in Dayton, Ohio, that existed about 800 years ago.

Investigate

Archaeologists divide a dig area into smaller work sites. Suppose you are working on an archaeological dig. Your job is to design work sites with different area models. What possible dimensions could you use for each site?

Archaeological Dig Sites	
Site	Area (in square feet)
A	20
B	24
C	30
D	36

GO ONLINE

Technology
Student pages are available in the Student eBook.

Check your understanding of important skills needed for success in Chapter 23.

▶ **Add Whole Numbers**

Find the sum.

1. $5 + 6 + 8 = $ ■

2. $9 + 4 + 2 + 7 = $ ■

3. $2 + 6 + 9 + 1 + 5 = $ ■

4. $11 + 27 + 18 = $ ■

5. $5 + 46 + 28 + 31 = $ ■

6. $53 + 21 + 66 + 34 = $ ■

▶ **Multiplication Facts**

Find the product.

7. $8 \times 3 = $ ■

8. $9 \times 8 = $ ■

9. $12 \times 5 = $ ■

10. $5 \times 6 = $ ■

11. $6 \times 6 = $ ■

12. $9 \times 7 = $ ■

13. $8 \times 5 = $ ■

14. $7 \times 4 = $ ■

▶ **Expressions and Variables**

Find the value of the expression.

15. $a \times 3$
  if $a = 9$

16. $7 + f + 18$
  if $f = 13$

17. $7 \times c$
  if $c = 5$

18. $s + 13 + 46$
  if $s = 8$

19. $26 + 34 + r + 78$
  if $r = 23$

20. $6 \times g$
  if $g = 12$

21. $38 + h + 51$
  if $h = 10$

22. $y \times 8$
  if $y = 8$

VOCABULARY POWER

CHAPTER VOCABULARY

area
cubic units (cu un)
formula
perimeter
square unit (sq un)
volume

WARM-UP WORDS

area the number of square units needed to cover a surface

formula a set of symbols that expresses a mathematical rule

perimeter the distance around a figure

volume the measure of the amount of space a solid figure occupies

1 Estimate and Measure Perimeter

OBJECTIVE: Estimate and measure perimeter.

 **Quick Review**

What is the length of the pen cap to the nearest centimeter?

Investigate

Materials ■ string ■ scissors ■ centimeter ruler ■ meterstick ■ 3 classroom objects

You can use string and a ruler to help you estimate and measure the perimeter of an object or a figure. **Perimeter** is the distance around a figure.

Vocabulary

perimeter

A Make a table to record the names, units, estimates, and actual measurements of 3 classroom objects.

Perimeter of Classroom Objects

Object	Unit	Estimate	Actual Measurement
?	■	■	■
?	■	■	■

B Choose the unit you would use to measure the perimeter of each object. Then estimate and record the estimated perimeter of each object.

C Now use string to measure the perimeter of each object. Place string around the outside of the object. Cut or mark the string to show the perimeter. Then measure and record the length of the string in the units you used to estimate.

Draw Conclusions

1. How did you estimate the perimeter of the objects?

2. How did you choose which unit to use to measure the perimeter of each object?

3. How do your measurements compare to your estimates? Were your estimates reasonable? Explain.

4. **APPLICATION** What unit would you use to meaure the perimeter of your classroom? Explain.

Connect

You can find the perimeter of a rectangle on a geoboard or dot paper by counting the number of units on each side.

This rectangle is 4 units long and 2 units wide. So, the perimeter of the rectangle is 4 units + 2 units + 4 units + 2 units, or 12 units.

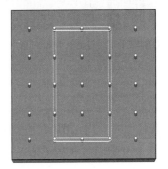

TALK Math

Explain how to find the perimeter of a square with sides 5 units long.

Practice

Use string to estimate and measure the perimeter of each object.

1. a sheet of paper   **2.** an index card   **3.** a chalkboard eraser ✓**4.** your desk

Find the perimeter of each figure.

5.    **6.**    **7.**    **8.**    ✓**9.**

Use dot paper or grid paper to draw a rectangle with the given perimeter. Then record the lengths of the sides.

10. 10 units   **11.** 20 units   **12.** 14 units   **13.** 12 units

14. 24 units   **15.** 16 units   **16.** 18 units   **17.** 26 units

Zach is helping his dad build a rectangular sandbox that has a perimeter of 24 feet.

18. On dot paper or grid paper, draw the different rectangular sandboxes that Zach and his dad could build. Label the length of each side.

19. **WRITE Math** Zach and his dad decide to make a sandbox that is square. What dimensions could they use? **Explain.**

ALGEBRA

Find Perimeter

OBJECTIVE: Use a formula to find perimeter.

Quick Review

1. $16 + 19 + 21$
2. $(2 \times 4) + (2 \times 10)$
3. $55 + 31 + 65 + 29$
4. $(2 \times 12) + (2 \times 11)$
5. $9 + 13 + 8 + 17 + 22$

Learn

PROBLEM Julio is putting a stone border around his garden. How many feet long is the border of Julio's garden?

To find how many feet of stones Julio needs, find the perimeter of the garden.

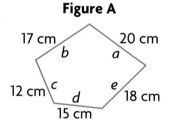

3 ft
3 ft
7 ft
5 ft
7 ft

Vocabulary

formula

ONE WAY **Add the lengths of the sides.**

$3 \text{ ft} + 3 \text{ ft} + 5 \text{ ft} + 7 \text{ ft} + 7 \text{ ft} = 25 \text{ ft}$

So, Julio needs 25 feet of stones.

A **formula**, or mathematical rule, can also be used to find perimeter. The number of variables used in a formula is the same as the number of sides in a figure.

ANOTHER WAY **Use a formula.**

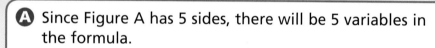

A Since Figure A has 5 sides, there will be 5 variables in the formula.

$P = $ sum of the lengths of the sides
$P = a + b + c + d + e$
$P = 20 + 17 + 12 + 15 + 18$
$P = 82$

Think: Use a variable to represent the length of each side.

Figure A

17 cm   20 cm
b   *a*
12 cm *c*   *e* 18 cm
d
15 cm

So, the perimeter of Figure A is 82 cm.

B Since Figure B has 6 sides, there will be 6 variables in the formula.

$P = $ sum of the lengths of the sides
$P = a + b + c + d + e + f$
$P = 15 + 12 + 16 + 20 + 17 + 10$
$P = 90$

Think: Use a variable to represent the length of each side.

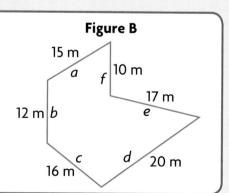

Figure B

15 m
a   *f* 10 m
17 m
12 m *b*   *e*
c   *d* 20 m
16 m

So, the perimeter of Figure B is 90 m.

Perimeter of Rectangles and Squares

You can use special formulas to find the perimeter of a rectangle
and a square.

Polygon	Perimeter	Formula
Rectangle 	Perimeter = length + width + length + width or Perimeter = 2 × length + 2 × width	$P = l + w + l + w$ or $P = (2 \times l) + (2 \times w)$
Square 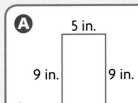	Perimeter = side + side + side + side or Perimeter = 4 × side	$P = s + s + s + s$ or $P = 4 \times s$

Examples Use a formula.

Ⓐ 5 in.   9 in.   9 in.   5 in.

$P = (2 \times l) + (2 \times w)$
$P = (2 \times 9) + (2 \times 5)$
$P = 18 + 10$
$P = 28$

The perimeter is 28 in.

Ⓑ 12 cm   12 cm

$P = 4 \times s$
$P = 4 \times 12$
$P = 48$

The perimeter is 48 cm.

- If you know the perimeter of a square, how can you find the
  length of each side?

Guided Practice

1. Add the lengths of the sides.
   What is the perimeter of this figure?

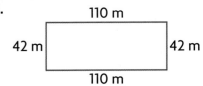

25 ft   13 ft   14 ft   13 ft   25 ft

Find the perimeter.

2.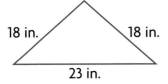
   18 in.   18 in.   23 in.

✅ 3.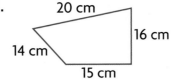
   20 cm   16 cm   14 cm   15 cm

✅ 4.
   110 m   42 m   42 m   110 m

5. **TALK Math** All the sides of a pentagon are 6 decimeters long.
   Explain how you can use multiplication to find the perimeter.

Independent Practice and Problem Solving

Find the perimeter.

6.
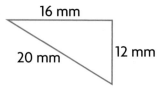
16 mm
20 mm
12 mm

7.
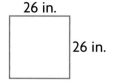
26 in.
26 in.

8.
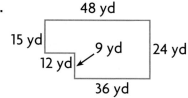
48 yd
15 yd
9 yd
12 yd
24 yd
36 yd

9.
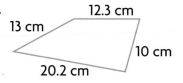
13 cm
12.3 cm
10 cm
20.2 cm

10.

9 ft   9 ft
13 ft   13 ft
9 ft   9 ft

11.
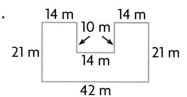
14 m   14 m
10 m
21 m   21 m
14 m
42 m

Use a formula to find the perimeter.

12.
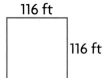
116 ft
116 ft

13.
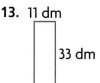
11 dm
33 dm

14.
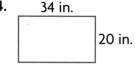
34 in.
20 in.

Measure with a centimeter ruler to find each perimeter.

15.
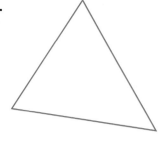

16.

17.
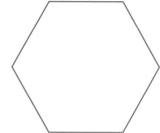

18. Reasoning A square and an equilateral triangle both have a perimeter of 36 centimeters. Draw and label the figures.

19. Reasoning The perimeter of a rectangle is 30 inches. The width of the rectangle is 5 inches. What is the length?

20. Mary is putting a brick edge around her patio. Her patio is shaped like a hexagon. Each side of the patio is 7 meters long. The bricks she is using are 50 centimeters long. How many bricks does Mary need? **Explain.**

21. **WRITE Math** ▸ **Sense or Nonsense** Tim wants to frame a square painting. One side of the painting is 4 feet long. He says 5 yards of frame is enough for the painting. Does this make sense? **Explain.**

CD ROM **Technology** Use Harcourt Mega Math, Ice Station Exploration, *Polar Planes*, Level P.

Learn About · Circumference of a Circle

The circumference of a circle is similar to the perimeter of a polygon. **Circumference** is the distance around the outside of the circle.

You can use a string to measure circumference.

Activity · **Materials** ▪ string ▪ circular lids ▪ ruler ▪ scissors

Step 1	Wrap the string around the outside of the can. Do not overlap the string.
Step 2	Mark the string where it meets the other end of the string. Cut it to show the distance around the can.
Step 3	Measure the string with a centimeter ruler. The length of the string is the circumference of the circle.

Try It

Copy and complete the table. Choose three circular objects to measure. Measure and record each circumference, using string and a centimeter ruler.

	Circular object	Measurement (in cm)
22.	?	▪
23.	?	▪
24.	?	▪

25. Compare the three circumferences. What is the difference between the largest circumference and the smallest circumference?

Mixed Review and Test Prep

26. Lynn is selecting outfits from the shirts and pants shown. She can select 1 shirt and 1 pair of pants. List all the different outfits Lynn can make. (Grade 3)

27. Jimmy cut 4 pieces of ribbon that were each 30 centimeters long. Does he have more or less than 1 meter of ribbon cut?

(p. 618)

28. **Test Prep** What is the perimeter of this figure?

    A 53 inches

    B 66 inches

    C 106 inches

    D 520 inches

    40 in.

    13 in.

29. **Test Prep** What is the perimeter of a square with sides 16 centimeters long? **Explain.**

Area of Plane Figures

OBJECTIVE: Estimate and find area.

Quick Review

1. 15 + 5 + 6
2. 8 ÷ 2
3. 9 + 5
4. 13 + 12 + 8
5. 10 ÷ 2

Vocabulary

area

square unit (sq un)

Learn

PROBLEM Mr. Hill is buying carpet for his bedroom. He used grid paper to make a diagram of his room to estimate and find the area. How can he use the grid to find the area of his bedroom?

Area is the number of square units needed to cover a surface. A **square unit (sq un)** is a square that is 1 unit long and 1 unit wide. You can use grid paper to estimate and find area.

Activity 1 Materials ■ grid paper ■ 2 different color pencils

- Copy the diagram on grid paper. Shade all the full squares in one color. Count them. 67 full squares
- Shade all the half-full squares in another color and count them. Two half-full squares equal one full square. Divide the sum of the squares by 2 to find the number of full squares. 10 half-full squares, 10 ÷ 2 = 5 full squares
- Find the sum of the squares counted. 67 + 5 = 72 squares

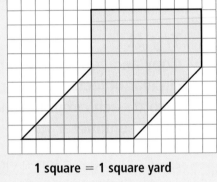

Mr. Hill's Diagram

1 square = 1 square yard

So, Mr. Hill can count the shaded squares in the grid to find that he needs 72 square yards of carpet.

Sometimes a figure on a grid has units that are almost-full or less than half-full. To estimate the area, you will need to count each square that is full, almost full, and half-full.

Activity 2 Materials ■ grid paper ■ 3 different color pencils

- Copy the figure on grid paper. Shade all the full squares in one color. Count them. Then shade the almost-full squares in another color. Count them. 42 full squares and 2 almost-full squares
- Now shade the half-full and almost half-full squares in a third color. Count them. Divide the sum of the squares by 2 to find the number of full squares. 4 half-full or almost half-full squares, 4 ÷ 2 = 2 full squares
- Find the sum of the squares counted. 42 + 2 + 2 = 46 squares

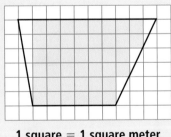

1 square = 1 square meter

So, the area is about 46 square meters.

Activity 3   Materials ■ grid paper ■ 3 different color pencils

- Copy the figure on grid paper. Shade all the full squares in one color and count them. Then shade the almost-full squares in another color and count them. 19 full squares and 9 almost-full squares

- Now shade the half-full and almost half-full squares in a third color and count them. Divide the sum of the squares by 2 to find the number of full squares. 8 half-full or almost half-full squares, 8 ÷ 2 = 4 full squares

- Find the sum of the squares counted. 19 + 9 + 4 = 32 squares

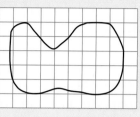

1 square = 1 square mile

So, the area is about 32 square miles.

- Why is your answer an estimate, rather than an exact answer? Explain.

More Examples Estimate the area.

A

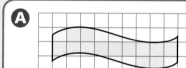

1 square = 1 square foot

The green squares are full.

There are 3 full squares.

The orange squares are almost full.

There are 10 almost-full squares.

The yellow squares are half-full or almost half-full. There are 6 half-full or about half-full squares. 6 ÷ 2 = 3 full squares

Find the sum of the squares.

3 + 10 + 3 = 16 squares

So, the area is about 16 square feet.

B

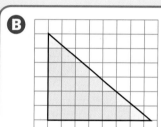

1 square = 1 square centimeter

The green squares are full.

There are about 17 full squares.

The orange squares are almost full.

There are 3 almost-full squares.

The yellow squares are half-full or almost half-full. There are 4 half-full or about half-full squares. 4 ÷ 2 = 2 full squares.

Find the sum of the squares. 17 + 3 + 2 = 22

So, the area is about 22 square centimeters.

Guided Practice

1. Find the area of the figure.

Estimate the area of each figure. Each unit is 1 sq cm.

2.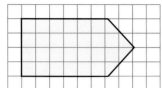

✓ 3.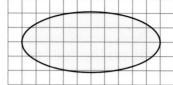

✓ 4.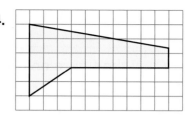

5. **[TALK Math]** Tommy drew a circle on grid paper and counted squares to find the area. Is the area he found an exact measurement or an estimate? **Explain.**

Independent Practice *(and Problem Solving*

Estimate the area of each figure. Each unit is 1 sq ft.

6.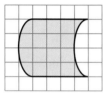

7.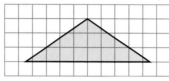

8.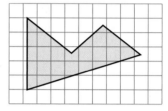

9.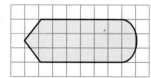

10.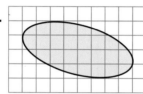

11.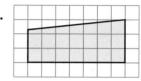

Draw each figure on grid paper. Then estimate its area in square units.

12. circle

13. triangle

14. oval

15. a figure with only straight line segments

16. a figure with curved paths and straight line segments

17. a figure with no straight line segments

USE DATA For 18–20, use the diagram.

18. About how many square yards is the area of the kitchen?

19. Which is greater, the area of the family room or the area of the living room? **Explain.**

20. **[WRITE Math]** ▸ **What's the Error?** Rosa says the total area of the part of her house shown is 96 square yards. Is Rosa correct? **Explain.**

Floor Plan

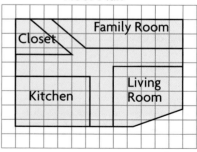

1 square = 1 square yard

Learn About Surface Area

The **surface area** of a figure is the number of square units that it takes to cover the outside of a figure. You can use grid paper to find the surface area of cubes and rectangular prisms.

Examples

Ⓐ Find the surface area of a cube.

Make a cube that is 3 centimeters by 3 centimeters by 3 centimeters.

Cover the cube with centimeter grid paper.

There are 9 grid squares on each face.

There are 6 faces, so it takes 6 × 9 = 54 centimeters to cover the cube.

So, the surface area of the cube is 54 square centimeters.

Ⓑ Find the surface area of a rectangular prism.

Make a rectangular prism that is 4 centimeters by 2 centimeters by 2 centimeters.

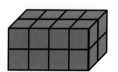

Cover the prism with centimeter grid paper.

There are 8 grid squares on 4 faces. 4 × 8 = 32
There are 4 grid squares on 2 faces. 2 × 4 = 8

It takes 32 + 8 = 40 centimeters to cover the prism.

So, the surface area of the prism is 40 square centimeters.

Try It

Make each figure. Then, find the surface area.

21. 4 cm by 5 cm by 3 cm   **22.** 4 cm by 4 cm by 4 cm   **23.** 2 cm by 3 cm by 5 cm

24. Audrey wrapped a package 10 centimeters long, 8 centimeters wide, and 5 centimeters high. What was the surface area of the package?

Mixed Review and Test Prep

25. What is the perimeter of this rectangle? (p. 636)

10 in.

27 in.

26. Mr. Wallace is putting packages of staples in boxes. He can pack 78 packages in one box. He packs 112 boxes. How many packages does he pack in all? (p. 254)

27. Test Prep In the figure below, each square is 1 square kilometer. What is the best estimate of the area of the figure?

A 21 square kilometers

B 18 square kilometers

C 16 square kilometers

D 12 square kilometers

ALGEBRA

Find Area

OBJECTIVE: Measure and find area by counting, multiplying, and using a formula.

Quick Review

1. 16×10
2. 12×21
3. 44×23
4. 8×13
5. 23×11

Learn

PROBLEM Danny is tiling the floor in his kitchen. The floor is a rectangle 8 feet long and 14 feet wide. How many square feet of tile does Danny need?

To find how many square feet of tile Danny needs, find the area of the floor. There are different ways to find the area of a rectangle.

Kitchen Floor Plan

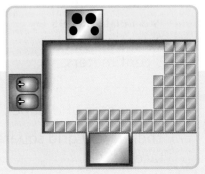

ONE WAY Count square units.

Step 1

To represent the floor, draw a rectangle 8 feet long and 14 feet wide on grid paper. Let each square represent 1 square foot.

Step 2

Estimate the number of squares inside the rectangle. Then count the squares. There are 112 squares, so the area of the floor is 112 feet.

So, Danny needs 112 square feet of tile.

- **What if** the rectangle was 12 feet long by 7 feet wide? How could you use grid paper to find the area?

OTHER WAYS

Ⓐ Use multiplication.

To find the area of a rectangle, multiply the number of rows by the number of units in each row.

number of rows		number in each row		area
↓		↓		↓
3	×	5	=	15 square units

3 rows of 5

So, the area is 15 square units.

Ⓑ Use a formula.

The formula for the area of a rectangle is Area = length × width, or $A = l \times w$.

Use the formula to find the area of the rectangle.

$A = l \times w$
$A = 3 \times 5$

$A = 15$

5 yd

3 yd   3 yd

5 yd

So, the area of the rectangle is 15 square yards.

Area of Rectangles and Squares

You can use a special formula to find the area of a rectangle that is a square.

Polygon	Area	Formula
Rectangle 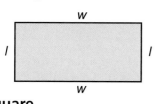	Area = length × width	$A = l \times w$
Square 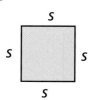	Area = length × width or $A = side \times side$	$A = l \times w$ or $A = s \times s$

Examples Use a formula.

A

12 cm / 4 cm / 4 cm / 12 cm

$A = l \times w$
$A = 4 \times 12$
$A = 48$

The area is 48 sq cm.

B

4 cm / 4 cm

$A = l \times w$
$A = 4 \times 4$
$A = 16$

The area is 16 sq cm.

Guided Practice

1. Use a formula to find the area of this square.

   $A = \blacksquare \times \blacksquare$

   12 cm / 12 cm

Find the area.

2.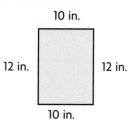
   10 in. / 12 in. / 12 in. / 10 in.

3.
   9 mi / 9 mi

4.
   16 m / 6 m

5. **TALK Math** Explain how can you find the area of a rectangle on grid paper without counting each individual square unit.

Find the area.

6.
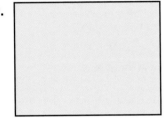
13 ft
5 ft   5 ft
13 ft

7.
6 km
6 km

8.
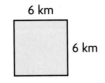
20 cm
2 cm

Use a centimeter ruler to measure each figure. Find the area and perimeter.

9.

10.

11.

⭐ **Algebra** Find the unknown length.

12. Area = 121 sq yd
?
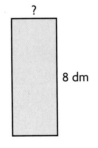
11 yd

13. Area = 24 sq dm
?
8 dm

14. Area = 80 sq mm
16 mm
?

USE DATA For 15–17, use the diagram.

15. The gray brick area is a square. How many square feet of gray bricks does Mark need for that area?

16. **Reasoning** The area surrounding the patio is grass. How many square feet of grass does Mark need? **Explain.**

17. **WRITE Math** ▸ **What's the Question?** Mark compared the number of square feet of gray bricks to the number of square feet of red bricks needed for the patio. The answer is red bricks.

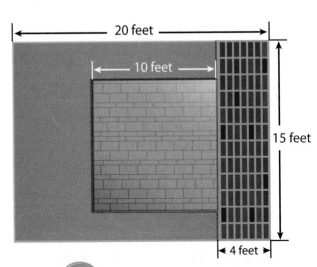
20 feet
10 feet
15 feet
4 feet

Technology
Use Harcourt Mega Math, Ice Station Exploration, *Polar Planes*, Level Q.

Extra Practice on page 659, Set C

ALGEBRA
Fractions and Area

You can use fractions to help you find the area of figures.

Figure A

Think of Figure A as $\frac{1}{2}$ of a whole figure. You can use what you know about fractions and area to draw what the whole figure might look like and find its area.

$\frac{1}{2}$ whole figure

Step 1

Find the area of Figure A.
  There are 28 full squares.
  There are 8 half-full squares. $8 \div 2 = 4$ full squares
  The area is $28 + 4 = 32$ square units.

Step 2

Find the area of the whole figure.
The whole figure is twice the size of Figure A.
So, the area of the whole figure is about $2 \times 32 = 64$ square units.
Draw the other half of the figure so the total area is 64 square units.

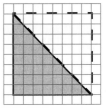

Try It

Draw the whole figure given each part. Find the area of the fraction of the figure given and whole figure.

18.

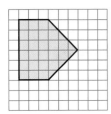

$\frac{1}{2}$ whole figure

19.

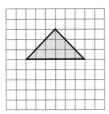

$\frac{1}{2}$ whole figure

20.

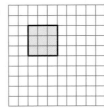

$\frac{1}{4}$ whole figure

21.

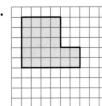

$\frac{2}{3}$ whole figure

Mixed Review and Test Prep

22. What is the value of $6 \times (9 + 12) - 85$?
(p. 126)

23. Test Prep What is the area of this figure?

  A 20 square centimeters

  B 40 square centimeters

  C 60 square centimeters

  D 96 square centimeters

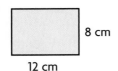

8 cm

12 cm

24. Kenny is framing a picture. The picture is 12 inches long and 14 inches wide. How many inches of framing material does Kenny need? (p. 636)

25. Test Prep Use a formula to find the area of a square with sides 7 feet in length. **Explain.**

LESSON 5 — Problem Solving Workshop
Skill: Use a Formula

OBJECTIVE: Solve problems by using the skill *use a formula*.

Use the Skill

PROBLEM Ellie and her mom are attending a sand castle building competition. The diagram shows two sections of a beach that will be roped off for the competition. What is the total area of both sections? How much rope will be needed to enclose the two sections?

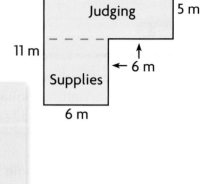

To find the perimeter and area of a complex figure, first divide the figure into sections. Then use formulas to find the area of each section and the perimeter of both sections.

Area of Each Section		Perimeter of Both Sections
Judging	**Supplies**	
$A = l \times w$	$A = l \times w$	$P = a + b + c + d + e + f$
$A = 5 \times 12$	$A = 6 \times 6$	$P = 12 + 5 + 6 + 6 + 6 + 11 = 46$
$A = 60$ sq m	$A = 36$ sq m	$P = 46$ m
Sum of the areas: $60 + 36 = 96$ sq m		

So, the total area is 96 square meters and 46 meters of rope is needed to enclose the two sections.

Think and Discuss

Use a formula to solve.

a. The competition staff decides to put only a fence around the judging section. How much fencing is needed?

b. The diagram at the right shows the floor plan of Mandy's sand castle. What is the total area of her sand castle?

c. Mandy is putting a moat around the outside of the castle. What will be the total length of the moat?

Mandy's Sand Castle

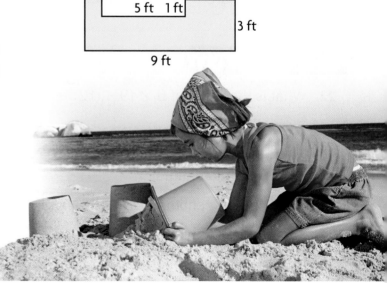

Guided Problem Solving

Use a formula to solve.

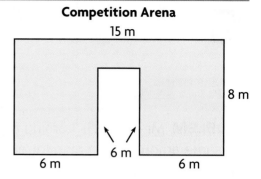

Competition Arena

1. George is competing in a sand castle competition. The diagram shows part of the competition arena. What is the area of this part of the arena?

   First, divide the competition arena into sections.
   Think: How can I divide the arena into rectangles and squares?

   Then, use a formula to find the area of each section.
   Think: What are the dimensions of each section?

   Finally, add the areas of the sections to get the total area.
   Think: What is the total area?

2. **What if** a rope was going to be placed around each section of the competition arena? How much rope would be needed?

3. A diagram of Ryan's sand castle in shown at the right. He decides to line the perimeter of his castle with shells. If each shell is two inches long, how many shells does Ryan need?

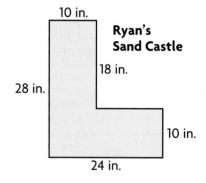

Ryan's Sand Castle

Mixed Applications

4. Casey is building a sand castle in a space with 4 sides of equal length and a perimeter of 80 feet. Sketch this space. What is the length of each side? What is the area of this space?

5. **≡FAST FACT** The weight of 1 cubic meter of dry sand is about 4,000 pounds. How many tons is this?

USE DATA For 6–9 use the table.

6. The Carter family bought 2 spades, 1 how-to book, and 3 castle tower molds. How much did they spend?

7. Megan buys 4 pails and 4 spades. Rob buys 7 shovels. Who spends more? How much more? **Explain.**

8. Janisa buys 22 how-to books for a sand castle building class she is teaching. Is $200 enough to buy all the books? **Explain** how you can use estimation to find out.

9. **WRITE Math** Devon buys a few of each type of supply. Is this enough information to find out how much money he spends? **Explain.**

Sand Castle Building Supplies	
Supply	Cost
Shovel	$3
Pail	$3
How-To Book	$9
Castle Tower Mold	$6
Spade	$2

LESSON 6
Relate Perimeter and Area

OBJECTIVE: Explore the relationship between perimeter and area.

Quick Review

1. $(2 \times 6) + (2 \times 10)$
2. 9×11
3. $14 + 16 + 14 + 16$
4. $(2 \times 10) + (2 \times 12)$
5. 8×19

Learn

PROBLEM Mr. Foster is framing three pictures. Does he need the same amount of framing for each picture? Does he need the same number of square inches of glass for each picture?

To find how much framing Mr. Foster needs, find the perimeter of each picture. To find how much glass he needs, find the area of each picture.

7 in.

3 in.

A

6 in.

5 in.

4 in.

B

5 in.

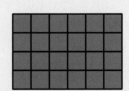

C

Activity 1 Materials ■ square tiles ■ grid paper

- Use square tiles to model Picture A. Make a rectangle 3 tiles long and 7 tiles wide. Trace the rectangle on grid paper.

- Copy the table and fill in the perimeter and area for Picture A.

- Repeat Steps 1 and 2 for the other pictures. Record your work in the table.

So, for each picture, Mr. Foster needs the same amount of framing but a different number of square inches of glass.

Perimeter and Area

Picture	Length	Width	Perimeter	Area
A	3 in.	7 in.	■	■
B	■	■	■	■
C	■	■	■	■

Activity 2 Materials ■ 24 square tiles ■ grid paper

- Use 24 square tiles to make a rectangle. Trace the rectangle onto grid paper. Copy the table and record the length and width. Find the perimeter and area, and record them in the table.

- Use the 24 tiles to make as many different rectangles as you can. Trace each rectangle and find the perimeter and area. Record each length, width, perimeter, and area in the table.

- Compare and contrast rectangles 1, 2, and 3.

Perimeter and Area

Rectangle	Length	Width	Perimeter	Area
1	4 un	6 un	20 un	24 sq un
2	■	■	■	■
3	■	■	■	■

Activity 3 Materials ■ square tiles ■ grid paper

Perimeter and Area				
Rectangle	Length	Width	Perimeter	Area
1	1 tile	12 tiles	■	■
2	2 tiles	■	■	■
3	3 tiles	■	■	■

- Use square tiles to make a rectangle 1 tile long and 12 tiles wide. Trace the rectangle on grid paper.
- Find the perimeter and area. Copy and complete the table.
- Continue to make rectangles with 12 tiles by decreasing the length and increasing the width. Make as many rectangles as you can. Trace each rectangle, find the perimeter and area, and record your work in the table.

- **Reasoning** When the area stays the same and the rectangle becomes more like a square, what happens to the perimeter?
- What is the difference between area and perimeter? Explain.

Math Idea
Two figures can have the same area but different perimeters or different areas but the same perimeter.

Guided Practice

1. How can you change this rectangle so that it has the same perimeter, but a greater area? Model and then record your answer.

6 cm
2 cm

Find the perimeter and area of each figure. Then draw another figure that has the same perimeter but a different area.

2.
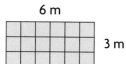
6 m
3 m

3.

9 mi
9 mi

✓4.
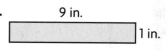
9 in.
1 in.

Find the area and perimeter of each figure. Then draw another figure that has the same area but a different perimeter.

5.

4 m
4 m

6.
9 ft
16 ft

✓7.
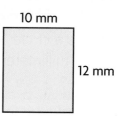
10 mm
12 mm

8. (TALK Math) **Explain** how knowing the factors of a number can help you find all the rectangles with an area of that number.

Find the perimeter and area of each figure. Then draw another figure that has the same perimeter but a different area.

9.
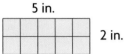
5 in.
2 in.

10.
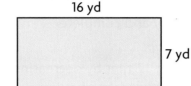
16 yd
7 yd

11.
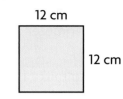
12 cm
12 cm

Find the perimeter and area of each figure. Then draw another figure that has the same area but a different perimeter.

12.

7 m
2 m

13.
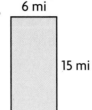
6 mi
15 mi

14.
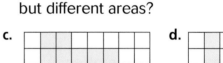
20 ft
2 ft

For 15–16, use figures a–d.

15. Which figures have the same area but different perimeters?

16. Which figures have the same perimeter but different areas?

a.
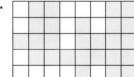

b.

c.

d.

17. Corynn paints a rectangular picture that has a perimeter of 22 centimeters. What are 3 possible areas for her picture?

18. **WRITE Math** ▸ Mia has two pictures, both with an area of 36 square inches. One is a rectangle, and one is a square. Which has the greater perimeter? **Explain.**

Mixed Review and Test Prep

19. Susie draws a circle. The diameter of the circle is 16 millimeters. What is the radius of the circle? (p. 530)

20. The length of a rectangle is 14 meters and the width is 11 meters. What is the area of the rectangle? (p. 644)

21. **Test Prep** The rectangles below have the same perimeter. Which has the greatest area?

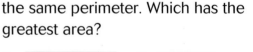
A

C

B

D

Extra Practice on page 659, Set D

Say Cheese!

Reading Skill Sequence

Linda loves photography. She uses a photo program on her computer to change the size of her photos. She increases the size of a 2-inch by 3-inch photo by doubling the length and width. Then she triples the original dimensions. She wants to know how the length, width, perimeter, and area change each time she changes the size of the photo.

Knowing the sequence, or order, of the changes made to the photo will help you solve the problem. Use grid paper and a table to find how the dimensions change.

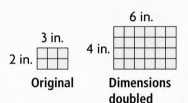
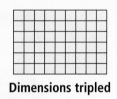

| 3 in. | 6 in. | |
| Original | Dimensions doubled | Dimensions tripled |

Perimeter and Area				
Photo	Length	Width	Perimeter	Area
Original	2 in.	3 in.	10 in.	6 sq in.
Doubled	4 in.	6 in.	20 in.	24 sq in.
Tripled	▪	▪	▪	▪

Problem Solving Track the sequence of the changes in each problem to solve. Use grid paper and a table to record.

1. Solve the problem above.

2. Abby has a photo that is 2 inches by 4 inches. She doubles the dimensions. Then she triples the dimensions. Then she halves the dimensions. How does the area of the photo change as the dimensions of the photo change?

7 Estimate and Find Volume of Prisms

OBJECTIVE: Estimate and find the volume of rectangular prisms.

Learn

Volume is the amount of space a solid figure occupies. Volume is measured using **cubic units**. Volume can be measured in units such as cubic centimeters, cubic inches, or cubic feet.

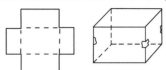
1 unit 1 unit
1 unit

Math Idea
To help estimate the volume of a prism, you can visualize the number of cubes that will fit along the length, width, and height of a prism.

Activity Estimate volume.

Materials ■ prism net ■ scissors ■ tape ■ centimeter cubes

| Step 1 | Cut out the net. Fold along the lines, and tape the sides to make an open box. |

| Step 2 | Estimate how many cubes will fill the box. Record your estimate. |

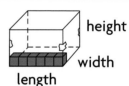
height
width
length

| Step 3 | Place as many cubes as you can in the box. Count the cubes you used. Record the number. |

• Is your estimate greater than or less than the actual number of cubes in the box? Explain.

Example Estimate volume.

Estimate the number of cubes that will fit along the length, width, and height of the prism.

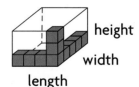
height
width
length

Think: About 4 cubes fit along the length, about 5 cubes fit along the width. So, the bottom layer has about 4×5, or 20 cubes. There are about 3 layers of 20 cubes each.

20 cubes + 20 cubes + 20 cubes = 60 cubes

So, the volume is about 60 cubic units.

• Fill an oatmeal container with cubes to estimate the volume. Will your estimate be greater than or less than the actual number of cubes in the container? Explain.

Find Volume

There are different ways to find volume.

ONE WAY Count cubic units.

Count the number of cubic units in a 7-unit by 3-unit by 4-unit rectangular prism.

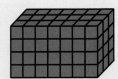

ANOTHER WAY Multiply length × width × height.

ERROR ALERT

Be sure to count all the cubes in each layer, even though you can't see them.

Step 1

Find the length.
Count the number of cubes in one row.
The length is 7 cubes.

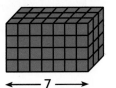

←— 7 —→

Step 2

Find the width.
Count the number of rows in one layer.
The width is 3 cubes.

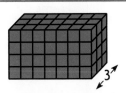

3

Step 3

Find the height.
Count the number of layers in the rectangular prism. The height is 4 cubes.

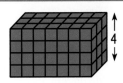

4

Step 4

Multiply length × width × height to find the volume.

$7 \times 3 \times 4 = 84$

So, the volume of the prism is 84 cubic units.

Guided Practice

1. How many cubes make up the bottom layer of the rectangular prism shown at right?

Count or multiply to find the volume.

2.

✓ 3.

✓ 4.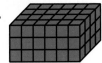

5. **TALK Math** Explain why you can use multiplication to find the volume of a rectangular prism.

Independent Practice and Problem Solving

Count or multiply to find the volume.

6.

7.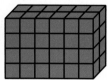

8.

9.

10.

11.

12.

13.

14.

⭐ **Algebra** Copy and complete the table.

	Length	Width	Height (number of layers)	Volume (cubic units)
15.	5 in.	2 in.	3 in.	◼
16.	6 cm	2 cm	10 cm	◼
17.	11 mm	2 mm	13 mm	◼

	Length	Width	Height (number of layers)	Volume (cubic units)
18.	5 cm	4 cm	◼	80 cu cm
19.	8 ft	◼	2 ft	64 cu ft
20.	◼	15 in.	2 in.	210 cu in.

Compare the volumes of the figures. Write <, >, or = for each ●.

21.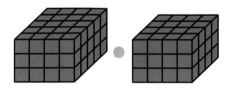

22.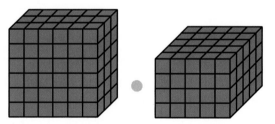

23. **Reasoning** What is the difference between an inch, a square inch, and a cubic inch? Name something you might measure with each unit and then draw a picture of each.

24. **Reasoning** Karla has 24 centimeter cubes. Name 3 different ways Karla can use all the cubes to build a rectangular prism.

25. **Pose a Problem** Look back at Problem 21. Write a similar problem by changing the number of cubes used.

26. **WRITE Math** ▸ **Explain** the difference between perimeter, area, and volume.

Extra Practice on page 659, Set E

Learn About) Relating Volume and Capacity

Solid volume and liquid capacity are related. Volume describes
the space a solid figure occupies. Capacity describes the amount
of liquid a container can hold when filled.

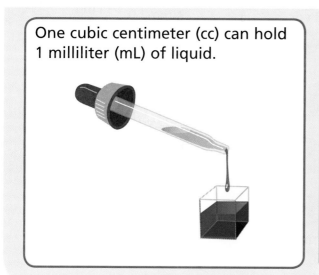

One cubic centimeter (cc) can hold
1 milliliter (mL) of liquid.

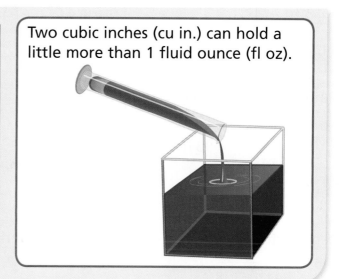

Two cubic inches (cu in.) can hold a
little more than 1 fluid ounce (fl oz).

Try It

Use what you know about volume and capacity to
complete each table of equivalent measures.

27.

Volume (in cubic inches)	Capacity (in milliliters)
1	1
10	▪
1,000	▪
10,000	▪

28.

Volume (in cubic inches)	Capacity (in fluid ounces)
1	▪
2	1
4	▪
9	▪

Mixed Review and Test Prep

29. An index card measures 3 inches by
5 inches. What is the area of the index
card? (p. 644)

30. Taylor, Sydney, and Jessie earned $8.55
running a lemonade stand. If they divide
the money evenly, how much will each
girl get? (p. 334)

31. **Test Prep** The volume of a rectangular
prism is 96 cubic inches. The height is
8 inches. What could the length and
width of the rectangular prism be?
Explain how you know.

Extra Practice

Set A Find the perimeter. (pp. 636–639)

1.   5 in.

2 in.

2.   17 yd

18 yd   18 yd

9 yd

3.   2 mm   2 mm

4 mm   →1 mm
        →1 mm

3 mm

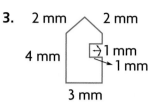

Use a formula to find the perimeter.

4.   18 ft

3 ft

5.   27 in.

39 in.

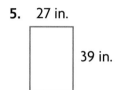

6.   32 yd

24 yd

Measure with a centimeter ruler to find each perimeter.

7.

8.

9.

Set B Estimate the area of each figure. Each square is 1 square foot. (pp. 640–643)

1.

2.

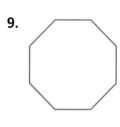

3.

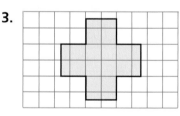

Draw each figure on grid paper. Then estimate its area in square units.

4. oval

5. square

6. rectangle

7. a figure with only
straight line segments

8. a figure with no
equal line segments

9. a figure with only
1 straight line segment

10. The fence around Caroline's garden is 12 feet
by 6 feet. What is the perimeter of her garden?

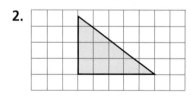

Set C Find the area. (pp. 644–647)

1.   11 in.

2 in.

2. 3 mm

3 mm

3.   12 yd
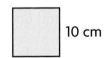
2 yd

Use a centimeter ruler to measure each figure. Find the area and perimeter.

4.

5.

6.
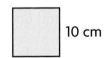

7. The dimensions of a twin-size blanket measure 90 inches long by 66 inches wide. What is the area?

Set D Find the perimeter and area of each figure. Then draw another figure that has the same perimeter but a different area. (pp. 650–653)

1. 3 ft
2 ft

2.   13 mi
 4 mi

3.   12 yd
1 yd

Find the perimeter and area of each figure. Then draw another figure that has the same area but a different perimeter.

4. 6 ft
 3 ft

5. 9 in.
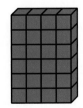11 in.

6. 10 cm

10 cm

Set E Count or multiply to find the volume. (pp. 654–657)

1.

2.

3.

4. Micah has 12 centimeter cubes. Name 2 different ways Micah can use all the cubes to build a rectangular prism.

MATH POWER Networks

Nifty Networks

You can use a network to help you solve word problems. A **network** is a graph made up of a set of points and paths joining them.

There are 6 children at the beach. Some of them are brothers and sisters. Which of the children are related? How many of the children are boys? How many are girls?

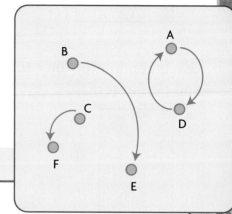

Example

Step 1

Use the arrows to see which children are pointing. The children who have arrows pointing to them are sisters.

- C is pointing to F, so F is the sister of C.
- B is pointing to E, so E is the sister of B.
- D is pointing to A, so A is the sister of D.
- A is pointing to D, so D is the sister of A.

Step 2

Use the relationships you found in Step 1 to figure out who is a boy and who is a girl.

- F is the sister of C, so F is a girl.
- No arrows point to C, so C is a boy.
- E is the sister of B, so E is a girl.
- No arrows point to B, so B is a boy.
- A and D are pointing to each other, which means they are sisters. Since they are sisters, A and D are both girls.

Step 3

Answer the questions using what you have learned.
- Which of the children are related?
  C and F, B and E, A and D
- How many of the children are boys? How many are girls?
  2 boys, C and B; 4 girls, F, E, A, D

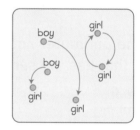

Try It

Use the network to solve the problem.

1. There are 3 children in one family. The arrows point to younger brothers or sisters. Write the letters of the children in order, from oldest to youngest.

2. **WRITE Math** ▶ There are 4 boys in one room. Each boy is pointing to the boys who are taller than he is. Who is the tallest boy in the room? **Explain.**

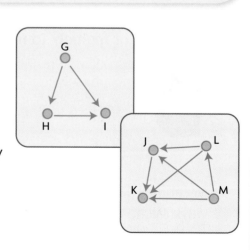

Chapter 23 Review/Test

Check Vocabulary and Concepts

Choose the best term from the box.

1. The distance around a figure is called __?__ . (p. 634)

2. A mathematical rule that can be used to find perimeter is called a __?__ . (p. 636)

3. The number of square units needed to cover a surface is called __?__ . (p. 640)

4. **Explain** how to find the perimeter of a square with sides 2 units long. (pp. 634–635)

> **VOCABULARY**
> area
> formula
> perimeter

Check Skills

Find the perimeter and area. (pp. 636–639, 644–647)

5. 105 in. | 23 in.

6. 68 mi | 68 mi

7. 14 yd | 42 yd

Find the perimeter and area of each figure. Then draw another figure that has the same perimeter but a different area. (pp. 650–653)

8. 9 cm | 4 cm

9. 5 yd | 12 yd

10. 18 in. | 3 in.

Count or multiply to find the volume. (pp. 654–657)

11.

12.

13.

Check Problem Solving

Solve. (pp. 648–649)

14. Shane is helping his grandparents plant a vegetable garden. The diagram shows the plot where the vegetables will be planted. What is its area? What is the perimeter of the plot?

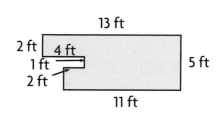

15. **WRITE Math ▸ Explain** how you can use a formula to find the area of a rectangle 12 meters long by 8 meters wide.

Standardized Test Prep
Chapters 1–23

Number and Operations

1. There are 192 students in the fourth grade. They are divided equally among 8 classes. How many students are in each class? (p. 356)

A 18

B 20

C 24

D 34

Test Tip

Eliminate Choices.

See Item 2. You need to multiply two whole numbers to find the answer. You can eliminate any answer choices that are less than the numbers in the problem.

2. Sarah bought 6 packs of erasers. There were 12 erasers in each pack. How many erasers did Sarah buy? (p. 102)

A 2

B 4

C 62

D 72

3. Nate had 312 baseball cards. He gave 148 to his brother. Which shows how many baseball cards Nate has left? (p. 48)

A 164 **C** 236

B 260 **D** 460

4. **WRITE Math** Which is greater, 5.82 or 5.19? **Explain** how you found your answer. (p. 470)

Algebraic Reasoning

5. Which number sentence is in the same fact family as $6 \times 9 = 54$? (p. 94)

A $6 \div 6 = 1$

B $9 \div 3 = 3$

C $54 \div 6 = 9$

D $54 \div 3 = 18$

6. Which correctly describes the relationship between the number of dogs and the number of tags in the table? (p. 386)

Dogs	6	7	8	9
Tags	12	14	16	18

A The number of tags is twice the number of dogs.

B The number of tags is 6 more than the number of dogs.

C The number of dogs is twice the number of tags.

D The number of tags is one-half the number of dogs.

7. What is the value of the expression? (p. 126)

$$4 \times (3 + 7)$$

A 11 **C** 19

B 14 **D** 40

8. **WRITE Math** Emily wants to find the product 4×500. **Explain** how she can use the basic fact $4 \times 5 = 20$ to help her. (p. 244)

Geometry

9. What kind of angle is shown? (p. 514)

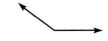

- **A** Obtuse
- **B** Right
- **C** Acute
- **D** Left

10. Hanna stores her CDs in a case like the one shown below. How many edges does the case have? (p. 570)

- **A** 6
- **B** 8
- **C** 12
- **D** 16

11. **WRITE Math** Rolando moved the arrow shape as shown below. What two transformations could Rolando have used to move the figure? **Explain** your answer. (p. 550)

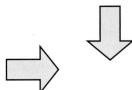

Data Analysis and Probability

12. The graph shows the number of coins students collected.

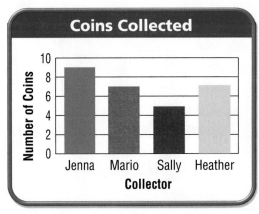

According to the graph, how many more coins did Jenna collect than Sally? (p. 204)

- **A** 14
- **C** 4
- **B** 9
- **D** 3

13. Which lists the possible outcomes of pulling a marble of equal size from the bag? (Grade 3)

- **A** Red, yellow, purple, black
- **B** Green, yellow, purple, black
- **C** Red, yellow, purple
- **D** Green, yellow

14. **WRITE Math** Jennifer took a survey of her classmates' favorite subjects. She made a bar graph showing the data she collected. The bars for Math and Reading were the same height. **Explain** what this means. (p. 204)

24 Probability

Investigate

Suppose you are waiting to take a Boston DUCK tour. The DUCK vehicles arrive in any order. Which color of DUCK is most likely to arrive next? What color of DUCK would you most like to ride in? What is the probability that it will come next? Explain how you know.

Boston DUCKs	
Color	**Number**
Black	🚤
Blue	🚤 🚤 🚤
Brown	🚤 🚤
Gray	🚤
Green	🚤 🚤 🚤 🚤 🚤
Orange	🚤 🚤
Pink	🚤
Purple	🚤 🚤
Red	🚤 🚤
White	🚤
Yellow	🚤 🚤
Multicolor	🚤 🚤 🚤

Key: Each 🚤 = 1 DUCK.

FAST FACT

The Boston DUCK Tour is an 80-minute tour. Visitors ride in a vehicle called a DUCK, which is a land-and-water vehicle—a boat with wheels. About 20 minutes of the tour takes place on the Charles River.

GO ONLINE

Technology
Student pages are available in the Student eBook.

Check your understanding of important skills needed for success in Chapter 24.

▶ **Make and Use a Tally Table**

Use the data to make a tally table. Then answer each question.

> Kailynn surveyed her class about favorite colors. There were 9 students who chose purple, 12 who chose green, 4 who chose blue, and 2 who chose yellow.

1. How many students were surveyed?

2. Which color was the least favorite?

3. How many more students chose green than blue?

4. How many students did not choose blue?

▶ **Possible Outcomes**

List the possible outcomes for each experiment.

5. pulling a marble from this bag

6. spinning the pointer of this spinner

7. tossing a coin

▶ **Compare Parts of a Whole and a Group**

Write a fraction for the part of the whole named.

8. green sections

9. purple sections

Write a fraction for the part of the group named.

10. circles

11. circles or squares

VOCABULARY POWER

CHAPTER VOCABULARY

arrangement	outcome
combination	predict
equally likely	tree diagram
event	unlikely
likely	

WARM-UP WORDS

event an outcome or a combination of outcomes in an experiment

outcome a possible result of an experiment

predict to make a reasonable guess about what will happen

1 List All Possible Outcomes

OBJECTIVE: List all possible outcomes of an experiment.

Quick Review

Write a fraction for the shaded part.

Vocabulary

outcome

Investigate

Materials ■ 4-part spinner colored red, blue, green, and yellow ■ coin

When you do an experiment, the **outcomes** are the results.

A Spin the pointer of the spinner with 4 equal parts.

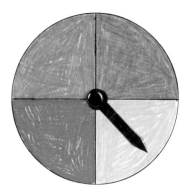

B Record your outcome.

C Repeat the activity for a total of 20 times. Record each different outcome.

Draw Conclusions

1. Explain how you found the outcome of each spin.

2. How many colors are on the spinner? How many possible outcomes are there for this experiment? Name the possible outcomes.

3. **Application** Emma has a bag with 2 green marbles, 3 red marbles, and 2 blue marbles that are all the same size. Without looking, she pulls out a marble. How many possible outcomes are there for this experiment?

Connect

This table shows the possible outcomes of spinning a pointer on a spinner with 4 equal parts and tossing a coin.

Coin	Color			
	Red	**Blue**	**Green**	**Yellow**
Heads	,	,	,	,
Tails	,	,	,	,

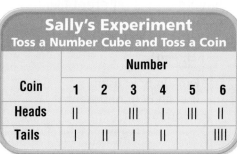

Do an experiment and record the results.

Activity

Materials ■ 4-part spinner colored red, blue, green, and yellow ■ coin

- Make a table like the one above.
- Toss a coin and spin the pointer.
- Record the outcome in the table by using a tally mark.
- Repeat a total of 20 times, recording the outcome after each toss and spin.

TALK Math

How would the number of possible outcomes change if the spinner had five colors?

Practice

USE DATA For 1–4, use the pictures. List all the possible outcomes for each experiment.

1. tossing the dime

2. tossing the cube labeled 1 to 6

3. tossing the cube labeled 1 to 6 and spinning the pointer on the spinner

✓ 4. tossing the dime and spinning the pointer

USE DATA For 5–7, use the table.

✓ 5. List all the possible outcomes for the experiment.

6. How many possible outcomes are there?

7. How many times did the outcome *Heads, 5* occur?

8. **WRITE Math** **Explain** how to find the number of possible outcomes for an experiment by looking at a table of results.

Sally's Experiment
Toss a Number Cube and Toss a Coin

Coin	Number					
	1	**2**	**3**	**4**	**5**	**6**
Heads	||		|||			|||	||
Tails			||			||		||||

Problem Solving Workshop
Strategy: Make an Organized List

OBJECTIVE: Solve problems by using the strategy *make an organized list.*

Learn the Strategy

Making an organized list is a good way to keep track of information. You can use different types of organized lists for different types of situations.

Make a list to sequence information.

Mr. Wong puts the daily schedule for his class on the board.

Make a list to organize information.

Each night, Kelly writes her homework assignments in a notebook. She organizes her homework by subject.

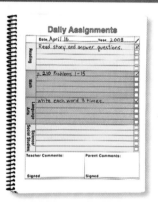

Make a list to find possible outcomes.

A bakery offers 3 different flavors and 2 different fillings for their layer cakes.

TALK Math

Explain how using a list can help represent information.

When you make a list, organizing the list into categories or parts can help you make sure you don't forget anything.

Use the Strategy

PROBLEM Molly is playing a game at the fair. Without looking, she reaches into a bag and pulls out a marble. Then, she reaches into a different bag and pulls out another marble. All the marbles are the same size. If both marbles are the same color, Molly wins a prize. List and count the possible outcomes of the game. Then, name the way Molly can win a prize.

Read to Understand

Reading Skill

- Summarize what you are asked to find.
- What information will you use?

Plan

- **What strategy can you use to solve the problem?**
  You can make an organized list.

Solve

- **How can you use the strategy to solve the problem?**
  Make a list of all the possible outcomes. Organize your list by showing the outcomes that could result if the first marble is green. Then, list the outcomes that could result if the first marble is another color.

green, black	red, black	yellow, black
green, purple	red, purple	yellow, purple
green, green	red, green	yellow, green

There is only one possible outcome in which both marbles are the same color, *green, green*.

So, of the nine outcomes, there is only one in which Molly can win a prize with the outcome *green, green*.

Check

- **What other ways could you solve the problem?**

Guided Problem Solving

Read to Understand
Plan
Solve
Check

1. Mason is playing a game that uses the two spinners shown. Each spinner has equal sections. He spins both pointers and adds the numbers. If the total is less than 4, he wins a prize. List the possible outcomes. Name the ways Mason can win a prize.

First, use a table to make an organized list.

Then, find the total for two spins.

Finally, find the totals that are less than 4.

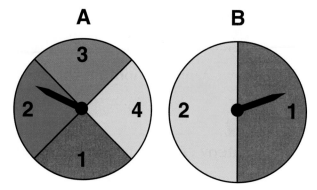

Spinner A	Spinner B	Total
1	1	2
1	2	3
2	1	3
2	▪	▪

✓ 2. **What if** Spinner A had two equal sections labeled 1 and 2? How would the number of possible outcomes change?

✓ 3. Yuri is playing a game using a coin and Spinner A. He tosses the coin and spins the pointer. List all the possible outcomes.

Problem Solving Strategy Practice

Make an organized list to solve.

4. Lyle is making tickets for the carnival. Each type of ticket will be a different color. There will be adult, child, and senior tickets. There will be one-day and two-day tickets. How many ticket colors will there be?

USE DATA For 5–6, use the information in the pictures.

5. Robin plays a game in which she spins the pointer and pulls one duck from the bag. How many possible outcomes are there?

6. For George to win a prize, the pointer must stop on a number that is greater than 3 and he must pull the green duck. Name the ways George can win.

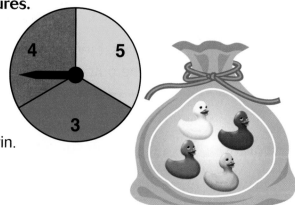

7. **WRITE Math** Shelly wants to find the total number of possible outcomes of spinning a pointer and tossing a coin. **Explain** how Shelly can organize a list of the possible outcomes.

670

Mixed Strategy Practice

USE DATA For 8–13, use the pictures.

8. **≡FAST FACT** The Kentucky State Fair was started in 1902. Which state fair was started 61 years before that?

9. The Illinois State Fair was started after the Michigan and Indiana State Fairs, but before the California State Fair. In what year was the Illinois State Fair started?

10. **Pose a Problem** The California State Fair was started in 1854. Use this information and the years in which other state fairs were started to write a problem.

11. **Open-Ended** Make a table that shows the number of state fairs started during each decade from the 1840s to the 1880s. Name one fact your table shows.

12. My year is even. The sum of the first two digits is less than the sum of the last two. The number formed by the sum of the last two digits is 2 more than the number formed by the sum of the first 2 digits. What state fair am I?

13. Make a list to organize the state fairs pictured. List them from earliest start date to latest start date.

CHALLENGE YOURSELF

One-day tickets to the California State Fair are $8 for adults and $5 for children.

14. An adult season pass is $4 more than 4 times the cost of a one-day ticket. A child season pass is $10 less than that. What is the cost of a season pass for a child?

15. **Algebra** A group of adults visited the California State Fair. Since they bought their tickets together, they got a $10 discount. What expression can you use to show the total cost of the group's tickets? **Explain** how to solve the problem.

Choose a STRATEGY

Draw a Diagram or Picture
Make a Model or Act It Out
Make an Organized List
Find a Pattern
Make a Table or Graph
Predict and Test
Work Backward
Solve a Simpler Problem
Write an Equation
Use Logical Reasoning

Nevada
Started: 1874

Gotta be there!
New York
Started: 1841

West Virginia
Started: 1854

California
Started: 1854

Indiana
Started: 1852

Arizona
Started: 1884

Michigan
Started: 1849

Texas
Started: 1886

Predict Outcomes of Experiments

OBJECTIVE: Predict outcomes of experiments.

Learn

You can predict the likelihood of events. When you **predict**, you make a reasonable guess about what might happen.

An **event** can be one outcome or a set of outcomes. Sometimes, one event is more likely than another, but not certain. An event is **likely** if it has a greater than even chance of happening. An event is **unlikely**, but not impossible, if it has a less than even chance of happening.

Vocabulary

predict	impossible
event	possible
likely	equally likely
unlikely	certain

Examples

Seven marbles of the same size are in a bag. What is the likelihood of each event?

A Pulling a yellow marble

An event is **impossible** if it is never able to happen. There are no yellow marbles in the bag, so pulling a yellow marble is impossible.
An event is **possible** if it is able to happen. There are green, red, and purple marbles in the bag, so pulling a red, green, or a purple marble is possible.

B Pulling a green or pulling a red marble

Two events are **equally likely** if they have the same chance of happening. There are the same number of red marbles as green marbles, so pulling a red marble and pulling a green marble are equally likely.

C Pulling a red, green, or purple marble

An event is **certain** if it will always happen. The bag has only red, green, and purple marbles, so pulling a red, green, or purple marble is certain.

• What is the difference between a certain and a likely event?

• This spinner has 3 equal sections. What is the likelihood of either spinning red or spinning yellow?

• There are 5 blue tiles, 2 red tiles, and 8 green tiles of the same size in a bag. Order the colors from least likely to be pulled to most likely.

Activity

Materials ■ equal-sized color tiles ■ bag

Step 1

Place 6 blue tiles, 3 red tiles, and 1 yellow tile of the same size in the bag.

Step 2

Copy the table. Predict the outcomes for pulling one tile out of the bag 30 times. Write tally marks in the Predicted Outcomes column to show the number of times you think you will pull each color.

Experiment Results

Color	Predicted Outcomes	Actual Outcomes
blue		
red		
yellow		

Step 3

Pull one tile from the bag. Record the outcome in the Actual Outcomes column of your table.

Step 4

Return the tile to the bag. Repeat 29 more times.

- How did your actual results compare to your predictions?
- List all possible outcomes. Which outcome is most likely? Explain.
- Which outcome is least likely? Explain.

Guided Practice

1. The bag has 7 marbles of the same size. Tim pulls one marble from the bag. Name an event that is likely, unlikely, and impossible.

Tell whether the event is *likely, unlikely, certain,* or *impossible.*

2. tossing a number greater than 1 on a cube labeled 1 to 6

3. spinning a multiple of 4 on a spinner with four equal parts labeled 4, 8, 12, and 16

4. **TALK Math** **Explain** the difference between an event that is possible and one that is impossible.

Independent Practice and Problem Solving

Tell whether the event is *likely, unlikely, certain,* or *impossible.*

5. tossing a number greater than 6 on a cube labeled 1 to 6

6. pulling a green marble from a bag that contains 22 red, 4 green, and 14 yellow marbles of the same size

 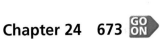

USE DATA For each experiment, tell whether Events A and B are *equally likely* or *not equally likely*. If they are not equally likely, name the event that is more likely.

7. Experiment: Toss a coin.

Event A: heads
Event B: tails

8. Experiment: Toss a cube numbered 1 to 6.

Event A: tossing a number less than 3
Event B: tossing an even number

9. Experiment: Spin the pointer.

Event A: red
Event B: yellow

10. Experiment: Pull one tile from the bag. All tiles are the same size.

Event A: green
Event B: red

USE DATA For 11–13, use the spinners. Each spinner has two equal sections. In the experiment, each pointer is spun and the outcomes are added.

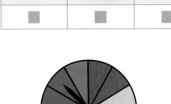

11. What are the possible sums? What is the most likely sum?

12. Copy the table. Record a prediction for how many times you will spin a sum of 3, if you do the experiment 20 times.

13. Make two spinners like the ones shown. Spin the pointers and add the results. Do the experiment 20 times. How do your results compare to the prediction you made in Problem 12?

Experiment Results		
Sum of 3	Predicted Outcomes	Actual Outcomes
■	■	■

USE DATA For 14–16, use the spinner. The spinner has equal sections.

14. Which two events are equally likely?

15. Name an event that is possible and an event that is impossible.

16. **WRITE Math** ▸ Harold is going to spin the pointer. Predict the outcome of his spin. **Explain** your choice.

Mixed Review and Test Prep

17. Shelly's school has 24 classes. Each class has 18 students. How many students are in Shelly's school? (p. 284)

18. What is the area of this figure? (p. 644)

10 in.

5 in.

19. **Test Prep** Nine marbles of the same size are in a bag. Which color marble are you most likely to pull?

A Blue

B Yellow

C Green

D Red

Technology
Use Harcourt Mega Math, Fraction Action, *Last Chance Canyon*, Level B.
CD ROM

Justify Your Answer

Sometimes you need to justify your answer by giving reasons to show that your answer is correct.

Meg's soccer coach will select one student to be team captain. She writes the names of each of the 23 players on separate index cards. Then, without looking, she pulls one card. Is it likely, unlikely, certain, or impossible that Meg's name will be pulled?

Meg wrote her answer and then gave reasons to justify it.

I think it is unlikely that my name will be pulled.

1. Since there are other possible outcomes, it is not certain that my name will be pulled.

2. Since my name is one of the possible outcomes, it is not impossible that it will be pulled.

3. Each student has an equal chance of being pulled. Since I have only a 1 out of 23 chance for my name to be pulled, it is not likely that my name will be pulled.

So, my reasons justify that it is unlikely my name will be pulled.

Tips

To justify an answer:

- First, state your answer.
- Next, write statements to explain why other possible answers can't be true.
- Use correct math terms in your statements.
- Finally, tell whether your reasons justify your answer.

Problem Solving
Solve. Justify your answer.

1. One October morning, Ms. Morters says, "It is impossible that it will snow today." Do you agree with Ms. Morters?

2. Oscar tosses a number cube labeled 1 to 6 and tosses a nickel. How many possible outcomes are there?

3. Rodney tosses a number cube labeled 1 to 6 and tosses a penny. Name two outcomes that are equally likely to occur.

4. Melinda is going to toss a coin 50 times. How many times do you predict the coin will land heads up?

4 Probability as a Fraction

OBJECTIVE: Express probability as a fraction.

Quick Review

Tim tosses a number cube labeled 1 to 6. How many possible outcomes are there?

Vocabulary

mathematical probability

Learn

PROBLEM Pauline spins the pointer. Each section of the spinner is equal. How can she describe the likelihood that the pointer will stop on green?

Mathematical probability is a comparison of a number of favorable outcomes to the number of possible outcomes when the outcomes are equally likely. The probability of an event occurring can be expressed as 0, 1, or a fraction between 0 and 1.

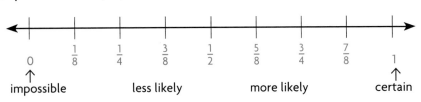

impossible   less likely   more likely   certain

So, Pauline can describe the likelihood that the pointer will stop on green as a fraction.

What is the mathematical probability of the pointer stopping on green?

$$\text{Probability of green} = \frac{\text{number of favorable outcomes (green)}}{\text{total number of possible outcomes (3 green, 4 red, 1 yellow)}} = \frac{3}{8}$$

So, the mathematical probability of the pointer stopping on green is $\frac{3}{8}$, or 3 out of 8.

The closer a probability is to 1, the more likely the event is to occur. The closer it is to 0, the more unlikely it is to occur. A probability of $\frac{1}{2}$ means that the event is just as likely to happen as not to happen.

Suppose you want to find the likelihood that the pointer will stop on yellow.

• Which is more unlikely to occur: the pointer stopping on red or the pointer stopping on yellow? Explain how you know.

• Which color on the spinner is most likely to have a probability near 1? Explain.

ERROR ALERT

The number of favorable outcomes is always the numerator. The total number of possible outcomes is always the denominator.

More Examples Find the probability of each event when all the marbles are the same size. Then, write the likelihood.

A Find the probability of pulling a marble that is not blue.

Probability of not blue $= \dfrac{5}{8} \begin{array}{l} \leftarrow \\ \leftarrow \end{array} \dfrac{\text{favorable outcomes (4 red, 1 green)}}{\text{total possible outcomes (3 blue, 4 red, 1 green)}}$

The probability of pulling a marble that is not blue is likely.

B Find the probability of pulling a green marble.

Probability of green $= \dfrac{0}{9} \begin{array}{l} \leftarrow \\ \leftarrow \end{array} \dfrac{\text{favorable outcomes (0 green)}}{\text{total possible outcomes (3 blue, 4 red, 2 yellow)}}$

The probability of pulling a green marble is impossible.

C Find the probability of pulling either a red or green marble.

Probability of red or green $= \dfrac{5}{7} \begin{array}{l} \leftarrow \\ \leftarrow \end{array} \dfrac{\text{favorable outcomes (2 red, 3 green)}}{\text{total possible outcomes (2 red, 3 green, 2 white)}}$

The probability of pulling either a red or green marble is likely.

D Find the probability of pulling a black marble.

Probability of black $= \dfrac{8}{8} \begin{array}{l} \leftarrow \\ \leftarrow \end{array} \dfrac{\text{favorable outcomes (8 black)}}{\text{total possible outcomes (8 black)}}$

The probability of pulling a black marble is certain.

Guided Practice

1. Use Spinner A, which has equal sections. What is the probability that the pointer will land on blue? Count the number of favorable outcomes. Count the total number of possible outcomes. Write the probability as a fraction.

A

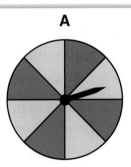

USE DATA For 2–7, use Spinner B. Spinner B has equal sections. Write the probability as a fraction.

2. spinning blue
3. spinning red or blue
4. spinning green
   ✓ 5. not spinning red
6. spinning red
   ✓ 7. not spinning blue or green

B

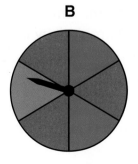

8. **TALK Math** Explain how you know that an event with the probability 11 out of 12 is likely to occur.

Independent Practice and Problem Solving

USE DATA For 9–13, use the equal-sized tiles. Write the probability as a fraction.

9. pulling a 1

10. pulling a 3

11. pulling a 5

12. pulling a 2 or 3

13. pulling a number that is not 6

USE DATA For 14–18, use the equal-sized cards. Write the probability as a fraction. Then, tell whether each event is *certain, impossible, likely,* or *unlikely.*

14. pulling a B

15. pulling an N or an A

16. pulling a T

17. pulling a B, A, N, or S

18. pulling a letter that is not A

★Algebra Find the value of *n*.

19. Ron filled a bag with 12 equal-sized marbles. There are *n* blue marbles. The probability of pulling a blue marble from the bag is $\frac{1}{4}$.

20. Eve spins a pointer that has 3 equally likely outcomes: red, green, and blue. The probability of spinning yellow is *n*.

USE DATA For 21–24, use the spinner. The spinner has equal sections.

21. What fraction shows the probability of spinning green?

22. Write the following outcomes in order from least likely to most likely and write the probability of each as a fraction: *spinning green, spinning a 6, spinning an even number.*

23. **Pose a Problem** Look back at Problem 21. Write a similar problem by changing the color.

24. **WRITE Math** ▸ **What's the Error?** Carlos says that the probability of spinning green is $\frac{1}{3}$ because green is one of three possible outcomes. Describe his error. Find the correct probability.

Extra Practice on page 686, Set B

CD ROM **Technology**
Use Harcourt Mega Math, Fraction Action, *Last Chance Canyon,* Level F.

Learn About Fair or Unfair

In probability, an experiment is **fair** if each outcome is equally likely to happen. An experiment is **unfair** if one or more outcomes are more likely than another.

Bob, Morgan, and Juanita are playing a game using a spinner. Each time the pointer stops on a player's name, that player gets 1 point.

Unfair	Fair
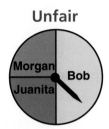	
This spinner is unfair. Bob has a greater chance of scoring than the other players.	This spinner is fair. Each player has the same chance of scoring.

Try It

Tell whether each game is *fair* or *unfair*. Explain.

25. John and Margie are tossing a number cube labeled 1 to 6. John wins if the outcome is 1, 2, or 3. Margie wins if the outcome is 4, 5, or 6.

26. Reggie and Pam are tossing a number cube labeled 1 to 6. Reggie wins if the outcome is less than 3. Pam wins if the outcome is greater than 3.

27. Lee and Walt are using the spinner at the right. Lee wins if the pointer stops on blue. Walt wins if the pointer stops on green or red.

Mixed Review and Test Prep

28. Camille has a paperweight in the shape of a square pyramid. How many vertices does it have? (p. 570)

29. Mr. Miller's patio is triangular. Classify the triangle by the length of its sides and by its angles. (p. 524)

30. **Test Prep** What is the probability of pulling a red marble when all the marbles are the same size?

A $\frac{1}{5}$ C $\frac{3}{5}$

B $\frac{2}{5}$ D $\frac{4}{5}$

31. **Test Prep** What is the likelihood that you will pull a blue crayon from a box of yellow crayons of the same size? **Explain.**

5 Experimental Probability

OBJECTIVE: Find experimental probability of events.

Investigate

Materials ■ coin

The **experimental probability** of an event can be found by conducting repeated trials. Compare the number of times an event actually occurs to the total number of trials, or times you repeat the activity.

Experimental probability $= \dfrac{\text{number of times event occurs}}{\text{total number of trials}}$

You can use experimental probability to predict future events.

Ⓐ Predict what you think will happen when you toss a coin 50 times. Then toss the coin.

Ⓑ Record the result in a tally table. Repeat 50 times.

Ⓒ Use your results to find the experimental probability of tossing heads.

$\dfrac{\text{number of times heads occurs}}{\text{total number of tosses}} = \dfrac{\blacksquare}{50}$ or ■ out of 50

Ⓓ Find the mathematical probability of tossing heads.

$\dfrac{\text{number of favorable outcomes (heads)}}{\text{total possible outcomes (heads, tails)}} = \dfrac{\blacksquare}{\blacksquare}$

Draw Conclusions

1. Compare your prediction with the outcomes shown in the tally table. Was your prediction close? Explain.

2. Compare your experimental probability with that of your classmates. Did everyone get the same answer? Why do you think this is so?

3. **Analysis** Is your experimental probability the same as the mathematical probability? Why do you think this is so?

Quick Review

Find the probability when a number cube labeled 1 to 6 is tossed.

1. even number
2. 2 or 3
3. not 6
4. 1
5. 4, 5, or 6

Vocabulary

experimental probability

Math Idea

The probability of tossing heads or tails does not depend on outcomes of previous tosses.

Connect

Experimental probability comes closer to the mathematical probability as the number of trials increases. You can combine your results with those of your classmates to see this.

Yuri and nine classmates combined their results. The total number of trials is now 500 instead of 50.

The mathematical probability of tossing heads is $\frac{1}{2}$. Look at the results for heads.

- Which experimental probability results for tossing heads came closer to $\frac{1}{2}$, Yuri's or the total combined results?

Think: Is $\frac{180}{500}$ or $\frac{230}{500}$ closer to $\frac{250}{500}$?

Coin Toss Experiment				
	Heads	Experimental Probability	Tails	Experimental Probability
Yuri	18	$\frac{18}{50}$, or $\frac{180}{500}$	32	$\frac{32}{50}$, or $\frac{320}{500}$
Total	230	$\frac{230}{500}$	270	$\frac{270}{500}$

TALK Math

Explain the difference between experimental probability and mathematical probability.

Practice

1. Toss a cube labeled 1 to 6 thirty times. Record the outcomes in a tally table. Write the experimental probability of tossing 1 as a fraction.

2. **Reasoning** Maryellen plans to spin the pointer of Spinner A, shown at the right, 30 times. Spinner A has equal sections. Maryellen predicts that the pointer will stop on red 3 times. Do you agree with Maryellen's prediction? Why or why not?

A

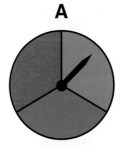

USE DATA For 3–6, use Spinner B and the table. Spinner B has equal sections.

3. How many times did Maryellen spin the pointer?

4. What is the experimental probability of the pointer stopping on red? What is the mathematical probability?

5. What is the experimental probability of the pointer not stopping on green? What is the mathematical probability?

6. **WRITE Math** **What's the Question?** Sue used the table to determine a probability. The answer is $\frac{14}{40}$.

B

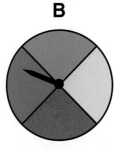

Maryellen's Results				
Outcomes	Blue	Red	Green	Yellow
Tally	卌 卌	卌 III	卌 III	卌 卌 IIII

Technology
Use Harcourt Mega Math, Fraction Action, *Last Chance Canyon*, Level I.

Combinations and Arrangements

OBJECTIVE: Find all possible combinations and arrangements in probability situations.

Learn

PROBLEM Lydia is at a sandwich shop. She can choose from 3 types of sandwiches: chicken, turkey, or ham. She can order milk, water, or apple juice with her sandwich. How many different combinations of sandwiches and drinks can Lydia choose?

A **combination** is a choice in which the order of the items does not matter.

One way to find the number of combinations for a set of given items is to use a tree diagram. A **tree diagram** is an organized list that shows all possible combinations. A tree diagram uses branches to connect the choices from groups of objects or of an event.

Sandwich	Drink	Combinations
chicken	milk	chicken sandwich with milk
	water	chicken sandwich with water
	apple juice	chicken sandwich with apple juice
turkey	milk	turkey sandwich with milk
	water	turkey sandwich with water
	apple juice	turkey sandwich with apple juice
ham	milk	ham sandwich with milk
	water	ham sandwich with water
	apple juice	ham sandwich with apple juice

So, Lydia can choose from 9 different sandwich and drink combinations.

- **Reasoning** How could Lydia have used multiplication to find the total number of combinations?

- **Reasoning** **What if** Lydia can also choose from cake, a cookie, or yogurt? How many combinations can you make now?

Arrangements

An **arrangement** is an ordering of items. In an arrangement, the order of items matters.

Joe is making a poster of fruit for his school project. He wants to show 3 separate pictures of an apple, an orange, and a banana in a row. How many different arrangements are possible?

In this problem, the order of the pictures is important.

ONE WAY **Make an organized list of all possible arrangements.**

This list is organized using the first letter of each fruit.

AOB	BAO	OAB
ABO	BOA	OBA

ANOTHER WAY **Multiply to find the total number of arrangements.**

Think: What choices are available for the three positions?

3 choices for the first picture	2 choices remain for the second picture	1 choice remains for the third picture

$$3 \times 2 \times 1 = 6$$

So, there are 6 possible arrangements.

- **What if** Josh had 4 pictures of fruit? How many possible arrangements could he make?

Guided Practice

1. Look at the tree diagram. How many possible combinations of shirts and pants does it show?

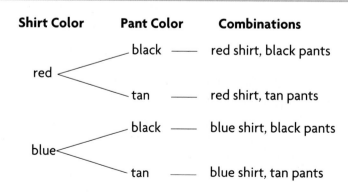

Make a tree diagram to list and find the number of possible combinations.

2. Sport choices
   Game: basketball, softball, soccer
   Day: Thursday, Friday, Saturday

3. Sundae choices
   Flavor: vanilla, strawberry, chocolate
   Topping: caramel, cherry

Make an organized list to find the number of possible arrangements.

4. tulips, daisies, roses

5. math, science, reading, art

6. **TALK Math** Explain the difference between an arrangement and a combination.

Independent Practice and Problem Solving

Make a tree diagram to list and find the number of possible combinations.

7. Outfit choices
   Pants: black, brown, blue, tan
   Shirt: red, green, yellow, purple

8. Sandwich choices
   Bread: white, wheat, roll
   Cheese: American, Swiss, Colby, Cheddar

Make an organized list to find the number of possible arrangements.

9. checkers, hopscotch, marbles, jump rope

10. markers, paint, crayons

USE DATA For 11–13, use the picture.

11. Tyler, Colin, Eric, and Maya are in a Geography Bee. Tyler sits in the first chair. List the different ways the students can sit in the chairs.

12. In how many different ways can the students be arranged if Colin is first and Tyler is second?

13. Each student receives a trophy or a ribbon. How many combinations of students and awards are there?

14. Rebecca, Toby, Jaclyn, and Madeline are lining up for school pictures. How many ways can they arrange themselves in line?

15. **WRITE Math** Explain how a tree diagram helps you list and organize all the possible combinations.

16. Nick can have potato soup, vegetable soup, or chicken soup for lunch. He can choose a brownie, a cookie, or frozen yogurt for dessert. To find the different lunch possibilities, do you need to find all possible arrangements or all possible combinations? **Explain.**

Learn About Combinations and Permutations

Another word for arrangement is permutation. **Permutations** are choices for which the order of the items is important. A permutation is different from a combination.

Example
Kaito, Mike, Annie and Thomas are starting a club.

Combination

They will draw names out of a hat to decide which 2 members will plan the first meeting.

The order is not important, so this is a combination. To show the ways to choose 2 names from 4 when order does not matter, make an organized list. Cross off the pairs that reverse the ones already listed.

KM	~~MK~~	~~AK~~	~~TK~~
KA	MA	~~AM~~	~~TM~~
KT	MT	AT	~~TA~~

So, there are 6 combinations.

Permutation

They will draw names out of a hat to assign the jobs of president and vice president.

The order is important, so this is a permutation. The first name chosen is the president and the second name chosen is the vice president. To show the ways to choose 2 names from 4 when order matters, make an organized list.

KM	MK	AK	TK
KA	MA	AM	TM
KT	MT	AT	TA

So, there are 12 permutations.

Try It

18. A club with 5 members is choosing a president and vice-president by pulling names from a hat. How many permutations are there?

19. Ronan has an apple, a banana, and an orange. He plans to pack 2 pieces of fruit in his lunch box. How many combinations of fruit are there?

Mixed Review and Test Prep

20. Bob caught 5 fish on Friday, 7 fish on Saturday, and 3 fish on Sunday. Find the mean number of fish Bob caught. (p. 186)

21 Robin rides a bike trail every weekend. The trail is 28 miles long. If she rode the trail once a week for 52 weeks, about how many miles did she ride in all? (p. 274)

22. Test Prep At summer camp, each camper chooses one arts & crafts activity from painting, woodworking, or ceramics and one sports activity from soccer, archery, or swimming. How many different combinations are possible?

Extra Practice

Set A Tell whether the event is *likely, unlikely, certain,* or *impossible.* (pp. 672–675)

1. pulling a blue tile from a bag that contains 26 green, 14 yellow, and 2 blue tiles of the same size

2. tossing a number less than 1 on a number cube labeled 1 to 6

For each experiment, tell whether Events A and B are equally likely or not equally likely. If they are not equally likely, name the event that is more likely.

3. Experiment: Spin the pointer.

   Event A: purple
   Event B: green

4. Experiment: Pull one marble from the bag of marbles of the same size.

   Event A: blue
   Event B: red

Set B For 1–6, use the spinner to find the probability of each event. The spinner has equal sections. (pp. 676–679)

1. spinning orange

2. spinning a color that is not blue

3. spinning red

4. spinning green or orange

5. spinning purple

6. spinning red or blue

For 7–12, use the equal-sized cards. Write the probability as a fraction. Then tell whether each event is *certain, impossible, likely,* or *unlikely.*

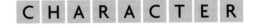

C H A R A C T E R

7. pulling an R

8. pulling an A or a C

9. pulling a H or a T

10. pulling a G

11. pulling an A, C, or R

12. pulling an A, C, H, E, R, or T

Set C Make a tree diagram to list and find the number of possible combinations. (pp. 682–685)

1. School play role choices
   Role: lead, friend, villain
   Person: Aria, Dan, Kim, Jorge

2. Activity choices
   Activity: swimming, running, swinging
   Day: Monday, Wednesday, Friday

Make an organized list to find the number of possible arrangements.

3. dog, cat, fish, turtle

4. chicken, spaghetti, pizza

Technology
Use Harcourt Mega Math, Fraction Action, *Last Chance Canyon,* Levels C, F, I.

TECHNOLOGY ★ CONNECTION

Spreadsheet: Spinner Probability

Ronnie conducted a probability experiment with the spinner shown at the right. Follow the steps below to conduct your own probability experiment.

Materials ■ spreadsheet program ■ spinner

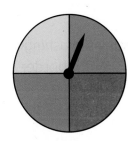

Step 1 Spin the pointer of a spinner with 4 equal sections 40 times.

Record each spin in a tally table like the one shown.

Then find the experimental probability for each color using the fraction shown below.

$$\frac{\text{number of times color occurs}}{\text{total number of spins}}$$

Ronnie's Spinner Results

Color	Tally	Probability
Red	卌 卌 I	$\frac{11}{40}$
Green	卌 III	$\frac{8}{40}$, or $\frac{1}{5}$
Yellow	卌 IIII	$\frac{9}{40}$
Blue	卌 卌 II	$\frac{12}{40}$, or $\frac{3}{10}$

Step 2 Record your spinner results in a spreadsheet. To move among cells in the spreadsheet, use the arrow keys or click on the desired cell.

	A	B
1	Ronnie's Spinner Results	
2	Color	Number
3	Red	11
4	Green	8
5	Yellow	9
6	Blue	12

Step 3 Make a bar graph of your results. Enter a title for the graph and labels for the axes.

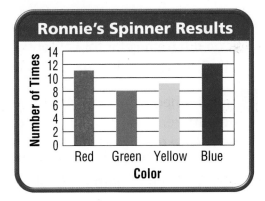

Try It

1. **Explore More** Repeat the experiment using the 3-color spinner shown at the right. Make predictions before you begin the experiment. Were your predictions reasonable? **Explain.**

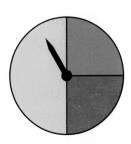

 **Explore Vertex-Edge Graphs**

Counting Colors

This map shows Washington, Oregon, Idaho, Nevada, and California. The states that share a border cannot be the same color. States that touch but do not share a border can be the same color. What is the least number of colors that you can use to color this map?

A vertex-edge graph can help answer the question. A **vertex-edge graph** is a system of points, or vertices, connected by line segments, or edges.

Example

Materials ■ tracing paper ■ color pencils

Step 1 Trace the outlines of each state. Draw a point to represent each state. Then connect the points if the states they represent share a border. Oregon shares a border with the most states. Choose a color for Oregon.	
Step 2 Washington shares a border with Oregon, so it cannot be the color you picked for Oregon. Pick a different color for Washington.	
Step 3 Nevada does not share a border with Washington, so Nevada can also be red.	
Step 4 The states that border California have all been colored, so pick a different color for California. Idaho does not share a border with California, so Idaho can also be yellow.	
Step 5 Check your map. Are the states that share a border colored with different colors? Count the total number of colors used. OR and NV are red, WA is orange, CA and ID are yellow.	

So, 3 is the least number of colors that you can use to color this map.

Try It

1. Make a vertex-edge graph to find the least number of colors needed to color the map of these states in the western United States.

2. **WRITE Math** ▸ Is this map of some states in the northeastern United States colored with the least number of colors? **Explain.**

Chapter 24 Review/Test

Check Vocabulary and Concepts

For 1–2, choose the best term from the box.

VOCABULARY

combination

outcome

tree diagram

1. An __?__ is the result of an experiment. (p. 666)

2. A __?__ is an organized list that shows possible combinations of groups of objects or of an event. (p. 682)

3. **Explain** the difference between experimental and mathematical probability. (pp. 680–681)

Check Skills

Tell whether the event is *likely, unlikely, certain,* or *impossible.* (pp. 672–675)

4. tossing a 0 on a number cube labeled 1 to 6

5. spinning an odd number on a spinner with three equal parts labeled 1 to 3

For 6–11, use the equal-size cards. Write the probability as a fraction. Then, tell whether each event is *certain, impossible, likely,* or *unlikely.* (pp. 676–679)

T R E A T M E N T

6. pulling a T

7. pulling an A

8. pulling an I

9. pulling an S

10. pulling a T, R, E, A, M, or N

11. pulling an M, E, or T

12. James has a blue shirt, a red shirt, and a white shirt. He has brown pants and black pants. How many different outfit combinations are possible? (pp. 682–685)

13. How many different ways can Mia, Liz, Benjamin, and Parker stand in line? (pp. 682–685)

Check Problem Solving

Solve. (pp. 668–671)

14. Amir is playing a game that uses two number cubes labeled 1 to 6. He earns an extra turn if he tosses 10 or greater. Name the ways Amir can earn an extra turn.

15. **WRITE Math** ▸ **Explain** how Amir can organize a list to find all the possible combinations of tossing two number cubes labeled 1 to 6.

Unit Review/Test
Chapters 22–24

Multiple Choice

1. Which unit of measurement would you most likely use to measure the weight of the dog shown below? (p. 608)

   A Ounce   **C** Pound

   B Foot   **D** Yard

2. Which is the best estimate of the length of a desk? (p. 606)

   A 3 inches

   B 3 feet

   C 30 feet

   D 3 miles

3. Susan has a pitcher that contains 6 pints of lemonade. How many 1-cup glasses of lemonade can she fill using the pitcher? (p. 610)

   A 3   **C** 10

   B 6   **D** 12

4. Which is a true statement? (p. 618)

   A 40 decimeters = 4 meters

   B 40 decimeters = 40 meters

   C 40 decimeters = 400 meters

   D 40 decimeters = 4,000 meters

5. What is the area of the patio shown below? (p. 644)

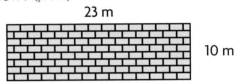
23 m   10 m

   A 230 square meters

   B 138 square meters

   C 66 square meters

   D 33 square meters

6. Which is a true statement? (p. 620)

   A 700 grams = 700 kilograms

   B 700 grams = 70 kilograms

   C 7,000 grams = 7 kilograms

   D 7 grams = 700 kilograms

7. What is the perimeter of the figure shown below? (p. 636)

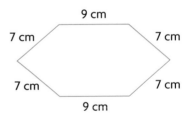
9 cm   7 cm   7 cm   7 cm   7 cm   9 cm

   A 63 centimeters   **C** 28 centimeters

   B 46 centimeters   **D** 16 centimeters

8. What is the probability of tossing a number greater than 1 on a number cube labeled 1 to 6? (p. 678)

   A $\frac{1}{6}$ **C** $\frac{2}{3}$

   B $\frac{1}{3}$ **D** $\frac{5}{6}$

GO ONLINE Technology Use *Online Assessment.*

9. A statue is 300 decimeters tall. How many meters tall is the statue? (p. 678)

 A 3,000 meters

 B 300 meters

 C 30 meters

 D 3 meters

10. The graph shows the results of pulling a marble of the same size from a bag 40 times. Which color marble is most likely to be pulled next? (p. 674)

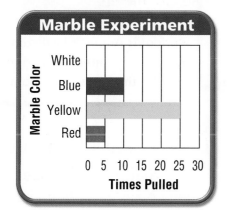

Marble Experiment

 A White

 B Yellow

 C Red

 D Blue

11. What is the volume of the rectangular prism shown below? (p. 654)

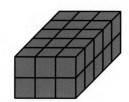

 A 6 cubic units

 B 10 cubic units

 C 30 cubic units

 D 90 cubic units

Short Response

12. The spinner below has equal sections. What is the probability, written as a fraction, that the pointer will stop on red? (p. 678)

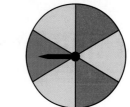

13. Ted measured the amount of iced tea in a pitcher. He found that the pitcher held 1,000 milliliters. How many liters of iced tea were in the pitcher? (p. 622)

14. Annemarie has 20 cups of juice. Jerry has 6 quarts of juice. Who has more juice? (p. 610)

Extended Response WRITE Math

15. What is the perimeter of the square shown below? **Explain** how you can use a formula to find the answer. (p. 636)

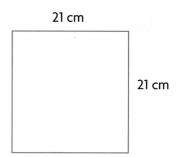

21 cm

21 cm

16. Taylor drew a rectangular prism measuring 3 inches long, 5 inches wide, and 4 inches tall. **Explain** how to find the volume of Taylor's rectangular prism. (p. 654)

17. Nancy has a stuffed bear, a game, and a puzzle on her shelf. How many ways can Nancy arrange her toys on the shelf? **Explain** your answer. (p. 684)

Birthday Rocks

Beautiful Birthstones

Did you know that many people buy jewelry based on the month they were born? Each month has its own birthstone. Many of the birthstones are found in mines. August's birthstone is mined in Arizona.

Peridot is August's birthstone. More people are born during August than any other month.

FACT·ACTIVITY

Birthstone Table

Month	Birthstone	Picture	Color
January	Garnet		Red
February	Amethyst		Purple
March	Aquamarine		Blue
April	Diamond		Clear
May	Emerald		Green
June	Pearl		White
July	Ruby		Red
August	Peridot		Green
September	Sapphire		Blue
October	Opal		White
November	Topaz		Yellow
December	Turquoise		Blue

For 1–4, use the Birthstone Table.

1. Make an organized list to see how many ways you can make a ring that includes these three birthstones: garnet, peridot, and topaz.

2. If one of each birthstone of the same size is in a bag, what is the probability of selecting a red stone? What is the probability of selecting either a blue or a green stone?

3. **WRITE Math** ▶ Survey and record 12 classmates' birthstones on small pieces of paper. If your results were placed in a bag, what would be the probability of pulling a green birthstone? **Explain.**

Likely Gems

Most gems are mined from deep within the Earth. Gems such as diamonds, emeralds, and pearls are called *precious gems* because they are very rare. Others, like opals and amethysts, are called *semiprecious* because they are found more often.

March
Aquamarine

September
Sapphire

February
Amethyst

December
Turquoise

This spinner shows some of the birthstone gems, grouped by color.

FACT·ACTIVITY

For 1–2, use the spinner above.

❶ How many possible color outcomes are there for the spinner? Name them.

❷ On which color is the pointer more likely to stop? **Explain.**

Make your own spinner and birthstone game.

► Make a spinner with 8 or more sections of the same size. Place the 3 birthstone colors you like best in any arrangement on the spinner.

► Make up and write out the rules for a birthstone board game that uses your spinner. For example, players might move ahead depending on the color they spin.

Student Handbook

Review the Key Concepts

These pages provide review of important ideas from each chapter.

Review the Key Concepts—Chapter 1

Whole Number Place Value

Key Concept The value of a digit depends on its place in a number. Numbers can be ordered by comparing digits in the same place-value position.

You can use place value to compare and order whole numbers with the same number of digits. If two whole numbers have different numbers of digits, the number with more digits is greater.

MILLIONS			THOUSANDS			ONES		
Hundreds	Tens	Ones	Hundreds	Tens	Ones	Hundreds	Tens	Ones
6	2	5,	7	2	3,	5	4	6
$6 \times 100{,}000{,}000$	$2 \times 10{,}000{,}000$	$5 \times 1{,}000{,}000$	$7 \times 100{,}000$	$2 \times 10{,}000$	$3 \times 1{,}000$	5×100	4×10	6×1
600,000,000	20,000,000	5,000,000	700,000	20,000	3,000	500	40	6

Examples

A Compare 845,027 and 8,453,027.

845,027 ← 6 digits

8,453,027 ← 7 digits

So, 845,027 < 8,453,027.

B Write these numbers in order from least to greatest: 531, 476, 479.

ONES		
Hundreds	Tens	Ones
5	3	1
4	7	6
4	7	9
5 > 4 531 is the greatest.	7 = 7 Same number of tens.	6 < 9 476 is the least.

So, 476 < 479 < 531.

ERROR ALERT

Always start at the left and compare digits in the same place-value position to compare and order.

Try It

Compare. Write <, >, or = for each ●.

1. 468,809 ● 46,809

2. 532,634 ● 532,346

3. 2,298,759 ● 20,307,213

Order the numbers from least to greatest.

4. 40,326,058; 4,365,925; 400,684,244

5. 16,548,848; 16,485,922; 16,854,033

6. Read the problem below. **Explain** why B cannot be the correct answer choice. Then choose the correct answer.

COMMON ERROR

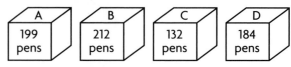

| A
199 pens | B
212 pens | C
132 pens | D
184 pens |

Which box has the least number of pens?

A Box A **B** Box B **C** Box C **D** Box D

Review the Key Concepts—Chapter 2

Add and Subtract 3-Digit and 4-Digit Numbers

Key Concept Addition and subtraction of multidigit numbers is based on single-digit addition and subtraction facts and on base-ten and place-value concepts.

Use addition to solve problems to find how many in all or how many altogether. Use subtraction to solve problems to find how many more, how many fewer, or how many left.

You can use place value to add and subtract numbers. Line up the digits by place value. Remember to regroup when necessary.

To add 487 + 356 line up the digits by place value.

$$\begin{array}{r} \text{H T O} \\ 4\ 8\ 7 \\ +\ 3\ 5\ 6 \\ \hline \end{array}$$

Examples

Ⓐ Add. 1,756 + 1,425

Step 1	Step 2	Step 3	Step 4
Add the ones. Regroup.	Add the tens.	Add the hundreds. Regroup.	Add the thousands.
$$\begin{array}{r} \overset{1}{1{,}75}6 \\ +1{,}425 \\ \hline 1 \end{array}$$	$$\begin{array}{r} \overset{1}{1{,}75}6 \\ +1{,}425 \\ \hline 81 \end{array}$$	$$\begin{array}{r} \overset{1}{1}{,}\overset{1}{7}56 \\ +1{,}425 \\ \hline 181 \end{array}$$	$$\begin{array}{r} \overset{1}{1}{,}\overset{1}{7}56 \\ +1{,}425 \\ \hline 3{,}181 \end{array}$$

So, 1,756 + 1,425 = 3,181.

Ⓑ Subtract. 2,502 − 1,246

Step 1	Step 2	Step 3	Step 4
Subtract the ones. Regroup.	Subtract the tens.	Subtract the hundreds.	Subtract the thousands.
$$\begin{array}{r} 4\,\overset{9}{\cancel{10}}\,12 \\ 2{,}\cancel{5}\cancel{0}\cancel{2} \\ -1{,}2\ 4\ 6 \\ \hline 6 \end{array}$$	$$\begin{array}{r} 4\,\overset{9}{\cancel{10}}\,12 \\ 2{,}\cancel{5}\cancel{0}\,2 \\ -1{,}2\ 4\ 6 \\ \hline 5\ 6 \end{array}$$	$$\begin{array}{r} 4\,\overset{9}{\cancel{10}}\,12 \\ 2{,}\cancel{5}\cancel{0}\,2 \\ -1{,}2\ 4\ 6 \\ \hline 2\ 5\ 6 \end{array}$$	$$\begin{array}{r} 4\,\overset{9}{\cancel{10}}\,12 \\ 2{,}\cancel{5}\cancel{0}\,2 \\ -1{,}2\ 4\ 6 \\ \hline 1{,}2\ 5\ 6 \end{array}$$

So, 2,502 − 1,246 = 1,256.

ERROR ALERT

Do not subtract the top number from the bottom.

INCORRECT:

$$\begin{array}{r} 52 \\ -\ 25 \\ \hline 33 \end{array}$$

Try It

Find the sum or difference.

1. 567 + 309
2. 498 + 294
3. 1,254 + 987
4. 4,567 + 1,098
5. 934 − 187
6. 704 − 256
7. 1,298 − 578
8. 2,087 − 1,567

9. Read the problem below. **COMMON ERROR**
   Explain why B cannot be the correct answer choice. Then choose the correct answer.

   There are 711 children at the game. If 423 are boys, how many are girls?

   A 1,134   **B** 312   **C** 308   **D** 288

Review the Key Concepts—Chapter 3

Algebra: Addition and Subtraction Equations

Key Concept Write addition and subtraction equations and use mental math to solve.

An equation is a number sentence stating that two amounts are equal. You can write an addition or subtraction equation with a variable to solve a problem.

Example 1 Write a subtraction equation.

Beatrice had 12 cat treats. Her cat ate some treats. Now she has 5 cat treats. How many treats did the cat eat?

Let e represent the number of treats eaten.

12 cat treats	minus	treats eaten	equals	5 treats
↓	↓	↓	↓	↓
12	−	e	=	5

So, the equation is $12 - e = 5$.

You solve an equation by finding the value of the variable the makes the number sentence true.

Example 2 Solve an equation using mental math.

Solve.	$12 - e = 5$	**Think:** 12 minus what
	$e = 7$	number equals 5?
Check:	$12 - 7 \overset{?}{=} 5$	Replace e with 7.
	$5 = 5 ✔$	The equation is true.

So, the value of e is 7.

ERROR ALERT

An equal sign (=) shows that two amounts are equal. An operation sign (+, −) tells you to compute.

Try It

Write an equation. Choose a variable for the unknown. Tell what the variable represents.

1. Ali had 8 eggs. He broke some. He has 3 eggs left. How many did he break?

Solve the equation.

2. $x + 8 = 12$

3. $10 - k = 2$

4. $h - 2 = 3$

5. $6 + y = 9$

6. Read the problem below. **Explain** why D cannot be the correct answer choice. Then choose the correct answer.

COMMON ERROR

Solve the equation.

$$w - 3 = 9$$

A $w = 3$ **C** $w = 12$

B $w + 9$ **D** $w = 27$

Review the Key Concepts—Chapter 4

Multiplication and Division Facts Through 12

Key Concept Use properties, patterns, and strategies to find products and quotients.

You can use the Zero Property of Multiplication or Identity Property of Multiplication, doubles, skip-counting, or the break apart strategy to help you learn the multiplication facts.

You can use a related multiplication fact to divide.

Examples

A Use the break apart strategy to find 11×12.

Think: $12 = 10 + 2$

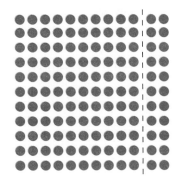

$11 \times 10 = 110$

$11 \times 2 = 22$

$110 + 22 = 132$

So, $11 \times 12 = 132$.

B Use a multiplication fact to find $24 \div 12$.

Think: $12 \times \blacksquare = 24$

$12 \times 2 = 24$, so $\blacksquare = 2$.

So, $24 \div 12 = 2$.

ERROR ALERT

Be sure to use the correct facts to solve a problem.

$24 \div 12$ does **NOT** equal 3 because 12×3 does **NOT** equal 24.

Try It

Find the product or quotient. Show the strategy you used.

1. 6×12
2. 7×11
3. 12×5
4. 2×12
5. $44 \div 11$
6. $84 \div 12$
7. $77 \div 7$
8. 11×10
9. 12×4
10. $120 \div 12$
11. $88 \div 11$
12. $99 \div 11$
13. 12×7
14. $48 \div 12$

15. Read the problem below. **COMMON ERROR**

Explain why D cannot be the correct answer choice. Then choose the correct answer.

Tomas made 12 equal stacks of pennies. There are 48 pennies in all. How many pennies are in each stack?

A 60   C 4

B 36   D 3

Review the Key Concepts—Chapter 5

Order of Operations

Key Concept Use the order of operations to find the value of an expression with more than one type of operation.

Follow the order of operations to find the value of the expression.

- First, perform any operations in parentheses.
- Next, multiply and divide from left to right.
- Then add and subtract from left to right.

Example

Find the value of $5 + 2 \times (6 - 2)$.

$$5 + 2 \times (6 - 2)$$
$$\downarrow$$
$$5 + 2 \times \quad 4$$
$$\downarrow$$
$$5 + \quad 8$$
$$\downarrow$$
$$13$$

Do what is in parentheses first.
Next multiply. Then add.

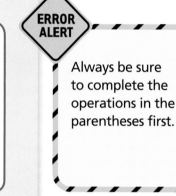

ERROR ALERT

Always be sure to complete the operations in the parentheses first.

So, $5 + 2 \times (6 - 2) = 13$.

Try It

Write *correct* if the operations are listed in the correct order. If not, write the correct order of operations.

1. $3 + 2 \times 30$ Add, multiply

2. $7 \times (5 - 3)$ Subtract, multiply

3. $12 \times 2 - (3 + 6)$ Add, multiply, subtract

4. $15 + 14 \div 7$ Add, divide

Find the value of each expression.

5. $40 + (9 - 6)$

6. $17 - (8 + 2)$

7. $(4 + 9) \times 3$

8. $5 \times (32 \div 8)$

9. $(35 - 15) \div 5 + 2$

10. $50 - (6 \times 7)$

11. $72 \div (3 \times 3)$

12. $24 + (15 - 2)$

13. $10 + 3 \times 6 - 5$

14. $(12 - 2) \times 5$

15. Read the problem below. **Explain** why C cannot be the correct answer choice. Then choose the correct answer.

    COMMON ERROR

    Find the value of the expression.

    $$5 + 3 \times (7 + 3)$$

    A 35   C 59

    B 45   D 61

Review the Key Concepts—Chapter 5

Multiplication and Division Equations

Key Concepts Use multiplication and division equations with a variable to solve problems.

You can write an equation with a variable to solve a problem.

Example 1 Write a multiplication equation.

Ms. Larson buys boxes of pens that hold 4 pens each. She buys a total of 32 pens. What equation can you write to find how many boxes she buys?

The number of boxes times 4 pens each is 32 pens.

$$b \times 4 = 32 \leftarrow b \text{ is the number of boxes.}$$

So, the equation is $b \times 4 = 32$.

Example 2 Write a division equation.

ERROR ALERT

Kelly has 24 crackers. She wants to share them equally among 4 friends. What equation can you write to find the number of crackers she should give each friend?

24 crackers divided into equal groups is 4 groups.

$$24 \div c = 4 \leftarrow c \text{ is the number of crackers in each group.}$$

So, the equation is $24 \div c = 4$.

Reread your equation to make sure you have used the correct operation.

Try It

Write an equation for each. Choose a variable for the unknown. Tell what the variable represents.

1. Ten students each in a number of groups is 40 students.

2. A number of crayons divided equally among 6 boxes is 9 crayons in each box.

3. 40 stickers divided equally among some pages is 8 stickers on each page.

4. Three T-shirts at an equal cost for each is a total cost of $36.

5. Read the problem below. **COMMON ERROR**

   Explain why C cannot be the correct answer choice. Then choose the correct answer.

   Six books each in a number of boxes is 18 books. If b is the number of boxes, which equation can be used to find b?

   A $6 \times b = 18$

   B $18 \times b = 6$

   C $6 \div b = 18$

   D $b \div 6 = 18$

Review the Key Concepts—Chapter 6

Elapsed Time

Key Concept Use a clock to find elapsed time.

To find elapsed time, count forward from the starting time to the end time.

Example 1 Find the elapsed time.

Soccer camp starts at 9:30 A.M. and ends at 1:15 P.M. How long will camp last?

Think: From 9:30 A.M. to 12:30 P.M., 3 full hours have passed.

Think: From 12:30 P.M. to 1:15 P.M., 45 minutes have passed.

3 hr + 45 min = 3 hr 45 min. So, camp lasts 3 hours 45 minutes.

Example 2 Find the end time.

Soccer camp starts at 9:30 A.M. After 1 hour 20 minutes, campers have a snack break. At what time do they have a snack?

1 hour after 9:30 A.M. is 10:30 A.M.

Count forward by 5 minutes at a time to 20 minutes.

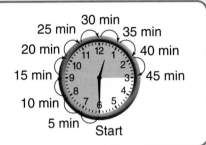

ERROR ALERT

To find the end time, be sure to count forward full hours first, and then minutes.

So, the campers get a snack at 10:50 A.M.

Try It

Find the elapsed time.

1. start: 6:05 A.M. end: 7:30 A.M.

2. start: 10:45 A.M. end: 11:20 A.M.

Find the end time.

3. start: 6:15 A.M. elapsed time: 4 hr 45 min

4. start: 7:35 P.M. elapsed time: 2 hr 30 min

5. Read the problem below. **COMMON ERROR** **Explain** why A cannot be the correct answer choice. Then choose the correct answer.

The piano recital began at 5:45 P.M. It lasted 2 hours 30 minutes. At what time did the recital end?

A 6:15 P.M.   C 8:15 P.M.

B 7:45 P.M.   D 8:30 P.M.

Review the Key Concepts—Chapter 6

Positive and Negative Numbers

Key Concept Use positive and negative numbers to represent real-world situations.

On a number line, negative numbers are to the left of 0. Positive numbers are to the right of 0. The number 0 is not positive or negative.

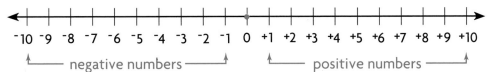

Positive and negative numbers can be used to represent situations.

Example 1

Write a positive or negative number to represent the situation.

A Carlos paid $8 for a model robot.

⁻8

B Margo climbed 1,112 feet up Sandia Mountain.

⁺1,112

ERROR ALERT Use negative numbers to show that someone has spent money, not earned money.

You can compare and order negative numbers.

Example 2

Use a number line to compare the numbers.

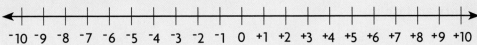

C Compare ⁺1 and ⁻5.

Since ⁺1 is to the right of ⁻5, ⁺1 > ⁻5.

D Compare ⁻9 and ⁻5.

Since ⁻5 is to the right of ⁻9, ⁻5 > ⁻9.

Try It

Write a positive or negative number to represent each situation.

1. The temperature dropped 9 degrees.

2. Angie owes $4.

3. Juan adds 4 cars to his collection.

Draw a number line and graph the numbers. Compare using < or >.

4. ⁻9 and ⁺9   5. ⁻1 and ⁻3

6. Read the problem below. **COMMON ERROR**
   Explain why B cannot be the correct answer choice. Then choose the correct answer.

   Jake earned $5 for walking the dog ten times. Which number best represents the money he earned?

   A ⁻10   **C** ⁺5

   B ⁻5   **D** ⁺10

Review the Key Concepts—Chapter 7

Mean, Median, and Mode

Key Concept Find the mean, median, and mode of a data set.

Bird Sightings	
Day	**Frequency (Number of Birds)**
1	12
2	11
3	17
4	9
5	8
6	9

A To find the mean of the data set in the table, first find the total number of birds seen.

$$12 + 11 + 17 + 9 + 8 + 9 = 66$$

Then divide by the number of days.

$$66 \div 6 = 11$$

B To find the median, or middle number, first order the data from least to greatest.

8, 9, 9, 11, 12, 17

Cross off numbers on each end until you reach the middle number or numbers.

8̶, 9̶, 9, 11, 1̶2̶, 1̶7̶

There are two middle numbers, 9 and 11.

Add the two middle numbers and divide by 2.

$$9 + 11 = 20 \qquad 20 \div 2 = 10$$

C To find the mode, find the number that occurs most often.

8, <u>9</u>, <u>9</u>, 11, 12, 17

There may be no mode, one mode, or more than one mode.

These data have one mode: 9.

ERROR ALERT

Be sure to order the data before you look for the middle number to find the median.

So, the mean number of birds is 11, the median is 10, and the mode is 9.

Try It

Find the mean, median, and mode.

1.

Megan's Hiking Trip					
Day	1	2	3	4	5
Number of Miles	6	7	16	6	10

2. Read the problem below. **COMMON ERROR** **Explain** why D cannot be the correct answer choice. Then choose the correct answer.

From Monday through Friday, Oscar sold 12, 21, 17, 12, and 13 bikes. What is the median number of bikes he sold?

A 12

B 13

C 15

D 17

Review the Key Concepts—Chapter 7

Line Plots

Key Concept A line plot is a graph that shows the frequency of data along a number line.

Ms. Clay's Class

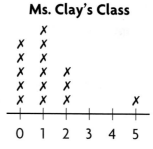

Number of Pets

In Ms. Clay's class, 5 students have no pets, 6 students have 1 pet, 3 students have 2 pets, and 1 student has 5 pets.

The range is the difference between the greatest and least values in the data set.

Examples

A What is the range of the data?

Greatest value: 5
Least value: 0

Range: 5 − 0 = 5

So, the range of the data is 5.

B How many students in Ms. Clay's class have 3 pets?

Find the 3 on the number line. Count the data points above the 3. There are no data points.

So, 0 students have 3 pets.

ERROR ALERT

Remember that the label on the number line tells you what each number shows.

Try It

For 1–6, use the table.

Free Throws Made	
Free Throws	Frequency (Number of Players)
1	5
2	3
3	4
4	2
8	1

1. Use the data to make a line plot.

2. What is the range of the data?

3. How many free throws did the greatest number of players make?

4. How many players made 3 or more free throws?

5. What is the median number of free throws made?

6. Would the range of the data change if 2 players made 7 free throws? **Explain.**

7. Read the problem below. **Explain** why A cannot be the correct answer choice. Then choose the correct answer.

COMMON ERROR

Use the line plot below.

Library Books Borrowed

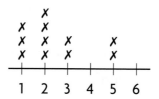

Number of Books

How many students borrowed more than two books?

A 3   **B** 4   **C** 9   **D** 11

Review the Key Concepts—Chapter 8

Choose an Appropriate Graph

Key Concept Use the appropriate type of graph to see trends, make predictions, and compare data to solve problems.

A bar graph or pictograph is used to compare data about different categories or groups.

A line graph is used to show how data change over time.

A circle graph is used to compare parts of a group to a whole group.

A line plot shows the frequency of data along a number line.

Example

Cole and Mason each made a graph to show the daily low temperature. Which is the better graph?

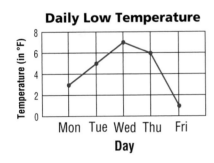

Daily Low Temperature

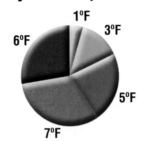

Daily Low Temperature

ERROR ALERT

Remember that you can compare categorical data, or data about different groups, using bar graphs, pictographs, or circle graphs.

Since the data change over time, the line graph is the better graph.

Try It

Choose the best type of graph or plot for the data. Explain your choice.

1. the growth of a bean plant over time

2. how Greg spends his weekly allowance

3. the number of students in each grade at an elementary school

4. how much weight a puppy gained each month for 6 months

5. how many students have different numbers of buttons on their clothes

6. Read the problem below. **Explain** why C cannot be the correct answer choice. Then choose the correct answer.

   COMMON ERROR

   Which type of graph would **NOT** be appropriate to use to compare the number of votes each of three students received in a school election?

   A Circle graph   **C** Bar graph

   B Line graph   **D** Pictograph

Review the Key Concepts—Chapter 9

Multiply 3-Digit and 4-Digit Numbers and Money

Key Concept Multiply greater numbers by using basic facts and place value.

When you multiply greater numbers, estimate first so you can check that your answer is reasonable.

Example 1 Use place value and regrouping.
Multiply. 5×387 **Estimate.** $5 \times 400 = 2,000$

Step 1	Step 2	Step 3
Multiply the ones. 5×7 ones $= 35$ ones	Multiply the tens. 5×8 tens $= 40$ tens	Multiply the hundreds. 5×3 hundreds $= 15$ hundreds
Regroup the 35 ones.	Add the regrouped tens. 40 tens $+ 3$ tens $= 43$ tens	Add the regrouped hundreds. 15 hundreds $+ 4$ hundreds $= 19$ hundreds
$\overset{3}{3}87$ $\times\ \ \ 5 \over 5$	Regroup the 43 tens. $\quad \overset{4\ 3}{3}87$ $\times\ \ \ 5 \over 35$	$\overset{4\ 3}{3}87$ $\times\ \ \ 5 \over 1,935$

So, $5 \times 387 = 1,935$. Since 1,935 is close to the estimate of 2,000 it is reasonable.

Example 2 Multiply dollars and cents.
Multiply. $4 \times \$28.05$ **Estimate.** $4 \times \$30 = \$120$

$$\$28.05 \quad\quad 2805$$
$$\times\ \ \ \ \ 4 \rightarrow \times\ \ \ 4$$

Multiply the same way you multiply whole numbers.

$$\rightarrow \quad \overset{3\ \ 2}{\$28.05}$$
$$\times\ \ \ \ \ \ \ 4 \over \$112.20$$

Write the product in dollars and cents.

ERROR ALERT

Be sure to place the decimal point to show dollars and cents.

So, $4 \times \$28.05 = \$112.20$. Since $112.20 is close to $120, the answer is reasonable.

Try It

Estimate. Then find the product.

1. $415 \atop \times\ \ 3$

2. $247 \atop \times\ \ 8$

3. $1,048 \atop \times\quad\ 9$

4. $7,293 \atop \times\quad\ 2$

5. 3×942

6. $7 \times \$6.83$

7. Read the problem below. **Explain** **COMMON ERROR** why A cannot be the correct answer choice. Then choose the correct answer.

Cate bought 6 albums. Each cost $4.35. How much did they cost in all?

A $2,610   C $26.10

B $261   D $2.61

Review the Key Concepts—Chapter 10

Multiply by 2-Digit Numbers

Key Concept Use place value to multiply by a two-digit number.

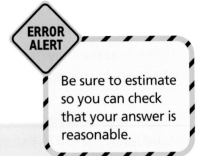

ERROR ALERT

Be sure to estimate so you can check that your answer is reasonable.

You can use place value to multiply by two-digit numbers. Always align the digits in place-value order. Remember to regroup when necessary.

Example Use place value.
Multiply. 46×378 **Estimate.** $50 \times 400 = 20,000$

Step 1	Step 2	Step 3
Multiply by the ones.	Multiply by the tens.	Add the partial products.
$\begin{array}{r} {}^{4\ 4} \\ 378 \\ \times\ \ 46 \\ \hline 2268 \leftarrow 6 \times 378 \end{array}$	$\begin{array}{r} {}^{3\ 3} \\ \cancel{4\ 4} \\ 378 \\ \times\ \ 46 \\ \hline 2685 \\ 15120 \leftarrow 40 \times 378 \end{array}$	$\begin{array}{r} {}^{3\ 3} \\ \cancel{4\ 4} \\ 378 \\ \times\ \ 46 \\ \hline 2685 \\ +\ 15\,120 \\ \hline 17,388 \end{array}$

So, $46 \times 378 = 17,388$.

Try It

Estimate. Then find the product.

1. $\begin{array}{r} 33 \\ \times 82 \end{array}$

2. $\begin{array}{r} 59 \\ \times 41 \end{array}$

3. $\begin{array}{r} 908 \\ \times\ 63 \end{array}$

4. $\begin{array}{r} 291 \\ \times\ 94 \end{array}$

5. $\begin{array}{r} 53 \\ \times 85 \end{array}$

6. $\begin{array}{r} 672 \\ \times\ 45 \end{array}$

7. $\begin{array}{r} 846 \\ \times\ 78 \end{array}$

8. $\begin{array}{r} 258 \\ \times\ 39 \end{array}$

9. 67×28

10. 183×96

11. 39×270

12. 47×72

13. Read the problem below.
Explain why B cannot be the correct answer choice. Then choose the correct answer.

COMMON ERROR

$\begin{array}{r} 286 \\ \times\ 39 \end{array}$

A 832

B 3,432

C 10,452

D 11,154

Review the Key Concepts—Chapter 10

Multiply Money by 2-Digit Numbers

Key Concept Multiply whole number amounts and decimal amounts of money by 2-digit numbers.

Multiply money the same way you multiply whole numbers. Then, write the product in dollars and cents.

Lionel sold 63 T-shirts for $8.95 each last week. What were his total sales for the T-shirts?

Example
Multiply. 63 × $8.95   **Estimate.** 60 × $9 = $540

Step 1	Step 2	Step 3
Multiply by the ones.	Multiply by the tens.	Add the partial products. Place the decimal point to write the product in dollar and cents.

Step 1

$$\begin{array}{r} \overset{2\ 1}{\$8.95} \\ \times\quad 63 \\ \hline 26\ 85 \end{array} \leftarrow 3 \times 895$$

Step 2

$$\begin{array}{r} \overset{5\ 3}{\cancel{2}\ \cancel{1}} \\ \$8.95 \\ \times\quad 63 \\ \hline 26\ 85 \\ 537\ 00 \end{array} \leftarrow 60 \times 895$$

Step 3

$$\begin{array}{r} \overset{5\ 3}{\cancel{2}\ \cancel{1}} \\ \$8.95 \\ \times\quad 63 \\ \hline 26\ 85 \\ +\ 537\ 00 \\ \hline \$563.85 \end{array}$$

ERROR ALERT

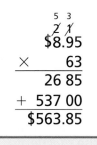

When multiplying money, you can estimate to help you place the decimal point in the product.

So, his total sales were $563.85. Since $563.85 is close to $540, the answer is reasonable.

Try It

Estimate. Then find the product.

1. $9.05
    × 28

2. $2.78
    × 36

3. $427
    × 61

4. $3.75
    × 58

5. $1.08
    × 49

6. $4.65
    × 37

7. $3.94
    × 51

8. $807
    × 23

9. Read the problem below. **Explain** why A cannot be the correct answer choice. Then choose the correct answer.

COMMON ERROR

School sweatshirts cost $11. How much do 198 sweatshirts cost?

A $21.78

B $217.80

C $2,178

D $21,780

Review the Key Concepts—Chapter 11

Divide by 1-Digit Divisors

Key Concept Divide 2-digit numbers by 1-digit numbers.

You can divide 2-digit numbers by 1-digit numbers to solve problems.

Ben wants to divide 89 baseballs equally among 7 teams. If he gives each team the same number of baseballs, how many baseballs will each team have?

Example

Divide 89 by 7. Write $89 \div 7$ or $7\overline{)89}$.

Step 1	**Step 2**	**Step 3**
Divide the 8 tens.	Bring down the 9 ones. Divide the 19 ones.	To check, multiply the quotient by the divisor. Then add the remainder.

Step 1

$$\begin{array}{r} 1 \\ 7\overline{)89} \\ -7 \\ \hline 1 \end{array}$$

Divide. $8 \div 7$
Multiply. 7×1
Subtract. $8 - 7$
Compare. $1 < 7$

Step 2

$$\begin{array}{r} 12 \text{ r5} \\ 7\overline{)89} \\ -7\downarrow \\ \hline 19 \\ -14 \\ \hline 5 \end{array}$$

Divide. $19 \div 7$
Multiply. 7×2
Subtract. $19 - 14$
Compare. $5 < 7$

Write the remainder next to the quotient.

Step 3

$$\begin{array}{r} 12 \\ \times 7 \\ \hline 84 \\ + 5 \\ \hline 89 \end{array}$$

quotient
divisor

remainder
dividend

ERROR ALERT

When solving a problem, decide if you need to use the remainder or not.

So, each team receives 12 baseballs; with 5 baseballs left over.

Try It

Divide.

1. $6\overline{)78}$
2. $5\overline{)62}$
3. $3\overline{)64}$
4. $4\overline{)63}$
5. $8\overline{)93}$
6. $7\overline{)85}$
7. $87 \div 5$
8. $72 \div 4$
9. $78 \div 7$
10. $46 \div 2$
11. $47 \div 5$
12. $82 \div 6$

13. Read the problem below. **COMMON ERROR**
Explain why A cannot be the correct answer choice. Then choose the correct answer.

There are 65 beads in a bag. Maggie needs 6 beads for each bracelet. If she uses all the beads in the bag, how many beads will she have left over?

A 10   C 5

B 8   D 2

Review the Key Concepts—Chapter 12

Practice Division

Key Concept When dividing greater numbers, you must decide where to place the first digit in the quotient.

You can use compatible numbers to determine where to place the first digit in the quotient.

Example Divide 171 by 7. Estimate. 200 ÷ 10 = 20

Step 1	Step 2	Step 3	Step 4
$7\overline{)171}$ **Think:** $\frac{20}{7\overline{)140}}$ or $\frac{30}{7\overline{)210}}$ The quotient is between 20 and 30. So, place the first digit in the tens place.	Divide the tens. $\begin{array}{r} 2 \\ 7\overline{)171} \\ -14 \\ \hline 3 \end{array}$ Divide. 17 ÷ 7 Multiply. 7 × 2 Subtract. 17 − 14 Compare. 3 < 7	Bring down the 1 one. Divide the 31 ones. $\begin{array}{r} 24\,r3 \\ 7\overline{)171} \\ -14\downarrow \\ \hline 31 \\ -28 \\ \hline 3 \end{array}$ Divide. 31 ÷ 7 Multiply. 7 × 4 Subtract. 31 − 28 Compare. 3 < 7	To check, multiply the quotient by the divisor. Then add the remainder. $\begin{array}{r} 24 \\ \times\ 7 \\ \hline 168 \\ +\ 3 \\ \hline 171 \end{array}$ quotient divisor remainder dividend

So, 171 ÷ 7 = 24 r3.

More Examples

A Divide 732 by 5.

Think: $\frac{100}{5\overline{)500}}$ or $\frac{200}{5\overline{)1,000}}$ The quotient is between 100 and 200. So, place the first digit in the hundreds place.

$\begin{array}{r} 146\,r2 \\ 5\overline{)732} \\ -5 \\ \hline 23 \\ -20 \\ \hline 32 \\ -30 \\ \hline 2 \end{array}$

B Divide $3.21 by 3.

Think: $\frac{\$1.00}{3\overline{)\$3.00}}$ or $\frac{\$2.00}{3\overline{)\$6.00}}$ The quotient is between $1.00 and $2.00. So place the first digit in the hundreds place.

$\begin{array}{r} \$1.07 \\ 3\overline{)\$3.21} \\ -3 \\ \hline 02 \\ -0 \\ \hline 21 \\ -21 \\ \hline 0 \end{array}$

ERROR ALERT

You can quickly check the reasonableness of your answer by comparing the quotient to your estimated quotient.

Try It

Divide.

1. 403 ÷ 8

2. $4.59 ÷ 9

3. $5.67 ÷ 9

4. 674 ÷ 3

5. 329 ÷ 9

6. 217 ÷ 4

7. 837 ÷ 5

8. 722 ÷ 3

9. $581 ÷ 7

10. $8.22 ÷ 6

11. Read the problem below. **Explain** why D cannot be the correct answer choice. Then choose the correct answer.

COMMON ERROR

Cassidy paid $1.80 for 5 erasers. How much did she pay for each eraser?

A $0.06 **B** $0.36 **C** $3.60 **D** $360

Review the Key Concepts—Chapter 13

Divide by 2-Digit Divisors

Key Concept When you divide by 2-digit numbers, estimate first to place the first digit in the quotient.

When you divide by 2-digit numbers, you can use compatible numbers to estimate the quotient.

ERROR ALERT

If your estimate for the first digit is not correct, adjust it by increasing or decreasing the digit.

Example 1 Divide 757 by 38. Estimate. $800 \div 40 = 20$

Step 1

Try the estimate, 20. So, place the first digit, 2, in the tens place.

$$\begin{array}{r} 2 \\ 38\overline{)757} \\ -76 \end{array}$$

Since $76 > 75$, the estimated digit is too high.

Step 2

Adjust. Try 1 in the tens place.

$$\begin{array}{r} 1 \\ 38\overline{)757} \\ -38 \\ \hline 37 \end{array} \quad 37 < 38$$

Step 3

Bring down the 7 ones. then divide 377 ones. Estimate the next digit in the quotient.

Think:
$360 \div 40 = 9$

Try 9.

$$\begin{array}{r} 19 \ r35 \\ 38\overline{)757} \\ -38\downarrow \\ \hline 377 \\ -342 \\ \hline 35 \end{array} \quad 35 < 38$$

So, $757 \div 38 = 19$ r35.

Example 2 Divide 611 by 15. Estimate. $600 \div 20 = 30$

Step 1

Try the estimate, 30. So, place the first digit 3, in the tens place.

$$\begin{array}{r} 3 \\ 15\overline{)611} \\ -45 \\ \hline 16 \end{array}$$

$16 > 15$
The estimated digit is too low.

Step 2

Adjust. Try 4 in the tens place.

$$\begin{array}{r} 4 \\ 15\overline{)611} \\ -60 \\ \hline 1 \end{array} \quad 1 < 15$$

Step 3

Bring down the 1 one. Divide the 11 ones.

$$\begin{array}{r} 40 \ r11 \\ 15\overline{)611} \\ -60\downarrow \\ \hline 11 \\ -0 \\ \hline 11 \end{array}$$

Since 11 is less than 15, write a zero in the quotient.

So, $611 \div 15 = 40$ r11.

Try It

Divide.

1. $53\overline{)289}$
2. $28\overline{)293}$
3. $48\overline{)319}$
4. $86\overline{)521}$
5. $271 \div 13$
6. $362 \div 45$
7. $113 \div 12$
8. $852 \div 21$
9. $311 \div 25$
10. $442 \div 72$

11. Read the problem below. **Explain** why A cannot be the correct answer choice. Then choose the correct answer.

COMMON ERROR

Brian put 966 photos into packs of 46. How many packs did he make?

A 15   **B** 20   **C** 21   **D** 40

Review the Key Concepts—Chapter 14

Factors and Multiples

Key Concept A factor is a number multiplied by another number to find a product. A multiple of a counting number is any product that has that number as a factor.

Every whole number has at least two factors—itself and 1. You can make an array to find all the factors of 9.

Example 1

Find the factors of 9.

To find all factors of 9, make as many different arrays as you can using 9 square tiles.

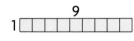

So, the factors of 9 are 1, 3, and 9.

To find multiples of any counting number, you can skip-count or multiply by the counting numbers 1, 2, 3, and so on.

Example 2

Find the first six multiples of 5.

Multiply by the counting numbers and make a list.

$1 \times 5 = 5$ $2 \times 5 = 10$ $3 \times 5 = 15$ $4 \times 5 = 20$
$5 \times 5 = 25$ $6 \times 5 = 30$

So, the first six multiples of 5 are 5, 10, 15, 20, 25, 30.

ERROR ALERT

Remember that 2 is a factor of every even number because every even number is a multiple of 2.

Try It

Find all the factors of each product.

1. 24   **2.** 36

3. 35   **4.** 12

5. 30   **6.** 64

List the first twelve multiples of each number.

7. 4   **8.** 6

9. 10   **10.** 12

11. 8   **12.** 7

13. Read the problem below.   **COMMON ERROR**

Explain why A cannot be the correct answer choice. Then choose the correct answer.

Which statement is true?

A The only factors of 6 are 1 and 6.

B The only factors of 15 are 1 and 15.

C The only factors of 19 are 1 and 19.

D The only factors of 21 are 1 and 21.

Review the Key Concepts—Chapter 15

Fractions and Mixed Numbers

Key Concept Fractions can describe parts of a whole or parts of a group.

A fraction names a part of a whole or part of a group.

Example 1

A What fraction of the counters are red?

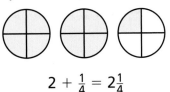

red counters $\longrightarrow 5 \longleftarrow$ numerator
total counters $\rightarrow \overline{8} \longleftarrow$ denominator

Five eighths of the counters are red.

B What fraction does point *W* represent?

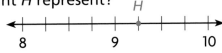

There are 6 equal parts between 0 and 1.

So, point *W* represents $\frac{5}{6}$.

A mixed number is an amount given as a whole number and a fraction.

Example 2

A Write the mixed number the picture represents.

$2 + \frac{1}{4} = 2\frac{1}{4}$

So, the mixed number is $2\frac{1}{4}$.

B What mixed number does point *H* represent?

Between the whole numbers, the number line is divided into 4 equal parts, or fourths.

So, point *H* represents $9\frac{1}{4}$.

> **ERROR ALERT**
>
> On a number line, count the number of equal parts between whole numbers to determine the denominator of the fraction.

Try It

1. What fraction of the counters are red?

2. Write the mixed number that the picture represents.

3. What fraction or mixed number do points *A* and *B* represent?

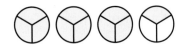

4. Read the problem below. **COMMON ERROR**

Explain why A cannot be the correct answer choice. Then choose the correct answer.

On the number line below, what mixed number does *R* represent?

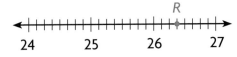

A $24\frac{3}{4}$ **B** $25\frac{1}{4}$ **C** $26\frac{3}{8}$ **D** $27\frac{1}{8}$

Review the Key Concepts—Chapter 16

Add and Subtract Fractions

Key Concept To add or subtract like fractions, add or subtract only the numerators. Use the same denominator as in the like fractions.

Add. $\frac{3}{10} + \frac{1}{10}$

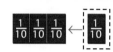

Think: There are four $\frac{1}{10}$ fraction bars.

$$\frac{3}{10} + \frac{1}{10} = \frac{4}{10}$$

Write the sum in simplest form.

$$\frac{4}{10} = \frac{2}{5}$$

So, $\frac{3}{10} + \frac{1}{10} = \frac{2}{5}$.

Subtract. $\frac{7}{12} - \frac{3}{12}$

Think: The difference is four $\frac{1}{12}$ bars.

$$\frac{7}{12} - \frac{3}{12} = \frac{4}{12}$$

Write the sum in simplest form.

$$\frac{4}{12} = \frac{1}{3}$$

So, $\frac{7}{12} - \frac{3}{12} = \frac{1}{3}$.

ERROR ALERT

With like fractions, be sure to add or subtract only the numerators. The denominator does not change.

Examples

Ⓐ $\frac{7}{8} + \frac{2}{8}$ The denominators are the same.

$\frac{7}{8} + \frac{2}{8} = \frac{9}{8}$ Add the numerators.

$\frac{9}{8} = 1\frac{1}{8}$ Write the sum as a mixed number.

Ⓑ $\frac{5}{6} - \frac{2}{6}$ The denominators are the same.

$\frac{5}{6} - \frac{2}{6} = \frac{3}{6}$ Subtract the numerators.

$\frac{3}{6} = \frac{1}{2}$ Write the difference in simplest form,

Try It

Find the sum or difference.

1. $\frac{7}{8} - \frac{2}{8}$

2. $\frac{3}{6} - \frac{1}{6}$

3. $\frac{1}{3} + \frac{1}{3}$

4. $\frac{1}{4} + \frac{3}{4}$

5. $\frac{9}{10} - \frac{3}{10}$

6. $\frac{5}{8} + \frac{3}{8}$

7. $\frac{5}{9} + \frac{1}{9}$

8. $\frac{11}{12} - \frac{5}{12}$

9. $\frac{4}{5} + \frac{2}{5}$

10. $\frac{7}{9} - \frac{2}{9}$

11. $\frac{3}{4} + \frac{2}{4}$

12. $\frac{6}{8} - \frac{3}{8}$

13. Read the problem below. **Explain** why B cannot be the correct answer choice. Then choose the correct answer.

COMMON ERROR

Jamie eats $\frac{5}{12}$ of a small pizza. Casey eats $\frac{3}{12}$ of the pizza. How much of the pizza do they eat altogether?

A $\frac{1}{6}$

B $\frac{8}{24}$

C $\frac{2}{3}$

D $\frac{3}{4}$

Review the Key Concepts—Chapter 17

Relate Fractions and Decimals

Key Concept Fractions can be written as decimals.

You can use models to show decimals.

Example 1

Write the fraction and decimal shown by each model.

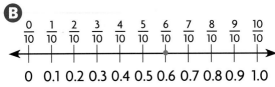

A

Read: fifty hundredths

Write: $\frac{50}{100}$, 0.50

B

0 0.1 0.2 0.3 0.4 0.5 0.6 0.7 0.8 0.9 1.0

Read: six tenths

Write: $\frac{6}{10}$, 0.6

C

Read: 3 hundredths

Write: $\frac{3}{100}$, 0.03 of a dollar, or $0.03

You can also write a decimal for a fraction that is not tenths or hundredths. First, write the fraction as tenths or hundredths. Then write the decimal.

ERROR ALERT

Make sure to find an equivalent fraction in tenths or hundredths before you write the decimal.

Example 2

A Write a decimal that shows the same amount as the fraction $\frac{1}{2}$.

$\frac{1}{2} = \frac{1 \times 5}{2 \times 5} = \frac{5}{10}$, or 0.5

So, $\frac{1}{2}$ is the same amount as $\frac{5}{10}$, or 0.5.

B Write a decimal that shows the same amount as the fraction $\frac{3}{4}$.

$\frac{3}{4} = \frac{3 \times 25}{4 \times 25} = \frac{75}{100}$, or 0.75

So, $\frac{3}{4}$ is the same amount as $\frac{75}{100}$, or 0.75.

Try It

Write the fraction and decimal shown by each model.

1.

2.

Write each fraction as a decimal. You may draw a picture.

3. $\frac{9}{10}$

4. $\frac{21}{100}$

5. $\frac{4}{5}$

6. $\frac{3}{25}$

7. Read the problem below. **COMMON ERROR**

Explain why A cannot be the correct answer choice. Then choose the correct answer.

Which decimal is the same as $\frac{1}{2}$?

A 0.1 **B** 0.2 **C** 0.5 **D** 1.0

Review the Key Concepts—Chapter 18

Add and Subtract Decimals

Key Concept You can add and subtract decimals as you add and subtract whole numbers.

You can draw models to add and subtract decimals.

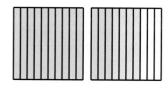

$$1.3 + 0.4 = 1.7$$

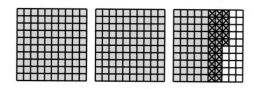

$$2.75 - 0.25 = 2.50$$

To add, shade the model to show the first decimal. Then shade it to show the second decimal. Count the total number of shaded parts to find the sum.

To subtract, shade the model to show the decimal. Then cross out the amount being subtracted. Count the number of shaded parts not crossed out to find what is left.

You can also use paper and pencil to add and subtract decimals.

Examples

A **Add.** 1.3 + 0.95

Estimate. 1 + 1 = 2

$$
\begin{array}{r}
\overset{1}{1}.30 \\
+\ 0.95 \\
\hline
2.25
\end{array}
$$

Place a zero to the right of the last digit after the decimal point.

So, 1.3 + 0.95 = 2.25. Since 2.25 is close to the estimate of 2, it is reasonable.

B **Subtract.** 4.5 − 1.95

Estimate. 5 − 2 = 3

$$
\begin{array}{r}
\overset{14}{3\ \cancel{4}}\,10 \\
\cancel{4}.5\cancel{0} \\
-\ 1.95 \\
\hline
2.55
\end{array}
$$

So, 4.5 − 1.95 = 2.55. Since 2.55 is close to the estimate of 3, it is reasonable.

ERROR ALERT

Make sure to line up the decimal points when you add or subtract.

Try It

Estimate. Then record the sum or difference.

1. 1.2 + 1.4

2. 0.7 + 1.33

3. 2.8 − 1.4

4. 3.33 + 0.79

5. 1.99 + 0.82

6. 3.5 − 1.22

7. 2.5 + 1.2

8. 3.47 + 1.2

9. 2.6 − 0.9

10. 5.45 − 0.8

11. Read the problem below. **COMMON ERROR** **Explain** why A cannot be the correct answer choice. Then choose the correct answer.

Find 1.3 + 0.06.

A 1.9   **C** 10.09

B 1.36   **D** 10.36

Review the Key Concepts—Chapter 19

Measure and Classify Angles

Key Concept A protractor can be used to measure and classify right, acute, obtuse, and straight angles.

You can use a protractor to measure the sizes of angles.

Place the center point of the protractor on the vertex of the angle.

Line up the center point and the 0° mark with $\overrightarrow{BC}$.

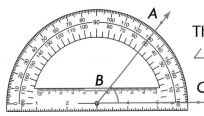

The measure of ∠ABC is 50°.

ERROR ALERT

Make sure you look at the angle *between* the rays.

An angle can be classified according to the size of the opening between its rays.

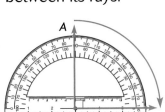 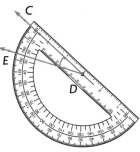 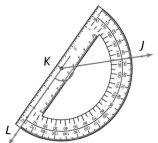 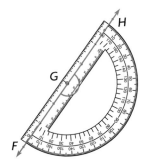

A **right angle** measures 90° and forms a square corner.

An **acute angle** measures greater than 0° and less than 90°.

An **obtuse angle** measures greater than 90° and less than 180°.

A **straight angle** measures 180°. A straight angle forms a line.

Try It

Trace each angle and extend the rays. Use a protractor to measure the angle. Then write *acute, right, straight,* or *obtuse*.

1.   2.

3.   4.

5.   6.

7. Read the problem below. **COMMON ERROR**
   Explain why C cannot be the correct answer choice. Then choose the correct answer.

   Is ∠RST right, acute, straight, or obtuse?

   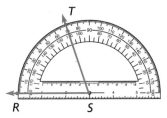

   A Acute   **C** Obtuse

   B Right   **D** Straight

Review the Key Concepts—Chapter 19

Classify Figures

Key Concept You can classify triangles and quadrilaterals by the characteristics of their sides and angles.

Triangles can be named by the lengths of their sides.

 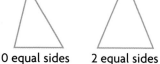

Scalene	Isosceles	Equilateral
0 equal sides	2 equal sides	3 equal sides

Triangles can be named by the measures of their angles.

   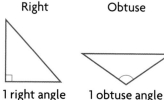

Acute	Right	Obtuse
3 acute angles	1 right angle	1 obtuse angle

Quadrilaterals can be named by the pairs of parallel sides they have.

Quadrilateral with no parallel sides

Quadrilateral with exactly 1 pair of parallel sides

Trapezoid

ERROR ALERT

Parallelograms have 1 pair of parallel sides, but they also have a second pair of parallel sides. So, trapezoids are not parallelograms.

Quadrilateral with 2 pairs of parallel sides

Parallelogram

The following figures each have 2 pairs of parallel sides and are parallelograms:

Square	Rhombus	Rectangle
4 equal sides	4 equal sides	

Try It

Classify each triangle. Write *isosceles,* *scalene,* **or** *equilateral.* **Then write** *right,* *acute,* **or** *obtuse.*

1. 3 in. 5 in. 4 in.

2. 3 in. 3 in. 3 in.

Classify each figure in as many of the following ways as possible. Write *quadrilateral, parallelogram, rhombus, rectangle, square,* **or** *trapezoid.*

3.

4.

5. Read the problem below. **COMMON ERROR** **Explain** why D cannot be the correct answer choice. Then choose the correct answer.

Which figure below is **NOT** a parallelogram?

A    C

B    D

Review the Key Concepts—Chapter 20

Transformations

Key Concept Transformations change the position of a figure. The size and shape of the figure remain the same.

A transformation is the movement of a figure by a reflection, rotation, or translation. A reflection, or a flip, flips a figure across a line. A rotation, or a turn, moves a figure around a point. A translation, or a slide, moves a figure to a new position along a straight line.

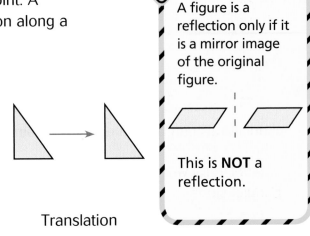

ERROR ALERT

A figure is a reflection only if it is a mirror image of the original figure.

This is **NOT** a reflection.

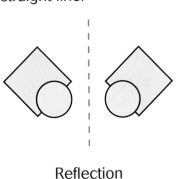

Reflection

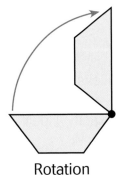

Rotation

Translation

Try It

Tell how each figure was moved. Write *translation, rotation,* **or** *reflection.*

1.

2.

3.

4.

5.

6.

7.

8.

9. Read the problem below. **COMMON ERROR**

   Explain why C cannot be the correct answer choice. Then choose the correct answer.

   Which of the following shows a reflection of the figure?

   A

   B

   C

   D

Review the Key Concepts—Chapter 21

Faces, Edges, and Vertices

Key Concept Three-dimensional figures can be classified by their faces, edges, and vertices.

Vertex

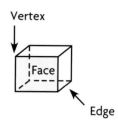

A polygon that is a flat surface of a solid figure is called a face. The line segment where two faces meet is an edge. The point where three or more edges meet is a vertex. The plural of *vertex* is *vertices*.

| cube | rectangular prism | triangular prism | triangular pyramid | square pyramid | cylinder | cone | sphere |

Examples

A Name a solid figure that is described.

5 faces, 9 edges, 6 vertices

Look at the solid figures above. A triangular prism has 5 faces, 9 edges, and 6 vertices.

B Name a solid figure that is described.

2 circular bases

Look at the solid figures above. A cylinder has 2 circular bases.

ERROR ALERT

Remember to count hidden faces, edges, or vertices.

A cube does **NOT** have 3 faces, 7 vertices, and 9 edges.

Try It

Name a solid figure that is described.

1. 6 square faces
2. 4 triangular faces
3. 5 vertices, 8 edges
4. 1 circular base

What solid figure do you see in each?

5.

6.

7. Read the problem below. **COMMON ERROR**

   Explain why A cannot be the correct answer choice. Then choose the correct answer.

   The difference between the number of faces and number of vertices of a figure is 1. What is the figure?

   A Square pyramid

   B Cube

   C Sphere

   D Triangular prism

Review the Key Concepts—Chapter 22

Change Units

Key Concept Multiply or divide to change units of measure.

To change from a larger unit to a smaller unit, multiply.

To change from a smaller unit to a larger unit, divide.

Customary Length	Metric Length
1 ft = 12 in.	1 cm = 10 mm
1 yd = 3 ft, or 36 in.	1 dm = 10 cm
1 mi = 5,280 ft	1 m = 100 cm, or 1,000 mm
1 mi = 1,760 yd	1 km = 1,000 m

ERROR ALERT

Be sure to choose the correct operation—multiplication or division—to change between units.

24 ft ÷ 12 is **NOT** 2 in.

6 ft × 3 is **NOT** 18 yd.

Example 1

A string is 108 inches long. How many yards long is it?

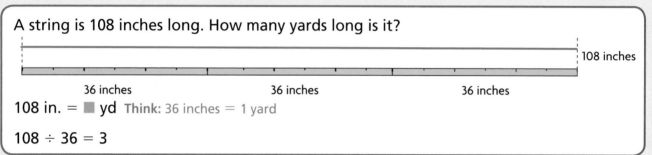

108 inches

36 inches   36 inches   36 inches

108 in. = ■ yd **Think:** 36 inches = 1 yard

108 ÷ 36 = 3

So, 108 inches equal 3 yards.

More Examples

Ⓐ How many feet equal 60 inches?

60 inches = ■ feet **Think:** 1 foot = 12 inches

Since inches are smaller than feet, divide.

60 ÷ 12 = 5

So, 60 inches equal 12 feet.

Ⓑ How many millimeters equal 8 meters?

8 meters = ■ millimeters **Think:** 1 meter = 1,000 millimeters

Since meters are larger than millimeters, multiply.

8 × 1,000 = 8,000

So, 8 meters equal 8,000 millimeters.

Try It

Complete. Tell whether you *multiply* or *divide*.

1. 8 yd = ■ ft

2. 3 m = ■ mm

3. 120 in. = ■ ft

4. 200 cm = ■ dm

5. 24 km = ■ m

6. 108 in. = ■ ft

7. 90 mm = ■ cm

8. 3 mi = ■ ft

9. Read the problem below. **COMMON ERROR** **Explain** why A cannot be the correct answer choice. Then choose the correct answer.

Mia measured 57 yards of material. How many feet of material did she measure?

A 19 ft   **B** 60 ft   **C** 171 ft   **D** 684 ft

Review the Key Concepts—Chapter 23

Perimeter and Area

Key Concept Perimeter is the distance around a figure. Area is the number of square units needed to cover a surface.

You can use formulas to find the perimeter and area of a rectangle.

Perimeter of a Rectangle	Area of a Rectangle
$P = (2 \times l) + (2 \times w)$	$A = l \times w$

To use the formulas, replace l with the length and w with the width.

Examples

A Find the perimeter.

8 in.

4 in.

$P = (2 \times l) + (2 \times w)$

$P = (2 \times 4) + (2 \times 8)$

$P = 8 + 16$

$P = 24$

So, the perimeter is 24 inches.

B Find the area.

12 cm

7 cm

$A = l \times w$

$A = 7 \times 12$

$A = 84$

So, the area is 84 square centimeters.

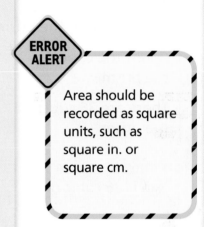

ERROR ALERT

Area should be recorded as square units, such as square in. or square cm.

Try It

Find the perimeter and area of each rectangle.

1.   20 ft

9 ft

2.   15 mi

18 mi

3.   3 m

11 m

4.   10 km

7 km

5. Read the problem below. **COMMON ERROR**
Explain why B cannot be the correct answer choice. Then choose the correct answer.

A table at the banquet was 9 feet long and 3 feet wide. What is the area of the table?

A 24 feet   **C** 24 square feet

B 27 feet   **D** 27 square feet

Review the Key Concepts—Chapter 23

Volume

Key Concept Volume is the amount of space a solid figure occupies. Volume is measured using cubic units.

To find the volume of a rectangular prism, you can count the cubes that fill it or multiply length, width, and height.

ERROR ALERT

Be sure to count all the cubes, including any hidden cubes, to find the volume.

ONE WAY Count cubes.

Count cubes to find the volume of the prism.

Count the cubes in the prism.

There are 36 cubes in the prism.

So, the volume of the prism is 36 cubic units.

ANOTHER WAY Multiply.

Multiply length × width × height to find the volume of the prism.

length = 3 cubes   width = 3 cubes   height = 4 cubes

$3 \times 3 \times 4 = 36$

So, the volume of the prism is 36 cubic units.

Try It

Count or multiply to find the volume.

1.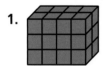

2.

3.

4.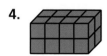

5. Read the problem below. **Explain** why C cannot be the correct answer choice. Then choose the correct answer.

COMMON ERROR

Sally built this prism. What is the volume of the prism?

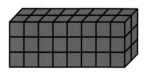

A 16 cubic units

B 24 cubic units

C 34 cubic units

D 48 cubic units

Review the Key Concepts—Chapter 24

Probability as a Fraction

Key Concept Mathematical probability is a comparison of the number of favorable outcomes to the number of possible outcomes. The probability of an event occurring is expressed as 0, 1, or a fraction between 0 and 1.

These marbles are all the same size.

You can use a fraction to express the probability of an outcome.

$$\text{Probability} = \frac{\text{number of favorable outcomes}}{\text{total number of possible outcomes}}$$

What is the probability of pulling a green marble from the bag?

$$\text{Probability of green} = \frac{\text{number of favorable outcomes (green)}}{\text{total number of possible outcomes (3 green, 5 blue, 2 yellow)}} = \frac{3}{10}$$

So, the probability of pulling a green marble is $\frac{3}{10}$.

Examples

ERROR ALERT

Ⓐ Use the bag of marbles above. What is the probability of pulling a marble that is not green?	**Ⓑ** Use the bag of marbles above. What is the probability of pulling a marble that is red?
There are 7 marbles that are not green.	There are no red marbles.
So, the probability of pulling a marble that is not green is $\frac{7}{10}$.	So, the probability of pulling a red marble is $\frac{0}{10}$, or 0.

Be sure to record the total number of possible outcomes as the denominator.

Try It

Equal-sized tiles are placed in a bag. Write the probability as a fraction.

1. pulling a 2

2. pulling a 5

3. pulling an odd number

4. pulling a 1 or a 2

5. pulling a number that is not 4

6. pulling a number less than 6

7. pulling a 9

$$\boxed{1}\ \boxed{3}\ \boxed{4}$$
$$\boxed{5}\ \boxed{2}\ \boxed{2}$$
$$\boxed{2}\ \boxed{3}\ \boxed{1}$$
$$\boxed{2}\ \boxed{1}\ \boxed{2}$$

8. Read the problem below. **Explain** why C cannot be the correct answer choice. Then choose the correct answer.

COMMON ERROR

The spinner has equal sections. What is the probability that the pointer will stop on red?

A $\frac{3}{8}$

B $\frac{1}{2}$

C $\frac{3}{5}$

D $\frac{5}{8}$

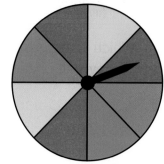

Test-Taking Strategies

Tips for Taking Math Tests

Being a good test-taker is like being a good problem-solver. When you answer test questions, you are solving problems. Remember to **Understand**, **Plan**, **Solve**, and **Check**.

Read to Understand

Read the problem

• Look for math terms and recall their meanings.

• Reread the problem and think about the question.

• Use the details in the problem and the question.

---

1. Exactly 15 students will go on the field trip to the art museum. There will be 3 students in each car. Which number sentence is in the same fact family as $15 \div 3 = \blacksquare$?

A $15 \times 3 = \blacksquare$ **C** $\blacksquare \times 3 = 15$

B $15 \times \blacksquare = 3$ **D** $3 \div \blacksquare = 15$

Test Tip **Understand the problem.**

The *fact family* for $15 \div 3 = \blacksquare$ has related multiplication and division number sentences with 15, 3, and 5. All of the answer choices have 15 and 3. So find the number sentence where the missing number is 5. The answer is **C**.

• Pay attention to words that are in **bold** type, all CAPITAL letters, or *italics* and words like **NOT**.

• If the answer choices include *Not here* and your answer is not given, make sure your work is correct and then mark *Not here*.

---

2. The table shows the money raised for computers by 4 elementary schools

Money Raised				
School	Emerson	King	Sunset	Valley View
Amount	$10,321	$9,864	$10,879	$12,009

Which is the best estimate of how much more money Valley View raised than King?

A $200   **C** $2,000

B $1,000   **D** $3,000

Test Tip **Look for important words.**

The word *estimate* is an important word. Round to the nearest thousand to estimate the amount of money Valley View and King raised. Then subtract. The answer is **C**.

Think about how you can solve the problem

- Can you solve the problem with the information given?

- Pictures, charts, tables, and graphs may have the information you need.

- You may need to recall information not given.

- The answer choices may have information you need.

3. The table below shows the regular prices of some backpacks and the sale prices. Find a rule that describes the relationship shown in the table.

Backpack Prices

Regular Price	Sale Price
$24	$12
$18	$9
$14	$7
$10	$5

A Take $12 off the regular price.

B Get 2 backpacks for $5.

C Divide the regular price by 2.

D Multiply the regular price by 2.

 Test Tip **Get the information you need.**

Use the table to find a rule that works for each regular price and sale price. Then find the rule in the answer choices. The answer is **C**.

- You may need to write a number sentence and solve it.

- Some problems have two steps or more.

- You may need to look at relationships rather than compute.

- If the path to the solution isn't clear, choose a problem solving strategy and use it to solve the problem.

4. Mr. Chow has 8 days left to address 165 envelopes for a party. He has already addressed 93 envelopes. How many envelopes should he address each day in order to finish on time?

A 5   C 8

B 6   D 9

Test Tip **Decide on a plan.**

You will need more than one step to answer some problems. First, subtract to decide how many envelopes he has left to address. Then divide the number of envelopes he has left by 8, to find how many he should address each day. The answer is **D**.

Solve

Follow your plan, working logically and carefully

- Estimate your answer. Are any answer choices unreasonable?

- Use reasoning to find the most likely choices.

- Make sure you solved all steps needed to answer the problem.

- If your answer does not match any of the answer choices, check the numbers you used. Then check your computation.

---

5. The array below has an area of 12 square units.

   Which shows another array with an area of 12 square units?

   A

   B ▯▯▯▯▯

   C ▯▯▯▯▯▯▯▯

   D

Test Tip — **Eliminate choices.**

You can eliminate choices **B** and **C** because you can see at a glance they are fewer than 12 square units. Answer choice **A** has 3 rows of 6 squares, so must be 18 square units. **D** has 2 rows of 6 squares, or 12 square units. The answer is **D**.

- If your answer still does not match, look for another form of the number such as a decimal instead of a fraction.

- If answer choices are given as pictures, look at each one by itself while you cover the other three.

- Read answer choices that are statements and relate them to the problem one by one.

- Change your plan if it isn't working. Try a different strategy.

---

6. In which number sentence does 4 make the equation true?

   A ▇ $\times 20 = 5$

   B $20 \times 5 =$ ▇

   C ▇ $\div 5 = 20$

   D $20 \div$ ▇ $= 5$

Test Tip — **Choose the answer.**

Use 4 as the missing number in each answer choice to see if the equation is true. You might be able to tell without solving the equation whether it is true. The answer is **D**.

Take time to catch your mistakes

- Be sure you answered the question asked.

- Check that your answer fits the information in the problem.

- Check for important words you might have missed.

- Be sure you used all the information you needed.

- Check your computation by using a different method.

- Draw a picture when you are unsure of your answer.

7. Look at the 2 sets of numbers below.

Set J	Set K
3	5
6	10
9	15
12	20

Which number belongs in Set J and Set K?

A 18   C 30

B 27   D 35

Test Tip **Check your work.**

Look at your answer choice. Does it fit a rule for **both** sets of numbers shown? If not, check all the answer choices to find one that fits in both sets of numbers. The answer is **C**.

Tips for Short-Answer and Extended-Response Items

- Plan to spend from 3 to 5 minutes on each Short-Answer item and from 5 to 15 minutes on each Extended-Response item.

- Read the problem carefully and think about what you are asked to do. Plan how to organize your response.

- Short-Answer items will ask you to find a solution to a problem. Extended-Response items will ask you to use problem solving and reasoning skills to apply something you have learned.

- Think about how you solved the problem. You may be asked to use words, numbers, or pictures to explain how you found you answer.

- Leave time to look back at the problem, check your answer, and correct any mistakes.

Addition Facts

	K	L	M	N	O	P	Q	R
A	6 +7	9 +6	3 +5	8 +9	0 +7	2 +8	6 +4	7 +7
B	1 +6	8 +4	5 +1	2 +7	3 +3	8 +2	4 +5	2 +6
C	6 +6	3 +7	7 +8	4 +6	9 +0	4 +2	10 +4	3 +8
D	6 +1	5 +9	10 +6	5 +7	3 +9	9 +8	8 +7	8 +1
E	7 +6	7 +1	6 +9	4 +3	5 +5	8 +0	9 +5	2 +9
F	9 +1	8 +5	7 +0	8 +3	7 +2	4 +7	10 +5	4 +8
G	5 +3	9 +9	3 +6	7 +4	0 +8	4 +4	7 +10	6 +8
H	8 +6	10 +7	0 +9	7 +9	5 +6	8 +10	6 +5	9 +4
I	9 +7	8 +8	1 +9	5 +8	10 +9	6 +3	6 +2	9 +10
J	9 +2	7 +5	6 +0	10 +8	5 +4	4 +9	9 +3	10 +10

Subtraction Facts

	K	L	M	N	O	P	Q	R
A	13 − 4	7 − 1	9 − 7	9 − 9	11 − 5	6 − 3	12 − 7	8 − 5
B	8 − 8	16 − 8	15 − 6	10 − 2	6 − 5	8 − 7	14 − 4	11 − 9
C	9 − 5	12 − 8	15 − 8	11 − 7	14 − 8	18 − 9	15 − 5	8 − 1
D	10 − 4	16 − 10	13 − 9	9 − 1	7 − 2	7 − 0	13 − 8	6 − 4
E	10 − 9	9 − 6	17 − 9	7 − 3	6 − 0	11 − 8	8 − 6	9 − 4
F	8 − 4	13 − 6	11 − 2	15 − 7	19 − 10	12 − 3	17 − 8	7 − 5
G	9 − 8	13 − 7	7 − 4	15 − 9	8 − 2	10 − 6	14 − 7	12 − 5
H	10 − 7	6 − 6	8 − 0	12 − 4	14 − 6	11 − 4	6 − 2	17 − 7
I	13 − 5	12 − 9	16 − 7	7 − 6	10 − 5	11 − 3	12 − 6	14 − 9
J	10 − 8	11 − 6	14 − 5	16 − 9	9 − 3	5 − 4	18 − 10	20 − 10

Multiplication Facts

	K	L	M	N	O	P	Q	R
A	5 ×6	5 ×9	7 ×7	9 ×10	7 ×5	12 ×2	10 ×6	6 ×7
B	6 ×6	0 ×6	2 ×7	12 ×8	9 ×2	3 ×5	5 ×8	8 ×3
C	7 ×0	5 ×1	4 ×5	9 ×9	6 ×8	8 ×11	11 ×7	10 ×5
D	1 ×7	9 ×4	0 ×7	2 ×5	9 ×7	10 ×9	3 ×3	12 ×7
E	5 ×7	1 ×9	4 ×3	7 ×6	11 ×3	3 ×8	4 ×2	10 ×10
F	10 ×12	5 ×5	6 ×4	9 ×8	0 ×8	9 ×6	11 ×2	12 ×6
G	5 ×3	4 ×6	6 ×3	7 ×9	12 ×5	0 ×9	5 ×4	12 ×11
H	7 ×1	6 ×9	1 ×6	4 ×4	3 ×7	11 ×11	4 ×8	12 ×9
I	7 ×4	2 ×4	8 ×6	3 ×4	11 ×5	2 ×9	8 ×9	7 ×8
J	8 ×0	3 ×9	12 ×12	8 ×5	4 ×7	6 ×2	9 ×5	8 ×8

Division Facts

	K	L	M	N	O	P	Q	R
A	$7\overline{)56}$	$5\overline{)40}$	$6\overline{)24}$	$6\overline{)30}$	$6\overline{)18}$	$7\overline{)42}$	$8\overline{)16}$	$9\overline{)45}$
B	$3\overline{)9}$	$10\overline{)90}$	$1\overline{)1}$	$1\overline{)6}$	$10\overline{)100}$	$3\overline{)12}$	$10\overline{)70}$	$8\overline{)56}$
C	$6\overline{)48}$	$12\overline{)60}$	$4\overline{)32}$	$6\overline{)54}$	$7\overline{)0}$	$3\overline{)18}$	$9\overline{)90}$	$11\overline{)55}$
D	$2\overline{)16}$	$3\overline{)21}$	$5\overline{)30}$	$3\overline{)15}$	$11\overline{)110}$	$9\overline{)9}$	$8\overline{)64}$	$9\overline{)63}$
E	$4\overline{)28}$	$2\overline{)10}$	$9\overline{)18}$	$1\overline{)5}$	$7\overline{)63}$	$8\overline{)32}$	$2\overline{)8}$	$9\overline{)108}$
F	$8\overline{)24}$	$4\overline{)4}$	$2\overline{)14}$	$11\overline{)66}$	$8\overline{)72}$	$4\overline{)12}$	$7\overline{)21}$	$6\overline{)36}$
G	$12\overline{)36}$	$5\overline{)20}$	$7\overline{)28}$	$7\overline{)14}$	$4\overline{)24}$	$11\overline{)121}$	$9\overline{)36}$	$11\overline{)132}$
H	$9\overline{)27}$	$3\overline{)27}$	$7\overline{)49}$	$4\overline{)20}$	$9\overline{)72}$	$5\overline{)60}$	$8\overline{)88}$	$10\overline{)80}$
I	$4\overline{)44}$	$8\overline{)48}$	$5\overline{)35}$	$8\overline{)40}$	$5\overline{)10}$	$2\overline{)12}$	$10\overline{)60}$	$9\overline{)54}$
J	$10\overline{)120}$	$12\overline{)72}$	$9\overline{)81}$	$4\overline{)16}$	$1\overline{)7}$	$12\overline{)60}$	$12\overline{)96}$	$12\overline{)144}$

Table of Measures

METRIC

Length

1 centimeter (cm) = 10 millimeters (mm)

1 decimeter (dm) = 10 centimeters

1 meter (m) = 10 decimeters

1 kilometer (km) = 1,000 meters

Capacity

1 liter (L) = 1,000 milliliters (mL)

1 metric cup = 250 milliliters

Mass/Weight

1 gram (g) = 1,000 milligrams (mg)

1 gram = 100 centigrams (cg)

1 kilogram (kg) = 1,000 grams

CUSTOMARY

Length

1 foot (ft) = 12 inches (in.)

1 yard (yd) = 3 feet, or 36 inches

1 mile (mi) = 1,760 yards, or 5,280 feet

Capacity

1 tablespoon (tbsp) = 3 teaspoons (tsp)

1 cup (c) = 8 fluid ounces (fl oz)

1 pint (pt) = 2 cups

1 quart (qt) = 2 pints

1 gallon (gal) = 4 quarts

Mass/Weight

1 pound (lb) = 16 ounces (oz)

1 ton (T) = 2,000 pounds

TIME

1 minute (min) = 60 seconds (sec)

1 quarter hour = 15 minutes

1 half hour = 30 minutes

1 hour (hr) = 60 minutes

1 day = 24 hours

1 week (wk) = 7 days

1 year (yr) = 12 months (mo), or about 52 weeks

1 year = 365 days

1 leap year = 366 days

MONEY

1 penny = 1¢, or $0.01

1 nickel = 5¢, or $0.05

1 dime = 10¢, or $0.10

1 quarter = 25¢, or $0.25

1 half dollar = 50¢, or $0.50

1 dollar = 100¢, or $1.00

SYMBOLS

$<$	is less than	$\perp$	is perpendicular to
$>$	is greater than	$\parallel$	is parallel to
$\leq$	is less than or equal to	$\overleftrightarrow{AB}$	line AB
$\geq$	is greater than or equal to	$\overrightarrow{AB}$	ray AB
$=$	is equal to	$\overline{AB}$	line segment AB
$\neq$	is not equal to	$\angle ABC$	angle ABC
$\approx$	is approximately equal to	°	degree
¢	cent	°F	degrees Fahrenheit
$	dollar	°C	degrees Celsius
(2,3)	ordered pair (x,y)	$^{+}8$	positive 8
%	percent	$^{-}8$	negative 8

FORMULAS

Perimeter of polygon = sum of length of sides

Perimeter of rectangle $P = (2 \times l) + (2 \times w)$

Perimeter of square $P = 4 \times s$

Area of rectangle $A = l \times w$

Volume of rectangular prism $V = l \times w \times h$

Glossary

A

A.M. [ā•em′] **a.m.** The time between midnight and noon (p. 152)

acute angle [ə•kyo͞ot′ ang′əl] **ángulo agudo** An angle that measures greater than 0° and less than 90° (p. 515)
Example:

acute triangle [ə•kyo͞ot′ trī′ang•əl] **triángulo acutángulo** A triangle with three acute angles (p. 524)
Example:

addend [a′dend] **sumando** A number that is added to another in an addition problem
Example: 2 + 4 = 6;
2 and 4 are addends.

addition [ə•di′shən] **suma** The process of finding the total number of items when two or more groups of items are joined; the opposite operation of subtraction

angle [ang′əl] **ángulo** A figure formed by two line segments or rays that share the same endpoint (p. 514)
Example:

area [âr′ē•ə] **área** The number of square units needed to cover a surface (p. 640)
Example:

area = 9 square units

arrangement [ə•rānj′mənt] **ordenación** A choice in which the order of items is important (p. 683)

array [ə•rā′] **matriz** An arrangement of objects in rows and columns (p. 98)
Example:

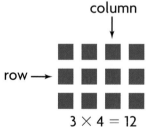

3 × 4 = 12

Associative Property of Addition [ə•sō′shē•ə•tiv prä′pər•tē əv ə•di′shən] **propiedad asociativa de la suma** The property that states you can group addends in different ways and still get the same sum (p. 64)
Example: 3 + (8 + 5) = (3 + 8) + 5

Associative Property of Multiplication [ə•sō′shē•ə•tiv prä′pər•tē əv mul•tə•plə•kā′shən] **propiedad asociativa de la multiplicación** The property that states you can group factors in different ways and still get the same product (p. 118)
Example: 3 × (4 × 2) = (3 × 4) × 2

bar graph [bär graf] **gráfica de barras** A graph that uses bars to show data (p. 204)
Example:

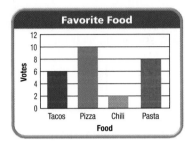

base [bās] **base** A polygon's side or a solid figure's face by which the figure is measured or named (p. 570)
Examples:

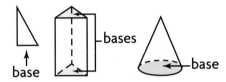

benchmark [bench'märk] **punto de referencia** A known number of things that helps you understand the size or amount of a different number of things (p. 15)

biased result [bī'əsed ri·zult'] **resultado parcial** A result of a survey is biased if some people are more likely to be asked to respond or a question suggests or leads to a specific response (p. 183)

billions [bil'yənz] **millardos** The period after millions

calendar [ka'lən·dər] **calendario** A table that shows the days, weeks, and months of a year (p. 158)

capacity [kə·pa'sə·tē] **capacidad** The amount a container can hold when filled (p. 610)
1 half gallon = 2 quarts

categorical data [ka·tə·gôr'i·kəl dā'tə] **datos categóricos** Data that can be sorted into different groups (p. 180)

center [sen'tər] **centro** The point inside a circle that is the same distance from each point on the circle (p. 530)
Example:

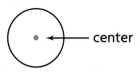

Word History

The word *center* comes from a Greek root, *kentron*, meaning "spur, or sharp, pointed object." A sharp point was used at a center point to fix the spot and a duller object was dragged around the center to draw the circle.

centigram (cg) [sen'tə·gram] **centigramo** A metric unit for measuring mass (p. 620)
100 centigrams = 1 gram

centimeter (cm) [sen'tə·mē·tər] **centímetro (cm)** A metric unit for measuring length or distance (p. 614)
100 centimeters = 1 meter
Example:

1 centimeter

certain [sər'tən] **seguro** An event is certain if it will always happen (p. 672)

chord [kôrd] **cuerda** A line segment with endpoints on a circle (p. 530)
Example:

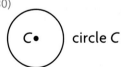

$\overline{AB}$ is a chord.

circle [sûr'kəl] **círculo** A closed figure made up of points that are the same distance from the center (p. 530)
Example:

circle C

circle graph [sûr'kəl graf] **gráfica circular** A graph in the shape of a circle that shows data as a whole made up of different parts (p. 208)
Example:

circumference [sər•kum'fər•əns] **circunferencia** The distance around a circle (p. 639)

clockwise [klok'wīz] **en el sentido de las manecillas del reloj** In the same direction in which the hands of a clock move (p. 546)

closed figure [klōzd fi'gyər] **figura cerrada** A figure that begins and ends at the same point
Examples:

clump [kləmp] **agrupamiento** A group of data values that are close together in a set of data (p. 190)

combination [käm•bə•nā'shən] **combinación** A choice in which the order of items does not matter (p. 682)

common multiple [kä'mən mul'tə•pəl] **múltiplo común** A number that is a multiple of two or more numbers (p. 375)

Commutative Property of Addition [kə•myoo'tə•tiv prä'pər•tē əv ədi'shən] **propiedad conmutativa de la suma** The property that states that when the order of two addends is changed, the sum is the same (p. 64)
Example: 4 + 5 = 5 + 4

Commutative Property of Multiplication [kə•myoo'tə•tiv prä'pər•tē əv mul•tə•plə•kā'shən] **propiedad conmutativa de la multiplicación** The property that states that when the order of two factors is changed, the product is the same (p. 98)
Example: 4 × 5 = 5 × 4

compare [kəm•pâr'] **comparar** To describe whether numbers are equal to, less than, or greater than each other (p. 12)

compass [kum'pəs] **compás** A tool used to construct circles (p. 530)

compatible numbers [käm•pa'tə•bəl num'bərz] **números compatibles** Numbers that are easy to compute mentally (p. 38)

composite number [kəm•pä'zət num'bər] **número compuesto** A whole number greater than 1 that has more than two factors (p. 378)
Example: 9 is composite since its factors are 1, 3, and 9.

cone [kōn] **cono** A solid, pointed figure that has a flat, round base (p. 570)
Example:

congruent [kən•groo'ənt] **congruente** Having the same size and shape (p. 542)
Example:

coordinate grid [kō•ôr'də•nət grid] **cuadrícula de coordenadas** A grid formed by a horizontal line called the *x*-axis and a vertical line called the *y*-axis (p. 210)
Example:

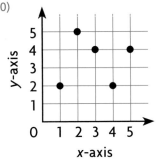

corner [kôr'nər] **esquina** See *vertex.*

counterclockwise [koun•ter•klok'wīz] **en sentido contrario a las manecillas del reloj** In the opposite direction in which the hands of a clock move (p. 546)

cube [kyoob] **cubo** A solid figure with six congruent square faces (p. 570)
Example:

cubic unit [kyoo'bik yoo'nət] **unidad cúbica** A unit of volume with dimensions of 1 unit × 1 unit × 1 unit (p. 654)

cup (c) [kup] **taza (t)** A customary unit used to measure capacity (p. 610)
8 ounces = 1 cup

cylinder [si'lən•dər] **cilindro** A solid figure that is shaped like a can (p. 570)
Example:

data [dā′tə] **datos** Information collected about people or things (p. 180)

decagon [de′kə•gän] **decágono** A polygon with ten sides and ten angles (p. 520)

decimal [de′sə•məl] **decimal** A number with one or more digits to the right of the decimal point (p. 458)

decimal point [de′sə•məl point] **punto decimal** A symbol used to separate dollars from cents in money amounts and to separate the ones and the tenths places in a decimal (p. 458)
Example: 6.4
↑ decimal point

decimeter (dm) [de′sə•mē•tər] **decímetro (dm)** A metric unit for measuring length or distance (p. 614)
10 decimeters = 1 meter

degree (°) [di•grē′] **grado (°)** The unit used for measuring angles and temperatures (p. 514)

degree Celsius (°C) [di•grē′ sel′sē•əs] **grado Celsius (°C)** A metric unit for measuring temperature (p. 164)

degree Fahrenheit (°F) [di•grē′ fâr′ən•hīt] **grado Fahrenheit (°F)** A standard unit for measuring temperature (p. 164)

denominator [di•nä′mə•nā•tər] **denominador** The number below the bar in a fraction that tells how many equal parts are in the whole or in the group (p. 402)
Example: $\frac{3}{4}$ ← denominator

diagonal [dī•a′gə•nəl] **diagonal** A line segment that connects two vertices of a polygon that are not next to each other (p. 586)

diameter [dī•am′ə•tər] **diámetro** A line segment that passes through the center of a circle and has endpoints on the circle (p. 530)
Example:

diameter

difference [di′fər•əns] **diferencia** The answer to a subtraction problem (p. 38)

digit [di′jət] **dígito** Any one of the ten symbols 0, 1, 2, 3, 4, 5, 6, 7, 8, or 9 used to write numbers (p. 4)

dimension [də•men′shən] **dimensión** A measure in one direction (p. 512)

Distributive Property [di•stri′byə•tiv prä′pər•tē] **propiedad distributiva** The property that states that multiplying a sum by a number is the same as multiplying each addend by the number and then adding the products (p. 118)
Example: 5 × (10 + 6) = (5 × 10) + (5 × 6)

divide [di•vīd′] **dividir** To separate into equal groups; the opposite operation of multiplication (p. 92)

dividend [di′və•dend] **dividendo** The number that is to be divided in a division problem (p. 94)
Example: 36 ÷ 6; 6)36; the dividend is 36.

divisible [də•vi′zə•bəl] **divisible** Capable of being divided so that the quotient is a counting number and the remainder is zero (p. 376)
Example: 21 is divisible by 3.

division [də•vi′zhən] **división** The process of sharing a number of items to find how many groups can be made or how many items will be in each group; the opposite operation of multiplication

divisor [də•vī′zər] **divisor** The number that divides the dividend (p. 94)
Example: 15 ÷ 3; 3)15; the divisor is 3.

double-bar graph [du′bəl bär graf] **gráfica de doble barra** A graph used to compare similar kinds of data (p. 206)
Example:

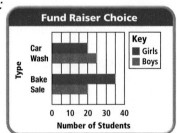

doubles [du′bəlz] **dobles** Two addends that are the same number

E

edge [ej] **arista** The line segment where two faces of a solid figure meet (p. 570)
Example:
edge

elapsed time [i·lapst′ tīm] **tiempo transcurrido** The time that passes from the start of an activity to the end of that activity (p. 154)

endpoint [end′point] **extremo** The point at either end of a line segment or the starting point of a ray (p. 512)

equal to (=) [ē′kwəl too͞] **igual a** Having the same value (p. 12)
Example: 4 + 4 is equal to 3 + 5.

equally likely [ē′kwə·lē lī′klē] **igualmente probable** Having the same chance of happening (p. 672)

equation [i·kwā′zhən] **ecuación** A number sentence which shows that two quantities are equal (p. 70)
Example: 4 + 5 = 9

equilateral triangle [ē·kwə·la′tə·rəl trī′ang·əl] **triángulo equilátero** A triangle with 3 equal, or congruent, sides (p. 524)
Example:

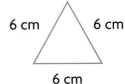

6 cm   6 cm

6 cm

equivalent [ē·kwiv′ə·lənt] **equivalente** Having the same value or naming the same amount

equivalent decimals [ē·kwiv′ə·lənt de′sə·məlz] **decimales equivalentes** Two or more decimals that name the same amount (p. 464)

equivalent fractions [ē·kwiv′ə·lənt frak′shənz] **fracciones equivalentes** Two or more fractions that name the same amount (p. 406)
Example: 3/4 and 6/8 name the same amount.

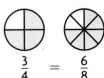

$$\frac{3}{4} = \frac{6}{8}$$

estimate [es′tə·māt] *verb* **estimar** To find an answer that is close to the exact amount (p. 38)

estimate [es′tə·mət] *noun* **estimación** A number close to an exact amount (p. 38)

even [ē′vən] **par** A whole number that has a 0, 2, 4, 6, or 8 in the ones place (p. 112)

event [i·vent′] **suceso** One outcome or a combination of outcomes in an experiment (p. 672)

expanded form [ik·span′dəd fôrm] **forma desarrollada** A way to write numbers by showing the value of each digit (p. 4)
Example: 253 = 200 + 50 + 3

experimental probability [ik·sper·ə·men′tal prä·bə·bil′ə·tē] **probabilidad experimental** The ratio of the number of times the event occurs to the total number of trials or times the activity is performed (p. 680)
experimental probability = $\frac{\text{number of times event occurs}}{\text{total number of trials}}$

expression [ik·spre′shən] **expresión** A part of a number sentence that has numbers and operation signs but does not have an equal sign (p. 66)

F

face [fās] **cara** A polygon that is a flat surface of a solid figure (p. 570)
Example:

— face

fact family [fakt fam′ə·lē] **familia de operaciones** A set of related multiplication and division, or addition and subtraction, equations (p. 32)
Example: 7 × 8 = 56; 8 × 7 = 56;
56 ÷ 7 = 8; 56 ÷ 8 = 7

factor [fak′tər] **factor** A number that is multiplied by another number to find a product (p. 94)

factor tree [fak′tər trē] **árbol de factores** A diagram that shows the prime factors of a number (p. 392)
Example:

30
5 × 6
5 × 2 × 3

fair [fâr] **equitativo** Each outcome is equally likely to happen (p. 679)

flip [flip] **inversión** See *reflection.*

fluid ounce (fl oz) [floo͞′əd ouns] **onza fluida** A customary unit used to measure liquid capacity (p. 610)
1 cup = 8 fluid ounces

foot (ft) [foot] **pie** A customary unit used for measuring length or distance (p. 602)
1 foot = 12 inches

formula [fôr′myə•lə] **fórmula** A set of symbols that expresses a mathematical rule (p. 636)
Example: $A = l \times w$

fraction [frak′shən] **fracción** A number that names a part of a whole or part of a group (p. 402)
Example:

$\frac{1}{3}$

frequency [frē′kwen•sē] **frecuencia** The number of times an event occurs (p. 180)

frequency table [frē′kwen•sē tā′bəl] **tabla de frecuencia** A table that uses numbers to record data about how often something happens (p. 180)
Example:

Favorite Color	
Color	Number
Blue	10
Red	7
Green	8

front-end estimation [frunt end es•tə•mā′shən] **estimación por el primer dígito** A method of estimating sums or differences by using the front digits of the numbers (p. 38)
Example:
$$\begin{array}{r} 245 \\ +\ 386 \\ \hline 500 \end{array}$$

function table [funk′shən tā′bəl] **tabla de funciones** A table that matches each input value with an output value. The output values are determined by the function. (p. 226)

gallon (gal) [ga′lən] **galón (gal)** A customary unit for measuring capacity (p. 610)
4 quarts = 1 gallon

gram (g) [gram] **gramo (g)** A unit for measuring mass (p. 620)
1,000 grams = 1 kilogram

greater than (>) [grā′tər than] **mayor que** A symbol used to compare two quantities, with the greater quantity given first (p. 12)
Example: 6 > 4

greater than or equal to (≥) [grā′tər than ôr ē•kwəl tōō] **mayor que o igual a** A symbol used to compare two quantities when the first is greater than or equal to the second (p. 136)
Example: 4 + 5 ≥ 7

grid [grid] **cuadrícula** Evenly divided and equally spaced squares on a figure or flat surface

Grouping Property of Addition [grōō′ping prä′pər•tē əv ə•di′shən] **propiedad de agrupación de la suma** See *Associative Property of Addition.*

Grouping Property of Multiplication [grōō′ping prä′pər•tē əv mul•tə•plə•kā′shən] **propiedad de agrupación de la multiplicación** See *Associative Property of Multiplication.*

H

half hour [haf our] **media hora** 30 minutes (p. 152)
Example: Between 4:00 and 4:30 is one half hour.

hexagon [hek′sə•gän] **hexágono** A polygon with six sides and six angles (p. 520)
Examples:

horizontal [hôr•ə•zän′təl] **horizontal** The direction from left to right

hour (hr) [our] **hora (hr)** A unit used to measure time (p. 152) 60 minutes = 1 hour

hundredth [hun′drədth] **centésimo** One of one hundred equal parts (p. 458)
Example:

hundredth

I

Identity Property of Addition [ī•den′tə•tē prä′pər•tē əv ə•di′shən] **propiedad de identidad de la suma** The property that states that when you add zero to any number, the sum is that number (p. 64)
Example: 16 + 0 = 16

Identity Property of Multiplication [ī·den′tə·tē prä′pər·tē əv mul·tə·plə·kā′shən] **propiedad de identidad de la multiplicación** The property that states that the product of any number and 1 is that number (p. 102)
Example: $9 \times 1 = 9$

impossible [im·pä′sə·bəl] **imposible** Never able to happen (p. 672)

improper fraction [imv·prä′pər frak′shən] **fracción impropia** A fraction greater than 1 (p. 414)

inch (in.) [inch] **pulgada (pulg)** A customary unit used for measuring length or distance (p. 602)
Example:

←——1 inch——→

inequality [in·i·kwol′ə·tē] **desigualdad** A mathematical sentence that uses the symbols $<$, $>$, $\le$, $\ge$, or $\ne$ and shows a relationship between two quantities that are not equivalent (p. 136)
Example: $4 < 9 - 3$

intersecting lines [in·tər·sek′ting līnz] **líneas secantes** Lines that cross each other at exactly one point (p. 518)
Example:

interval [in′tər·vəl] **intervalo** The distance between one number and the next on the scale of a graph (p. 192)

inverse operations [in′vərs ä·pə·rā′shənz] **operaciones inversas** Operations that undo each other. Addition and subtraction are inverse operations. Multiplication and division are inverse operations. (pp. 32, 94)
Example: $6 \times 8 = 48$ and $48 \div 6 = 8$

isosceles triangle [ī·sä′sə·lēz trī′ang·əl] **triángulo isósceles** A triangle with two equal, or congruent, sides (p. 524)
Example:

10 in. ╱╲ 10 in.
7 in.

Word History

When you look at the sides of an *isosceles* triangle, you see that two sides are equal in length. The Greek root *iso-* means "same or equal," and *skelos* means "leg."

K

key [kē] **clave** The part of a map or graph that explains the symbols

kilogram (kg) [ki′lə·gram] **kilogramo (kg)** A metric unit for measuring mass (p. 620)
1 kilogram = 1,000 grams

kilometer (km) [kə·lä′mə·tər] **kilómetro (km)** A metric unit for measuring length or distance (p. 614) 1,000 meters = 1 kilometer

L

leaf [lēf] **hoja** A ones digit in a stem-and-leaf plot (p. 198)

less than (<) [les ŧħan] **menor que** A symbol used to compare two numbers, with the lesser number given first (p. 12)
Example: $3 < 7$

less than or equal to (≤) [les ŧħan ôr ē′kwəl tōō] **menor que o igual a** A symbol used to compare quantities, when the first is less than or equal to the second (p. 136)
Example: $8 \le 14 - 5$

like fractions [līk frak′shənz] **fracciones semejantes** Fractions with the same denominator (p. 432)

likely [līk′lē] **probable** Having a greater than even chance of happening (p. 672)

line [līn] **línea** A straight path of points in a plane that continues without end in both directions with no endpoints (p. 512)
Example:
←•————————•→
S   T

line graph [līn graf] **gráfica lineal** A graph that uses line segments to show how data changes over a period of time (p. 214)
Example:

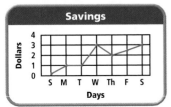
Savings

line plot [līn plät] **diagrama de puntos** A graph that shows the frequency of data along a number line (p. 190)
Example:

```
              X
      X   X       X
      X   X   X   X   X
      ├───┼───┼───┼───┼───┤
      1   2   3   4   5
          Books Read
```

line segment [līn seg'mənt] **segmento** A part of a line that includes two points called endpoints and all the points between them (p. 512)
Example:

```
      ●───────────────────●
      A                   B
```

line symmetry [līn si'mə•trē] **simetría axial** What a figure has if it can be folded about a line so that its two parts match exactly (p. 547)
Example:

line of symmetry ⟶ △

linear units [li'nē•ər yoo'nəts] **unidades lineales** Units that measure length, width, height, or distance (p. 602)

liter (L) [lē'tər] **litro (L)** A metric unit for measuring capacity (p. 622)
1 liter = 1,000 milliliters

mass [mas] **masa** The amount of matter in an object (p. 620)

mathematical probability [math•ma'ti•kəl prä•bə•bi'lə•tē] **probabilidad matemática** A comparison of the number of favorable outcomes to the number of possible outcomes of an event (p. 676)

mean [mēn] **media** The number found by dividing the sum of the set by the number of addends (p. 186)

median [mē'dē•ən] **mediana** The middle number in an ordered set of data (p. 186)

meter (m) [mē'tər] **metro (m)** A metric unit for measuring length or distance (p. 614)
100 centimeters = 1 meter

mile (mi) [mīl] **milla (mi)** A customary unit for measuring length or distance (p. 602)
5,280 feet = 1 mile

milligram (mg) [mi'lə•gram] **miligramo (mg)** A metric unit for measuring mass (p. 620)
1,000 milligrams = 1 gram

milliliter (mL) [mi'lə•lē•tər] **mililitro (mL)** A metric unit for measuring capacity (p. 622)
1,000 milliliters = 1 liter

millimeter (mm) [mi'lə•mē•tər] **milímetro (mm)** A metric unit for measuring length or distance (p. 614) 1 centimeter = 10 millimeters

millions [mil'yənz] **millones** The period after thousands (p. 8)

minute (min) [mi'nət] **minuto (min)** A unit to measure short amounts of time (p. 152)
60 seconds = 1 minute

mixed number [mikst num'bər] **número mixto** An amount given as a whole number and a fraction (p. 414)

mode [mōd] **moda** The number(s) or item(s) that occur most often in a set of data (p. 186)

multiple [mul'tə•pəl] **múltiplo** The product of two counting numbers is called a multiple of each of those numbers (p. 104)

multiplication [mul•tə•plə•kā'shən] **multiplicación** A process to find the total number of items in equal-size groups, or to find the total number of items in a given number of groups when each group contains the same number of items; multiplication is the inverse of division

multiply [mul'tə•plī] **multiplicar** When you combine equal groups, you can multiply to find how many in all; the opposite operation of division (p. 92)

multistep problem [mul'ti•step prä'bləm] **problema de varios pasos** A problem requiring more than one step to solve

negative numbers [ne'gə•tiv num'bərz] **números negativos** All the numbers to the left of zero on the number line; negative numbers are less than zero (p. 168)

net [net] **plantilla** A two-dimensional pattern that can be folded to make a three-dimensional figure (p. 578)
Example:

network [net′wərk] **gráfica de red** A graph made up of a set of points and paths joining them (p. 660)

not equal to (≠) [nät ē′kwəl tōō] **no igual a** A symbol that indicates one quantity is not equal to another (p. 13)
Example: 12 × 3 ≠ 38

number line [num′bər līn] **recta numérica** A line on which numbers can be located
Example:

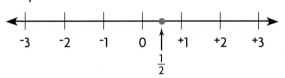

numerator [nōō′mə•rā•tər] **numerador** The number above the bar in a fraction that tells how many parts of the whole or group are being considered (p. 402)

Example: $\frac{2}{3}$ ← numerator

numerical data [nōō•mer′i•kəl dā′tə] **datos numéricos** Data that can be counted or measured (p. 180)

obtuse angle [äb•tōōs′ ang′əl] **ángulo obtuso** An angle that measures greater than 90° and less than 180° (p. 515)
Example:

> **Word History**
>
> The Latin prefix *ob-* means "against." When combined with *-tuse*, meaning "to beat," the word *obtuse* means "to beat against." This makes sense when you look at an obtuse angle because the angle is not sharp or acute. The angle has been beaten against and become blunt and rounded.

obtuse triangle [äb•tōōs′ trī′ang•əl] **triángulo obtusángulo** A triangle with one obtuse angle (p. 524)
Example:

octagon [äk′tə•gän] **octágono** A polygon with eight sides and eight angles (p. 520)
Examples:

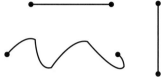

odd [od] **impar** A whole number that has a 1, 3, 5, 7, or 9 in the ones place (p. 112)

one-dimensional [wən′ də•men(t)′shə•nəl] **unidimensional** A measure in only one direction, such as length (p. 512)
Examples:

open figure [ō′pən fi′gyər] **figura abierta** A figure that does not begin and end at the same point
Examples:

order [ôr′dər] **orden** A particular arrangement or placement of things one after the other (p. 16)

order of operations [ôr′dər əv ä•pə•rā′shənz] **orden de las operaciones** A special set of rules that gives the order in which calculations are done in an expression (p. 126)

Order Property of Addition [ôr′dər prä′pər•tē əv ə•di′shən] **propiedad de orden de la suma** See *Commutative Property of Addition*.

Order Property of Multiplication [ôr′dər prä′pər•tē əv mul•tə•plə•kā′shən] **propiedad de orden de la multiplicación** See *Commutative Property of Multiplication*.

ordered pair [ôr′dərd pâr] **par ordenado** A pair of numbers used to locate a point on a coordinate grid. The first number tells how far to move horizontally, and the second number tells how far to move vertically. (p. 210)

origin [ôr′ə•jən] **origen** The point where the *x*-axis and the *y*-axis in the coordinate plane intersect, (0,0) (p. 210)

ounce (oz) [ouns] **onza** A customary unit for measuring weight (p. 608)
16 ounces = 1 pound

outcome [out′kum] **resultado** A possible result of an experiment (p. 666)

overestimate [ō•vər•es′tə•mət] **sobrestimar** An estimate that is greater than the exact answer (p. 41)

P.M. [pē•em′] **p.m.** The time between noon and midnight (p. 152)

parallel lines [par′ə•lel līnz] **líneas paralelas** Lines in the same plane that never intersect and are always the same distance apart (p. 518)
Example:

Word History

Euclid, an early Greek mathematician, was one of the first to explore the idea of parallel lines. The prefix *para-* means "beside or alongside." This prefix helps you understand the meaning of the word *parallel*.

parallelogram [par•ə•lel′ə•gram] **paralelogramo** A quadrilateral whose opposite sides are parallel and equal, or congruent (p. 526)
Example:

parentheses [pə•ren′thə•sēz] **paréntesis** The symbols used to show which operation or operations in an expression should be done first (p. 64)

partial product [pär′shəl prä′dəkt] **producto parcial** A method of multiplying in which the ones, tens, hundreds, and so on are multiplied separately and then the products are added together (p. 248)

pattern [pat′ərn] **patrón** An ordered set of numbers or objects; the order helps you predict what will come next (p. 8)
Example: 2, 4, 6, 8, 10

pattern unit [pat′ərn yōō′nət] **unidad de patrón** The part of a pattern that repeats (p. 386)
Example:

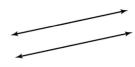

pattern unit

pentagon [pen′tə•gän] **pentágono** A polygon with five sides and five angles (p. 520)
Examples:

percent [pər•sent′] **porcentaje** The ratio of a number to 100; *percent* means "per hundred" (p. 478)

perimeter [pə•ri′mə•tər] **perímetro** The distance around a figure (pp. 78, 634)

period [pir′ē•əd] **período** Each group of three digits separated by commas in a multidigit number (p. 4)
Example: 85,643,900 has three periods.

permutation [pûr•myōō•tā′shən] **permutación** A choice in which the order of items is important (p. 685)

perpendicular lines [pər•pən•di′kyə•lər līnz] **líneas perpendiculares** Two lines that intersect to form four right angles (p. 518)
Example:

perspective [pur•spək′tiv] **perspectiva** A drawing or painting technique used to make three-dimensional objects on a flat surface appear to have depth and distance; a way of seeing and judging objects in relation to one another (p. 577)

pictograph [pik′tə•graf] **pictografía** A graph that uses symbols to show and compare information (p. 362)
Example:

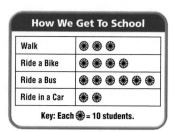

pint (pt) [pīnt] **pinta (pt)** A customary unit for measuring capacity (p. 610)
2 cups = 1 pint

place value [plās val′yōō] **valor posicional** The value of a digit in a number, based on the location of the digit (p. 12)

plane [plān] **plano** A flat surface that extends without end in all directions (p. 512)
Example:

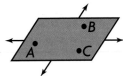

plane figure [plān fi′gyər] **figura plana** A figure that lies in a plane

point [point] **punto** An exact location in space (p. 512)

polygon [pä′lē·gän] **polígono** A closed plane figure formed by three or more straight sides that are line segments. (p. 520)
Examples:

Polygons   Not Polygons

positive numbers [pä′zə·tiv num′bərz] **números positivos** All the numbers to the right of zero on the number line; positive numbers are greater than 0 (p. 168)

possible [pos′ə·bəl] **posible** Having a chance of happening (p. 672)

pound (lb) [pound] **libra (lb)** A customary unit for measuring weight (p. 608)
16 ounces = 1 pound

predict [pri·dikt′] **predecir** To make a reasonable guess about what will happen (p. 672)

prime factor [prīm fak′tər] **factor primo** A factor that is a prime number (p. 392)

prime number [prīm num′bər] **número primo** A whole number greater than 1 that has only two factors: 1 and itself (p. 378)
Examples: 2, 3, 5, 7, 11, 13, 17, and 19 are prime numbers. 1 is not a prime number.

probability [prä·bə·bi′lə·tē] **probabilidad** The likelihood that an event will happen

product [prä′dəkt] **producto** The answer to a multiplication problem (p. 94)

proportion [prə·pôr′shən] **proporción** An equation that shows that two ratios are equal (p. 426)
Examples: $\frac{1}{3} = \frac{3}{9}$

protractor [prō′trak·tər] **transportador** A tool for measuring the size of an angle (p. 514)

pyramid [pir′ə·mid] **pirámide** A solid figure with a polygon base and triangular sides that meet at a single point
Example:

Q

quadrilateral [kwä·drə·la′tə·rəl] **cuadrilátero** A polygon with four sides and four angles (p. 520)

quart (qt) [kwôrt] **cuarto (ct)** A customary unit for measuring capacity (p. 610)
2 pints = 1 quart

quarter hour [kwôr′tər our] **cuarto de hora** 15 minutes (p. 152)
Example: Between 4:00 and 4:15 is one quarter hour

quotient [kwō′shənt] **cociente** The number, not including the remainder, that results from dividing (p. 94)
Example: 8 ÷ 4 = 2; 2 is the quotient.

R

radius [rā′dē·əs] **radio** A line segment with one endpoint at the center of a circle and the other endpoint on the circle (p. 530)
Example:

range [rānj] **rango** The difference between the greatest and the least number in a set of data (p. 190)

ratio [rā′shē·ō] **razón** The comparison of two numbers by division (p. 406)

ray [rā] **rayo** A part of a line; it has one endpoint and continues without end in one direction (p. 512)
Example:

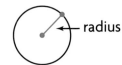

rectangle [rek'tang·gəl] **rectángulo** A parallelogram with opposite sides that are equal, or congruent, and with four right angles (p. 526)
Example:

rectangular prism [rek·tang'gyə·lər pri'zəm] **prisma rectangular** A solid figure in which all six faces are rectangles (p. 570)
Example:

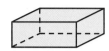

rectangular pyramid [rek·tang'gyə·lər pir'ə·mid] **pirámide rectangular** A pyramid with a rectangular base and with four triangular faces (p. 570)
Example:

reflection (flip) [ri·flek'shən] **reflexión (inversión)** A movement of a figure to a new position by flipping the figure over a line (p. 542)

regroup [rē·grŏŏp'] **reagrupar** To exchange amounts of equal value to rename a number
Example: 5 + 8 = 13 ones or 1 ten 3 ones

regular polygon [reg'yə·lər pä'lē·gän] **polígono regular** A polygon that has sides that are equal in length and all angles equal in measure (p. 520)
Examples:

remainder [ri·mān'dər] **residuo** The amount left over when a number cannot be divided equally (p. 306)

rhombus [räm'bəs] **rombo** A parallelogram with four equal, or congruent, sides (p. 526)
Example:

right angle [rīt ang'əl] **ángulo recto** An angle that forms a square corner and has a measure of 90° (p. 514)
Example:

right triangle [rīt trī'ang·əl] **triángulo rectángulo** A triangle with one right angle (p. 524)
Example:

rotation (turn) [rō·tā'shən] **rotacion (giro)** A movement of a figure to a new position by rotating the figure around a point (p. 550)
Example:

point of rotation

rotational symmetry [rō·tā'shən·əl si'mə·trē] **simetría rotacional** What a figure has if it can be turned about a central point and still look the same in at least two positions (p. 547)

round [round] **redondear** To replace a number with another number that tells about how many or how much (p. 34)

S

scale [skāl] **escala** A series of numbers placed at fixed distances on a graph to help label the graph (p. 192)

scalene triangle [skā'lēn trī'ang·əl] **triángulo escaleno** A triangle with no equal, or congruent, sides (p. 524)
Example:

13 cm   30 cm   18 cm

second (sec) [se'kənd] **segundo (seg)** A small unit of time (p. 152)
60 seconds = 1 minute

similar [si'mə·lər] **semejante** Having the same shape but possibly different size (p. 542)
Example:

simplest form [sim'pləst fôrm] **mínima expresión** A fraction is in simplest form when 1 is the only number that can divide evenly into the numerator and the denominator (p. 406)

slide [slīd] **traslación** See *translation.* (p. 542)

solid figure [so'ləd fi'gyər] **cuerpo geométrico** A three-dimensional figure

sphere [sfēr] **esfera** A round object whose curved surface is the same distance from the center to all its points (p. 570)
Example:

square [skwâr] **cuadrado** A parallelogram with four equal, or congruent, sides and four right angles (p. 526)
Example:

square number [skwâr num'bər] **número cuadrado** The product of a number and itself (p. 104)
Example: 2 × 2 = 4, so 4 is a square number.

square pyramid [skwâr pir'ə•mid] **pirámide cuadrada** A pyramid with a square base and with four triangular faces (p. 570)
Example:

square unit (sq un) [skwâr yoo'nət] **unidad cuadrada** A unit of area with dimensions of 1 unit × 1 unit (p. 640)

standard form [stan'dərd fôrm] **forma normal** A way to write numbers by using digits (p. 4)
Example: 3,540 ← standard form

stem [stem] **tallo** A tens digit in a stem-and-leaf plot (p. 198)

stem-and-leaf plot [stem ənd lēf plot] **diagrama de tallo y hojas** A data display that shows groups of data arranged by place value (p. 198)
Example:

Number of Tickets Sold

Stem	Leaves			
1	1	2	4	
2	0	3	4	5
3	4	5	7	

straight angle [strāt ang'el] **ángulo llano** An angle whose measure is 180° (p. 515)
Example:

subtraction [səb•trak'shən] **resta** The process of finding how many are left when a number of items are taken away from a group of items; the process of finding the difference when two groups are compared; the opposite operation of addition

sum [sum] **suma o total** The answer to an addition problem (p. 38)

surface area [sur'fəs âr'ē•ə] **área total** The sum of the areas of all the faces of a solid figure (p. 643)

survey [sûr'vā] **encuesta** A method of gathering information (p. 180)

T

tablespoon (tbsp) [tā'bəl•spoon] **cucharada (cda)** A customary unit used for measuring capacity 3 teaspoons = 1 tablespoon (p. 610)

tally table [ta'lē tā'bəl] **tabla de conteo** A table that uses tally marks to record data (p. 180)

Word History

Some people keep score in card games by making marks on paper (IIII). These marks are known as tally marks. The word *tally* is related to *tailor*, from the Latin *talea*, meaning "one who cuts." In early times, a method of keeping count was by cutting marks into a piece of wood or bone.

teaspoon (tsp) [tē'spoon] **cucharadita (cdta)** A customary unit used for measuring capacity 1 tablespoon = 3 teaspoons (p. 610)

tenth [tenth] **décimo** One of ten equal parts (p. 458)
Example:

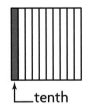
tenth

tessellation [tes•ə•lā'shən] **teselación** A repeating pattern of closed figures that covers a surface with no gaps and no overlaps (p. 558)

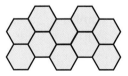

thousandth [thou'zəndth] **milésimo** One of one thousand equal parts (p. 462)

three-dimensional [thrē·də·men'shən·əl] **tridimensional** Measured in three directions, such as length, width, and height (p. 570)
Example:

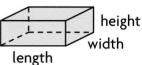

time line [tīm līn] **línea cronológica** A schedule of events or an ordered list of historic moments (p. 162)

ton (T) [tun] **tonelada (T)** A customary unit for measuring weight (p. 608)
2,000 pounds = 1 ton

transformation [trans·fər·mā'shən] **transformación** The movement of a figure by a translation, reflection, or rotation (p. 550)

translation [trans·lā'shən] **traslación** A movement of a figure to a new position along a straight line (p. 550)
Example:

trapezoid [tra'pə·zoid] **trapecio** A quadrilateral with exactly one pair of parallel sides (p. 526)
Examples:

tree diagram [trē dī'ə·gram] **diagrama de árbol** An organized list that shows all possible outcomes of an event (p. 682)
Example:

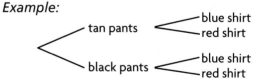

trends [trendz] **tendencias** On a graph, areas where the data increase, decrease, or stay the same over time (p. 214)

triangle [trī'ang·gəl] **triángulo** A polygon with three sides and three angles (p. 520)
Examples:

triangular prism [trī·ang'gyə·lər pri'zəm] **prisma triangular** A solid figure that has two triangular bases and three rectangular faces (p. 570)
Example:

triangular pyramid [trī·ang'gyə·lər pir'ə·mid] **pirámide triangular** A pyramid that has a triangular base and three triangular faces (p. 570)
Example:

turn [tûrn] **giro** See *rotation.*

24-hour clock [twen·tē·fōr our klok'] **reloj de 24 horas** A clock that measures time from midnight and is divided into 24 hours; does not use A.M. or P.M. (p. 174)
Example:

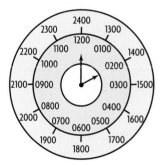

two-dimensional [tōō·də·men'shən·əl] **bidimensional** Measured in two directions, such as length and width (p. 512)
Example:

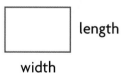

 U

unbiased result [un·bi'əsed ri·zult'] **resultado imparcial** A result of a survey is unbiased if every person has an equal chance of being asked to respond or a question does not suggest or lead to a specific response (p. 183)

underestimate [un·dər·es'tə·mət] **subestimar** An estimate that is less than the exact answer (p. 41)

unfair [un•far, fer] **no equitativo** One or more outcomes are more likely to happen then another (p. 679)

unit fraction [yo͞o′nit frak′shən] **fracción unitaria** A fraction that has a numerator of one (p. 402)

unlike fractions [un•līk′ frak′shənz] **fracciones no semejantes** Fractions with different denominators (p. 448)
Examples: $\frac{3}{4}$ and $\frac{2}{5}$ are unlike fractions.

unlikely [un•lī′klē] **poco probable** Having a less than even chance of happening (p. 672)

variable [vâr′ē•ə•bəl] **variable** A letter or symbol that stands for a number or numbers (p. 66)

Venn diagram [ven dī′ə•gram] **diagrama de Venn** A diagram that shows relationships among sets of things (p. 184)
Example:

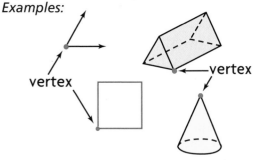

vertex [vûr′teks] **vértice** The point at which two rays of an angle meet or two (or more) line segments meet in a plane figure, or where three or more edges meet in a solid figure; the top point of a cone (p. 570)
Examples:

vertex

vertex

vertex

vertex-edge graph [vûr′teks ej graf] **gráfica de vértices** A graph made up of a set of points and paths joining them (p. 688)

vertical [vûr′ti•kəl] **vertical** The direction from top to bottom

volume [väl′yo͞om] **volumen** The measure of the amount of space a solid figure occupies (p. 654)

weight [wāt] **peso** How heavy an object is (p. 608)

whole number [hōl num′bər] **número entero** One of the numbers 0, 1, 2, 3, 4 . . . ; the set of whole numbers goes on without end

word form [wûrd fôrm] **en palabras** A way to write numbers by using words (p. 4)
Example: Sixty-two million, four hundred fifty-three thousand, two hundred twelve

x-axis [eks′ak•səs] **eje de la x** The horizontal line on a coordinate grid or plane (p. 210)

x-coordinate [eks•kō•ôr′də•nət] **coordenada x** The first number in an ordered pair; it tells the distance to move horizontally (p. 210)

y-axis [wī′ak•səs] **eje de la y** The vertical line on a coordinate grid or plane (p. 210)

y-coordinate [wī•kō•ôr′də•nət] **coordenada y** The second number in an ordered pair; it tells the distance to move vertically (p. 210)

yard (yd) [yärd] **yarda (yd)** A customary unit for measuring length or distance (p. 602)
3 feet = 1 yard

Zero Property of Multiplication [zē′rō prä′pər•tē əv mul•tə•plə•kā′shən] **propiedad del cero de la multiplicación** The property that states that the product of 0 and any number is 0 (p. 118)
Example: $0 \times 8 = 0$

Index

estimating and measuring in, 602–605, 608–609, 610–611

Fahrenheit temperature, 164–167

length/distance
  feet, 602–605
  inches, 602–605
  miles, 602–605
  yards, 602–605

weight
  ounces, 608–609
  pounds, 608–609
  tons, 608–609

See also Measurement

Cylinders, 570–573

D

Data
analyzing, 180–183, 184–185, 190–191, 192–193, 204–205, 206–207, 208–209, 214–215, 222–225
categorical, 180–183, 218–221, 222–225
clumps, 190
collecting, 180–183
comparing, 189, 206–207
frequency tables, 180–183, 186–189
graphing, 206–207, 216–217, 218–221, 226–229, 230–231
graphs
  bar, 204–205, 206–207, 218–221, 222–225
  circle, 208–209, 222–225, 234
  coordinate. See Coordinate grids
  double-bar, 206–207
  line, 214–215, 216–217, 218–221, 222–225
  one variable, 204–205, 208–209, 214–215, 222–225
  pictographs, 218–221, 222–225
  two variables, 206–207
interpreting, 184–185, 204–205, 206–207, 208–209, 214–215, 216–217
intervals, 192–193, 206–207, 216–217
line plots, 190–191, 218–221, 222–225
making tables, 133, 379, 498, 532, 612, 624–625
mean of, 186–189, 191
median of, 186–189, 191
mode of, 186–189, 191
numerical, 180–183, 222
organized lists, 20, 313, 498, 668–671
organizing, 180–183, 218–221, 230
outcomes, 666–667, 672–675
range and, 190–191
representing, 190–191, 198, 204–205, 206–207, 208–209, 214–215, 216–217, 222–225, 666–667, 676–679, 680–681, 682–685
review, H10–H12
scale and, 192–193, 206–207, 216–217
schedules, 668

surveys, 180–183, 234
tally tables, 180–183
tree diagrams, 682–685
Venn diagrams, 20, 184–185, 374, 473
See also Problem solving activities, Use Data

Days, 152–153, 158–159, 160–161

Decagons, 520–523

Decimal fractions. *See* Decimals

Decimal point, 458

Decimals, 458
adding, 486–487, 488–489, 492–495, 501
comparing and ordering, 470–473, 474–475, 477
division, 502
equivalent, 464–467, 493
estimating sums and differences, 486–487, 492–495
and fractions, 458–461, 466–469
  modeling equivalencies, 458–459, 462, 470, 478
  relating on a number line, 459
greater than one, 466–469
hundredths, 458–461, 462–463, 464
mixed numbers and, 466–468
modeling, 458–459, 462, 464–465, 466–467, 470–471, 474, 478, 484, 488–489, 490–491, 492, 502
money and, 458–461, 470, 493, 496–497
multiplying, 502
on a number line, 459, 467, 471, 484, 486, 492
place value in, 458–461, 462–463, 467, 470–471, 474, 484
point, 458
reading and writing, 458–461, 462–463
review H22–H23
rounding, 484–485, 486
subtracting, 486–487, 490–491, 492–495, 496
tenths, 458–461, 462–463, 464
thousandths, 462–463
writing, as fractions, 458–461, 462–463, 478
See also Money

Decimeters, 614–617

Degrees
in angles, 514–517
Celsius, 164–167
Fahrenheit, 164–167

Denominator, 402, 410, 415, 418, 422, 426, 432, 436–437

Describe, 9, 36, 40, 166, 188, 275, 284, 312, 423, 513, 572, 588, 589

Diagonal, 586

Diagrams
drawing, 184–185, 313, 314–317
tree, 682–685
Venn, 20, 184–185, 374, 473
See also Data

Diameters, 530–531

Differences, 38–41, 48–51

Digits, place value of, 4–7, 8–9, 10–11, 458–461, 462–463

F

Inequalities, 136
  graphing, 136–137
Input/output tables, 78–79, 81, 136–139
  See also Function tables
Integers
  compare and order, 169
  negative, 168–171
  on a number line, 169
  positive, 168–171
Interpreting remainders, 332–333
Intersecting lines, 518–519
Intervals, 192–193, 206–207, 216–217
Inverse operations, 32–33, 94–95
Investigate, 2, 30, 62, 90, 116, 150, 178, 202, 242,
  268, 304, 330, 350, 370, 400, 430, 456, 482, 510,
  540, 568, 600, 632, 664
Isosceles triangles, 524–525

Key, of graph, 219, 222
Kilograms, 620–621
Kilometers, 614–617

Learn About, 7, 15, 19, 37, 41, 51, 55, 69, 131, 157,
  167, 183, 189, 229, 253, 341, 361, 375, 385, 405,
  409, 413, 417, 447, 461, 495, 573, 577, 605, 617,
  639, 643, 647, 657, 679, 685
Length. *See* Coordinate grids *and* Measurement
Less than symbol, 136
Like fractions, 432–433, 434–435, 436–439
Likely events, 672–675
Line graphs, 214–215, 216–217, 218–221, 222–225
Line plots, 190–191, 218–221, 222–225
Line segments, 512–513
Line symmetry, 546–549
Linear equations, graphing, 226–229
Linear units
  changing, 602–605, 614–617
  choosing, 602–605, 614–617
  customary units, 602–605
  fractions with, 602–605
  metric units, 614–617
  See also Measurement *and* Perimeter
Lines, 512–513
  diagonal, 586
  intersecting, 518–519
  parallel, 518–519
  perpendicular, 518–519
  of symmetry, 546–549
Lists, organized, 20, 313, 498, 668–671
Liters, 622–623
Logical reasoning, 20–23, 58, 532

See also Reasoning

Make a Graph strategy, 218–221
Make a Model strategy, 582–585
Make an Organized List strategy, 313, 668–671
Make a Table strategy, 498, 532, 612, 624–625
Making decisions, 20–23, 46–47, 74–77, 106–107,
  132–135, 162–163, 194–195, 218–221, 230–231,
  260–261, 276–279, 292–293, 314–317, 332–333,
  362–363, 386–389, 422–423, 440–443, 474–475,
  498–499, 532–533, 554–557, 582–585, 612–613,
  624–625, 648–649, 668–671
Making generalizations, 194–195, 624
Manipulatives and visual aids
  balances, 620
  base-ten blocks, 4, 12, 16, 249, 263, 280, 308–309,
    354, 376
  centimeter cubes, 584, 591, 643, 654
  coins, 25, 365, 666, 667, 680
  compasses, 530
  connecting cubes, 186
  counters, 108, 111, 118, 173, 306, 325, 391, 410,
    591
  decimal models, 458, 459, 462, 464, 466–467, 470,
    488, 490, 492, 502
  dot paper, 521, 526, 542, 575, 635
    isometric, 574, 575
  Equabeam™ balances, 71, 129, 136
  fraction bars, 406–409, 410, 411, 415, 418, 425,
    436, 449, 451
  geoboards, 526
  geometric solids, 580, 587
  geostrips, 546
  grid paper, 8, 98, 190, 216, 248, 280, 372, 640,
    641, 643, 650, 651, 653
  measuring cups, 610, 622
  multiplication tables, 99, 102–103, 104
  nets, 654
  number cubes, 173, 325, 451
  number lines, 12, 16, 34, 49, 51, 69, 136, 169, 375,
    403, 406, 410, 411, 413, 414, 418, 419, 422, 432,
    435, 459, 467, 470, 471, 484, 486, 492
  pattern blocks, 78, 122, 123, 414, 432, 434, 448,
    547, 550, 551, 559, 586, 589
  patterns, 206, 216, 589, 654
  protractors, 514
  rulers, 417, 521, 530, 542, 543, 558, 602, 603, 614,
    615, 624, 634
  spinners, 666, 667, 687
  spreadsheet programs, 81, 687
  spring scales, 608
  stopwatches, 155
  thermometers, 165
  tiles, 81, 119, 372, 378, 379, 650, 651, 673

place value in, 4–7, 8–9, 10–11
prime, 378–380, 381
reading and writing, 4–7, 8–9, 10–11
rounding, 34–37, 484–485
square, 104–105
standard form, 4–7, 8–9, 10–11, 459, 462, 467
uses of, 19
word form, 4–7, 10–11, 459, 462, 467
Numeration systems, 26
Numerator, 402

O

Obtuse angles, 514–517
Obtuse triangles, 524–525
Octagons, 520–523
Odd numbers, 112, 185, 376
One-digit numbers
  dividing by, 306–307, 308–309, 310–312, 314–317, 318–319, 320–321, 334–337, 338–341
  multiplying by, 244–245, 248–249, 250–253, 254–257, 258–259
One-dimensional, 512
Open-Ended problems, xxi, 23, 77, 127, 135, 221, 279, 317, 389, 423, 443, 544, 557, 585, 671
Operations, choosing, 106–107, 440–443
Order of operations, 126–127
Order Property, *See* Commutative Property of Addition *and* Commutative Property of Multiplication
Ordered pairs, 81, 210–213, 226–229
Ordering
  decimals, 470–473
  fractions, 410–413
  greater numbers, 16–19
  integers, 169–170
  measurements, 603, 614, 620, 622
  on a number line, 16–19
  whole numbers, 16–19
Organized lists, 20, 313, 668–671
Origin, 210–213
Ounces, 608–609
Outcomes, 666–667, 672–675

P

Palindrome, 55
Parallel lines, 518–519
Parallelograms, 526–529
Parentheses, 64–65, 66–69
Patterns
  analyzing, 78–79, 104–105, 138–139, 386–389, 560–561
  describing, 78–79, 138–139, 382–385, 386–389, 560–561
  comparing, 105, 560–561

in division, 99, 103, 318–319, 320–321, 339, 346, 352
extending, 382–385, 386–389, 560–561
finding, 276, 382–385, 386–389
geometric, 558–559, 560–561, 563
input/output, 78–79, 138–139
linear, 78–79
making, 370, 382–385, 558–559, 560–561
with multiples, 104–105, 318–319, 352
in multiplication, 102–103, 104–105, 244–245, 270–271, 276, 346
number, 104–105, 382–385, 386–389
repeating, 104–105, 386, 560–561
for solid figures, 578–579, 592
visual, 386–389, 560–561
writing a rule, 78–79, 138–139, 382–385, 386–389, 560–561
Pentagons, 520–523
Percent, 478
Perimeter
  estimating, 634–635
  formulas, 636–639, 648–649
  measuring, 634–635
  of polygons, 634–635, 636–639, 650–653
  of rectangles, 636–639
    same area, different perimeter, 650–653
    same perimeter, different area, 650–653
  relating to area, 650–653
  of squares, 636–639
Periods, 4–7, 9, 10–11
Permutations, 685. *See also* Arrangements
Perpendicular lines, 518–519
Perspective, 577
Pictographs, 218–221, 222–225
Pints, 610–611
Place value
  charts, 5, 9, 10, 13, 17, 462, 470
  composing 4–7, 9–10, 458–461, 462–463, 465, 466–469
  decomposing 4–7, 9–10, 458–461, 462–463, 465, 466–469
  hundred millions, 8–9, 10–11
  hundred thousands, 4–7, 9
  hundreds, 4–7
  hundredths, 458–461, 462–464
  millions, 8–9, 10–11
  modeling, 4–7, 8–9, 12
  ones, 4–7
  periods, 4–7, 9, 10–11
  placing first digit in quotient, 322–323, 334–335, 338, 342, 356
  tens, 4–7
  tenths, 458–461, 462–463, 464–465
  thousands, 4–7
  thousandths, 462–463
  using in rounding, 34
Plane
  defined, 512–513

R

Yards, 602–605
y-**axis,** 210–213
y-**coordinate,** 210–213
Years, 160–161

Zero
  in division, 338–341
  in multiplication, 258–259
  in subtraction, 49
Zero Property, 102, 118–121

Photo Credits

KEY: (t) top, (b) bottom, (l) left, (r) right, (c) center, (bg) background, (fg) foreground

Front Cover: (l) Georgette Douwma/Getty Images; (r) John Foxx/Getty Images.
Back Cover: (l) John Foxx/Getty Images; (r) Roy Ooms/Masterflie.

Front Endsheets: Page 1 & 2, Caroline Warren/Getty Images; Page 3, Photodisc/Getty Images.
Back Endsheets: Page 1, J. A. Kraulis/Masterfile; Page 2 & 3, Digital Vision/Getty Images.

Title Page: (l) Georgette Douwma/Getty Images; (r) John Foxx/Getty Images.

Copyright Page: J. A. Kraulis/Masterfile.

Table of Contents: iv Ambient Images Inc./Alamy; vi Dorney Park & Wildwater Kingdom; viii AP Photo/James A. Finley; x AP Photo/Kathy Willens; xii Garry D. McMichael/Photo Researchers, Inc.; xiv NPS Volunteer, Bruce Douglas; xvi AP Photo/The Pioneer of Bemidji, Minn., Monte Draper; xviii Boston Duck Tours; xx-xxi (bg) Robin Smith/Getty Images.

Unit 1: 1 (t) The Futures Channel, Inc; 1 (c) The Futures Channel; 1 (b) The Futures Channel; 2 Momatiuk-Eastcott/Corbis; 4 Peter Titmuss/Alamy; 5 Medioimages/Alamy; 6 (t) Stockdisc Classic/Alamy; 6 (tc) GK Hart/Vikki Hart/ Getty Images (Royalty-free); 6 (bc) Juniors Bildarchiv/ Alamy; 6 (b) Dave King/ Dorling Kindersley; 12 Gibson Stock Photography; 13 Garry Black/ Masterfile; 16 Julie Mowbray/Alamy; 21 Jeff Gentner/Icon SMI/Corbis; 23 (tl) Kit Kittle/Corbis; 23 (bg) Getty/Harcourt; 26 (bg) Corbis/Harcourt; 30 Ambient Images Inc./Alamy; 32 Unicorn Stock Photos L.L.C.; 34 Jim Watson/AFP/Getty Images; 36 Getty/Harcourt; 37 Nancy Kaszerman/ NewsCom; 38 Jeremy Woodhouse/digital vision/Getty Images; 42 Syracuse Newspapers/Dick Blume/The Image Works; 45 Alamy; 46 Tim Heneghan/Index Stock imagery; 47 Jon Armstrong/ Lonely Planet Images; 48 Stephen Dalton /Animals Animals - Earth Scenes; 52 NASA; 53 NASA; 62 [Photo by Jason Clarke, IRELAND OUT]; 62 (inset) Patti McConville/Getty Images; 64 Photo Network/Alamy; 65 Getty Images/Harcourt; 67 Tony Freeman/PhotoEdit; 70 Courtesy of Canine Companions for Independence; 71 Stella Davis/Associated Press; 72 Getty/Harcourt; 73 Mark E. Gibson; 75 Jupiter Images; 76 (t) Tannen Maury/Associated Press; 76 (b) ABPL/HAAGNER, CLEM/Animals Animals - Earth Scenes; 77 Galen Rowell/Corbis; 81 (bg) Court Mast/Taxi/Getty Images; 86 Jose Luis Pelaez/Corbis; 87 Sheila Terry/Photo Researchers.

Unit 2: 89 (t) The Futures Channel; 89 (c) The Futures Channel; 89 (b) The Futures Channel; 90 Dorney Park & Wildwater Kingdom; 92 Jennifer Crites Photography; 96 Michael P. Gadomski; 97 (tr) iStockPhoto; 97 (br) Cathy Melloan/Photo Edit; 98 PhotoSpin, Inc/Alamy; 101 AP Photo/Edis Jurcys; 112 (bg) Royalty-Free/Corbis; 116 Frans Lanting/Corbis; 122 (t) The Granger Collection, New York; 124 Randall K. Roberts; 125 Lauren Victoria Burke/AP Photo; 126 AP Photo/Nathan K. Martin; 135 AP Photo/The Janesville Gazette, Adam Lasker; 136 (bg) GardenWorld Images/Alamy; 137 Roger McClean/iStockPhoto; 138 (tr) Holly Kuper/ AGStockUSA; 138 (b) Robert Warren/Getty Images; 141 (bg) Court Mast/Taxi/Getty Images; 142 (tr) Rob Howard/Corbis; 146 (tr) SuperStock/Alamy; 146 (c) Joseph Sohm; Visions of America/ Corbis; 146 (cr) Alamy; 146 (br) MCT/NewsCom; 146-147 (bg) G. Biss/Masterfile; 147 (tr) Alamy; 147 (bl) SuperStock; 147 (bcl) Robert Fried/Alamy; 147 (bcr) Cristina Fumi/Alamy.

Unit 3: 149 (t) The Futures Channel; 149 (c) The Futures Channel; 149 (b) The Futures Channel; 150 AP Photo/James A. Finley; 152 (tr) Spencer Grant/PhotoEdit; 154 Tony Freeman/Photo Edit; 157 Getty Images; 158 (t) Joseph A. Rosen/New York Stock Photo; 158 (br) Matisse, Henri (1869-1954), *"Interior with a Phonograph"*. 1924. Oil on canvas, 34 5/8 x 31 1/2 in (100.5 x 81 cm). Pinacoteca Gianni e Marella Agnelli, Turin, Italy/© Succession H. Matisse, Paris/Artists

Rights Society (ARS), New York.; 160 Hans Reinhard/Bruce Coleman, Inc.; 161 Johnny Johnson/ Animals Animals - Earth Scenes; 162 (t) Sasha/Getty Images; 162 (cr) Bettmann/Corbis; 162 (cr) Brown Brothers, Sterling, Pennsylvania; 162 (b) Pictorial Parade/Getty Images; 164 Scott Olson/ Getty Images; 168 Macduff Everton/The Image Works; 171 Jane Faircloth/TRANSPARENCIES, Inc.; 174 (tr) Lourens Smak/Alamy; 174 (bg) José Fuste Raga/zefa/Corbis; 178 Doug Menuez/ Getty Images; 182 Getty/Harcourt; 186 Courtesy Cattaraugus County Tourism; 190 NASA; 192 Chris Trotman/Duomo/Corbis; 194 Michael Newman/Photo Edit; 197 (bg) Court Mast/Taxi/Getty Images; 198 (bg) Alamy; 202 WorldSat International/Photo Researchers, Inc.; 204 NASA; 205 Masterfile Royalty Free ; 207 (tr) Jules Frazier/Getty Images; 207 (br) Tony Freeman/PhotoEdit; 208 (tr) Image Source/Getty Images; 208 (br) Envision/Corbis; 210 S. T. Yiap/Age Fotostock; 213 Dennis MacDonald/PhotoEdit; 214 Alamy; 220 Super Stock/Age Fotostock; 221 Rudy Sulgan/ Age Fotostock; 223 (tr) iStockphoto; 225 Nicole Katano/Age Fotostock; 227 (t) Zedcor Wholly Owned/PhotoObjects.net/Jupiter Images; 227 (b) Bruce Davidson/Nature Picture Library; 229 J. A. Kraulis/Masterfile; 231 Greg Nicholas/iStockphoto; 238-239 Masterfile; 239 (br) Jupiter Images.

Unit 4: 241 (t) The Futures Channel; 241 (c) The Futures Channel; 241 (b) The Futures Channel; 242 Martin Harvey/Gallo Images/Corbis; 246 Robert Winslow/Animals Animals - Earth Scenes; 247 Photodisc Green/Getty Images; 250 (cr) Victoria Mc Cormick/Animals Animals - Earth Scenes; 250 (b) Royalty-Free/Corbis; 252 (tc) Jonathan Blair/Corbis; 252 (bc) David A. Northcott/ Corbis; 254 Kim Karpeles/Alamy; 257 Photo by Pat & Chuck Blackley; 259 Joe Sohm/The Image Works; 260 Masterfile; 261 Jason Kirk/Online USA, Inc./NewsCom; 263 (tr) Nicole Katano/Age Fotostock; 263 (bg) Court Mast/Taxi/Getty Images; 264 (tr) White Cross Productions/The Image Bank/Getty Images; 268 AP Photo/Kathy Willens; 270 Kim Taylor/Dorling Kindersley; 271 James King-Holmes/Science Photo Library; 277 BIOS Ferry Eric & Oertel Bruno/Peter Arnold, Inc.; 278 Warren Stone/Bruce Coleman USA; 279 (tc) Arco Images/Alamy; 279 (tr) Joe McDonald/Corbis; 279 (c) Rod Planck/Dembinsky Photo Associates; 279 (bc) Alan G. Nelson/Dembinsky Photo Associates; 279 (bg) Getty/Harcourt; 280 (tr) Jerry and Marcy Monkman/EcoPhotography. com/Alamy; 280 (b) Dennis MacDonald/PhotoEdit; 282 Kevin Dodge/Masterfile; 284 Holger Wulschlaeger/iStockPhoto; 286 Hulton-Deutsch Collection/Corbis; 287 Digital Vision Ltd./ SuperStock; 289 Bob Daemmrich/The Image Works; 290 Susan Van Etten/PhotoEdit; 292 (tr) Corbis; 292 (br) Graham French/ Masterfile; 293 Larry Mulvehill/Photo Researchers, Inc.; 296 (bg) Benjamin Rondel/Corbis; 300 (t) MPI/Getty Images; 300 (b) Bettmann/Corbis; 300-301 (bg) STScI/NASA/Corbis; 301 (fg) Bettmann/Corbis.

Unit 5: 303 (t) Movin' On Livestock; 303 (c) The Futures Channel; 303 (b) The Futures Channel; 304 Garry D. McMichael/Photo Researchers, Inc.; 307 S.T. Yiap/Alamy; 310 The Granger Collection, New York; 311 Photo File/MLB Photos via Getty Images; 313 Andy Mead/Icon SMI/NewsCom; 315 Linda Kennedy/Alamy; 316 (tr) ML Harris/Getty Images; 317 (t) Yann Arthus-Bertrand/Corbis; 317 (tc) Imagebroker/Alamy; 317 (c) Imagebroker/Alamy; 317 (bc) DK Limited/Corbis; 317 (b) vario images GmbH & Co.KG/Alamy; 318 Kelly-Mooney Photography/ Corbis; 320 Michael & Patricia Fogden/Minden Pictures; 321 (tc) MichaelL Durham/Minden Pictures; 321 (c) Stephen Dalton/Minden Pictures; 321 (c) Tim Oram/Alamy; 321 (bc) Arco Images/Alamy; 322 Philip Krejcarek/JupiterImages; 323 Philip Krejcarek/JupiterImages; 326 (tl) PhotoDisc/Getty Images/Harcourt; 326 (tc) PhotoDisc/Getty Images/Harcourt; 326 (tr) Richard Hamilton Smith/Corbis; 326 (bg) Danita Delimont/Alamy; 330 Masa Ushioda/Bruce Coleman, Inc.; 332 Richard T. Nowitz/Corbis; 333 Sandro Vannini/Corbis; 334 Bettmann/Corbis; 335 (br) Ryan McVay/Getty Images ; 336 Chuck Eckert/Alamy; 337 Liu Liqun/Corbis; 338 (tl), (tc) Getty/ Harcourt; 339 (tl) Brand X Pictures/Alamy; 339 (tr) Jack Cox-Travel Pics Pro/Alamy; 339 (br) Getty/Harcourt; 341 AM Corporation/Alamy; 342 Florian Graner/Nature Picture Library; 345 (bg) Court Mast/Taxi/Getty Images; 350 Associated Press/AP; 352 Paul A. Souders/Corbis; 353 Dave King/Getty Images; 356 U.S. Mint; 362 Corbis; 366 (tr) Corbis; 366 (br) foodfolio/Alamy; 370 AP Photo/Jeff Roberson; 375 Harcourt /Corel Stock Photo Library -royalty free; 378 (all) Lake County Museum/Corbis; 382 John Birdsall/age fotostock; 384 photolibrary.com pty. ltd./ Index Stock; 385 (tl) Getty/Harcourt; 385 (tr) Scott Camazine/Photo Researchers, Inc.; 386 Jeff Gynane/iStockPhoto; 387 Dynamic Graphics/Jupiterimages; 388 (t) Chris Lisle/Corbis; 388 (cr) iStockphoto; 388 (cl) Tyler Olson/ShutterStock.com; 388 (br) Nancy Nehring/iStockphoto; 396 (tl) Alamy; 396 (tr) francesco survara/Alamy; 396 (cr) Rob Lacey/vividstock.net/Alamy; 396 (cl),

572 (cr) Artefaqs Corporation; 572 (r) Ambient Images Inc./Alamy; 576 (tc) Michael Newman/ Photoedit; 577 (tr) Jupiter Images; 577 (c) Corbis; 580 (r) Rodolfo Arpia/Age Fotostock; 583 SuperStock; 585 (t) Klaus Hackenberg/zefa/Corbis; 585 (b) Stefano Bianchetti/Corbis; 586 ***"Unfoldings"***, 05-PB21 © Jae Hahn 2005; 587 (tr) William Manning Photography/Alamy; 587 (cr) Robert Llewellyn; 587 (br) ***"Incomplete Open Cubes"***, 1974, 12 in. x 120 in. x 216 in. (30.48 cm x 304.8 cm x 548.64 cm). Collection San Francisco Museum of Modern Art. Accessions Committee Fund: gift of Emily L. Carroll and Thomas Weisel, Jean and James E. Douglas, Jr., Susan and Robert Green, Evelyn Haas, Mimi and Peter Haas, Eve and Harvey Masonek, Elaine McKeon, the Modern Art Council, Phyllis and Stuart G. Moldaw, Christine and Michael Murray, Danielle and Brooks Walker Jr., and Phyllis Wattis; © Estate of Sol LeWitt/Artists Rights Society (ARS), New York"; 588 (l) Paul Eekhoff/Masterfile; 588 (cl) Emmanuel Lattes Photography; 588 (cr) Lee Foster/Bruce Coleman; 588 (r) Cindy L Manieri Photography; 589 M.C. Escher's ***"Metamorphosis II"***, © 2007 The M.C. Escher Company-Holland. All rights reserved. www. mcescher.com/Art Resource, NY; 590 (tl) Dynamic Graphics Group/Creatas/Alamy; 590 (tcl) Elvele Images/Alamy; 590 (tcr) Alex Bramwell/iStockPhoto; 590 (tr) P. Narayan/age fotostock; 592 (tr) © Oxford Science Archive, Oxford, Great Britain/HIP/Art Resource, NY; 592 (bg) Comstock Images/Alamy; 593 (l) Carolyn Ross/Jupiter Images; 593 (cr) Christopher O Driscoll; 593 (r) SuperStock/Alamy; 596 (tr) Time Life Pictures/Getty Images; 596 (cl) Getty Images; 596 (c) Handout/NewsCom; 596 (cr) Steve Gorton/Getty Images; 596-597 (bg) World Almanac Books; 597 (tr) Getty/Harcourt; 597 (c) Getty/Harcourt; 597 (cr) Glenn Mitsui/Photodisc/Getty Images.

Unit 8: 598 Larry Gatz/Photographer's Choice/Getty Image; 599 (t) The Futures Channel; 599 (c) The Futures Channel; 599 (b) The Futures Channel; 600 Joe McNally; 602 (tlc) Ron Chapple Stock/Corbis; 605 (bl) Jim Cole, Photographer/Alamy; 605 (bc) Thomas Stevenson Grant/PhotographersDirect; 605 (br) ST-images/Alamy; 609 age fotostock/SuperStock; 611 Judd Pilossof/JupiterImages; 612 (tr) Lee Hacker/Alamy; 614 Steve Hamblin/Alamy; 616 (cl) WoodyStock/Alamy; 616 (cr) Rick & Nora Bowers/Alamy; 616 (bl) Jim Brandenburg/Minden Pictures; 616 (br) Don Farrall/Getty Images; 617 Gordon & Cathy Illg/ AnimalsAnimals; 618 O.S.F./Animals Animals - Earth Scenes; 621 (tr) iStockphoto; 621 (cl) Getty Images/Photodisc/ Harcourt Index; 621 (br) Getty Images/PhotoDisc /Harcourt Index; 622 (b) Paul Poplis/Jupiter Images; 625 David Reed/Alamy; 626 (bc) Getty Images; 627 (tl) Corbis/Harcourt; 627 (tr) Luis Carlos Torres/iStockPhoto; 627 (c) Thomas Northcut/Getty Images (Royalty-free); 627 (bl) Masterfile Royalty Free; 627 (bc) David Bishop/JupiterImages; 627 (br) DK Limited/Corbis; 629 (cr) Hemera Technologies/ JupiterImages; 631 (cr) C Squared Studios/Getty Images; 631 (b) Image Source/Jupiter Images; 632 Sunwatch Indian Village and Archaeological Site; 635 Imagebroker/Alamy; 648 Corbis; 649 Stockdisc/Getty Images; 650 (tr) Thomas Henderson ABEL/Getty Images; 650 (cl) Mike Powell/Getty Images; 650 (cr) Alberto Biscaro/Masterfile; 653 Altrendo Images/Getty Images; 660 Getty Images/PhotoDisc/Harcourt; 663 iStockphoto; 664 Boston Duck Tours; 671 (tl) Courtesy of Nevada State Fair; 671 (tr) Courtesy of New York State Fair; 671 (cl) Swim Ink 2, LLC/Corbis; 671 (cr) California State Fair; 671 (bl) Courtesy of Michigan State Fair; 671 (br) Courtesy of Arizona State Fair; 671 (bl) Courtesy of Indiana State Fair Commission; 671 (br) Courtesy of the Michigan State Fair; 671 (br) Courtesy of the State Fair of Texas; 687 Court Mast/Taxi/Getty Images; 688 Maps.com/Corbis; 690 age fotostock; 692 (tr) Harry Taylor/Getty Images; 692 Garnet: Harry Taylor/Getty Images; 692 Amethyst: Lawrence Lawry/Photo Researchers; 692 Aquamarine: Lawrence Lawry/Photo Researchers; 692 Diamond: Charles D. Winters/Photo Researchers; 692 Emerald: Harry Taylor/Getty Images; 692 Pearl: Chip Forelli/Getty Images; 692 Ruby: Harry Taylor/Getty Images; 692 Peridot: Harry Taylor/Getty Images; 692 Sapphire: Wayne Scherr/Photo Researchers; 692 Opal: Lawrence Lawry/Photo Researchers; 692 Topaz: Lawrence Lawry/Photo Researchers; 692 Turquoise: Lawrence Lawry/ Photo Researchers; 692-693 (bg) Sandro Sodano/Getty Images; 693 (tl) Vaughan Fleming/ Science Photo Library; 693 (tr) Ian Pilbeam/Alamy;

Student Handbook: page H, Jim Brandenburg/ Minden Pictures; H1, GK Hart/Vikki Hart/Getty Images.

All other photos © Harcourt School Publishers. Harcourt photographers; Weronica Ankarorn, Eric Camden, Don, Couch, Doug Dukane, Ken Kinzie, April Riehm, and Steve Williams.

Each section of a nautilus shell is called a chamber. The sizes of the chambers form a pattern.

The shell of an adult nautilus can have about 30 chambers.

There are about **1,000** types of sea anemones, but the clownfish can live among only 10 of those varieties.

Clownfish are the only fish that do not get stung by the tentacles of these sea anemones.